2019 release

Adobe Illustrator, Photoshop, & InDesign CC

Graphic Design Portfolio

AGAINST THE CLOCK

mastering graphic technology

Managing Editor: Ellenn Behoriam
Cover & Interior Design: Erika Kendra

The fonts utilized in these training materials are the property of Against The Clock, Inc. and are supplied to the
legitimate buyers of the Against The Clock training materials solely for use with the exercises and projects provided in the
body of the materials. They may not be used for any other purpose, and under no circumstances may they be transferred to
another individual, nor copied or distributed by any means whatsoever.

Against The Clock and the Against The Clock logo are trademarks of Against The Clock, Inc., registered in the
United States and elsewhere. References to and instructional materials provided for any particular application program, operating system, hardware platform, or other commercially available product or products do not represent
an endorsement of such product or products by Against The Clock, Inc.

Photoshop, Acrobat, Illustrator, InDesign, Flash, Dreamweaver, and PostScript are trademarks of Adobe Systems Incorporated.
Macintosh is a trademark of Apple Computer, Inc. Word, Excel, Office, Microsoft, and Windows are either registered trademarks or trademarks of Microsoft Corporation.

Other product and company names mentioned herein may be the trademarks of their respective owners.

Cover image by Ricardo Gomez Angel on Unsplash.com.

10 9 8 7 6 5 4 3 2 1

Print ISBN: 978-1-946396-26-6
Ebook ISBN: 978-1-946396-27-3

AGAINST THE CLOCK
mastering graphic technology

4710 28th Street North, Saint Petersburg, FL 33714
800-256-4ATC • www.againsttheclock.com

ACKNOWLEDGEMENTS

About Against The Clock

Against The Clock, long recognized as one of the nation's leaders in courseware development, has been publishing educational materials for the graphic and computer arts industries since 1990. The company has developed a solid and widely respected approach to teaching people how to effectively use graphics applications while maintaining a disciplined approach to real-world problems.

Having developed the *Against The Clock* and the *Essentials for Design* series with Prentice Hall/Pearson Education, ATC drew from years of professional experience and instructor feedback to develop *The Professional Portfolio Series*, focusing on the Adobe Creative Suite. These books feature step-by-step explanations, detailed foundational information, and advice and tips from professionals that offer practical solutions to technical issues.

About the Author

Erika Kendra holds a BA in History and a BA in English Literature from the University of Pittsburgh. She began her career in the graphic communications industry as an editor at Graphic Arts Technical Foundation, and has been a full-time professional graphic designer since 1999.

Erika is the author or co-author of more than forty books about Adobe graphic design software. She has also written several books about graphic design concepts such as color reproduction and preflighting and dozens of articles for graphics and print industry journals. Working with Against The Clock for almost twenty years, Erika was a key partner in developing *The Professional Portfolio Series* of software training books.

Contributing Editors and Artists

A big thank you to the people whose comments and expertise contributed to the success of these books:

- **Dan Christensen,** technical editor
- **Tony Cowdrey,** technical editor
- **Roger Morrissey,** technical editor
- **Gary Poyssick**, technical editor
- **Joseph A. Staudenbaur**, technical editor
- **Matthew Woodring,** technical editor
- **Amanda Gambill**, copy editor
- **Jaclyn Garver,** copy editor

Images used in the projects throughout this book are in the public domain unless otherwise noted. Individual artists' credit follow:

Project 4:
Sunrise.jpg photo by Stefan Kunze on Unsplash.com.
Lightning.jpg photo by David Mourn on Unsplash.com
Tornado.jpg photo by Jean Beaufort on Publicdomainpictures.net

Project 5:
amg.jpg photo by Mike on Pexels.com
inset1.jpg photo by Kyle Murfin on Unsplash.com
inset2.jpg photo by Jake Weirick on Pexels.com
inset3.jpg photo by Sergiusz Rydosz on Publicdomainpictures.net
tires.jpg photo by Imthaz Ahamed on Pexels.com

Project 6:
Museum images in this project are courtesy of the Getty's Open Content Program: getty.edu/about/whatwedo/opencontentfaq.html
HDR image exposures by Charlie Essers.

Project 7:
coffee.tif photo by Polymanu on Pixabay.com
creampuffs.tif photo by la-fontaine on Pixabay.com
fruit.tif photo by Luke Michael on Unsplash.com
peppers.tif photo by DXT_91 on Pexels.com
spices.tif photo by Akhil Chandran on Unsplash.com

Project 8:
guitar.jpg photo by Suvan Chowdhury on Pexels.com

Project 9:
U.S. Navy Blue Angels photos copyright Erika Kendra

Moon-landing photo is a NASA photo in the public domain. Scanning by NASA Johnson and post-processing by Kipp Teague

Aircraft images used in the supplied PDF ad were taken by government employees and as such are in the public domain:
B-2: U.S. Navy photo/Jordon R. Beesley
F-117: Bobbi Zapka
F-22: U.S. Air Force photo/Staff Sgt. Samuel Rogers
SR-71: U.S. Air Force photo/Tech. Sgt. Michael Haggerty

Project 10:
Images used in this project are copyright Against The Clock, Inc.

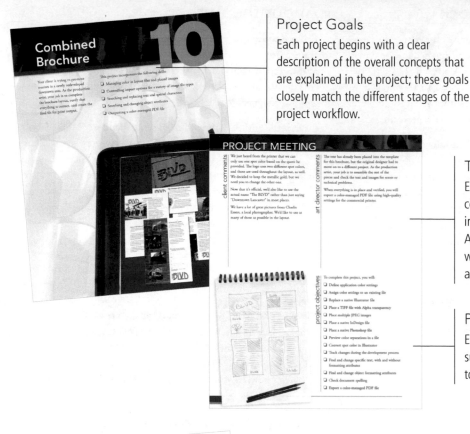

Project Goals

Each project begins with a clear description of the overall concepts that are explained in the project; these goals closely match the different stages of the project workflow.

The Project Meeting

Each project includes the client's initial comments, which provide valuable information about the job. The Project Art Director, a vital part of any design workflow, also provides fundamental advice and production requirements.

Project Objectives

Each Project Meeting includes a summary of the specific skills required to complete the project.

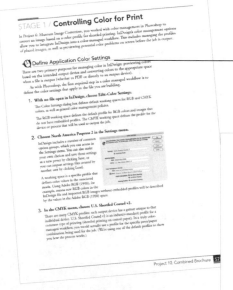

Real-World Workflow

Projects are broken into logical lessons, or "stages," of the workflow. Brief introductions at the beginning of each stage provide vital foundational material required to complete the task.

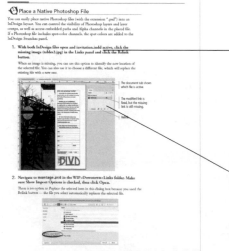

Step-By-Step Exercises

Every stage of the workflow is broken into multiple hands-on, step-by-step exercises.

Visual Explanations

Wherever possible, screen captures are annotated so students can quickly identify important information.

Design Foundations
Additional functionality, related tools, and underlying graphic design concepts are included throughout the book.

Advice and Warnings
Where appropriate, sidebars provide shortcuts, warnings, or helpful tips.

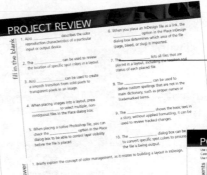

Project Review
After completing each project, students can complete these fill-in-the-blank and short-answer questions to test their understanding of the concepts in the project.

Portfolio Builder Projects
Each step-by-step project is accompanied by a freeform project, allowing students to practice skills and creativity, resulting in an extensive and diverse portfolio of work.

Visual Summary
Using an annotated version of the finished project, students can quickly identify the skills used to complete different aspects of the job.

PROJECTS AT A GLANCE

Against The Clock's *The Professional Portfolio Series* teaches graphic design software tools and techniques entirely within the framework of real-world projects; we introduce and explain skills where they would naturally fall into a real project workflow.

The project-based approach in *The Professional Portfolio Series* allows you to get in-depth with the software beginning in Project 1 — you don't have to read several chapters of introductory material before you can start creating finished artwork.

Our approach also prevents "topic tedium" — in other words, we don't require you to read pages and pages of information about text (for example); instead, we explain text tools and options as part of larger projects.

Clear, easy-to-read, step-by-step instructions walk you through every phase of each job, from creating a new file to saving the finished piece. Wherever logical, we also offer practical advice and tips about underlying concepts and graphic design practices that will benefit you as you enter the job market.

The projects in this book reflect a range of different types of print design jobs using Adobe Illustrator, Photoshop, and InDesign. When you finish the ten projects in this book (and the accompanying Portfolio Builder exercises), you will have a solid foundational knowledge of the three most popular applications in the print design market — and a substantial body of work that should impress any potential employer.

CONTENTS

CONTENTS

CONTENTS

Project 9
Aerospace Newsletter
509

Project 10
Combined Brochure
573

GETTING STARTED

Prerequisites

The Professional Portfolio Series is based on the assumption that you have a basic understanding of how to use your computer. You should know how to use your mouse to point and click, as well as how to drag items around the screen. You should be able to resize and arrange windows on your desktop to maximize your available space. You should know how to access drop-down menus, and understand how check boxes and radio buttons work. It also doesn't hurt to understand how your operating system organizes files and folders, and how to navigate your way around them. If you're familiar with these fundamental skills, then you know all that's necessary to use the Portfolio Series.

Resource Files

All the files you need to complete the projects in this book — except, of course, the Adobe application files — are on the Student Files Web page at againsttheclock.com. See the inside back cover of this book for access information.

Each archive (ZIP) file is named according to the related project (e.g., **Camping_Print19_RF.zip**). At the beginning of each project, you must download the archive file for that project and expand that archive to access the resource files that you need to complete the exercises. Detailed instructions for this process are included in the Interface chapter.

Files required for the related Portfolio Builder exercises at the end of each project are also available on the Student Files Web page; these archives are also named by project (e.g., **Airborne_Print19_PB.zip**).

ATC Fonts

You must download and install the ATC fonts from the Student Files Web page to ensure that your exercises and projects will work as described in the book. Specific instructions for installing fonts are provided in the documentation that came with your computer. You should replace older (pre-2013) ATC fonts with the ones on the Student Files Web page.

System Requirements

The Professional Portfolio Series was designed to work on both Macintosh or Windows computers; where differences exist from one platform to another, we include specific instructions relative to each platform.

One issue that remains different from Macintosh to Windows is the use of different modifier keys (Control, Shift, etc.) to accomplish the same task. When we present key commands, we always follow the same Macintosh/Windows format — Macintosh keys are listed first, then a slash, followed by the Windows key commands.

Software Versions

This book was written and tested using the 2019 release of the Adobe Creative Cloud (CC) software:

- Adobe InDesign — v 14.0
- Adobe Illustrator — v 23.0
- Adobe Photoshop — v 20.0

(You can find the specific version number of your applications in the Splash Screen that appears while an application is launching.)

Because Adobe has announced periodic upgrades rather than releasing new full versions, some features and functionality might have changed since publication. Please check the Errata section of the Against The Clock Web site for any significant issues that might have arisen from these periodic upgrades.

Explore the InDesign Interface

Adobe InDesign is a robust publishing application that allows you to integrate text and graphics, either prepared in the program or imported from other sources, to produce files that can be printed or published digitally.

The user interface (UI) is what you see when you launch the application. The specific elements that you see depend on what was done the last time the application was open. The first time you launch an application, you see the default workspace settings defined by Adobe. When you relaunch after you or another user has quit, the workspace defaults to the last-used settings.

1. **Create a new empty folder named WIP (Work In Progress) on any writable disk (where you plan to save your work in progress).**

2. **Download the Interface_Print19_RF.zip archive from the Student Files web page.**

3. **Macintosh users: Place the ZIP archive in your WIP folder, then double-click the file icon to expand it.**

   Windows users: Double-click the ZIP archive file to open it. Click the folder inside the archive and drag it into your primary WIP folder.

   This **InterfaceCC19** folder contains all the files you need to complete this introduction.

| **Macintosh:** | **Windows:** |
| Double-click the archive file icon to expand it. | Open the archive file, then drag the InterfaceCC19 folder from the archive to your WIP folder. |

4. **Macintosh users: While pressing Command-Control-Option-Shift, launch InDesign. Click Yes when asked if you want to delete Preference files.**

   Windows users: Launch InDesign, and then immediately press Control-Alt-Shift. Click Yes when asked if you want to delete the Preference files.

5. Macintosh users: Open the Window menu and make sure the Application Frame option is toggled on.

Many menu commands and options in InDesign are **toggles**, which means they are either on or off; when an option is already checked, that option is toggled on (visible or active). You can toggle an active option off by choosing the checked menu command, or toggle an inactive option on by choosing the unchecked menu command.

Note:

On Windows, the Application Frame menu command is not available; you can't turn it off on the Windows OS.

This option should be checked.

Understanding the Application Frame FOUNDATIONS

On Windows, each running application is contained within its own frame; all elements of the application — including the Menu bar, panels, tools, and open documents — are contained within the Application frame. You can't turn off the Application Frame on the Windows OS.

On Macintosh, the Application frame contains all elements of the workspace, excluding the menu bar. The Macintosh Application frame is active by default, but you can toggle it off by choosing Window>Application Frame. If the menu option is checked, the Application frame is active; if the menu option is not checked, it is inactive.

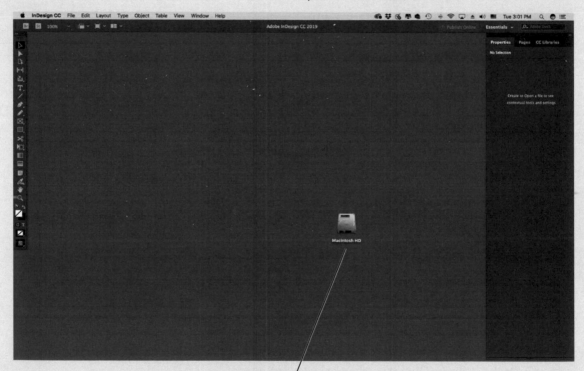

When the Application frame is not active, the desktop is visible behind the workspace elements.

6. Review the options in the Start screen.

The default user interface shows a stored "Start" workspace. No panels are visible in this workspace. Instead, you have one-click access to a list of recently opened files (if any), buttons to create a new file or open an existing one, and links to additional functionality provided by the Adobe Creative Cloud suite.

This workspace appears whenever InDesign is running, but no actual file is open. As soon as you open or create a file, the interface reverts to show the last-used workspace arrangement.

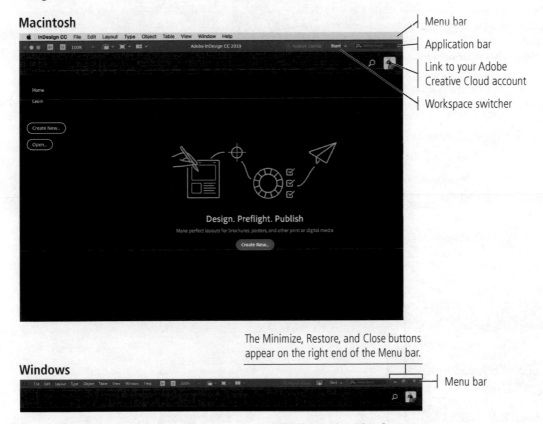

The Minimize, Restore, and Close buttons appear on the right end of the Menu bar.

The Macintosh and Windows workspaces are virtually identical, with a few primary exceptions:

- On Macintosh, the application's title bar appears below the Menu bar; the Close, Minimize, and Restore buttons appear on the left side of the title bar, and the Menu bar is not part of the Application frame.

- On Windows, the Close, Minimize, and Restore buttons appear at the right end of the Menu bar, which is part of the overall Application frame.

- Macintosh users have two extra menus, consistent with the Macintosh operating system (OS) structure. The Apple menu provides access to system-specific commands. The InDesign menu follows the Macintosh system-standard format for all applications; this menu controls basic application operations such as About, Hide, Preferences, and Quit.

7. Open the Workspace switcher in the top-right corner of the workspace and choose Essentials from the menu.

Saved **workspaces** provide one-click access to a defined group of panels.

8. Open the Workspace switcher again and choose Reset Essentials.

This step might or might not do anything, depending on what was done in InDesign before you started this project. If you or someone else changed anything, and then quit the application, those changes are remembered when InDesign is relaunched. Because we can't be sure what your default settings show, by completing this step you are resetting the user interface to one of the built-in, default workspaces so your screen captures will match ours.

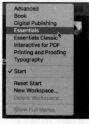

Step 7   Step 8

9. Macintosh users: Choose InDesign>Preferences>Interface.

Windows users: Choose Edit>Preferences>Interface.

Remember that on Macintosh systems, the Preferences dialog box is accessed in the InDesign menu; Windows users access the Preferences dialog box in the Edit menu.

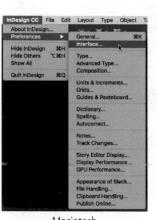

Macintosh   Windows

Note:

As you work your way through the projects in this book, you'll learn not only what you can do with these different collections of preferences, but also why and when you might want to use them.

Preferences customize the way many of the program's tools and options function. When you open the Preferences dialog box, the active pane is the one you chose in the Preferences submenu. Once open, however, you can access any of the Preference categories by clicking a different option in the left pane; the right side of the dialog box displays options related to the active category.

10. In the Appearance section, choose any Color Theme option that you prefer.

You might have already noticed the rather dark appearance of the panels and interface background. InDesign uses the medium-dark "theme" as the default. (We used the Light option throughout this book because text in the interface elements is easier to read in printed screen captures.)

11. In the Panels section, check the option to Auto-Collapse Icon Panels.

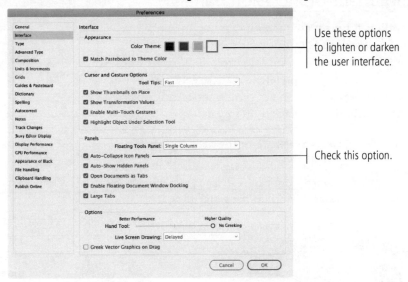

Use these options to lighten or darken the user interface.

Check this option.

12. Click OK to close the Preferences dialog box.

13. Continue to the next exercise.

Menus in Adobe Applications

If a specific menu command can be accessed with a keyboard shortcut, those shortcuts are listed to the right of the related command.

Some menu commands are toggles, which means a feature can be turned on or off, or an option is either visible or hidden. A check mark indicates that the command is currently active.

Some menu commands include the "Show" or "Hide" indicator at the beginning of the menu command. When visible, the command appears as "Hide [Option];" when not already visible, the command appears as "Show [Option]."

Finally, if a specific menu command is grayed out (it can't be selected), that command does not apply in the current context (usually, depending on what is selected in the document).

The image here shows the View menu in InDesign. The concepts identified here apply to menus in all Adobe applications.

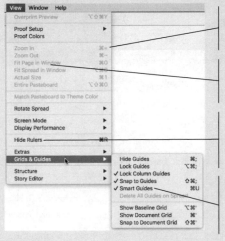

Keyboard shortcuts (if available) are listed on the right side of the menu.

If a menu command is grayed out, it is not available for the current selection.

Some commands appear as Hide [Option] when visible or Show [Option] when not visible.

Many menu commands are toggles; the check mark indicates that an option is visible or toggled on.

Explore the Arrangement of InDesign Panels

InDesign includes a number of options for managing the numerous panels, so you can customize and personalize the workspace to suit your specific needs. We designed the following exercise to give you an opportunity to explore different ways of controlling InDesign panels. Because workspace preferences are largely a matter of personal taste, the projects in this book instruct you to use certain tools and panels, but where you place those elements within the interface is up to you.

1. **With InDesign open, review the options available in the user interface.**

   The default Essentials workspace includes the Tools panel on the left side of the screen, the Control panel at the top of the screen, and a set of panels attached to the right side of the screen. The area where the panels are stored is called the **panel dock**.

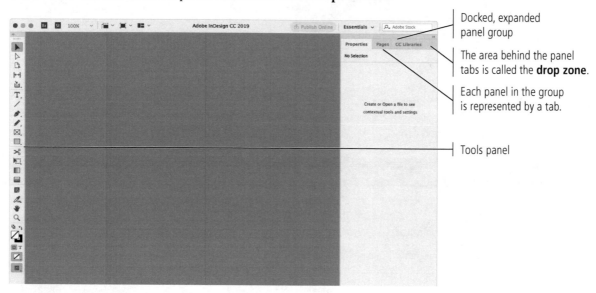

Docked, expanded panel group

The area behind the panel tabs is called the **drop zone**.

Each panel in the group is represented by a tab.

Tools panel

2. **Choose Window>Stroke.**

   All InDesign panels can be toggled on and off from the Window menu.

   - If you choose a panel that's already open but iconized, the panel expands to the left of its icon.

   - If you choose a panel that's already open in an expanded group, but is not the active panel, that panel comes to the front of the group.

   - If you choose a panel that isn't currently open, it opens in the same place it was when it was last closed.

When you expand a panel that is part of a panel group, the entire group expands.

The panel you selected is the active panel in the expanded group.

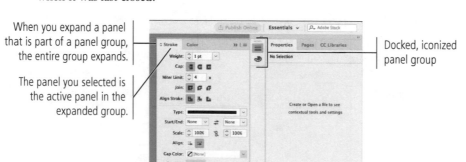

Docked, iconized panel group

3. Control/Right-click the Color panel tab and choose Close from the contextual menu.

Control/Right-clicking opens a contextual menu, which provides options specific to the thing on which you click. In this case, you access commands related to the Color panel because you clicked on that panel tab. You can choose to close the individual panel or close all tabs in the active panel group. The lower three options in the menu relate to the behavior of all panels, not only the specific panel in which you opened the contextual menu.

Control/Right-click to access contextual menus.

The Stroke panel remains open after closing the Color panel.

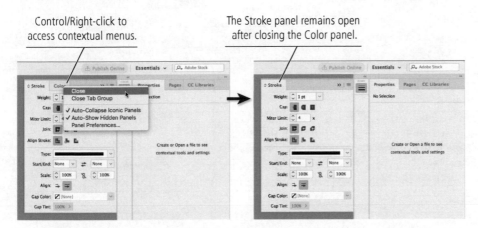

Note:

Macintosh users who do not have right-click mouse capability can press the Control key and click to access the contextual menu. You do not have to press Control and right-click to access the menus.

Note:

A panel group is still technically considered a group even if it has only one panel.

4. Click away from the expanded panel group to collapse it.

By default, expanded panels remain open until you manually close them or expand another panel in the same dock column. Because you activated the Auto-Collapse Iconic Panels option in the previous exercise, the expanded panel collapses as soon as you click away from it.

5. Choose Window>Layers.

6. Click the drop zone behind the Layers/Links panel tabs and drag left away from the dock.

Panels and panel groups can be **floated** by clicking a panel tab and dragging away from the dock. By clicking the panel group's drop zone, you can move the entire group at once.

Note:

If a panel group is floating, you can also click the group's close button to close all panels in that groups.

Macintosh

Windows

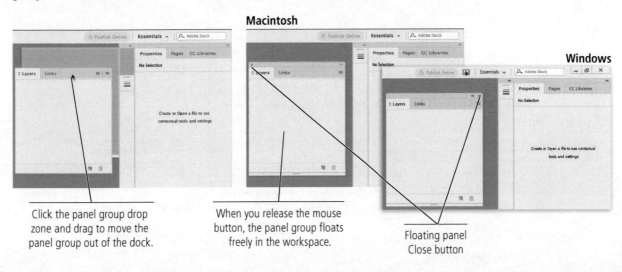

Click the panel group drop zone and drag to move the panel group out of the dock.

When you release the mouse button, the panel group floats freely in the workspace.

Floating panel Close button

Nested Tools and Keyboard Shortcuts

Any tool with an arrow in the bottom-right corner includes related tools below it. When you click a tool and hold down the mouse button (or Control/right-click a tool), the **nested tools** appear in a pop-up menu. When you choose one of the nested tools, that variation becomes the default choice in the Tools panel.

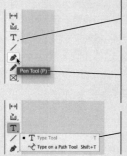

This arrow means the tool has other nested tools.

Hover the mouse cursor over the tool to see a tool tip with the name of the tool.

Click and hold down the mouse button to show the nested tools.

Most of the default InDesign tools can be accessed with a keyboard shortcut. When you hover the mouse cursor over a tool, the pop-up **tool tip** shows the name of the tool and a letter in parentheses. Pressing that letter on the keyboard activates the associated tool (unless you're working with type). If you don't see tool tips, check the Interface pane of the Preferences dialog box and set the Tool Tips menu to Fast or Normal.

Finally, if you press and hold a tool's keyboard shortcut, you can temporarily call the appropriate tool (called **spring-loaded keys**); after releasing the shortcut key, you return to the tool you were using previously.

To the right is a quick reference of nested tools, as well as the keyboard shortcut (if any) for each tool. Nested tools are shown indented.

Tools Panel Options

In addition to the basic tool set, the bottom of the Tools panel includes options that control the fill and stroke colors, options for the attribute being affected by color changes, and which screen preview mode to use.

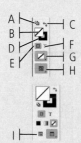

A	Fill color
B	Stroke color
C	Swap Fill and Stroke
D	Default Fill and Stroke
E	Formatting Affects Container
F	Formatting Affects Text
G	Apply Color/Gradient/None menu
H	Preview Mode menu
I	Normal view mode

In the two-column Tools panel, the position of some elements is slightly different. In addition to the position of certain elements, the Apply Color/Gradient/None options appear as individual buttons instead of consolidated into a menu, and the Normal viewing mode has a separate button from the Preview Mode menu button.

Tool Hints

The Tool Hints panel (Window>Utilities>Tool Hints) provides useful tips about the active tool, including a brief description of the tool and an explanation of the tool's behavior if you press one or more modifier keys and the tool's keyboard shortcut.

- ▶ Selection tool (V)
- ▷ Direct Selection tool (A)
- ⬚ Page tool (Shift-P)
- ↔ Gap tool (U)
- Content Collector tool (B)
  - Content Placer tool
- T. Type tool (T)
  - Type on a Path tool (Shift-T)
- / Line tool (\)
- Pen tool (P)
  - Add Anchor Point tool (=)
  - Delete Anchor Point tool (-)
  - Convert Direction Point tool (Shift-C)
- Pencil tool (N)
  - Smooth tool
  - Erase tool
- ⊠ Rectangle Frame tool (F)
  - ⊗ Ellipse Frame tool
  - ⊗ Polygon Frame tool
- ▢ Rectangle tool (M)
  - ○ Ellipse tool (L)
  - ○ Polygon tool
- ✂ Scissors tool (C)
- Free Transform tool (E)
  - ↻ Rotate tool (R)
  - Scale tool (S)
  - Shear tool (O)
- ▣ Gradient Swatch tool (G)
- Gradient Feather tool (Shift-G)
- 🗒 Note tool
- Color Theme tool (Shift-I)
  - Eyedropper tool (I)
  - Measure tool (K)
- ✋ Hand tool (H)
- 🔍 Zoom tool (Z)

7. Click the drop zone behind the floating Layers/Links panel tabs and drag right until a blue line appears at the right edge of the user interface.

Panels and panel groups can be dragged to different locations (including into different groups) by dragging the panel's tab. The target location — where the panel will reside when you release the mouse button — is identified by the blue highlight.

Note:

Drag a panel tab onto a panel group's drop zone to make the dragged panel part of the target group.

The blue line indicates where the panel group will be placed when you release the mouse button.

The expanded panel group is added as a third column in the dock.

8. Click the Properties panel tab in the left dock column. Drag the Properties panel tab until a blue line appears above the Layers/Links panel group.

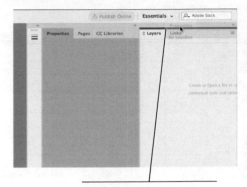
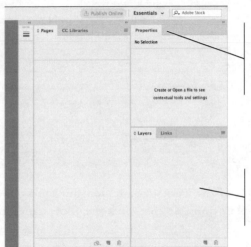

When you release the mouse button, the moved panel becomes a separate panel group in the right dock column.

Other docked panel groups expand or contract to make room for the new panel.

The blue line indicates where the panel will be placed when you release the mouse button.

9. In the right dock column, click the line separating the two panel groups and drag down until the Properties panel occupies approximately two-thirds of the space in the column.

Dragging the bottom edge of a docked panel group changes the height of that panel group. Other panels in the same column expand or shrink as necessary to fit the column.

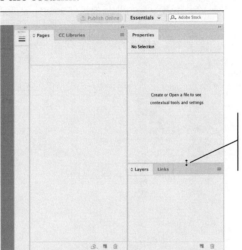

When the cursor is a double-headed arrow, click and drag to resize panel groups vertically.

Note:

Each column of the dock can be made wider or narrower by dragging the left edge of the column.

Dragging the left edge of a dock column changes the width of all panels in that column.

10. Double-click the title bar above the right dock column to collapse it to icons.

Double-clicking the dock title bar expands a collapsed column or collapses an expanded column.

Collapsed panels are referred to as **iconized** or **iconic**. When panels are iconized, they default to show only the panel icon. You can move your mouse cursor over an icon to see the panel name in a pop-up tool tip.

Double-click the title bar at the top of the dock column to collapse or expand it independently of other dock columns.

Each dock column, technically considered a separate dock, can be expanded or collapsed independently of other columns. You can also independently iconize or expand each floating panel (group).

11. Choose Window>Control.

The Control panel, which appears at the top of the workspace below the Application/Menu bar, is context sensitive, which means it shows different options depending on what is selected in the layout. You will use the Control panel extensively throughout this book.

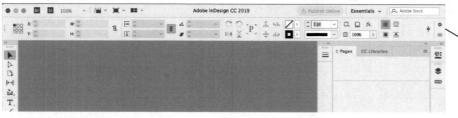

The Control panel appears immediately below the Application/Menu bar, above all other interface elements.

12. On the left side of the workspace, review the Tools panel. If you don't see all of the panel options, double-click the Tools panel title bar.

The Tools panel can be displayed as either one or two columns; double-clicking the Tools panel title bar toggles between these two modes.

Some monitors — especially laptops — might be too small to display the number of tools that are available in InDesign's Tools panel. If this is the case, you should use the two-column mode.

The Tools panel can also be floated (moved out of the dock) by clicking its title bar and dragging away from the edge of the screen. To re-dock the floating Tools panel, simply click the panel's title bar and drag back to the left edge of the screen. When a blue line highlights the edge of the workspace, releasing the mouse button places the Tools panel back in the dock. If the Tools panel is floating, you can toggle through three different modes — one-column vertical, two-column vertical, and one-row horizontal.

Double-click the Tools panel title bar to toggle between the one- and two-column layouts.

Note:

You can click the left edge of an iconized dock column and drag left to show the panel name, as well as the icon.

Note:

Double-clicking the drop zone behind an expanded panel group minimizes that group, or collapses it down to show only the panel tabs.

You can click any tab in a minimized panel group to expand the group and make the selected panel active.

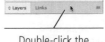

Double-click the drop zone to minimize a panel group.

Customizing Keyboard Shortcuts and Menus

Adobe CC applications have several sophisticated options for customizing the user interface, including the ability to define the available menu options and the keyboard shortcuts associated with various commands.

InDesign

At the bottom of the InDesign Edit menu, two options (Keyboard Shortcuts and Menus) open different dialog boxes for modifying the respective commands.

In the Menu Customization dialog box, clicking the visibility (eye) icon for any menu command hides it in the application menu. You can also use the Color option to define a colored background for a specific item in a menu.

In the Keyboard Shortcuts dialog box, **Product Area** lists categories of options that can be modified (primarily menu commands, but also some task-specific commands, such as manipulating objects or text).

The **Commands** window lists all options (in the selected product area) for which you can assign a keyboard shortcut.

Current Shortcuts for the selected command are listed immediately below the commands. You can use the **New Shortcut** field to assign an alternative shortcut.

If you edit the default options in these dialog boxes, you see a message asking you to save changes as a new set. You cannot override the application's default options in the Default set.

Photoshop

At the bottom of the Photoshop Edit menu, two options (Keyboard Shortcuts and Menus) open different tabs of the same dialog box.

Options in the Menus tab are the same in Photoshop as they are in the InDesign dialog box.

In the Keyboard Shortcuts tab, you can simply select an item in the command list, and then press the keys you want to use as the new shortcut. After you define custom keyboard shortcuts, you can use the Save All Changes... ( ) or Create a New Set... button ( ) to save your custom keyboard shortcuts. (You can't save changes to the Photoshop Defaults set; either button opens a dialog box where you can name the new set you are saving.)

Illustrator

In Illustrator, choosing Edit>Keyboard Shortcuts opens a dialog box where you can modify the shortcuts for menu commands and tools. If you assign a shortcut that isn't part of the default set, you have to save a custom set of shortcuts (Illustrator won't let you modify the default set of keyboard shortcuts).

Create a Saved Workspace

Over time you will develop personal preferences — for example, the Colors panel always appears at the top — based on your work habits and project needs. Rather than re-establishing every workspace element each time you return to InDesign, you can save your custom workspace settings so you can recall them with a single click.

1. Click the Workspace switcher in the Application/Menu bar and choose New Workspace.

Again, keep in mind that we list differing commands in the Macintosh/Windows format. On Macintosh, the Workspace switcher is in the Application bar; on Windows, it's in the Menu bar.

The Workspace switcher shows the name of the last-called workspace.

Note:

The Delete Workspace option opens a dialog box where you can choose a specific user-defined workspace to delete. You can't delete the default workspaces that come with the application.

2. In the New Workspace dialog box, type Portfolio. Make sure the Panel Locations option is checked and click OK.

You didn't define custom menus, so that option is not relevant in this exercise.

After saving the current workspace, the Workspace switcher shows the name of the newly saved workspace.

3. Open the Window>Workspace menu and review the options.

Saved workspaces can be accessed in the Window>Workspace submenu, as well as the Workspace switcher on the Application/Menu bar.

Keyboard shortcuts (if available) are listed on the right side of the menu.

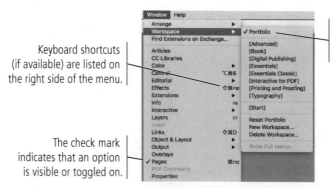

User-defined workspaces appear at the top of the menu.

The check mark indicates that an option is visible or toggled on.

Note:

If you are using a shared computer, you might want to also include your own name in the workspace name.

Note:

If a menu option is grayed out, it is not available for the active selection.

Keep in mind that calling a saved workspace restores the panels exactly as they were the last time you used that workspace. For example, if you close a panel that is part of a saved workspace, the closed panel will not be reopened the next time you call the same workspace. To restore the saved state of the workspace, including opening closed panels or repositioning moved ones, you have to use the Reset option.

4. Continue to the next exercise.

Explore the InDesign Document Views

There is far more to using InDesign than arranging panels around the workspace. What you do with those panels — and even which panels you need — depends on the type of work you are doing in a particular file. In this exercise, you open an InDesign file and explore the interface elements you'll use to create documents.

1. **In InDesign, choose File>Open. Navigate to your WIP>InterfaceCC19 folder and select sfaa1.indd in the list of available files.**

   The Open dialog box is a system-standard navigation dialog box.

2. **Press Shift, and then click sfaa5.indd in the list of files.**

   Pressing Shift allows you to select multiple contiguous (consecutive) files in the list. You can also press Command/Control to select and open non-contiguous files.

Note:

Press Command/Control-O to access the Open dialog box.

Note:

On Windows, file extensions might not be visible in the Open dialog box.

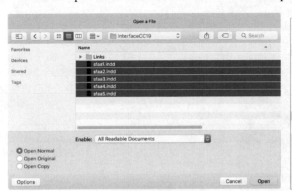
Macintosh

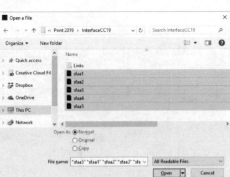
Windows

One final reminder: we list differing commands in the Macintosh/Windows format. On Macintosh, you need to press the Command key; on Windows, press the Control key. (We will not repeat this explanation every time different commands are required for the different operating systems.)

3. **Click Open to open all five selected files. If you get any warnings about modified images, click the Update Links button.**

   This warning sometimes occurs when opening files that were compressed in a zip archive (especially on Windows systems). You might not see this warning.

   The concept of linked files will be explained in depth in later projects. For now, simply click the Update Links button.

4. **If you see any Profile or Policy Mismatch warnings, click OK.**

   InDesign files open in the document window. Across the top of the document window, each open document is represented by a separate tab; the document tabs show the file name and current view percentage.

Note:

If the file name includes the word "(Converted)" in the document tab, it was created in a previous version of InDesign.

The active file tab is lighter than the others.

5. **Click the sfaa2.indd tab to make that document active.**

6. **Click the Zoom Level field in the Application/Menu bar and change the view percentage to 200.**

    Different people prefer larger or smaller view percentages, depending on a number of factors (eyesight, monitor size, and so on). As you complete the projects in this book, you'll see our screen captures zoom in or out as necessary to show you the most relevant part of a particular file. In most cases, we do not tell you the specific view percentage to use, unless it is specifically required for the work being done.

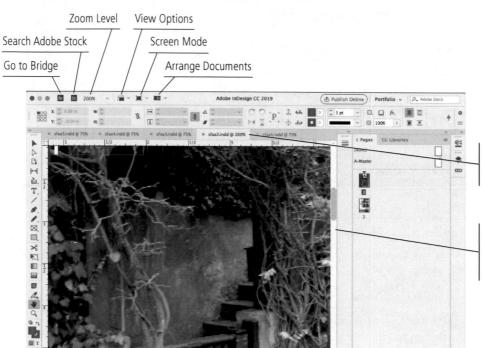

Search Adobe Stock — Zoom Level — View Options — Screen Mode — Go to Bridge — Arrange Documents

Click the tab to activate a specific file in the document window.

Changing the view percentage of the file does not affect the size of the document window.

7. **Choose View>Fit Page in Window.**

    Fit Page in Window automatically calculates view percentage based on the size of the document window.

These six options affect the view percentage of a file.

8. **Click the Zoom tool in the Tools panel. Click in the document window and drag a marquee around the logo in the top-left corner.**

Dragging a marquee with the Zoom tool enlarges the selected area to fill the document window.

The area of the marquee enlarges to fill the document window.

Summing up InDesign View Options

Most InDesign projects require some amount of zooming in and out to various view percentages, as well as navigating around the document within its window. As we show you how to complete various stages of the workflow, we usually won't tell you when to change your view percentage, because that's largely a matter of personal preference. However, you should understand the different options for navigating an InDesign file so you can easily, and efficiently, get to what you want.

View Menu

The View menu provides options for changing the view percentage. You should also become familiar with the keyboard shortcuts for these commands:

Zoom In	Command/Control-equals (=)
Zoom Out	Command/Control-minus (-)
Fit Page in Window	Command/Control-0 (zero)
Fit Spread in Window	Command-Option-0/Control-Alt-0
Actual Size (100%)	Command/Control-1
Entire Pasteboard	Command-Option-Shift-0/Control-Alt-Shift-0

Zoom Level Field/Menu

You can use the Zoom Level field in the Application/Menu bar to type a specific view percentage, or you can use the attached menu to choose from the predefined view percentage steps.

Zoom Tool

You can click with the **Zoom tool** to increase the view percentage in specific, predefined intervals (the same intervals you see in the View Percentage menu in the bottom-left corner of the document window). Pressing Option/Alt with the Zoom tool allows you to zoom out in the same predefined percentages. If you drag a marquee with the Zoom tool, you can zoom into a specific location; the area surrounded by the marquee fills the available space in the document window.

Hand Tool

Whatever your view percentage, you can use the **Hand tool** to drag the file around in the document window, including scrolling from one page to another. The Hand tool only changes what is visible in the window; it has no effect on the actual content of the file.

9. With the Zoom tool selected, Option/Alt-click in the document window.

One final reminder: When commands are different for the Macintosh and Windows operating systems, we include the different commands in the Macintosh/Windows format. In this case, Macintosh users should press the Option key while clicking; Windows users should press the Alt key.

Clicking with the Zoom tool enlarges the view percentage in specific, predefined steps. Pressing Option/Alt while clicking with the Zoom tool reduces the view percentage in the reverse sequence of the same percentages.

Note:

You can set the view-ing percentage of an InDesign document to any value from 5% to 4000%.

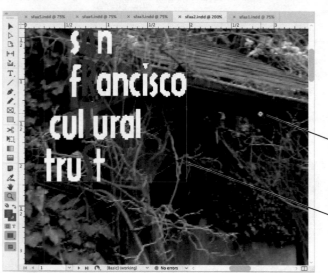

With the Zoom tool active, pressing Option/Alt changes the cursor to the Zoom Out icon.

Option/Alt-clicking with the Zoom tool reduces the view percentage in the predefined sequence of percentages.

10. Click the Hand tool near the bottom of the Tools panel.

11. Click in the document, hold down the mouse button, and drag around.

The Hand tool is a very easy and convenient option for changing the visible area of an image in the document window.

Note:

Press the Z key to access the Zoom tool.

Press the H key to access the Hand tool.

Hand tool cursor

Note:

If you click and hold down the mouse button when the Hand tool is active, the page zooms out, and a red "view box" appears. You can drag the view box and release the mouse button to recenter the view on the area inside the view box.

12. **Choose View>Display Performance>High Quality Display.**

You might have noticed that the images in this file look very bad (they are badly bitmapped). This is even more evident when you zoom in to a high view percentage. By default, InDesign displays a low-resolution preview of placed images to save time when the screen redraws (i.e., every time you change something). Fortunately, however, you have the option to preview the full-resolution images placed in a file.

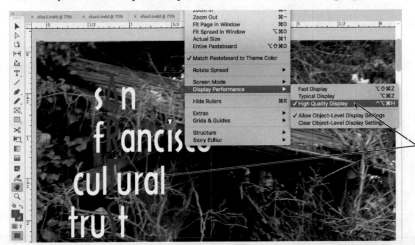

Using the High Quality Display, images do not show the bitmapping of the default low-resolution previews.

Controlling Display Performance   FOUNDATIONS

By default, files display in the document window using the Typical display performance settings. In the Display Performance pane of the Preferences dialog box, you can change the Default View settings (Fast, Typical, or High Quality). In the Adjust View Settings section, individual sliders control the display of raster images, vector graphics, and objects with transparency.

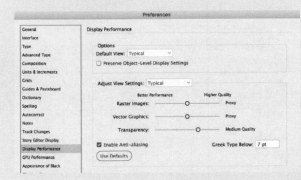

In the layout, you can change the document display performance using the View>Display Performance menu.

If **Allow Object-Level Display Settings** is checked in the View>Display Performance submenu, you can also change the preview for a specific image in the Object>Display Performance submenu or (using the object contextual menu).

To remove object-level settings, choose **Clear Object-Level Display Settings**. (Object-level display settings are maintained only while the file remains open; if you want to save the file with specific object-level display settings, check the **Preserve Object-Level Display Settings** option in the Preferences dialog box.)

Fast displays gray boxes in place of graphics.

Typical shows the low-resolution proxy images.

High-quality shows the full resolution of placed files.

13. **Using the Selection tool, click the background image to select it. Control/right-click the selected image and choose Display Performance> Typical Display from the contextual menu.**

Control/right-clicking an object on the page opens a contextual menu, which make it easy to access item-specific options.

In the View menu, the Allow Object-Level Display Settings option is active by default (see the image in the previous step); this means you can change the display of individual objects on the page.

Note:

Macintosh users who do not have right-click mouse capability can press the Control key and click to access the contextual menu. You do not have to press Control and right-click to access the menus.

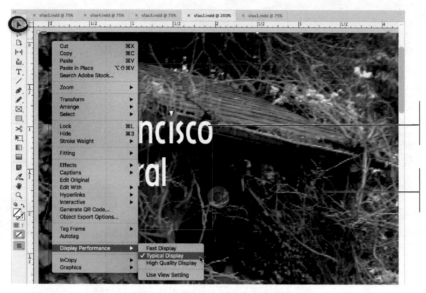

High-Quality Display is especially evident where sharp lines exist.

Typical Display uses a low-resolution preview of placed images.

14. **Choose View>Fit Page in Window to see the entire page.**

15. **In the Pages panel, double-click the Page 2 icon to show that page in the document window.**

The Pages panel is the easiest way to move from one page to another in a multi-page document. You will use this panel extensively as you complete the projects in this book.

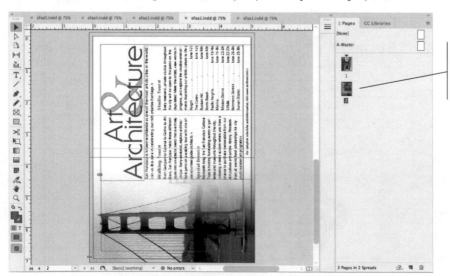

Double-click a page icon to display that page in the document window.

16. **Control/right-click the Page 2 icon in the Pages panel and choose Page Attributes>Rotate Spread View>90° CW from the contextual menu.**

Rotating the view only changes the display of the page; the actual page remains unchanged in the file. This option allows you to work more easily on objects or pages that are oriented differently than the overall document. In this example, the front side of the postcard has portrait orientation, but the mailer side has landscape orientation.

Note:

You can also rotate page views using the options in the View>Rotate Spread menu.

Pages with a rotated view are identified in the Pages panel.

The rotated display makes it easier to work on pages with orientations different from the document definition.

17. **Continue to the next exercise.**

Explore the Arrangement of Multiple Documents

In many cases, you will need to work with more than one layout at the same time. InDesign incorporates a number of options for arranging multiple documents. We designed the following simple exercise so you can explore these options.

1. **With sfaa2.indd active, choose Window>Arrange>Float in Window.**

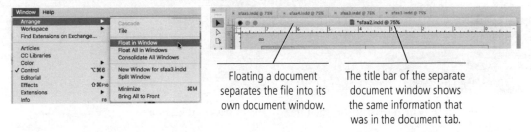

Floating a document separates the file into its own document window.

The title bar of the separate document window shows the same information that was in the document tab.

When multiple document windows are open, two options in the Window>Arrange menu allow you to cascade or tile the document windows. You can separate all open files by choosing Window>Arrange>Float All in Windows.

2. **In the Application/Menu bar, click the Arrange Documents button to open the panel of defined arrangements.**

If the Application Frame is not active on a Macintosh, the Application bar must be visible to access the Arrange Documents button.

3. Click the 2 Up button in the Arrange Documents panel.

The defined arrangements provide a number of options for tiling multiple open files within the available workspace. These arrangements manage all open files, including those in floating windows.

The Consolidate All button (top left) restores all floating documents into a single tabbed document window. The remaining buttons in the top row separate all open files into separate document windows ,and then arrange the different windows as indicated.

The lower options use a specific number of floating documents (2-Up, 3-Up, etc.). If more files are open than an option indicates, the extra files are consolidated as tabs in the first document window.

The Arrange Documents panel includes a number of tiling options for arranging multiple open files in the workspace.

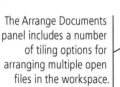

The appearance of each icon suggests the result of that option.

Rolling your mouse cursor over an icon shows the arrangement name in a tool tip.

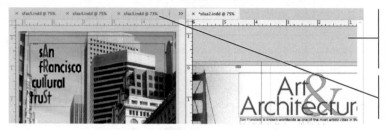

The 2-Up arrangement divides the document window in half, as indicated by the button icon.

Extra documents remain as tabs in the left document window.

4. Click the sfaa2.indd document tab and drag left until a blue highlight appears around the document tabs in the other panel.

When you release the mouse button, all of the open files are again part of the same document window.

5. **Click the Screen Mode button in the Application/Menu bar and choose Preview.**

The files you explored in this project were saved in Normal screen mode. In Normal mode, you can see all nonprinting elements, including guides and frame edges (if those are toggled on). You can now also see the pasteboard surrounding the defined page area; your development work is not limited by the defined page size.

Preview screen mode surrounds the page with a neutral gray background. Page guides, frame edges, and other nonprinting areas are not visible in the Preview mode.

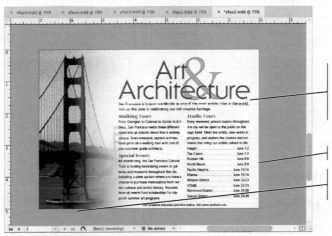

In Preview mode, all nonprinting elements (frame edges, guides, etc.), are hidden.

Page edge

All elements past the page edge are hidden.

6. **Click the Screen Mode button at the bottom of the Tools panel and choose Bleed from the pop-up menu.**

This menu has the same options as the button in the Application/Menu bar. As you will learn throughout this book, there is almost always more than one way to accomplish a particular goal in InDesign.

The Bleed screen mode is an extension of the Preview mode; it shows an extra area (which was defined when the document was originally set up) around the page edge. This bleed area is a required part of print document design — objects that are supposed to print right up to the edge of the page must extend past the page edge, usually 1/8″ or more. (Bleed requirements and setup are explained in Project 7: Letterhead Design.)

Note:

By default, the pasteboard matches the color of that you defined for the user interface in the Interface pane of the Preferences dialog box. If you uncheck the Match Pasteboard to Theme Color option, the pasteboard is white.

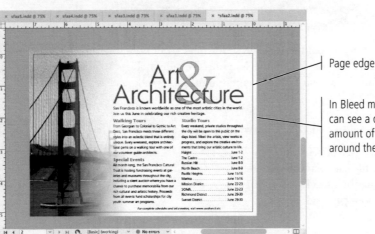

Page edge

In Bleed mode, you can see a defined amount of space around the page edge.

7. Using either Screen Mode button, choose the Presentation mode.

Presentation mode fills the entire screen with the active spread. By default, the area around the page is solid black. You can press W to change the surrounding area to white, or press G to change it to neutral gray. In Presentation mode, clicking anywhere on the screen shows the next spread; Shift-clicking shows the previous spread.

In Presentation mode, the page, surrounded by solid black, fills the entire screen.

8. Press ESC to exit Presentation mode.

9. Click the Close button on the active document tab.

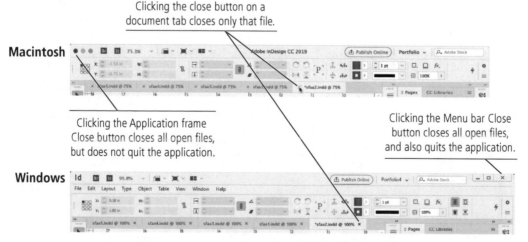

Clicking the close button on a document tab closes only that file.

Macintosh

Clicking the Application frame Close button closes all open files, but does not quit the application.

Clicking the Menu bar Close button closes all open files, and also quits the application.

Windows

Closing the Macintosh Application frame closes all open files, but does not quit the application. Clicking the Close button on the Windows Menu bar closes all open files *and* quits the application. To close open files without quitting, you have to manually close each open file.

10. Click Don't Save/No when asked if you want to save changes to sfaa2.indd.

In the document tab, an asterisk before the file name indicates that the file has been changed, but not yet saved. By rotating the spread view on Page 2, the file has technically been changed. InDesign automatically asks if you want to save any file that has been changed before closing it.

11. Close (without saving) all but the sfaa5.indd file.

12. Continue to the next exercise.

Note:

An asterisk before the file name in the document tab indicates that the file has been changed and not yet saved.

Note:

You can also close the active file by pressing Command/Control-W.

Explore the Illustrator User Interface

Illustration is a very broad career path, with potential applications in virtually any industry. In other words, mastering the tools and techniques of Adobe Illustrator can significantly improve your range of career options. Within the general category of illustration, many Illustrator experts specialize in certain types of work — logo design, technical drawing, and editorial illustration are only a few of the subcategories of artwork you can create with Illustrator.

Adobe Illustrator is the industry-standard application for creating digital drawings or **vector images** (graphics composed of mathematically defined lines instead of pixels). Although not intended as a page-layout application, you can also use the tools in Illustrator to combine type, graphics, and images into a single cohesive design. Many people create flyers, posters, and other one-page projects entirely within Illustrator. With the ability to work with multiple artboards (explained in Project 3: Identity Package), we will likely see more of this type of Illustrator work in the future.

1. **With sfaa5.indd open (from your WIP>InterfaceCC19 folder), use the Selection tool (the black arrow) to select the "SFCT" graphic on Page 1.**

2. **Control/right-click the selected object and choose Edit Original from the contextual menu.**

   Choosing Edit Original opens the placed file in its native application. This graphic is a native Adobe Illustrator file (with the extension ".ai"), so it opens in the latest possible version of Adobe Illustrator. If Adobe Illustrator is not already running on your computer, it might take a moment while the application launches.

   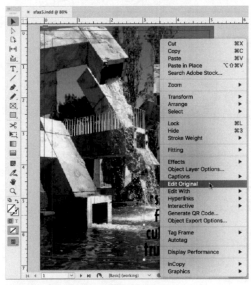

3. **Macintosh users: Open the Window menu in Illustrator. If Application Frame is not checked (active), choose that command in the menu.**

   This option should be checked.

Note

You can press Command-Option-Shift/Control-Alt-Shift while launching the application to reset the Illustrator preferences.

4. **Choose Essentials in the Workspace switcher, then choose Reset Essentials.**

Remember that in InDesign, calling a workspace restores it to its last-used state; to restore the saved state of a workspace, you have to choose Reset [Workspace] in the Workspace switcher. The same is true of Illustrator.

Note:

The Manage Work-spaces option opens a dialog box where you can rename or delete user-defined custom workspaces. You can't alter the default work-spaces that come with the application.

Illustrator panels are arranged and accessed using the same techniques you already learned, and saved workspaces in Illustrator serve the same function as those in InDesign. The Essentials workspace includes the Tools panel on the left of the screen, the Control panel at the top, and a set of docked panels on the right. (The Tools panel defaults to one- or two-column mode, depending on the size of your screen.)

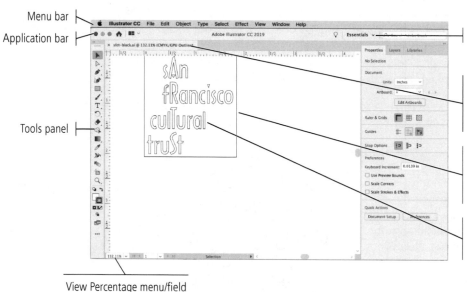

Menu bar

Application bar

Tools panel

Workspace switcher

The document tab shows the active file name, view percentage, color space, and current viewing mode.

The **artboard** is essentially the digital page, or the area in which artwork should be created or placed.

In Outline viewing mode, only the object's wireframe is visible.

View Percentage menu/field

5. **With nothing selected in the open file, review the options in the Properties panel.**

The Properties panel is context sensitive, which means it provides access to different options, depending on which tool is active and what is selected in the document.

When nothing is selected in the file, you can use the Properties panel to change a number of settings related to the overall file. The most important options open the Document Setup and Preferences dialog boxes (more about these specific elements in the projects).

Document and application specific options are available when nothing is selected.

6. **With the sfct-black.ai file open, choose File>Open.**

In many cases, you will open Illustrator files from directly within an InDesign file (as you did for the sfct-black.ai file). Of course, you can also simply open a file from directly within Illustrator. How you open a file does affect what happens to instances that are placed in an InDesign layout. In Project 10 you will see how opening a file from within an InDesign layout offers distinct advantages in an integrated workflow.

7. **Navigate to the WIP>InterfaceCC19>Links folder. Click sfaa.ai to select that file, and then click Open.**

This file was saved in Preview mode, which shows the artwork in color.

Note:

Macintosh users: If you turn off the Application frame, the new document will have its own title bar.

Note:

You can zoom an Illustrator document from 3.13% to 6400%.

8. **Click the Selection tool at the top of the Tools panel to make that tool active, then click any of the black letter shapes at the bottom of the artwork.**

The Selection tool (the black arrow) is used to select entire objects in the file. The Properties panel shows the attributes of the selected object (in this case, a group).

Selection tool

The Properties panel shows options for the selected object.

Selected object (indicated by **bounding-box handles** on all four sides of the object)

Bounding-box handles

9. **Choose Window>Control to open the Control panel.**

The Control panel, which appears at the top of the interface, is another context-sensitive tool that shows options related to the selected object. In this case, the entire set of black letter shapes is a group, so the Control panel shows options related to groups.

The Control panel shows options and attributes of the selected group.

10. **Click anywhere in the area outside the artboard to deselect the text group.**

11. **Click the button at the bottom of the Tools panel to show the screen mode options.**

Illustrator has three **screen modes**, which change the way the document window displays on the screen. The default mode, which you saw when you opened these three files, is called Normal Screen mode.

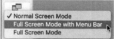

12. **Choose Full Screen Mode with Menu Bar from the Screen Mode menu.**

All open files are listed at the bottom of the Window menu. You can use those options to navigate from one file to another, which is particularly useful if you're working in Full Screen Mode with Menu Bar because document tabs are not visible in this mode.

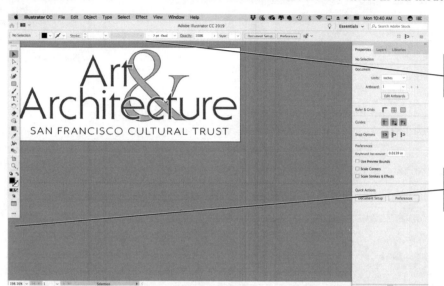

In Full Screen Mode with Menu Bar, the document tabs are hidden.

The document window extends behind the docked panels.

More About the Illustrator Control Panel

What you see in the Control panel depends on the size of your monitor (or the size of your Application frame if you've made it smaller than your monitor). When working with a smaller space, some options are not available directly in the panel; instead, you have to use the hot-text links (identified by an underline) to open pop-up versions of the related panel.

In the images below, for example, you have to click the Paragraph hot-text link in the top version to open the pop-up panel and access the paragraph alignment options. In the wider version, you can access three paragraph alignment options directly in the Control panel.

Regardless of your interface width, options in the Control panel are a limited subset related to the selected object. You can click any hot-text link to open the related pop-up panel and access additional options. Clicking the Y link, for example, opens the Transform panel with additional object transformation options.

Click these hot-text links to open the related pop-up panel.

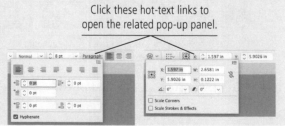

Customizing Illustrator Tools Panels

The Tools panel can be customized to show only certain tools, making it easier and quicker to find what you need to complete a given task. The built-in Essentials workspace, for example, includes only the more commonly used drawing tools.

The Find More Tools button at the bottom of the Tools panel provides access to the entire toolset, regardless of which tools are currently available in the Tools panel.

Find More Tools

Tools that are already in the Tools panel appear grayed out in the pop-up menu. You can drag additional tools into the Tools panel from the menu. A blue line between existing tools shows where the tool will be added as a new, first-level tool. A blue highlight around an existing tool indicates it will be added as a new nested tool in that location.

You can also drag to reposition existing tools within the panel. As with adding new tools, the blue highlight identifies the new location of the tool.

You can remove a tool from the Tools panel by simply dragging it away from the panel (as indicated by the minus sign in the cursor icon).

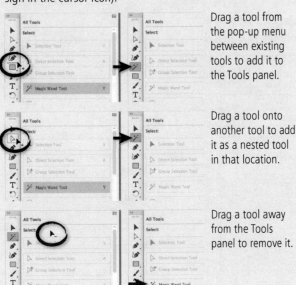

Drag a tool from the pop-up menu between existing tools to add it to the Tools panel.

Drag a tool onto another tool to add it as a nested tool in that location.

Drag a tool away from the Tools panel to remove it.

In addition to modifying the built-in Tools panels, you can also create custom Tools panels that you can recall at any time.

The New Toolbar option in the Find More Tools panel menu opens a dialog box where you can name the new panel. (You can also choose Window>Toolbars>New Toolbar.)

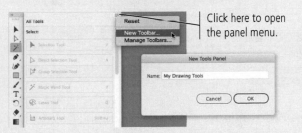

Click here to open the panel menu.

Clicking OK creates a new empty Tools panel; the large plus-sign icon indicates that you have not yet added any tools to it. You can click the Find More Tools button at the bottom of the new panel to add tools. The process is the same as adding reorganizing, and removing tools from the basic Tools panel.

Find More Tools

Changes to a custom Tools panel are saved automatically. If you close a custom panel (by clicking the panel's Close button), the same tools appear in the same position when you reopen it. Existing custom Tools panels can always be opened in the Window>Toolbars submenu.

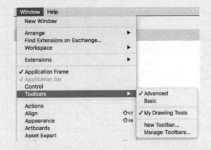

Choosing Window>Toolbars>Manage Toolbars opens a dialog box where you can rename or delete custom panels.

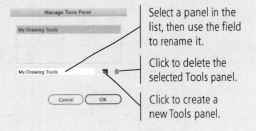

Select a panel in the list, then use the field to rename it.

Click to delete the selected Tools panel.

Click to create a new Tools panel.

In the Illustrator Tools panel, tool icons that show a small black arrow in the lower-right corner have **nested tools**. You can access nested tools by clicking the primary tool and holding down the mouse button until a pop-up menu shows the nested variations, or Control/right-clicking the tool in the panel.

If you hover your mouse over a tool, a pop-up **tool tip** shows the name of the tool, as well as

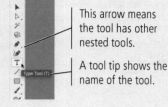

This arrow means the tool has other nested tools.

A tool tip shows the name of the tool.

the associated keyboard shortcut if one exists. If a tool has a defined shortcut, pressing that key activates the associated tool. (If you don't see tool tips, check the Show Tool Tips option in the General pane of the Preferences dialog box.)

If you drag the mouse cursor to the bar on the right of the nested-tool menu, the nested-tool options separate into their own floating toolboxes, so you can more easily access the nested variations. (The primary tool is not removed from the main Tools panel.)

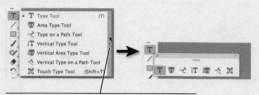

Hold down the mouse button, drag to here, then release the mouse button to tear off a separate panel with all the related tools.

The chart below offers a quick reference of nested tools, as well as the keyboard shortcut (if any) for each tool. Nested tools are shown indented.

- ▶ Selection tool (V)
  - ▷ Direct Selection tool (A)
  - ▷⁺ Group Selection tool
- ⁒ Magic Wand tool (Y)
- ⌦ Lasso tool (Q)
- ✎ Pen tool (P)
  - ✎⁺ Add Anchor Point tool (+)
  - ✎⁻ Delete Anchor Point tool (-)
  - ⌐ Anchor Point tool (Shift-C)
- ✐ Curvature tool (Shift-`)
- T Type tool (T)
  - ⊞ Area Type tool
  - ⌁ Type on a Path tool
  - ⌄T Vertical Type tool
  - ⌄⊞ Vertical Area Type tool
  - ⌄ Vertical Type on a Path tool
  - ꒰ꓬ Touch Type tool (Shift-T)
- / Line Segment tool (\)
  - ⌒ Arc tool
  - ◎ Spiral tool
  - ⊞ Rectangular Grid tool
  - ⊕ Polar Grid tool

- ▢ Rectangle tool (M)
  - ▢ Rounded Rectangle tool
  - ◯ Ellipse tool (L)
  - ◯ Polygon tool
  - ☆ Star tool
  - ◎ Flare tool
- ✏ Paintbrush tool (B)
  - ✑ Blob Brush tool (Shift-B)
- ✑ Shaper tool (Shift-N)
  - ✎ Pencil tool (N)
  - ⸝ Smooth tool
  - ✎ Path Eraser tool
  - ⤜ Join tool
- ◆ Eraser tool (Shift-E)
  - ✂ Scissors tool (C)
  - ✎ Knife tool
- ↻ Rotate tool (R)
  - ▷◁ Reflect tool (O)
- ⊡ Scale tool (S)
  - ✎ Shear tool
  - ꒰ Reshape tool

- ⌇ Width tool (Shift-W)
  - ◤ Warp tool (Shift-R)
  - ✦ Twirl tool
  - ✳ Pucker tool
  - ✦ Bloat tool
  - ◣ Scallop tool
  - ✦ Crystallize tool
  - ◣ Wrinkle tool
- ✦ Puppet Warp tool
- ⊡ Free Transform tool (E)
- ⌖ Shape Builder tool (Shift-M)
  - ◪ Live Paint Bucket tool (K)
  - ◪ Live Paint Selection tool (Shift-L)
- ◫ Perspective Grid tool (Shift-P)
  - ⌐ Perspective Selection tool (Shift-V)
- ▦ Mesh tool (U)
- ▮ Gradient tool (G)
- ✒ Eyedropper tool (I)
  - ✎ Measure tool
- ⌾ Blend tool (W)

- ◳ Symbol Sprayer tool (Shift-S)
  - ◌ Symbol Shifter tool
  - ◌ Symbol Scruncher tool
  - ◌ Symbol Sizer tool
  - ◌ Symbol Spinner tool
  - ◌ Symbol Stainer tool
  - ◌ Symbol Screener tool
  - ◌ Symbol Styler tool
- ▦ Column Graph tool (J)
  - ▦ Stacked Column Graph tool
  - ▬ Bar Graph tool
  - ▬ Stacked Bar Graph tool
  - ⬈ Line Graph tool
  - ⬈ Area Graph tool
  - ⬚ Scatter Graph tool
  - ◕ Pie Graph tool
  - ◎ Radar Graph tool
- ◳ Artboard tool (Shift-O)
- ✎ Slice tool (Shift-K)
  - ⤢ Slice Selection tool
- ✋ Hand tool (H)
  - ⬚ Print Tiling tool
- 🔍 Zoom tool (Z)

13. **Click the Screen Mode button at the bottom of the Tools panel and choose Full Screen Mode.**

Note:

Press F to switch between screen modes.

In Full Screen Mode, the Menu bar, title bar, and all panels are hidden.

Move your mouse cursor to the edges of the screen to temporarily show docked panels.

14. **Press the Escape key to exit Full Screen Mode and return to Normal Screen Mode.**

15. **Click the Close button on the sfaa.ai tab to close that file.**

As in InDesign, all open Illustrator files can be accessed and closed using the document tabs

at the top of the document window. A file does not need to be active before you close it using the document tab.

16. **Click the Close button on the sfct-black.ai document tab. If asked to save changes, click Don't Save in the warning message.**

17. **Return to the open InDesign file (sfaa5.indd) and then continue to the next exercise.**

As we show you how to complete different stages of the workflow, we usually won't tell you when to change your view percentage because that's largely a matter of personal preference. However, you should understand the different options for navigating around an Illustrator file so you can efficiently get to what you want.

To change the file view percentage, you can type a specific percent in the **View Percentage field** of the document window or choose from the predefined options in the menu.

You can also click with the **Zoom tool** to increase the view percentage in specific, predefined intervals (the same intervals you see in the View Percentage menu in the bottom-left corner of the document window). Pressing Option/Alt with the Zoom tool allows you to zoom out in the same defined percentages.

By default, Animated Zoom is active when GPU Preview is enabled; clicking and dragging with the Zoom tool dynamically changes the view percentage depending on which way you drag (right to enlarge or left to reduce).

If you turn off Animated Zoom in the Performance pane of the Preferences dialog box, you can drag a marquee with the Zoom tool to zoom into a specific location; the area surrounded by the marquee fills the available space in the document window.

The **View menu** also provides options for changing view percentage. (The Zoom In and Zoom Out options step through the same predefined view percentages as clicking with the Zoom tool.)

Zoom In	Command/Control-plus (+)
Zoom Out	Command/Control-minus (-)
Fit Artboard in Window	Command/Control-0 (zero)
Fit All in Window	Command-Option-0/Control-Alt-0 (zero)
Actual Size (100%)	Command/Control-1

Whatever your view percentage, you can use the **Hand tool** to drag the file around in the document window. The tool changes what is visible in the window; it has no effect on objects in the file. If the insertion point is not flashing, you can press the Spacebar to temporarily access the Hand tool; when the insertion point is placed, you can press the Option/Alt key to temporarily access the Hand tool.

Using the Navigator Panel

The **Navigator panel** (Window>Navigator) is another method of adjusting what you see, including the view percentage and the specific area that is visible in the document window. The Navigator panel shows a thumbnail of the active file; a red rectangle (called the Proxy Preview Area) represents exactly how much of the document shows in the document window. You can drag the proxy in the panel to change the visible portion of the image in the document window.

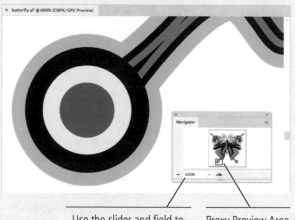

Use the slider and field to change the view percentage.

Proxy Preview Area

Working with Saved Views

Named views can be helpful if you repeatedly return to the same area and view percentage. By choosing View>New View, you can save the current view with a specific name.

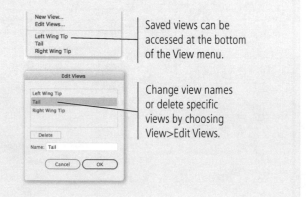

Saved views can be accessed at the bottom of the View menu.

Change view names or delete specific views by choosing View>Edit Views.

Explore the Photoshop User Interface

Adobe Photoshop is the industry-standard application for working with pixels — both manipulating existing ones and creating new ones. Many Photoshop experts specialize in certain types of work. Photo retouching, artistic painting, image compositing, color correction, and website design are only a few subcategories of work you can create with Photoshop. Our goal in this book is to teach you how to use the available tools to create different types of work that you might encounter in your professional career.

Although not intended as a layout-design application, you can also use the Photoshop tools to combine type, graphics, and images into a finished design. Many people create advertisements, book covers, and other projects entirely in Photoshop. Others argue that Photoshop should never be used for layout design, maintaining that InDesign is the preferred page-layout application.

Project 4: Music CD Artwork, and Project 5: Car Magazine Cover result in finished composite designs. We do not advocate doing *all* or even *most* layout composite work in Photoshop. However, because many people use the application to create composite designs, we feel the projects in this book portray a realistic workflow. Project 6: Museum Image Correction, focuses specifically on image manipulation or creation — which is the true heart of the application.

As you move forward in your career, it will be your choice to determine which application is appropriate for which task; it is our job to teach you how to use the tools so you can make the best possible decision when that need arises.

1. **With sfaa5.indd open in InDesign, use the Selection tool (the black arrow) to select the background image on Page 1.**

2. **Control/right-click the selected image and choose Edit With>Adobe Photoshop CC 2019 in the contextual menu.**

   If you have more than one version of an application installed on your machine, each version is listed in the Edit With menu (as you can see in our screen capture).

   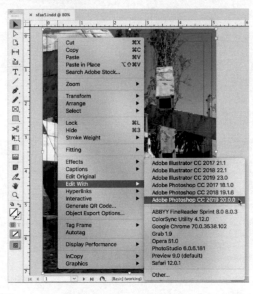

3. **If you see any Profile Mismatch messages, click OK.**

   You will learn about color managing Photoshop images in Project 6: Museum Image Correction.

4. **Macintosh users: Open the Window menu. If Application Frame is not checked (active), choose that command in the menu.**

5. **Choose Essentials in the Workspace switcher, then choose Reset Essentials to restore the default user interface settings.**

   Photoshop panels are arranged and accessed using the same techniques you already learned, and saved workspaces in Photoshop serve the same function as those in InDesign. Also like InDesign, calling a saved workspace calls the last-used version of it; you have to use the Reset option to call the saved version of the workspace.

Menu bar

Application title bar

Options bar

Workspace switcher

Tools panel

View Percentage field

6. **Highlight the current value in the View Percentage field (in the bottom-left corner of the document window). Type 45, then press Return/Enter.**

Changing the view percentage of the file does not affect the size of the document window.

Note:

In Photoshop, the Arrange Documents options are available in the Window>Arrange submenu.

7. Choose View>100%.

These options affect the file's view percentage.

8. Click the Hand tool (near the bottom of the Tools panel). Click in the document window, hold down the mouse button, and drag around.

The Hand tool is a very easy and convenient option for changing the area of an image that is currently visible in the document window.

If the Scroll All Windows option is checked in the Options bar, dragging in one window affects the visible area of all open files.

Hand tool cursor

Note:

Depending on what you or a previous user did in Photoshop, the Hand tool might be nested under the Rotate View tool. Both tools appear in the spot immediately above the Zoom tool near the bottom of the Tools panel.

9. **Click the Zoom tool in the Tools panel. Press Option/Alt, and then click anywhere in the document window.**

Clicking with the Zoom tool enlarges the view percentage in specific, predefined percentage steps. Pressing Option/Alt while clicking with the Zoom tool reduces the view percentage in the reverse sequence of the same percentages.

When the Zoom tool is active, pressing Option/Alt changes the cursor to the Zoom Out icon.

10. **In the Options bar, click the Fit Screen button.**

The Options bar appears by default at the top of the workspace below the Menu bar. It is context sensitive, which means it provides different options depending on which tool is active. When the Zoom tool is active:

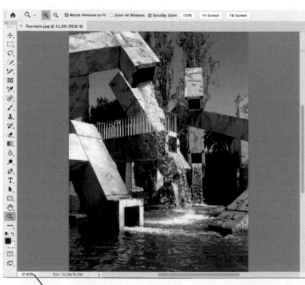

- If Resize Windows to Fit is checked, zooming in a floating window affects the size of the actual document window.

- If Zoom All Windows is checked, zooming in one window affects the view percentage of all open files.

- Scrubby Zoom enables dynamic image zooming depending on the direction you drag in the document window.

- The 100% button changes the view percentage to 100%.

- The Fit Screen option changes the image view to the percentage necessary to show the entire image in the document window. This has the same effect as choosing Window>Fit on Screen.

- The Fill Screen button changes the image view to the percentage necessary to fill the available space in the document window.

The Fit Screen command automatically calculates view percentage based on the size of the document window.

11. **In the Tools panel, choose the Rotate View tool (nested under the Hand tool). Click in the top half of the document window and drag right to turn the document clockwise.**

The Rotate View tool turns an image without permanently altering the orientation of the file; the actual image data remains unchanged. This tool allows you to more easily work on objects or elements that are not oriented horizontally — for example, working with text that appears on an angle in the final image.

In the Options bar, you can type a specific angle in the Rotation Angle field or click the rotation proxy icon to dynamically rotate the view. At any time, you can click the Reset View button to restore the original rotation (0°) of the image. If Rotate All Windows is checked, dragging in one window affects the view angle of all open files.

Note:

If you are unable to rotate the image view, your graphics processor does not support OpenGL — a hardware/software combination that makes it possible to work with complex graphics operations. If your computer does not support OpenGL, you will not be able to use a number of Photoshop features (including the Rotate View tool).

Rotate View tool cursor

The red arrow of the compass indicates the image's original North.

12. **In the Options bar, click the Reset View button.**

As we said, the Rotate View tool is **nondestructive** (i.e., it does not permanently affect the pixels in the image). You can easily use the tool's options to define a specific view angle or to restore an image to its original orientation.

Resetting the view restores the image's original orientation.

Note:

*Like Illustrator, Photoshop has three **screen modes** that change the way the document window displays on the screen. In Photoshop, you can access these options using the Screen Mode button in the Tools panel.*

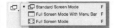

13. **Click the Close button on the fountain.jpg tab.**

14. **Return to InDesign. Close the sfaa5.indd file without saving, and then continue to Project 1.**

In the Tools panel, tools with a small mark in the lower-right corner have **nested tools**.

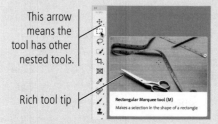

This arrow means the tool has other nested tools.

Rich tool tip

If you hover your mouse over a tool, a rich **tool tip** shows the name of the tool, keyboard shortcut (if any), a small animation related to that tool, and a link to video tutorials related to the specific tools.

You can disable overall tool tips or rich tool tips in the Tools pane of the Preferences dialog box. If you disable only rich tool tips, you would see only the tool name and keyboard shortcut when you hover over a tool.

You can access nested tools by clicking the primary tool and holding down the mouse button, or by Control/ right-clicking the primary tool to open the menu of nested options.

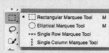

If a tool has a defined shortcut, pressing that key activates the associated tool. Most nested tools have the same shortcut as the default tool. By default, you have to press Shift plus the shortcut key to access the nested variations. You can change this behavior in the Tools pane of the Preferences dialog box by unchecking the Use Shift Key for Tool Switch option; when unchecked, you can simply press the shortcut key multiple times to cycle through variations.

Finally, if you press and hold a tool's keyboard shortcut, you can temporarily call that tool (called **spring-loaded keys**). After releasing the shortcut key, you return to the previous tool. For example, you might switch temporarily from the Brush to the Eraser tool while painting.

The following chart offers a quick reference of nested tools, as well as the shortcut (if any) for each tool. Nested tools are shown indented.

- Move tool (V)
  - Artboard tool (V)
- Rectangular Marquee tool (M)
  - Elliptical Marquee tool (M)
  - Single Row Marquee tool
  - Single Column Marquee tool
- Lasso tool (L)
  - Polygonal Lasso tool (L)
  - Magnetic Lasso tool (L)
- Quick Selection tool (W)
  - Magic Wand tool (W)
- Crop tool (C)
  - Perspective Crop tool (C)
  - Slice tool (C)
  - Slice Select tool (C)
- Frame tool (I)
- Eyedropper tool (I)
  - 3D Material Eyedropper tool (I)
  - Color Sampler tool (I)
  - Ruler tool (I)
  - Note tool (I)
  - Count tool (I)
- Spot Healing Brush tool (J)
  - Healing Brush tool (J)
  - Patch tool (J)
  - Content Aware Move tool (J)
  - Red Eye tool (J)
- Brush tool (B)
  - Pencil tool (B)
  - Color Replacement tool (B)
  - Mixer Brush tool (B)
- Clone Stamp tool (S)
  - Pattern Stamp tool (S)
- History Brush tool (Y)
  - Art History Brush tool (Y)

- Eraser tool (E)
  - Background Eraser tool (E)
  - Magic Eraser tool (E)
- Gradient tool (G)
  - Paint Bucket tool (G)
  - 3D Material Drop tool (G)
- Blur tool
  - Sharpen tool
  - Smudge tool
- Dodge tool (O)
  - Burn tool (O)
  - Sponge tool (O)
- Pen tool (P)
  - Freeform Pen tool (P)
  - Curvature Pen tool (P)
  - Add Anchor Point tool
  - Delete Anchor Point tool
  - Convert Point tool
- Horizontal Type tool (T)
  - Vertical Type tool (T)
  - Horizontal Type Mask tool (T)
  - Vertical Type Mask tool (T)
- Path Selection tool (A)
  - Direct Selection tool (A)
- Rectangle tool (U)
  - Rounded Rectangle tool (U)
  - Ellipse tool (U)
  - Polygon tool (U)
  - Line tool (U)
  - Custom Shape tool (U)
- Hand tool (H)
  - Rotate View tool (R)
- Zoom tool (Z)

Customizing the Photoshop Tools Panel

Near the bottom of the Tools panel, the Edit Toolbar button ⋯ provides access to a dialog box where you can customize the options that appear in the Tools panel. If you click and hold on this button, you can choose the Edit Toolbar option in the pop-up menu.

In the Customize Toolbar dialog box, you can select and move individual tools or entire groups of tools into the Extra Tools window. Any tools in that window are moved from their regular position in the default Tools panel to a single position, nested under the Edit Toolbar option.

You can toggle the buttons in the bottom-left corner of the dialog box to show or hide several options in the Tools panel. From left to right:

- Edit Toolbar
- Default Foreground and Background Colors
- Edit in Quick Mask Mode
- Change Screen Mode

If you choose to hide the Edit Toolbar option, any tools in the Extra Tools list are simply hidden; you will not be able to access them unless you customize the Tools panel again. (In this case, you can accomplish this task by choosing Edit>Toolbar.)

Clicking the Restore Defaults button in the Customize Toolbar dialog box resets all tools and options in the panel to their original default positions and visibility.

Click and drag tools from the Toolbar list to the Extra Tools list.

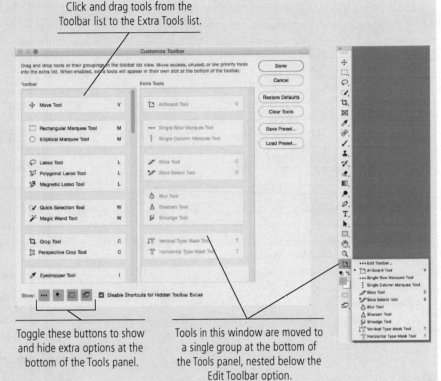

Toggle these buttons to show and hide extra options at the bottom of the Tools panel.

Tools in this window are moved to a single group at the bottom of the Tools panel, nested below the Edit Toolbar option.

Summing Up the Photoshop View Options

Most Photoshop projects require some amount of zooming in and out to various view percentages, as well as navigating around the document within its window. As we show you how to complete different stages of the workflow, we usually won't tell you when to change your view percentage because that's largely a matter of personal preference. However, you should understand the different options for navigating around a Photoshop file so you can easily and efficiently get to what you want, when you want to get there.

View Percentage Field

You can type a specific percentage in the View Percentage field in the bottom-left corner of the document window.

View Menu

The View menu also provides options for changing the view percentage, including the associated keyboard shortcuts. The Zoom In and Zoom Out options step through the same predefined view percentages the Zoom tool uses.

Zoom In	Command/Control-plus (=)
Zoom Out	Command/Control-minus (-)
Fit On Screen	Command/Control-0 (zero)
Actual Pixels (100%)	Command/Control-1

Zoom Tool

You can click with the **Zoom tool** to increase the view percentage in specific, predefined intervals. Pressing Option/Alt with the Zoom tool allows you to zoom out in the same predefined percentages. If you drag a marquee with the Zoom tool, you can zoom into a specific location; the area surrounded by the marquee fills the available space in the document window.

When the Zoom tool is active, you can also activate the Scrubby Zoom option in the Options bar. This allows you to click and drag left to reduce the view percentage, or drag right to increase the view percentage. The Scrubby Zoom option does not follow predefined stepped percentages.

Hand Tool

At any view percentage, you can use the **Hand tool** to drag the file around in the document window. The Hand tool changes only what is visible in the window; it has no effect on the actual pixels in the image.

Mouse Scroll Wheel

If your mouse has a scroll wheel, rolling the scroll wheel up or down moves the image up or down within the document window. If you press Command/Control and scroll the wheel, you can move the image right (scroll up) or left (scroll down) within the document window. You can also press Option/Alt and then scroll the wheel up to zoom in down to zoom out.

In the General pane of the Preferences dialog box, the Zoom with Scroll Wheel option is unchecked by default. If you check this option, scrolling up or down with no modifier key zooms in or out and does not move the image within the document window.

Navigator Panel

The **Navigator panel** is another method of adjusting how close your viewpoint is, and what part of the page you're currently viewing if zoomed in close enough that you're only seeing a portion of the image. The Navigator panel shows a thumbnail of the active file. A red rectangle represents exactly how much of the document shows in the document window.

Drag the red rectangle to change the visible portion of the file.

Use the slider and field at the bottom of the panel to change the view percentage.

Campground Icons

Cooper's Lake Campground is a family-oriented campground that hosts individual camping, as well as large planned events at their grounds. The owner has hired you to create a digital collection of icons that they can use to create signs, print on a variety of collateral, and place on their website.

This project incorporates the following skills:

❏ Placing raster images into an Illustrator file to use as drawing templates

❏ Creating and managing simple shapes and lines

❏ Using various tools to transform objects' color, position, and shape

❏ Cloning objects to minimize repetitive tasks

❏ Using sublayers and groups to organize and manage artwork

❏ Drawing complex shapes by combining simple shapes

PROJECT MEETING

client comments

We have a set of icons on our website, but we need to use the same artwork in other places as well — signs throughout the park, flyers that we hand out to new guests, and so on.

Our printer told us that the symbols on our website are "low res," so they can't be used for print projects. The printer also said he needs vector graphics that will scale larger and still look good. The printer suggested we hire a designer to create digital versions of the icons so we can use them for a wide variety of purposes, from large signs to small cards, to anything else that might come up.

We need you to help us figure out exactly what we need, and then create the icons for us.

art director comments

Basically, we have the icons, but they're low-resolution raster images, so they only work for the web, and they can't be enlarged. The good news is that you can use the existing icons as templates and, more or less, trace them to create the new icons.

The client needs files that can be printed cleanly and scaled from a couple of inches up to several feet. Illustrator vector files are perfect for this type of job. In fact, vector graphics get their resolution from the printer being used for a specific job, so you can scale them to any size you want without losing quality.

project objectives

To complete this project, you will:

- [ ] Use a variety of tools and techniques to create, align, and transform basic shapes

- [ ] Control objects' fill and stroke attributes

- [ ] Import raster images to use as artwork templates

- [ ] Use sublayers and groups to manage complex artwork

- [ ] Use the Line Segment tool to create a complex object from a set of straight lines

- [ ] Edit properties of Live Shapes to create finished icon artwork

- [ ] Draw and combine basic Live Shapes using the Shaper tool

- [ ] Draw complex artwork with the Pencil tool

STAGE 1 / Setting up the Workspace

There are two primary types of digital artwork: raster images and vector graphics. (**Line art**, sometimes categorized as a third type of image, is actually a type of raster image.)

Raster images are pixel-based, made up of a grid of individual **pixels** (**rasters** or **bits**) in rows and columns (called a **bitmap**). Raster files are **resolution dependent**; their resolution is determined when you scan, photograph, or create the file. As a professional graphic designer, you should have a basic understanding of the following terms and concepts:

- **Pixels per inch (ppi)** is the number of pixels in one horizontal or vertical inch of a digital raster file.

- **Lines per inch (lpi)** is the number of halftone dots produced in a linear inch by a high-resolution imagesetter, which simulates the appearance of continuous-tone color.

- **Dots per inch (dpi)** or **spots per inch (spi)** is the number of dots produced by an output device in a single line of output.

Drawing objects that you create in Illustrator are **vector graphics**, which are composed of mathematical descriptions of a series of lines and points. Vector graphics are **resolution independent**; they can be freely scaled and are output at the resolution of the output device.

 ## Create a New Document

In this project, you work with the basics of creating vector graphics in Illustrator, using a number of different drawing tools, adding color, and managing various aspects of your artwork. The first step is to create a new document for building your artwork.

1. **Download Camping_Print19_RF.zip from the Student Files web page.**

2. **Expand the ZIP archive in your WIP folder (Macintosh) or copy the archive contents into your WIP folder (Windows).**

   This results in a folder named **Camping**, which contains all of the files you need for this project. You should also use this folder to save the files you create in this project.

   If necessary, refer to Page 1 of the Interface chapter for specific information on expanding or accessing the required resource files.

3. **In Illustrator, choose File>New.**

   You have several options for creating a new file:
   - Choose File>New;
   - Use the associated keyboard shortcut, Command/Control-N; or
   - Click the Create New button in the Home workspace.

If the Home workspace is visible, click the Create New button to open the New Document dialog box.

4. Click the Print option at the top of the resulting New Document dialog box.

The New Document dialog box offers a number of preset sizes and prebuilt starter templates, broken into categories based on the intended output.

When you choose the Print category, you see common page sizes such as Letter and Legal. The Print presets automatically default to the CMYK color mode and 300 ppi raster effects, which are required for commercial printing applications. For all other categories of presets (Mobile, Web, Film & Video, and Art & Illustration), the new document defaults to the RGB color mode and 72 ppi raster effects. (You will learn more about the importance of those options in later projects.)

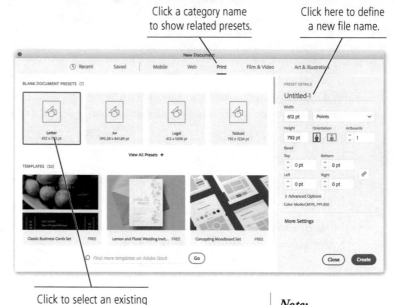

Click a category name to show related presets.

Click here to define a new file name.

Click to select an existing preset or template.

5. On the right side of the dialog box, type icons in the Name field.

6. Choose Points in the Units menu, and choose Portrait Orientation.

Although inches is the standard unit of measurement in the United States, the default **points** option is a standard unit of measurement for graphic designers. There are 72 points in an inch. Don't worry, though, about being able to define everything in points; Illustrator can make the calculations for you.

7. Make sure the Number of Artboards field is set to 1.

Options on the right side of the dialog box, such as artboard orientation and units of measurement, default to the last-used settings.

Illustrator includes the ability to create multiple **artboards** (basically, Illustrator's version of "pages"). For this project, you need only a single artboard.

8. Set all four bleed values to 0.

Bleed is the amount an object needs to extend past the edge of the artboard or page to meet the mechanical requirements of commercial printing.

Note:

You can change the color mode and raster effects settings by expanding the Advanced Options in the right side of the New Document dialog box.

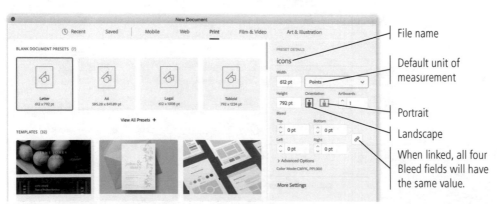

File name

Default unit of measurement

Portrait

Landscape

When linked, all four Bleed fields will have the same value.

9. **Click Create to create the new file. Immediately choose View>Fit Artboard in Window.**

In the resulting document window, the letter-size "page" (or artboard) is represented by a dark black line.

The color of the pasteboard (the area around the artboard) defaults to match the brightness of the user interface. You can change this setting to show a white pasteboard in the User Interface pane of the Preferences dialog box.

As we explained in the Interface chapter, the panels you see depend on what was done the last time you (or someone else) used the application. Because workspace arrangement is such a personal preference, we tell you what panels you need to use, but we don't tell you where to place them.

Note:

Our screenshots show the Macintosh OS using the Application frame.

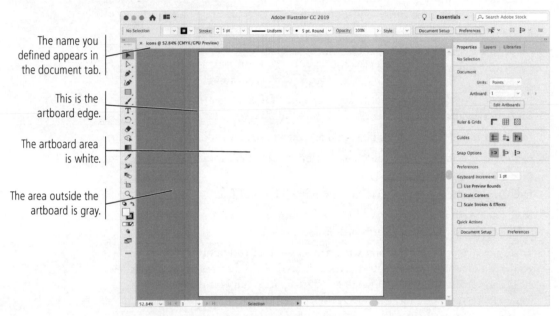

The name you defined appears in the document tab.

This is the artboard edge.

The artboard area is white.

The area outside the artboard is gray.

10. **Choose File>Save As and navigate to your WIP>Camping folder.**

If you assign a name in the New Document dialog box (as you did in Step 5), that name becomes the default file name in the Save As dialog box.

The dialog box defaults to Adobe Illustrator (.ai) format, and the extension is automatically added to the name you defined.

Note:

Feel free to work with whatever workspace settings you are most comfortable using as you complete the projects in this book.

Note:

Press Command/Control-S to save a document, or press Command/Control-Shift-S to open the Save As dialog box.

11. **Click Save in the Save As dialog box. Review the options in the resulting Illustrator Options dialog box.**

This dialog box determines what is stored in the resulting file. The default options are adequate for most files.

- Use the **Version** menu to save files to be compatible with earlier versions of the software. (Keep in mind that many features are not supported by earlier versions; if you save a file for an earlier version, some file information will probably be lost.)

- **Subset Fonts when Percent of Characters Used Is Less Than** determines when to embed an entire font instead of just the characters that are used in the file. Embedding the entire font can significantly increase file size.

- Make sure **Create PDF Compatible File** is checked if you want to use the file with other Adobe applications (such as placing it into an InDesign layout). This does not create a separate PDF file; it simply includes PDF preview data in the file.

- **Include Linked Files** embeds files that are linked to the artwork.

- **Embed ICC Profiles** stores color information inside the file for use in a color-managed workflow.

- **Use Compression** compresses PDF data in the Illustrator file.

- **Save Each Artboard to a Separate File** saves each artboard as a separate file; a separate master file with all artboards is also created.

- **Transparency** options determine what happens to transparent objects when you save a file for Illustrator 9.0 or earlier. Preserve Paths discards transparency effects and resets transparent artwork to 100% opacity and Normal blending mode. Preserve Appearance and Overprints preserves overprints that don't interact with transparent objects; overprints that interact with transparent objects are flattened.

12. **Click OK to save the file, and then continue to the next exercise.**

Define Smart Guide Preferences

Adobe Illustrator provides many tools to help you create precise lines and shapes. **Smart Guides** are dynamic snap-to guides that help you create, align, and transform objects. Smart Guides also show you when the cursor is at a precise angle relative to the original position of the object or point you're moving. In this exercise, you will make sure the correct Smart Guides are active.

1. **With icons.ai open, make sure the Control panel is visible (Window>Control).**

2. **Click the Preferences button in the Control panel or Properties panel.**

   When nothing is selected in the file, you can access the Preferences dialog box directly from either panel. If something is selected in the file, you have to choose from the Illustrator>Preferences (Macintosh) or Edit>Preferences (Windows) submenu.

3. **Choose Smart Guides in the list of categories on the left.**

4. **In the Display section, check all but the Construction Guides option.**

   The Display options determine what is visible when Smart Guides are active:

   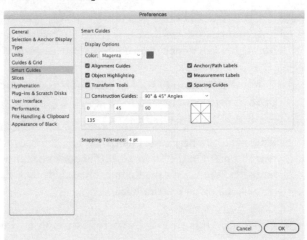

   - When **Alignment Guides** is active, Smart Guides show when a new or moved object aligns to the center or edge of a nearby object.

   - When **Object Highlighting** is active, moving the mouse over any part of an unselected object shows the anchors and paths that make up that object.

   - When **Transform Tools** is active, Smart Guides display when you scale, rotate, or shear objects.

   - When **Anchor/Path Labels** is active, Smart Guides include labels that show the type of element (path or anchor) under the cursor.

   - When **Measurement Labels** is active, Smart Guides show the distance and angle of movement.

   - When **Construction Guides** is active, Smart Guides appear when you move objects in the file at or near defined angles (0°, 45°, 90°, and 135° are the default angles). A number of common angle options are built into the related menu, or you can type up to six specific angles in the available fields.

5. **Click OK to close the Preferences dialog box.**

6. **Choose View>Smart Guides to make sure that option is toggled on (checked).**

   If the option is already checked, simply move your mouse away from the menu and click to dismiss the menu without changing the active option.

7. **Continue to the next exercise.**

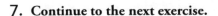

Draw Rounded Rectangles

Illustrator includes a number of tools that make it easy to create basic shapes — rectangles (or squares), ellipses (or circles), and so on.

Using any of the basic shape tools, you can click and drag with the tool cursor to create a shape of any size. Pressing Shift while dragging constrains the shape to equal height and width — for example, an exact square or circle. Pressing Option/Alt while you drag creates the shape so that the center appears where you first click. In the images to the right, the red dot identifies where we first clicked to create the new shape; the yellow circle identifies the current location of the cursor.

You can also single-click using a basic shape tool to open a dialog box, where you can define settings specific to the shape. In this case, the top-left corner of the new shape will be positioned at the place where you click.

In this exercise, you are going to draw a set of simple rectangles with rounded corners to contain the icon artwork that you create throughout this project. We introduce you to a number of techniques for creating these shapes so you can be better aware of the options as you continue your professional career using Illustrator.

Click and drag

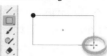

Shift-click and drag

Option/Alt-click and drag

1. **With icons.ai open, choose Window>Toolbars>Advanced.**

   This command shows the entire Illustrator toolset, including all nested variations. Throughout this book, we assume you are using the Advanced Tools panel.

2. **Click the Rectangle tool in the Tools panel and hold down the mouse button until the nested tools appear. Choose the Rounded Rectangle tool from the list of nested tools.**

   When you choose a nested tool, that variation becomes the default option in the Tools panel. You don't need to access the nested menu to select the Rounded Rectangle tool again as long as the application remains open.

	Rectangle Tool	(M)
	Rounded Rectangle Tool	
	Ellipse Tool	(L)
	Polygon Tool	
	Star Tool	
	Flare Tool	

3. **Click the Default Fill and Stroke button at the bottom of the Tools panel.**

   In Illustrator, the default fill is white and the default stroke is 1-pt black. The button appears in a slightly different location depending on whether your Tools panel is in one- or two-column mode.

One-Column mode — Default Fill and Stroke / Swap Fill and Stroke

Two-Column mode — Default Fill and Stroke / Swap Fill and Stroke

Note:

You can also press D to restore the default fill and stroke colors.

4. **With the Rounded Rectangle tool active, click anywhere on the artboard.**

   In the case of the Rounded Rectangle tool, you can define the size of the shape you want to create, as well as the corner radius. The default measurement system is points, which you defined when you created this file.

   Rounded Rectangle
   Width: 214.4 pt
   Height: 141.6 pt
   Corner Radius: 12 pt
   Cancel   OK

   The Width field is highlighted when the dialog box opens.

   When the dialog box first opens, the Width field is automatically highlighted. You can simply type to replace the highlighted value.

5. Type 1.75″ in the Width field, then press Tab to move to the Height field.

Regardless of which unit of measurement you see in the dialog box, you can enter values in whatever system you prefer, as long as you remember to type the correct unit in the dialog box fields (use ″ for inches, mm for millimeters, and pt for points). Illustrator automatically translates one unit of measurement to another.

When you move to the next field, Illustrator calculates the conversion of 1.75 inches (the value you typed in the Width field) to 126 pt (the value that automatically appears in the Width field after you move to the Height field).

The value in inches is converted to the default measurement (points).

Pressing Tab automatically highlights the next field value.

6. Type 1.75″ in the Height field.

Because you are making a shape with the same height and width, you could also click the Constrain icon (the broken chain) on the right side of the dialog box to make the Height field match the modified Width field.

7. Make sure the corner radius field is set to 12 pt.

A rounded-corner rectangle is simply a rectangle with the corners cut at a specific distance from the end (the corner radius). The two sides are connected with one-fourth of a circle, which has a radius equal to the amount of the rounding.

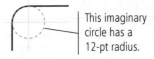

This imaginary circle has a 12-pt radius.

8. Click OK to create the new shape.

A shape appears on the artboard with its top-left corner exactly where you clicked with the Rounded Rectangle tool. (If you Option/Alt-click with any of the shape tools, the place where you click becomes the center of the new shape.)

9. Zoom in so you can clearly see the entire rectangle.

As a general rule, we don't tell you what view percentage to use unless we want to highlight a specific issue. As you work through the projects in this book, we encourage you to zoom in and out as necessary to meet your specific needs.

10. Click the Selection tool (the black arrow) at the top of the Tools panel. If the rounded rectangle is not already selected, click to select the shape.

The Selection tool is used to select entire objects.

When the object is selected, the rectangular **bounding box** marks the outermost edges of the shape. **Bounding-box handles** mark the corners and exact horizontal and vertical center of the shape. (If you don't see the bounding box, choose View>Show Bounding Box.) Because this shape has rounded corners, the corner bounding-box handles actually appear outside the shape edges.

Four small circles inside each corner of the shape are Live Corner widgets, which allow you to click and drag to change the shape of object corners.

Note:

You can choose View>Hide Corner Widget to toggle the visibility of live corner widgets, or use the Show/Hide Shape Widgets button in the Control panel when a rectangle or polygon live shape is selected.

The Selection tool is active.

The top-left corner of the new shape is placed where you clicked.

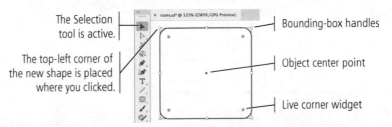

Bounding-box handles

Object center point

Live corner widget

11. **Click the Rounded Rectangle tool in the Tools panel and hold down the mouse button until the nested tools appear. Choose the Rectangle tool from the list of nested tools.**

12. **Move the cursor to the right of the top edge of the existing shape. When you see a guide line connected to the top edge of the first shape, click, hold down the mouse button, and drag down and right.**

The line is a function of the Smart Guides feature, which provides instant feedback while you draw.

Note:

If you do something wrong, or aren't happy with your results, press Command/Control-Z to undo the last action you took.

13. **When cursor feedbacks show both Width and Height values of 126 pt, release the mouse button to create the second shape.**

As you drag, cursor feedback shows the size of the new shape. Smart Guides identify when the new shape's bottom edge aligns with the bottom of the previous shape. The diagonal guide identifies when the shape has equal height and width, making it easy to draw a perfect square. (You can also press Shift while dragging to create a shape with equal height and width.)

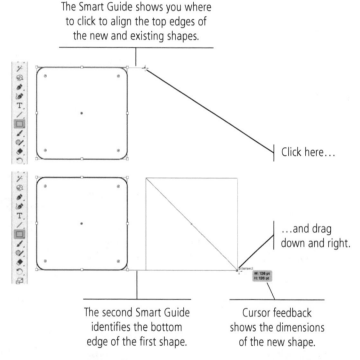

The Smart Guide shows you where to click to align the top edges of the new and existing shapes.

Click here…

…and drag down and right.

The second Smart Guide identifies the bottom edge of the first shape.

Cursor feedback shows the dimensions of the new shape.

Because you are using the Rectangle tool instead of the Rounded Rectangle tool, the second shape does not have rounded corners; the bounding-box handles match the actual shape corners.

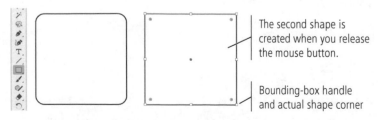

The second shape is created when you release the mouse button.

Bounding-box handle and actual shape corner

14. Click one of the Live Corner widgets and drag toward the center of the shape. When cursor feedback shows a corner radius of approximately 12 pt, release the mouse button.

The Live Corner widgets allow you to manually adjust the corner radius for all corners on the selected shape. Dragging in toward the shape center increases the corner radius; dragging out toward the corner decreases the corner radius.

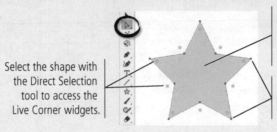

Dragging the Live Corner widget affects the shape of all selected corners.

Cursor feedback shows the corner radius as you drag.

Because the entire object is selected, dragging any of the widgets applies the same change to all corners on the shape. To change only certain corners, you can use the Direct Selection tool to select the corner points you want to affect before dragging a Live Corner widget.

More about Working with Live Corners

If a shape is an actual rectangle (with all 90° corners), the Live Corner widgets appear whenever the shape is selected with either Selection tool. For any other shape, including a four-cornered polygon with different-angled corners, the widgets appear only when the shape is selected with the Direct Selection tool.

Select the shape with the Direct Selection tool to access the Live Corner widgets.

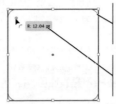

Click inside the shape to select the entire object (and all shape corners).

Click specific corner points to select only those corners.

If the entire object is selected, dragging any one Live Corner widget affects all corners on the same shape (below left). If you want to affect only specific corners, you can select those points first, and then drag any of the visible widgets to change only the selected corners (below right).

Option/Alt-clicking a Live Corner widget toggles through the available corner shapes — round, inverted round, and chamfer/beveled. Again, only selected corners are affected by the shape change.

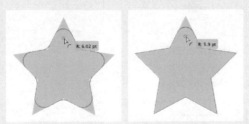

|Round|Inverted Round|Chamfer|

If you have a wide enough application frame, you can also use the Corner Shape button in the Control panel to change the corner shapes.

Click this button to open the Corner Shape menu.

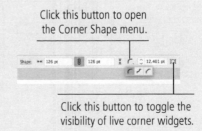

Click this button to toggle the visibility of live corner widgets.

15. **With the adjusted shape still selected, open the Transform panel (Window>Transform).**

    When a rectangle is selected, the Transform panel shows the corner radius of all four corners on the shape. If you find it difficult to achieve an exact radius by dragging, you can always use these fields to adjust the corner radius to specific values.

16. **Make sure the Constrain icon between the Corner Radius fields is active (highlighted). Highlight any of the Corner Radius fields and type 12. Press Return/Enter to finalize the change.**

    Because you are using the default unit of measurement (points), you don't need to type the unit.

    Corner radius fields are only available in the Transform panel if the shape is a rectangle (with four 90° corner angles).

    Corner Radius fields can also be accessed by clicking the Shape hot-text link in the Control panel, or by clicking the More Options button in the Transform section of the Properties panel.

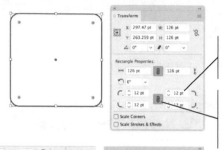

These fields adjust the corner radius of each corner on the shape.

When this icon is active (highlighted), changing one Corner Radius field changes all four fields.

More Options button

17. **Choose the Selection tool in the Tools panel.**

18. **Using the Selection tool, press Option/Alt, then click the second shape and drag right.**

    When you drag an object with the Selection tool, you move it to another location. If you press Option/Alt while dragging, you clone (make a copy of) the original object and move the clone.

    Again, Smart Guides make it easy to align objects. You can see the horizontal guide connecting the center of the original object to the center of the one you are cloning. Smart Guides also identify distances between objects, so you can place multiple objects at the same distances from one to the next. (Don't worry about the exact spaces between the objects; you will define precise object spacing in a later exercise.)

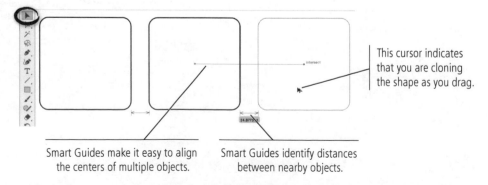

This cursor indicates that you are cloning the shape as you drag.

Smart Guides make it easy to align the centers of multiple objects.

Smart Guides identify distances between nearby objects.

19. **Save the file and continue to the next exercise.**

Understanding Selection Basics

Most Illustrator objects (including shapes like rounded-corner rectangles) contain two basic building blocks: anchor points and paths. You don't need to worry about the geometric specifics of vectors because Illustrator manages them for you — but you do need to understand the basic concept of how Illustrator works with anchor points and paths. You should also understand how to access those building blocks so you can do more than create basic shapes.

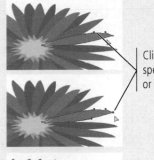

Path (line) segment

Curve handle controls the shape of the path

Anchor point

If you select an object with the **Selection tool** (the black arrow), you can see the bounding box that identifies the outermost dimensions of the shape. Bounding-box handles, which you can use to resize the shape, appear at the edges of the bounding box. (Press Command/Control-Shift-B to show or hide the bounding box of selected objects.)

When you select an object with the **Direct Selection tool** (the white arrow), you can see the anchor points and paths that make up the selected object. As you work with Illustrator, keep this distinction in mind: use the Selection tool to select an entire object; use the Direct Selection tool to edit the points and paths of an object.

Selection tool

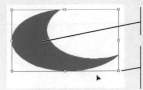

Click any part of an object to select the entire object.

Bounding-box handles mark the outer dimensions of the selection.

Click any part of a group to select the entire group.

Direct Selection tool

Click to select a specific line segment or point on a shape.

Click an object's fill to select the entire object, even if it is part of a group.

Clicking and dragging to draw a marquee with the Selection tool…

…selects any object touched by the marquee.

Clicking and dragging to draw a marquee with the Direct Selection tool…

…selects only points within the marquee.

Control Fill and Stroke Attributes

At the beginning of the previous exercise, you clicked the Default Fill and Stroke button in the Tools panel to apply a white fill and 1-pt black stroke to the objects you created. Obviously, most artwork requires more than these basic attributes.

As you complete the projects in this book, you will learn about styles, patterns, gradients, effects, and other attributes that can take an illustration from flat to fabulous. In this exercise, you learn about a number of options for changing the basic fill, stroke, and color attributes for objects on the page.

1. **With icons.ai open, choose the Selection tool in the Tools panel. Click the left rectangle on the artboard to select it.**

2. **Choose View>Hide Corner Widget.**

   These widgets can be distracting, so it's useful to turn them off when they are no longer needed.

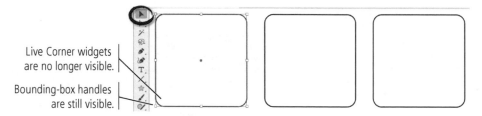

Live Corner widgets are no longer visible.

Bounding-box handles are still visible.

3. **Choose Window>Swatches to open the Swatches panel. If the panel is docked, float it away from the dock.**

   If the panel shows a list of items including the color names, open the Swatches panel Options menu and choose Small Thumbnail View.

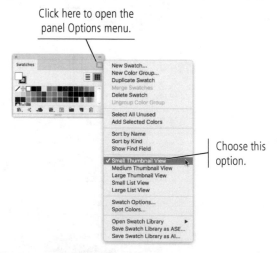

Click here to open the panel Options menu.

Choose this option.

Note:

Remember, panels can always be accessed in the Window menu.

The Swatches panel includes a number of predefined and saved colors, which you can use to change the color of the fill and stroke of an object. You can also save custom swatches to more efficiently apply specific colors as you create artwork.

4. At the top of the Swatches panel, click the Stroke icon to bring it to the front of the stack.

The fill and stroke icons in the Swatches panel are used to determine which attribute is active — in other words, which would be changed by clicking a swatch in the Swatches panel. Clicking one of these buttons brings it to the front of the stack, making it active, so you can change the color of that attribute.

You can also use the same icons at the bottom of the Tools panel to change the active attribute.

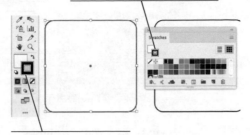

Click an icon to bring it to the top and make that attribute active.

The same options are available in the Tools panel.

5. In the Swatches panel, click the light brown swatch in the third row.

Because the Stroke icon is active in the Tools panel, the color of the selected object's stroke (border) changes to light brown.

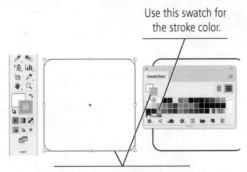

Use this swatch for the stroke color.

The top icon determines what attribute will be changed when you click a swatch in the panel.

6. In the Tools or Swatches panel, click the Fill icon to bring it to the front of the stack. In the Swatches panel, click the black swatch in the first row.

Because the Fill icon is the active attribute, clicking the black color swatch changes the fill color of the selected object.

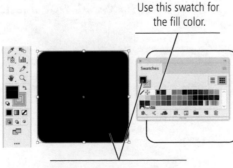

Use this swatch for the fill color.

Because the Fill icon is on top, clicking a swatch changes the object's fill color.

Note:

You can press the X key to switch the active attribute between Stroke and Fill.

Note:

It is very easy to forget to check which icon (fill or stroke) is on top of the stack. If you forget and accidentally change the color of the wrong attribute, simply undo the change (press Command/Control-Z), and then bring the correct attribute to the front before changing colors.

7. **With the rounded rectangle selected, change the Stroke Weight field in the Control panel to 3 pt. Press Return/Enter to apply the change.**

The Stroke icon in the Tools panel does not need to be active to change the stroke weight. The Tools panel icons relate only to color changes made with the stand-alone Swatches or Color panels.

Change the Stroke Weight field to 3 pt.

The Stroke icon doesn't need to be on top to change an object's stroke weight.

8. **With the rectangle still selected, click the Swap Fill and Stroke button in the Tools panel.**

This button makes it easy to reverse the fill and stroke colors of an object; the stroke weight remains unaffected when you swap the colors.

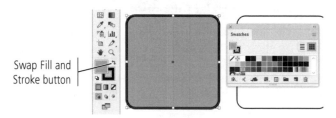

Swap Fill and Stroke button

Note:

You can press Shift-X to swap the active Stroke and Fill colors.

9. **Using the Selection tool, click the second rectangle on the artboard.**

The Fill and Stroke icons change to reflect the colors of the selected objects.

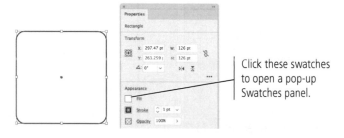

Click these swatches to open a pop-up Swatches panel.

Note:

Fill Color, Stroke Color, and Stroke Weight fields are also available in the Control panel.

10. **In the Appearance section of the Properties panel, change the Stroke Weight value to 3 pt.**

11. **Click the Fill color swatch to open the pop-up Swatches panel. Choose the light brown swatch in the third row to change the fill color for the selected object.**

When an object is selected with the Selection tool, the Properties panel provides quick access to the stroke and fill colors for the selected object; you don't need to worry about which icon is active in the Tools panel.

Clicking the Fill color swatch opens an attached Swatches panel so you can change the fill for the selected object without opening the separate Swatches panel.

12. **Using the Selection tool, click the third rectangle on the artboard.**

Again, the Fill and Stroke icons in the Tools panel change to reflect the colors of the selected object.

13. **Select the Eyedropper tool in the Tools panel, and then click the first or second rectangle on the artboard.**

The Eyedropper tool copies fill and stroke attributes from one object (the one you click) to another (the one you first selected).

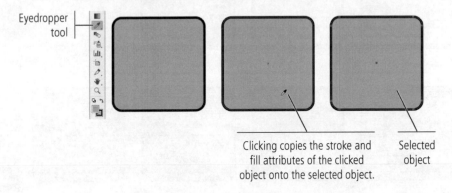

Eyedropper tool

Clicking copies the stroke and fill attributes of the clicked object onto the selected object.

Selected object

Note:

You can double-click the Eyedropper tool in the Tools panel to define which attributes are picked up and applied by clicking with the tool.

14. **Press and hold the Command/Control key, and click anywhere on the artboard away from the three rectangles.**

Pressing Command/Control temporarily switches to the last-used Selection tool (Selection or Direct Selection). By clicking on the empty artboard area while holding down the modifier key, you can quickly deselect the selected object(s). When you release the Command/Control key, the tool reverts to the one you last used — in this case, the Eyedropper tool.

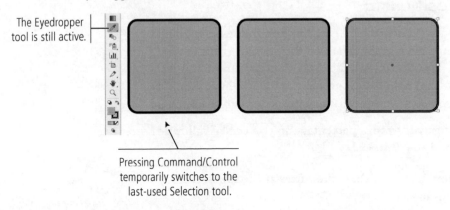

The Eyedropper tool is still active.

Pressing Command/Control temporarily switches to the last-used Selection tool.

15. **Release the Command/Control key.**

16. **Choose the Rounded Rectangle tool in the Tools panel.**

17. **To the right of the third shape on the artboard, draw a fourth rounded rectangle that is 126 pt square.**

The Fill and Stroke swatches remember the last-used options, so the new rectangle has the same heavy black stroke and brown fill as the others. Don't worry if your shapes aren't entirely on the artboard; you will define their precise positions in the next exercise.

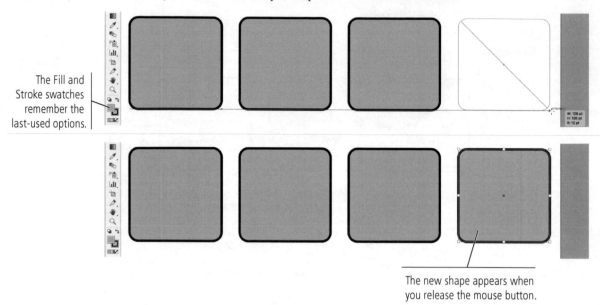

The Fill and Stroke swatches remember the last-used options.

The new shape appears when you release the mouse button.

18. **Save the file (File>Save or Command/Control-S) and continue to the next exercise.**

Control Object Positioning

The ability to move objects around on the artboard is one of the advantages of digital drawing. On paper, you have to manually erase items and then redraw them in their new locations. Illustrator offers a number of tools that make it easy to move objects around the artboard, either as isolated objects or in relation to other elements on the page. In this exercise, you learn several techniques for moving objects on the artboard.

1. **With icons.ai open, change your zoom percentage so you can see all four shapes and the entire top of the artboard.**

2. **Choose View>Rulers>Show Rulers to show the rulers at the top and left edges of the document window.**

Because you created this file using points as the default unit of measurement, the rulers — and fields in dialog boxes and panels — show measurements in points.

Note:

The Change to Global Rulers option is only relevant when you work with multiple artboards.

3. **Control/right-click the top ruler and choose Inches from the contextual menu.**

Rulers on the top and left edges show measurements in the default units of measurement.

4. **Choose the Selection tool at the top of the Tools panel, then click the left rectangle on the artboard to select it.**

5. **In the Properties panel, review the Transform options for the active selection.**

Transform options in the Properties panel are the same as those that are available in the stand-alone Transform panel (Window>Transform).

The **reference points** correspond to the bounding box handles of the selected object. The selected square in this icon identifies which point of the object is being measured.

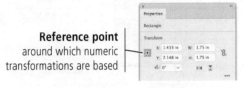

Reference point around which numeric transformations are based

If you use the W or H fields to resize an object, you can constrain the object's height-to-width aspect ratio by clicking the chain icon (to the right of the W and H fields in the Transform panel, or between the W and H fields in the Control panel).

In Illustrator, the default **zero point** (the source of measurements) is the top-left corner of the artboard; the X and Y positions of an object are measured relative to that location. The X axis is the horizontal value and the Y axis is the vertical value. You can change the zero point by clicking where the horizontal and vertical rulers meet, and dragging to a new position; if you do reposition the zero point, you can double-click the intersection of the rulers to restore the default zero point.

Keep these ideas in mind when you move something in an Illustrator file:

- Moving up requires subtracting from the Y value.
- Moving down requires adding to the Y value.
- Moving left requires subtracting from the X value.
- Moving right requires adding to the X value.

6. **Click the top-left reference point to select it.**

The X and Y fields now show the exact position of the top-left bounding box handle for the selected object.

7. **Highlight the X field and type .25. Press Return/Enter to apply the change.**

You don't need to type the measurement unit (″) or the preceding zero (0). Because the rulers are showing inches, Illustrator automatically applies inches as the unit of value.

Note:

If you have a wide monitor, the reference point proxy and the X, Y, W, and H fields are available directly in the Control panel.

If you have a smaller application frame, the Control panel includes a hot-text link to a pop-up Transform panel.

The top-left reference point is selected.

Measurements correspond to this point of the selected shape.

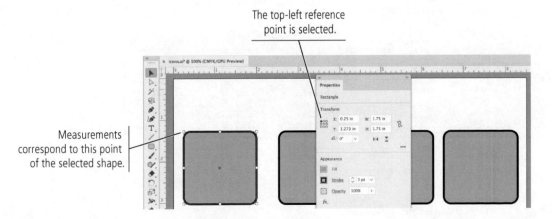

8. **Highlight the Y field and type .25. Press Return/Enter to apply the change.**

The top-left handle of the selected object is now 1/4″ from the top and left edges. The numbers you typed correspond to the measurements you see on the rulers.

Rulers show that the selected point of the object is at the position you just defined.

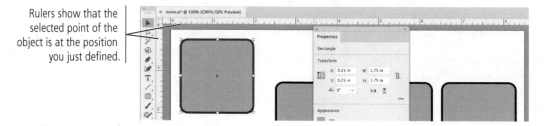

9. **Using the Selection tool, click the second rectangle and drag until a guide line appears, connecting the center points of the first and second shapes.**

As you drag, the cursor feedback shows the relative position of the object. In other words, you can see the change (<u>difference</u>) in the object's position, both horizontally (<u>X</u>) and vertically (<u>Y</u>) — hence the "dX" and "dY" values.

As we explained previously, Smart Guides can be very useful for aligning objects on the artboard. Illustrator identifies and highlights relative alignment as you drag, and snaps objects to those alignment points.

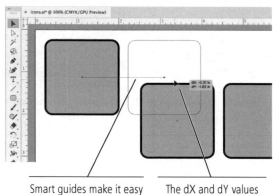

Smart guides make it easy to align multiple objects.

The dX and dY values show the changes to the object's X and Y values.

Note:

The X position is an object's horizontal position on the artboard; the Y position is the object's vertical position.

10. **Release the mouse button while the center Smart Guide is visible.**

If you don't see the alignment guides as you drag, make sure that option is checked in the Smart Guides preferences.

11. **Click the fourth shape on the page. Select the top-right reference point, type 8.25 in the X field, and type .25 in the Y field.**

Because you changed the reference point, you defined the X/Y position for the top-right bounding-box handle of the fourth rectangle.

Note:

When a field value is highlighted in a panel or dialog box, you can use the Up Arrow and Down Arrow keys to increase or decrease (respectively) the highlighted value.

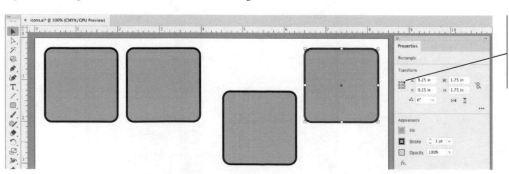

The top-right reference point means the X and Y values refer to the top-right corner of the selected shape.

12. **Save the file and continue to the next exercise.**

As you have already seen, there is almost always more than one way to accomplish a specific task. Although Smart Guides make alignment very easy, the Align panel is useful for certain functions that are not enabled by Smart Guides. You can use the Align panel to align multiple objects relative to one another within a selection, to a specific object in the selection, or to the active artboard.

The **Align Object options** are fairly self explanatory; when multiple objects are selected, the objects align based on the edge(s) or center(s) you click. Icons on the various buttons indicate the function of each.

- ▣ Align Left Edges
- ▦ Align Horizontal Centers
- ▤ Align Right Edges
- ▥ Align Top Edges
- ▦ Align Vertical Centers
- ▦ Align Bottom Edges

The **Distribute Objects options** enable you to control the positions of multiple objects relative to each other. By default, objects are equally distributed within the dimensions of the overall selection.

- ▤ Distribute Top Edges
- ▧ Distribute Vertical Centers
- ▤ Distribute Bottom Edges
- ▥ Distribute Left Edges
- ▦ Distribute Horizontal Centers
- ▥ Distribute Right Edges

You can use the Align To menu to determine how selected objects will align. If you don't see the Align To menu, open the panel Options menu and choose Show Options.

The **Align To Selection** option aligns selected objects to one another based on the outermost edge of the entire selection. In other words, aligning the top edges moves all objects to the same Y position as the highest selected object.

If you use the **Key Object** option, you can click any object in the selection to designate it as the key. (The key object shows a heavier border than other objects in the selection.)

Because you can align objects relative to the document, the align buttons are also available when only one object is selected, allowing you to align any single object to a precise location on the page or spread.

By default, Align options apply based on the outermost edge of the active selection. In the following image, dashed lines indicate the original top edges of the objects:

Using the **Align To Key Object** option, the middle image was selected as the key. The Align options apply to the edges of the defined key object:

The following images show the original placement, followed by the result of applying the Distribute Vertical Centers and Distribute Horizontal Centers options to evenly space the three fish.

You can use the Distribute Spacing option to align objects to one another by a specific amount based on the selected key object. To access the measurement field for these options, you must first click one of the selected objects to define the key. You can then type a value in the field, then click the Horizontal or Vertical options (or both, as we did in the following image):

If you don't see the Distribute Spacing options, open the panel Options menu and choose Show Options.

Align and Distribute Objects

In addition to dragging objects around the artboard, the Illustrator Align panel makes it very easy to align and distribute selected objects relative to one another, to a specific key object in the file, or to the overall artboard. In this exercise, you learn how to use the Align panel to align shapes.

Note:

When multiple objects are selected, you can access the basic Align options in the Properties panel. Click the More Options button to access the full pop-up panel.

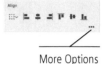

More Options

1. **With icons.ai open, click and drag with the Selection tool to draw a marquee that touches some part of all four objects on the artboard.**

   The Selection tool selects objects, so the selection marquee only needs to touch the objects you want to select. The marquee doesn't need to surround the objects entirely.

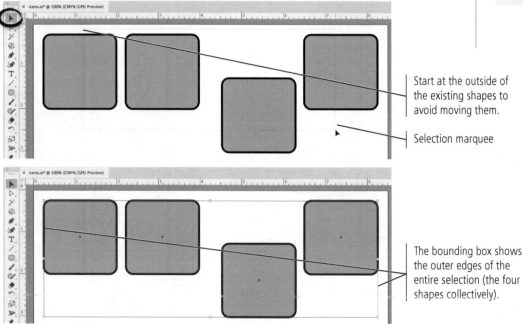

Start at the outside of the existing shapes to avoid moving them.

Selection marquee

The bounding box shows the outer edges of the entire selection (the four shapes collectively).

2. **Open the Align panel (Window>Align) and click the Vertical Align Top button.**

   By default, alignment and distribution functions occur relative to the selected objects. In other words, when you click the Vertical Align Top button, Illustrator determines the topmost edge of the selected objects, and then moves the top edges of all other selected objects to that position.

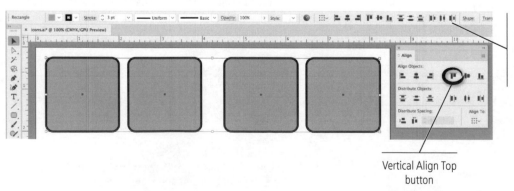

Depending on your monitor width, Align options might also be available in the Control panel.

Vertical Align Top button

3. **With all four objects selected, click the Horizontal Distribute Center button.**

   By default, the distribution functions create equal distance between the selected point of the selected objects. In this case, Illustrator distributes the center points along the horizontal axis by determining the center positions of the outermost selected objects, and then moving the middle two objects to create equal distance between the centers of all four selected objects; the positions of the two outer objects remain unchanged.

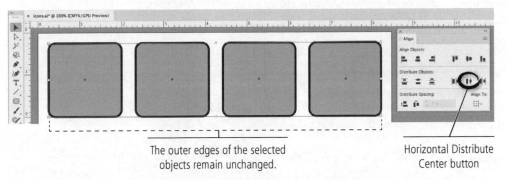

The outer edges of the selected objects remain unchanged.

Horizontal Distribute Center button

4. **Click inside any of the selected objects. While still holding down the mouse button, press Option/Alt and drag down.**

5. **Use the Smart Guides and cursor feedback to drag exactly vertical (the dX value should be 0). When the dY value in the cursor feedback is 2 in, release the mouse button.**

   Remember, pressing Option/Alt while you drag clones the original selection.

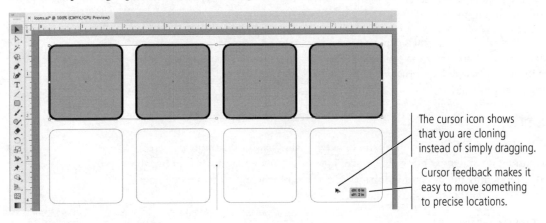

The cursor icon shows that you are cloning instead of simply dragging.

Cursor feedback makes it easy to move something to precise locations.

6. **Click anywhere outside the selected shapes to deselect all objects.**

7. **Save the file and continue to the next exercise.**

Import Template Images

Many Illustrator projects require you to start with something that has already been captured — a sketch, for example, or low-resolution image (which is the case in this project). In this exercise you will place files to use as templates for your new artwork.

1. **With icons.ai open, choose File>Place. Navigate to your WIP>Camping folder and click picnic.jpg to select that file.**

2. **Macintosh users: If you don't see a series of check boxes across the bottom of the dialog box, click the Options button.**

   The dialog box button remembers the last-used state, so the actual options might already be visible. We do not repeat the instruction to click the Options button whenever you place a file throughout the projects in this book.

3. **At the bottom of the Place dialog box, check the Link and Template options.**

   When you check the Link option, the placed file does not become a part of the actual file where you're working; for the file to output properly, Illustrator must be able to locate the linked file in the same location (hard drive, flash drive, etc.) as when you placed it. If the Link option is *not* checked, the placed file is **embedded** — it becomes part of the file where it's placed; the original external file is not necessary for the artwork to output properly.

   In the case of this project, you are going to delete the template images after you create the artwork; it doesn't matter if the images are embedded.

   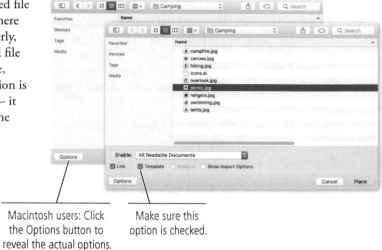

   Macintosh users: Click the Options button to reveal the actual options.

   Make sure this option is checked.

4. **Click Place.**

   When you place an object into Illustrator as a Template, it is automatically centered in the current document window. In our example, you can see that the placed image is mostly hidden by the background shapes; regardless of where your template images appear, you will correct this issue in the next exercise.

   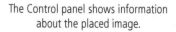
   The Control panel shows information about the placed image.

   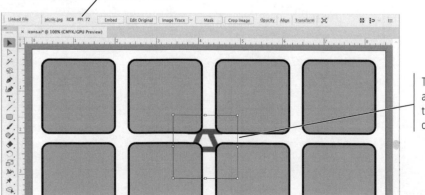

   Template images are automatically placed in the center of the document window.

5. **Choose File>Place a second time. Select hiking.jpg in the list, check the Template option, and click Place.**

The Place dialog box remembers the last-used location, so you don't have to re-navigate to the Camping folder. The Link option also remembers the last-used settings. The Template option, however, always defaults to off, so you have to manually check this box for each template object.

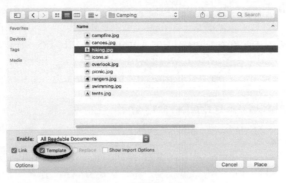

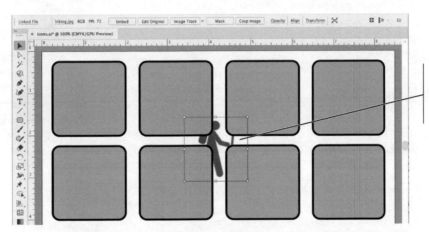

This image is also placed in the center of the document window, directly on top of the first placed image.

6. **Repeat Step 5 to place campfire.jpg and tents.jpg into your file as template images.**

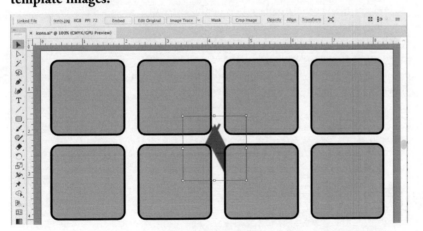

Note:

If you change the view percentage or scroll the document in the window before placing the second image, the second file will not be centered over the first. Instead, it will be centered in the document window based on the current view.

7. **Click an empty area of the artboard to deselect the last-placed template image.**

8. **Save the file and continue to the next exercise.**

Manage Multiple Layers

When you create artwork in Illustrator, you almost always end up with more than one object on the artboard. In many cases, a completed file has dozens or hundreds of objects, arranged in specific order on top of one another. As files become more and more complex, it can be difficult to find and work with exactly the pieces you need. Illustrator layers are one of the most powerful tools available for solving this problem.

1. **In the open icons.ai file, open the Layers panel.**

    By default, all files have a single layer, named Layer 1.

    When you place an object as a template, it's added to the file on a separate, non-printing layer that is partially grayed, making it easier to work with. Below Layer 1, your file has four additional layers — the template layers. Template layers are locked by default, which means you can't select or modify objects on those layers.

    Note:

    If you don't see all four locked template layers, you forgot to check the Template option when you placed one of the images. You can select and delete the placed file from the artboard, and then replace the necessary image as a template.

Click in this column to show or hide a layer.

Click in this column to lock or unlock a layer.

Double-click the layer thumbnail to open the Layer Options dialog box.

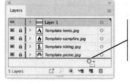

2. **In the Layers panel, click the Layer 1 name and drag it below all four template layers in the stack.**

    The top-to-bottom position of objects or layers is called the **stacking order**. Objects and layers typically appear in the stack based on the order in which they are created — the first-created is at the bottom, the last-created is at the top, and so on, in between.

    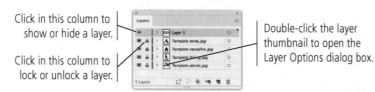

    Click and drag a layer to move it in the stacking order.

    Placed template objects are the exception; these layers are placed *below* the currently selected layer (i.e., lower in the stacking order). In this case, the rectangle shapes are filled with a color, which obscures the template images on the underlying layers. To see the template images, you need to move the template object layers above the layer containing the background shapes. Rather than moving four layers above Layer 1, you can save a few clicks by moving Layer 1 below all of the template layers.

    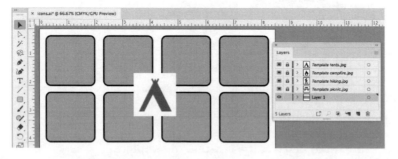

    Note:

    For a template layer, the Visibility icon is a small square instead of an eye.

3. **In the Layers panel, click the Lock icon for the Template picnic.jpg layer to unlock that layer.**

    Because you need to move the placed template object into the correct position, you first need to unlock the layer where that object resides.

    Click here to unlock the template layer.

    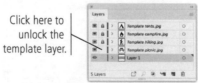

4. **Using the Selection tool, click the top-left rounded rectangle to select it.**

5. **With the Selection tool active, press Shift and click anywhere inside the area where the template images are placed.**

   Pressing Shift allows you to add objects to the current selection. The first rectangle and the image should both be selected. (Remember, the other three template object layers are still locked. Even though you can't see it, you can select the picnic.jpg image by clicking in the area where it is placed.)

6. **With both objects selected, click the Align To button in the Control panel.**

   The Align and Distribute options in the Control panel are the same as the options in the Align panel.

Click this button to access the Align To options.

The placed template images are stacked on top of each other in the order in which you placed them.

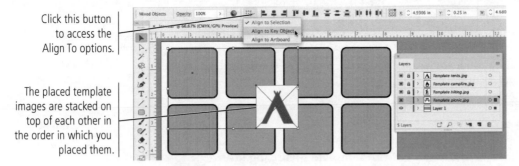

7. **Choose Align to Key Object in the menu.**

The default key object is identified with a heavy border.

8. **Click the selected rounded rectangle on the artboard.**

   Key Object alignment allows you to define where you want other objects to align. By selecting the key object, you're telling Illustrator which object to use as the basis for alignment.

Click any selected object to define the key object for the alignment.

The border colors match the defined layer colors.

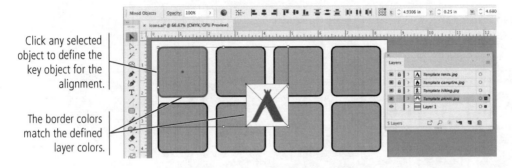

9. **Click the Horizontal Align Center and Vertical Align Center buttons in the Control panel.**

   Because you selected the rounded rectangle as the key object, the placed template image moves to the horizontal and vertical center of the rounded rectangle; the rectangle — the key object — remains in the same place.

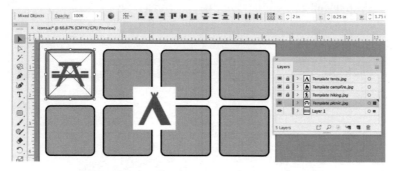

10. **In the Layers panel, click the empty space to the left of the Template picnic.jpg layer to relock that layer.**

    Now that the template object is in place, it's a good idea to lock it again so you don't accidentally move the object.

11. **Double-click the layer thumbnail of the Template picnic.jpg layer.**

    Double-clicking a layer thumbnail opens the Layer Options dialog box for that layer, where you can change a number of attributes for the selected layer.

12. **Change the Dim Images To field to 30, and then click OK to close the Layer Options dialog box.**

    Dimming the template image will make it easier to see your artwork when you draw.

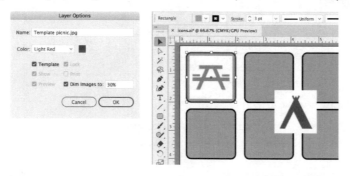

Note:

The Color menu in the Layer Options dialog box determines the color of bounding box handles and other visual indicators for objects on a layer.

13. **Repeat Steps 3–12 to position the other three template images in the first-row rectangles (as shown in the following image).**

14. **In the Layers panel, double-click the Layer 1 name to highlight it. Type Backgrounds to change the layer name, then press Return/Enter.**

Whenever you have more than one working layer, it's a good idea to use names that tell you what is on each layer. Doing so prevents confusion later when you or someone else needs to change a particular item.

Double-click the layer name to highlight it.

Type a new layer name, then press Return/Enter to finalize it.

15. **In the Layers panel, click the empty space immediately left of the Backgrounds layer.**

This step — locking the Backgrounds layer — is simply a safeguard to avoid accidentally changing the background rectangles while you're drawing the icon artwork.

Lock the Backgrounds layer to protect the objects on that layer.

16. **In the Layers panel, click the Create New Layer button.**

In the next stage of the project, you will start tracing the objects in the templates. The completed icon will be a series of black icons on top of the rounded rectangles with the brown background color.

Create New Layer button

At this point, most of the brown color in the background shapes is obscured by the placed images, because the template layers are above the layer containing the rectangles. If you tried to draw the icon shapes on the existing non-template layer, you would be drawing *behind* the template — in other words, you wouldn't be able to see what you were drawing. Instead, you need a layer above the template layers, where you can create the icon artwork.

17. **In the Layers panel, drag Layer 6 to the top of the layer stack.**

New layers are automatically placed immediately above the selected layer. You need this new layer to be above the template layers so you can see what you're drawing.

18. **Double-click the Layer 6 name in the Layers panel. Type Icon Art and press Return/Enter to finalize the new layer name.**

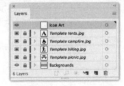

19. **Save the file and continue to the next stage of the project.**

STAGE 2 / Drawing with Basic Shapes

A number of tools and utilities can be used to create complex Illustrator artwork. Creating the icons in this project gives you an opportunity to experiment with some of these options. As you complete the other projects in this book, you will dig deeper into complex drawing techniques.

 ## Numerically Transform Drawing Objects

Basic shapes, such as rectangles, can be used as the basis for a wide variety of drawings. In the next two exercises, you will use basic rectangles to create the picnic table art.

1. **With icons.ai open, make sure the Icon Art layer is active, and then zoom into the picnic table template image.**

2. **Choose the Rectangle tool in the Tools panel.**

3. **With nothing selected on the artboard, change the fill color to black and the stroke color to None.**

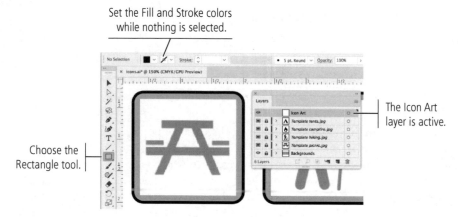

Set the Fill and Stroke colors while nothing is selected.

Choose the Rectangle tool.

The Icon Art layer is active.

4. **Click and drag to create the shape that represents the top of the picnic table.**

5. **Click and drag again to create the second horizontal shape in the artwork.**

6. **Using the Selection tool, click the top rectangle to select it.**

7. **Open the Transform panel (Window>Transform). Make a note of the H (height) field in the Transform panel.**

    We use the stand-alone Transform panel in this exercise because it eliminates the need to constantly reopen the panel using the Control panel hot-text link.

Note:

We changed the layer color of the Icon Art layer to magenta so that the visual indicators on the layer will be more visible in our printed screen captures.

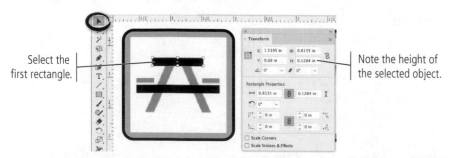

Select the first rectangle.

Note the height of the selected object.

8. Click to select the second shape (from Step 5).

9. **If necessary, click the Constrain Width and Height Proportions button in the Transform panel to turn off that option.**

   When this button is active, changing the height or width field makes a proportional change to the other dimension. When it is inactive, you can change one dimension of a shape without affecting the other dimension.

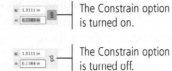

The Constrain option is turned on.

The Constrain option is turned off.

10. **With the second shape selected, change the H (height) field to the same value that you noted in Step 7.**

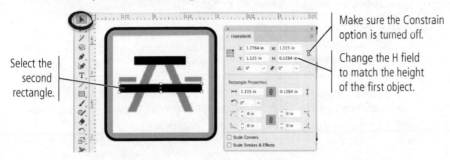

Select the second rectangle.

Make sure the Constrain option is turned off.

Change the H field to match the height of the first object.

11. **Using the Rectangle tool, click and drag to create the seat shape on the left side of the template.**

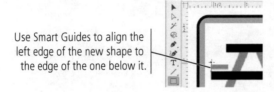

Use Smart Guides to align the left edge of the new shape to the edge of the one below it.

12. **Choose the Selection tool. Press Option/Alt, then click the new shape and drag right to clone it.**

13. **Continue dragging until Smart Guides show the right edge of the cloned shape aligned to the right edge of the bottom rectangle (as shown here).**

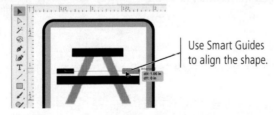

Use Smart Guides to align the shape.

14. **Save the file and continue to the next exercise.**

Shear and Reflect Drawing Objects

Illustrator includes four transformation options — Rotate, Reflect, Scale, and Shear. Each of these transformations can be applied either by hand, using the related tool in the Tools panel; or numerically, using either the fields in the Transform panel or the appropriate dialog box from the Object>Transform menu. In this exercise, you will use these methods to finish the picnic table artwork.

1. **With `icons.ai` open, choose the Rectangle tool in the Tools panel.**

2. **Draw a vertical rectangle beginning at the bottom of the artwork and ending at the bottom edge of the top horizontal shape (as shown after Step 3).**

   Illustrator recognizes certain basic shapes, including rectangles, ellipses, and lines. When one of these shapes — called Live Shapes — is selected, the lower half of the Transform panel includes properties specific to the type of shape. For a rectangle, you can change the height, width, rotation angle, and corner radius for each corner.

3. **With the Constrain option turned off, change the W field in the Transform panel to the same value you used for the height of the horizontal shapes in the previous exercise.**

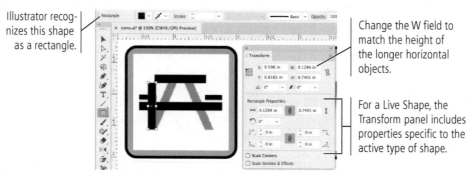

Illustrator recognizes this shape as a rectangle.

Change the W field to match the height of the longer horizontal objects.

For a Live Shape, the Transform panel includes properties specific to the active type of shape.

4. **Select the Shear tool (nested under the Scale tool) in the Tools panel.**

   When you select one of the transformation tools, an **origin point** appears by default at the center of the selected object. This origin point acts as an anchor when using the transformation tools; it is the point around which transformations occur. You can single-click anywhere to define a different origin point.

5. **Move the cursor to the bottom-right anchor point of the vertical rectangle. When you see the word "anchor" in the cursor icon, click to reposition the origin point.**

   The word "anchor" is another function of Illustrator's Smart Guides. When you move the cursor near an existing anchor point, Illustrator identifies that point so you can click exactly on the existing point.

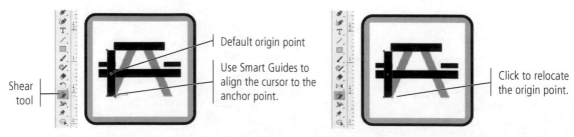

Shear tool

Default origin point

Use Smart Guides to align the cursor to the anchor point.

Click to relocate the origin point.

6. **Click the top edge of the selected shape and drag right until the shape matches the table leg shape in the template image.**

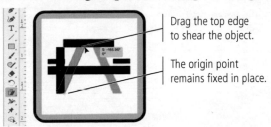

Drag the top edge to shear the object.

The origin point remains fixed in place.

After you shear a Live Shape, it is no longer recognized as the original Live Shape; the specific shape properties are no longer available in the Transform panel.

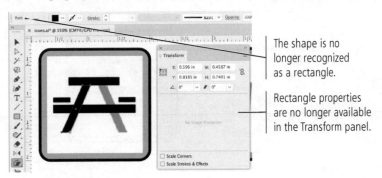

The shape is no longer recognized as a rectangle.

Rectangle properties are no longer available in the Transform panel.

Note:

The Illustrator trans- formation tools all use this same origin point concept as the basis for transformations. You can click without dragging to reposition the origin point before applying the transfor- mation.

7. **Choose the Reflect tool (nested under the Rotate tool) in the Tools panel.**

8. **Double-click the Reflect tool in the Tools panel.**

   Double-clicking a transformation tool in the Tools panel opens a dialog box, where you can numerically define the transformation. (This dialog box is the same one you would see by choosing Object>Transform>Reflect.)

9. **Check the Preview option at the bottom of the dialog box.**

   When the Preview option is active, you can see the result of your choices before finalizing them.

10. **Choose the Vertical option in the Axis section.**

    Reflecting vertically flips the object around the Y axis. Reflecting horizontally flips the object around the X axis.

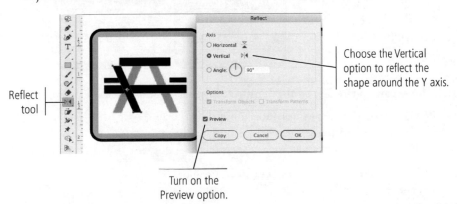

Reflect tool

Choose the Vertical option to reflect the shape around the Y axis.

Turn on the Preview option.

Note:

Transformation dialog boxes default to the last-used settings for that transformation.

11. Click Copy.

If you simply clicked OK, the original object would have been reflected. By clicking Copy, you create the second table leg shape; the original remains in place.

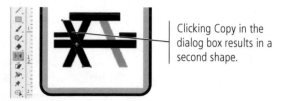

Clicking Copy in the dialog box results in a second shape.

12. Using the Selection tool, click the reflected shape and drag right. Use Smart Guides to keep the dragged shape aligned to the original.

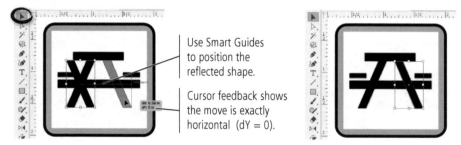

Use Smart Guides to position the reflected shape.

Cursor feedback shows the move is exactly horizontal (dY = 0).

13. Save the file and continue to the next exercise.

Manage Artwork with Groups

The artwork for this icon consists of six separate shapes (seven, if you count the background rectangle). Because these distinct objects make up one piece of artwork, you should create a group so that all pieces can be treated as a single unit.

1. With **icons.ai** open, select the Template picnic.jpg layer in the Layers panel.

2. Click the panel's Delete Selection button. When asked to confirm the deletion, click Yes.

Since the picnic table artwork is complete, you no longer need the template image.

Delete Selection button

3. In the Layers panel, click the arrow to the left of the Icon Art layer.

When you expand a layer in the panel, you can see the individual objects that exist on that layer (called **sublayers**). You drew six shapes in the previous exercise; the expanded Icon Art layer lists each of those objects separately.

Objects are listed in the order you created them; the first object you create appears at the bottom of the list and the last object appears at the top. This bottom-to-top arrangement is called **stacking order**.

4. With the Selection tool active, choose Select>All.

This command selects all unlocked objects in the file. Because the Backgrounds layer is locked, the rectangle behind the artwork is not selected.

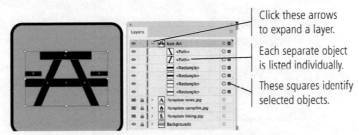

Click these arrows to expand a layer.

Each separate object is listed individually.

These squares identify selected objects.

5. With all the objects selected, choose Object>Group.

The six individual objects are components of a single thing — the "picnic" icon. Grouping them allows all the pieces to be treated as a single object on the artboard.

Grouping allows you to treat the icon artwork as a single object.

6. Click the arrow to the left of the Backgrounds layer to expand that layer.

Because you locked the entire layer, all objects on that layer are also locked.

Because the parent layer is locked, all objects on that layer are also locked.

7. Click the Lock icon for the Backgrounds layer to unlock it.

When you unlock a layer, all objects on that layer are also unlocked.

8. Using the Selection tool, Shift-click the brown background shape to add it to the active selection.

If you used the Select All method, you would select all eight background shapes because the Backgrounds layer is now unlocked. Manually clicking is a better choice to select only the one you want.

Objects on multiple layers can be selected at the same time.

9. **Choose Object>Group.**

10. **In the Layers panel, click the arrow to the left of the resulting group.**

When you group objects that exist on different layers, all objects in the group are moved to the top-most layer in the selection. In this case, the background rectangle is moved from the Backgrounds layer to the group on the Icon Art layer.

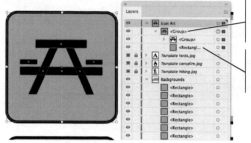

The parent group contains the icon group and the background rectangle.

All grouped objects are moved to the top-most layer in the selection.

Note:

You can choose Object>Ungroup, or press Command/Control-Shift-G, to ungroup objects in a group.

11. **Click the arrow to collapse the Backgrounds layer, and then click the empty space to the left of the Backgrounds layer to relock that layer.**

12. **With the group on the Icon Art layer selected, choose Object>Lock>Selection.**

The lock icon in the Layers panel shows that the group is locked, but the parent Icon Art layer is not. You can draw more artwork on the same layer without accidentally affecting the existing artwork.

Click this space to lock or unlock only a specific sublayer.

13. **In the Layers panel, double-click the parent <Group> name to highlight it.**

14. **Type Picnic Table, then press Return/Enter to finalize the new name.**

You can assign specific names to sublayers, just as you do to regular layers. Meaningful names for each group will make it easier to manage the various icons if you need to make changes at a later date.

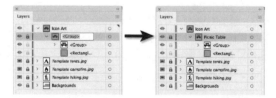

15. **Click the arrows to collapse the Picnic Table sublayer and the Icon Art layer.**

16. **Save the file and continue to the next exercise.**

Using the Group Selection Tool

You can create more than one level of group, called **nesting**, by selecting an existing group, and then grouping it with other objects or groups. You can use the **Group Selection tool** to help navigate complex levels of nested groups.

The first click with the Group Selection tool selects an individual object in a group. The second click selects that object's containing group. The third click adds the next containing group to the selection, and so on, until the entire parent group is selected.

Group Selection tool

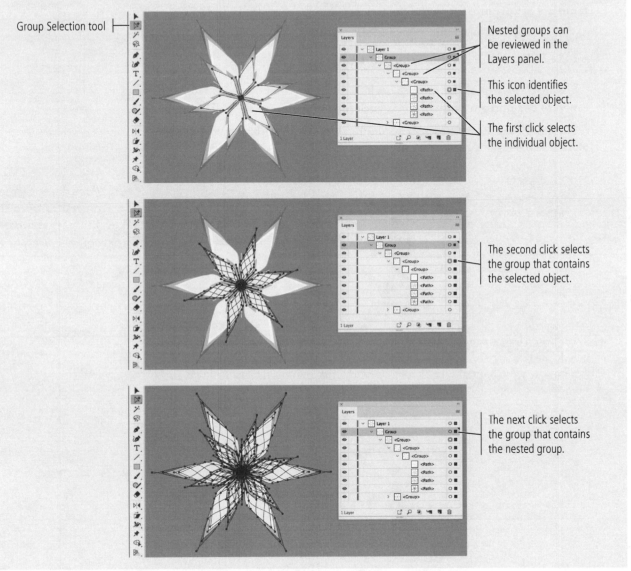

Nested groups can be reviewed in the Layers panel.

This icon identifies the selected object.

The first click selects the individual object.

The second click selects the group that contains the selected object.

The next click selects the group that contains the nested group.

Create Artwork with Lines

The Hiker icon is a perfect candidate for drawing with lines — which makes it ideal for introducing the Line Segment tool. In this exercise, you combine simple lines with other basic shapes to create the final icon.

1. **With icons.ai open, make sure the Icon Art layer is active. Make the hiker template art prominent in the document window.**

2. **Choose the Line Segment tool in the Tools panel. Using the Control panel, set the Fill to None and the Stroke to 1-pt Black.**

3. **Click near the top of the figure's neck, hold down the mouse button, and drag down to the bottom of the figure's back leg (as shown in the following image).**

   As you drag, the cursor feedback shows the distance (D) or length, as well as the angle of the line you're drawing.

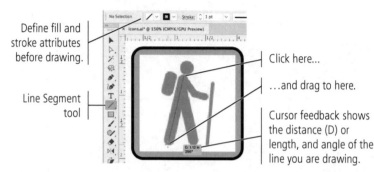

Define fill and stroke attributes before drawing.

Line Segment tool

Click here...

...and drag to here.

Cursor feedback shows the distance (D) or length, and angle of the line you are drawing.

Note:

If you don't see the cursor feedback, choose View>Smart Guides to toggle on that option.

When you release the mouse button, the line appears with the 1-pt black stroke that you defined in Step 2. The Control panel shows that Illustrator recognizes this object as a Line — a function of Live Shapes capability. The Transform panel includes Line Properties of length and rotation.

The object is recognized as a Line.

You can use the Properties panel to change the length and angle of a Line.

4. **Using the Control panel, change the Stroke Weight field to 12 pt.**

5. **Open the Stroke panel (Window>Stroke). If you only see the Stroke Weight field, open the panel's Options menu and choose Show Options.**

   Stroke properties are not limited to simply the stroke weight. The panel includes a number of options for customizing the appearance of a line.

Click here to open the panel Options menu.

6. **With the line selected on the artboard, choose the Round cap style in the Stroke panel.**

By default, lines have flat ends that stop at the anchor points that mark the ends of the lines. If you choose the Round or Square cap styles, the caps extend beyond the ending anchor points by one half the defined stroke weight.

In this case, you defined a 12-pt stroke, so the caps extend 6 points beyond the ending anchor points. Because the round caps essentially make the line longer, you have to change the line length to match the icon artwork.

Round caps extend beyond the actual endpoints of the line.

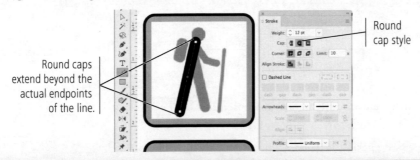

Round cap style

The Stroke Panel in Depth

The **Cap** options define the appearance of a stroke beyond the endpoint of the line.

None cap style

Round cap style

Square cap style

The **Corner** options define the appearance of corners where two lines meet. When Miter Join is selected, you can define a miter limit in the Limit field. A miter limit controls when the corner switches from a pointed joint to a beveled joint as a factor of the stroke weight. If you define a miter limit of 2 for a 2-point line, the corner is beveled if the pointed corner extends beyond 4 points (2 × 2).

Miter join   Round join   Bevel join

The **Align Stroke** options determine where the stroke is placed relative to the actual path.

Align Stroke to Center   Align Stroke to Inside   Align Stroke to Outside

When the **Dashed Line** option is checked, you can define a specific pattern of dashes and gaps in the related fields. The two buttons to the right of the check box determine how a dash pattern is stretched (or not) so that line ends or object corners have the same appearance.

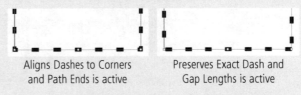

Aligns Dashes to Corners and Path Ends is active   Preserves Exact Dash and Gap Lengths is active

The **Arrowheads** options can be used to control end treatments on each end of a line. You can choose an arrowhead shape from the menus, and change the scale of applied arrowheads (relative to the applied stroke weight).

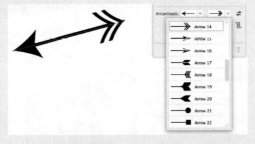

The Align [Arrowheads] options determine how arrowhead treatments are positioned relative to the path endpoint.

Place Arrow Tip at End of Path   Extend Arrow Tip Beyond End of Path

7. **Using the Transform panel, change the Line Length field to 1 in. Press Return/Enter to finalize the change.**

When you use the Line Properties options, the change always orients around the center of the line. The selected reference point at the top of the panel has no effect on the change.

The line length is changed from the middle, so both ends align to the template.

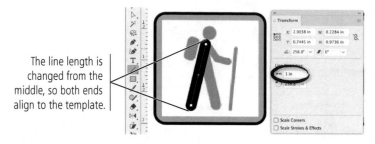

8. **Press Command/Control to temporarily access the Selection tool and click away from the active line to deselect it.**

If you don't deselect the first line, clicking at the same spot as an existing, selected anchor point would actually drag the existing point instead of drawing a new line. This function of Live Shapes means you can edit existing line points and properties without switching tools, but it also means you can't begin a new line at the same point without first deselecting the original line.

Press Command/Control to temporarily access the last-used Selection tool.

The Line Segment tool is still technically active.

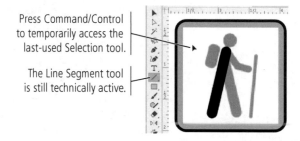

9. **With the Line Segment tool still active, move the cursor over the top end of the existing line until you see the word "anchor" in the cursor.**

The "anchor" label, a function of Smart Guides, indicates that clicking will create a new point at the same location as the existing one. Because you are using the Line Segment tool, the two lines will remain separate; they are not connected at the overlapping anchor points.

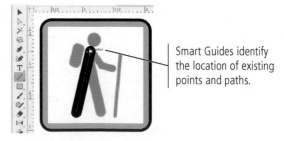

Smart Guides identify the location of existing points and paths.

10. **Click and drag down to the bottom of the front leg in the template artwork. When the cursor feedback shows the line is 1 in long, release the mouse button.**

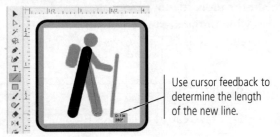

Use cursor feedback to determine the length of the new line.

11. **Command/Control-click away from the selected line to deselect it.**

12. **Click again at the point where the lines meet, and drag to create the figure's top arm segment.**

   The new line uses the same stroke attributes as the previous ones unless you change those settings before drawing. In this case, the 12-pt stroke is too heavy, so you need to reduce it.

13. **Using the Control panel or the Stroke panel, change the line weight to 8 pt.**

14. **Deselect the new line, then draw the lower segment of the figure's arm.**

15. **Using the Line Segment tool, click and drag to create the walking stick. Define the line to have a 4-pt stroke with round caps.**

16. **Save the file and continue to the next exercise.**

Draw with Live Shapes

In addition to using the Transform panel to edit the properties of Live Shapes, you can also use the tool cursor to edit those shapes without the need to constantly switch tools. In this exercise, you will create and edit two more live shapes to complete the Hiking icon artwork.

1. **With icons.ai open, deselect everything on the artboard.**

2. **Choose the Rectangle tool, and define a 1-pt black stroke with no fill.**

3. **Click and drag to create a rectangle that is approximately the same size as the backpack in the template art.**

Note:

Zooming in to the artwork can be helpful for completing the next two exercises.

The shape is recognized as a Rectangle.

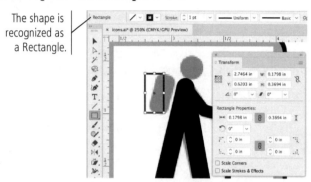

4. **Click the object's center point and drag to move the shape until its center approximately matches the center of the shape in the template art.**

    Because this is a Live Shape, you do not need to change tools to rotate, move, or transform the shape.

Click the center point and drag to move the Live Shape.

The Rectangle tool is still active.

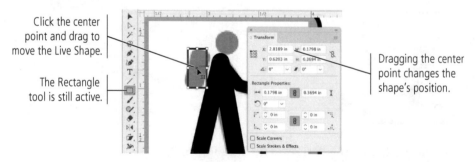

Dragging the center point changes the shape's position.

5. **Move the cursor near the corner of the resulting shape. When you see the rotation cursor, click and drag to rotate the shape to match the angle of the same shape in the template art.**

Click just outside a corner point and drag to rotate the Live Shape.

The Rectangle tool is still active.

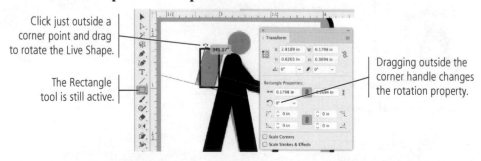

Dragging outside the corner handle changes the rotation property.

6. **Click and drag any of the bounding-box handles until the shape's height and width matches the template art.**

Click and drag any of the bounding-box handles to resize the Live Shape.

The Rectangle tool is still active.

Dragging the bounding-box handles changes the shape's size properties.

7. **In the Transform panel, make sure the link between the Corner Radius fields is active, then change any of the fields to 0.05 in.**

Remember, you hid the Corner Widgets in an earlier exercise. If they were visible, you could drag the live widgets to change the shape's corner radius.

Note:

To show corner widgets, choose View>Show Corner Widgets.

The Rectangle tool is still active.

Use these fields to change the corner radius if the on-screen widgets are not visible.

8. **With the object selected, click the Swap Fill and Stroke button at the bottom of the Tools panel.**

Swap Fill and Stroke button

9. **Choose the Ellipse tool (nested under the Rectangle tool).**

10. **Press Option/Alt, then click at the center of the figure's head and drag out. Use the Smart Guides to create a shape with equal height and width.**

Pressing Option/Alt while you draw creates the new shape with its center at the point where you click. You can press Shift to constrain the new shape to a circle, or simply use the Smart Guides.

Again, ellipses are recognized by Illustrator's Live Shapes functionality. The Transform panel shows options that are relative to an ellipse.

Option/Alt-click the center of the figure's head to draw out from the center.

Ellipse tool

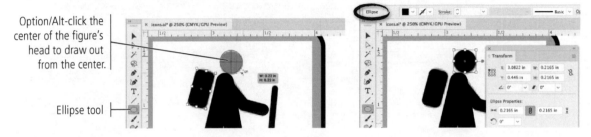

11. **If necessary, adjust the circle's size and position until you are satisfied with the results.**

12. **Save the file and continue to the next exercise.**

Transforming Objects with the Bounding Box

Bounding-box handles make it easy to transform an object on the artboard. When the Selection tool is active, you can resize an object by dragging any handle, and even rotate an object by placing the cursor directly outside a corner handle. If Smart Guides are active, cursor feedback helps if you want to make specific transformations, or you can work freestyle and drag handles until you're satisfied with the results.

Drag a left- or right-center handle
to change the object's width.

Shift-drag to maintain an object's original
height-to-width aspect ratio as you transform it.

Drag a top- or bottom-center handle
to change the object's height.

Option/Alt-drag a handle to transform
the object around its center point.

Drag a corner handle to change both the
height and shape of an object at once.

Click directly outside an object's
corner handle to rotate the object.

Artwork used in these examples is taken from the built-in Adobe symbol libraries.

Understanding the Free Transform Tool

The Free Transform tool allows you to change the shape of selected objects by dragging transformation handles.

The **Touch widget**, which you can use to change the active transformation mode, appears when the Free Transform tool is active. To move the Touch bar in the workspace, click away from the three buttons and drag to another location.

Moving the cursor over a handle shows the transformation that can be made by dragging that handle. Clicking one of the handles shows a larger icon to indicate the possible transformation.

Transformation handles

Constraint

Free Transform

Perspective Distort

Free Distort

When the cursor is over a transformation handle, the icon shows which distortions can be made.

When you first select the Free Transform tool, the widget shows that the **Free Transform** mode is active. Larger transformation handles appear over all eight of the selected object's bounding-box handles. In this case, most of the available transformations are the same as those you can make when the Selection tool is active.

Drag a corner handle diagonally in or out to scale the selection horizontally and vertically at the same time.	Drag a center handle perpendicular to the bounding box edge to scale the selection in one direction.	Drag a center handle parallel to the bounding box edge to skew the selection.
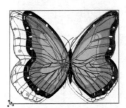	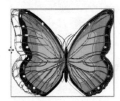	
Click a corner handle and drag around to rotate the selection.	Press Option/Alt to apply the transformation around the center point.	Press Shift, or activate the Constraint option, to transform the selection proportionally (maintaining the original height-to-width aspect ratio).

If you activate the **Perspective Distort** option in the Touch widget, you can drag the object's corner transformation handles to change the object's perspective. (The Constraint option is not available when Perspective Distort is active.)

When the Free Transform mode is active, you can accomplish the same goal by clicking a corner handle, then pressing Command-Option-Shift/Control-Alt-Shift and dragging.

If you activate the **Free Distort** option, you can drag the corner transformation handles to distort the selection. When Constraint is active, you can only drag the corner exactly horizontal or vertical from its previous position.

When the Free Transform mode is active, you can accomplish the same goal by clicking a corner handle, then pressing Command/Control and dragging.

Explore Artwork Outlines

As you develop complex artwork, it can be helpful to view the basic artwork structure without applied fill and stroke attributes. Illustrator's Outline mode makes this possible.

1. **With icons.ai open, deselect everything in the file.**

2. **Choose View>Outline.**

    Regardless of the defined stroke weight, lines are still just lines. Outline mode shows you a wireframe of your artwork; fill and stroke attributes are not visible.

In Outline viewing mode, the Layers panel shows a hollow eye icon for non-template layers.

In Outline mode, you can't see the objects' fill or stroke attributes.

Note:

By default, objects on template layers remain visible in outline mode. You can convert a template layer to outlines by Command/Control-clicking the template layer icon.

3. **Choose the Join tool in the Tools panel (nested under the Shaper tool).**

    The Join tool is an easy way to connect open line segments.

4. **Click and drag with the Join tool to paint an area over the point where the figure's elbow meets.**

    Because these lines have rounded caps, outline mode makes it easier to see the actual ends of the lines.

Paint over the open endpoints to join them.

Note:

You can also select open endpoints and choose Object>Path>Join. If the selected points overlap, as in this exercise, the two points are simply combined into a single corner endpoint. If the selected endpoints do not overlap, this command creates a straight, connecting segment between the points.

5. **Choose the Selection tool in the Tools panel, and click either of the arm segments to select them.**

    You can now see the bounding box of the selected object — both angled lines, which have been joined into a single Path object (as you can see in the Control panel). After joining the endpoints of the two lines, they no longer function independently.

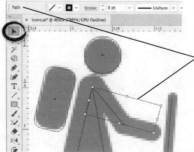

Joining the endpoints combines the two separate lines into a single path with multiple segments.

6. With the new Path object selected, choose Object>Lock>Selection.

When an object is locked, you can't select or change it — just as locking a layer protects the objects on that layer.

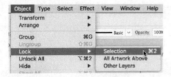

7. Choose the Join tool again. Click and drag over the top endpoints of the lines that make up the figure's legs.

This shape is locked, so the upper endpoint of this line segment is not affected.

8. Choose View>Preview or View>Preview on CPU to exit Outline mode and display the normal artwork.

The available options depend on whether GPU Performance is enabled on your device.

- If GPU Performance is enabled, you can use the View menu to toggle between the Outline and Preview mode. A separate menu option allows you to choose View Using CPU, which does not use the GPU to display graphics.

- If GPU Performance is not enabled, you can only toggle between Outline and Preview on CPU mode.

When Outline mode is turned off, you can see the result of joining the endpoints. By default, connected line segments use the Miter Join method. This is obviously not appropriate for the icon artwork in this exercise.

9. **Click either unlocked line with the Selection tool to select the Path object.**

   Again, joining the open endpoints combined the two Lines into a single Path object.

10. **With the Path object selected, click the Round Join Corner option in the Stroke panel.**

11. **In the Layers panel, expand the Icon Art layer.**

   As you can see, the Picnic Table artwork group is locked from the earlier exercise. The second path object that makes up the figure's arm is also locked from Step 6.

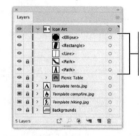

These five objects make up the Hiker artwork.

Working with GPU Preview

The Graphics Processing Unit (GPU) is a specialized processor that can quickly execute commands for displaying images, which allows faster artwork rendering in Illustrator.

If your computer meets the hardware and software requirements*, GPU Performance is enabled by default. You can temporarily disable Illustrator's GPU Preview mode by choosing View>Preview on CPU. You can also permanently disable the feature in the GPU Performance pane of the Preferences dialog box.

When GPU Performance is enabled and the Zoom tool is active, you can also use the animated zoom feature:

- Hold down the mouse button to dynamically zoom in on the spot where you click.
- Click and drag right to dynamically zoom in.
- Click and drag left to dynamically zoom out.

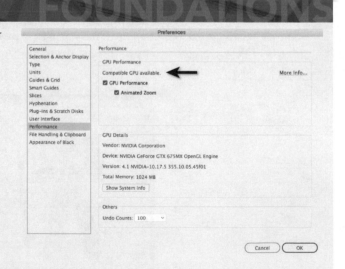

*A complete list of requirements can be found at https://helpx.adobe.com/illustrator/kb/gpu-performance-preview-improvements.html

12. **Click the Lock icon for the Path object to unlock only that object.**

The Object>Unlock All menu command unlocks all individually locked objects on unlocked layers (it does not affect objects on locked layers). When a layer is expanded, however, you can use the Lock column in the Layers panel to lock and unlock individual objects without unlocking everything.

Use this column to lock or unlock specific objects on a layer.

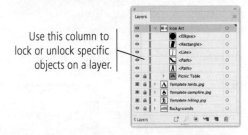

13. **Use what you learned in the previous exercise to finalize the icon artwork:**

- **Delete the Template hiking.jpg layer**
- **Choose Select>All**
- **Choose Object>Group**
- **Unlock the Backgrounds layer**
- **Press Shift, then click the background shape to add it to the active selection**
- **Choose Object>Group**
- **Lock the Backgrounds layer**
- **Rename the parent group** `Hiker` **in the Layers panel**
- **Lock the Hiker sublayer**

14. **Save the file and continue to the next exercise.**

 ## Draw with the Shaper Tool

The Shaper tool allows you to easily create basic shapes, almost as you would with a pencil on paper. The software automatically translates your drawing into rectangles, polygons with other than four sides, ellipses, or straight lines. In this exercise you will use this tool to create the tent artwork.

1. **With `icons.ai` open, expand the Icon Art layer, and then zoom into the tent template artwork.**

2. **Make sure the Icon Art layer is active, then choose the Shaper tool in the Tools panel.**

If you continued directly from the previous exercise, the tool is nested under the Join tool.

3. **If you see a window appear with advice on using the Shaper tool, click the window's Close button.**

Illustrator includes a number of these pop-up "helper" dialog boxes that explain certain features. Feel free to explore those dialog boxes when they appear.

4. **Click and drag to draw a triangle that represents the outer shape of the tent.**

For some reason, the Shaper tool always defaults to a light gray fill, even if you define a different fill color before drawing.

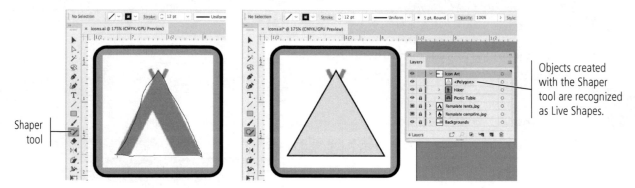

Shaper tool

Objects created with the Shaper tool are recognized as Live Shapes.

5. **Click and drag again to draw the inner triangle.**

6. **Click and drag again to draw two straight lines that represent the tent poles.**

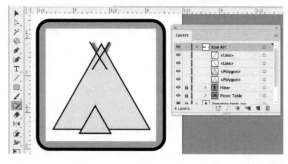

7. **Using the Shaper tool, scribble a path that begins below both rectangles and touches the overlapping area of the two triangles.**

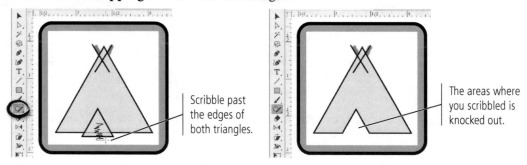

Scribble past the edges of both triangles.

The areas where you scribbled is knocked out.

8. **In the Layers panel, expand the Shaper Group sublayer.**

Scribbling over an area of overlapping objects converts those objects into a Shaper Group. All overlapping objects become part of the group, even if they were not affected by the scribbling motion.

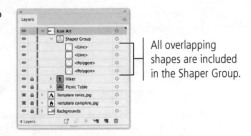

All overlapping shapes are included in the Shaper Group.

How you scribble with the tool determines what will happen:

- Scribble past the outer edges of the shapes to remove (knock out) both the fill and stroke attributes of the area.

- Scribble entirely within an overlap area to knock out that area.

- Scribble from an overlap area to a non-overlap area to merge the shapes where you scribble. The resulting shape is the color of the front shape in the stacking order.

- Scribble from a non-overlap area to an overlap area to create shapes that depend on where you start to scribble:

    - Start in the back object to create a merged shape with the same color as the back shape.

    - Start in the front object to knock out the areas where you scribble.

9. **Move the Shaper tool cursor over overlapping shapes to reveal the overlapping paths.**

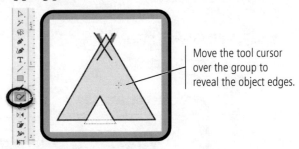

Move the tool cursor over the group to reveal the object edges.

10. **Click the group to select it.**

Clicking inside a Shaper Group selects the entire group object. It is surrounded by a single bounding box, and an arrow widget appears on the right edge. When the entire Shaper Group is selected, changes to the fill or stroke attributes affect all visible elements of the group.

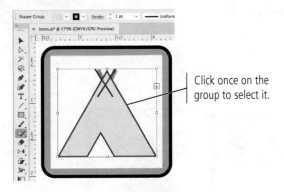

Click once on the group to select it.

11. **In the Control panel, change the Stroke color to None.**

Because the entire group is selected, this affects all objects in the group — including the two lines that are supposed to represent the tent poles.

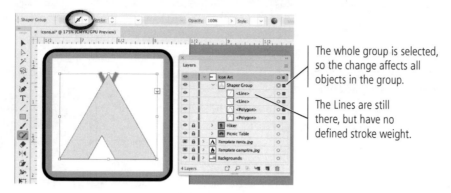

The whole group is selected, so the change affects all objects in the group.

The Lines are still there, but have no defined stroke weight.

12. **Click once on the surface of the visible (back) triangle shape.**

Clicking any of the filled shapes in the Shaper Group enters into Face Selection mode, in which the selected surface is identified with a crosshatch overlay. You can use this method to edit the fill color — but not the stroke color — of only the selected element within the group.

13. **Using the Control panel, change the selected shape's fill color to Black.**

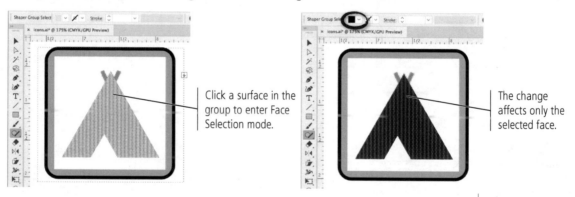

Click a surface in the group to enter Face Selection mode.

The change affects only the selected face.

14. **Click the arrow icon in the top-right corner of the shaper group's bounding box to enter Construction mode.**

Clicking the arrow widget on the Shaper Group bounding box enters Construction mode, in which you can access and edit the individual shape properties of the component shapes of a shaper group.

Note:

If the arrow widget on group's bounding box is pointing up, you are in Construction mode.

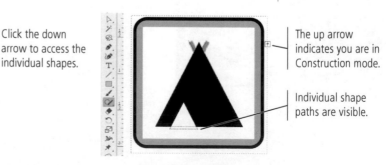

Click the down arrow to access the individual shapes.

The up arrow indicates you are in Construction mode.

Individual shape paths are visible.

15. Click the black filled area again to reveal the triangle's bounding box. Adjust the bounding-box handles until it approximately matches the outer shape in the template image.

It is important to realize that Shaper Groups maintain the original shapes, even after you knock out or merge specific areas of those shapes.

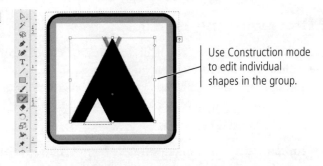

Use Construction mode to edit individual shapes in the group.

16. Click the edge of the inner triangle to select that element of the group. Adjust the bounding-box handles until you are satisfied with the inner shape's size and position relative to the template artwork.

Because that shape has no fill, you have to click the edge to select it.

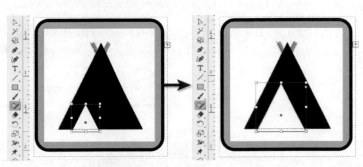

17. Select each of the tent pole lines and define a 4-pt black stroke.

You can edit the lines individually, or Shift-click to select both before changing the stroke weight.

18. Click away from the Shaper Group to exit Construction mode and deselect the group.

Note:

You can also single-click an object's stroke or double-click an object's fill to enter into Construction mode.

19. Delete the Template tents.jpg layer from the file.

20. Use what you learned in previous exercises to create a final locked group named Campsites for the tent artwork and its background.

In this case you do not need to create a separate group for the icon because it is already combined in a special Shaper Group.

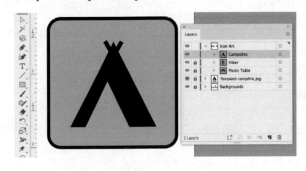

Note:

To remove an object from a Shaper Group, enter into Construction mode for that group. Click the center point of the shape you want to remove, then drag it out of the Shaper Group's bounding box.

21. Save the file and continue to the next exercise.

Draw with the Pencil Tool

As you might already realize, not all artwork can be created from basic shapes and lines. Illustrator includes everything you need to create artwork in any form, including irregular shapes. The Pencil tool is one method for creating custom shapes. Like a regular pencil on a piece of paper, the Pencil tool creates lines that follow the path of your cursor.

Note:

If you have a digital drawing tablet, the Pencil tool can be particularly useful for drawing custom artwork.

1. **With icons.ai open, make sure the Icon Art layer is selected in the Layers panel. Zoom in to the campfire template artwork.**

2. **Choose the Pencil tool (nested under the Shaper tool) in the Tools panel, and click the Default Fill and Stroke button in the Tools panel.**

Pencil tool

3. **Double-click the Pencil tool in the Tools panel.**

   Double-clicking certain tools in the Tools panel opens an Options dialog box, where you can control the behavior for the selected tool. The Pencil tool options include:

   - **Fidelity.** This option determines how far apart anchor points are added as you drag. Smooth results in fewer points and smoother curves, but also less accuracy matching the path you draw. More accurate means more anchor points and a path closer to what you draw (this can make the lines appear choppy).

   - **Fill New Pencil Strokes.** By default, pencil paths are not filled, regardless of the fill color defined in the Tools panel.

   - **Keep Selected.** If this option is checked, the line you draw is automatically selected when you release the mouse button.

   - **Option Key Toggles to Smooth Tool.** As the name suggests, this allows you to quickly and temporarily switch to the Smooth tool while drawing with the Pencil tool. The Smooth tool can be used to remove unnecessary points along a pencil-drawn path, removing small or jagged jumps in the path.

   - **Close Paths when Ends are within __ Pixels.** When this option is active, dragging back near the original starting point creates a closed path when you release the mouse button. If this option is not checked, dragging near the original point does not create a closed path.

   - **Edit Selected Paths.** If this option is checked, drawing near a selected path (based on the Within value) can change the existing path. This is an important distinction — especially when Keep Selected is checked — because you can accidentally edit the first path instead of creating a second shape.

4. Define the following settings in the Pencil Tool Options dialog box:
    - **Set the Fidelity slider to the midpoint.**
    - **Check the Close Paths... option**
    - **Uncheck all other options**

5. Click OK to apply your changes and return to the artboard.

6. Click at the bottom-left point of the fire icon. Hold down the mouse button and begin dragging around the shape of the fire.

7. When you get near your original starting point and a hollow circle appears in the cursor icon, release the mouse button.

    As you drag, a colored line indicates the path you're drawing. Don't worry if the path isn't perfect; when you release the mouse button, Illustrator automatically smooths the path.

    When you release the mouse button, the shape shows the defined stroke color, but not the fill color, because you unchecked the Fill New Pencil Strokes option in Step 4.

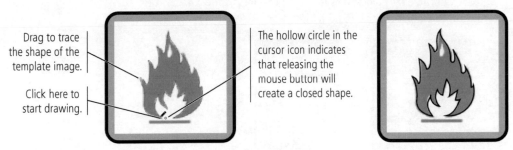

Drag to trace the shape of the template image.

Click here to start drawing.

The hollow circle in the cursor icon indicates that releasing the mouse button will create a closed shape.

8. Click near the top point of the white flame area (inside the first path) and drag to create the white inner shape in the fire icon.

Use the Pencil tool to draw this shape.

9. Using the Rectangle tool, draw the gray bar below the fire shape.

10. In the Layers panel, delete the Template campfire.jpg layer.

11. Expand the Icon Art layer if necessary.

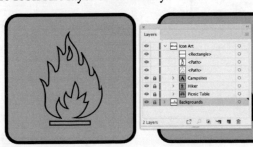

Note:

Pressing the Option/Alt key while you drag with the Pencil tool places an anchor point at the location of the cursor when you press the key.

If you hold down the Option/Alt key while dragging, you can draw a straight line. When you release the modifier key, an anchor point ends the straight segment; continuing to drag resumes drawing a path in whatever shape you drag.

12. **Use the Selection tool to select all three shapes of the icon art. Change the fill color to black and the stroke color to None.**

    When all three objects are filled, you can't see the inner shape at the top of the flame.

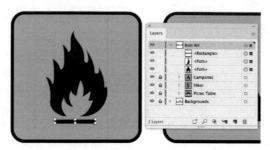

13. **Choose Object>Compound Path>Make.**

    A **compound path** is a single shape made up of more than one path. Compound paths usually have inner "empty" areas, such as the letter O or Q.

    This option combines all three selected shapes into one; the area of the smaller top shape is removed from the larger shape behind it.

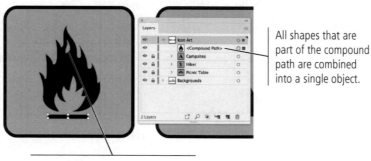

    All shapes that are part of the compound path are combined into a single object.

    As a compound path, the top shape is knocked out from the bottom shape.

14. **Use what you learned in previous exercises to create a locked group named Campfire for the final icon artwork.**

    In this case you do not need to create a separate group for the icon because it is already combined in the Compound Path object.

15. **Save the file and continue to the final exercise.**

Edit Individual Grouped Elements

The client has decided that the icons should be white artwork on green backgrounds, so the final step in this exercise requires changing the colors of both the background shapes and the icon artwork. This is a fairly easy process, but because each of the icons are grouped, it will require a few extra steps.

1. **With icons.ai open, change your view percentage so you can see all the artwork in the file.**

2. **In the Layers panel, unlock all layers and sublayers in the file.**

3. **Choose the Selection tool, then click the picnic table artwork.**

   Because the artwork is grouped, the Selection tool selects the entire group. You need to use a different method to select only certain elements within the group.

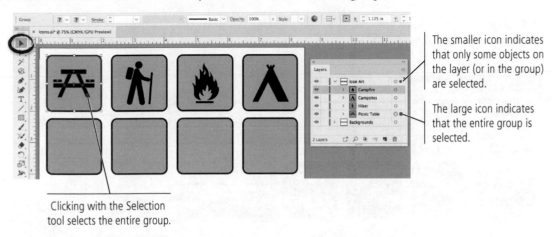

The smaller icon indicates that only some objects on the layer (or in the group) are selected.

The large icon indicates that the entire group is selected.

Clicking with the Selection tool selects the entire group.

4. **Click anywhere outside the rectangle shapes to deselect the group, then choose the Direct Selection tool in the Tools panel.**

   The Direct Selection tool selects pieces of an object — specific paths, anchor points, or individual elements in a grouped object.

5. **Click the brown fill of the background shape behind the picnic table artwork to select it.**

   Because you clicked the fill, you selected the entire object. If you had clicked along the object's stroke, you would have selected that particular segment of the shape's edge.

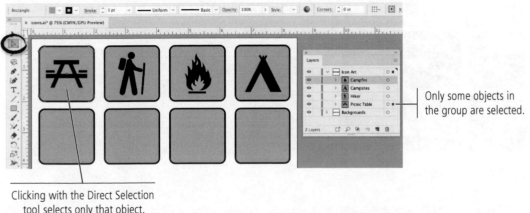

Only some objects in the group are selected.

Clicking with the Direct Selection tool selects only that object.

6. **Choose Select>Same>Fill Color.**

   The options in this menu are very useful for finding objects that share specific attributes. They select all similar unlocked objects on the entire artboard. The Select>Same menu options select objects regardless of which layer they occupy.

7. **With all eight brown shapes selected, use the Control panel to change the Stroke color to None and the Fill color to a medium green.**

Note:

You can also use the Select Similar Objects menu in the Control panel to select objects with like attributes.

8. **Using the Direct Selection tool, click any of the black shapes that make up the picnic table icon.**

9. **Choose Select>Same>Fill Color.**

10. **With all the black-filled objects selected, change the Fill color to White.**

    As you can see, there are two problems. First, the lines in the Hiker icon are still black because they are lines and not filled shapes. Second, the elements in the Campsite icon are still black because the Select>Same commands cannot access individual pieces of a Shaper Group.

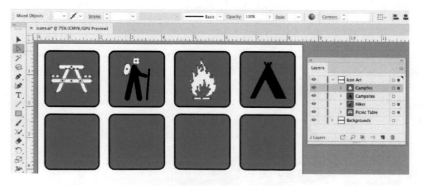

11. **Choose the Selection tool in the Tools panel, and click away from all artwork to deselect everything.**

12. **Double-click the Hiker artwork. In the Layers panel, expand the Hiker group.**

   Double-clicking a group enters into **Isolation mode**, where only objects within the selected group are available. Basically, Isolation mode provides access to objects in the group without ungrouping the objects on the main artboard. Other elements outside the group are dimmed and visible, but you can't access or edit them.

13. **Using the Selection tool, click to select the Hiker artwork.**

   Remember, you created a group from the icon artwork, and then grouped that with the background shape. Because there are two levels of grouping, you have to enter into Isolation mode for the second (nested) group to access the individual paths that make up the actual icon artwork.

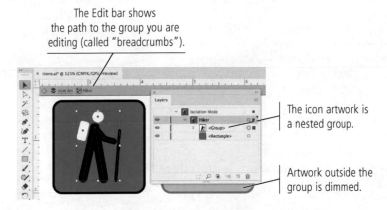

The Edit bar shows the path to the group you are editing (called "breadcrumbs").

The icon artwork is a nested group.

Artwork outside the group is dimmed.

14. **Double-click the icon artwork on the artboard to enter into the nested group. In the Layers panel, expand the Group sublayer.**

15. **Shift-click to select the two Path objects and the Line object.**

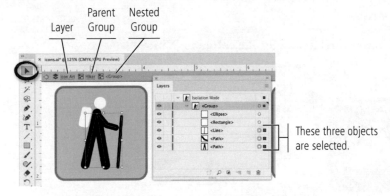

Parent Group | Nested Group

Layer

These three objects are selected.

16. Choose Object>Path>Outline Stroke.

This command converts lines to filled shapes. You can no longer access the actual paths that made up the original Line or Path objects.

17. With all three shapes selected, change the Fill color to White.

18. At the top of the document window, click the arrow button three times to return to the main artboard.

The first click closes the nested group. The second click closes the Hiker group. The third click exits the layer and returns to the main artboard.

19. Using the Shaper tool, click to select the Campsite icon artwork.

The Shaper tool selects the Shaper Group, even though it is grouped with the background rectangle.

20. Using the Control panel, change the Fill and Stroke colors to White.

21. Save the file and close it.

Note:

You can also press the ESC key, or double-click an area outside the group, to exit Isolation mode.

Editing Similar Shapes with Global Edit

In this project, you used the Select>Similar menu to select and edit all shapes with the same fill color at one time. Illustrator includes a related option to identify similar shapes based on their appearance, size, or both.

When an object is selected on the artboard, you can click the Start Global Edit button in the Quick Actions section of the Properties panel, or click the Start Editing Similar Shapes Together button in the Control panel to find other objects that match the current selection.

Clicking the arrow button to the right of either button opens a pop-up panel of preferences, where you can define the attributes you want to include in the search.

Appearance refers to attributes listed in the Appearance panel — fill and stroke, opacity, effects, and so on. Size refers to the physical dimensions (height and width) of the object. You can also determine which artboards to include in the search, as well as whether to include objects on the canvas (pasteboard) outside the artboard boundaries

Start Editing Similar Shapes Together

Click the arrow button to define the parameters of the search.

When you enter the Global Edit mode, the software highlights other shapes that match the attributes of the original selection. (The highlight can be difficult to see, depending on the actual artwork you are building.) Changes to the selected object are also reflected in the highlighted shapes.

When you are finished editing, you can click the Stop Global Edit button or simply click away from the original selection to exit this mode.

In this example, we selected Shape 1 and chose the Match Appearance option. Five objects are not highlighted:

Shapes 2 and 6	Different fill color
Shape 7	Different stroke weight
Shape 9	Different shape
Shape 11	Applied drop shadow

Note that Shape 5 is selected even though it is a different size than Shape 1.

Shape 6 is not selected because different types of objects are not considered to match; a 1″ × 1″ ellipse will not be identified if the original selection is a 1″ × 1″ rectangle.

Changing the fill color of the selected shape also changes the fill color of all highlighted shapes.

Match Appearance is active

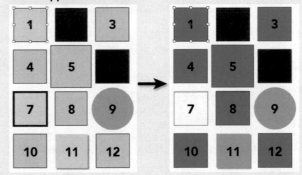

In this second example, we selected Shape 1 and chose the Match Size option. Only Shapes 6 and 11 are not highlighted.

Because the identified objects have different appearance attributes in this case, a warning notes that attributes of the selected item will be copied to all highlighted objects.

After changing the fill color of Shape 1 and dismissing the warning message, all highlighted objects now have a green fill color and no stroke color. The drop shadow effect that was previously applied to Shape 11 has been removed because Shape 1 has no applied drop shadow.

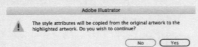

Match Size is active

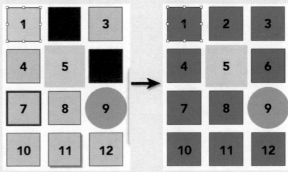

PROJECT REVIEW

1. _____ are composed of mathematical descriptions of a series of lines and points; they are resolution independent, can be freely scaled, and are automatically output at the resolution of the output device.

2. _____ are pixel-based, made up of a grid of individual pixels (rasters or bits).

3. The _____ is a rectangle that marks the outermost edges of an object, regardless of the actual object shape.

4. _____ is the relative top-to-bottom order of objects on the artboard, or of layers in the Layers panel.

5. The _____ is used to select entire objects or groups.

6. The _____ is used to select individual paths and points of a shape, or to select component pieces within a group.

7. The _____ is used to draw freeform paths defined by dragging the mouse cursor.

8. Press _____ to temporarily access the Selection tool; releasing the modifier key restores the previously selected tool.

9. A(n) _____ combines multiple Live Shapes, but maintains the original shapes in a special group.

10. A(n) _____ is a single object that is made up of more than one shape.

1. Briefly explain the difference between vector graphics and raster images.

2. Briefly explain the difference between the Selection tool and the Direct Selection tool.

3. Briefly explain how the Fill and Stroke icons at the bottom of the Tools panel affect your work.

PORTFOLIO BUILDER PROJECT

Use what you have learned in this project to complete the following freeform exercise.
Carefully read the art director and client comments, then create your own design to meet the needs of the project.
Use the space below to sketch ideas. When finished, write a brief explanation of the reasoning behind your final design.

art director comments

The client is pleased with the first four icons, and they want you to complete the rest of the set. They also want you to create an additional set of icons for athletic activities that they offer during their special holiday weekend events.

To complete this project, you should:

❏ Complete the remaining campsite icons. The bitmap versions are in your WIP>Camping folder.

❏ Carefully consider the best approach for each icon and use whichever tool (or tools) you feel is most appropriate.

❏ Create a second Illustrator file for the five new tournament icons.

client comments

Holidays are one of our busiest times, and we host a number of family-oriented special events during those weekends. To help keep everyone happy, we always set up organized tournaments for families with children of all ages, and we want to be able to post signs directing guests to those activities.

Since you did such a good job on the first four icons, we would like you to finish those first.

For the second set, we need icons for badminton, bocce, relay races, horseshoes, and volleyball. We don't have the images for these ones, so we would like you to come up with something. Remember, icons need to be easily recognizable, so they should clearly convey each activity.

project justification

PROJECT SUMMARY

The skills that you learned in this project will serve as the foundation for most work you create in Illustrator. You learned how to place raster images as templates, from which you created scalable vector graphics that will work in virtually any printed application. You learned a number of techniques for selecting objects and component pieces of objects, as well as various options for aligning objects relative to one another and to the artboard.

You learned how to draw primitive geometric shapes, and how to control the color of objects' fill and stroke attributes. You used a number of transformation options, including cloning methods to copy existing objects. Finally, you learned how to draw freeform shapes to suit more complex needs. As you move forward in this book, you will build on the basic skills you learned in this project to create increasingly complex artwork.

Draw, shear, reflect, and clone basic shapes

Use stroke properties to create unique artwork

Create and align basic rectangles with rounded corners

Use various techniques to select objects, groups, and the component pieces of those objects and groups

Use the Shaper tool to combine and manage Live Shapes

Use the Pencil tool and compound paths to draw complex shapes

Regatta Artwork

Your client is the marketing director for the Long Beach Regatta, which attracts tens of thousands of visitors to the beach community throughout the four-day event. You have been hired to create the primary artwork for this year's event, which will be used in a variety of different products (ads, posters, etc.).

This project incorporates the following skills:

❏ Drawing complex custom shapes with the Pen tool

❏ Editing points and handles to control the position of vector paths

❏ Drawing irregular shapes by painting with the Blob Brush tool

❏ Creating a custom color scheme using saved swatches

❏ Adding interest and depth with color gradients

❏ Adjusting color, both globally and in specific selections

❏ Saving a PDF file for print distribution

client comments

The poster to promote the Regatta is basically the "play bill," and we will place it in store windows, public sites, and on bulletin boards all over the city. It will also be placed in local newspapers and entertainment magazines, and used as the cover for the souvenir program that we produce for the event.

We want the artwork to be very colorful and vivid, so the main focus — and most of the poster real estate — should be on the graphics. The only text for the poster is the event name, date, and location.

art director comments

I sketched a mock-up of a sailboat that you can use as the basis for the artwork. You should use the Pen tool to draw the necessary paths because simple shapes won't work and the Pencil tool doesn't provide fine enough control to efficiently achieve what you need.

I assigned the ocean background artwork to another designer, so you will have to incorporate your artwork into that file. This is going to be a complex piece of artwork, so you should pay close attention to the layer content when you organize the various pieces. That will make it far easier to edit specific components as necessary if the client decides to make changes.

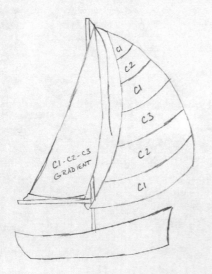

project objectives

To complete this project, you will:

- ❏ Use the Pen tool to draw precise curves
- ❏ Adjust anchor points and handles to precisely control the shape of vector objects
- ❏ Reshape line segments with the Anchor Point tool
- ❏ Use the Blob Brush tool to "paint" the area of vector shapes
- ❏ Define custom color swatches to allow easy universal changes
- ❏ Create color gradients to blend multiple colors in a single object
- ❏ Adjust gradients in context on the artboard
- ❏ Manage artwork with sublayers
- ❏ Save the file as a PDF

STAGE 1 / Drawing Complex Artwork

Much of the artwork you create will require far more complexity than simple lines and geometric shapes. When you need to produce custom artwork — whether from scratch or by tracing a hand-drawn sketch or photo — Illustrator includes a powerful set of tools to create and manipulate every point and path in the illustration. In the first stage of this project, you begin exploring the Pen tool, as well as other options for building and controlling custom shapes.

 ## Prepare the Drawing Workspace

As with any project, setting up the workspace is an important first step. This project requires a single artboard to contain the entire illustration.

1. Download **Regatta_Print19_RF.zip** from the Student Files web page.

2. **Expand the ZIP archive in your WIP folder (Macintosh) or copy the archive contents into your WIP folder (Windows).**

   This results in a folder named **Regatta**, which contains the files you need for this project. You should also use this folder to save the files you create in this project.

3. **In Illustrator, choose File>New. Choose the Print option at the top of the dialog box, and choose the Letter document preset.**

   Remember, using the Print category of presets automatically applies the CMYK color mode and 300 ppi raster effects.

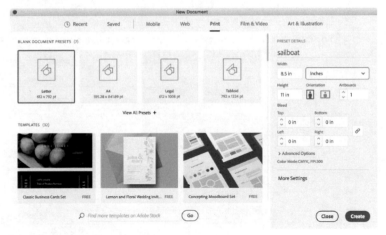

4. **Define the following settings in the Preset Details section:**

Name:	**sailboat**
Units:	Inches
Orientation:	Portrait
Artboards:	1

5. **Click Create to create the file.**

6. **Choose View>Fit Artboard in Window.**

   On Macintosh, the artboard of a new file is automatically centered in the document window. On some Windows systems, the artboard might be slightly off-center. The Fit Artboard in Window command centers the artboard in the document window, so the template image you place in the next step will be automatically centered on the artboard.

7. **Choose File>Place. Navigate to the file `sketch.jpg` in your WIP>Regatta folder. Check the Link and Template options at the bottom of the dialog box, and then click Place.**

Macintosh users: remember, you might have to click the Options button to reveal the options check boxes at the bottom of the Place dialog box.

You will use this client-supplied sketch to create the primary artwork for this illustration.

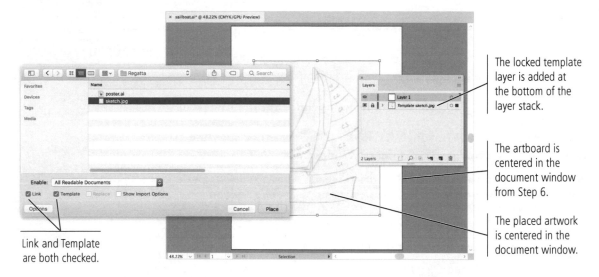

The locked template layer is added at the bottom of the layer stack.

The artboard is centered in the document window from Step 6.

The placed artwork is centered in the document window.

Link and Template are both checked.

8. **Double-click the template layer icon in the Layers panel to open the Layer Options dialog box. Uncheck the Dim Images option and click OK.**

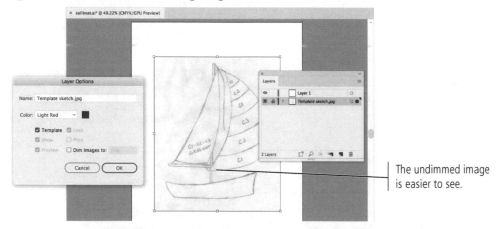

The undimmed image is easier to see.

9. **Double-click the Layer 1 name in the Layers panel to highlight it. Rename the layer `Boat Drawing`, then press Return/Enter to finalize the new name.**

10. **Click away from the placed sketch image to deselect it.**

11. **Save the file as an Illustrator file named `sailboat.ai` in your WIP>Regatta folder using the default Illustrator options, and then continue to the next exercise.**

Use the Pen Tool to Trace the Sketch

In this project, you use the Pen tool, which provides far more power to control the precise position of every line in a drawing. In fact, many believe the Pen tool is the most powerful and important tool in the Illustrator Tools panel.

An **anchor point** marks the end of a line **segment**, and the point **handles** determine the shape of that segment. That's the basic definition of a vector, but there is a bit more to it than that. Fortunately, you don't need to be a mathematician to master the Pen tool because Illustrator handles the underlying geometry for you.

Note:

The lines you create by connecting anchor points and pulling handles are called **Bézier curves**.

Understanding Anchor Points and Handles

Each segment in a path has two anchor points, and can have two associated handles.

You can create corner points by simply clicking with the Pen tool instead of clicking and dragging. Corner points do not have their own handles; the connected segments are controlled by the handles of the other associated points. (Using the Convert Direction Point tool, click a smooth point to convert it to a corner point; click and drag from a corner point to add handles, converting it to a smoother point.)

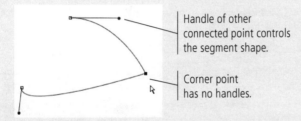

Handle of other connected point controls the segment shape.

Corner point has no handles.

In the image to the right, we clicked to create Point A and dragged (without releasing the mouse button) to create Handle A1. We then clicked and dragged to create Point B and Handle B1; Handle B2 was automatically created as a reflection of B1 (Point B is a **symmetrical point**).

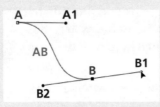

The next image shows the result of dragging Handle B1 to the left instead of to the right when we created the curve. Notice the difference in the curve here and the curve above. When you drag a handle, the connecting segment arcs away from the direction you drag.

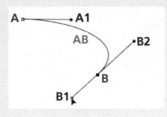

It's important to understand that every line segment is connected to two handles. In this example, Handle A1 and Handle B2 determine the shape of Segment AB. Dragging either handle affects the shape of the connected segment.

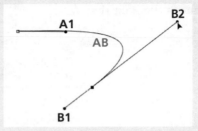

When you use the Pen tool, clicking and dragging a point creates a symmetrical (smooth) point; both handles start out at equal length, directly opposite one another. Changing the angle of one handle of a symmetrical point also changes the opposing handle of that point. In the example here, repositioning Handle B1 also moves Handle B2, which affects the shape of Segment AB. You can, however, change the length of one handle without affecting the length of the other handle.

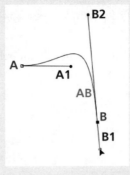

1. **With sailboat.ai open, zoom in so you can clearly see the shape of the boat in the sketch.**

2. **Open the View menu. If the menu command near the bottom of the menu says "Hide Corner Widget," choose that option.**

   This menu command toggles between "Show" and "Hide." If the command already says "Show Corner Widget," then these widgets are already hidden; you can simply click away from the menu to dismiss it.

   Live Corner widgets can be distracting when you don't need them; turning them off allows you to focus on only what you need to see to complete these exercises.

Note:

As you draw, zoom in as necessary to view different parts of the sketch.

3. **Choose the Pen tool in the Tools panel. Using the Control panel, set the stroke to 1-pt black and the fill to None.**

4. **Click with the Pen tool to place the first anchor point on the top-left corner of the boat shape.**

   We typically find it easier to start drawing at a corner (if one exists).

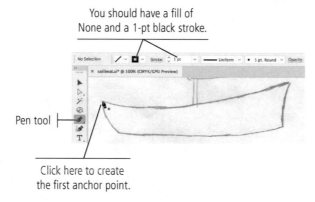

You should have a fill of None and a 1-pt black stroke.

Pen tool

Click here to create the first anchor point.

5. **Click again at the bottom-left corner of the boat shape and immediately drag down and right to create handles for the second point. When the preview of the connecting segment matches the sketch, release the mouse button.**

   When you click and drag without releasing the mouse button, you create symmetrical handles, which determine the shape of the segment that connects the two points.

Note:

When we say "click and drag," you should hold down the mouse button until the end of the step.

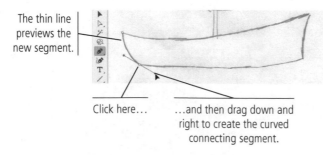

The thin line previews the new segment.

Click here... ...and then drag down and right to create the curved connecting segment.

6. Click and drag again from the bottom-right corner of the boat shape.

Again, clicking and dragging creates a smooth, symmetrical point. Equal-length, exactly opposing handles are created on both sides of the point.

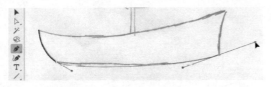

Note:

Don't worry if the connecting segment doesn't exactly match the sketch. The bottom of the boat will be obscured by other artwork in the final poster.

7. Click again on the third anchor point and release the mouse button without dragging.

Clicking a smooth point as you draw converts it to a corner point, removing the outside handle from the point; the inside handle that defines the shape of the connecting segment remains in place. This allows you to change direction as you draw.

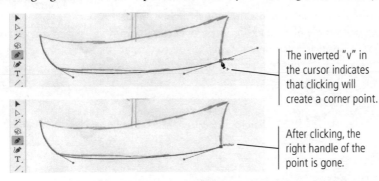

The inverted "v" in the cursor indicates that clicking will create a corner point.

After clicking, the right handle of the point is gone.

Note:

While drawing with the Pen tool, you can Option/Alt-click an anchor point, hold down the mouse button, and drag to add a non-symmetrical handle to one side of a corner point.

8. Click and drag to create a new point (with handles) from the top-right corner of the boat shape. Drag the handles until the connecting segment matches the shape of the sketched line.

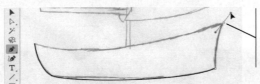

Click here and drag up and right until the connecting segment matches the shape of the sketched line.

9. Click the original point without dragging to close the shape.

When you return to the original point, the cursor shows a small hollow circle. This indicates that clicking the existing point will close the shape.

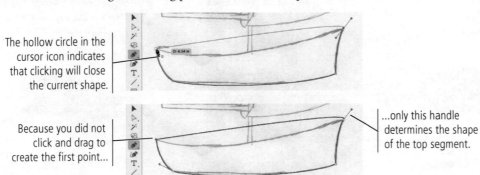

The hollow circle in the cursor icon indicates that clicking will close the current shape.

Because you did not click and drag to create the first point...

...only this handle determines the shape of the top segment.

Note:

The words "anchor" and "path" near the cursor icon are a function of Illustrator Smart Guides.

10. **Using the Direct Selection tool, click the top-right point on the shape to select only that anchor point.**

   You can use the Direct Selection tool to edit any specific anchor point or segment.

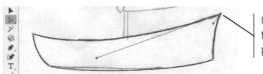

   Unselected anchor points are hollow.

   Selected anchor points are solid.

   The handles related to the selected point are visible.

   Note:

   You can change the size of anchor points and handles in the Selection and Anchor Display pane of the Preferences dialog box.

11. **Press Option/Alt, then click and drag the top handle of the selected point. Drag the handle left until the top segment matches the line in the sketch.**

   Remember, the Direct Selection tool allows you to adjust individual anchor points and handles. Option/Alt-dragging one handle of a smooth point converts the point to a corner point, but leaves both handles in place. This method allows you to change the direction of an existing point, but leaves the opposite curve intact.

   Option/Alt-dragging the handle converts the point to a corner point.

   Note:

   A diagonal line in the Pen tool cursor icon indicates that clicking will connect to an open endpoint so you can continue drawing the shape.

12. **Save the file and continue to the next exercise.**

Understanding Anchor Point and Bézier Curve Tools

Keep the following points in mind as you work with the Pen tool (and its nested variations) and Bézier curves.

Using the Direct Selection tool:

Click a specific anchor point to select it and show all handles that relate to that point.

Option/Alt drag a handle of a smooth point to convert it to a corner point.

Click a segment on a selected path and drag to bend the path; connected segments might also be affected.

Using the Pen tool:

Place the cursor over an existing point to temporarily access the Delete Anchor Point tool.

Place the cursor over an existing segment to temporarily access the Add Anchor Point tool.

Press Option/Alt and place the cursor over an existing point to temporarily access the Anchor Point tool.

Reshape Line Segments

In Illustrator, you have numerous options to create, select, and modify shapes — or parts of shapes — so you can create exactly what you need, regardless of what is already on the artboard. In this exercise you use a convenient method to easily bend line segments into the shapes you need.

1. **With sailboat.ai open, make the right sail in the sketch visible in the document window.**

2. **Using the Pen tool, click to place three connected anchor points at the corners of the sail.**

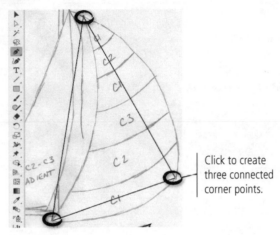

Click to create three connected corner points.

Note:

As a general rule, use as few points as necessary to create a shape with the Pen tool.

3. **Press the Option/Alt key to temporarily access the Anchor Point tool.**

The Anchor Point tool, nested under the Pen tool, can be used to change anchor points from corner to smooth (or vice versa):

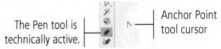

The Pen tool is technically active.

Anchor Point tool cursor

- Click a smooth point to convert it to a corner point.
- Click and drag a corner point to convert it to a smooth point with symmetrical handles.
- Option/Alt-click a handle to move only that handle, even if the point has an opposing handle; a smooth point is converted to a corner point as you drag.

4. **While holding down the Option/Alt key, click the right segment of the sail and drag until the segment matches the sketch.**

You can click and drag a segment to bend it into a different shape; handles are added to, or adjusted as necessary for the related points. This method of reshaping a line segment makes it very easy to edit your artwork without manually manipulating anchor points or handles.

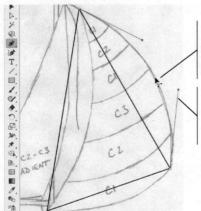

Using the Anchor Point tool, click a segment and drag to push it into a different shape.

Handles are added or adjusted as necessary when you reshape a line segment.

5. **Still holding down the Option/Alt key, adjust the other two lines that make up the sail shape.**

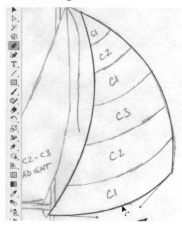

6. **Repeat Steps 2–4 to create the shape of the left sail.**

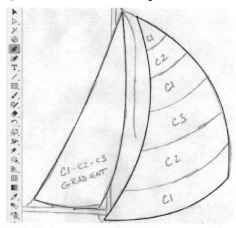

Editing Anchor Points with the Control Panel

When you are working with Bézier paths, the Control panel provides options for editing selected anchor points.

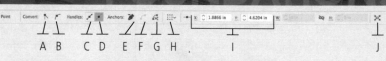

A **Convert Selected Anchor Points to Corner** removes direction handles from both sides of the selected point(s).

B **Convert Selected Anchor Points to Smooth** adds symmetrical handles to both sides of the selected point(s).

C **Show Handles for Multiple Selected Anchor Points.** If this option is toggled on, direction handles display for all selected points.

D **Hide Handles for Multiple Selected Anchor Points.** If this option is toggled on, direction handles are not visible when more than one point is selected.

E **Remove Selected Anchor Points** removes the selected point from the path. If the removed point was between two other points, the connecting segment is not removed.

F **Connect Selected End Points** has the same effect as the Object>Path>Join command.

G **Cut Path at Selected Anchor Points** results in two overlapping, open endpoints where the selected point was previously a single point.

H **Align To.** Use this menu to align a selected point to the active selection or relative to the artboard.

I **Point Position.** Use the X and Y fields to define a specific position for the selected point. You can also use mathematical operations to move a point relative to its current position (e.g., move it left by typing "-1" after the X value).

J **Isolate Selected Object** enters isolation mode with the object containing the selected point(s). If points are selected on more than one object, this button is not available.

7. **Using the Pen tool, click to place a new anchor point to the left of the bottom horizontal line in the right sail, starting and stopping past the edges of the sail shape (as shown in the following image).**

You are going to use the Shape Builder tool to divide the sail into the necessary shapes. For this process to work properly, the dividing lines need to be at least on top of the outside shape; to be sure, you should extend the lines farther than they need to be.

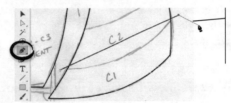

The Pen tool preview shows that clicking again will create another connected segment.

When you move the mouse cursor away from the last point you created, a thin line previews the segment that would be created by clicking again. You can turn this preview on and off using the Enable Rubber Band for Pen Tool option in the Selection and Anchor Display pane of the Preferences dialog box.

8. **Press Option/Alt, then use the Anchor Point tool to reshape the segment to match the line in the sketch.**

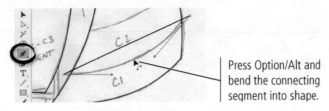

Press Option/Alt and bend the connecting segment into shape.

9. **While the Pen tool is still active, press Command/Control to temporarily access the Selection tool and click away from the line to deselect it.**

You can simply click away from selected objects with the Selection or Direct Selection tool to deselect the current selection. You can also press Command/Control-Shift-A to deselect the current selection.

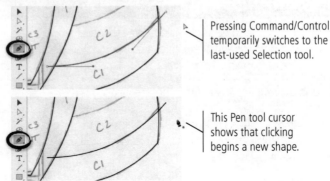

Pressing Command/Control temporarily switches to the last-used Selection tool.

Pressing Command/Control while drawing temporarily switches to the last-used Selection tool. This technique allows you to easily deselect the current path, and then continue to draw another unconnected path, all without manually switching tools.

This Pen tool cursor shows that clicking begins a new shape.

10. **Still using the Pen tool, draw the second horizontal line on the sail.**

If you don't deselect the previous path before clicking to draw the next line, the third click would create a segment that is connected to the last place you clicked (on the first line). In the context of this exercise, a single line with multiple anchor points is much more difficult to control than two separate lines with open endpoints.

11. **Press Option/Alt, then use the Anchor Point tool to reshape the segment to match the line in the sketch.**

12. **Move the cursor away from the existing line, then press the ESC key.**

When drawing with the Pen tool, this key disconnects your drawing from the current shape. You can then click to begin a new shape that is not part of the previously suggested shape.

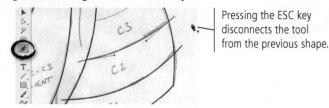

Pressing the ESC key disconnects the tool from the previous shape.

13. **Repeat Steps 10–12 to draw the rest of the curved horizontal lines on the sail.**

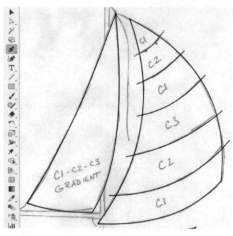

14. **Save the file and continue to the next exercise.**

Drawing with the Curvature Tool

The Curvature tool can be used to create and edit complex paths without manually manipulating anchor points.

Using the Curvature tool, begin by clicking to place points in a new path. As you drag after creating the first two points, the software shows a rubber-band preview of the path that will be created by clicking again. (You can turn this preview behavior off in the Selection and Anchor Display pane of the Preferences dialog box.)

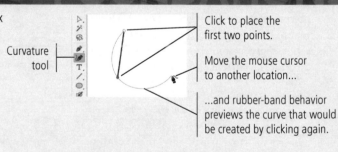

Curvature tool

Click to place the first two points.

Move the mouse cursor to another location...

...and rubber-band behavior previews the curve that would be created by clicking again.

As long as the Curvature tool is active, you do not need to change tools to edit the path:

- Option/Alt-click click to create a corner point.
- Click anywhere along an existing path to add a new anchor point.
- Double-click any point to toggle it between a smooth and corner point.
- Click a point to select it.
- Drag a selected point to move it.
- Press Delete to remove the selected point; the existing curve is maintained.
- Press the Esc key to stop drawing the current shape.

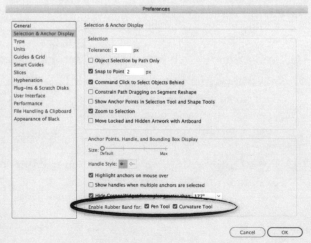

Build Shapes from Overlapping Paths

The Shape Builder tool makes it easy to break apart overlapping objects into component pieces. This tool offers similar functionality as the Pathfinder, but on a piece-by-piece basis, rather than for entire selected shapes. In this exercise, you will use the Shape Builder tool to break the sail into the individual strips that are shown on the sketch.

1. **With sailboat.ai open, use the Selection tool to draw a marquee that selects all lines that make up the right sail.**

2. **Choose the Shape Builder tool in the Tools panel, and then reset the default fill and stroke colors.**

3. **Move the cursor over the bottom section of the sail.**

The Shape Builder tool identifies overlapping areas of selected objects, which is why you had to select the pieces in Step 1.

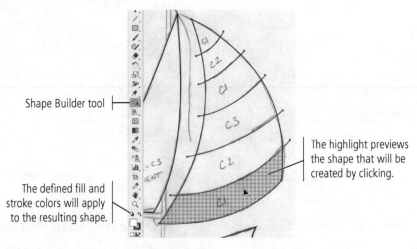

Shape Builder tool

The defined fill and stroke colors will apply to the resulting shape.

The highlight previews the shape that will be created by clicking.

4. **Click the highlighted area to create the new shape.**

Clicking with the Shape Builder tool changes the fill of the resulting shape to the active fill color — white, in this case, because you reset the default fill and stroke colors in Step 2. The resulting shape now obscures the sketch behind it; this helps to identify which pieces you have already created.

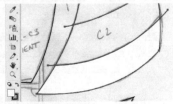

5. **Repeat Steps 3–4 for the remaining five strips on the sail.**

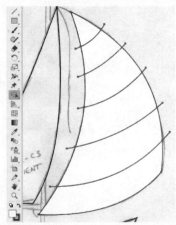

Note:

When the Shape Builder tool divides the objects into separate shapes, it creates anchor points as necessary at the intersections, and also maintains the original points.

6. **Press Option/Alt, and move the cursor over the bottom line segment outside the right sail edge. When the line segment is highlighted and the cursor shows a minus sign in the icon, click the segment to remove it.**

The Shape Builder tool can be used to both create and remove shapes. Pressing Option/Alt switches the tool into Erase mode so you can remove paths or shapes.

The area that will be removed is highlighted.

After clicking, the segment is gone.

7. **Repeat Step 6 to remove the remaining extraneous line segments.**

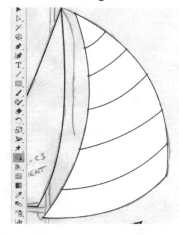

8. **Command/Control-click away from the sail to deselect everything.**

9. **Using the Direct Selection tool, click the right edge of the top shape to select that segment. Click the selected segment and drag slightly out to create a slightly bulged appearance.**

When the Direct Selection tool is active, you can click and drag a selected segment on a closed path to access the same path-reshaping functionality as you have using the Anchor Point tool.

10. **Repeat Step 9 to adjust the right edges of the other shapes in the sail.**

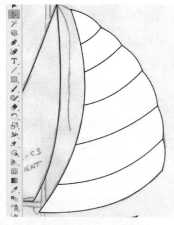

11. **Save the file and continue to the next exercise.**

More about the Shape Builder Tool

Click and drag with the Shape Builder tool to combine multiple pieces into a single shape:

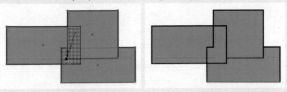

Option/Alt-click and drag with the Shape Builder tool to remove multiple pieces at once:

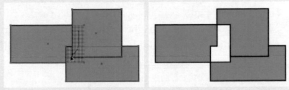

When In Merge Mode, Clicking Stroke Splits the Path is active, click a path to cut apart the path at the nearest anchor points:

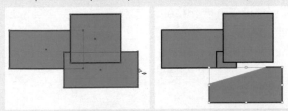

When Cursor Swatch Preview is active, three available swatches appear above the tool cursor. Use the Left and Right Arrow keys to move through those swatches:

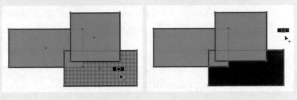

Double-clicking the Shape Builder tool in the Tools panel opens the Shape Builder Tool Options dialog box, where you can change the tool's behavior.

If a small opening exists in a path, you can activate **Gap Detection** settings to overlook small, medium, large, or custom-sized gaps in open paths. This option is especially useful if the Consider Open Filled Paths as Closed option is not checked.

The **Pick Color From** menu determines whether the tool recognizes all swatches in the file or only colors that are actually used in the artwork.

The **Selection** option defines how you can click and drag to connect shapes. The default option (Freeform) means you can drag in any direction to select objects to join. If Straight Line is active, you can only drag a straight path to combine shapes.

You can also use the **Highlight** options to determine what, if anything, is highlighted when you move the tool cursor over a shape.

 Use the Draw Behind Mode

Illustrator's three drawing modes allow you to create new shapes in different ways relative to other existing shapes. In the Draw Normal method (the default), new objects are simply created on top of one another in sequential order; you can rearrange them using commands in the Object>Arrange submenu, or drag them in the Layers panel. Alternatively, you can use the Draw Behind mode to automatically create new shapes behind existing objects, which eliminates a few steps in reaching the accurate object stacking order.

1. **With sailboat.ai open, use any method you prefer to fill the left sail with white and fill the boat shape with black.**

2. **Deselect everything on the artboard.**

3. **Choose the Pen tool in the Tools panel. In the Control panel, set the fill color to a dark brown from the built-in swatches and the stroke to None.**

4. **At the bottom of the Tools panel, choose the Draw Behind option.**

If your Tools panel is in one-column mode, the Drawing Mode options are available in a pop-up menu. If your Tools panel is in two-column mode, the Drawing Mode options are presented as three buttons (from left to right: Draw Normal, Draw Behind, and Draw Inside).

When you use the Draw Behind mode, new objects are automatically placed behind the selected object(s), or at the bottom of the stacking order if nothing is selected.

5. **Using the sketch as a guide, use the Pen tool to click four times without dragging to create the mast shape (use the following image as a guide).**

Remember, when you see a small round circle in the cursor icon, clicking creates a closed shape. Because you aren't dragging when you click to place the anchor points, you are creating four corner points and a closed polygon shape.

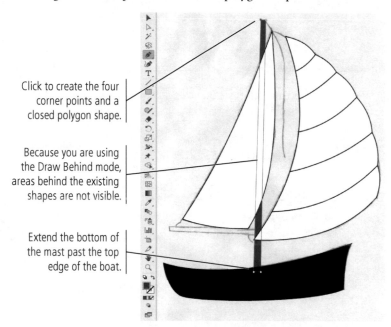

Click to create the four corner points and a closed polygon shape.

Because you are using the Draw Behind mode, areas behind the existing shapes are not visible.

Extend the bottom of the mast past the top edge of the boat.

6. **Use the Pen tool to create the boom (the horizontal pole sticking out from the mast).**

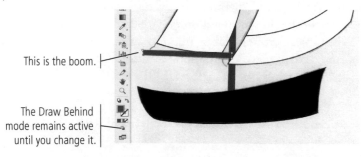

This is the boom.

The Draw Behind mode remains active until you change it.

7. **Deselect the shape you just created.**

8. **At the bottom of the Tools panel, choose the Draw Normal option.**

   The drawing mode remains at the last-used setting. To draw the rope shapes in font of the sails and mast, you need to restore the Draw Normal mode.

9. **Choose the Pencil tool in the Tools panel. In the Control panel, change the fill color to None, choose a medium brown swatch as the stroke color, and define a stroke weight of 2 pt.**

10. **Use the Pencil tool to draw the ropes on the sketch.**

11. **If necessary, adjust the anchor points of the ropes until you are satisfied with the results.**

    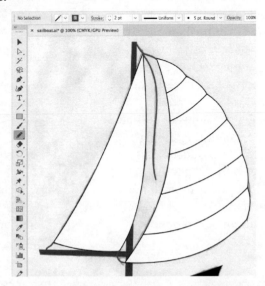

12. **Save the file and continue to the next stage of the project.**

Using the Draw Inside Mode

The Draw Inside mode, which is only available when an existing object is selected, is an easy way to create new objects inside a **clipping path** (a shape that defines areas of other objects that will be visible; anything outside the area of the clipping path is not visible).

If you select the clipped object with the Selection tool, you can use the Edit Clipping Path and Edit Contents buttons in the Control panel to edit either shape without ungrouping and without entering isolation mode.

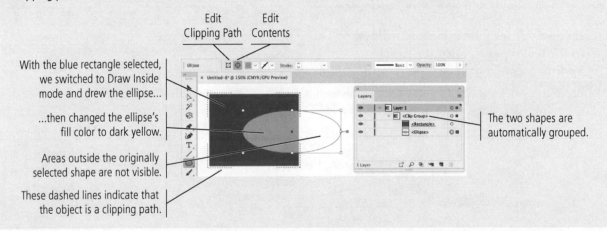

Edit Clipping Path   Edit Contents

With the blue rectangle selected, we switched to Draw Inside mode and drew the ellipse...

...then changed the ellipse's fill color to dark yellow.

Areas outside the originally selected shape are not visible.

These dashed lines indicate that the object is a clipping path.

The two shapes are automatically grouped.

STAGE 2 / Coloring and Painting Artwork

The CMYK color model, also called "process color," recreates the range of printable colors by overlapping layers of cyan, magenta, yellow, and black inks in varying (0–100) percentages.

Using theoretically pure pigments, a mixture of equal parts of cyan, magenta, and yellow would produce black. Real pigments, however, are not pure; the actual result of mixing these three colors usually appears as a muddy brown. The fourth color, black (K), is added to cyan, magenta, and yellow to extend the range of printable colors and allow purer blacks to be printed. Black is abbreviated as "K" because it is the "key" color to which others are aligned on the printing press. Using K for black also avoids confusion with blue in the RGB color model, which is used for digitally distributed files.

In process-color printing, each of the four process colors — cyan, magenta, yellow, and black — is imaged, or separated, onto an individual printing plate. Each color separation is printed on a separate unit of a printing press. When printed on top of each other in varying percentages, the semi-transparent inks produce the range of colors in the CMYK **gamut**. Other special colors (called spot colors) are printed using specifically formulated inks as additional color separations.

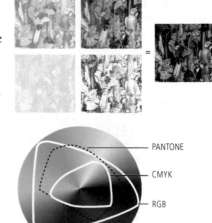

Different color models have different ranges or gamuts of possible colors. A normal human visual system is capable of distinguishing approximately 16.7 million different colors; color reproduction systems, however, are far more limited. The RGB model has the largest gamut of the output models. The CMYK gamut is much more limited; many of the brightest and most saturated colors that can be reproduced using light (in the RGB model) cannot be reproduced using CMYK inks.

PANTONE

CMYK

RGB

Create Global Custom Color Swatches

As you saw in the original sketch, the sail in this project will be filled using three different colors (indicated as C1, C2, and C3). In this exercise, you are going to create these colors and then save them as swatches that can be changed at any time to dynamically modify the colors in the artwork.

1. **With sailboat.ai open, deselect everything on the artboard.**

2. **Open the Color and Swatches panels.**

   If you don't see four color fields/sliders in the Color panel, open the panel options menu and choose Show Options.

   Click here to open the panel Options menu.

   Because you defined CMYK as the color mode for this document, the Color panel shows ink value sliders for those four primary colors.

   Show List View

   Show Tile View

   The default Swatches panel includes a number of default swatches.

3. **Open the Swatches panel Options menu and choose Select All Unused.**

The default Swatches panel includes a number of basic swatches that provide a good starting point for some artwork; you already used two of these to color the mast, boom, and rope shapes. When you build custom swatches, it can be a good idea to delete any default swatches that you don't need so your panel isn't too cluttered.

Note:

The default swatches appear in every new file you create, even if you delete them from a specific file.

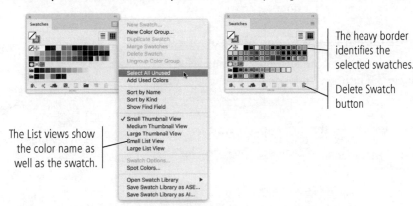

The heavy border identifies the selected swatches.

Delete Swatch button

The List views show the color name as well as the swatch.

4. **Click the Swatches panel Delete button, and then click Yes in the resulting warning dialog box.**

You used two of the built-in swatches to create the mast and ropes, so those swatches remain in the panel and file.

Note:

If you delete a swatch that you applied to objects in a project, there is no effect on the existing objects; you simply can't apply that color to any new objects in the project.

5. **Using Selection tool, click to select any of the white-filled shapes and then choose Select>Same>Fill Color.**

Alternatively, you can Shift-click each white-filled object to select them individually.

6. **With all the white shapes selected, change the Opacity field in the Control panel to 50%.**

Opacity defines the transparency of the selected object. In this case, you're reducing the opacity from 100% (entirely solid or opaque) so you can see the color indicators on the original sketch.

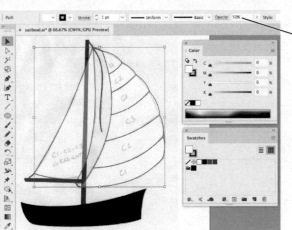

Change the shapes' opacity to 50%.

7. **Deselect everything, and then use the Selection tool to select only the top stripe in the sail (labeled C1 in the sketch).**

8. **Press Shift and click the other two C1 shapes to add them to the selection.**

   By pressing Shift, you can click to add other objects to the current selection. Shift-clicking an object that is already selected removes it from the active selection.

9. **In the Color panel, make sure the Fill icon is on top of the Stroke icon.**

   Like the options in the Tools panel, the Fill and Stroke icons determine which attribute you are currently changing. Whichever icon is on top will be affected by changes to the color values.

10. **In the Color panel, click a green area in the color spectrum bar.**

    All three selected objects fill with the green color you clicked. They seem lighter because they are still semi-transparent.

Note:

Press Shift while dragging any of the sliders in the Color panel to drag all four sliders at once. Their relative relationship to each other remains the same while you drag.

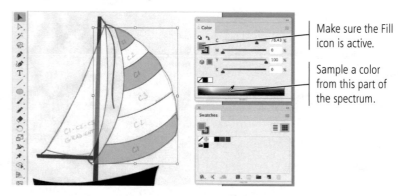

Make sure the Fill icon is active.

Sample a color from this part of the spectrum.

11. **With the Fill icon still active in the Swatches panel, click the New Swatch button at the bottom of the panel.**

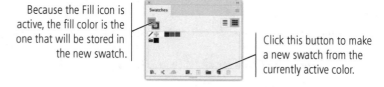

Because the Fill icon is active, the fill color is the one that will be stored in the new swatch.

Click this button to make a new swatch from the currently active color.

12. **Check the Global option in the New Swatch dialog box.**

13. **Uncheck the Add to My Library option, then click OK.**

Note:

If you have an individual user account for the Adobe Creative Cloud, CC Libraries are a way to share assets between Adobe applications. They are explained in Project 4: Ski Resort Map.

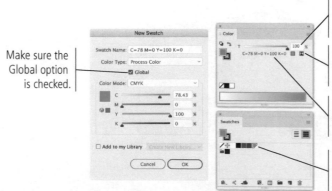

Make sure the Global option is checked.

Use this option to apply percentages of a global color swatch.

Click this button to convert the color to CMYK sliders (not linked to the global swatch).

The Color panel switches to a single slider of the defined swatch value.

The global color swatch has a small white corner in the swatch.

14. **Select the two shapes marked C2 in the sketch.**

15. **Repeat the process from Steps 9–13 to fill the C2 shapes with a blue color and then create a global swatch from the color.**

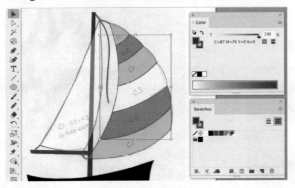

16. **Select the shape marked C3 in the sketch, fill it with a purple color, and then create a third global swatch from the color.**

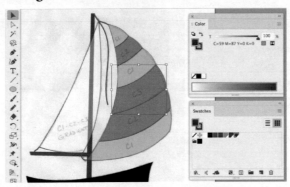

17. **With the purple shape still selected, choose Select>Same>Opacity. Return the selected objects' opacity to 100%.**

    You no longer need to see the color markers on the sketch, so you can return these objects to full opacity.

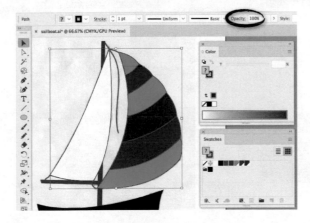

18. **Deselect all objects in the file, save the file, and then continue to the next exercise.**

Add a Color Gradient

Illustrator supports three types of gradient fills. When an object is selected, clicking one of the gradient types at the top of the Gradient panel (Window>Gradient) applies the default gradient to the active attribute (fill or swatch). The Gradient panel remembers the last-used gradient as the default sample, so that gradient is applied to the selected object when you apply a gradient.

Note:

A fourth type, called a gradient mesh, is explained in Project 3: Identity Package.

Linear gradient

Radial gradient

Freeform gradient

Default gradient   Fill is the active attribute

When a linear or radial gradient is applied, you can use the Gradient panel to change the gradient colors. Defined stops appear as large circles below the ramp. You can change the stop colors, move stops along the gradient, change the midpoints between adjacent stops, and add new stops. To remove a stop, simply drag it off the gradient ramp. You can also use the Gradient panel to change the angle of the applied gradient, as well as the aspect ratio of radial gradients.

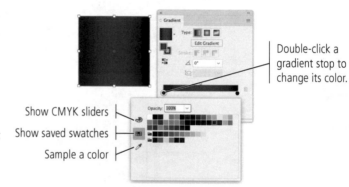

Double-click a gradient stop to change its color.

Show CMYK sliders

Show saved swatches

Sample a color

Drag a stop to move the color along the gradient.

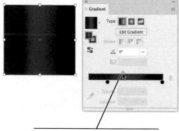

Drag these markers to move the midpoint between stops.

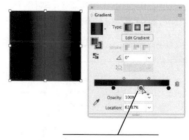

Click below the ramp to add a new stop.

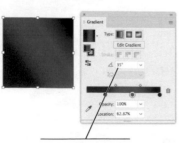

Change the angle of a linear gradient.

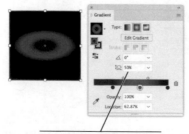

Change the aspect ratio to make a radial gradient oval instead of perfectly round.

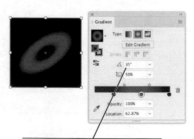

When the aspect ratio is less than 100%, you can change the angle of the radial gradient.

When a linear or radial gradient is applied, you can click the Edit Gradient button in the Gradient panel to automatically activate the Gradient tool and show the Gradient Annotator controls. You can use this on-screen widget to dynamically change the applied gradient in immediate relation to the selected object.

When the Gradient tool is active, you can click and drag to change the position and angle of the gradient. The place where you first click is the beginning of the gradient, or the left end of the ramp in the Gradient panel; the end color of the gradient, or the right end of the ramp, exists where you release the mouse button.

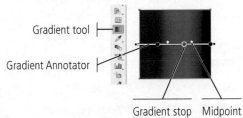

Gradient tool

Gradient Annotator

Gradient stop   Midpoint

The same color stop controls you see on the ramp in the Gradient panel appear on the Gradient Annotator. You can also change the gradient angle and aspect ratio (for radial gradients) by dragging the annotator handles.

Note:

You can also click the Edit Gradient button in the Gradient panel to access the Gradient Annotator.

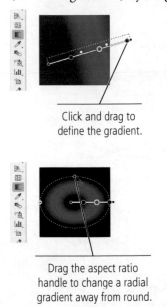

Click and drag to define the gradient.

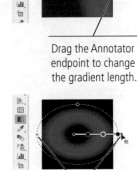

Drag the Annotator endpoint to change the gradient length.

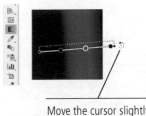

Move the cursor slightly away from the endpoint to rotate the gradient.

Drag the aspect ratio handle to change a radial gradient away from round.

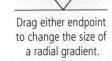

Drag either endpoint to change the size of a radial gradient.

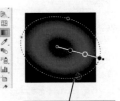

Drag the radial gradient boundary to rotate the gradient.

Note:

You can turn off the Gradient Annotator in the View menu (View>Hide Gradient Annotator).

The original sketch shows that the left sail needs to be a gradient of the three colors in the other sail. Because the sketch shows the look of a sail billowing in the wind, a straight linear gradient would not accurately reflect the way blended colors would appear in a real sail. Instead, you will use the third type of gradient— a freeform gradient — to create the necessary effect.

1. **With sailboat.ai open, use the Selection tool to select the left sail shape.**

2. **Open the Gradient panel (Window>Gradient). If you see only a gradient sample in the panel, open the panel Options menu and choose Show Options.**

3. **If you see a pop-up window about working with Gradients, click the Skip Tour button.**

4. **With the left sail shape selected, click the Freeform Gradient button at the top of the Gradient panel.**

Freeform gradients use color points to define the location of various colors in the gradient. When you first apply a freeform gradient, the software evaluates the shape and adds stop points where it determines they might be needed.

By default, freeform gradients are created in [Draw] Points mode, which means the individual color points in the gradient are not connected.

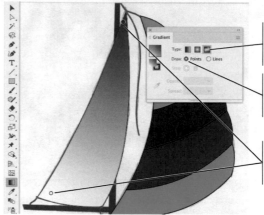

Click here to apply a freeform gradient.

Draw Points mode is active by default.

Color points are automatically added to the selected shape.

5. **Click to select the top color point in the sail shape.**

When a color point is selected, you can drag it to a new location, or press the Delete key to remove it from the gradient. You can also click the Delete button in the Gradient panel to remove the selected point.

Click to select a specific color point in the gradient.

The spread control widget appears when the cursor hovers over a gradient point.

If you move the cursor over a selected point, the dotted line identifies the spread of that point's color within the overall gradient. You can click the dotted line and drag to change the spread percentage.

6. **Press the Delete key to remove the selected point from the gradient.**

7. **Click to select the remaining point in the gradient. Double-click the selected stop to open the pop-up color selector for that stop.**

You can change the color of stops by double-clicking the circles, which opens the color panel for that stop (the same as when you change the color for a linear or radial gradient).

8. **Choose the custom green swatch, then press Return/Enter to dismiss the panel.**

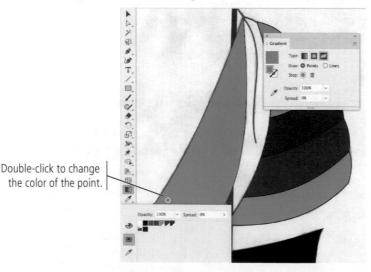

Double-click to change the color of the point.

Note:

You can change the opacity of the selected gradient point in the Gradient panel.

9. **Choose the Lines option in the Gradient panel.**

   The Lines option allows you to draw a path that defines the precise shape of a gradient, rather than simply blending from one point to another.

10. **Click the existing color point to connect to it, then move the cursor halfway up the left edge of the sail. Click near the left edge of the shape to place a new color point.**

    Although it can be difficult to see on the green background a thin blue line connects each color point on the same line. This preview shows the curve that will be created when you click to place a new point.

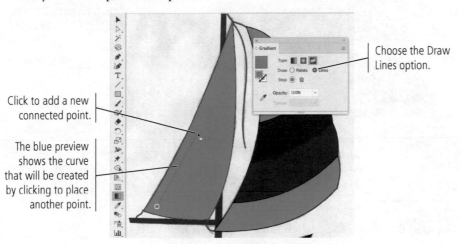

Click to add a new connected point.

The blue preview shows the curve that will be created by clicking to place another point.

Choose the Draw Lines option.

11. **Move the cursor to the top of the sail shape. Click just inside the sail shape to place a third color point on the same line.**

    Color points in a gradient line are automatically created with smooth points; you can Option/Alt-click a point on the gradient line to convert it to a corner point.

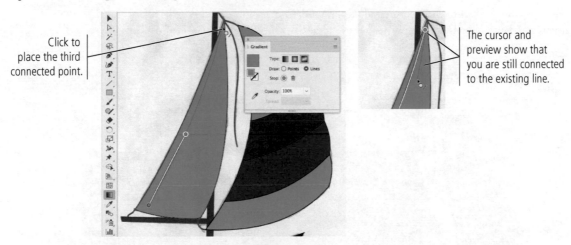

Click to place the third connected point.

The cursor and preview show that you are still connected to the existing line.

12. **Press the ESC key to disconnect from the current gradient line.**

    As with the Pen tool, the cursor remains connected to the existing line until you intentionally disconnect.

The cursor shows that clicking creates a new point not connected to the previous line.

13. **Click near the middle of the bottom line in the sail shape to create a new color point.**

14. **Double-click the new point to open the color selector. Choose the custom blue swatch as the stop color, then press Return/Enter to dismiss the panel.**

15. **Move the cursor to the middle of the shape, then click to place a new point.**

16. **Move the cursor near the top of the shape, then click to place a third point on the middle line.**

    Make sure you don't click directly on top of the top point of the left line; doing so would actually connect to the existing line, which is not what you want.

    You can always use the Undo command (Command/Control-Z) to undo the last click if you accidentally connect to another existing point.

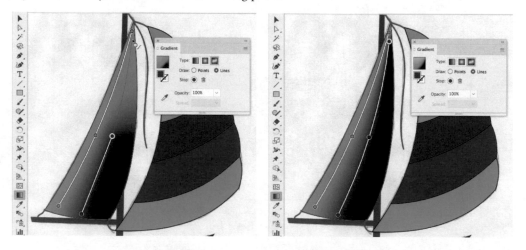

17. **Press the ESC key to disconnect from the current gradient line.**

18. **Repeat Steps 13–17 on the right side of the shape to add a third gradient line, using the custom purple swatch as the color for the stops.**

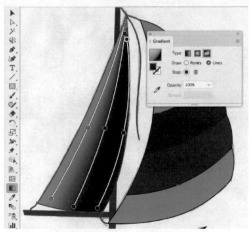

19. **Save the file and continue to the next exercise.**

Edit Global Color Swatches

Global swatches offer a particular advantage when you need to change the colors used in your artwork. In the case of this project, you are going to place this artwork into a stylized ocean illustration, in which blues are the predominant color. To make the boat more prominent in the final poster, you are going to use a yellow-orange scheme — complementary colors to blue — for the boat sails.

1. **With sailboat.ai open, deselect all objects on the artboard.**

2. **In the Swatches panel, double-click the green custom swatch.**

3. **In the resulting Swatch Options dialog box, make sure the Preview option is checked.**

4. **Change the color values to C=0 M=75 Y=75 K=10, and then click OK to change the swatch definition.**

   Because this is a global color swatch, any objects that use the color (including the gradient) reflect the new swatch definition. Locked objects are also affected by the change.

Note:

Complementary color refers to opposing colors on a color wheel.

Everything that was colored with the green swatch is now orange.

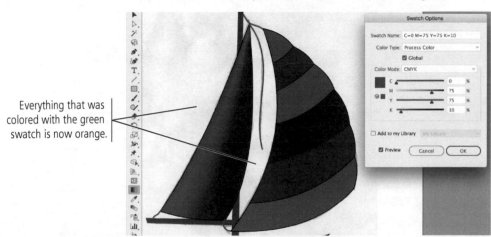

5. Repeat Steps 2–4 to change the blue swatch definition to C=0 M=10 Y=100 K=0.

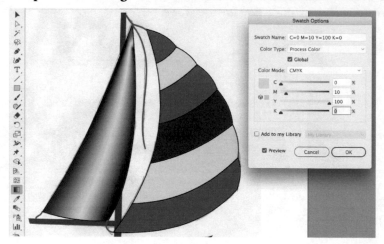

6. Repeat Steps 2–4 to change the purple swatch definition to C=0 M=60 Y=100 K=0.

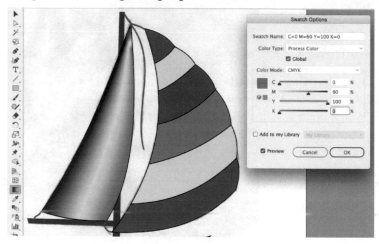

7. Save the file and continue to the next exercise.

Understanding Color Terms

Many vague and technical-sounding terms are mentioned when discussing color. Is hue the same as color? The same as value? As tone? What's the difference between lightness and brightness? What is chroma? And where does saturation fit in?

This problem has resulted in several attempts to normalize color communication. A number of systems have been developed to define color according to specific criteria, including Hue, Saturation, and Brightness (HSB); Hue, Saturation, and Lightness (HSL); Hue, Saturation, and Value (HSV); and Lightness, Chroma, and Hue (LCH). Each of these models, or systems, plots color on a three-dimensional diagram, based on the elements of human color perception — hue, intensity, and brightness.

Hue is what most people think of as color — red, green, purple, and so on. Hue is defined according to a color's position on a color wheel, beginning at red (0°) and traveling counterclockwise around the wheel.

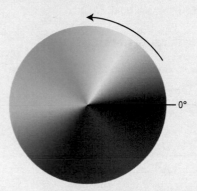

Saturation (also called "intensity") refers to the color's difference from neutral gray. Highly saturated colors are more vivid than those with low saturation. Saturation is plotted from the center of the color wheel. Color at the center is neutral gray and has a saturation value of 0; color at the edge of the wheel has the most intense saturation value (100) of that hue.

If you bisect the color wheel with a straight line, the line creates a saturation axis for two complementary colors. A color is dulled by the introduction of its complement. Red, for example, is neutralized by the addition of cyan (blue and green). Near the center of the axis, the result is neutral gray.

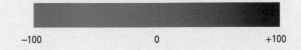

-100   0   +100

Chroma is similar to saturation, but chroma factors in a reference white. In any viewing situation, colors appear less vivid as the light source dims. The process of chromatic adaptation, however, allows the human visual system to adjust to changes in light and still differentiate colors according to the relative saturation.

Brightness is the amount of light reflected off an object. As an element of color reproduction, brightness is typically judged by comparing the color to the lightest nearby object (such as an unprinted area of white paper).

Lightness is the amount of white or black added to pure color. Lightness (also called "luminance" or "value") is the relative brightness based purely on the black-white value of a color. A lightness value of 0 means there is no addition of white or black. Lightness of +100 is pure white; lightness of −100 is pure black.

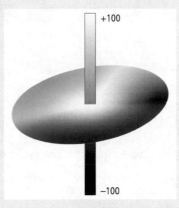

All hues are affected equally by changes in lightness.

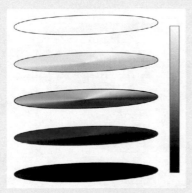

The final step in the process is to place your finished sailboat in the background illustration that was created by a colleague; this type of collaborative workflow is common in the graphic design world. Although there are many ways to accomplish this task, you are going to use the most basic — copying and pasting — in this project. When all of the pieces are together in the same file, you will make necessary adjustments to make all pieces of the file work together as a single composition.

 ## Manage Artwork with Sublayers

In the first stage of this project you created the entire sailboat on a single layer. When you paste it into the background artwork, you need to be able to manage the sailboat as a single object. In this exercise, you work with sublayers to accomplish this goal.

1. **With sailboat.ai open, make the Section tool active and make sure nothing is selected on the artboard.**

2. **In the Layers panel, click the arrow to the left of the Boat Drawing layer to reveal the sublayers.**

   Individual objects are listed as sublayers in the Layers panel. Because you created all of the artwork in this file on a single layer, every object appears as a sublayer of the Boat Drawing layer.

Click this arrow to expand the layer.

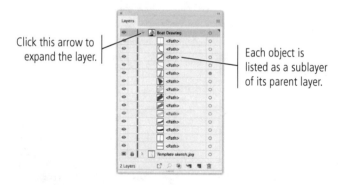

Each object is listed as a sublayer of its parent layer.

3. **Click the empty space to the right of any of the available sublayers.**

   You can use sublayers to select individual objects on a specific layer; the Selected Art icon (the larger rectangle) identifies selected objects. The parent layer of selected art shows a smaller Selected Art icon, which makes it easier to identify which layer contains a specific object.

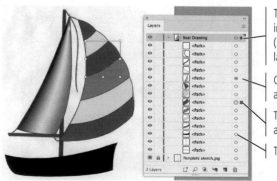

The smaller rectangle indicates that one or more (but not all) objects on the layer are selected.

Click this space to select a specific sublayer.

This icon identifies a selected object.

Target icon

Note:

This technique also works to select individual components of a group.

Note:

You can also click the Target icon for a specific layer or sublayer to select specific objects.

4. Choose Select>All.

This command selects all unlocked objects on the artboard. The Layers panel now shows a Selected Art icon for all objects on the Boat Drawing layer. The Selected Art icon for the parent layer is now larger, which means all objects on that layer are selected.

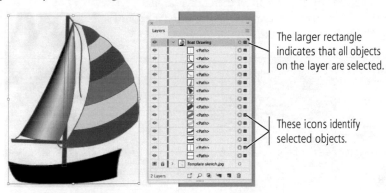

The larger rectangle indicates that all objects on the layer are selected.

These icons identify selected objects.

Note:

Press Command/Control-A to select all objects in the file.

Note:

You can click the space to the right of a specific layer name to select all objects on that layer.

5. Choose Object>Group. In the Layers panel, click the arrow to expand the Group.

Grouping multiple objects creates a second level of nesting: the Boat Drawing layer is the parent of the Group, which is the parent of the individual objects in the artwork. You can use the Selected Art icons in the Layers panel to select individual objects in a group, just as you can to select those objects when they are not grouped.

6. In the Layers panel, double-click the <Group> name to highlight it. Type Sailboat to rename the group, then press Return/Enter to finalize the new name.

You can rename sublayers — including groups and individual objects — just as you would rename actual layers. This type of descriptive naming can help you to better organize and manage the elements in a complex file.

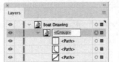

7. With the group selected on the artboard, choose Edit>Copy.

8. Save the sailboat.ai file, then choose File>Open. Navigate to poster.ai in the WIP>Regatta folder and click Open.

9. Choose View>Fit Artboard in Window.

This command not only shows you the entire artboard, but also centers the artboard in the active document window.

Note:

You can press Command/Control-C to copy the selected objects.

10. **Choose Edit>Paste.**

The group you copied in Step 7 is pasted into the poster file, in the center of the document window.

Because you grouped the sailboat objects before you copied them, they are pasted as a group. If you had not grouped them, each object that makes up the sailboat artwork would be pasted as a separate sublayer in the poster file.

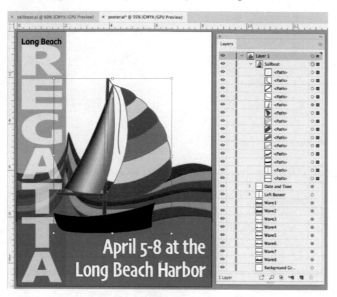

11. **In the Layers panel, click the arrow to the left of the Sailboat sublayer to collapse it (if necessary).**

12. **Using the Selection tool, drag the selected group into the empty space at the top-right section of the poster (use the following image as a guide).**

The arrow indicates that this is a group, containing more than one object.

13. **In the Layers panel, drag the Sailboat sublayer down. When a heavy line appears below the Wave6 sublayer, release the mouse button.**

When you use the Edit>Paste command, the pasted objects are placed at the top of the stacking order on the active layer. You can use this method to easily reorder sublayers as necessary.

Changing the stacking-order position of the sublayer means the bottom of the Sailboat group is hidden by sublayers higher in the stack.

14. **If necessary, adjust the position of the sailboat artwork so the entire bottom edge is hidden by the third wave from the top.**

15. **Save the file and continue to the next exercise.**

Lock and Hide Artwork

The final required adjustment for this poster is to change the shape of the highest wave so it looks like a splash. If you review the existing artwork and Layers panel, you can see that the wave nearest the top of the artboard is also the lowest in the sublayer stacking order — Wave8, according to the object names assigned in the Layers panel. To make this task easier, you are going to lock and hide certain sublayers to avoid accidentally changing elements that you don't want to change.

1. **With poster.ai open, click the empty space to the left of the Date and Time sublayer. Hold down the mouse button and drag down the same column to lock all other sublayers.**

Individual objects in a file can be locked by clicking the empty space immediately left of the object name in the Layers panel. If a Lock icon already appears in that space, you can click the lock icon to unlock a specific object.

You can also select an object on the artboard and choose Object>Lock.

Click here and drag down over the empty space to lock all sublayers.

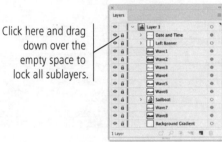

2. Click the Lock icon to the left of the Wave8 sublayer to unlock only that element.

The Object>Unlock All menu command is an all-or-nothing option; it unlocks all locked objects on all layers. The Layers panel allows you to unlock only certain objects, which provides better control over your workflow.

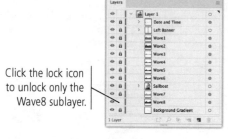

Click the lock icon to unlock only the Wave8 sublayer.

Because all other objects in the file are locked, you can now edit the Wave8 shape without affecting the other elements.

3. In the Layers panel, click the Eye icon for the Left Banner sublayer.

The Eye icons identify visible layers and sublayers. You can click any Eye icon to hide an entire layer, or hide only specific sublayers. If an element is already hidden, you can click the empty space in the Layers panel to show that element.

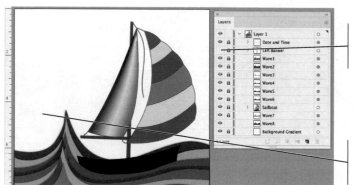

Click an Eye icon to hide a specific layer or sublayer.

Hidden artwork is no longer visible on the artboard.

You can also select an object on the artboard and choose Object>Hide>Selection. The Object>Show All command, however, shows all hidden objects on all layers in the file. As with locking and unlocking objects, it is often better to use the icons in the Layers panel to show and hide exactly (and only) the elements you need.

4. Choose Select>All.

Because all the other sublayers are locked and/or hidden, you selected only the artwork on the Wave8 sublayer.

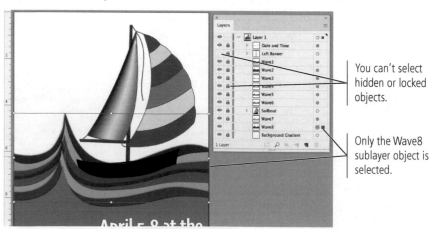

You can't select hidden or locked objects.

Only the Wave8 sublayer object is selected.

5. Save the file and continue to the next exercise.

Create Shapes with the Blob Brush Tool

The Blob Brush tool is used to paint filled shapes, which you can manipulate just as you would any other shape made up of anchor points and handles. In this exercise, you use the Blob Brush tool to paint a splashing wave shape, which you will then merge with the top wave shape to create a single object.

1. **With sailboat.ai open, deselect everything on the artboard.**

2. **Choose the Blob Brush tool (nested under the Paintbrush tool).**

3. **Double-click the Blob Brush tool in the Tools panel to open the Blob Brush Tool Options dialog box.**

4. **Check the Keep Selected option and uncheck Merge Only with Selection.**

   Overlapping Blob Brush strokes merge to create a single object. If Merge Only with Selected is active, overlapping strokes will not merge unless the previous strokes are selected.

Blob Brush tool

5. **Set the Fidelity slider to the halfway point.**

   Like the Pencil tool, the Blob Brush tool Tolerance options determine the accuracy of the resulting shape. Fidelity settings nearer the Accurate end of the scale result in more points to better match the path you drag with the tool; a setting closer to the Smooth end of the scale results in fewer points and smoother edges on the shape you draw.

6. **Leave the remaining options at their default values, then click OK.**

   The lower half of the dialog box defines the size, angle, and roundness of the brush cursor.

7. **Reset the default fill and stroke colors, then move the Blob Brush tool cursor near the peak of the top wave shape. Align the right side of the brush to the right side of the wave peak, as shown here:**

Note:

Press the right bracket key ( ]) to increase the brush size by one point. Press the left bracket key ([ ) to decrease the brush size by one point.

Reset the default fill and stroke colors.

When you draw with the Blob Brush tool, the cursor shows the size and shape of the defined brush.

Align the right edge of the cursor to the right edge of the wave shape.

8. **Click and drag to create an arch shape that approximately matches the curve of the existing wave.**

You are essentially painting a shape that matches the brush stroke you see while you drag. As you paint, the path might look a bit sketchy; however, the resulting path is smoothed based on the Fidelity setting defined in the tool options.

When you release the mouse button, the result is a single shape that fills the entire area where you drew. The shape is still selected because you activated the Keep Selected option in the tool options.

It is important to note that the resulting path is filled with the default *stroke* color you defined in Step 7. When you "paint" with the Blob Brush tool, the defined fill color

The previous Stroke color becomes the Fill color of the resulting shape.

When you release the mouse button, the result is a filled shape based on where you dragged the brush cursor.

Anchor points are automatically created to define the outside edge of the shape.

has no effect on the resulting shape unless the stroke color is set to None.

9. **With the path still selected, click and drag to create another path near the top of the splash, using a slightly different arch.**

As you complete the rest of this exercise, use our images as a guide. You do not have to match the exact shape you see in our images, but your end result should be similar.

Draw a second arched shape that braches off of the first shape.

The second path is merged with the previous (selected) path.

10. **Continue adding brush strokes to the selected path to create more branches off the splash shape.**

As you draw, you can press the right bracket key ( ]) to increase the brush size by one point; press the left bracket key ([ ) to decrease the brush size by one point. Feel free to enlarge or reduce the brush size to create different thicknesses throughout the shape.

11. **Where the splash shape meets the top wave, make sure the left edge of the splash shape matches the left edge of the wave shape.**

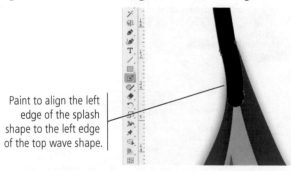

Paint to align the left edge of the splash shape to the left edge of the top wave shape.

12. **Paint several shapes that do not overlap the main splash shape.**

When you paint a shape that does not overlap the existing selection, it is created as a new, separate shape.

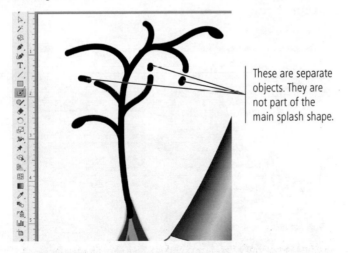

These are separate objects. They are not part of the main splash shape.

13. **Deselect everything in the layout.**

14. **Save the file and continue to the next exercise.**

Combine Shapes with the Pathfinder

Using the Illustrator Pathfinder panel, you can combine multiple shapes in a variety of ways, or you can use one object as a "cookie cutter" to remove or separate one shape from another. As you work with more complicated artwork in Illustrator, you will find many different ways to use the Pathfinder functions, alone or in combination.

1. **With `poster.ai` open, open the Pathfinder panel (Window>Pathfinder).**

2. **In the Layers panel, click the top <Path> sublayer to select it in the panel. Press Shift and click the bottom <Path> object to add it, and all in-between sublayers, to the previous selection.**

Selecting an element in the Layers panel is not the same as selecting it on the artboard. The right side of the panel shows no Selected Art icons, which means nothing is selected on the artboard.

Note:

You can Command/Control-click to select multiple, nonconsecutive layers or sublayers in the Layers panel.

3. **In the Layers panel, click any of the selected elements and drag them below the Wave8 sublayer.**

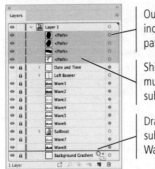

Our splash shape includes four separate paths (objects).

Shift-click to select multiple consecutive sublayers in the panel.

Drag all selected sublayers below the Wave8 sublayer.

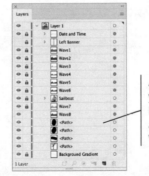

All the path objects you created with the Blob Brush tool should appear below the Wave8 layer.

4. **Choose Select>All.**

   Because most objects are locked, only the top wave and splash shapes are selected.

5. **In the Pathfinder panel, click the Unite button.**

   Options in the Pathfinder panel allow you to cut shapes out of other shapes and merge multiple shapes into a single shape.

   The Unite function merges overlapping shapes into a single object; non-overlapping objects are grouped with the merged shape. All elements affected by the unification adopt the appearance attributes (fill color, opacity, etc.) of the top-most selected object — which is why you reordered the sublayers in Step 3.

Unite button

The resulting group contains all objects in the wave shape.

6. **Choose Select>Deselect to turn off any active selection.**

7. **In the Layers panel, click the empty space to the left of the Left Banner sublayer to show that layer.**

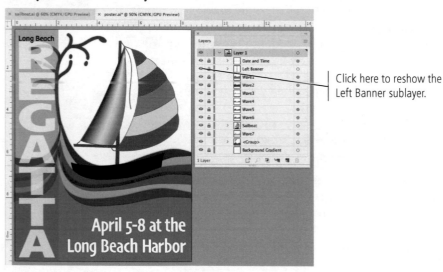

Click here to reshow the Left Banner sublayer.

8. **Save the file and continue to the final exercise.**

The Pathfinder Panel in Depth

In the Pathfinder panel, the top row of buttons — the Shape Modes — create complex shapes by combining the originally selected shapes. You can press Option/Alt and click a Shape Mode to maintain the paths from the original objects.

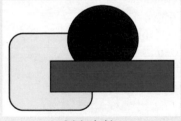

Original objects

Unite combines all selected objects into a single shape. By default, the Shape options result in a single new object.

If you Option/Alt-click a shape mode button, the result maintains the original paths unless you manually expand it.

Minus Front removes overlapping areas from the backmost shape in the selection.

Intersect creates a shape of only areas where all selected objects overlap.

Exclude removes any areas where two objects overlap.

The second row of options — the Pathfinders — do exactly that. The resulting shapes are some combination of the paths that made up the originally selected objects.

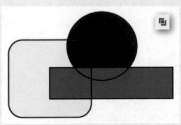

Divide creates separate shapes from all overlapping areas of selected objects.

Trim removes underlying areas of overlapping objects. Objects of the same fill color are not combined.

Merge removes underlying areas of overlapping objects. Objects of the same fill color are combined.

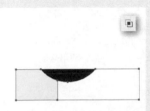

Crop returns the areas of underlying objects that are within the boundary of the topmost object.

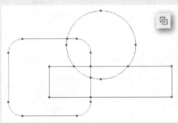

Outline divides the selected objects, then returns unfilled, open paths.

Minus Back removes the area of underlying objects from the front object.

Save the File as PDF

Adobe PDF (or simply PDF, for Portable Document Format) has become a universal method of moving files to virtually any digital destination. One of the most important uses for the PDF format is the ability to create perfectly formatted digital documents, exactly as they would appear if printed on paper. You can embed fonts, images, drawings, and other elements into the file so all the required bits are available on any computer. The PDF format can be used to move your artwork to the web as a low-resolution RGB file or to a commercial printer as a high-resolution CMYK file.

1. **With `poster.ai` open, choose File>Save As.**
   If necessary, navigate to your WIP>Regatta folder as the target location.

2. **Choose Adobe PDF in the Format/Save As Type menu and click Save.**

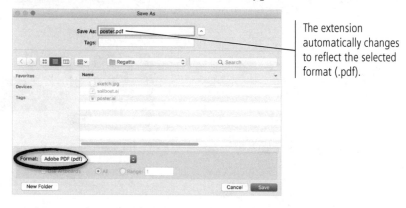

The extension automatically changes to reflect the selected format (.pdf).

3. **Choose Illustrator Default in the Adobe PDF Preset menu.**

4. **Review the options in the General pane.**

   Read the description area to see what Adobe has to say about these options.

Use this menu to call a group of saved settings (called a preset).

Choose a category from this menu to see related options.

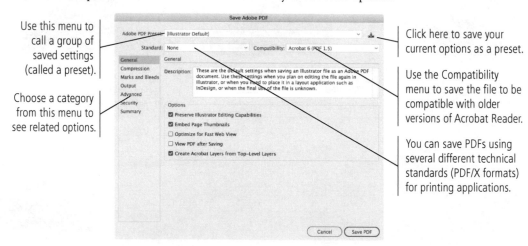

Click here to save your current options as a preset.

Use the Compatibility menu to save the file to be compatible with older versions of Acrobat Reader.

You can save PDFs using several different technical standards (PDF/X formats) for printing applications.

5. **Click Compression in the list of categories on the left and review the options.**

   These options allow you to reduce the resulting file size by compressing color, grayscale, and/or monochrome bitmap (raster) images. You can also compress text and line art by clicking the check box at the bottom.

   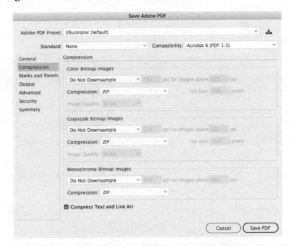

6. **Review the Marks and Bleeds options.**

   These options add different marks to the output page:

   - **Trim marks** indicate the edge of the page, where a page printed on a larger sheet will be cut down to its final size. You can also define the thickness (weight) of the trim marks, as well as how far from the page edge the lines should appear (offset).

   - **Registration marks** resemble a small crosshair. These marks are added to each ink unit on a printing press to make sure the different inks are properly aligned to one another.

   - **Color bars** are rows of small squares across the sheet, used to verify press settings for accurate color reproduction.

   - **Page information** adds the file name, date, and time of output.

   - **Bleeds** define how much of elements outside the page boundaries will be included in the final output. Most printers require at least a 0.125″ bleed on each side, but you should always ask before you create the final file.

Note:

Most printers require trim marks to be created outside the bleed area. Always check with your service provider when saving a PDF for commercial output.

   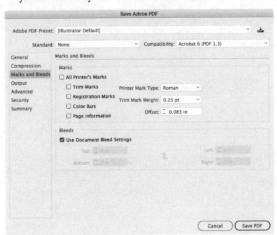

Note:

The other categories of options are explained in later projects that discuss transparency and color management.

7. **Click Save PDF.**

8. **Close any open Illustrator files.**

PROJECT REVIEW

fill in the blank

1. The _____ tool is used to place anchor points that are connected by line segments.

2. The _____ tool is used to change a smooth anchor point to a corner anchor point (and vice versa).

3. The _____ tool is used to edit individual anchor points (and their related handles) on a vector path.

4. _____ is the range of possible colors within a specific color model.

5. _____ are the four component colors in process-color output.

6. The _____ panel includes value sliders for each component in the defined color model.

7. The _____ is used to paint shapes of solid color based on the defined brush size and the area you drag with a single mouse click.

8. The _____ appears over a gradient-filled object when selected with the Gradient tool; you can use it to control the position and direction of color in the gradient-filled object.

9. Changes made to a _____ color swatch are reflected in all elements where that color is applied.

10. Individual objects on a layer appear as _____ in the Layers panel.

short answer

1. Describe three ways to deselect the current selection on the artboard.

2. Briefly explain the significance of "process color" related to Illustrator artwork.

3. Briefly explain the advantage of using the PDF format for creating printable files.

PORTFOLIO BUILDER PROJECT

Use what you have learned in this project to complete the following freeform exercise.
Carefully read the art director and client comments, then create your own design to meet the needs of the project.
Use the space below to sketch ideas. When finished, write a brief explanation of the reasoning behind your final design.

art director comments

Your local animal shelter hosts an annual fundraising gala on the first Saturday in October. You have been hired to create a poster advertising this year's theme — a classic, black-tie masquerade ball.

❑ Design an 11″ × 17″ poster to promote the event in local storefronts and public venues.

❑ Develop a creative type treatment for the event name: "Barking Mad for the Masquerade."

❑ Find or create imagery and graphics to support the event theme.

❑ Include the event date (look at this year's calendar to find the exact date) prominently in the poster design.

❑ Include the contact information (phone number and web address) for your local animal shelter.

client comments

We raise a considerable portion of our annual operating budget during this annual event. This year, the theme is a very classic masquerade in the style of Victorian-England opulence — think "Phantom of the Opera," the state dining room on the Titanic, that sort of thing. Men in tuxes and women in flowing gowns, everyone masked in some fashion until the traditional "reveal" at midnight.

Every year, the event includes a silent auction with some incredible prizes that are donated by local businesses, as well as a gourmet four-course meal prepared by a celebrity chef.

If there is any way you could tastefully incorporate a couple of animal photos in the poster, we would like that. However, it isn't really a requirement as long as the shelter's name and contact information is clearly displayed.

project justification

PROJECT SUMMARY

This project incorporated more advanced drawing techniques that allow you to exercise precise control over every point and path in a file. The Pen tool is arguably one of the most important tools you will use throughout your career as an illustrator; although it can be challenging at first, practice is the best way to master this skill.

This project also explored working with color in Illustrator: applying color, saving global color swatches to make changes more efficiently, and using gradients to add visual interest.

Finally, you saved your artwork in a file format that is commonly used to share Illustrator artwork with other applications. The PDF format is an invaluable part of design workflows using software applications that can't import native Illustrator files.

Use the Pen tool to create custom artwork based on lines in a hand-drawn sketch

Use the Anchor Point tool to reshape specific line segments

Use the Blob Brush tool to paint the outline of custom shapes

Use the Shape Builder tool to divide overlapping objects into individual shapes

Create a freeform gradient to blend colors in a non-linear shape

Use global swatches to allow universal changes to all objects where that color is applied

Use layers and sublayers to manage the various elements in a complex file

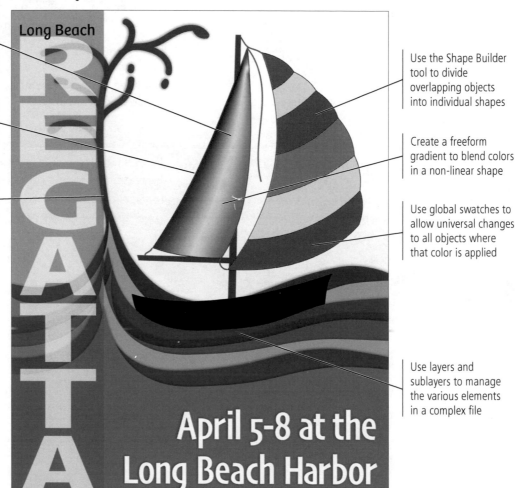

Identity Package

3

Your client is rebranding and relaunching a local cafe that has been open since 1982. She has hired you to create a logo for the establishment's new name, as well as stationery that can be used for various purposes throughout the business operations.

This project incorporates the following skills:

❏ Developing custom logo artwork based on an object in a photograph

❏ Using a gradient mesh to create realistic color blends

❏ Manipulating letter shapes to create a finished logotype

❏ Using layers to easily manage complex artwork

❏ Creating multiple artboards to contain specific projects and layouts

❏ Building various logo versions to meet specific output requirements

❏ Printing desktop proofs of individual artboards

PROJECT MEETING

client comments

In six weeks, Home Town Diner will officially become Cafe Limon. First, we need a logo for the new name. I want the words to be clearly styled — not just regular type — using a lemon in place of the letter "o."

We want to have everything in place for the Grand Reopening, so we need to make things as versatile as possible. Once the logo is created, we need a letterhead-style page that we're going to have printed in large quantities. We'll use those preprinted blanks for everything, including daily menus, invoices, and correspondence.

The printer I spoke with said I could do this for less money if I go "four-color" for the letterhead, but "two-color" for the envelope; I really don't know what that means — I'm hoping you do.

art director comments

The logo is the first part of this project because you will use it on the other two pieces. The client told you exactly what she wants, so that part is done. I had our photographer take a good picture of a lemon; use that as the basis for the one you draw in the logo art.

The client wants to print the letterhead in four-color and the envelope in two-color, so you will have to create two different versions of the logo. Since logos are used on far more than just these two jobs in this one application, you should also create a one-color version because the client will inevitably ask for it at some point.

project objectives

To complete this project, you will:

- ❑ Use the Pen tool to trace the outline of a photograph
- ❑ Create a gradient mesh
- ❑ Use Smart Guides to manage a gradient mesh
- ❑ Use effects to add object highlights
- ❑ Create and control point-type objects
- ❑ Convert text to outlines so you can manipulate the letter shapes
- ❑ Use the Appearance panel to revert gradient mesh objects back to regular paths
- ❑ Apply spot-color inks for special printing applications
- ❑ Create versions of the final logo for one-color, two-color, and four-color printing
- ❑ Print desktop proofs of the completed identity pieces

STAGE 1 / Working with Gradient Meshes

There are several important points to keep in mind when you design a logo. First, logos need to be scalable. A company might place its logo on the head of a golf tee or on the side of a building. Vector graphics — the kind you typically create in Illustrator — can be scaled as large or small as necessary without losing quality. Photographs are raster images, and they typically can't be greatly enlarged or reduced without losing quality. That's why you're converting a photograph (a raster image) into a vector graphic in this project.

Second, you almost always need more than one version of a logo. Different kinds of output require different formats (specifically, one set of files for print and one for the web), and some types of jobs require special options saved in the files, such as the four-color, two-color, and one-color versions that you will create in this project.

Set up the Workspace

Illustrator includes a number of tools ideally suited for creating lifelike illustrations. In this project, you will work from a photograph to create a vector-based lemon graphic that will be part of your client's logo. You will start with the full-color version, and then work from there to create variations that are part of a typical logo package.

1. **Download `Cafe_Print19_RF.zip` from the Student Files web page.**

2. **Expand the ZIP archive in your WIP folder (Macintosh) or copy the archive contents into your WIP folder (Windows).**

    This results in a folder named **Cafe**, which contains the files you need for this project. You should also use this folder to save the files you create in this project.

3. **In Illustrator, choose File>New. Choose the Print option at the top of the dialog box, and then choose the Letter document preset.**

    Remember, using the Print category of presets automatically applies the CMYK color mode and 300 ppi raster effects.

    Because the CMYK gamut is smaller than the RGB gamut, you are starting with the smaller gamut to avoid the color shift that could occur if you started with RGB and converted the colors to CMYK. You are also creating the file to meet the high-resolution requirements of commercial printing.

4. **Define the following settings in the Preset Details section:**

Name:	cafe-logo
Units:	Inches
Orientation:	Portrait
Artboards:	1

    You are simply using this artboard as a drawing space, so you only need to make it large enough to draw. Later, you will adjust the artboard to meet the specific needs of the finished logo. You will also add multiple artboards to hold various versions of the logo.

5. **Click Create to create the file.**

6. **Choose View>Fit Artboard in Window.**

   The Fit Artboard in Window command centers the artboard in the document window, so the template image you place in the next step will be automatically centered on the artboard.

7. **Choose File>Place. Navigate to lemon.jpg in your WIP>Cafe folder. Make sure the Template option is checked, and then click Place.**

   Macintosh users might need to click the Options button to access the actual Options at the bottom of the dialog box.

8. **In the Layers panel, double-click the template layer icon to open the Layer Options dialog box. Uncheck the Dim Images option, then click OK.**

   Choosing the Template option places an image onto a template layer that is automatically dimmed. You want the photograph to appear at full visibility so you can extract colors from the photo.

   Uncheck this option.

   For most of the drawing process, you will use the lemon photo as the basis of your artwork. You will draw on other layers, and then delete the template layer when your lemon graphic is complete. You're starting with a letter-size artboard. After you finish the logo graphic, you will resize the artboard to fit the artwork.

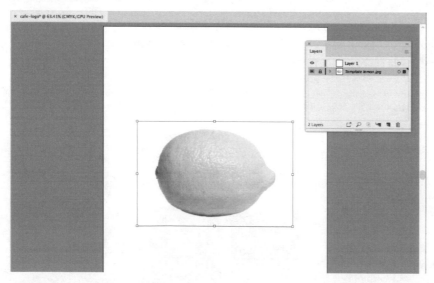

9. **Save the file as a native Illustrator file named cafe-logo.ai in your WIP>Cafe folder, and then continue to the next exercise.**

Note:

Whenever you save an Illustrator file throughout this book, use the default Illustrator options.

Create a Gradient Mesh

A gradient mesh is basically a special type of fill. Each point in the mesh can have a different color value. Areas between mesh lines are gradients of the surrounding point colors; connecting lines between mesh points control the shape of related gradients.

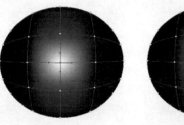

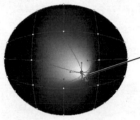

Moving a mesh point or changing its handles affects the position and shape of the associated gradient areas.

1. **With `cafe-logo.ai` open, double-click the Layer 1 name and type `Lemon`. Press Return/Enter to finalize the new layer name.**

2. **Using the Pen tool with a 1-pt black stroke and no fill, draw the outline of the lemon in the template image.**

3. **If necessary, use the Direct Selection tool to adjust the anchor points and handles until the outline matches the lemon shape.**

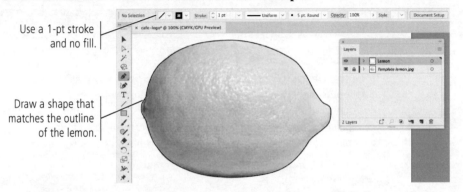

Use a 1-pt stroke and no fill.

Draw a shape that matches the outline of the lemon.

Note:

Refer back to Project 2: Regatta Artwork for details about drawing and editing Bézier curves.

4. **Using the Selection tool, select the outline shape on the Lemon layer.**

5. **Using the Eyedropper tool, click a medium-yellow color in the template image to fill the selected shape with the sampled color.**

   You can add a gradient mesh to a path without filling it with color first, but if you don't choose a color, the mesh will automatically fill with white.

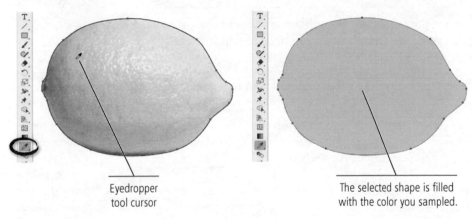

Eyedropper tool cursor

The selected shape is filled with the color you sampled.

6. **Choose Object>Create Gradient Mesh.**

7. **In the Create Gradient Mesh dialog box, activate the Preview option. Set the Rows value to 8 and the Columns value to 7, and make sure the Appearance menu is set to Flat.**

   The Rows and Columns settings determine how many lines make up the resulting mesh.

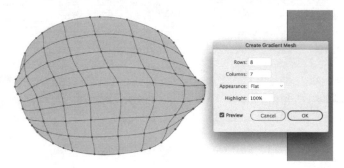

Note:

When you convert a path to a mesh, the shape is no longer a path. You cannot apply a stroke attribute to a gradient mesh object.

8. **Click OK to create the mesh.**

9. **Save the file and continue to the next exercise.**

Understanding Gradient Mesh Options

The Appearance option in the Create Gradient Mesh dialog box determines how colors affect the mesh you create.

Flat spreads a single color to all points in the mesh. If you don't fill the shape with a color before creating the mesh, the mesh object will fill with white.

To Center creates a white highlight at the center and spreads the highlight color outward toward the object edges. The Highlight (%) field controls the strength of white in the resulting mesh.

To Edge is essentially the opposite of the To Center option; the white highlight appears around the edges of the mesh, blending to the solid color in the center of the mesh object.

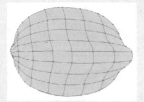

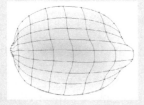

Work in Outline Mode

Outline mode allows you to see the points and paths of an object without the colors and fills. This viewing mode can be very useful when you need to adjust anchor points of one shape while viewing the underlying objects.

1. **With `cafe-logo.ai` open, choose View>Smart Guides to make sure that option is turned on.**

   When Smart Guides are active, you can see the entire mesh wireframe as soon as your cursor touches any part of the object —even if that object is not selected. The cursor feedback also identifies specific points along the mesh.

2. **Make sure the Snap to Point option is toggled off in the View menu.**

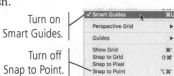

Turn on Smart Guides.

Turn off Snap to Point.

Note:

When using Smart Guides, make sure the Snap to Point option is toggled off. If Snap to Point is active, Smart Guides will not work (even if you have the command selected in the menu).

3. **Choose View>Outline.**

In Outline mode, you see only the edges, or **wireframes**, of the objects in the file.

Template layers are not affected when you view the file in Outline mode. You can now see the mesh wireframe and the actual pixels of the lemon image, enabling you to sample colors directly from the lemon image, and then use those colors to paint the mesh points.

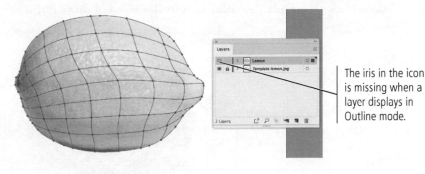

The iris in the icon is missing when a layer displays in Outline mode.

4. **Using the Direct Selection tool, click the left anchor point on the bottom horizontal mesh line to select only that mesh point.**

Your mesh might appear different than ours, based on where you placed your anchor points on the shape edges. You will still be able to achieve the same overall effect as what you see in our examples.

5. **With the mesh point selected, choose the Eyedropper tool in the Tools panel, and then click next to the selected mesh point to sample the color from the lemon photo.**

Because the mesh object is still displayed in Outline mode, you can't see the effect of the color sampling.

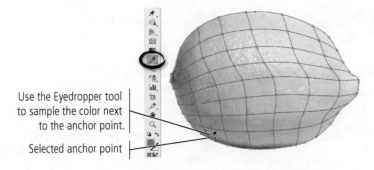

Use the Eyedropper tool to sample the color next to the anchor point.

Selected anchor point

6. **Press and hold the Command/Control key to temporarily access the Direct Selection tool, and then click to select the next point along the bottom line of the mesh.**

Remember, pressing Command/Control with another tool selected temporarily accesses the last-used Selection tool.

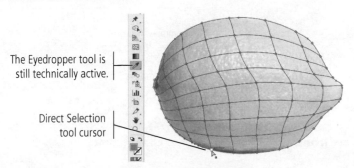

The Eyedropper tool is still technically active.

Direct Selection tool cursor

Note:

In our screen shots, we have the bounding box turned off to better show only the mesh points. You can turn off the bounding box by choosing View>Hide Bounding Box.

7. **Release the Command/Control key to return to the Eyedropper tool, and then click to sample the color next to the selected mesh point.**

   When you release the Command/Control key, you return to the previously active tool.

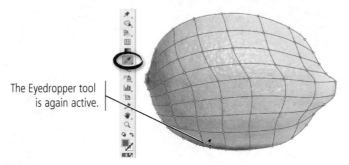

The Eyedropper tool is again active.

8. **Continue this process to change the color of all mesh points on the bottom three rows of points on the mesh.**

   As you progress, keep an eye on which point is actually selected when you click with the Direct Selection tool. The handles of one mesh point might overlap the actual anchor point; you might actually be clicking the handle of another point and, ultimately, selecting the point related to the handle instead of the point you want to affect. If this is the case, you can click and drag a marquee to select the actual mesh point instead of simply clicking.

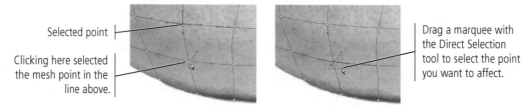

Selected point

Clicking here selected the mesh point in the line above.

Drag a marquee with the Direct Selection tool to select the point you want to affect.

9. **Command/Control-click the eye icon for the Lemon layer to change only that layer back to Preview mode.**

   When working in Outline mode, Command/Control-clicking a layer's visibility icon (the eye icon) returns only that layer to Preview mode.

10. **Deselect the mesh object and review your progress.**

    When you change the color of a mesh point, you change the way surrounding colors blend into that point's color. After painting only the bottom three rows of mesh points, you can already see how the shadows and highlights are starting to blend naturally.

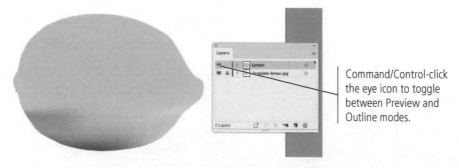

Command/Control-click the eye icon to toggle between Preview and Outline modes.

11. **Command/Control-click the eye icon for the Lemon layer to change that layer back to Outline mode.**

12. **Using the same technique from the previous steps, finish painting all the mesh points in the mesh object.**

This task might seem tedious because there are so many points in the mesh, but with this process, you can create realistic depth in a flat vector object in a matter of minutes. To accomplish the same result using manual techniques would require many hours of time and a high degree of artistic skill.

13. **Deselect the mesh object. Command/Control-click the Lemon layer eye icon to return that layer to Preview mode, then review your results.**

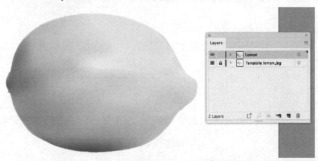

14. **Select the template layer in the Layers panel, then click the Delete Selection button at the bottom of the panel to remove the template layer. When asked to confirm the deletion, click Yes.**

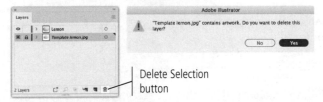

Delete Selection button

15. **Save the file and continue to the next exercise.**

Edit the Gradient Mesh Lines

In addition to simply painting the points that were created when you defined the mesh, you can add to or remove lines from the mesh, move existing points, and even adjust the point handles to change the blending direction. In this exercise, you will adjust the mesh to manipulate the shadows that appear in the lemon artwork.

1. **With cafe-logo.ai open, make sure the Direct Selection tool is active.**

2. **Click to select the center point along the bottom internal mesh line (as shown in the following image).**

You are going to add a new mesh line to the bottom of the lemon shape to minimize the shadow that appears on the shape's bottom edge.

Selecting a point changes the Fill color to match the color of the selected point. This color will become the color for the new point you add in the next few steps.

Selecting the point changes the active Fill color.

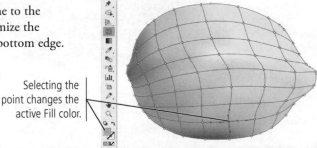

3. **Click away from the shape to deselect it, then choose the Mesh tool in the Tools panel.**

   The Mesh tool adds new gridlines to an existing mesh, or it creates a mesh if you click inside a basic shape that doesn't currently have a mesh. You can also press Option/Alt and click an existing gridline to remove it from the mesh.

4. **Move the cursor over the center vertical gridline, between the bottom edge and the first internal horizontal gridline.**

   Because Smart Guides are active, you can see the mesh lines as soon as the tool cursor enters the shape area.

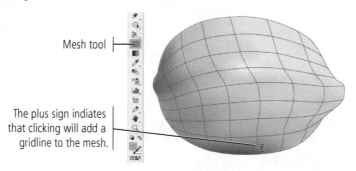

Mesh tool

The plus sign indiates that clicking will add a gridline to the mesh.

Note:

If you don't see the plus sign in the Mesh tool cursor, clicking simply selects an existing point or handle on the mesh.

5. **When you see a plus sign in the tool cursor, click to add a new gridline to the mesh.**

   When you see the plus sign in the cursor, clicking adds a new line to the mesh. Clicking a horizontal gridline adds a new vertical one; clicking a vertical gridline adds a new horizontal one.

   The point where you click uses the fill color you defined in Step 2. The darker color on the bottom edge now only extends as far as the new line; you have effectively reduced the shadow area in half by adding the new gridline.

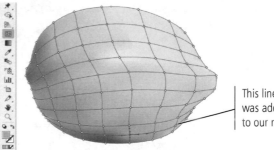

This line was added to our mesh.

6. **Using the Eyedropper method from the previous exercise, change the color of each mesh point on the new row to match the point immediately above it.**

7. **Using the Direct Selection tool, move down the points in the new horizontal mesh line to further reduce the shadow distance on the shape's bottom edge.**

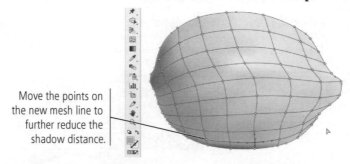

Move the points on the new mesh line to further reduce the shadow distance.

8. **Continue adjusting the positions and colors of the mesh points until you are satisfied with the result.**

9. **Save the file and continue to the next stage of the project.**

STAGE 2 / Working with Type

In this stage of the project, you will use some of Illustrator's basic type formatting options to set your client's company name. You will also use illustration techniques to manipulate the individual letter shapes in the company name to create the finished logotype.

Before you begin the exercises in the second stage of this project, you should understand the terms that are commonly used when people talk about type. Keep the following terms in mind as you work through the next exercises.

Baseline ⊦ Never tell people how to do things. ⊣ Serif font

Tell them what to do and they will

Leading ⊦ surprise you with their ingenuity. ⊐⊣ Body clearance

– George Smith Patton, *War as I Knew It*, 1947 ⊣ Sans-serif font

Type is typically divided into two basic categories: serif and sans serif. **Serif type** has small flourishes on the ends of the letterforms; **sans-serif** has no such decorations (*sans* is French for "without"). There are other categories of special or decorative fonts, including script, symbol, dingbat, decorative, and image fonts.

The actual shape of letters is determined by the specific **font** you use; each character in a font is referred to as a **glyph**. Fonts can be monospaced or proportionally spaced. In a monospace font, each character takes up the same amount of space on a line; in other words, a lowercase i and m occupy the same horizontal space. In a proportionally spaced font, different characters occupy different amounts of horizontal space as necessary.

The **x-height** of type is the height of the lowercase letter x. Elements that extend below the baseline are called **descenders** (as in g, j, and p); elements that extend above the x-height are called **ascenders** (as in b, d, and k).

The size of type is usually measured in **points**; there are approximately 72 points in an inch. When you define type size, you determine the distance from the bottom of descenders to the top of ascenders (plus a small extra space above ascenders called the **body clearance**).

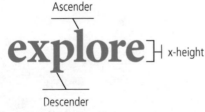

Ascender

Descender

x-height

When you set type, it rests on a non-printing line called the **baseline**. If a type element has more than one line in a single paragraph, the distance from one baseline to the next is called **leading** (pronounced "ledding"). Most applications set the default leading as 120% of the type size.

Create Point-Type Objects

Creating type in Illustrator is fairly simple; just click with the Type tool and begin typing. Many advanced options are also available, such as importing type from an external file, using type areas to control long blocks of text, and so on. In this project, you concentrate on the basic type formatting controls.

1. **With `cafe-logo.ai` open (from your WIP>Cafe folder), choose View>GPU Preview.**

   Although you changed the Lemon layer back to the Preview mode in the previous exercise, the overall file is still technically in Outline mode.

2. **Lock and hide the Lemon layer. Create a new layer named `Type` at the top of the layer stack, and make sure the new layer is selected.**

Note:

If you can't use GPU preview, choose View>Preview on CPU.

3. **Choose the Type tool in the Tools panel, and then click an empty area of the artboard to create a new point-type object.**

   When you single-click with the Type tool, you create **point type**. The type object is automatically filled with placeholder text, which is highlighted. The type automatically defaults to black fill and no stroke, set with the last-used character and paragraph formatting options.

   Depending on the width of your application frame, basic character and paragraph formatting options might be available in the Control panel. If not, you can use the Character and Paragraph hot-text links to open the pop-up panels.

   You can also access character and paragraph formatting options in the Properties panel whenever a type object is selected.

Note:

You can turn off the automatic placeholder text in the Type Preferences dialog box by unchecking the Fill New Type Objects with Placeholder Text option.

Highlighted placeholder text

The Control panel might include basic text formatting options.

Type tool

Click the More Options button to access additional type formatting options.

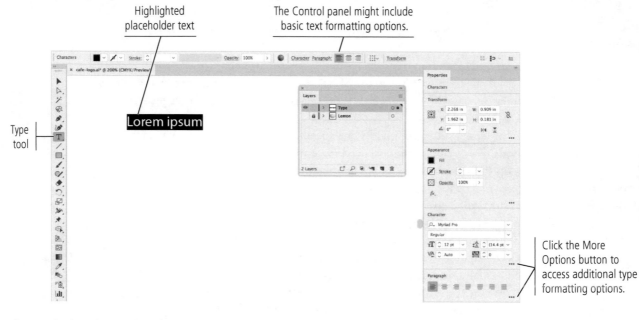

4. **With the placeholder text highlighted, type cafe.**

   When the type tool is active and text is not highlighted, the insertion point flashes in the type object. This insertion point marks the location where text will be added if you continue typing.

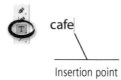

cafe

Insertion point

5. **Choose the Direct Selection tool in the Tools panel.**

   When selected with the Direct Selection tool, you can see the point and path that make up the type object.

6. **Open the Character panel (Window>Type>Character).**

   The Character panel provides access to all character formatting options that can be applied in Illustrator. Character formatting options can also be accessed in the Properties panel, or by clicking the Character hot-text link in the Control panel.

Note:

Hot text *is any text in the user interface that appears underlined in a panel. Clicking these hot-text links opens a panel or dialog box where you can change the related settings.*

Point Type vs. Area Type

You can create two basic kinds of type (or text) objects in Illustrator: **point-type objects** (also called **path type**), where the text usually resides on a single line or path, and **area-type objects**, where the text fills a specific shape (usually a rectangle).

Clicking with the Type tool creates a point-type object. Clicking and dragging with the Type tool creates an area-type object.

Point type (or path type) starts at a single point and extends along or follows a single path. **Area type** fills up an area (normally a rectangle).

The difference between the two kinds of type becomes obvious when you try to resize them or otherwise modify their shapes using the Selection tool. Area type is contained within an area. If you resize that area, the type doesn't resize; it remains within the area but simply flows (or wraps) differently. If you scale or resize point type by dragging a bounding box handle, the type within the object resizes accordingly.

Point-Type Objects

When selected with the Direct Selection tool, you can see the paths that make up the type object.

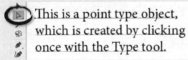

When selected with the Selection tool, you can see the object's bounding-box handles.

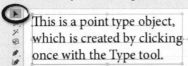

Using the Selection tool, resizing the bounding box resizes the text in the point-type object.

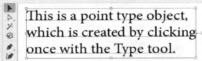

Area-Type Objects

When selected with the Direct Selection tool, you can see the edges of the type object, but no bounding-box handles appear.

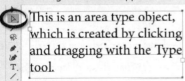

You can see the edges of the type object, as well as the object's bounding-box handles.

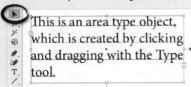

Using the Selection tool, resizing the bounding box resizes the object; the text rewraps inside the new object dimensions.

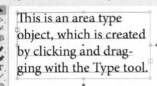

Path Alignment

Another consideration is where the "point" sits on the type path. When you change the paragraph alignment of point type, the point remains in the same position; the text on the point moves to the appropriate position, relative to the fixed point.

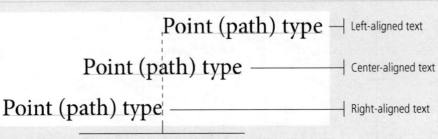

The point for path type is determined by where you click to place the object.

Converting Type Objects

When the Selection tool is active, the handle on the right side of the type-object bounding box indicates whether that object contains point type or area type. A hollow handle identifies a point-type object; a solid handle identifies an area-type object. When you move the cursor over a type object, an icon in the cursor indicates that double-clicking will convert the object to the other kind of type object.

Double-click the hollow handle to convert to an area-type object.

Double-click the solid handle to convert to a point-type object.

7. **Click the Font Family field to highlight the active font. Type atc.**

When you type in the Font Family field, a menu shows all fonts that include the letters you type. By default, the menu includes any font containing those letters, regardless of the position of the letters within the font name. In other words, typing "gar" would show fonts named both "Garamond" and "Adobe Garamond."

If you click the Magnifying Glass icon to the left of the field, you can choose Search First Word Only. In that case, the letters you type automatically scroll the Font Family list to the first font with the typed letters at the beginning of the name; typing "gar" would scroll to Garamond and skip over Adobe Garamond.

8. **Move your mouse cursor over various fonts in the menu.**

You can use this method in the font menu to show a live preview of various fonts before actually applying them to the selected text.

Individual characters do not need to be selected to change text formatting. Changes made while a type *object* is selected apply to all text in that type object.

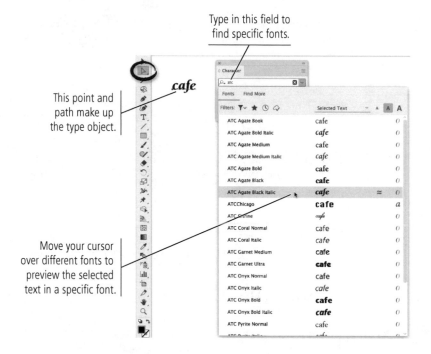

Type in this field to find specific fonts.

This point and path make up the type object.

Move your cursor over different fonts to preview the selected text in a specific font.

9. **Click ATC Garnet Medium in the Font menu to select that font.**

After you select the font, you should notice that the Font Family menu shows "ATC Garnet" and the secondary Font Style menu shows "Medium." When you use the Font Search option (as in Step 7), the resulting menu shows all font variations that include the letters you type — including different styles within the same family.

Font Family

Font Style

10. **Click the Selection tool in the Tools panel.**

When the Selection tool is active, you can see the bounding-box handles of the type object. (If you don't see the bounding box, choose View>Show Bounding Box to toggle it on.) Like any other object, you can use the handles to stretch, scale, or rotate the type object.

11. **Click any of the type object's corner handles and drag out to make the type larger. When the cursor feedback shows the object's height of approximately 0.5 in, release the mouse button.**

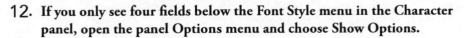

You can press Shift after you begin dragging to constrain the object's original proportions.

We turned Smart Guides on (View>Smart Guides) to show the cursor feedback in our screen shots.

12. **If you only see four fields below the Font Style menu in the Character panel, open the panel Options menu and choose Show Options.**

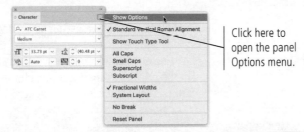

Click here to open the panel Options menu.

13. **Review the extended character formatting options in the Character panel.**

The Size menu shows the new size that results from resizing the object by dragging its bounding-box handles. If you do not constrain the resizing, you might have a horizontal or vertical scale other than 100%.

14. **In the Character panel, change the Size field to 72. Make sure both the horizontal and vertical scale values are set to 100%.**

Pressing Tab moves through the panel fields; as soon as you move to a new field, your changes in the previous field are reflected in the document. You can also press Return/Enter to finalize a change.

15. **Using the Type tool, double-click the word "cafe" to select all the letters in the word.**

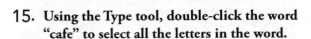

16. **In the Character panel, change the Tracking field to -10 to tighten the space between all selected letters.**

Tracking and kerning are two terms related to the horizontal spacing between characters in a line of text. **Kerning** is the spacing between two specific characters; **tracking** refers to the spacing between all characters in a selection.

Smaller type does not usually pose tracking and kerning problems; when type is very large, however, spacing often becomes an issue. To fix spacing problems, you need to adjust the kerning and/or tracking values.

You can change the field manually, choose a pre-defined value from the Tracking menu, or click the up- or down-arrow button to change the tracking by 1 unit with each click.

The Character Panel in Depth

The Character panel includes all the options you can use to change the appearance of selected text characters.

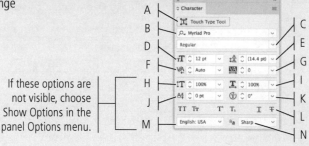

If these options are not visible, choose Show Options in the panel Options menu.

A The **Touch Type tool** is used to change the shape and position of individual characters in a text object. If this tool is not visible at the top of the panel, you can choose Show Touch Type Tool in the panel Options menu.

B **Font Family** is the general font that is applied, such as Minion or Warnock Pro.

C **Font Style** is the specific variation of the applied font, such as Italic, Bold, or Light.

D **Font Size** is the size of the type in points.

E **Leading** is the distance from one baseline to the next. Adobe applications treat leading as a character attribute, even though leading controls the space between lines of an individual paragraph. (Space between paragraphs is controlled using the Space Before and Space After options in the Paragraph panel.) To change leading for an entire paragraph, you must first select the entire paragraph.

If you change the leading for only certain characters in a line, keep in mind that the adjusted leading applies to the entire line where adjusted characters exist; for example:

> In this sentence, we changed the leading
>
> for only the underlined word; all text in the same line moves to accommodate the adjusted leading of the characters.

F **Kerning** increases or decreases the space between pairs of letters. Kerning is used in cases where particular letters in specific fonts need to be manually spread apart or brought together to eliminate a too-tight or too-spread-out appearance. Manual kerning is usually necessary in headlines or other large type elements. Many commercial fonts have built-in kerning pairs, so you won't need to apply much hands-on intervention with kerning. Adobe applications default to the kerning values stored in the **font metrics**.

G **Tracking**, also known as "range kerning," refers to the overall tightness or looseness across a range of characters. Tracking and kerning are applied in thousandths of an **em** (or the amount of space occupied by an uppercase "M," which is usually the widest character in a typeface).

H, I **Vertical Scale** and **Horizontal Scale** artificially stretch or contract the selected characters. This scaling is a quick way of achieving condensed or expanded type if those variations of a font don't exist. Type that has been artificially condensed or expanded too much looks bad because the scaling destroys the type's metrics. If possible, use a condensed or expanded version of a font before resorting to horizontal or vertical scaling.

J **Baseline Shift** moves the selected type above or below the baseline by a specific number of points. Positive numbers move the characters up; negative values move the characters down.

K **Character Rotation** rotates only selected letters, rather than rotating the entire type object.

L Type Styles — **All Caps**, **Small Caps**, **Superscript**, **Subscript**, **Underline**, and **Strikethrough** — change the appearance of selected characters.

M **Language Dictionary** defines the language that is used to check spelling in the story.

N **Anti-aliasing** can be used to help smooth the apparent edges of type that is exported to a bitmap format that does not support vector information.

17. **Click with the Type tool to place the insertion point between the "c" and the "a".**

    This is a good example of a **kern pair** that needs adjustment. The Auto setting built into the font leaves a little too much space between the two characters, even after you have tightened the tracking considerably.

18. **Change the Kerning value to -20.**

    Like tracking, you can change this value manually, choose a value from the pop-up menu, or use the Kerning field buttons to change kerning by 1 unit.

    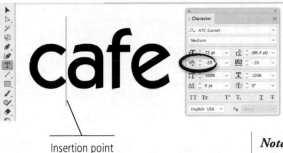

    These slight modifications to tracking and kerning improve the overall appearance and readability of the logo. Later in the project, you will use a different technique to adjust letter spacing. For now, however, you should become familiar with making this type of manual adjustment.

    Insertion point

    Note:

    Kerning and tracking are largely matters of personal preference. Some people prefer much tighter spacing than others.

19. **Save the file and continue to the next exercise.**

 ## Manipulate Type Objects

When you work with type in Illustrator, you need to be aware of a few special issues that can affect the way you interact with the application. This exercise explores some common problems that can arise when you work with type, as well as some tricks you can use to work around them.

1. **With cafe-logo.ai open, select the Type tool in the Tools panel. Click anywhere in the existing type object to place the insertion point.**

2. **Move the Type tool cursor away from the existing type object. Click to deselect the existing type object.**

   When the insertion point is already flashing in a type object, the exact position of the cursor determines what happens if you click. When the cursor is within the bounds of the existing type object, clicking simply places the insertion point where you click. If you move the cursor outside the bounds of the active type object (where the insertion point is flashing), clicking deselects the previously active type object; you can then click again to create a new point-type object.

   This cursor moves the insertion point.

   This cursor deselects the current type object.

   Note:

   When the insertion point is flashing in a type object, you can't use the keyboard shortcuts to access tools; instead, pressing a key adds that letter to the current type object, at the location of the insertion point.

More about Working with Fonts

You can click the arrow to the right of the Font Family menu to open the Font panel, which provides a number of options for finding fonts you want to use in your design. (The same options are available wherever you see a Font Family menu — the Character panel, the Control panel, and the Properties panel.)

The top section of the menu lists up to ten most recently used fonts. These appear in the order in which they were used, with the most recent at the top of the menu. (You can change the number of displayed fonts in the Type pane of the Preferences dialog box.)

The second and third sections list Variable and SVG fonts, respectively. The fourth section lists all other fonts that are available to Illustrator.

The font family names in each section appear in alphabetical order. An arrow to the left of a font name indicates that a specific font family includes more than one style. You can click the arrow to show all possible styles in the panel.

If you apply a font that includes more than one style, the style you choose appears in the Font Style menu. You can open the Font Style menu to change the style without changing the font family.

Each font in the panel includes a sample of the font, which defaults to show the currently selected text. If no text is selected, the sample text simply shows the word "Sample." You can choose a different sample text from the menu at the top of the panel. You can also change the size of the sample text using the three icons to the right of the menu

Clear the Font Family field

Open the Font menu

Click here to change the search behavior when you type in the Font Family field.

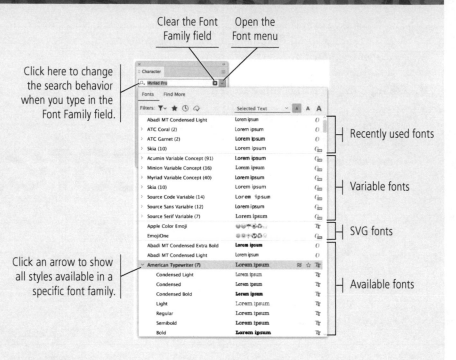

Recently used fonts

Variable fonts

SVG fonts

Click an arrow to show all styles available in a specific font family.

Available fonts

Change the sample text size

Click to change the sample text

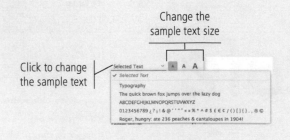

The right column in the Font menu shows an icon to identify the type of font:

a **PostScript (Type 1) fonts** have two file components (outline and printer) that are required for output.

Tr **TrueType fonts** have a single file, but (until recently) were primarily used on the Windows platform.

O **OpenType fonts** are contained in a single file that can include more than 60,000 glyphs (characters) in a single font. OpenType fonts are cross-platform; the same font can be used on both Macintosh and Windows systems.

Csvg **OpenType SVG fonts** allow font glyphs to be created as SVG (scalable vector graphics) artwork, which means glyphs can include multiple colors and gradients. These fonts, which are relatively new, are most commonly used for emojis.

Cvar **OpenType Variable fonts**, introduced in 2016, were developed jointly by Adobe, Apple, Google, and Microsoft to allow a single font file to store a continuous range of variants. If you apply a variable font, you can adjust the width and weight of the applied font without the need for different font files for variations such as Bold, Black, Condensed, or Extended.

↷ **Typekit fonts** are those that have been activated from Adobe Typekit through your Creative Cloud account.

Above the list of fonts in the Font panel, you can use the Filters options to show only certain fonts in the panel. Clicking the Filter Fonts by Classification button opens a menu where you can find fonts of a certain style (serif, sans serif, etc.), as well as fonts with specific properties:

▼˅ Filter Fonts by Classification

★ Show Favorite Fonts

🕘 Show Recently Added Fonts

☁ Show Activated (Typekit) Fonts

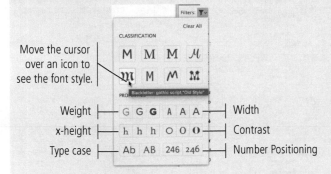

Move the cursor over an icon to see the font style.

Weight — G G **G** A A — Width
x-height — h h h O O — Contrast
Type case — Ab AB 246 246 — Number Positioning

– Weight, or the thickness of strokes in the letterforms
– Width of the individual letterforms
– x-height, or the ratio of lowercase letter height compared to uppercase
– Contrast, or the ratio of thin strokes compared to thick strokes in individual letterforms
– Type case, or whether a font includes both upper- and lowercase, or all capitals/small caps and all caps
– Number positioning, which refers to whether numbers all align to the baseline or extend above or below the baseline

When you use any of the filtering options, the Font panel shows only fonts that match the selected filter. You can click the Clear All link in the top-right corner of the panel to restore the default font list.

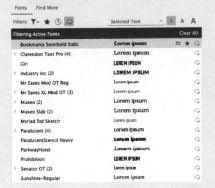

When the mouse cursor hovers over a font in the list, two additional icons appear on the right side of the panel for the highlighted font.

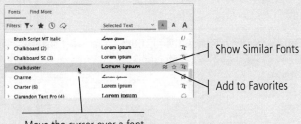

Show Similar Fonts

Add to Favorites

Move the cursor over a font to reveal additional options.

You can click the Show Similar Fonts ≈ button to show only fonts similar to one you selected; clicking the Back hot-text link returns to the full Font panel.

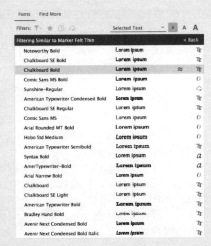

Clicking the Add to Favorites ☆ button designates a font as a Favorite. Favorite fonts are identified by a solid star icon even when the cursor is not hovering over that particular font. You can also use the Filtering option at the top of the panel to show only Favorite fonts.

Adobe Typekit is an online library of high-quality fonts. The Typekit Portfolio Plan, which provides access to the full font library and allows you to sync up to 100 fonts at a time to your desktop, is included in your individual user subscription to the Adobe Creative Cloud.

The Find More option at the top of the Font panel provides a link to Adobe Typekit fonts from directly in the Illustrator interface.

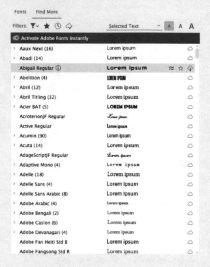

When you find a font you want to use, move your mouse over that font to show the Activate icon ☁; click that icon to activate it in your Creative Cloud account. (A separate icon shows that a particular font is currently being activated ☁.) Synced fonts will be available for use in any application on your device.

If only certain fonts in a family are active, you can click the Active Remaining icon ☁ to activate all fonts in that family.

If a font is already active, move your mouse over the Active icon ☁ to access the Deactivate icon ☁; click that icon to unsync that font.

Verifying your Adobe ID

To use Typekit fonts in an Adobe application, you must first verify that you are signed in using the username and password that is associated with your individual user subscription. (Typekit functionality is not available if you are working on a computer that has an Adobe software Device license instead of an individual user subscription.)

If you open the Help menu, you will see an option to either Sign In or Sign Out. If you see the words "Sign Out," the

menu option also shows the email address (username) that is currently signed in.

If you see your own username, you are already signed in, and can use the Typekit functionality. If you see a different username, you should choose the Sign Out option, and then sign in with your own username. If you see the words "Sign In," you should choose that menu option and follow the on-screen directions to sign in with your own username.

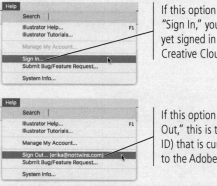

If this option shows "Sign In," you are not yet signed in to your Creative Cloud account.

If this option shows "Sign Out," this is the email (Adobe ID) that is currently signed in to the Adobe Creative Cloud.

Using the Adobe Creative Cloud Application

On Macintosh, the Adobe Creative Cloud application is accessed on the right side of the Menu bar at the top of the screen. On Windows, it is accessed on the right side of the Taskbar at the bottom of the screen.

Macintosh

Windows

Font syncing through Adobe Typekit is managed through the Assets:Fonts pane of the application. Any fonts that are already synced in your account are listed in this pane. (If you have not yet synced fonts in your account, you see a default screen.)

3. **With the Type tool active, click to create a new point-type object.**

When you add a new type object, the placeholder text is automatically set using the last formatting options that you defined in the Character panel. (Settings that were altered by scaling the type object, such as font size and horizontal scale, are not maintained.)

Note:

You can press the ESC key to switch to the Selection tool, which effectively removes the insertion point and selects the type object.

4. **With the placeholder text highlighted, type Limon.**

5. **With the insertion point flashing, press Command/Control.**

As you know, this modifier key temporarily switches the active tool to the last-used Selection tool. The bounding box of the type object remains visible as long as you hold down the Command/Control key. If you release the Command/Control key, you return to the previously active tool (in this case, the Type tool).

6. **While still holding down the Command/Control key, click within the bounding box of the type object.**

When you click, you select the actual type object. The point and path become active, and the insertion point no longer flashes. You can use this method to move or modify a type object without switching away from the Type tool.

Pressing Command/Control temporarily accesses the last-used Selection tool and reveals the type object's bounding box.

7. **Press Command/Control. Click the second type object and drag it until the "i" in Limon aligns with the "f" in cafe.**

You might want to zoom in to better align the two type objects. Use the following image as a guide.

The layer color previews the new position of the type object.

Note:

When you're working with type, it can be easier to work with bounding boxes turned off. You can turn off the bounding boxes for all objects — including type objects — by choosing View>Hide Bounding Box.

Managing Missing Fonts

It is important to understand that fonts are external files of data that describe the font for the output device. The fonts you use in a layout need to be available on any computer that opens the file. Illustrator stores a reference to used fonts, but it does not store the actual font data.

When you open a file that uses fonts you don't have installed on your computer, a Missing Fonts dialog box shows which fonts should be installed.

The software scans the Typekit library to locate missing fonts; missing fonts that exist in the Typekit library are automatically checked in the list. Clicking the Activate Fonts button syncs the required Typekit fonts in your Creative Cloud (CC) account, making them available in your desktop version of Illustrator.

Fonts available in Typekit are checked in the list.

Click here to sync fonts checked in the list.

Using the Find Font Dialog Box

You can also use the Find Font dialog box (accessed by clicking the Find Fonts button in the Missing Fonts dialog box or by choosing Type>Find Font) to replace one font with another throughout a layout.

The top half of the dialog box lists every font used in the file; missing fonts are identified by a warning icon in the list. If a missing font is available in the Typekit library, it is automatically checked in the top list. You can click the Activate Fonts button to sync those fonts in your CC account.

The lower half shows fonts that can be used to replace fonts in the top list. Document shows only fonts used in the file. Recent shows fonts you have recently used in Illustrator. System shows all fonts that are active on your computer.

If you click the Change or Change All button, the font selected in the top list will be replaced with the font selected in the bottom list. You can also use the Find button to locate instances of the selected font without making changes.

8. **Release the mouse button to reposition the type object.**

9. **Press the Command/Control key again, click the type object, then press Shift and drag up or down until there is only a small space between the bottom of the "e" in cafe and the top of the "m" in Limon.**

10. **Release the Command/Control key to return to the Type tool.**

11. **Save the file and continue to the next exercise.**

Convert Type to Outlines

In Illustrator, fonts — and the characters that compose them — are like any other vector objects. They are made up of anchors and paths, which you can modify just as you would any other vector object. To access the anchor points, however, you must first convert the text to outlines.

1. **With `cafe-logo.ai` open, expand the Type layer in the Layers panel.**

   Each type object exists as a separate sublayer.

2. **Use the Selection tool to select both type objects in the file.**

3. **Choose Type>Create Outlines.**

   When you convert the type to outlines, the anchor points and paths that make up the letter shapes appear. Each type object (in this case, one for "cafe" and one for "Limon") is a separate group of letter shapes.

   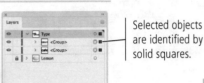

   Selected objects are identified by solid squares.

Note:

Press Command/Control-Shift-O to convert type to outlines.

Note:

If the Properties panel is open, you can also click the Create Outlines button in the Quick Actions section of the panel..

4. **In the Layers panel, click the arrow to the left of the each group on the Type layer to expand them.**

By expanding the individual layers and sublayer groups, you can use the Layers panel to access and work with individual objects in a group, without ungrouping the objects.

5. **In the Layers panel, click the space to the right of the Target icon of the "m" to select only that object.**

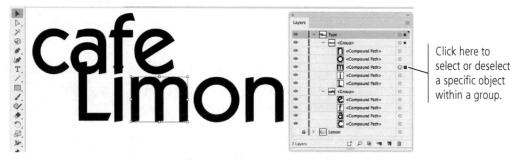

Click here to select or deselect a specific object within a group.

6. **With the Selection tool active, press the Left Arrow key three times to nudge the selected object left, narrowing the space between the letter shapes.**

You can open the General pane of the Preferences dialog box to change the distance an object moves when you press the arrow keys (called the **keyboard increment**). Press Shift and an arrow key to move an object 10 times the default keyboard increment.

You could have fine-tuned the letter spacing with tracking and kerning before you converted the letters to outlines. Since you're working with these letters as graphics, you are nudging individual pieces of a group to adjust the spacing in the overall logotype.

7. **Repeat Steps 5–6 to move the "o" and "n" shapes closer to the other letters in the same word.**

As mentioned previously, letter spacing is largely a matter of personal preference. You might prefer more or less space between the letters than what you see in our images.

8. **Repeat Steps 5–6 to move the "e" closer to the "f" in the word cafe.**

9. **In the Layers panel, click the space to the right of the Target icon of the "a" to select only that object.**

10. **Press Shift, and click the same space for the "c" to add that object to the active selection.**

You can Shift-click the icons in the panel to add or subtract sublayers from the active selection. In this case, however, Shift-clicking does not select all in-between sublayers when you add more than one object to the selection.

You can also Shift-click the icon for a selected object to remove it from the active selection.

11. **Press the Right Arrow key one time to nudge both selected objects closer to the "f" in the same word.**

Shift-click to select multiple sublayers.

12. Use the Layers panel to select only the "L" in Limon, then drag it until the vertical section appears immediately below the vertical line in the "a" (use the following image as a guide).

Although the individual letter shapes are parts of various groups, selecting sublayers in the Layers panel means you don't need to switch to the Direct Selection tool to move only the selected objects.

13. Save the file and continue to the next exercise

Create Custom Graphics from Letter Shapes

Because you converted the letter shapes to outlines, the logo text no longer behaves as type. You can now apply your drawing skills to adjust the vector shapes and create a unique appearance for your client's logotype. Remember, you can use the Add Anchor Point tool to add points to a vector path, use the Delete Anchor Point tool to remove points from a vector path, and use the Anchor Point tool to convert smooth points to corner points (and vice versa). All three of these tools are nested below the Pen tool in the Tools panel.

1. With `cafe-logo.ai` open, click the Eye icon to hide the "cafe" sublayer.

2. Select only the "i" object, and then choose Object>Compound Path>Release.

A compound path is simply a single object that is made up of more than one path. Where multiple objects overlap, the top object knocks out (removes) underlying objects without destructively changing the underlying shapes.

In this case, releasing the compound path simply breaks the two shapes that make up the "i" into separate objects.

Letter shapes become compound paths.

Releasing the compound path separates the various shapes into distinct objects.

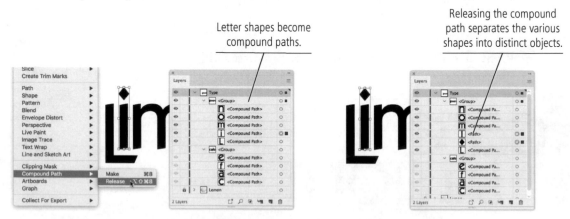

3. Using what you know about anchor points, edit the dot over the "i" to resemble a leaf character.

We converted the bottom, left, and right points to smooth points, then adjusted the position of the top point to achieve the leaf shape.

4. **Change the fill color of the selected object to a medium green from the built-in swatches.**

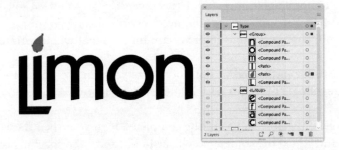

5. **Show the "cafe" sublayer, then edit the bottom of the "f" to align with the leaf shape you just created.**

6. **Using the Direct Selection tool, select the two right anchor points on the "L" shape. Drag them right until the shape creates an underline below all the other letters in the word "Limon."**

7. **Select and delete the "o" object from the "Limon" sublayer.**

8. **Show and unlock the Lemon layer. Transform the gradient-mesh object and move it to fill the space left by deleting the "o" letter shape.**

9. **Save the file and continue to the next stage of the project.**

For all intents and purposes, the Cafe Limon logo is now complete. However, you still need to create the alternate versions that can be used in other applications. You need a two-color version for jobs that will be printed with spot colors, and you need a one-color version for jobs that will be printed with black ink only.

Rather than generating multiple files for individual versions of a logo, you can use Illustrator's multiple-artboard capabilities to create a single file that manages the different logo variations on separate artboards.

In this stage of the project, you adjust the artboard to fit the completed logo. You then duplicate the artwork on additional artboards, and adjust the colors in each version to meet the specific needs of different color applications.

Adjust the Default Artboard

When you place an Illustrator file into another file (for example, a page-layout file in InDesign or even another Illustrator file) you can decide how to place that file — based on the artwork boundaries (the outermost bounding box), on the artboard boundaries, or on other specific dimensions. To make the logo artwork more placement-friendly, you should adjust the Illustrator artboard to fit the completed logo artwork.

1. **With `cafe-logo.ai` open, make the Selection tool active, then choose Select>All to select all elements on the artboard.**

2. **Using the Properties panel, choose the top-left reference point in the Transform section. Change the X and Y positions to 0.125 in.**

Position the selection based on the top-left reference point.

3. **Make sure the W and H fields are linked, then type 250% in the W field.**

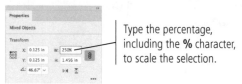

Type the percentage, including the **%** character, to scale the selection.

Note:

Your W and H values might be slightly different than what you see in our screenshots, but they should be in the same general ballpark.

4. **Press Return/Enter to finalize the transformation.**

When you press Return/Enter (or simply click away from the panel field), the selection is scaled proportionally to 250% of its original size.

5. **Select the Artboard tool in the Tools panel.**

   When the Artboard tool is active, the artboard edge is surrounded by marching ants; you can drag the side and corner handles to manually resize the artboard in the workspace.

Drag the handles to manually resize the artboard.

Artboard tool

6. **Click the bottom-right handle of the artboard, then drag up and left until the artboard is approximately 1/8″ larger than the artwork on all four sides.**

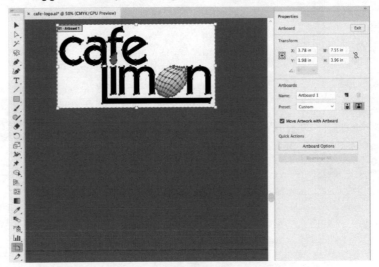

7. **Click the Selection tool to exit the Artboard-editing mode.**

8. **Save the file and continue to the next exercise.**

Managing Artboard Options

When the Artboard tool is active, the Control panel presents a number of options for adjusting the active artboard.

A   B C D E   F   G H I   J   K   L

A Use this menu to change the artboard to a predefined size (letter, tabloid, etc.).

B Click to change the artboard to portrait orientation.

C Click to change the artboard to landscape orientation.

D Click to add a new artboard at the currently defined size. The cursor is "loaded" with the new artboard; you can click to place the new artboard in the workspace.

E Click to delete the active artboard.

F Type here to define a name for the active artboard.

G Click to toggle the Move/Copy Artwork with Artboard option. When active, objects on the artboard move along with the artboard being moved (or cloned).

H Click to open the Artboard Options dialog box.

I Choose a registration point for changes in size or position.

J Use these fields to define the position of the artboard. (The first artboard always begins at X: 0, Y: 0.)

K Use these fields to change the size of the artboard. If the link icon is active, the height and width will be constrained.

L If a file includes more than one artboard, you can click this button to open a dialog box in which you can define a grid pattern for all existing artboards. You can determine the number of columns in the grid, as well as the exact space between individual artboards.

Clicking the Artboard Options button opens a dialog box where you can further manage and control the selected artboard. Most of these options (Preset, Width, Height, Orientation, and Position) are the same as those available in the Control panel.

The remaining choices are explained here:

- **Constrain Proportions** maintains a consistent aspect ratio (height to width) if you resize the artboard.
- **Show Center Mark** displays a point in the center of the crop area.
- **Show Cross Hairs** displays lines that extend into the artwork from the center of each edge.
- **Show Video Safe Areas** displays guides that represent the areas inside the viewable area of video.

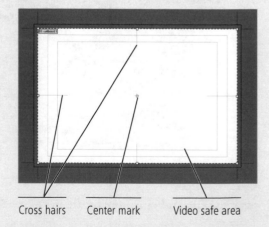

Cross hairs   Center mark   Video safe area

- **Video Ruler Pixel Aspect Ratio** specifies the pixel aspect ratio used for artboard rulers.
- **Fade Region Outside Artboard** displays the area outside the artboard darker than the area inside the artboard.
- **Update While Dragging** keeps the area outside the artboard darker as you move or resize the artboard.

Use the Layers Panel to Organize Artwork

Your goal is to create three separate versions of the logo — the four-color version that's already done, a two-color version for spot-color applications, and a one-color version that will be used in jobs that are printed black-only.

As you created the artwork, you used two layers and a variety of sublayers to manage the arrangement and stacking order of the various elements. Now that the drawing is complete, however, you will use layers for a different purpose — to create, isolate, and manage multiple versions of the logo in a single file.

1. **With cafe-logo.ai open, choose Select>All to select all objects on the artboard.**

2. **Choose Object>Group. In the Layers panel, expand the resulting group.**

   When you group objects, the resulting group is placed on the top-most layer in the active selection. All objects in the group are moved to the same layer containing the group. The original stacking order is maintained, so the mesh object from the Lemon layer still appears at the bottom of the list in the resulting group

The new group exists on the top-most layer in the previous selection.

The mesh object is moved from its original layer into the group.

The mesh object is still below other objects in the stacking order.

3. **Collapse the Type layer in the panel to hide the sublayers.**

4. **Double-click the Type layer name to highlight it. Type Four-Color Logo, then press Return/Enter to finalize the new name.**

5. **Select the Lemon layer in the Layers panel, then click the Delete Selection button.**

   Because this layer no longer has any artwork, you are not asked to confirm the deletion.

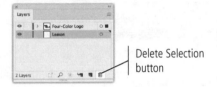

Delete Selection button

6. **Save the file and continue to the next exercise.**

Copy the Artboard and Artwork

The final step in this project is to create the two alternate versions of the logo. This process is largely a matter of cloning the existing artboard and artwork — but you need to complete a few extra steps to convert the mesh objects to standard filled paths.

1. **With** `cafe-logo.ai` **open, choose the Artboard tool in the Tools panel.**

2. **With the only artboard currently active, highlight the contents of the Name field in the Control panel and type** `Four Color`**.**

3. **Make sure the Move/Copy Artwork with Artboard option is toggled on.**

The Artboard name appears in the Name field and in the artboard tag.

The Move/Copy Artwork with Artboard option should be toggled on.

Note:

You might want to zoom out so you can see the entire original artboard and the empty space below it.

4. **Place the cursor inside the artboard area. Press Option/Alt and then click and drag down to clone the existing artboard.**

Pressing Option/Alt clones the existing artboard, just as you would clone a regular drawing object.

Because Move/Copy Artwork with Artboard is toggled on, the logo artwork and the artboard are cloned at the same time.

5. **When the new artboard/artwork is entirely outside the boundaries of the first artboard, release the mouse button.**

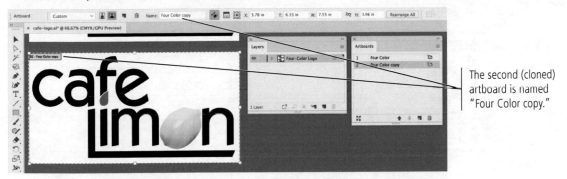

The second (cloned) artboard is named "Four Color copy."

6. **With the second artboard active, change the Name field to Two Color.**

7. **In the Layers panel, click the Create New Layer button.**

New layers are added above the previously selected layer. Because the Four Color layer was the only layer in the file, the new layer is added at the top of the layer stack.

Create New Layer button

8. **Double-click the new layer name in the panel, then type Two-Color Logo to rename the layer.**

9. **Using the Selection tool, drag a marquee to select all the objects on the second artboard.**

10. **In the Layers panel, drag the Selected Art icon from the Four-Color Logo layer to the Two-Color Logo layer.**

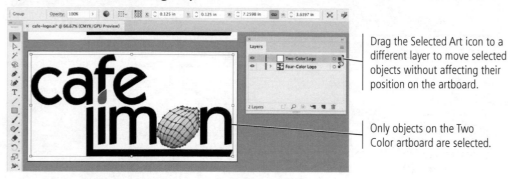

Drag the Selected Art icon to a different layer to move selected objects without affecting their position on the artboard.

Only objects on the Two Color artboard are selected.

When you release the mouse button, the selected objects are moved to the Two-Color Logo layer.

11. **Save the file and continue to the next exercise.**

Convert Mesh Objects to Regular Paths

When you created the gradient meshes in the first stage of this project, you saw that adding the mesh removed the original path you drew. When you worked on the mesh, you might have noticed that the Control panel showed that the selected object was transformed from a path object to a mesh object.

To create the flat two-color version of the logo, however, you need to access the original paths you drew to create the mesh objects. There is no one-step process to convert the mesh object back to a flat path object, so you need to take a few extra steps to create the flat version of the logo.

Because the black-only version of the logo is also flat, you are going to create the flat two-color version first, and then clone it. Doing so avoids unnecessary repetition of the process presented in this exercise.

1. **With cafe-logo.ai open, deselect everything in the file and then open the Artboards panel (Window>Artboards).**

The Artboards panel can be used to access and arrange the various artboards in a file.

2. **In the Artboards panel, double-click the Two Color artboard (away from the artboard name).**

   This forces the selected artboard to fill the space available in the document window.

3. **Expand the Two-Color Logo layer in the Layers panel. If necessary, expand the first group so you can see the three sublayers in the group.**

4. **Use the Layers panel to select the mesh object on the Two-Color Logo layer.**

5. **Open the Appearance panel (Window>Appearance).**

6. **With the mesh object selected, click the Add New Stroke button at the bottom of the Appearance panel.**

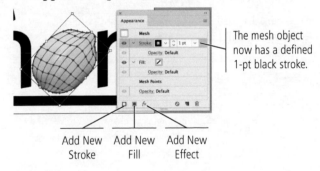

The mesh object now has a defined 1-pt black stroke.

Add New Stroke   Add New Fill   Add New Effect

The Appearance Panel in Depth

The Appearance panel allows you to review and change the appearance attributes of objects, including stroke, fill, transparency, and applied effects.

As you know, the last-used settings for fill color, stroke color, and stroke weight are applied to new objects. Other attributes, such as the applied brush or effects, are not automatically applied.

A   Add New Stroke
B   Add New Fill
C   Add New Effect
D   Cear Appearance
E   Duplicate Selected Item
F   Delete

If you need to create a series of objects with the same overall appearance, you can turn off the **New Art Has Basic Appearance** option in the Appearance panel Options menu.

Clicking the **Clear Appearance** button reduces the selected object to a fill and stroke of None.

Choosing **Reduce to Basic Appearance** in the panel Options menu resets an object to only basic fill and stroke attributes; fill color and stroke weight and color are maintained, but all other attributes are removed.

You can use the **Duplicate Selected Item** button to create multiple versions of the same attribute for an object, such as two stroke weights/colors, allowing you to compound the effect without layering multiple objects.

New appearance attributes are created on top of the currently selected appearance. You can drag the appearance names in the panel to change their stacking sequence, which can have a significant impact on the end result.

If you want to remove a specific attribute, simply select that item and click the panel's **Delete** button.

7. **With the mesh object still selected, choose Object>Expand Appearance.**

   This command converts the selected object into separate constituent objects — one path for the shape's stroke attribute and one for the object's mesh fill — which are automatically grouped together.

8. **In the Layers panel, expand the new group.**

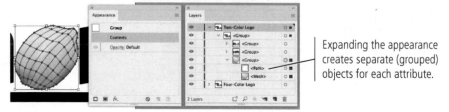

Expanding the appearance creates separate (grouped) objects for each attribute.

9. **Use the Layers panel to select only the mesh object in the group.**

10. **Press Delete/Backspace to remove the selected mesh object.**

    You now have a simple path object that is essentially the lemon shape. However, you need to complete one more step because the path is still part of the group that was created by the Expand Appearance command.

After deleting the mesh, the remaining path is still part of the group.

11. **Use the Layers panel to select the path in the group, and then choose Object>Ungroup.**

After ungrouping, the selected path is a regular sublayer (it is not grouped).

12. **Save the file and continue to the next exercise.**

Add Spot Color to the Two-Color Logo

Spot colors are created with special premixed inks that produce a certain color with one ink layer; they are not built from the standard CMYK process inks. Each spot color appears on its own separation. Spot inks are commonly used to reproduce colors you can't get from a CMYK build, in two- or three-color documents, or as additional separations when exact colors are needed.

You can choose a spot color directly from the library on your screen, but you should look at a printed swatch book to verify that you're using the color you intend. Special inks exist because many of the colors can't be reproduced with process inks, nor can they be accurately represented on a monitor. If you specify spot colors and then convert them to process colors later, your job probably won't look exactly as you expect.

Note:

In the United States, the most popular collections of spot colors are the Pantone Matching System (PMS) libraries. TruMatch and Focoltone are also used in the United States. Toyo and DICColor (Dainippon Ink & Chemicals) are used primarily in Japan.

1. **With `cafe-logo.ai` open, choose Window>Swatch Libraries>Color Books>Pantone+ Solid Coated.**

Illustrator includes swatch libraries of all the common spot-color libraries. You can open any of these libraries to access the various colors available in each collection.

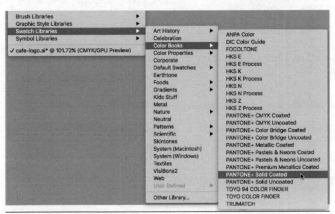

2. **In the Pantone+ Solid Coated library Options menu, choose Small List View to show the color names for each swatch.**

It is often easier to view swatches with their names and samples, especially when you need to find a specific swatch (as in this exercise).

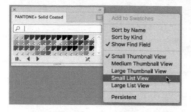

Note:

The View options in the panel Options menu are available for all swatch panels, including colors, patterns, and brushes.

Note:

To restore all spot color to the panel, simply delete the characters from the panel's Search field.

3. **On the Two Color artboard/layer, select the path that represents the lemon.**

4. **In the Find field of the color library panel, type 102.**

You could simply scroll through the panel to find the color you want, but typing a number in the Find field shows only colors that match what you type.

5. **Make sure the Fill icon is active in the Tools panel, and then click Pantone 102 C in the swatch Library panel.**

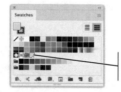

The Fill is the active attribute.

6. **Review the Swatches panel (Window>Swatches).**

When you apply a color from a swatch library, that swatch is added to the Swatches panel for the open file.

This is the Pantone color swatch.

7. **Using whichever method you prefer, change the stroke color of the selected object to None.**

8. **Select only the leaf shape that you created from the dot over the "i."**

Use the Direct Selection tool or the icons in the Layers panel to select only that shape.

9. **Change the fill color to None and change the stroke to 2-pt Black.**

10. **Choose the Artboard tool. With the Move/Copy Artwork with Artboard option still active, press Option/Alt and then click and drag down to clone the flat version. Rename the new artboard One Color.**

11. **Move the artwork on the third artboard to a new layer named One-Color Logo. Change the lemon shape to a fill of None with a 2-pt Black stroke.**

12. **Save the file, close it, and then continue to the next stage of the project.**

STAGE 4 / Combining Text and Graphics

The final stage of this project requires two additional layouts: a letterhead and a business envelope. Rather than adding more artboards to the logo file, you are going to create a new file that will contain both pieces of stationery. This means you must place the logos from the original cafe-logo.ai file, and understand how to work with objects that are placed from external files.

Work with Placed Graphics

Some production-related concerns dictate how you design a letterhead. In general, there are two ways to print a letterhead: commercially in large quantities, or one-offs on your desktop laser or inkjet printer. The second method includes a letterhead template, which you can use to write and print your letters from directly within a page-layout program; while this method is common among designers, it is rarely done using Illustrator.

If your letterhead is being printed commercially, it's probably being printed with multiple copies on a large press sheet, from which the individual letterhead sheets will be cut. Most commercial printing happens this way. This type of printing typically means that design elements can run right off the edge of the sheet; this is called **bleeding**. If you're using a commercial printer, always ask the output provider whether it's safe (and cost-effective) to design with bleeds, and find out how much bleed allowance to include.

If you're designing for a printer that can only run letter-size paper, you need to allow enough of a margin area for your printer to hold the paper as it moves through the device (called the **gripper margin**); in this case, you can't design with bleeds.

1. **Open the New Document dialog box (File>New). Define the following settings:**

Intent:	Print
Preset:	Letter
Name:	stationery
Units:	Inches
Orientation:	Portrait
Artboards:	1
Bleed:	0.125 in (all four sides)

   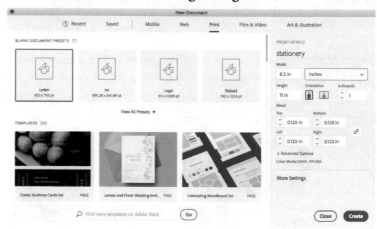

2. **Click Create to create the new file.**

   The red line indicates the defined bleed (1/8″ outside the artboard edge).

   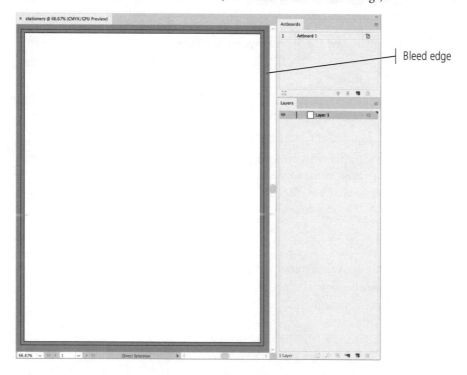

   Bleed edge

3. **Choose File>Place. Navigate to the file cafe-logo.ai in your WIP>Cafe folder, and make sure Link and Template are both unchecked. Check the Show Import Options box, then click Place.**

   Until now, you have placed raster images in the JPEG format. Different types of files, however, have different options that determine what is imported into your Illustrator file.

4. **Review the options in the Place PDF dialog box.**

Although you're placing a native Illustrator (.ai) file, the dialog box shows options for placing PDF files. Illustrator files use PDF as the underlying structure (which is what enables multiple artboard capability), so the options are the same as those you would see if you were placing a PDF file.

Use these arrows to select which artboard you want to place.

The **Crop To** option determines exactly what is placed into an Illustrator file. (If you are placing an Illustrator file, many of these options produce the same result.)

- The **Bounding Box** setting places the file's bounding box, or the minimum area that encloses the objects on the page or artboard.

- The **Art** setting crops incoming files relative to the size and position of any objects selected at the time of the cropping. For example, you can create a frame and use it to crop an incoming piece of artwork.

- Use the **Crop** setting when you want the position of the placed file to be determined by the location of a crop region drawn on the page, when placing an Illustrator file, this refers to the defined artboard.

- The **Trim** setting identifies where the page will be physically cut in the production process, if trim marks are present.

- The **Bleed** setting places only the area within bleed margins (if a bleed area is defined). This is useful if the page is being output in a production environment. The printed page might include page marks that fall outside the bleed area.

- The **Media** setting places the area that represents the physical paper size of the original PDF document (for example, the dimensions of an A4 sheet of paper), including printers' marks.

Note:

If Show Import Options is not checked in the Place dialog box, the Illustrator file is placed based on the last-used Crop To option.

5. **Choose Bounding Box in the Crop To menu, and then click OK to place the four-color logo.**

6. **If you get a warning about an unknown image construct, click OK to dismiss it.**

For some reason, gradient mesh objects *created in Illustrator* are unrecognized *by Illustrator*, which is the case with this logo file. Gradient meshes are imported into the new file as "non-native art" objects that can't be edited in the new file unless you use the Flatten Transparency command to turn them into embedded raster objects.

After dismissing the warning message, the selected file is loaded into the Place cursor. A small preview of the loaded file appears in the cursor.

The selected file is loaded into the Place cursor.

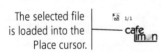

7. **Click near the top-left corner of the artboard to place the loaded image.**

8. **Open the General pane of the Preferences dialog box. Make sure the Scale Strokes & Effects option is checked, and then click OK.**

Note:

On Macintosh, open the Preferences dialog box in the Illustrator menu. On Windows, open the Preferences dialog box in the Edit menu.

If this option is checked, scaling an object also scales the applied strokes and effects proportionally to the new object size. For example, reducing an object by 50% changes a 1-pt stroke to a 0.5-pt stroke. If this option is unchecked, a 1-pt stroke remains a 1-pt stroke, regardless of how much you reduce or enlarge the object.

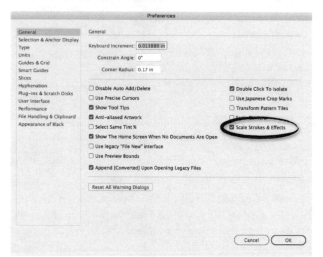

9. **With the placed artwork selected, use the Transform panel to scale the artwork to 3 in wide (constrained). Using the top-left reference point, position the artwork 0.25 in from the top and left edges (as shown in the following image).**

Constrain the width and height before changing the object size.

10. **Using the Type tool, click to create a new point-type object. Type 47653 Main Street, Pittsburgh, PA 05439. Format the type as 9-pt ATC Coral Normal.**

11. **Using the Selection tool, position the type object directly below the stylized L (use the following image as a guide).**

Note:

Remember, your original artwork might be a slightly different size than ours, so your resized height might also be slightly different than what is shown here.

12. **Activate the Selection tool, then choose File>Place. Navigate to the file leaves.ai in your WIP>Cafe folder and click Place.**

The Show Import Options check box remembers the last-used setting, so it should still be checked. After clicking Place, the Place PDF dialog box automatically appears.

The Place PDF dialog box also defaults to the last-used option, so Bounding Box should already be selected in the Crop To menu.

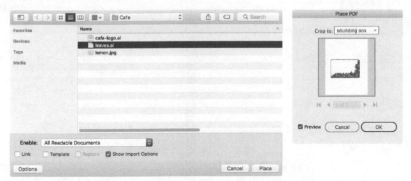

13. **Click OK to close the Place PDF dialog box.**

Again, the selected file is loaded into the Place cursor.

14. **Click the loaded Place cursor to place the leaves.ai file.**

15. **Using the Selection tool, drag the placed graphic so the edges of the artwork align with the bottom and right bleed guides.**

Areas outside the bleed guide would not be included in the output.

Areas outside the artboard edge will be trimmed from the press sheet.

16. Choose View>Trim View.

The Trim view hides any elements that extend beyond the artboard edge. This allows you to more accurately preview the finished job as it will appear when output.

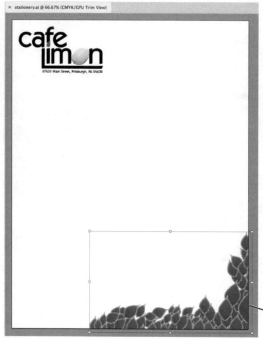

Areas outside the trim edge are hidden.

17. Choose View>Trim View to toggle off that option.

18. Save the file as an Illustrator file named stationery.ai in your WIP>Cafe folder, and then continue to the next exercise.

Create the Envelope Layout

In general, printed envelopes can be created in two ways. You can create and print the design on a flat sheet, which will be specially **die cut** (stamped out of the press sheet), and then folded and glued into the shape of the finished envelope. Alternatively (and usually at less expense), you can print on pre-folded and -glued envelopes.

Both of these methods for envelope design have special printing requirements, such as ensuring no ink is placed where glue will be applied (if you're printing on flat sheets), or printing far enough away from the edge (if you're printing on pre-formed envelopes). Whenever you design an envelope, consult with the output provider that will print the job before you get too far into the project.

In this case, the design will be output on pre-folded #10 business-size envelopes (4-1/8″ by 9-1/2″). The printer requires a 1/4″ gripper margin around the edge of the envelope where you cannot include any ink coverage.

1. With stationery.ai open, zoom out until you can see the entire artboard and an equal amount of space to the right.

2. Choose the Artboard tool. With the current artboard active, type Letterhead in the Name field of the Control panel.

Note:

*The **live area** is the "safe" area inside the page edge, where important design elements should remain. Because printing and trimming are mechanical processes, there will always be some variation, however slight. Elements too close to the page edge run the risk of being accidentally trimmed off.*

3. **Place the cursor to the right of the existing artboard, then click and drag to create a new artboard.**

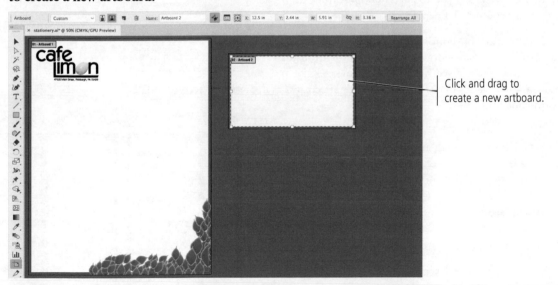

Click and drag to create a new artboard.

4. **With the second artboard active, type Envelope in the Name field of the Control panel.**

5. **With the second artboard active, use the fields in the Control panel to change the artboard dimensions to W: 9.5 in, H: 4.13 in.**

   If the W and H fields are not visible in your Control panel, click the Artboard Options button in the Control panel and use the resulting dialog box to change the artboard size.

   Depending on where you created the second artboad, and which reference point was active when you changed the artboard size, your two artboards might end up overlapping.

6. **Click the Rearrange All button in the Control panel.**

This dialog box allows you to align multiple artboards to one another in a specific, defined grid.

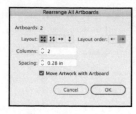

The Grid-by-Row (⊞) option aligns the top edge of each artboard in a single row. If the number of artboards is greater than the allowed number of columns (in the Columns field), additional rows of artboards are created as necessary to accommodate all artboards in the file.

The Grid-by-Column (⊞) option aligns the left edge of each artboard in a single row. If the number of artboards is greater than the allowed number of rows (in the Rows field), additional columns of artboards are created as necessary to accommodate all artboards in the file.

The Spacing field determines how much space appears between individual artboards in a row or column.

The Arrange by Row (↔) and Arrange by Column (↕) options place all artboards in a single row or column, respectively.

Grid by Column

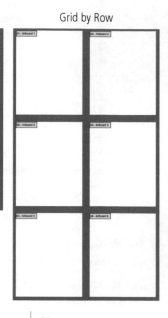

Grid by Row

The Layout Order defaults to use the Left-to-Right (→) option, which places artboards left-to-right (for example, Artboard 1, then 2, then 3). If you select the Change to Right-to-Left Layout option (←), artboards are placed in reverse order (for example, Artboard 3, then 2, then 1).

7. **Change the Spacing field to 0.25 in and click OK.**

The top edges of the two artboards are aligned, with 0.25″ between the two artboards.

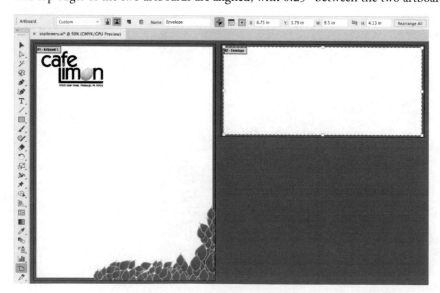

Note:

Press Shift and drag a marquee to select multiple artboards in the document window.

8. Choose File>Place. Navigate to the file `cafe-logo.ai` in your WIP>Cafe folder. Make sure Show Import Options is checked, then click Place.

9. In the Place PDF dialog box, click the right-arrow button to show 2 of 3, then click OK.

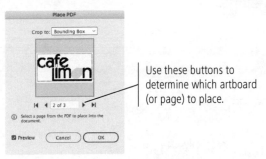

Use these buttons to determine which artboard (or page) to place.

10. Click with the loaded Place cursor to place the loaded file on the Envelope artboard.

11. Make the Selection tool active. If rulers are not visible in your document window, choose View>Rulers>Show Rulers.

12. Choose View>Rulers and make sure the menu option reads "Change to Global Rulers".

    When Artboard rulers are active — which you want for this exercise — the menu command reads "Change to Global Rulers."

    Artboard rulers show all measurements from the zero-point of the active artboard. Global rulers show all measurements from the zero-point of Artboard 1 (unless you reset the zero-point when a different artboard is active).

Note:

You can't switch between Artboard and Global rulers while the Artboard tool is active.

13. Select the placed object with the Selection tool. Scale it to 2.5 in wide (constrained) and place it 0.25 in from the top and left edges of the envelope artboard.

Because Artboard rulers are active, each artboard has its own zero point.

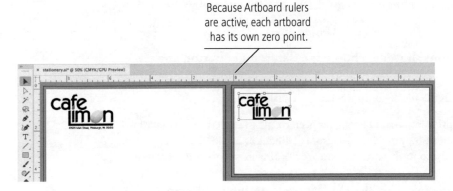

14. **Copy the type object from the letterhead and paste it onto the envelope layout. Change the size of the type in the pasted object to 7.5 pt.**

15. **Save the file and continue to the next exercise.**

 Print Desktop Proofs of Multiple Artboards

Before you send a file to a commercial output provider, it's a good idea to print a sample to see how the artwork looks on paper. Illustrator provides a large number of options for outputting files.

There are two important points to remember about using inkjet and laser proofs. First, inkjet printers are usually not PostScript driven. Because the commercial output process revolves around the PostScript language, proofs should be created using a PostScript-compatible printer, if possible. Second, inkjet and laser printers typically do not accurately represent color.

1. **With stationery.ai open, choose File>Print.**

   The Print dialog box is divided into eight sections or categories, which display in the window on the left side of the dialog box. Clicking one of the categories in the list shows the associated options on the right side of the dialog box.

2. **In the Printer menu, choose the printer you want to use, and then choose the PPD for that printer in the PPD menu (if possible).**

   If you are using a non-PostScript printer, complete as much of the rest of this exercise as possible based on the limitations of your output device.

   The most important options you'll select are the Printer and PPD (PostScript printer description) settings at the top of the dialog box. Illustrator reads the information in the PPD to determine which of the specific print options are available for the current output.

3. **With the General options showing, choose the Range radio button and type 1 in the field.**

   By default, all artboards in the file are output when you click Print.

   If your printer can only print letter-size paper, you need to tile the letterhead artboard to multiple sheets, so you can output a full-size proof. Tiling is unavailable when printing multiple artboards, so in this exercise you are printing each artboard separately.

4. **In the Options section, make sure the Do Not Scale option is selected.**

   As a general rule, proofs — especially final proofs that would be sent to a printer with the job files — should be output at 100%.

Note:

A print preset is a way to store many different settings in a single menu choice. You can create a print preset by making your choices in the Print dialog box, and then clicking the Save Preset button.

5a. **If your printer is capable of printing oversize sheets, choose Tabloid/ A3/11×17 in the Media menu. Choose the Portrait orientation option.**

5b. **If you can only print to letter-size paper, turn off the Auto-Rotate option and choose the Landscape orientation option. Choose Tile Full Pages in the Scaling menu and define a 1 in Overlap.**

To output a letter-size page at 100% on letter-size paper, you have to tile to multiple sheets of paper. Using the landscape paper orientation allows you to tile to 2 sheets instead of 4 (as shown in the preview area).

Note:

The Tile options are not available if you are printing multiple artboards at one time.

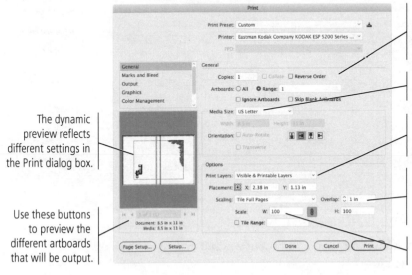

Use these options to print more than one copy and reverse the output order of the multiple artboards (last to first).

Define the paper size used for the output.

The dynamic preview reflects different settings in the Print dialog box.

Use this menu to output visible and printable layers, visible layers, or all layers.

Use these buttons to preview the different artboards that will be output.

When tiling a page to multiple sheets, you can define a specific amount of space that will be included on both sheets.

Use these options to scale the output (if necessary).

6. **Click the Marks and Bleed option in the list of categories on the left. Activate the All Printer's Marks option, and then change the Offset value to 0.125 in.**

If you type the value in the Offset field, Illustrator rounds up to the nearest two-decimal value. Since 0.13″ is larger than the 0.125″ bleed, this offset position is fine.

7. **In the Bleeds section, check the Use Document Bleed Settings option.**

When you created the stationery file, you defined 1/8″ bleeds on all four sides of the artboard. Checking this box in the Print dialog box includes that same 1/8″ extra on all four sides of the output.

Note:

The Auto-Rotate option is useful if you are printing multiple artboards; when this option is active, the application automatically positions each artboard to take best advantage of the available paper.

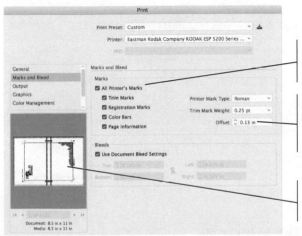

Use these options to select individual printer's marks or print all marks.

The Offset value determines how far from the page edge the printer's marks will be placed.

The preview now includes all selected printer's marks and the defined bleed area.

Note:

Some output providers require printer's marks to stay outside the bleed area, which means the offset should be at least the same as or greater than the defined bleed area.

8. **Click the Output option in the list of categories on the left.**

   Depending on the type of output device you are using, you can print all colors to a single sheet by choosing Composite in the Mode menu, or print each color to an individual sheet by choosing Separations (Host-based). The third option — In-RIP Separation — allows the file data to be separated by the output device instead of by the software.

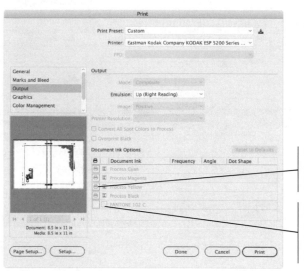

When printing separations, click any of these icons to stop that ink separation from outputting.

If a job includes spot colors, click the icon in this column to convert the spot color to process color for the output.

9. **Click Print to output the artwork.**

10. **Choose File>Print again. Choose the Range radio button and type 2 in the field to print the envelope layout.**

11. **Choose US Letter in the Size menu and choose the Landscape orientation option. Choose Do Not Scale in the Scaling menu.**

    In this case, a letter-size sheet is large enough to print the envelope artboard without scaling. Some of the printer's marks might be cut off by the printer's gripper margin, but that is fine for the purpose of a desktop proof.

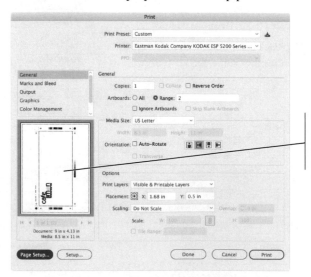

The preview area shows that the envelope artboard will fit on a letter-size page at 100% if you use landscape orientation.

12. **Click Print to output the envelope proof.**

13. **When the document comes back into focus, save and close it.**

PROJECT REVIEW

1. The _____ provides access to handles that you can use to manually resize the artboard in the workspace.

2. Press _____ and click the eye icon on a specific layer to switch only that layer between Preview and Outline mode.

3. When _____ are active, moving your cursor over an unselected object reveals the paths that make up that object.

4. The _____ tool is used to sample colors from an object already placed in the file.

5. The _____ is used to monitor and change the individual attributes (fill, stroke, etc.) of the selected object.

6. The _____ is the imaginary line on which the bottoms of letters rest.

7. _____ is the spacing between specific pairs of letters (where the insertion point is placed).

8. The _____ command makes the vector shapes of letters accessible to the Direct Selection tool.

9. A _____ is a special ink used to reproduce a specific color, typically used for one- or two-color jobs.

10. Click the _____ in the Layers panel to select a specific sublayer.

1. Explain the advantages of using a gradient mesh, compared to a regular gradient.

2. Briefly explain two primary differences between point-type objects and area-type objects.

3. Explain the potential benefits of using multiple artboards rather than different files for different pieces.

PORTFOLIO BUILDER PROJECT

Use what you have learned in this project to complete the following freeform exercise.
Carefully read the art director and client comments, then create your own design to meet the needs of the project.
Use the space below to sketch ideas. When finished, write a brief explanation of the reasoning behind your final design.

art director comments

The Cincinnati Zoo has hired you to create a series of graphics that will be used to rebrand the facility at next spring's Grand Reopening. Your work will be used for everything from printed collateral and park signage, to the zoo's website, and even embroidery on clothing.

❏ Create a new logo to identify the redesigned zoo.

❏ Create a series of icons for each of the zoo's seven main sections: Tropics, Desert, Arctic, Forest, Ocean, Sky, and Kids Kingdom.

❏ Create an invitation for the Grand Reopening celebration incorporating the new logo. Research the best size for a printed invitation that will be sent through the U.S. Postal Service. Include placeholder text for the date and time of the event, as well as the zoo's phone number and web address.

client comments

Our facility received a significant grant from an anonymous donor to update the entire facility — everything from the animal enclosures and guest facilities, to the walking paths and water fountains. Basically, we've rebuilt from the ground up, and are very excited to reveal our efforts to the public next spring at the Grand Reopening.

Since everything is new, we felt it was also time to update our corporate identity. The previous logo was designed more than 20 years ago and is little more than the words, "Cincinnati Zoo." We want something fresh that incorporates more than just two words in a fancy typeface. Remember though, it has to look good on a 15-foot sign or embroidered on the pocket of a T-shirt.

For the section icons, try to keep them simple. We don't want visitors to have to work to figure out what they mean. You can include the actual words, but we're an international facility, so not everyone will be able to read the English explanations.

project justification

PROJECT SUMMARY

Logos are one of the most common types of artwork that you will create in Illustrator. These can be as simple as text converted to outlines, or as complex as a line drawing based on an object in a photograph. Most logos will actually be some combination of drawing and text-based elements. As you learned throughout this project, one of the most important qualities of a logo is versatility. A good logo can be used in many different types of projects, and output in many different types of print processes. To accomplish this goal, logos should work equally well in grayscale, four-color, and spot-color printing.

By completing this project, you worked with complex gradients to draw a realistic lemon, then added creative type treatment to build the finished logotype. After completing the initial logo, you converted it to other variants that will work with different output processes (two-color and one-color). Finally, you incorporated the logo artwork into completed stationery for your client's communication needs as he expands his business.

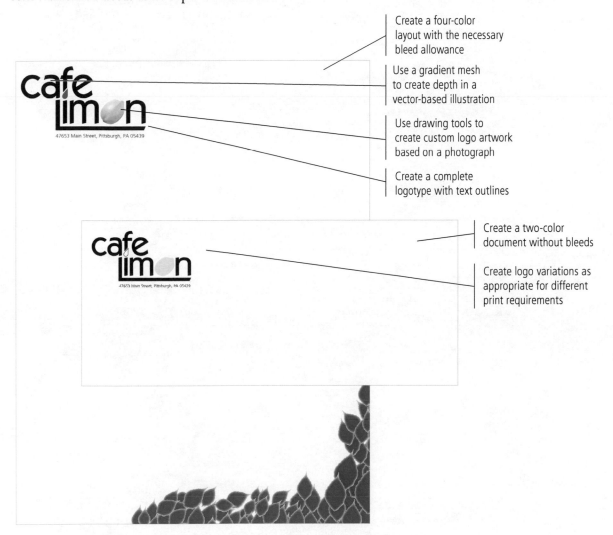

Create a four-color layout with the necessary bleed allowance

Use a gradient mesh to create depth in a vector-based illustration

Use drawing tools to create custom logo artwork based on a photograph

Create a complete logotype with text outlines

Create a two-color document without bleeds

Create logo variations as appropriate for different print requirements

Music CD Artwork

4

You have been hired to create the artwork for a local band's new CD release. The final artwork will be used for an album sleeve, in CD cases, on digital music libraries, as well as in advertisements in a variety of printed media (newspapers, magazines, and so on).

This project incorporates the following skills:

❑ Creating a single composite ad from multiple supplied images

❑ Compositing multiple photographs, using various techniques to select the focal object in each image

❑ Incorporating graphics as rasterized layers and Smart Object layers

❑ Moving and transforming layer content in relation to the page, and to each other

❑ Managing individual layout elements using layers and layer groups

❑ Saving versions of a file to meet different output requirements

STORM FRONT CONSPIRACY

HIGH HANDED THIEVERY

PROJECT MEETING

Our new CD, Storm Front Conspiracy, kind of tells a story across the 11 tracks. The husband goes away on military service, the wife waits for him, he comes home but doesn't remember her, and she looks for answers to his amnesia.

Our band is a combination of rock, country, and alternative/punk. We want the artwork for the new CD to be dramatic, and reflect both our personalities, and the story we are telling.

We're actually releasing this first as a limited-edition album on vinyl. The sleeve for that version is 10″, square. We also need files for a standard-size printed CD insert, and for digital libraries like iTunes.

The band loved the initial concept sketch I submitted last week, so we're ready to start building the files. In addition to the band's logo, I've gathered the photographs I want to use. I also already created a title treatment in Photoshop, so I'll send you that file as well.

The special edition LP will be 10″, square, but you need to incorporate a 1/8″ bleed allowance and a 1/4″ margin since the cover sleeve will be printed.

The 10″ file should be large enough for most print advertising applications, so we can just use the same file for those projects.

A standard CD insert is 4.75″, square. That version needs to incorporate 1/8″ bleeds as well, but it only needs 1/8″ safe margin according to our printer.

For digital media, use the current standards for iTunes music cover art. They require artwork to be at least 3000 × 3000 pixels, and delivered as high-quality JPEG or PNG files. That format should be sufficient for most other online catalogs.

To complete this project, you will:

- ❏ Resize a raster image to change resolution

- ❏ Composite multiple images into a single background file

- ❏ Incorporate both raster and vector elements into the same design

- ❏ Transform and arrange individual layers to create a cohesive design

- ❏ Create layer groups to easily manage related layer content

- ❏ Use selection techniques to isolate images from their backgrounds

- ❏ Save different types of files for different ad requirements

STAGE 1 / Compositing Images and Artwork

Technically speaking, **compositing** is the process of combining any two or more objects (images, text, illustrations, etc.) into an overall design. The ad you're building in this project requires compositing three digital photographs, as well as title treatment and logo files that were created in Adobe Illustrator by other designers. The various elements that make up the finished artwork are fairly representative of the type of work you can (and probably will) create in Photoshop.

Types of Images

There are two primary types of digital artwork: vector graphics and raster images.

Vector graphics are composed of mathematical descriptions of a series of lines and shapes. Vector graphics are **resolution independent**; they can be freely enlarged or reduced, and they are automatically output at the resolution of the output device. The shapes that you create in Adobe InDesign, or in drawing applications, such as Adobe Illustrator, are vector graphics.

Raster images, such as photographs, are made up of a grid of independent pixels (rasters or bits) in rows and columns (called a **bitmap**). Raster files are **resolution dependent**; their resolution is fixed, and is determined when you scan, photograph, or otherwise create the file. You can typically reduce raster images, but you cannot significantly enlarge them without losing image quality.

Line art (also called a **bitmap image**) is actually a type of raster image, made up entirely of 100% solid areas. The pixels in a line-art image have only two options: they can be all black or all white. Examples of line art are UPC bar codes or pen-and-ink drawings.

Screen Ruling

The file that you will be building in this project is intended to be printed, so you have to build the new file with the appropriate settings for commercial printing. When reproducing a photograph on a printing press, the image must be converted into a set of printable dots that fool the eye into believing it sees continuous tones. Prior to image-editing software, pictures that were being prepared for printing on a press were photographed through a screen to create a grid of **halftone dots** that simulate continuous tone, resulting is a **halftone image**. Light tones in a photograph are represented as small halftone dots; dark tones become large halftone dots.

> **Note:**
>
> *Despite their origins in pre-digital print work-flows, these terms persist in the digital environ-ment.*

The screens used to create the halftone images had a finite number of available dots in a horizontal or vertical inch. That number was the **screen ruling**, or **lines per inch (lpi)** of the halftone. A screen ruling of 133 lpi means that in a square inch; there are 133×133 (17,689) possible locations for a halftone dot. If the screen ruling is decreased, there are fewer total halftone dots, producing a grainier image. If the screen ruling is increased, there are more halftone dots, producing a clearer image.

Line screen is a finite number based on a combination of the intended output device and paper. You can't randomly select a line screen. Ask your printer what line screen will be used before you begin creating your images. If you can't find out ahead of time or, if you're unsure, follow these general guidelines:

- Newspaper or newsprint: 85–100 lpi

- Magazine or general commercial printing: 133–150 lpi

- Premium-quality-paper jobs (such as art books or annual reports): 150–175 lpi; some specialty jobs might use 200 lpi or more

Image Resolution

When an output device creates halftone dots, it calculates the average value of a group of pixels in the raster image and generates a spot of appropriate size. A raster image's resolution — measured in **pixels per inch (ppi)** — determines the quantity of pixel data the printer can read. Images need to have sufficient resolution so the output device can generate enough halftone dots to create the

appearance of continuous tone. In the images above, the same raster image is reproduced at 72 ppi (left) and 300 ppi (right). Notice the obvious degradation in quality in the 72-ppi version.

Ideally, the printer will have four pixels for each halftone dot created. In the image to the right, each white square represents a pixel. The highlighted area shows the pixel information used to generate a halftone dot. If an image only has 72 pixels per inch, the output device has to generate four halftone dots per pixel, resulting in poor printed quality.

The relationship between pixels and halftone dots defines the rule of resolution for raster-based images — the resolution of a raster image (ppi) should be two times the screen ruling (lpi) that will be used for printing.

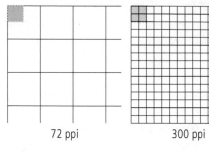

72 ppi   300 ppi

Open and Resize an Image

Every raster image has a defined, specific resolution that is established when the image is created. If you scan an image to be 3″ high by 3″ wide at 150 ppi, that image has 450 pixels in each vertical column and 450 pixels in each horizontal row. Simply resizing the image stretches, or compresses, those pixels into a different physical space, but does not add or remove pixel information. If you resize the 3″ × 3″ image to 6″ × 6″ (200% of the original), the 450 pixels in each column or row are forced to extend across 6″ instead of 3″, causing a marked loss of quality.

The **effective resolution** of an image is the resolution calculated after any scaling is taken into account. This number is equally (perhaps more so) as important as the original image resolution. The effective resolution can be calculated with a fairly simple equation:

Original resolution ÷ (% magnification ÷ 100) = Effective resolution

If a 300-ppi image is magnified 150%, the effective resolution is:

300 ppi ÷ 1.5 = 200 ppi

In other words, the more you enlarge a raster image, the lower its effective resolution becomes. In general, you can make an image 10% or 15% larger without significant adverse effects. The more you enlarge an image, however, the worse the results. Even Photoshop, which offers very sophisticated formulas (called "algorithms") for sizing images, cannot guarantee perfect results.

Effective resolution can be a very important consideration when working with client-supplied images, especially those that come from consumer-level digital cameras. Many of those devices capture images with a specific number of pixels rather than a number of pixels per inch (ppi). In this exercise, you will explore the effective resolution of an image to see if it can be used for a full-page printed magazine ad.

Note:

For line art, the general rule is to scan the image at the same resolution as the output device. Many laser printers and digital presses image at 600–1200 dots per inch (dpi). Imagesetters used to make printing plates for a commercial press typically output at much higher resolution — possibly 2400 dpi or more.

1. Download **Music_Print19_RF.zip** from the Student Files web page.

2. **Expand the ZIP archive in your WIP folder (Macintosh) or copy the archive contents into your WIP folder (Windows).**

   This results in a folder named **Music**, which contains all of the files you need for this project. You should also use this folder to save the files you create in this project.

   If necessary, refer to Page 1 of the Interface chapter for specific information on expanding or accessing the required resource files.

3. **Choose File>Open and navigate to your WIP>Music folder. Select Sunrise.jpg and click Open.**

4. **If the rulers are not visible on the top and left edges, choose View>Rulers (or press Command/Control-R).**

5. **Control/right-click the horizontal ruler and make sure Inches is checked as the default unit of measurement.**

   As you can see in the rulers, this image has a very large physical size.

Note:

We are intentionally overlooking issues of color space for the sake of this project. You will learn about color spaces and color management in Project 6: Museum Image Correction.

Note:

You can change the default unit of measurement in the Units & Rulers pane of the Preferences dialog box. Double-clicking either ruler opens the appropriate pane of the Preferences dialog box.

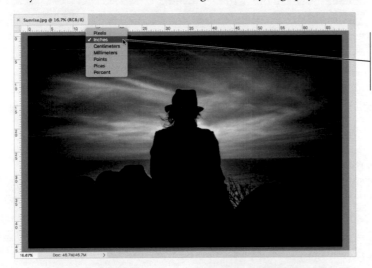

Use the contextual menu to make sure rulers are displayed in Inches.

6. **Choose Image>Image Size.**

   The Image Size dialog box shows the number of pixels in the image, as well as the image dimensions and current resolution. You can change any value in this dialog box, but you should understand what those changes mean before you do so.

   As you can see, this image is approximately 69″ wide and 46″ high, but it was captured at 72 pixels/inch. For most commercial printing, you need at least 300 ppi. You can use the principle of effective resolution to change the file to a high enough resolution for printing.

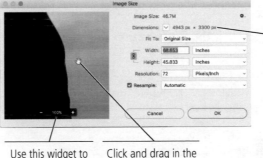

The actual number of pixels in the image is the most important information.

Use this widget to change the preview percentage.

Click and drag in the preview window to show a different area.

Note:

Press Command-Option-I/Control-Alt-I to open the Image Size dialog box.

7. **Check the Resample option at the bottom of the dialog box (if necessary).**

The options in this dialog box remember the last-used choices. The Resample option might already be checked in your dialog box.

Resampling means maintaining the existing resolution in the new image dimensions; in other words, you are either adding or deleting pixels to the existing image. When this option is turned on, you can change the dimensions of an image without affecting the resolution, or you can change the resolution of an image (useful for removing excess resolution or **downsampling**) without affecting the image size.

8. **Change the Resolution field to 300 pixels/inch.**

When you change the resolution with resampling turned on, you do not change the file's physical size. To achieve 300-ppi resolution at the new size, Photoshop needs to add a huge number of pixels to the image. You can see at the top of the dialog box that this change would increase the total number of pixels from 4943 × 3300 to 20596 × 13750.

You can also see that changing the resolution of an image without affecting its physical dimensions would have a significant impact on the file size. Changing the resolution to 300 ppi at the current size would increase the file size to over 810 megabytes.

When Resample is checked, changing the Resolution value adds or removes pixels.

Higher resolution means larger file sizes, which translates to longer processing time for printing, or longer download time over the Internet. When you scale an image to a smaller size, simply resizing can produce files with far greater effective resolution than you need. Resampling allows you to reduce physical size without increasing the resolution, resulting in a smaller file size.

The caveat is that once you delete pixels, they are gone. If you later try to re-enlarge the smaller image, you will not achieve the same quality as the original file before it was reduced. You should save reduced images as copies instead of overwriting the originals.

9. **Press Option/Alt and click the Reset button to restore the original image dimensions in the dialog box.**

In many Photoshop dialog boxes, pressing the Option/Alt key changes the Cancel button to Reset. You can click the Reset button to restore the original values that existed when you opened the dialog box.

Pressing Option/Alt changes the Cancel button to Reset.

10. **Uncheck the Resample option at the bottom of the dialog box.**

11. **Change the Resolution field to 300 pixels/inch.**

Resizing *without* resampling basically means distributing the same number of pixels over a different amount of physical space. When you resize an image without resampling, you do not change the number of pixels in the image. In fact, those fields in the dialog box become simple text; the fields are unavailable and you cannot change the number of pixels in the image.

You can see how changing one of the linked fields (Resolution) directly affects the other linked fields (Width and Height). By resizing the image to be 300 ppi — enough for commercial print quality — you now have an image that is approximately 16.5″ × 11″.

When the Resample option is unchecked, these three fields are all linked.

Note:

Although many magazines are printed at 133 lpi, some are printed at 150 lpi. By setting the resolution to 300, your file will work for any magazine that prints at 133 or 150 lpi.

12. **Click OK to apply the change and return to the document window.**

The rulers change to reflect the new dimensions of the file.

Because you did not resample the image, the screen display does not change.

13. **Choose File>Save As. If necessary, navigate to your WIP>Music folder as the target location. Change the file name (in the Save As/File Name field) to cd-artwork.**

Since this is a basic image file with only one layer (so far), most of the other options in the Save As dialog box are grayed out (not available).

14. **Choose Photoshop in the Format/Save As Type menu and then click Save.**

You can save a Photoshop file in a number of different formats, all of which have specific capabilities, limitations, and purposes. While you are still working on a file, it's best to keep it as a native Photoshop (PSD) file. When you choose a different format, the correct extension is automatically added to the file name.

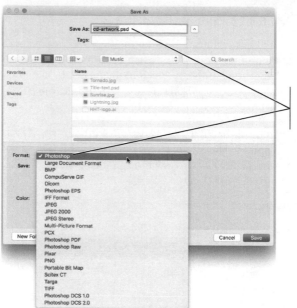

Files saved in the native Photoshop format display a ".psd" extension.

15. **Continue to the next exercise.**

Note:

Also called "native," the PSD format is the most flexible format to use while building files in Photoshop.

 ## Crop the Canvas and Place Ruler Guides

The final step in preparing the workspace is defining the live area of the page. **Trim size** is the actual size of a page once it has been cut out of the press sheet. According to your client, the final required artwork has a trim size of 10″ × 10″.

Any elements that print right to the edge of a page (called **bleeding**) must actually extend beyond the defined trim size. The **bleed allowance** is the amount of extra space that should be included for these bleed objects. Most applications require at least a 1/8″ bleed allowance on any bleed edge.

Because of inherent variation in the mechanical printing and trimming processes, most printing projects also define a safe or **live area**. All important design elements — especially text — should stay within this live area. The live area for this project is 9.5″ × 9.5″ (leaving a 0.25″ safe margin on each edge of the artwork).

1. **With cd-artwork.psd open, choose the Crop tool in the Tools panel.**

When you choose the Crop tool, a crop marquee appears around the edges of the image. The marquee has eight handles, which you can drag to change the size of the crop area.

Note:

You should familiarize yourself with the most common fraction-to-decimal equivalents:

1/8 = 0.125

1/4 = 0.25

3/8 = 0.375

1/2 = 0.5

5/8 = 0.625

3/4 = 0.75

7/8 = 0.875

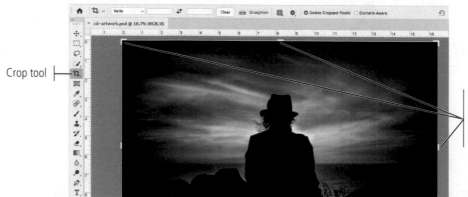

Crop tool

Marquee handles allow you to resize the crop area before finalizing the crop.

Understanding File Saving Preferences

You can control a number of options related to saving files in the File Handling pane of the Preferences dialog box.

Image Previews. You can use this menu to always or never include image thumbnails in the saved file. If you choose Ask When Saving in this menu, the Save As dialog box includes an option to include the preview/thumbnail.

On Macintosh, you have an additional option to include a thumbnail in the saved file. If checked, the image thumbnail appears in dialog boxes instead of the Photoshop file icon.

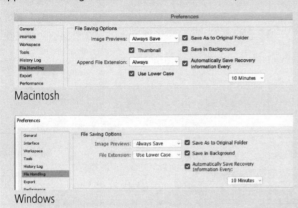

Macintosh

Windows

Append File Extension. On Macintosh, you can use this menu to always or never include the file extension in the saved file. If the Ask When Saving option is selected in this menu, the Save As dialog box includes options to append the file extension (in lowercase or not).

On Windows, file extensions are always added to saved files. This preference menu has only two options: Use Upper Case and Use Lower Case.

Save As to Original Folder. When this option is checked, choosing File>Save As automatically defaults to the location where the original file is located.

Save in Background. The Save process occurs by default in the background. In other words, you can continue working even while a file is being saved. Especially when you work with large files, this can be a significant time saver because you don't have to sit and wait the several minutes it might take to save a very large file. The only thing you can't do while a file is being saved is use the Save As command; if you try, you will see a warning advising you to wait until the background save is complete.

> When a file is being saved in the background, the completed percentage appears in the document tab.
>
> × aftermath.psd @ 16.7% (Layer 6, RGB/8) – Saving 25%

Automatically Save Recovery Information Every... When checked, this option means that your work is saved in a temporary file, every 10 minutes, by default. If something happens — such as a power outage — you will be able to restore your work back to the last auto-saved version. In other words, the most you will lose is 10 minutes of work!

2. In the Options bar, make sure the Delete Cropped Pixels option is checked.

When this option is checked, areas outside the crop area are permanently removed from all layers in the file. If this option is not checked, cropped pixels remain in the file, but exist outside the edges of the canvas. The Background layer, if one exists, is converted to a regular layer (you'll learn more about Background layers later).

This is an important distinction — by maintaining cropped pixels, you can later transform or reposition layers to reveal different parts of the layer within the newly cropped canvas size.

3. Click the right-center handle of the crop marquee and drag left until the cursor feedback shows W: 10.250 in.

When you drag certain elements in the document window, live cursor feedback (also called "heads-up display") shows information about the transformation. When dragging a side crop marquee handle, for example, the feedback shows the new width of the area.

You might need to zoom into at least 33.3% or 66.67% view percentage to achieve the exact dimensions needed for this project.

Use the cursor feedback to find the appropriate measurement.

Click and drag the marquee handle to resize the marquee area.

4. Repeat Step 3 with the top-center handle until feedback shows the area of H: 10.250 in.

Remember, the defined trim size is 10″ × 10″ for this ad. Anything that runs to the page edge has to incorporate a 0.125″ bleed allowance, so the actual canvas size must be large enough to accommodate the bleed allowance on all edges:

[Width] $10'' + 0.125'' + 0.125'' = 10.25''$

[Height] $10'' + 0.125'' + 0.125'' = 10.25''$

Note:

You can press the Escape key to cancel the crop marquee and return to the uncropped image.

Note:

You can rotate a crop marquee by placing the cursor slightly away from a corner handle.

Note:

At the time of this writing, a bug in the software causes rulers to disappear when you begin dragging a crop handle.

Note:

It might be helpful to toggle off the Snap feature (View>Snap), which causes certain file elements to act as magnets when you move a marquee or drag a selection.

5. **Zoom out until you can see the entire canvas in the document window.**

6. **Click inside the crop area and drag to reposition the image so that the woman's silhouette is on the left side of the crop area (use the following image as a guide).**

   When you change the marquee size, the area outside the marquee is "shielded" by a darkened overlay so you can get an idea of what will remain after you finalize the crop.

   You can drag the image inside the crop area to change the portion that will remain in the cropped image. By default, the crop area remains centered in the document window; instead, the image moves behind the crop area.

Note:

You can also use the Arrow keys on your keyboard to "nudge" the image in a specific direction.

Note:

The X coordinate refers to an object's horizontal position and Y refers to the vertical position.

Click and drag inside the crop area to change the portion of the image inside the crop.

Areas outside the crop marquee are partially obscured.

7. **Press Return/Enter to finalize the crop.**

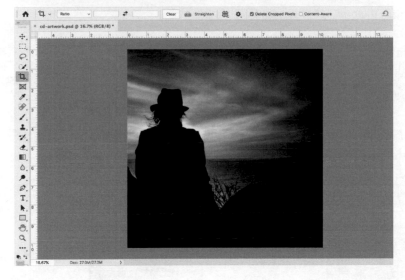

8. Choose View>New Guide Layout.

This dialog box makes it very easy to define a page grid using non-printing guides. The dialog box defaults to add 8 columns with a 20-pixel (0.067 in) gutter. In the document window, you can see the guides (blue lines) that will be created based on the active settings in the New Guide Layout dialog box.

9. Uncheck the Columns option and check the Margin option. Change all four margin field values to 0.125.

You can use the Margin fields to place guides at specific distances from each edge of the canvas. You don't need to type the unit of measurement because the default unit for this file is already inches. Photoshop automatically assumes the value you type is in the default unit of measurement.

10. Click OK to return to the document and add the required margin guides.

At this point you should have four guides – two vertical and two horizontal, each 1/8″ from the file edges. These mark the trim size of your final 10″ × 10″ file.

11. Choose View>100%.

It helps to zoom in to a higher view percentage if you want to precisely place guides. To complete the following steps accurately, we found it necessary to use at least 100% view.

12. In the top-left corner of the document window, click the zero-point crosshairs and drag to the top-left intersection of the guides.

You can reposition the zero point to the top-left corner of the bleed allowance by double-clicking the zero-point crosshairs.

Zero-point crosshairs

Drag to here to change the 0/0 point of the rulers.

This new zero point will be the origin for measurments.

13. Choose the Move tool, and then open the Info panel (Window>Info).

As we explained in the Interface chapter, the panels you see depend on what was done the last time you (or someone else) used the Photoshop application. Because workspace arrangement is such a personal preference, we tell you what panels you need to use, but we don't tell you where to put them.

Remember, for this file, the live area should be a 0.25" inset from the trim edge. In the next few steps you will add guides to identify that live area.

14. Click the horizontal page ruler at the top of the page and drag down to create a guide positioned at the 1/4" (0.25") mark.

If you watch the vertical ruler, you can see a marker indicating the position of the cursor. In addition to the live cursor feedback, the Info panel also shows the precise numeric position of the guide you are dragging.

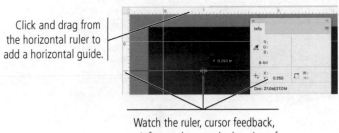

Click and drag from the horizontal ruler to add a horizontal guide.

Watch the ruler, cursor feedback, or Info panel to see the location of the guide you're dragging.

15. Click the vertical ruler at the left and drag right to place a guide at the 0.25" mark.

Watch the marker on the horizontal ruler to judge the guide's position.

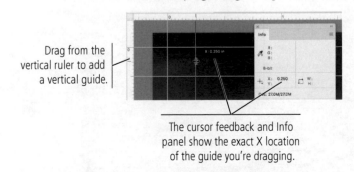

Drag from the vertical ruler to add a vertical guide.

The cursor feedback and Info panel show the exact X location of the guide you're dragging.

16. Double-click the intersection of the two rulers.

This resets the file's zero point to the original position (the top-left corner of the canvas).

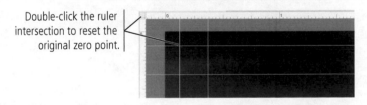

Double-click the ruler intersection to reset the original zero point.

17. Zoom out so you can see the entire canvas in the document window.

Note:

Use the Move tool to reposition placed guides. Remove individual guides by dragging them back onto the ruler.

If you try to reposition a guide and can't, choose View>Lock Guides. If this option is checked, guides are locked; you can't move them until you toggle this option off.

Note:

Press Option/Alt and click a guide to change it from vertical to horizontal (or vice versa). The guide rotates around the point where you click, which can be useful if you need to find a corner based on the position of an existing guide.

Note:

You can press Command/Control-; to toggle the visibility of page guides.

18. **Choose View>New Guide. In the resulting dialog box, choose the Horizontal option, type 9.875 in the field, and click OK.**

    This dialog box always measures the position of guides from the canvas's top-left corner, regardless of the zero point as reflected in the rulers.

19. **Choose View>New Guide again. Choose the Vertical option and type 9.875 in the field. Click OK.**

    Step 18

    Step 19

20. **Click the View menu and make sure a check mark appears to the left of Lock Guides. If no check mark is there, choose Lock Guides to toggle on that option.**

    After you carefully position specific guides, it's a good idea to lock them so you don't accidentally move or delete them later. If you need to move a guide at any point, simply choose View>Lock Guides to toggle off the option temporarily.

    The outside guides mark the trim edge.

    The inside guides mark the live area.

    The option should be checked.

    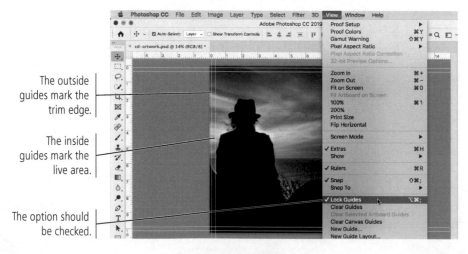

21. **Save the file and continue to the next exercise.**

    Because you have already saved this working file with a new name, you can simply choose File>Save, or press Command/Control-S to save without opening a dialog box. If you want to change the file name, you can always choose File>Save As.

When the Crop tool is selected, the Options bar can be used to define a number of settings related to the cropped area.

The first menu includes a number of common aspect ratio presets. If you choose one of these, the crop marquee is constrained to the specified aspect ratio. It's important to note that these presets define only the aspect ratio of the crop, not the actual size.

You can also choose the **W x H x Resolution** option to define custom settings for the result of a crop. For example, if you define the width and height of a crop area as 9″ × 9″ at 300 ppi, when you click and drag to draw, the crop area will be restricted to the same proportions defined in the Width and Height fields (in this example, 1:1).

When you finalize the crop, the resulting image will be resized to 9″ × 9″, regardless of the actual size of the crop marquee. This presents a problem if you remember the principles of resolution.

Enlarging a 3″ × 3″ area (for example) to 9″ × 9″ means the application needs to create enough pixels to fill in the 6 extra inches. At 300 ppi, Photoshop needs to create ("interpolate") more than 1800 pixels per linear inch. Although Photoshop can enlarge images with reasonable success, such a significant amount of new data will not result in the best possible quality. As a general rule, you should avoid enlarging raster images by such a large percentage.

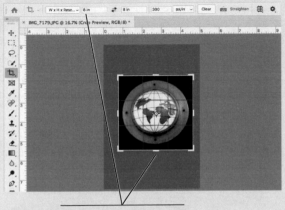

The crop area is constrained
to the aspect ratio of the
defined width and height.

The resulting cropped image is the
actual size defined in the Crop
Image Size & Resolution dialog box.

You can use the **Set Overlay Options** menu (⊞) to show a variety of overlays within the crop area; these follow basic design principles, such as the Rule of Thirds and the Golden Spiral.

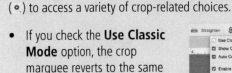

You can also use the commands in this menu to turn the overlay on or off. If you choose Auto Show Overlay, the selected overlay only appears when you drag the marquee handles or click inside the marquee area to move the image inside the crop area.

You can also click the **Set Additional Crop Options** button (✿) to access a variety of crop-related choices.

- If you check the **Use Classic Mode** option, the crop marquee reverts to the same appearance and behavior as in previous versions of Photoshop.

- When **Show Cropped Area** is checked, the area outside the crop marquee remains visible in the document window until you finalize the crop.

- When **Auto Center Preview** is checked, the crop area will always be centered in the document window. The image dynamically moves as you resize the crop area.

- When **Enable Crop Shield** is checked, areas outside the crop marquee are partially obscured by a semi-transparent solid color. You can use the related options to change the color and opacity of the shielded area.

The Crop Tools in Depth (continued)

When the Crop tool is selected, you can click the **Straighten** button in the Options bar, and then draw a line in the image to define what should be a straight line in the resulting image. The image behind the crop marquee rotates to show what will remain in the cropped canvas. The line you drew is adjusted to be perfectly horizontal or vertical.

Click the Straighten button, then draw a line representing what you want to be "straight" in the cropped image.

The image is rotated behind the crop marquee to be "straight" based on the line you drew.

You can draw a crop area larger than the existing canvas to effectively enlarge the canvas.

Using the default settings, new areas outside the original canvas size become transparent on regular layers, or filled with the background color on the locked Background layer.

If you check the **Content-Aware** option in the Options bar, Photoshop generates new pixels based on the existing image, filling the new pixels with content that better matches the previous image edges.

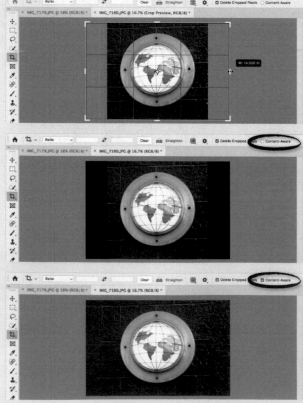

The **Perspective Crop tool** (nested under the Crop tool) can be used to draw a non-rectangular crop area. To define the area you want to keep, simply click to place the four corners of the area, then drag the corners in any direction as necessary. When you finalize the crop, the image inside the crop area is straightened to a front-on viewing angle. You should use this option with care, however, because it can badly distort an image.

In the following example, we used apparent lines in the photograph to draw the perspective crop marquee. After finalizing the crop, the building appears to be straight, rather than the original viewing angle at which it was photographed.

Copy and Paste Selected Pixels

Like many processes in Photoshop, there are various methods for compositing multiple images into a single file. In this exercise, you will use the most basic selection tool — the Rectangle Marquee tool.

1. **With cd-artwork.psd open, choose View>Fit on Screen to show the entire image centered in the document window.**

2. **Open the file Tornado.jpg from your WIP>Music folder.**

   If you see a profile mismatch warning when opening the files for this project, choose the option to use the embedded profile. Color management will be explained in Project 3: Museum Image Correction.

3. **With Tornado.jpg the active file in the document window, open the Image Size dialog box (Image>Image Size).**

   This image is only 150 ppi, but it has a physical size much larger than the defined size for the CD artwork. As with the original image, the principle of effective resolution might make this image usable in the composite ad.

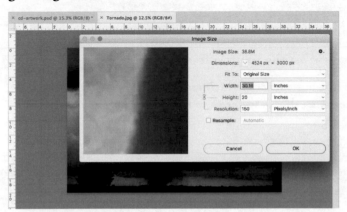

Note:

When you created the background file for this project, you created a raster image that contains pixels. Digital photographs and scans are also pixel-based, which is why you use Photoshop to edit and manipulate those types of files.

Note:

You can press Command-Option-I/Control-Alt-I to open the Image Size dialog box.

4. **Click Cancel to close the Image Size dialog box.**

5. **Choose the Rectangular Marquee tool in the Tools panel and review the options in the Options bar.**

   By default, dragging with a marquee tool creates a new selection. You can use the buttons on the left end of the Options bar to define what happens if you draw more than one marquee.

   Rectangular Marquee tool

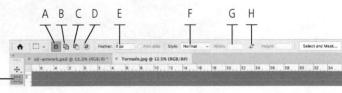

   A. **New Selection** creates a new selection each time you create a new marquee.

   B. **Add to Selection** adds the area of a new marquee to the existing selected area.

   C. **Subtract from Selection** removes the area of a new marquee from the existing selection.

   D. **Intersect with Selection** results in a selection only where a new marquee overlaps an existing selection.

   E. **Feather** softens the edges of a selection by a specified number of pixels.

   F. Use the **Style** menu to choose a normal selection, a fixed-ratio selection, or a fixed-size selection.

   G. When Fixed Ratio or Fixed Size is selected, enter the size of the selection in the **Width** and **Height** fields.

   H. Click this button to reverse the Width and Height fields.

6. **Choose the New Selection option in the Options bar. Click outside of the top-left corner, drag down past the bottom edge of the image, and drag right to create a selection area that is approximately 20.5" wide.**

   You can't select an area larger than the current canvas, so the top, left, and bottom edges of the selection snap to the canvas edges. The live cursor feedback, as well as the mark on the horizontal ruler, help to determine the selection area's width.

Selection marquee

Rectangular Marquee tool cursor

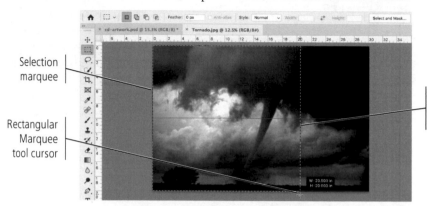

"Marching ants" identify the selected area.

Note:

Press Shift while dragging a new marquee to constrain the selection to a square (using the Rectangular Marquee tool) or circle (using the Elliptical Marquee tool).

7. **In the Options bar, choose the Subtract from Selection option.**

8. **Click outside the top-left corner of the image, and drag down and right to create a selection area that is wider than the original selection area and approximately 2" high.**

Subtract from Selection is active.

The cursor shows a minus sign because you are subtracting from the existing selection.

Click here...   ...and drag to here.

When you release the mouse button, the area you drew in this step is removed from the original selection area:

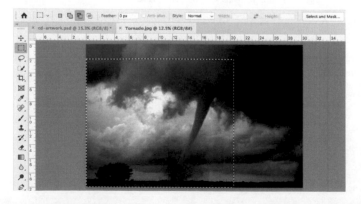

Note:

Command/Control-clicking a layer thumbnail results in a selection around the contents of that layer.

Note:

When the New Selection option is active, you can move a selection marquee by clicking inside the selected area with the Marquee tool and dragging to the desired area of the image.

The live cursor feedback shows how far you have moved the area. The pink horizontal lines that appear as you drag are smart guides, which help you to reposition objects (including selection marquees) relative to other objects or to the canvas.

9. Choose Edit>Copy.

The standard Cut, Copy, and Paste options are available in Photoshop, just as they are in most applications. Whatever you have selected will be copied to the Clipboard, and whatever is in the Clipboard will be pasted.

10. Click the Close button on the Tornado.jpg document tab to close that file.

11. With the cd-artwork.psd file active, choose Edit>Paste.

The copied selection is pasted in the center of the document window. If you remember from the Image Size dialog box, the tornado image was approximately 30″ × 20″ at 150 ppi. Photoshop cannot maintain multiple resolutions in a single file. When you paste the copied content into the cd-artwork file, it adopts the resolution of the target file (in this case, 300 ppi). The concept of effective resolution transforms the selected area (20.5″ × 18″) of the tornado image to approximately 10.25″ × 9″ at 300 ppi.

12. Open the Layers panel (Window>Layers).

The original cd-artwork.psd file had only one layer — Background. When you copy or drag content from one file into another, it is automatically placed on a new layer with the default name "Layer *n*," where "n" is a sequential number.

The document tab shows the
name of the active layer.

A new layer (Layer 1) is added to contain the contents that you pasted from the Tornado.jpg file.

The Background layer contains the original Sunrise.jpg file content.

13. Choose File>Save, and then read the resulting message.

Because this is the first time you have saved the file after adding new layers, you should see the Photoshop Format Options dialog box with the Maximize Compatibility check box already activated. It's a good idea to leave this check box selected so that your files will be compatible with other Adobe applications and other versions of Photoshop.

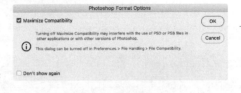

14. Make sure the Maximize Compatibility check box is selected, click OK, and then continue to the next exercise.

Note:

If you want to move a marquee, make sure the Marquee tool is still selected. If the Move tool is active, clicking inside the marquee and dragging will actually move the contents within the selection area.

Note:

When creating a new selection with a marquee tool, pressing Option/Alt places the center of the selection marquee at the point where you click; when you drag out, the marquee is created around that point.

Note:

When the New Selection option is active, press Shift to add to the current selection or press Option/Alt to subtract from the current selection.

Note:

If you don't see this warning, check the File Handling pane of the Preferences dialog box. You can set the Maximize PSD and PSB File Compatibility menu to Always, Never, or Ask.

Create a Feathered Selection

The Marquee tool you used in the previous exercise created a basic rectangular selection. The basic Lasso tool works like a pencil, following the path where you drag the mouse; you will use that method in this exercise.

1. **With cd-artwork.psd open, open Lightning.jpg from your WIP>Music folder.**

2. **Choose the Lasso tool in the Tools panel. In the Control panel, choose the New Selection option.**

   Most options in the Control panel are the same for the Lasso tool as they are for the Marquee tools.

3. **Click at the top edge of the canvas, just to the left of the lightning bolt. Hold down the mouse button and drag around the general lightning shape in the image. Keep the following points in mind as you drag:**

   - **Avoid dragging past the bottom edge of the canvas.**

   - **Drag past the right image edge and up to the top of the image.**

     When you drag past the image edge, the marquee follows the image edge instead of the actual cursor position.

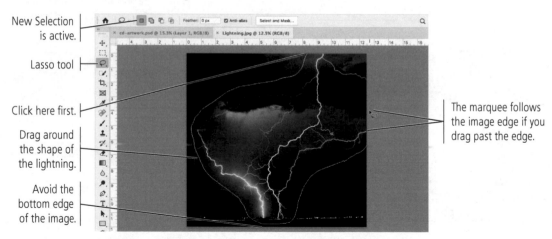

New Selection is active.

Lasso tool

Click here first.

Drag around the shape of the lightning.

Avoid the bottom edge of the image.

The marquee follows the image edge if you drag past the edge.

4. **Release the mouse button.**

   When you release the mouse button, the software automatically connects the first point you clicked with the last location of the mouse cursor with a straight line.

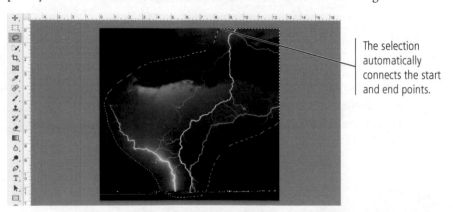

The selection automatically connects the start and end points.

Note:

It isn't uncommon for a mouse to unexpectedly jump when you don't want it to. If you aren't happy with your Lasso selection, choose Select>Deselect, and then try again.

5. **With the marching ants active, choose Select>Modify>Feather.**

Photoshop offers a number of options for modifying an exiting selection marquee.

- **Select>Grow** expands the selection to include all adjacent pixels that fall within the tolerance defined for the Magic Wand tool.

- **Select>Similar** expands the selection to include all pixels throughout the image that fall within the tolerance range, even if they are not adjacent to the active selection.

- **Select>Transform Selection** shows bounding-box handles around the selection marquee, which you can use to transform the selection as you would transform layer content.

In the Select>Modify menu:

- **Border** creates a selection of a defined number of pixels around the edge of the active marquee.

- **Smooth** helps to clean up stray pixels at the edge of a selection. Within a defined radius from the selection edge, pixels with less than half of the surrounding pixels are excluded from the selection.

- **Expand** and **Contract** enlarge and shrink, respectively, a selection by a defined number of pixels.

- **Feather** creates a blended edge to the active selection area.

6. **In the resulting dialog box, type 100 in the Feather Radius field. Make sure Apply Effect at Canvas Bounds is not checked, then click OK.**

Feathering means to soften the edge of a selection so the image blends into the background instead of showing a sharp line around the edge. The Feather Radius defines the distance from solid to transparent.

If the Apply Effect... check box is active, the feathering will be applied at the top and right edges of the canvas, where you dragged past the image edge while making the selection. You want these edges to remain hard, so the option should remain unchecked.

Note:

*You could also create a feathered selection by typing in the Feather field of the Options bar **before** drawing the selection marquee.*

Keep in mind, however, that if you draw a feathered selection (using the tool option setting), you can't undo the feather without also undoing the selection area.

7. **Click the Edit in Quick Mask button at the bottom of the Tools panel to toggle into Quick Mask mode.**

Marching ants do not show degrees of transparency. Quick Mask mode creates a temporary red overlay (called an Alpha channel) that shows the feathered selection. By default, the overlay is semi-transparent, which allows you to see the underlying image.

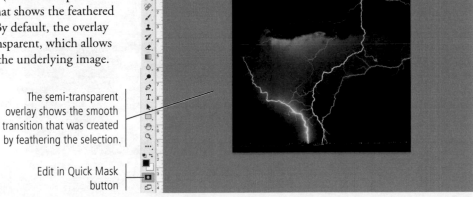

The semi-transparent overlay shows the smooth transition that was created by feathering the selection.

Edit in Quick Mask button

8. **Click the Edit in Standard Mode button at the bottom of the Tools panel to toggle off the Quick Mask.**

   When Quick Mask mode is active, the Edit in Quick Mask mode toggles to become the Edit in Standard Mode button.

9. **Choose Edit>Copy to copy the active selection.**

10. **Click the Close button on the Lightning.jpg document tab to close that file. Click Don't Save when asked.**

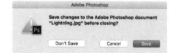

11. **With cd-artwork.psd active, choose Edit>Paste.**

    The feathered selection is pasted into the file as a new layer.

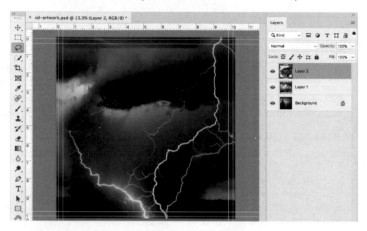

12. **Save the file, then continue to the next exercise.**

Understanding the Lasso Tool Variations

The **Polygonal Lasso tool** creates selections with straight lines, anchoring a line each time you click. To close a selection area, click the first point in the selection.

The **Magnetic Lasso tool** snaps to high-contrast edges. You can use the Options bar to control the way Photoshop detects edges:

- **Width** is the distance from the edge the cursor can be and still detect edges; set this higher to move the cursor farther from edges.

- **Contrast** is how different the foreground can be from the background and still be detected; if there is a sharp distinction between the foreground and background, you can set this value higher.

- **Frequency** is the number of points that will be created to make the selection; setting this number higher creates finer selections, while setting it lower creates smoother edges.

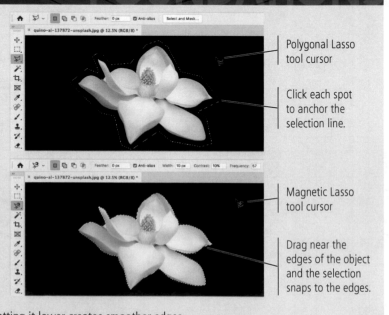

Polygonal Lasso tool cursor

Click each spot to anchor the selection line.

Magnetic Lasso tool cursor

Drag near the edges of the object and the selection snaps to the edges.

Rasterize a Vector File

Logos and title treatments — such as the ones you will use in this project — are commonly created as vector graphics. Although Photoshop is typically a pixel-based application, you can also open and work with vector graphics created in illustration programs like Adobe Illustrator.

1. **With cd-artwork.psd open, choose File>Open. Select HHT-logo.ai (in your WIP>Music folder) and then click Open.**

   This is an Adobe Illustrator file of the band's logo. When you open a vector file (Illustrator, EPS, or PDF) in Photoshop, it is rasterized or converted to a raster graphic. The resulting Import PDF dialog box allows you to determine exactly what and how to rasterize the file. (Illustrator uses PDF as its underlying file structure.)

   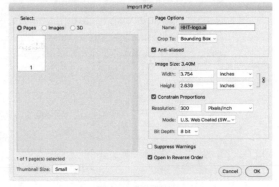

   The Crop To options determine the outside dimensions of the opened file. Depending on how the file was created, some of these values might be the same as others:

   - **Bounding Box** is the outermost edges of the artwork in the file.
   - **Media Box** is the size of the paper as defined in the file.
   - **Crop Box** is the size of the page/artboard, including printer's marks.
   - **Bleed Box** is the trim size, plus any defined bleed allowance.
   - **Trim Box** is the trim size as defined in the file.
   - **Art Box** is the area of the page as defined in the file.

   The Image Size fields default to the settings of the bounding box you select. You can change the size, resolution, color mode, and bit depth by entering new values. You can check the Constrain Proportions option to keep the height and width proportional to the original dimensions.

2. **Make sure Bounding Box is selected in the Crop To field, and the Resolution field is set to 300 pixels/inch.**

3. **Click OK.**

   The logo file opens in Photoshop. The checkered area behind the text indicates that the background is transparent. If you look at the Layers panel, you will see that Layer 1 isn't locked; because it's transparent, it is not considered a background layer.

Note:

If you're opening a multi-page PDF or an Illustrator file with more than one artboard, the preview window on the left side of the dialog box shows thumbnails of each "page" in the file. You can click a specific thumbnail to select anything other than Page 1. Press Shift and click to select multiple consecutive pages, or press Command/Control and click to select multiple, nonconsecutive pages.

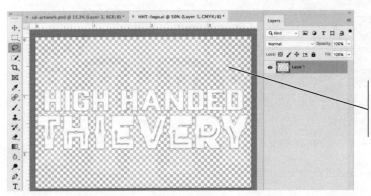

The gray-and-white checked pattern identifies areas of transparency in the layer content.

4. **Open the Window>Arrange menu and choose 2-up Vertical to show both open files at one time.**

As you saw in the Interface chapter, these options are useful for arranging and viewing multiple open files within your workspace.

5. **Choose the Move tool in the Tools panel.**

6. **Click in the HHT-logo.ai image window and drag into the cd-artwork.psd image window, then release the mouse button.**

Basic compositing can be as simple as dragging a selection from one file to another. If no active selection appears in the source document, this action moves the entire active layer from the source document.

Move tool

Note:

On Windows, the cursor shows a plus sign to indicate that you are adding the image as a new layer in the document to which you dragged.

This cursor shows that you are dragging a layer. In this case, you're dragging it into another document window.

7. **Click the Close button on the HHT-logo document tab to close that file. Click Don't Save when asked.**

After closing the logo file, the cd-artwork.psd document window expands to fill the available space.

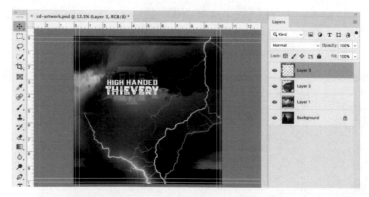

8. **Save cd-artwork.psd and continue to the next exercise.**

Place Files as Smart Object Layers

As you have seen in the last few exercises, copying layer content from one file to another results in new regular layers for the pasted content. Photoshop also supports Smart Object layers, in which you place one file into another instead of pasting layer content. Smart Objects provide a number of advantages over regular layers, which you will explore later in this project. In this exercise, you will create a Smart Object layer for the remaining image element.

Note:

Smart Objects enable tight integration between Photoshop and Illustrator. You can take advantage of the sophisticated vector-editing features in Adobe Illustrator, and then place those files into Photoshop without losing the ability to edit the vector information.

1. **With `cd-artwork.psd` open, choose File>Place Embedded.**

   Two options in the File menu — Place Embedded and Place Linked — give you the option to embed the placed file data into the active file, or to place smart objects as links to the original placed file. (See Page 226 for more about placing linked files.)

2. **Choose the `Title-text.psd` file (in your WIP>Music folder) and click Place.**

   The placed file appears centered in the document window, with bounding-box handles and crossed diagonal lines. The placement isn't final until you press Return/Enter. You can press the Escape key to cancel the placement. If you check Skip Transform when Placing in the General pane of the Preferences dialog box, you will not see the diagonal lines and handles when you place a Smart Object layer.

   In the Options bar, you can see that the placed image has been scaled to approximately 70% to fit into the document where it is being placed.

The placed image is centered in the document window.   It has been scaled to fit into the active canvas.

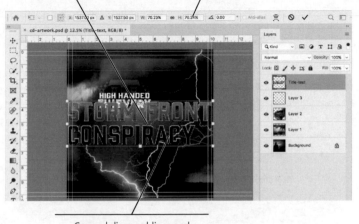

Crossed diagonal lines and bounding-box handles indicate that the placement is not yet final.

3. **Press Return/Enter to finalize the placement.**

   After you finalize the placement, the bounding-box handles and crossed diagonal lines disappear. In the Layers panel, the placed file has its own layer. This layer, however, is automatically named, based on the name of the placed file.

   The layer's thumbnail indicates that this layer is a **Smart Object**. Because you placed this file using the embedded option, it is not dynamically linked to the original file. Instead, Photoshop maintains the

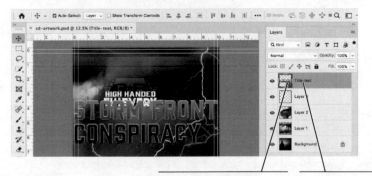

This icon identifies an embedded Smart Object layer.   The layer adopts the name of the placed file.

original file data within the Smart Object layer. The advantages of this technique will become clear in the next stage of this project.

4. **Save the file and continue to the next stage of the project.**

In this project you used the Place Embedded option to create Smart Object layers containing the placed file data. In this case the embedded file data becomes a part of the parent file.

If you double-click the thumbnail icon of an embedded Smart Object, the embedded file opens in an application that can edit the stored data — AI files open in Illustrator; PSD, TIFF, and JPEG files open in Photoshop.

When you first open a Smart Object file, the application provides advice for working with Smart Objects:

After you make necessary changes, you can save the file and close it, and then return to Photoshop (if necessary). Your changes in the Smart Object file will automatically reflect in the parent file where the Smart Object layer is placed.

Important note: Do not use the Save As option when editing Smart Object layers. The changes will not reflect in the parent file if you save changes with a different file name.

If you choose the Place Linked option in the File menu, Smart Object layer stores a link to the original file data rather than embedding that data inside the parent file.

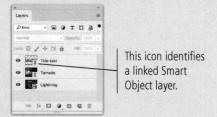

This icon identifies a linked Smart Object layer.

This provides an opportunity for maintaining consistency because you only need to change one instance of a file to reflect those changes anywhere the file is placed.

Say you place a logo created in Illustrator into a Photoshop file. The same logo is also placed as a link in an InDesign file. If you open the logo in Illustrator and change the main color (for example), when you save the changes in the original logo file, the new color automatically reflects in any file — whether InDesign or Photoshop — that is linked to the edited logo.

If you use the Place Embedded option in Photoshop, the Smart Object layer is not linked to the original, edited logo file; you would have to open the embedded Smart Object and make the same color change a second time.

Linked files also have potential disadvantages. As we mentioned previously, double-clicking a Smart Object layer thumbnail opens the linked or embedded file in an application that can edit the relevant data. If you are working with *linked* Smart Object layers, any changes you make affect the original file data. This means your changes appear not only in the parent Photoshop file where it is linked, but also in any other file that links to the same data.

For a file to output properly, linked Smart Object layers must be present and up to date at the time of output.

If the linked file has been modified while the parent file is open, the changes automatically reflect in the parent file when you return to that document. If the parent file is not open in Photoshop when the linked file is edited, you will see a Modified icon for the linked Smart Object layer.

If the linked file is deleted or moved to another location after it has been placed, the parent file will show a Missing icon for the linked Smart Object layer.

If a linked Smart Object has been moved while the parent file is not open, you will see a warning dialog box when you open the parent Photoshop file. You can use that dialog box to locate the missing link, or close it and use the options in the Layers panel to correct the problem.

Control/right-clicking a linked Smart Object layer name opens a contextual menu with options to update modified content and resolve broken links.

This icon identifies a linked, modified Smart Object layer.

This icon identifies a linked, missing Smart Object layer.

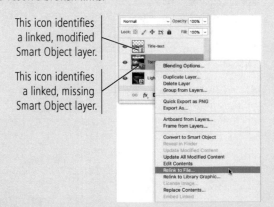

To avoid potential problems with missing linked files, you can use the File>Package command to create a job folder. The parent file is copied to a new folder, along with a Links subfolder containing any files placed as linked Smart Object layers.

STAGE 2 / **Managing Layers**

Photoshop includes a number of options for managing layers: naming layers for easier recognition, creating layer groups so multiple layers can be manipulated at once, moving layers around on the canvas, transforming layers both destructively and nondestructively, controlling individual layer visibility, and arranging the top-to-bottom stacking order of layers to determine exactly what is visible. You will use all of these options in this stage of the project.

 ## Name Layers and Layer Groups

It's always a good idea to name your layers because it makes managing the file much easier — especially when you work with files that include dozens of layers. Even with only four unnamed layers in this file (counting the Background layer), it would be tedious to have to toggle each layer on to find the one you want.

1. **With cd-artwork.psd open, review the Layers panel.**

2. **Option/Alt-click the eye icon for Layer 1 to hide all other layers.**

   Toggling layer visibility is an easy way to see only what you want to see at any given stage in a project.

   Clicking the Eye icon for a specific layer hides that layer. Clicking the empty space where the Eye icon should be shows the hidden layer. To show or hide a series of consecutive layers, click the visibility icon (or empty space) for the first layer you want to affect, hold down the mouse button, and drag down to the last layer you want to show or hide.

The checked pattern shows transparent areas of the visible layer(s).

Click an empty space to show a hidden layer.

Click the Eye icons to hide individual layers.

Option/Alt-click an Eye icon to hide all other layers.

3. **Double-click the Layer 1 layer name, and then type Tornado. Press Return/Enter to finalize the new layer name.**

   You can rename any layer by simply double-clicking the name and typing.

Double-click the layer name to access it.

Press Return/Enter after typing to finalize the new name.

4. **Click the Eye icon to hide the renamed Tornado layer, and then click the empty space to the left of Layer 2 to show only that layer.**

5. **Double-click the Layer 2 name, then type Lightning. Press Return/Enter to finalize the new layer name.**

6. **Repeat Steps 4–5 to rename Layer 3 as Logo.**

7. **Click the spaces on the left side of the Layers panel (where the Eye icons were) to show all hidden layers.**

8. **In the Layers panel, click the Title-text layer to select it.**

9. **Press Shift and click the Logo layer to select that layer as well.**

Press Shift and click to select consecutive layers in the Layers panel. Press Command/Control and click to select nonconsecutive layers in the Layers panel.

10. **With the two layers selected, click the Create a New Group button at the bottom of the panel.**

This button creates a group that automatically contains the selected layers. The new group is named "Group N" (where N is simply a sequential number). Of course, you can rename a layer group just as you can rename a layer. You can also choose New Group from Layers in the panel Options menu.

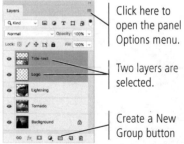

Click here to open the panel Options menu.

Two layers are selected.

Create a New Group button

The new group automatically contains the selected layers.

To create a new empty layer group, make sure nothing is selected in the Layers panel before clicking the Create a New Group button. Alternatively, choose New Group in the panel Options menu; this results in an empty layer group even if layers are selected.

11. **Double-click the Group 1 name in the Layers panel to highlight it, then type Logotypes. Press Return/Enter to finalize the new layer group name.**

As with any other layer, you should name groups based on what they contain so you can easily identify them later.

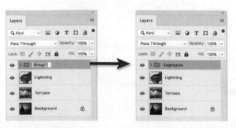

Note:

Deselect all layers by clicking in the empty area at the bottom of the Layers panel.

Note:

You can create up to ten levels of nested layer groups (groups inside of other groups).

12. **Click the arrow to the left of the Logotypes group name to expand the layer group.**

You have to expand the layer group to be able to access and edit individual layers in the group. If you select the entire layer group, you can move all layers within the group at the same time. Layers in the group maintain their position relative to one another.

Note:

You can click the Eye icon for a layer folder to hide the entire layer group (and all layers inside the folder).

13. **Save the file and continue to the next exercise.**

 ## Move and Transform a Smart Object Layer

Photoshop makes scaling, rotating, and other transformations fairly easy to implement, but it is important to realize the potential impact of your transformations.

1. **With cd-artwork.psd open, click the Title-text layer (in the Logotypes folder) in the Layers panel to select only that layer.**

2. **Choose the Move tool in the Tools panel.**

As the name suggests, the Move tool is used to move a selection around on the canvas. You can select a specific area, and then click and drag to move only the selection on the active layer. If there is no active selection area, you can click and drag to move the contents of the entire active layer.

3. **In the Options bar, make sure the Auto-Select option is not checked.**

When Auto-Select is checked, you can click in the image window and drag to move the contents of the layer containing the pixels where you click; you do not need to first select the layer in the Layers panel before moving the layer content. This is very useful in some cases, but not so much in others — for example, when the contents of multiple layers are stacked on top of each other (as is the case with your file as it exists now).

4. **Click in the image window and drag until the Title-text layer content snaps to the top and left live-area guides.**

If you toggled off the Snap feature when you used the Crop tool, you should turn it back on now by choosing View>Snap.

Uncheck this option.

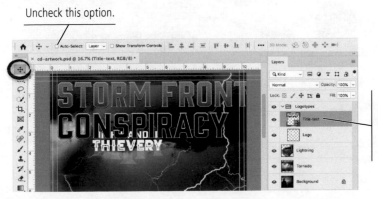

Select the layer you want to move, then click and drag in the document window to move the layer content.

As you dragged the layer in the previous exercise, you might have noticed a series of pink lines appearing in different locations. These lines are a function of Smart Guides, which make it easier to align layer content to other layers or the overall canvas.

Smart Guides are active by default, but you can toggle them on and off in the View>Show submenu.

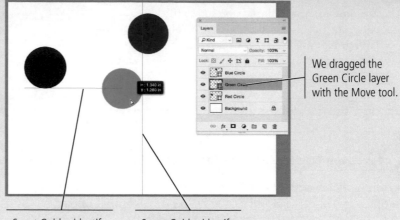

We dragged the Green Circle layer with the Move tool.

Smart Guides identify the center and edges of content on other layers.

Smart Guides identify the center and edges of the overall canvas.

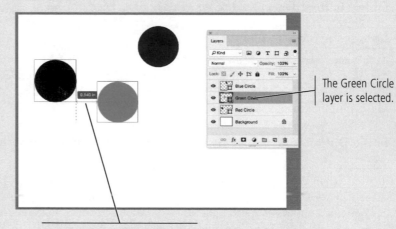

The Green Circle layer is selected.

Press Command/Control and hover over an object to find the distance between it and the selected layer.

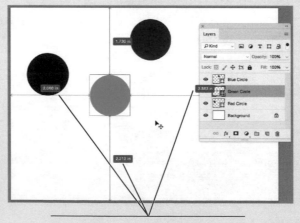

Press Command/Control and hover over the canvas to find the distance between the selected layer content and the canvas edges.

5. With the Title-text layer still active, choose Edit>Free Transform.

When you use the transform options, bounding-box handles surround the selection in the document window. The Options bar gives you a number of options for controlling the transformations numerically:

Bounding box handles surround the content that is being transformed.

A Reference Point Location. This point determines the point around which transformations are made. It always defaults to the center point. To choose a different reference point, you have to check the related box.

B Set Horizontal Position of Reference Point. This is the X position of the reference point for the content being transformed. If the center reference point is selected, for example, this is the X position of the center point of the active content.

C Use Relative Positioning for Reference Point. If this option is active, the Set Horizontal Position and Set Vertical Position fields default to 0; changing these values moves the reference point by the value you type. For example, typing "–25" in the Set Horizontal Position field moves the active content 25 pixels to the left.

D Set Vertical Position of Reference Point. This is the Y position of the reference point for the content being transformed.

E Set Horizontal Scale. Use this field to change the horizontal scale percentage of the transformed content.

F Maintain Aspect Ratio. When active, the horizontal scale and vertical scale fields are locked to have the same value.

G Set Vertical Scale. Use this field to change the vertical scale percentage of the transformed content.

H Rotate. Use this field to rotate the transformed content by a specific angle.

I Switch Between Free Transform and Warp Modes. If available, click this button to apply a built-in warp to the active selection.

J Cancel Transform. Click this button (or press the Esc key) to exit Free Transform mode without applying any transformation.

K Commit Transform. Click this button (or press Return/Enter) to finalize the transformation that you applied while in Free Transform mode. You can also simply click away from the area in the bounding box to finalize the transformation.

6. **Click the bottom-right bounding-box handle, and then drag up and left until the title treatment fits inside the live area guides on both sides of the canvas.**

The selection (in this case, the entire Title-text layer) dynamically changes as you scale the layer.

When you drag handles to transform a selection, Photoshop automatically constrains the selection's aspect ratio (height-to-width proportions).

You can press Shift while you drag a handle to transform the selection nonproportionally. This behavior is new in the 2019 release; in prior releases you had to press Shift to maintain the aspect ratio while transforming.

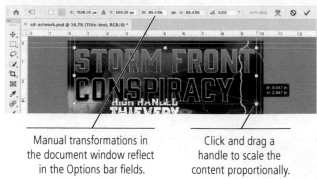

Manual transformations in the document window reflect in the Options bar fields.

Click and drag a handle to scale the content proportionally.

When you release the mouse button, the handles remain in place until you finalize ("commit") the transformation.

7. **Press Return/Enter to finalize the transformation.**

After finalizing the transformation, the bounding-box handles disappear.

8. **With the Title-text layer still active, press Command/Control-T to enter Free Transform mode again and look at the Options bar.**

Because the rating layer is a Smart Object layer, the W and H fields still show the scaling percentage based on the original.

It is not uncommon for a placed image to have slightly different height and width percentages when

it is placed. The change will be slight, but it's a good idea to check this issue so that you maintain the integrity of the placed artwork.

9. **In the Options bar, make sure the Maintain Aspect Ratio button is active, then change the W field to 65%.**

You can type in Options bar fields to apply specific numeric transformations.

When the Maintain Aspect Ratio option is active, the X and Y percentage fields are forced to the same values; changing the W value also changes the value in the H field.

Click to activate this option.

The W and H percentages are now the same value.

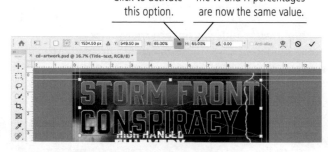

10. **Click the Commit Transform button on the Options bar (or press Return/Enter) to finalize the transformation.**

If you press Return/Enter, you have to press it twice to finalize the transformation. The first time you press it, you apply the change to the active field; the second time, you finalize the transformation and exit Free Transform mode.

11. **Save the file and continue to the next exercise.**

Move and Transform Regular Layers

Smart Object layers enable nondestructive transformations, which means those transformations can be changed or undone without affecting the quality of the layer content. Transforming a regular layer, on the other hand, is destructive and permanent.

1. **With cd-artwork.psd open, hide all but the Tornado layer. Click the Tornado layer in the Layers panel to select it.**

2. **Using the Move tool, drag the layer content up so there is no transparent area at the top of the canvas.**

3. **Choose Edit>Transform>Flip Horizontal.**

   The Transform submenu commands affect only the selected layer.

Note:

When the Move tool is active, you can move the selected object or layer 1 pixel by pressing the Arrow keys. Pressing Shift with any of the Arrow keys moves the selected object/layer by 10 pixels.

Note:

You can also use the Edit>Transform submenu to apply specific transformations to a layer or selection.

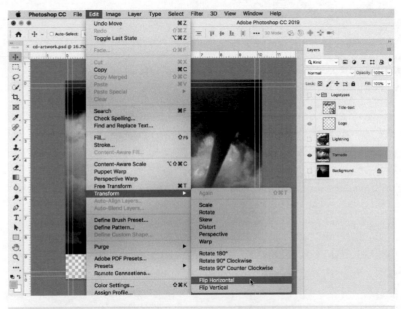

4. **Show and select the Lightning layer, then press Command/Control-T to enter Free Transform mode.**

Some handles might not be visible within the boundaries of the document window. If necessary, zoom out so you can see all eight handles of the layer content.

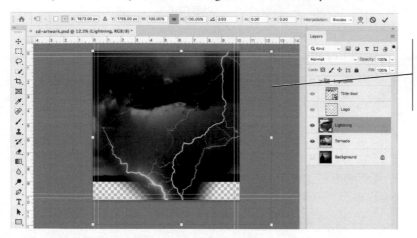

The edge of the bounding box shows that some parts of the layer do not fit within the current file dimensions.

5. **Click inside the bounding-box area and drag until the layer content snaps to the top and right canvas edges.**

6. **On the left side of the Options bar, check the box for the Reference Point option and then choose the top-right reference point.**

The reference point, which defaults to the center point, is the point around which numeric transformations are made. To choose a different reference point, you must first activate the check box in the Option bar, and then choose the desired point in the 9-square proxy.

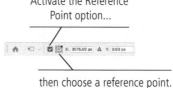

Activate the Reference Point option...

then choose a reference point.

7. **Place the cursor over the W field label to access the scrubby slider for that field.**

When you see the scrubby slider cursor, you can drag right to increase or drag left to decrease the value in the related field.

Place the cursor over a field label to access the "scrubby slider" for that field.

8. **Click and drag left until the W field shows approximately 75%.**

Because you selected the top-right reference point, the top-right corner of the layer remains in place when you scale the selection. The bottom-left corner moves based on the scaling you define.

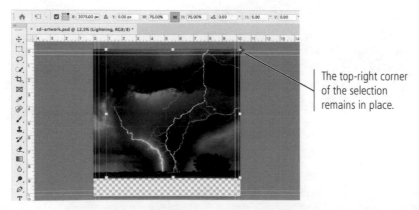

The top-right corner of the selection remains in place.

9. **Press Return/Enter to finalize the transformation.**

10. **With the Lightning layer still active, press Command/Control-T to re-enter Free Transform mode.**

    Once you commit the transformation on a regular layer, the transformation is final. Looking at the Options bar now, you can see that it shows the layer at 100%, instead of the 75% from Step 8.

    If you transform a Smart Object layer, the scale percentage is maintained even after you finalize the change, unlike scaling a regular layer, where the layer recalibrates so the new size is considered 100% once you finalize the scaling.

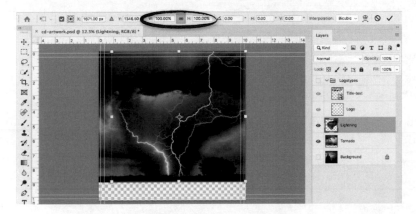

11. **Press Esc to exit Free Transform mode without changing anything.**

12. **Save the file and continue to the next exercise.**

Transform the Background Layer

Your file currently has a number of layers, most of which were created by pasting or placing external files into the original file. Because every photograph and scan (and some images that you create from scratch in Photoshop) begins with a default locked Background layer, it is important to understand the special characteristics of that layer:

- You can't apply layer transformations, styles, or masks to the Background layer.

- You can't move the contents of the Background layer around in the document.

- If you delete pixels from the Background layer, you must determine the color that will be used in place of the deleted pixels.

- The Background layer cannot include transparent pixels, which are necessary for underlying layers to be visible.

- The Background layer is always the bottom layer in the stacking order. You can't add or move layers lower than the Background layer.

    In the final composite file for this project, you need to flip the woman's silhouette from left to right, and remove the sunset from the image background. For either of these options to work properly, you need to convert the default Background layer to a regular layer.

Note:

If you crop an image that includes a Background layer, the Background layer is automatically converted to a regular layer if the Delete Cropped Pixels option is not checked.

1. **With cd-artwork.psd open, show only the Background layer.**

2. **Click the Background layer to select it and then choose Edit>Transform.**

   The Transform submenu commands are not available for the locked Background layer.

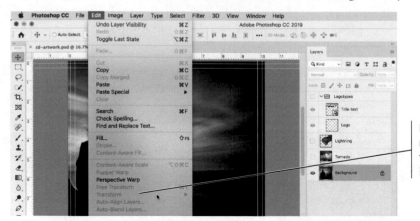

Many commands are not available because the Background layer is locked.

3. **With the Background layer still selected, choose Image>Image Rotation> Flip Canvas Horizontal.**

   To affect the locked background layer, you have to flip the actual canvas.

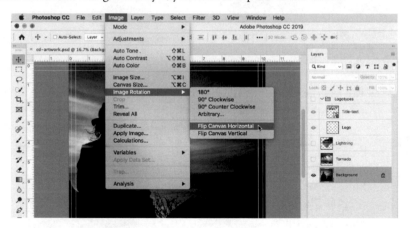

Note:

Although the Background layer exists by default in many files, it is not a required component.

4. **Show the Logotypes layer group.**

   Because you flipped the canvas, the Title-text and Logo layers are also flipped left-to-right. Rotating or flipping the entire canvas affects all layers in the file; this is obviously not what you want to do.

Because you flipped the canvas, the logos are now backward.

Showing the layer group shows all layers in that group.

5. **Choose Edit>Undo Layer Visibility.**

   The Undo command affects the last action you performed. The actual Undo menu command changes to reflect the action that will be undone.

Note:

You can press Command/Control-Shift-Z to redo the last undone action.

6. **Choose Edit>Undo Flip Canvas Horizontal.**

   Beginning with the 2019 release, Photoshop now supports multiple Undo commands. You can use the Undo command to step back through multiple actions.

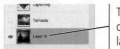

7. **In the Layers panel, click the Lock icon on the Background layer.**

   Clicking the Lock icon unlocks the layer and immediately converts the previous Background layer to a regular layer named "Layer 0."

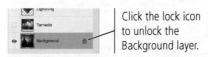

Click the lock icon to unlock the Background layer.

The layer is automatically converted to a regular layer named Layer 0.

8. **Double-click the Layer 0 layer name to highlight it, then type Sunrise to rename the layer. Press Return/Enter to finalize the new layer name.**

9. **With the Sunrise layer selected, choose Edit>Transform>Flip Horizontal.**

   Because the layer is no longer locked, you can now access and apply the transform commands that affect only the selected layer.

10. **Show the Logos layer group again.**

    Because you flipped only the selected layer, the Title-text and Logo layers are not flipped; they appear in the correct position and orientation.

11. **Choose the Logo layer in the Layers panel.**

12. **Using the Move tool, move the Logo layer content until it snaps to the bottom and right live area guides.**

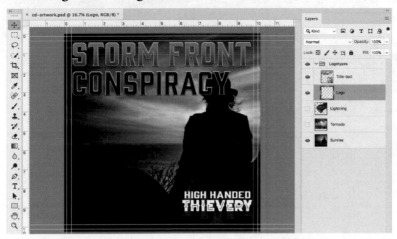

13. **Save the file and continue to the next stage of the project.**

Navigating the Photoshop File History

In addition to using the Undo command to step back through each previous action, you can use the use the History panel (Window>History) to navigate back to earlier stages.

Every action you take is recorded as a state in the History panel. You can click any state to return to that particular point in the document progression. You can also delete specific states or create a new document from a particular state using the buttons at the bottom of the panel.

By default, the History panel stores the last 50 states; older states are automatically deleted. You can change that setting in the Performance pane of the Preferences dialog box. Keep in mind, however, that storing a larger number of states will increase the memory that is required to work with a specific file.

Keep the following in mind when using the History panel:

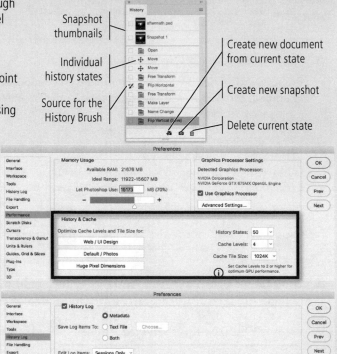

- The default snapshot is the image state when it was first opened.

- The oldest state is at the top of the list. The most recent state appears at the bottom.

- You can save any particular state as a snapshot to prevent it from being deleted when that state is no longer within the number of states that can be stored.

- The history is only stored while the file is open. When you close a file, the history and snapshots are not saved.

- When you select a specific state, the states below it are dimmed so you can see which changes will be discarded if you go back to a particular history state.

- Selecting a state, and then changing the image eliminates all states that come after it.

- Deleting a state deletes that state and those after it. If you choose Allow Non-Linear History in the History Options dialog box (accessed in the History panel Options menu), deleting a state deletes only that state.

If you need to keep a record of a file's history even after you close the file, you can activate the History Log option in the History Log pane of the Preferences dialog box. When this option is checked, you can save the history log as metadata, in a text file, or both. You can also determine the level of detail that will be recorded in the history log.

- Sessions Only records each time you launch or quit, and each time you open and close individual files.

- Concise adds the text that appears in the History panel to the Sessions information.

- Detailed gives you a complete history of all changes made to files.

STAGE 3 / **Creating Complex Selections**

Photoshop includes a number of options for making selections based on the color content of an image. The method you use will vary depending on the actual content of your image, as well as what you hope to accomplish.

The **Magic Wand tool** is an easy way to select large areas of solid color.

- The first options in the Options bar are the same as those for the Marquee tools (New, Add To, Subtract From, and Intersect).

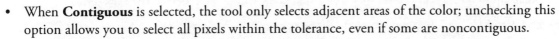

- **Tolerance** is the degree of variation between the color you click and the colors Photoshop will select. Higher tolerance values select a larger range based on the color you click.

- The **Anti-alias** check box allows edges to blend more smoothly into the background, preventing a jagged appearance. Anti-aliasing is the process of blending shades of pixels to create the illusion of sharp lines.

- When **Contiguous** is selected, the tool only selects adjacent areas of the color; unchecking this option allows you to select all pixels within the tolerance, even if some are noncontiguous.

- By default, selections relate to the active layer only. You can check **Sample All Layers** to make a selection of all layers in the file.

- The **Select Subject** button allows Photoshop to automatically make a selection based on what it determines to be the main "subject" of the photo.

- The **Select and Mask** button opens a special workspace where you can use a number of tools to fine-tune the selection edge.

The **Quick Selection tool** essentially allows you to "paint" a selection. As you drag, the selection expands and automatically finds the edges in the image.

- In the Options bar, you choose to create a new selection, add to, or subtract from the current selection.

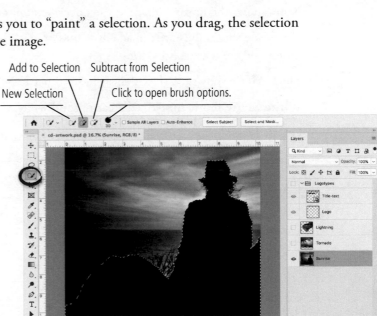

- Open the Brush Options to change the brush size, so that your selection includes a smaller or wider range of color.

- **Auto-Enhance** allows the software to refine the edges of the selection based on internal algorithms. (Although many "auto" features in the software are very useful starting points, never rely entirely on this type of automatic result.)

The **Select>Color Range** menu command opens a dialog box that you can use to select areas of an image based on sampled colors.

- On the right side of the dialog box, the **Eyedropper tool** is selected by default. You can click a color in the image, either in the document window or in the dialog box preview window, to define the color range you want to select (called **sampling**). You can then use the Add to Sample and Subtract from Sample eyedroppers to refine your selection.

- The **Select** menu at the top of the dialog box includes several presets for isolating specific ranges of primary colors (Reds, Yellows, Greens, Cyans, Blues, or Magentas), or specific ranges of color (highlights, midtones, or shadows).

- If you select the Skin Tones preset, you can then activate the **Detect Faces** option at the top of the dialog box. By adjusting the Fuzziness slider, you can use this dialog box to make reasonably good selections of people's skin. (Again, remember that no automatic option is a perfect substitute when subjective decision-making is required. Other tones in an image might be similar enough to a "skin tone" that unwanted areas will be included in the selection.)

- The **Localized Color Clusters** option can be used to select specific areas of a selected color. When this option is checked, the Range slider defines how far away (in physical distance) a color can be located from the point you click and still be included in the selection.

- **Fuzziness** is similar to the Tolerance setting for the Magic Wand tool. Changing the Fuzziness value expands (higher numbers) or contracts (lower numbers) the selection. Be careful, though, as higher fuzziness values can eliminate fine lines and detail.

- The Selection Preview menu determines how the selection appears in the document window:

  - **None** shows the normal image in the document window.

  - **Grayscale** shows the entire image in shades of gray. Selected areas are solid white and unselected areas are solid black.

  - **Black Matte** shows unselected areas in solid black. Selected areas appear in color.

  - **White Matte** shows unselected areas in solid white. Selected areas appear in color.

  - **Quick Mask** adds a partially transparent overlay to unselected areas.

- You can check the **Invert** box to return a selection that is the opposite of the color range you select. This is useful if you want to isolate (select) the background instead of the actual areas you selected in the dialog box.

Create and Refine a Color-Based Selection

Many images have both hard and soft edges, and/or very fine detail that needs to be isolated from its background (think of a model's blowing hair overlapping the title on the cover of a magazine). In this exercise, you are going to use two techniques to isolate the woman's silhouette and the ground on which she is sitting in the Sunrise image layer.

1. **With cd-artwork.psd open, hide all but the Sunrise layer. Click the Sunrise layer to make it active.**

2. **Choose View>Show>Guides.**

   Now that the file elements are in place, you can turn off the guides so that they do not distract from the work you will do in the rest of this project.

   You can also press Command/Control-; to toggle the visibility of guides.

3. **Choose the Quick Selection tool in the Tools panel.**

4. **In the Options bar, make sure the Sample All Layers option is not checked.**

   You only want to select an area based on the Sunrise layer content, so you do not want to make a selection based on the content of other layers in the file.

5. **Click near the bottom-left corner of the image, then drag right and up into the woman's head.**

   The resulting selection marquee shows that the software does a good job of isolating the obvious foreground elements of the image (the ground and the woman's silhouette). If you look closely, however, areas of fine detail — the woman's hair and the grass in front of her — are not included. You will need to use a different method to refine the selection edge and add the areas of detail.

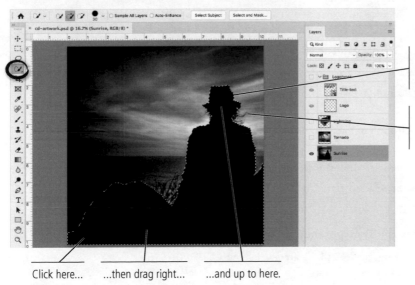

Marching ants surround the selected area.

Areas of fine detail are not included in the quick selection.

Click here...   ...then drag right...   ...and up to here.

6. Click the Select and Mask button in the Options bar.

The Select and Mask workspace is a specialized workspace that contains only the tools you need to refine a complex selection.

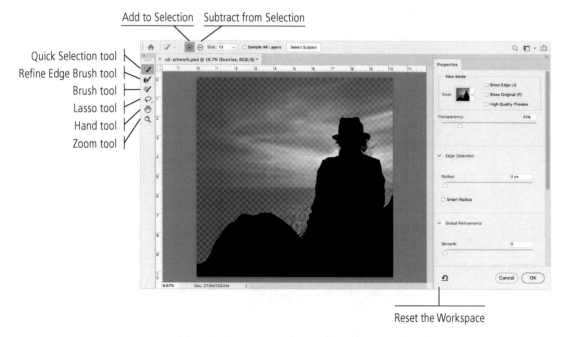

Add to Selection   Subtract from Selection

Quick Selection tool
Refine Edge Brush tool
Brush tool
Lasso tool
Hand tool
Zoom tool

Reset the Workspace

7. In the Properties panel, open the View menu and make sure Onion Skin is selected.

The different types of preview change the way your image appears while you refine the edges within the workspace.

- **Onion Skin**, the default, shows unselected (masked) areas as semi-transparent, based on the value in the Transparency slider. You can make the masked areas more or less transparent by increasing or decreasing (respectively) the Transparency value.

- **Marching Ants** shows the basic standard selection.

- **Overlay** shows the unselected areas with a Quick Mask overlay.

- **On Black** shows the selection in color against a black background.

- **On White** shows the selection in color against a white background.

- **Black & White** shows the selected area in white and the unselected area in black.

- **On Layers** shows only the selected area. Unselected areas are hidden so that underlying layers are visible in masked areas in the preview.

8. In the Properties panel, set the Transparency slider to 50%.

Using the 50% transparency setting, masked pixels are partially visible, so that you can see the areas you want to add to the selection.

9. **Zoom into the woman's head in the image, then choose the Refine Edge Brush tool.**

   This tool has edge detection capabilities, which means you can simply "paint" over areas to identify edges of very small areas of detail.

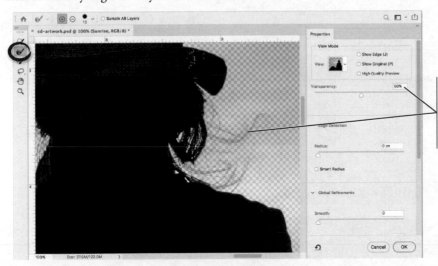

Changing the onion skin transparency allows you to see the unselected areas of the image layer.

Note:

You can use the Zoom and Hand tools, as well as their associated shortcuts, to change the image preview in the Select and Mask workspace.

10. **Click and drag over the wispy areas of the woman's hair.**

    You might not see much of a difference as you drag, but when you release the mouse button, you should see some of the thin details appear solid (selected) instead of transparent (not selected).

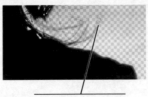 

Paint over the detail areas that are currently unselected.

Details appear solid (selected) after you paint over them and release the mouse button.

11. **Continue to drag over the details on both sides of the woman's head until you are satisfied with the results.**

    You don't need to be precise when you drag over the details, although dragging approximately over the details generally does produce better results.

Original Selection

Refined Selection

12. **Repeat this process to add the grass (near the woman's arm) to the selection.**

It might be helpful in this area to reduce the onion skin transparency, so that you can better see the details in this portion of the image.

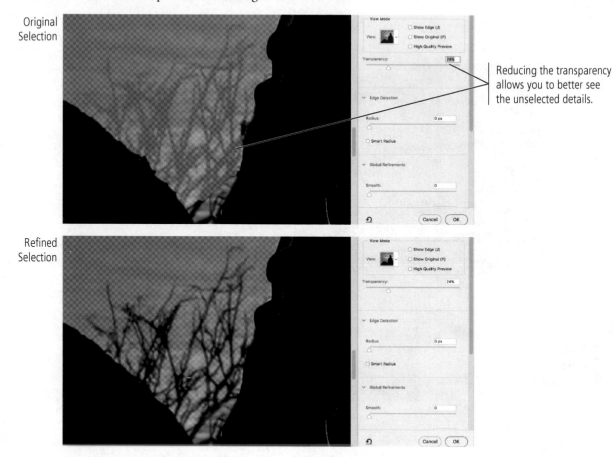

Original Selection

Refined Selection

Reducing the transparency allows you to better see the unselected details.

13. **If necessary, expand the Edge Detection and Global Refinements sections of the Properties panel, then review those options.**

- **Radius** is the number of pixels around the edge that are affected. Higher radius values result in softer edges and lower values result in sharper edges.

- **Smart Radius** automatically adjusts the radius for hard and soft edges found in the border region. You should turn off this option if your selection area has all hard edges or all soft edges, or if you prefer to manually control the Radius.

- **Smooth** reduces the number of points that make up your selection and, as the name suggests, makes a smoother edge. You can set smoothness from 0 (very detailed selection) to 100 (very smooth selection).

- **Feather** softens the selection edge, resulting in a transition that does not have a hard edge (in other words, blends into the background). You can feather the selection up to 250 pixels.

- **Contrast** is the degree of variation allowed in the selection edge. Higher Contrast values (up to 100%) mean sharper selection edges.

- **Shift Edge** shrinks or grows the selection edge by the defined percentage (from –100% to 100%).

- **Invert** reverses the mask; selected areas become unselected and vice versa.

14. **Experiment with the adjustments until you're satisfied with the selection edge.**

    We increased the Smooth value to 10 to reduce jagged effects at the selection edge.

15. **Expand the Output Settings in the Properties panel and choose the Layer Mask option in the Output To menu.**

    This menu can be used to create a new layer or file (with or without a mask) from the selection. You want to mask the existing layer, so you are using the Layer Mask option.

Note:

Decontaminate Colors *can be checked to remove a certain percentage of color from the edge of a selection.*

16. **Click OK to accept your refined selection.**

    When you pasted the feathered selection from the original Lightning.jpg file, you pasted only the pixels inside the selection area; unselected pixels from the original image are not a part of the composite file.

    Rather than actually excluding or deleting pixels, a **layer mask** hides unwanted pixels. The mask you just created is a raster-based pixel mask. Unselected (masked) areas are hidden but not deleted, so you can later edit the mask to change the visible part of the image. This is a nondestructive way to hide certain elements of a layer without permanently deleting pixels. You can edit or disable the layer mask at any time.

Note:

A layer mask is basically an Alpha channel that is connected to a specific layer.

The resulting layer mask hides areas that were not selected.

17. **Control/right-click the mask thumbnail and choose Disable Layer Mask from the contextual menu.**

    When you disable the mask, the background pixels are again visible. This is one advantage of using masks — masked pixels are not removed, they are simply hidden.

Control/right-click the thumbnail to open the mask's contextual menu.

When the mask is disabled, the masked pixels are visible.

A red X indicates that the mask is disabled.

18. **Control/right-click the mask thumbnail and choose Apply Layer Mask from the contextual menu.**

    This option applies the mask to the attached layer, permanently removing the masked pixels from the layer.

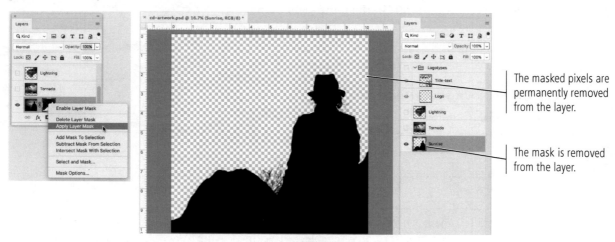

The masked pixels are permanently removed from the layer.

The mask is removed from the layer.

19. **Choose Edit>Undo Apply Layer Mask to restore the layer mask.**

    As you saw in the previous step, applying a mask permanently removes the masked pixels. This essentially defeats the purpose of a mask, so you are restoring it in this step.

20. **Control/right-click the mask thumbnail and choose Enable Layer Mask from the contextual menu.**

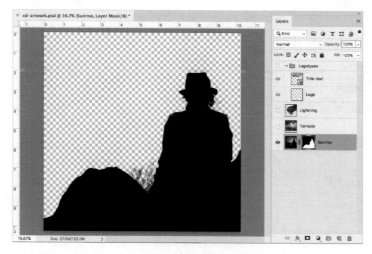

21. **Save the file and continue to the next exercise.**

Understanding Channels

You need a bit of background about channels to understand what's happening in the Quick Mask you will use in the next exercise. (You will use channels extensively in later projects.)

Every image has one channel for each component color. Each channel contains the information for the amount of that component color in any given pixel. An RGB image has three channels: Red, Green, and Blue (right top). A CMYK image has four channels: Cyan, Magenta, Yellow, and Black (right bottom).

In RGB images, the three additive primaries can have a value of 0 (none of that color) to 255 (full intensity of that color). Combining a value of 255 for each primary results in white. A value of 0 for each primary results in black.

In CMYK images, the three subtractive primaries plus black are combined in percentages from 0 (none of that color) to 100 (full intensity of that color) to create the range of printable colors. Channels in a CMYK image represent the printing plates or separations required to output the job.

Understanding Alpha Channels

An Alpha channel is a special type of channel, in which the value determines the degree of transparency of a pixel. In other words, a 50% value in the Alpha channel means that area of the image will be 50% transparent.

When working in Quick Mask mode, a temporary Quick Mask channel stores the degree of transparency based on the current selection. A semi-transparent red overlay shows areas being masked (i.e., the areas that are not included in the current selection).

Quick Masks are useful when you need to work with a temporary selection, or if you are still defining the exact selection area. As long as you stay in Quick Mask mode, the temporary Alpha channel remains in the Channels panel (listed as "Quick Mask"). If you return to Standard mode, the Quick Mask disappears from the window and the panel.

You can save a Quick Mask channel as a permanent Alpha channel by dragging the Quick Mask channel onto the New

Channel button at the bottom of the Channels panel. This adds a channel named "Quick Mask copy," which becomes a permanent part of the file even if you exit Quick Mask mode. You can then double-click the Alpha channel name in the panel to rename it, as we did in the following image (naming the channel "Baby Face").

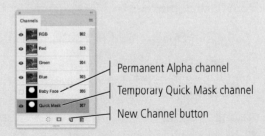

Permanent Alpha channel

Temporary Quick Mask channel

New Channel button

You can change the appearance of an Alpha channel mask by double-clicking a channel thumbnail in the Channels panel. In the top half of the resulting dialog box, you can change the overlay to show selected areas instead of the default masked areas.

Clicking the Color swatch opens a Color Picker, where you can change the color of the Quick Mask overlay. You can also use the Opacity field to change the transparency of the overlay (the default is 50%). Keep in mind that these settings only affect the appearance of the mask in Photoshop; the density of the selection is not affected by changing the overlay opacity.

Edit Layer Mask Properties

The most important thing to understand in this series of exercises is that layer masks are nondestructive. You can change the mask to change the visible area of the layer, temporarily hide the mask to show the entire layer, or even delete the mask entirely if you decide you don't want or need it. You can also edit a number of mask properties to further refine the mask and its effect on the masked layer contents.

1. **With cd-artwork.psd open, open the Channels panel (Window>Channels).**

2. **In the Channels panel, click the empty space on the left side of the panel to make the Sunrise Mask channel visible.**

   Layer masks are not visible by default; you have to turn them on in the Channels panel to see them. This isn't strictly necessary, since you can edit a mask without seeing it, but it is easier (at least when you're first learning) to be able to see what you're doing.

   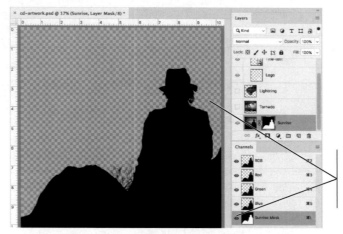

   Making the mask channel visible allows you to see the red overlay in the image.

3. **Double-click the Sunrise Mask channel icon in the Channels panel.**

4. **Change the Opacity field to 100%, then click OK.**

   Remember, this change only affects the transparency of the mask, not the degree of transparency applied to the layer.

   By setting the mask opacity to 100%, you will be better able to see the results of your choices in the following steps.

   Anything solid red will be hidden and anything with no red will be visible; shades of red will be partially transparent.

   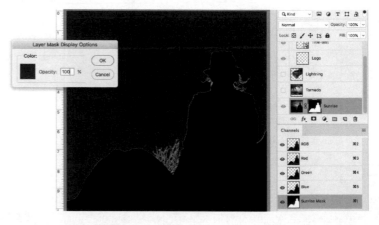

5. **In the Layers panel, click the Sunrise layer mask thumbnail to select it.**

   These corner icons indicate that the base layer is selected.

   Clicking the layer mask thumbnail selects the mask so you can edit it.

6. **Open the Properties panel (Window>Properties).**

Like the Options bar, the Properties panel is contextual. Different options are available in the panel depending on what is selected in the Layers panel. When a layer mask is selected, you can manipulate a variety of properties related to the selected mask.

The layer mask must be selected in the Layers panel.

The Properties panel can be used to edit the selected mask.

Note:

The Select and Mask button opens the Select and Mask workspace. The Color Range button opens the [Select] Color Range dialog box.

The Density slider changes the opacity of the overall mask. If you reduce the density to 80%, for example, underlying layers will be 20% visible through the mask. (Don't confuse this with the opacity of an alpha channel, which only affects the appearance of the mask onscreen.)

7. **In the Properties panel, change the Feather value to 25 px.**

If you feather a selection and then make a layer mask from that selection, the feathering becomes a permanent part of the mask. The Properties panel allows you to adjust the feathering of a hard-edge mask, and then later change or even remove the feathering if necessary, without painting on the mask.

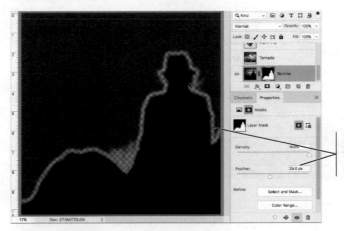

Use the Properties panel to feather the mask edge nondestructively.

8. **Change the Feather value to 1 px.**

This small feathering value will help to remove (or at least minimize) any remaining background artifacts around the edges of your mask.

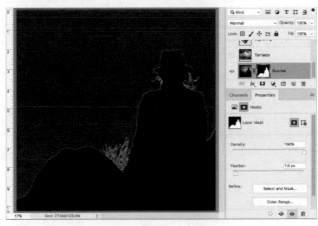

9. **Double-click the Sunrise Mask channel icon in the Channels panel.**

10. **Change the Opacity field back to 50%, then click OK.**

Remember, the Layer Mask Display Options setting only affects the mask's visibility in the document window. This does *not* affect the degree to which the mask affects pixels on the masked layer.

11. **In the Channels panel, click the eye icon for the Sunrise Mask channel.**

Even when the actual mask channel is not visible, the mask remains in tact on the layer.

The mask remains in tact and enabled, even though the mask channel is not visible.

12. **Save the file and continue to the next exercise.**

Arrange Layer Position and Stacking Order

The ad is almost final, but a few pieces are still not quite in position. You already know you can use the Move tool to move the contents of a layer around on the canvas. You can also move a layer to any position in the **stacking order** (the top-to-bottom position of a layer) by simply dragging it to a new position in the Layers panel.

1. **With cd-artwork.psd open, make all layers visible.**

2. **Click the Sunrise layer in the Layers panel and drag up. When a heavy bar appears above the Lightning layer, release the mouse button.**

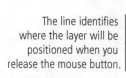

The line identifies where the layer will be positioned when you release the mouse button.

Note:

Be careful when dragging layers near a layer group. If the border appears around a layer group, releasing the mouse button would place the dragged layer inside of the group.

After you restack the layers, you can see that a small blank space appears in the bottom-left corner. (Yours might be slightly different, depending on how you painted the mask in the previous exercise.)

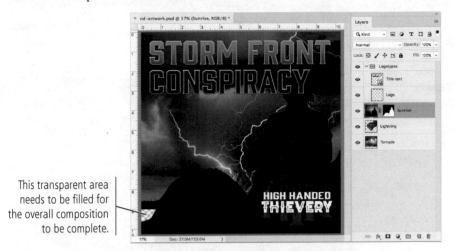

This transparent area needs to be filled for the overall composition to be complete.

Note:

Press Command/Control-[(left bracket) to move a layer down in the stacking order.

Press Command/Control-] (right bracket) to move a layer up in the stacking order.

3. **In the Layers panel, select the Tornado layer as the active one.**

4. **Press Command/Control-T to enter Free Transform mode.**

5. **Drag the bottom-right corner handle of the layer until the transparent area in the bottom-left corner is filled.**

   Keep in mind that you are enlarging a raster-image layer, which can cause loss of detail. Because this is a very small increase, and because the layer is the background image behind several other elements, you can make this enlargement without ruining the integrity of the composition.

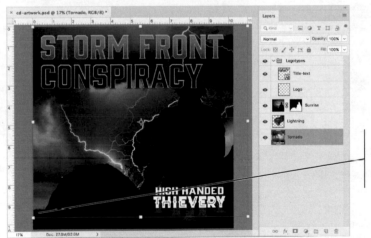

Drag the bottom-right handle to enlarge the active layer until this area is filled.

6. **Press Return/Enter to finalize the transformation.**

When you work with complex files, you might find yourself with dozens — or even hundreds — of layers. Descriptive names can help you navigate through the layers, but you still have to scroll through the panel to find what you need.

Layer filtering, available at the top of the Layers panel, allows you to narrow down the panel to only layers that meet certain criteria, making it much easier to locate a specific layer.

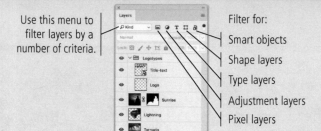

Use this menu to filter layers by a number of criteria.

Filter for:
Smart objects
Shape layers
Type layers
Adjustment layers
Pixel layers

When **Kind** is selected in the menu, you can use the associated buttons to show only certain types of layers (adjustment layers, smart objects, etc.).

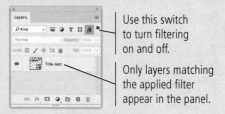

Use this switch to turn filtering on and off.

Only layers matching the applied filter appear in the panel.

When **Name** is selected, you can type in the attached field to find layers with names that include the text you enter in the field. The defined text string does not need to be at the beginning of the layer name. For example, typing "r" would return both Sunrise and Tornado layers in the file for this project.

When **Effect** is selected, you can use the secondary menu to find only layers with a specified effect (applied using the Layer>Layer Style submenu).

When **Attribute** is selected, you can choose from a number of layer attributes (visible, linked, clipped, masked, etc)..

When **Color** is selected, you can choose any of the built-in colors from the secondary menu. These colors, which appear around the layer's visibility icon, can be assigned to individual layers in each layer's contextual menu.

When **Mode** is selected, you can use the secondary menu to find only layers to which a certain blending mode has been assigned.

When **Smart Object** is selected, you can use the buttons at the top of the panel to find linked layers, layers with modified source data, layers with missing source data, or embedded layers. These buttons are nonexclusive, which means you can select more than one option at a time (for example, all layers with missing and modified source data).

The **Selected** option shows a subset of layers that exist in Isolation mode. To create a subset, select one or more layers in the Layers panel, and then choose Select>Isolate Layers. The Layers panel automatically shows a subset of only the selected layers, and Selected appears in the Filter By menu.

7. **Select the Lightning layer in the Layers panel, then change the layer opacity to 35%.**

   Layer opacity is the degree to which you can see underlying layers through the layer you are editing. Because you made the lightning only 35% opaque, the underlying tornado image is strongly visible through the lightning.

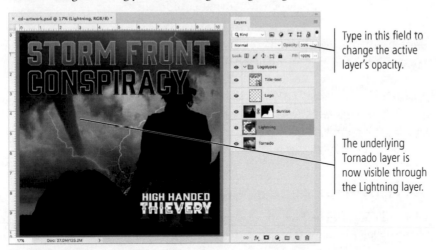

   Type in this field to change the active layer's opacity.

   The underlying Tornado layer is now visible through the Lightning layer.

8. **Save the file and then continue to the final stage of the project.**

STAGE 4 / Saving Files for Multiple Media

Many Photoshop projects require saving the completed file in more than one format. Many artists prefer to leave all files in the native PSD format, as there is then only one file to track. Others prefer to send only flattened TIFF files of their artwork because the individual elements can't be changed. Ultimately, the formats you use will depend on where and how the file is being placed.

Many Photoshop projects are pieces of a larger composition, and the overall project defines the format you need. The ad you just created, for example, will be placed in magazine layouts, which will be built in a page-layout application, such as Adobe InDesign. Although the current versions of industry-standard page-layout applications can support native layered PSD files, older versions can't import those native files. As the Photoshop artist, you have to save your work in a format that is compatible with the process being used by the magazine designer.

As you know, the artwork you created will be used in a variety of ways. You need to save three different versions of the artwork to meet those requirements.

Photoshop can save files in a number of common formats, including:

- **Photoshop**, with the extension PSD, is the native format.

- **JPEG** is a lossy compressed file format that does not support transparency.

- **Photoshop PDF** can contain all required font and image information in a single file, which can be compressed to reduce file size.

- **PNG** is a raster-based format that supports both continuous-tone color and transparency. It is more commonly used in digital publishing (specifically, web design), and does not support CMYK color, which is required for commercial printing.

- **TIFF** is a raster-based image format that supports layers, alpha channels, and file compression.

Save a Flattened TIFF File

The TIFF format is commonly used for print applications. Although the format can include layers, many designers prefer to send flattened files for output to avoid any potential problems that might be caused by older output devices, which is still an issue, as many service providers do not update very expensive output equipment until it becomes absolutely necessary.

In this exercise you will save the finished artwork as a flattened TIFF file that can be used for the album cover sleeve, as well as for most print advertising requirements.

1. **With `cd-artwork.psd` open, choose File>Save As.**

   The CD artwork is complete in the native Photoshop file. In the next few exercises you are going to make changes that you don't want to become a permanent part of the file. Saving it now, if you haven't already, means the finished artwork file won't be compromised in the following exercises.

2. **If necessary, navigate to your WIP>Music folder as the target location.**

   The Save As dialog box defaults to the last-used location. If you continued the entire way through this project without stopping, you won't have to navigate.

3. **In the Save As/File Name field, type `-album` at the end of the current file name (before the .psd extension).**

4. **Click the Format/Save As Type menu and choose TIFF.**

5. **In the bottom half of the dialog box, uncheck the Layers option.**

   Because this file contains layers, the Layers option was checked by default.

   The As a Copy box is now selected by default. A warning shows that the file must be saved as a copy when the Layers option is unchecked. This is basically a failsafe built into Photoshop that prevents you from overwriting your layered file with a flattened version.

   If your file contained alpha channels, annotations, or spot colors, those check boxes would also be available.

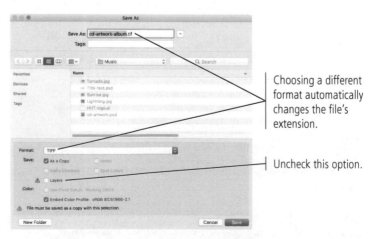

Choosing a different format automatically changes the file's extension.

Uncheck this option.

6. **Leave the remaining options at their default values and click Save.**

7. **In the resulting TIFF Options dialog box, make sure the None image compression option is selected.**

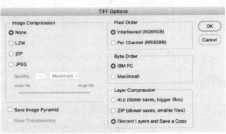

TIFF files can be compressed (made smaller) using three methods:

- **None** applies no compression to the file. This option is safe if file size is not an issue, but digital file transmission often requires files to be smaller than a full-page, multilayered Photoshop file.

- **LZW** (Lempel-Ziv-Welch) compression is **lossless**, which means all file data is maintained in the compressed file.

- **ZIP** compression is also lossless, but is not supported by all desktop-publishing software (especially older versions).

- **JPEG** is a **lossy** compression scheme, which means some data will be thrown away to reduce the file size. If you choose JPEG compression, the Quality options determine how much data can be discarded. Maximum quality means less data is thrown out and the file is larger; minimum quality discards more data and results in a smaller file size.

8. **Leave the Pixel Order radio button at the default value, and choose the Byte Order option for your operating system.**

Pixel Order determines how channel data is encoded. The Interleaved (RGBRGB) option is the default. Per Channel (RRGGBB) is called "planar" order.

Byte Order determines which platform can use the file on older versions of desktop publishing software. This option is largely obsolete because most modern software can now read either byte order.

Save Image Pyramid creates a tiered file with multiple resolution versions; this isn't widely used or supported by other applications, so you can typically leave it unchecked.

If your file contains transparency, the **Save Transparency** check box will be available. If you don't choose this option, transparent areas will be white in the saved file.

Note:

Some experts argue that choosing the order for your system can improve print quality, especially on desktop output devices.

9. **In the Layer Compression area, make sure Discard Layers is selected.**

These three options explain — right in the dialog box — what they do.

10. **Click OK to save the file, then continue to the next exercise.**

Reduce the Physical File Size

The CD insert artwork needs to be approximately half the size of the album artwork. Reducing the file's physical size is an easy process, although you need to check the positioning of various elements to make sure they meet the output requirements. In this exercise you will reduce the file's physical size, and then make necessary layer adjustments to meet the needs of the CD insert.

1. **With cd-artwork.psd open in Photoshop, choose Image>Image Size.**

2. **Make sure the Resample option is checked.**

You are resizing this image, which means you are changing the physical dimensions (and the actual number of pixels in the file). If Resample was not checked, you would simply be redistributing the same number of pixels across a different physical space.

3. **With Inches selected in the Width and Height Units menus, type 5 in the Width field.**

The CD insert is 4.75″ square, but it requires 1/8″ bleeds on all four sides:

$$4.75″ + 0.125″ + 0.125″ = 5″$$

Because the width and height are constrained by default, changing one value applies a proportional change to the other value.

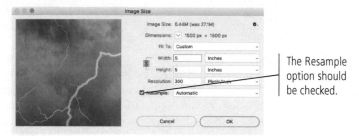

The Resample option should be checked.

4. **Click OK to change the file size.**

5. **Choose View>Show>Guides. Zoom in to the top-left corner and review the position of the guides.**

Reducing the file size affects all elements of the file, including guides. As you can see, the position of the various guides is reduced by approximately half (for example, the bleed guides are near the 1/16″ mark instead of the 1/8″ mark).

Guides are moved proportionally based on the reduced file size.

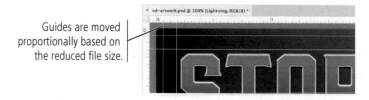

6. **Choose View>Clear Guides.**

Rather than manually dragging each guide on the page, you are going to simply replace them with new ones. This command removes all existing guides from the canvas.

7. **Choose View>New Guide Layout.**

8. **With the Margin option checked, set all four fields to 0.125 in. Click OK to add the new guides.**

This set of guides defines the trim size of the CD insert, marking a 1/8″ bleed allowance on all four edges of the file.

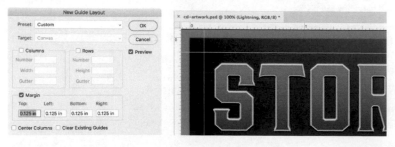

9. **Choose View>New Guide Layout again.**

10. **With the Margin option checked, change all four fields to 0.25 in. Click OK to add the new guides.**

   This second set of guides defines the live area, marking the required 1/8″ safe margin. Although they are 1/4″ from the canvas edge, they are 1/8″ from the trim guides.

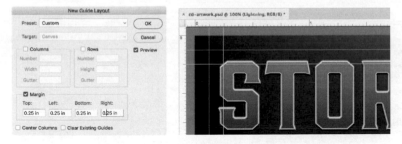

11. **Zoom out so you can see the entire top of the artwork.**

12. **Choose the Move tool in the Tools panel. In the Options bar, make sure the Auto-Select option is checked and Layer is selected in the attached menu.**

   When active, clicking in the document window automatically selects the layer containing the layers where you click.

   Because Layer is selected in the menu, only the relevant layer will move, even if it is part of a layer group. If you want all layers in a group containing the selected layer to move, you can choose Group in the menu.

13. **Click any of the letters in the album title and drag until the layer snaps to the top and left margin guides.**

   Auto-Select is active.   Layer is selected in the menu.

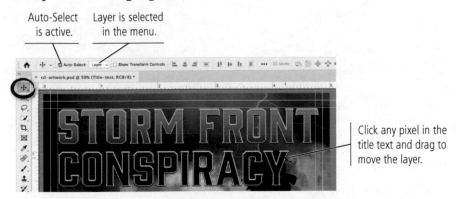

   Click any pixel in the title text and drag to move the layer.

14. **Press Command/Control-T to enter Free Transform mode. Click and drag the bottom-right bounding-box handle until the title fits inside the margin guides in the reduced file.**

   Drag the bottom-right handle to fit the title into the live area.

15. Press Return/Enter to finalize the transformation.

16. With the Move tool still active, click any pixel in the logo and drag until it snaps to the bottom and right margin guides.

Because the Auto-Select option is active, you don't need to first select the target layer in the Layers panel to move the content.

Click any pixel in the logo artwork and drag to move the layer content.

17. Choose File>Save As. Using the same method as in the previous exercise, save this file as a flat TIFF file named cd-artwork-insert.tif. Click OK to accept the default TIFF options.

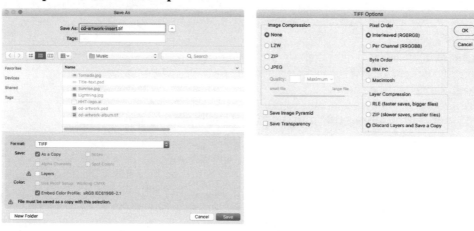

18. With cd-artwork.psd still active, choose File>Revert.

This command restores the file to the last-saved version. Because you saved the completed artwork at the beginning of this stage, the command restores the artwork to its original, 10.25″ file size.

Because enlarging a raster image to such a degree (more than 200% to go from 5″ to 10.25″) would almost certainly cause image degradation, you are restoring the larger version instead of saving the smaller one.

19. Continue to the next exercise.

Save a JPEG File for Digital Media

The final file required for this project is a 3000 x 3000 pixel, high-quality JPEG file.

1. **With cd-artwork.psd open and restored to its last-saved state, choose Image>Image Size.**

2. **Choose Pixels in the Width menu.**

3. **With the Resample option checked, change the Width field to 3000.**

   Again, you are defining the actual number of pixels to include in the file. If the resample was not checked, changing the width or height would only change the distribution of pixels instead of changing the actual number of pixels in the file.

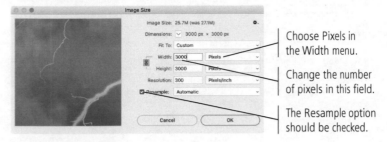

Choose Pixels in the Width menu.

Change the number of pixels in this field.

The Resample option should be checked.

4. **Click OK to finalize the new size.**

   This file is not being printed, so you don't need to worry about the bleed and margin areas. Because the size reduction is slight in this case, no further adjustment is required before saving the JPEG file for digital music libraries.

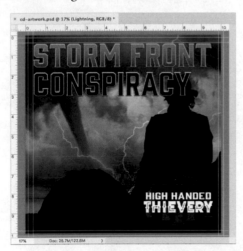

5. **Choose File>Save As.**

6. **Choose JPEG in the Format/Save As Type menu, then change the file name to `cd-artwork-digital.jpg`.**

   The JPEG format does not support layers, alpha channels, or spot colors, so those options are unavailable in the bottom of the dialog box.

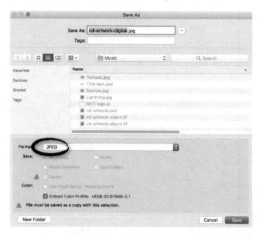

7. **Click Save.**

8. **In the resulting JPEG Options dialog box, choose High in the Image Options Quality menu.**

   This menu determines how much compression will be used in the resulting file:

   - Higher values mean less compression, better quality, and larger file size.
   - Lower values mean more compression, lower quality, and smaller file size.

Type a quality level (1–12) in this field...

...or choose a quality level in this menu.

9. **Click OK to save the JPEG file.**

10. **Close the `cd-artwork.psd` file without saving.**

PROJECT REVIEW

fill in the blank

1. _____ is likely to cause degradation of a raster image when it's reproduced on a printing press.

2. A _____ is a linked file that you placed into another Photoshop document.

3. The _____ is context sensitive, providing access to different functions depending on which tool is active.

4. The _____ is the final size of a printed page.

5. The _____ tool is used to draw irregular-shaped selection marquees.

6. The _____ tool is used to select areas of similar color by clicking and dragging in the image window.

7. The _____ tool can be used to drag layer contents to another position within the image, or into another open document.

8. When selecting color ranges, the _____ value determines how much of the current color range falls into the selection.

9. A _____ can be used to non-destructively hide certain areas of a layer.

10. _____ is a lossy compression method that is best used when large file size might be a problem.

short answer

1. Briefly describe the difference between raster images and vector graphics.

2. Briefly explain three methods for isolating an image from its background.

3. Briefly explain the concept of a layer mask.

PORTFOLIO BUILDER PROJECT

Use what you have learned in this project to complete the following freeform exercise.
Carefully read the art director and client comments, then create your own design to meet the needs of the project.
Use the space below to sketch ideas. When finished, write a brief explanation of the reasoning behind your final design.

art director comments

Your client's friend liked your work on the new CD artwork. She would like to hire you again to create the ad concept and final files for a new movie that they're releasing early next year.

To complete this project, you should:

❏ Download the **Airborne_Print19_PB.zip** archive from the Student Files web page to access the client-supplied title artwork and rating placeholder file.

❏ Find appropriate background and foreground images for the movie theme (see the client's comments at right).

❏ Incorporate the title artwork, logos, and rating placeholder that the client provided.

❏ Composite the different elements into a single completed file; save both a layered version and a flattened version.

client comments

The movie is titled, *Above and Beyond*. Although the story is fictionalized, it will focus on the men who led the first U.S. Airborne unit (the 501st), which suffered more than 2,000 casualties in the European theater of World War II.

We don't have any other images in mind, but the final ad should reflect the time period (the 1940s) of the movie. The 501st Parachute Infantry Battalion was trained to parachute into battle, so you should probably incorporate some kind of parachute image.

This movie is a joint venture between Sun and Tantamount, so both logos need to be included in the new ad. It isn't rated yet, so please use the "This Movie Is Not Yet Rated" artwork as a placeholder.

Create this ad big enough to fit on an 8.5″ × 11″ page, but keep the live area 1″ inside the trim so the ad can be used in different-sized magazines.

project justification

PROJECT SUMMARY

Making selections is one of the most basic — and most important — skills that you will learn in Photoshop. Selections are so important that Photoshop dedicates an entire menu to the process.

As you created the music CD artwork in this project, you used a number of techniques that you will apply in many (if not all) projects you build in Photoshop. You learned a number of ways to make both simple and complex selections, and you will learn additional methods in later projects. You also learned how to work with multiple layers, which will be an important part of virtually every Photoshop project you create, both in this book and throughout your career.

Unify multiple files into a single composition

Transform a Smart Object layer

Transform a regular layer

Move layer content around on the canvas

Incorporate vector graphics into a raster image

Make a basic selection with a Marquee tool

Create a feathered selection to blend one layer into another

Create and refine a selection based on colors in the image

Use a layer mask to hide pixels on a layer

Car Magazine Cover

5

Your client publishes a monthly magazine for car enthusiasts. Your agency has been hired to take over the magazine design and you have been tasked with designing the cover for the next issue.

This project incorporates the following skills:

❑ Resizing and resampling supplied images

❑ Creating complex vector paths and shape layers

❑ Compositing images as Smart Objects

❑ Applying nondestructive styles, effects, and filters

❑ Developing a custom artistic background

PROJECT MEETING

client comments

Every month, the magazine cover includes one main featured car, and three smaller images related to other articles in the issue. In addition to those images and the magazine title, we also always include several text blurbs with teasers for secondary articles in the issue, and a QR code that links to the website.

We're looking for a new way to present these elements. Once we finalize a general layout, we'll use that layout going forward for every new issue.

The only thing we're fixed on is the trim size, which is 8″ × 10″, with a 1/8″ bleed allowance.

art director comments

The client sent me the main car image for the first redesign. It's a little bit small, so we'll have to do some manipulation to make it large enough to fill the cover space. The car also needs to be knocked out of its background so it can be more prominent. A vector path will work well to meet this goal because you can edit it at any time without losing quality.

You're going to use a combination of styles, filters, and effects on the background and inset images. Photoshop's Smart Object capabilities will be a significant advantage in this task because we can edit the effects and filters if the client isn't thrilled with the initial effort.

I've also already created a template in Illustrator with the magazine nameplate and text elements; we'll repurpose the same file every month with the different text for each issue. You can place that file directly into Photoshop as a linked file so that any last-minute changes in the file will automatically appear in the final composite cover.

project objectives

To complete this project, you will:

- ❏ Resize and resample an existing source image
- ❏ Edit the canvas size
- ❏ Create a vector-based layer mask
- ❏ Create a vector shape layer
- ❏ Create a clipping mask
- ❏ Add texture to a shape layer
- ❏ Apply custom layer effects
- ❏ Use the Filter Gallery
- ❏ Liquify a layer
- ❏ Use the Eyedropper tool
- ❏ Create a custom gradient
- ❏ Print a composite proof

STAGE 1 / **Enlarging Source Files**

Any project that you build in Photoshop requires some amount of zooming in and out to various view percentages, as well as navigating around the document within its window. As we show you how to complete different stages of the workflow, we usually won't tell you when to change your view percentage because that's largely a matter of personal preference. Nonetheless, you should understand the different options for navigating around a Photoshop file so you can easily and efficiently get to what you want, when you want to get there.

To review information from the Interface chapter, keep in mind that you have a number of options for navigating around a document:

- Click with the Hand tool to drag the image around in the document window.

- Click with the Zoom tool to zoom in; Option/Alt-click to zoom out.

- Use the View Percentage field in the bottom-left corner of the document window.

- Use the options in the View menu (or the corresponding keyboard shortcuts).

- Use the Navigator panel.

Resize and Resample the Existing Source Image

This project — like many others you will build throughout your career — starts with an existing image, which you will open and use as the basis for the rest of the project. Whenever you start with an existing file, it's best to evaluate what you already have before you make any changes.

1. **Download Cars_Print19_RF.zip from the Student Files web page.**

2. **Expand the ZIP archive in your WIP folder (Macintosh) or copy the archive contents into your WIP folder (Windows).**

   This results in a folder named **Cars**, which contains the files you need for this project. You should also use this folder to save the files you create in this project.

3. **In Photoshop, choose File>Open. Navigate to the file amg.jpg in the WIP>Cars folder and click Open.**

4. **Choose View>Fit on Screen so you can see the entire image, and make sure rulers are visible (View>Rulers).**

5. **Choose Image>Image Size.**

   The amg.jpg file is 25″ wide by 18.75″ high, with a resolution of 72 pixels/inch. Commercial printing typically requires 300 pixels/inch, so this image would not be considered "print quality" at its current size.

   The first step is to resize the image using the principle of effective resolution to achieve the 300 pixels/inch required for commercial printing.

6. **At the bottom of the dialog box, uncheck the Resample option and change the Resolution field to 300.**

   Remember, when resampling is not active, the image retains the same number of pixels when you change the size or resolution fields. The image's physical size is now smaller since you compressed 300 pixels into an inch instead of the original 72 ppi.

Uncheck the Resample option.

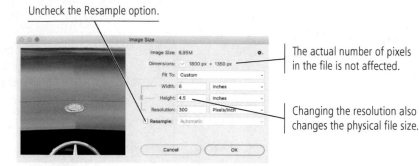

The actual number of pixels in the file is not affected.

Changing the resolution also changes the physical file size.

7. **Click OK to resize the source image.**

   As you can see, the image view in the document window does not change because the image still has the same number of pixels. The rulers at the left and top edges of the document window show the new measurements that are associated with the resized image.

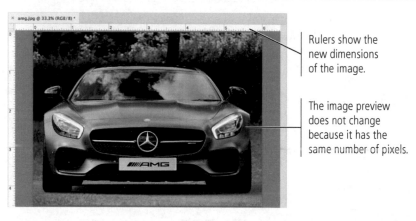

Rulers show the new dimensions of the image.

The image preview does not change because it has the same number of pixels.

8. **Choose Image>Image Size again.**

   Because you already defined the appropriate resolution for this image, you now need to make the image large enough to meet the overall job requirements.

   Resampling adds or removes pixels to create the size you define, without affecting the defined resolution.

9. **Click in the Preview window and drag until the logo on the car's grill is visible.**

   Areas of greater detail are the most prone to distortion when you enlarge an image. The Image Size preview area allows you to review the results before finalizing the process.

10. **At the bottom of the dialog box, check the Resample option.**

    When the Resample option is checked, you can change the actual number of pixels in the image without affecting its resolution.

11. **Open the Resample menu and choose Preserve Details (enlargement).**

Although you should try to capture images at the size you will need them, this is not always possible when working with client-supplied images. The Preserve Details option significantly improves the results of artificially enlarging an existing image.

12. **Make sure the Constrain option is active.**

13. **With the units menus set to Inches, change the Width field to 8.25.**

The overall project requires a finished image that is 8.25″ wide by 10.25″ high. If you enlarged the picture to match the required height, it would be too wide for the entire car to fit into the composition. Instead, you are enlarging the image to match the required width; you will later adjust the canvas to suit the project's height requirement.

As you can see, increasing the image's physical size with resampling adds more pixels to the image. This also significantly increases the file weight (its size in bytes).

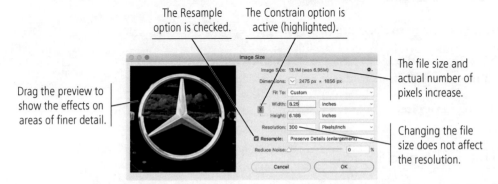

The Resample option is checked.

The Constrain option is active (highlighted).

Drag the preview to show the effects on areas of finer detail.

The file size and actual number of pixels increase.

Changing the file size does not affect the resolution.

14. **Drag in the Preview window to show an area with flat areas of color near a high-contrast edge.**

Artificially enlarging an image often results in small pixels of varying color, especially in areas of solid color and near high-contrast edges. When you choose the Preserve Details option, you can use the Reduce Noise slider to help reduce those artifacts.

15. **Change the Reduce Noise slider to 20%.**

The Preview window shows the results that will be achieved when you finalize the resampling.

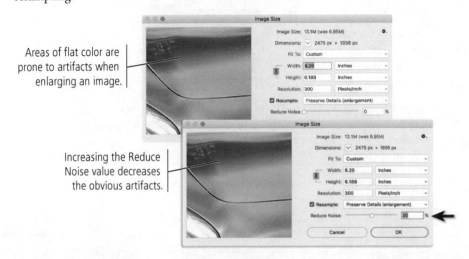

Areas of flat color are prone to artifacts when enlarging an image.

Increasing the Reduce Noise value decreases the obvious artifacts.

16. **Click OK to finalize the resampling.**

    Resampling the image (enlarging) adds pixels to the file. The image no longer fits in the document window at the current view percentage.

The image now has more pixels, so less of the image is visible in the document window.

Note:

You're adding a sizeable amount of information to this file, so the resampling process might take a few seconds. Depending on the power and speed of your computer, you might see a progress bar as the image size is remapped.

17. **Choose View>Fit On Screen to show the entire image.**

18. **Choose File>Save As. Save the file as a native Photoshop file named magazine.psd in your WIP>Cars folder.**

19. **Continue to the next exercise.**

Sharpen the Enlarged Image

When you enlarge an image in Photoshop, the application must generate new data. The algorithm underlying the Preserve Details option does a significantly better job of generating new pixels than was available in previous versions, but the pixels are still not original to the image. This can result in a loss of detail, especially near apparent edges or areas of high contrast. Whenever you enlarge an image, **sharpening** can help to restore detail and make the image appear more crisp.

1. **With magazine.psd open, choose Filter>Sharpen>Unsharp Mask.**

2. **Make sure the Preview check box is active in the dialog box.**

   Unsharp masking sharpens an image by increasing contrast along apparent edges in th image.

   - **Amount** determines how much the contrast in edges will increase. Typically, 150–200% creates good results in high-resolution images.

   - **Radius** determines how many pixels will be included in the edge comparison. Higher radius values result in more pronounced edge effects.

   - **Threshold** defines the difference that is required for Photoshop to identify an edge. A threshold of 15 means that colors must be more than 15 levels different.

Note:

The Sharpen, Sharpen More, and Sharpen Edges filters apply sharpening with no user control.

Drag here or click in the document window to change the visible area in the preview window.

3. **Change the Amount to 100%, the Radius to 2.0 pixels, and the Threshold to 3 levels.**

4. **Toggle the Preview option off and on to review the results in the document window.**

Sharpening is most obvious in areas of high contrast.

5. **Click OK to apply the Unsharp Mask filter.**

6. **Save the file and continue to the next exercise.**

Edit the Canvas Size

As you learned in the project meeting, the final artwork for this project needs to be 8.25" wide by 10.25" high. You already accomplished the required width when you resampled the source file. In this exercise, you are going to enlarge the canvas to meet the project's height requirement.

1. **With magazine.psd open, make the Layers panel visible.**

   Photos and scans almost always default to exist on the Background layer when you first open them.

2. **Choose Image>Canvas Size.**

   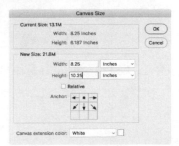

   In Photoshop, **canvas** refers to the overall image area — like the surface of a canvas used by traditional artists. It is not directly connected to the content of most layers (except for the Background layer, as you will see shortly).

   You can use this dialog box to change the size of the canvas to specific measurements.

3. **Choose the top-center anchor option.**

   The Anchor area shows the reference point around which the canvas will be enlarged or cropped. Using this option, all new pixels will be added at the bottom of the image.

4. **Change the Height field to 10.25 [Inches], and choose White in the Canvas Extension Color menu.**

   This menu defines what color will appear in the new pixels on the Background layer.

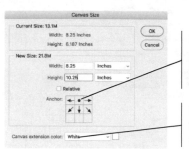

Anchoring the top edge means new pixels will be added to the bottom of the existing canvas.

Use this menu to define the color of new pixels on the Background layer.

Note:

If you define smaller measurements, you are basically accomplishing the same thing as using the Crop tool.

Note:

If you reduce the canvas size, clicking OK in the Canvas Size dialog box results in a warning that some clipping will occur.

Content on the Background layer that is outside the new canvas size is permanently removed from the layer. Content on other layers is maintained.

5. **Click OK to apply the change, then choose View>Fit On Screen.**

   As you can see, new pixels were added to the bottom of the canvas. Because the existing image content exists on the Background layer, and the Background layer cannot contain transparent pixels, the new pixels are filled with white.

Because the photo existed on the locked Background layer, new pixels are filled with white.

6. **Choose Edit>Undo Canvas Size.**

   Press Command/Control-Z to undo the previous action.

7. **In the Layers panel, click the Lock icon to unlock the Background layer.**

8. **Double-click the Layer 0 name, type Car to rename the layer, then press Return/Enter.**

9. **Choose Image>Canvas Size again. Select the top-center Anchor option, then change the Height field to 10.25 [Inches].**

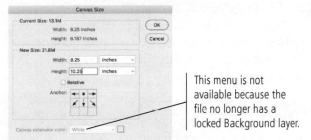

This menu is not available because the file no longer has a locked Background layer.

Note:

If you check the Relative option, you can change the canvas size by specific amounts. For example, to make the canvas one inch narrower, you would type −1 in the Width field. Photoshop automatically calculates the resulting canvas size based on the selected Anchor position.

10. **Click OK to apply the change.**

   Regular layers support transparency, so the new pixels are not filled with a solid color. The gray-and-white checked pattern identifies transparent areas of the visible layer.

Because regular layers can include transparency, no color appears in the area of the new pixels.

11. **Save the file. With Maximize Compatibility checked, click OK in the Photoshop Format Options dialog box.**

   Because you converted the Background layer to a regular image layer, you see the dialog box that asks if you want to maximize compatibility the first time you save the file.

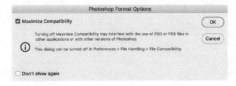

12. **Continue to the next stage of the project.**

STAGE 2 / **Working with Vector Tools**

Vector paths, also called Bézier curves, are defined mathematically based on the position of anchor points and the length and angle of direction handles that are connected to those anchor points. Unlike the pixels in a raster image, vector paths do not have a defined resolution until they are output. Because of this, vector paths can be edited at any time without any loss of quality.

Photoshop includes a number of tools for creating vector paths:

- The **Pen tool** places individual anchor points each time you click; line segments connect each point. If you click and drag, you create a point with direction handles, which precisely control the shape of the connecting segments.

- The **Freeform Pen tool** draws vector paths wherever you drag, just as you would draw with a pencil on paper.

- The **Rectangle** and **Ellipse tools** create shapes that you would expect based on the tool names. If you press Shift while you click and drag, you create a shape with equal height and width (a square or circle, respectively).

> **Note:**
>
> *The Type tool is also technically a vector-based tool because digital type uses vectors to define the character shapes.*

- The **Polygon tool** creates a shape with any number of sides. Clicking once opens a dialog box where you can define the number of sides.

Polygon created with all options unchecked

Polygon created with the Star option checked

  If you check the **Smooth Corners** option, each anchor point has direction handles that make the corners rounded instead of sharp.

  If you choose the **Star** option, the **Indent Sides By** value determines where the inner points of the star appear relative to the overall shape diameter.

  You can also check the **Smooth Indents** option to create smooth curves on the inside points of the shape, instead of corner points.

Polygon (star) created with the Smooth Corners option checked

Polygon (star) created with the Smooth Corners and Smooth Indents options checked

- The **Line tool** creates open straight lines with two points — one at each end. When first created, the points have no direction handles and the connecting segment is a straight line.

- The **Custom Shape tool** creates vector-based shapes from built-in or external libraries.

When you use the vector drawing tools, you have the option to create a new shape, path, or pixels.

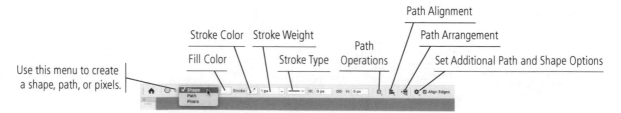

Use this menu to create a shape, path, or pixels.

Fill Color | Stroke Color | Stroke Weight | Stroke Type | Path Operations | Path Alignment | Path Arrangement | Set Additional Path and Shape Options

- If you choose Shape, the shape is placed on a vector-based shape layer.

- If you choose Path, the shape exists only as a work path in the Paths panel.

- If you choose Pixels, the resulting shape is created as pixels on the previously selected layer. No vector path is created.

> **Note:**
>
> *The Pixels option is not available when you are using the Pen tools.*

Use the Freeform Pen Tool

The Freeform Pen tool creates a vector path based on where you drag the cursor. The application creates anchor points and direction handles as necessary to create the shape that you draw.

1. **With magazine.psd open, show the image at 100% in the document window.**

   Ideally, you should work at 100% while you complete this exercise.

2. **Choose the Freeform Pen tool (nested under the Pen tool) in the Tools panel.**

3. **In the Options bar, choose the Path option in the left menu.**

   When you choose Path in the tool mode menu, the vector path that you draw is stored in the Paths panel.

4. **Open the Path Operations menu and choose the Combine Shapes option.**

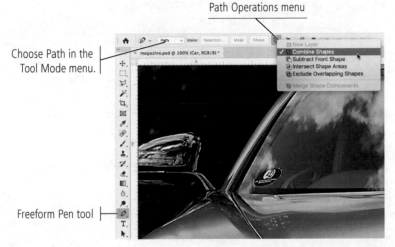

Path Operations menu

Choose Path in the Tool Mode menu.

Freeform Pen tool

Note:

The Pen Pressure option only applies if you have a pressure-sensitive graphics tablet. When this option is turned on, higher pressure decreases the Width tolerance.

These options define how a new path will interact with any existing paths. (Illustrator and InDesign users might recognize these as options from the Pathfinder panel.)

- **New Layer**, available when Layer is selected in the Tool Mode menu, creates a new shape layer every time you draw a new path.

- **Combine Shapes** adds new paths to an already selected path or shape layer. Each path's shape is maintained as a separate vector path. If you want a new path to include only areas inside the path you draw, you should choose this option before you begin drawing a new path.

- **Subtract Front Shape** removes the area of secondary shapes from existing shapes.

- **Intersect Shape Areas** results in a shape that is only the area where a new shape overlaps an existing shape.

- **Exclude Overlapping Shapes** is similar to Subtract; overlapping areas are removed from the existing shape, but nonoverlapping areas of the new shape are filled with the shape color.

- The **Merge Shape Components** option, available when a single path contains more than one shape, results in a single (possibly compound) shape. Any overlapping paths are combined into one shape/path.

5. **Check the Magnetic option in the Options bar, then click the Set Additional Path and Shape Options button.**

When you draw with the Pen tool, the default path appears in the document window as a thin, medium blue line. You can use the Thickness and Color options to change the appearance of the path. (The settings here do not affect the actual stroke color and width of a path; they refer only to the appearance of paths in the document window.)

- **Curve Fit** determines how closely the curves will match the path that you drag with the mouse cursor. When the Magnetic option is active, you can also define settings that control how the magnetic function behaves:

- **Width** determines how far from an edge you have to drag (1–256 pixels) for Photoshop to still find the edge.

- **Contrast** determines how much variation (1–100%) must exist between pixels for Photoshop to define an edge.

- **Frequency** determines the rate at which Photoshop places anchor points. Higher values (up to 100) create anchor points faster than lower values (down to 0).

6. **Define the following settings in the pop-up menu, then press Return/ Enter to apply them:**

Thickness:	2 px
Color:	**Light Red**
Curve Fit:	2 px
Width:	15 px
Contrast:	10%
Frequency:	25

Open this menu.   Check this option.

7. **Click at the corner where the left side mirror meets the car to place the first anchor point. Drag up and around the car shape.**

You don't have to hold down the mouse button when you draw with the Freeform Pen tool in Magnetic mode.

As you drag, the magnetic function creates anchor points to define a vector path around obvious edges where you drag.

Magnetic Freeform Pen tool cursor

The path snaps to the high-contrast edges near where you drag.

Click here to place the first anchor point for the path.

8. **Continue dragging around the car shape to create the initial outline.**

Skip the tires for now, and don't worry if the path is not perfect as you outline the car shape. You will fine-tune the path in the next few exercises.

9. **If you can't see the entire car in the document window, press the Spacebar to temporarily access the Hand tool, then click and drag to move the image so you can see the edges that you need to follow.**

The Spacebar temporarily switches to the Hand tool, so you can drag the image in the window, even while working on another task. When you release the Spacebar, you return to the previously selected tool, so you can continue drawing the path of the car's shape.

If you drag past the edge of the document window, Photoshop automatically scrolls the visible area of the image. Manually repositioning with the Hand tool gives you better control over exactly what you see.

Note:

Some users report processor-related issues when temporarily switching to the Hand tool while drawing with the Freeform Pen tool in Magnetic mode.

If you experience performance problems, try zooming out and in with the keyboard commands instead of dragging with the Hand tool.

Press the Spacebar to temporarily access the Hand tool.

10. **When you reach an obvious corner in the car's outline, click to place a specific anchor point.**

Although Photoshop automatically creates anchor points based on the defined magnetic behavior, you can also click to place anchor points in specific locations.

Click to manually place an anchor point at apparent corners.

11. **Continue outlining the car shape. When you get back to your original starting point, click to create a closed path.**

When the tool cursor is over the original starting point, a hollow circle in the icon indicates that clicking will close the path.

The hollow circle indicates that clicking will close the path.

12. Open the Layers and Paths panels.

As you can see, no layer has been added. The path you drew is stored in the Paths panel as the Work Path, which is a temporary path that exists only until you create another path.

Some parts of the car are not included inside the path.

No layer is added to the file.

The path you drew is stored as the Work Path.

13. With the Work Path selected in the Paths panel, open the panel Options menu and choose Save Path.

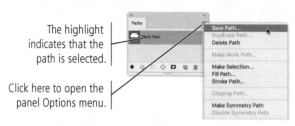

The highlight indicates that the path is selected.

Click here to open the panel Options menu.

More about Working with the Paths Panel

In the Paths panel options menu, you can choose **Make Selection** to make a marching-ants selection based on the path shape. You can use the resulting dialog box to define the details of the selection.

If you choose **Fill Path** in the Options menu, you can use the resulting dialog box to determine how the fill will be created. You can choose a color or pattern, blending mode and opacity, and whether to feather the edge of the fill so it blends smoothly into underlying layers.

If you choose the **Stroke Path** option, you must also choose which tool will create the stroke. The applied stroke will have the last-used settings for the selected tool. In other words, you have to define the tool options (brush size, hardness, etc.) that you want before using this option.

The Fill Path and Stroke Path options add the resulting pixels to the currently active layer — an important distinction from the Shape Layer option, which creates a new layer when you begin drawing the vector path. It is also important to remember that although the path remains a vector path, color applied to the fill or stroke of the path is raster-based and it does not have the same scalability as a vector shape layer.

If you choose the **Clipping Path** option, the selected path will become a clipping path, which is essentially a vector mask that can define the visible area of an image. The white area in the path thumbnail defines the visible areas.

Buttons across the bottom of the panel provide quick access to many of the available options. They are, from left:

- Fill Path with Foreground Color
- Stroke Path with Brush
- Load Path as a Selection
- Make Work Path from Selection
- Add Layer Mask
- Create New Path
- Delete Path

14. Type Car Outline in the resulting dialog box, then click OK.

After you save the path, the new name appears instead of "Work Path;" this path will remain in the file even if you create a different temporary Work Path.

The saved path is permanent.

15. Click the bottom area of the Paths panel to deselect the path.

When the path is not selected, you can't see its anchor points and connecting segments in the document window.

When the path is not selected, you can't see it in the document window.

16. Save the file and continue to the next exercise.

Add to an Existing Path

In the previous exercise, you intentionally skipped the wheels in the image because the Freeform Pen tool's magnetic properties perform better with higher-contrast edges than what is evident where the tires meet the pavement. In this exercise, you will use the Pen tool to add the wheels to the existing path.

In this exercise, you will use the Pen tool to add the wheels to the existing path. The Photoshop Pen tool (and its variants) work in the same manner as the Pen tool in Illustrator. If necessary, refer to Project 2: Regatta Artwork for a refresher.

1. With magazine.psd open, make sure the view percentage is 100% and position the image so the right wheel is entirely visible.

2. Choose the Pen tool (nested under the Freeform Pen tool) in the Tools panel.

When you choose a nested tool, it becomes the default option in that position of the Tools panel. To access the original default tool — the Pen tool, in this case — you have to click the tool and hold down the mouse button to access the nested tools menu.

3. In the Paths panel, click the Car Outline path to make it visible in the document window.

You want to add more shapes to the existing path, so the path needs to be selected and visible in the document window.

4. In the Options bar, choose Path in the Tool Mode menu.

5. **Click the Path Operations button and choose Combine Shapes (if it is not already selected).**

Clicking the path name selects it.

The selected path is visible in the document window.

6. **Click the Pen tool in the Tools panel to hide the anchor points of the existing path (if necessary).**

If the existing path's anchor points are visible, you can use the Pen tool to add anchor points to the existing path. You want to create a second shape in the same path, so you need to turn off the existing path's anchor points.

If the existing path's anchor points are visible, clicking would add a new point to the existing path.

If the existing path's anchor points are not visible, clicking creates a new shape that is part of the same path.

7. **Click with the Pen tool cursor where the rear tire meets the car undercarriage.**

Clicking once with the Pen tool creates a corner anchor point with no direction handles.

8. **Move the cursor down and right along the tire edge (as shown in Step 9).**

9. **Click to create an anchor point, hold down the mouse button, and drag down and right to create direction handles for the point.**

Click here to place the first point.

Click and drag to create a new point with direction handles.

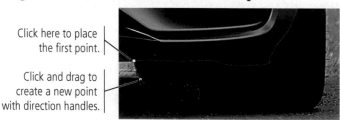

Note:

Don't worry if the curve isn't quite perfect — you will learn how to edit anchor points and handles in the next exercise.

10. **When the shape of the connecting segment between the two points matches the shape of the tire, release the mouse button.**

When you click and drag with the Pen tool, you create a smooth point with symmetrical direction handles. As you drag, you can see the handles extend equal distances from both sides of the point you just created. The length and angle of the direction handles control the shape of segments that connect two anchor points.

As long as you hold down the mouse button, you can drag to change the length and angle of the point's handles, which also changes the shape of the connecting segment.

11. **Move the cursor to the right, following the bottom edge of the rear tire. Click and drag to create another anchor point with symmetrical direction handles. When the connecting segment matches the shape of the tire, release the mouse button.**

When you click-drag to create a smooth point, the point is automatically symmetrical. In other words, the handles on each side of the point are the same length.

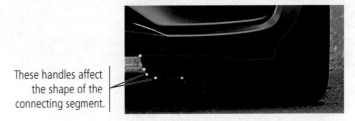

These handles affect the shape of the connecting segment.

12. **Click without dragging where the rear tire meets the front tire.**

Click without dragging to create a corner point.

13. **Continue adding symmetrical smooth points to the path, placing the final point where the front tire meets the body of the car.**

Add a point where the tire meets the body.

14. Click and drag to place another smooth point inside the area of the bumper.

You are intentionally overlapping the new path with the existing one. Later, you will combine the multiple separate shapes into a single path.

15. Move the cursor over the original starting point. When you see a hollow circle in the cursor icon, click to close the path.

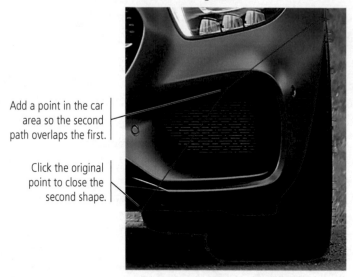

Add a point in the car area so the second path overlaps the first.

Click the original point to close the second shape.

16. Repeat the process from this exercise to add a path around the left wheels.

Remember, clicking without dragging creates a corner point, which does not have direction handles.

The Car Outline path is still selected.

17. Change your view percentage so you can see the entire car in the document window.

18. With the Car Outline path selected in the Paths panel, make sure the Pen tool is still active.

19. **Open the Path Operations menu in the Options bar and choose Merge Shape Components.**

The three original paths are combined into a single shape. Photoshop adds anchor points where necessary and removes overlapping segments from the original paths.

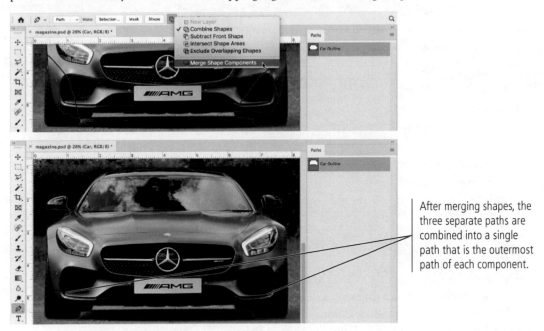

After merging shapes, the three separate paths are combined into a single path that is the outermost path of each component.

20. **Save the file and continue to the next exercise.**

Edit Vector Paths

You probably noticed that the path you created in the previous exercises is not a perfect outline of the car. The Freeform Pen tool can be a very good starting point for creating odd-shaped paths, but you will almost always need to edit and fine-tune the results to accurately reflect the path you want. Fortunately, Photoshop offers a number of options for editing vector paths.

You can use the **Path Selection tool** (▶.) to select an entire path or the **Direct Selection tool** (▷.) to select a specific anchor point or segment.

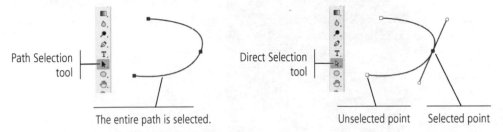

Path Selection tool

The entire path is selected.

Direct Selection tool

Unselected point   Selected point

The **Add Anchor Point tool** (✐.) adds a new anchor point to an existing path. Photoshop automatically creates handles for the new point and adjusts handles for existing points to maintain the existing path shape.

You can use the **Delete Anchor Point tool** (✐.) to remove an existing point from a path. Photoshop removes the selected point and adjusts the handles of remaining points to try to maintain the original path shape.

Clicking a smooth point with the **Convert Point tool** (⌃.) converts that point to a corner point by removing its handles (below left). Clicking and dragging from a corner point with this tool converts it to a smooth, symmetrical point (below right).

You can add a handle to only one side of a corner point by Option/Alt-clicking a point with the Convert Point tool and dragging (below left). You can also click a handle with the Convert Point tool and drag to move only one handle of the point, resulting in a corner point with asymmetrical handles (below right).

Note:

When the Pen tool is active, placing the cursor over an existing selected path automatically shows the Add Anchor Point tool cursor.

Note:

When the Pen tool is active, placing the cursor over an existing point on a selected path automatically shows the Delete Anchor Point tool cursor.

Note:

When the Pen tool is active, you can press Option/Alt to temporarily access the Convert Point tool cursor.

1. **With magazine.psd open, set your view percentage to at least 100%.**

2. **Drag around the image to review the Car Outline path.**

   Although your results might differ from our screen captures, the path almost certainly does not accurately outline the car. You must use what you learned in the introduction to this exercise to edit the path to exactly match the car's shape.

The Magnetic Freeform Pen tool path excluded some areas that must be inside the path.

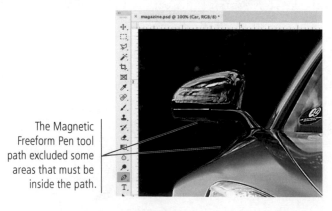

3. Use the following information to fine-tune your Car Outline path.

In this instance, we can't give you specific instructions because everyone's path will be a bit different. Keep the following points in mind as you refine your shape:

- Use the Direct Selection tool to select and edit specific segments or points on the path. You can move points to a new position by dragging (or using the Arrow keys) or moving their handles to change segment shapes.
- Use the Add Anchor Point tool to add a point to the path.
- Use the Delete Anchor Point tool to remove a point from the path.
- Use the Convert Point tool to change a corner point to a smooth point and vice versa.

4. Save the file and continue to the next exercise.

Drawing with the Curvature Pen Tool

The Curvature Pen tool, nested under the regular Pen tool, can be used to create and edit complex paths, without manually manipulating anchor points.

Using the Curvature Pen tool, begin by clicking to place points in a new path. As you drag after creating the first two points, the software shows a rubber-band preview of the path that will be created by clicking again.

If you don't see the rubber-band behavior, open the Set Additional Pen and Path Options menu in the Options bar and make sure Rubber Band is checked.

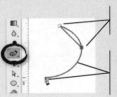

Click to place the first two points.

Rubber-band behavior previews the curve that would be created by clicking again.

Make sure Rubber Band is checked.

As long as the Curvature Pen tool is active, you do not need to change tools to edit the path:

- Option/Alt-click to create a corner point.
- Click anywhere along an existing path to add a new anchor point.
- Double-click any point to toggle it between a smooth and corner point.
- Click a point to select it.
- Drag a selected point to move it.
- Press Delete to remove the selected point. The existing curve is maintained.
- Press the Esc key to stop drawing the current shape.

Create a Vector-Based Layer Mask

Now that your car outline shape is nearly complete, you are going to use the path to create a vector-based layer mask, which will remove the car from the surrounding background. The edges of a vector mask are defined by a vector path, which means they cannot have degrees of transparency. To edit the mask edge, you have to edit the vector path.

1. **With magazine.psd open, set your view percentage so you can see the entire car in the document window.**

2. **Select the Car Outline path in the Paths panel and select the Car layer in the Layers panel.**

3. **Choose Layer>Vector Mask>Current Path.**

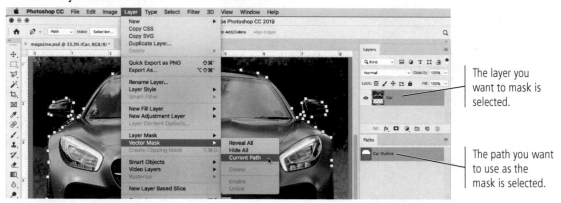

The layer you want to mask is selected.

The path you want to use as the mask is selected.

As you can see, a new path is added to the Paths panel. The name, "Car Vector Mask" identifies this path as a vector mask for the layer named, "Car." This temporary path only appears in the panel when the masked layer is selected.

Nothing is added to the Channels panel because channels are raster-based; they do not store vector-based path information.

The mask thumbnail is added to the masked layer.

The mask path is visible in the Paths panel when the masked layer is selected.

No alpha channel is added to the file.

4. **Click the empty area at the bottom of the Layers panel to deselect the layer.**

When the masked layer is not selected, the mask path does not appear in the Paths panel. This is an important distinction — if you want to edit the mask path, you have to make sure the correct path is selected first. Editing the original Car Outline path will have no effect on the mask path.

When the masked layer is not selected, the mask path does not appear in the Paths panel.

5. **Save the file and continue to the next exercise.**

Create a Vector Shape Layer

A shape layer is a special type of Photoshop layer that retains vector path information. The vector shape functions as a mask, revealing the defined fill color for the shape. Any vector paths can have defined stroke properties (color, width, and type/style), and can be edited using the same tools that you used to edit the paths in the previous exercises.

In this exercise, you will build a compound vector shape that will provide a background for the magazine's "In This Issue" text.

1. **With magazine.psd open, hide the Car layer.**

2. **In the Tools panel, choose the Rounded Rectangle tool (nested under the Rectangle tool).**

Note:

If a tool is missing from its default spot in the Tools panel, check in the Edit Toolbar menu ⬛ *at the bottom of the Tools panel. You can also reset the Essentials workspace to show all tools in their default locations.*

3. **In the Options bar, choose Shape in the Tool Mode menu.**

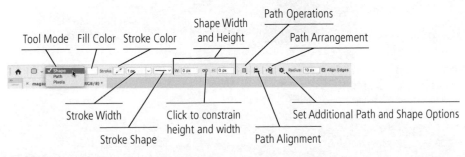

4. **Click the Fill color swatch to open the pop-up Swatches panel. Click the CMYK Blue swatch to select it as the fill color.**

You can define separate fill and stroke colors of a vector shape layer, just as you might do for an object you create in Adobe Illustrator or InDesign. Clicking the Fill or Stroke color swatch opens a pop-up panel, where you can select a specific swatch to use as the attribute's color. Four buttons at the top of the panel change the attribute to (from left): None, Solid, a Gradient, or a Pattern. You can also click the Color Picker button to define any color that is not already in the Swatches panel.

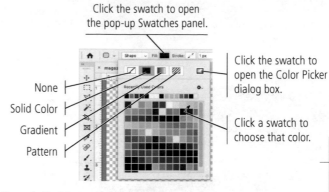

Click the swatch to open the pop-up Swatches panel.

None
Solid Color
Gradient
Pattern

Click the swatch to open the Color Picker dialog box.

Click a swatch to choose that color.

Note:

The color you are using here is temporary, because you will later apply a built-in graphic style to this shape.

5. **Click the Stroke swatch and choose No Color in the pop-up Swatches panel.**

6. **Change the Radius field to 50 px.**

A rounded-corner rectangle is simply a rectangle with the corners cut at a specific distance from the end (the corner radius). The two sides are connected with one-fourth of a circle, which has a radius equal to the amount of the rounding.

This imaginary circle has a 50-px radius.

7. **Click in the top-right area of the canvas, then drag down and right to create the new shape.**

When you release the mouse button, the shape you drew fills with the defined Fill color. Because you chose None as the Stroke color, the shape you drew has no applied stroke. The red color you see around the shape is the color you defined earlier as the path color when you drew the car path.

When you use the Shape option in the Tool Mode menu, the resulting vector shape exists by default on its own layer.

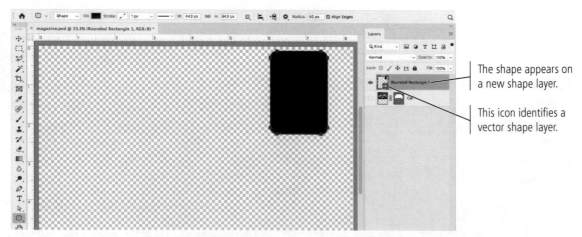

The shape appears on a new shape layer.

This icon identifies a vector shape layer.

8. **Click the empty space at the bottom of the Layers panel to deselect the Rounded Rectangle layer.**

When you deselect the layer, you can see the actual shape without the heavy red vector path. You can now see that the shape you created has no defined stroke color.

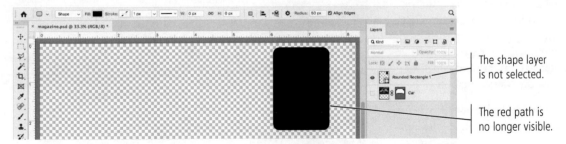

The shape layer is not selected.

The red path is no longer visible.

9. **Click the Rounded Rectangle 1 layer to select it again.**

When the shape layer is selected, you can again see the vector path that makes up the shape.

10. **Make sure the rulers are visible (View>Rulers), then review the information in the Properties panel.**

This panel automatically appears when you create a new shape with one of the vector shape tools. It shows the dimensions and position of the resulting shape, as well as other properties that were not available in the Options bar before you created the shape.

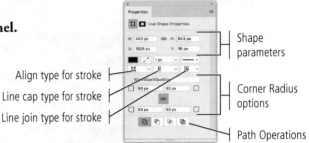

Shape parameters

Align type for stroke

Line cap type for stroke

Line join type for stroke

Corner Radius options

Path Operations

11. **Highlight the current W field and type 500. Press Tab to highlight the H field, then type 1230. Press Return/Enter to apply the change.**

The W and H fields define the object's physical dimensions.

The Properties panel defaults to use pixels for shape layers, regardless of the default units for the active file. You can, however, type values in other units of measurement, as long as you include the appropriate unit in the value you type (for example, "2 in" or "4 cm").

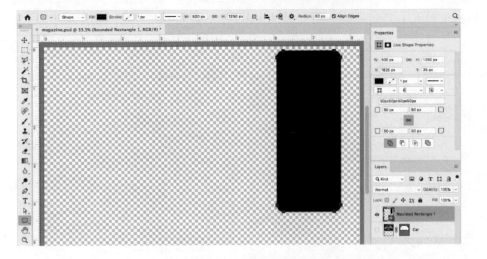

Note:

Because you are creating a vector shape, you can edit its properties at any time, without losing quality or pixel integrity (as would happen for pixel-based, raster data).

12. **Place the Mouse cursor over the X field until you see the scrubby slider cursor. Click and drag right or left until the X field shows 1865 px (the shape is approximately 3/8″ from the right edge of the canvas).**

The X and Y fields in the Properties panel define the object's position based on its top-left corner. Unlike transforming objects in the Options panel, you cannot select a different reference point around which to anchor the transformation.

Scrubby sliders, available in most Photoshop panels, offer a dynamic way to change field values. You can click the field name and drag left to decrease the value, or drag right to increase the value.

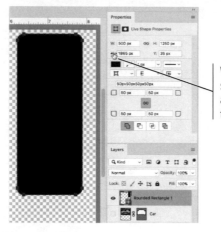

When you see this scrubby slider, click and drag to change the related field value.

13. **Using either the scrubby slider or the field, change the Y position to 0 px.**

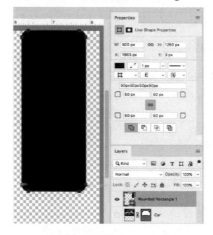

14. **Click the Rounded Rectangle tool in the Tools panel to deselect the existing vector shape and hide the path's anchor handles.**

Although the actual vector path is deselected, the shape layer is still selected in the Layers panel.

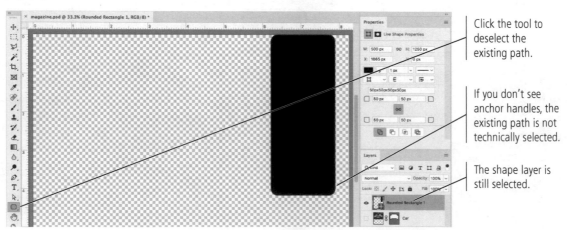

Click the tool to deselect the existing path.

If you don't see anchor handles, the existing path is not technically selected.

The shape layer is still selected.

15. **In the Options bar, open the Path Operations menu and choose Subtract Front Shape.**

    If no shape layer is currently selected, the Path Operations menu defaults to New Layer. As long as a shape layer is selected and one of the shape layer tools is active, the menu retains the last-used option. You can continue subtracting as many new shapes as you like until you switch to a different tool — the Direct Selection tool, for example, to modify a specific anchor point.

Note:

The Path Operations menu retains the last-used selection, as long as the same tool remains active. If you switch to a different tool, the path operation reverts back to the New Layer option.

16. **Click and drag to create another rectangle inside the area of the first.**

    Using the Subtract Front Shape option, the second shape removes the overlapping area of underlying shapes, creating a compound path that results in a "window" effect.

    Options for the basic Shape tools remember the last-used settings, so the new shape automatically has the 50-px corner radius that you defined for the first shape.

Note:

*A **compound path** is any single shape made up of more than one closed path.*

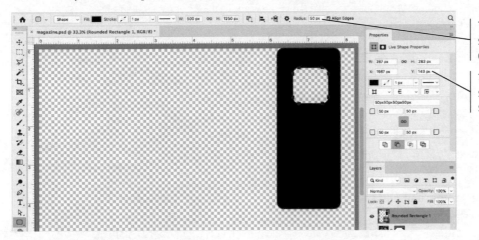

The Options panel shows options for the overall shape layer.

The Properties panel shows options for the selected vector path.

17. **In the Properties panel, change the new shape's parameters to:**

    W: 300 px   H: 300 px
    X: 1965 px   Y: 135 px

More about Vector Shape Options

Stroke Types

When a vector drawing tool is active, you can use the Stroke Type menu in the Options bar to choose a preset stroke style (solid, dashed, or dotted).

- The Align menu changes the stroke's alignment relative to the path. The icons in the menu suggest the result.
- The Caps menu determines how the stroke aligns to the ends of the path.
- The Corners menu defines the way the stroke appears at corners on the path.

If you click the More Options button, you can define a custom dash pattern.

Align
- Align stroke to inside of path
- Align stroke to center of path
- Align stroke to outside of path

Caps
- No end cap
- Rounded end cap
- Square end cap

Corners
- Miter join
- Rounded join
- Beveled join

Path Alignment

You can use the **Path Alignment** to align or distribute multiple shapes on the same layer. For these options to work properly, you must use the Path Selection tool to select the paths you want to align, and then choose an option from the menu. When Canvas is selected in the Align To menu, you can align one or more paths in relation to the overall canvas.

Geometry Options

Pen Tool

For the Pen tool, you can check the Rubber Band option in the Geometry Options menu to show a preview of the path curve as you move the cursor.

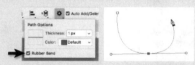

Rectangle, Rounded Rectangle, and Ellipse Tools

When **Unconstrained** is selected, you can simply click and drag to create a rectangle of any size.

If you choose the **Square** option (or Circle for the Ellipse tool), the shape you draw will be constrained to equal width and height (1:1 aspect ratio).

Rectangle/Rounded Rectangle tool

You can use the **Fixed Size** option to create a shape at a specific width and height. When you click in the canvas, you see a preview of the shape that will be created. You can drag around to determine where the shape will be placed when you release the mouse button.

Ellipse tool

You can also use the **Proportional** option to define the aspect ratio of the shape you will create. When you click and drag, the shape is constrained to the proportions you define.

If you choose the **From Center** option, the center of the shape you create will be placed where you first click.

Polygon Tool

Geometry options for this tool are the same as those that are available when you click the tool to define the shape you want to create (see Page 274).

Line Tool

When you draw with the Line tool, you can use the Geometry Options menu to add arrowheads to the start and/or end of the line. The Width and Length fields define those attributes of the arrowheads as a percentage of the line weight. The Concavity field defines the arrowheads' inset as a percentage of its length.

Custom Shape Tool

The Custom Shape tool makes it easy to create custom vector shapes from one of several defined libraries. You can open the Shape panel in the Options bar to access the built-in libraries of shapes.

Geometry options for the Custom Shape tool are the same as those for the Rectangle and Ellipse tools.

Understanding Vector Path Operations

New Layer

When you first choose one of the vector drawing tools — Pen, Freeform Pen, or one of the Shape tools — the Path Operations menu defaults to **New Layer**. When this option is active, every new path will be created on a separate layer.

Combining Shapes

Combine Shapes creates the new path on the existing (selected) shape layer.

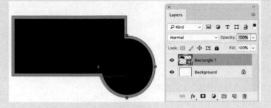

Subtract Front Shape creates the new path on the existing (selected) layer and removes overlapping areas of the new shape from the existing shape.

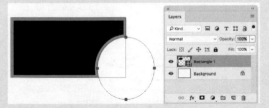

Intersect Shape Areas results in the shape of only overlapping areas in the existing and new shapes.

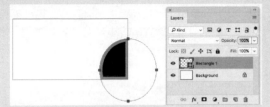

Exclude Overlapping Areas removes overlapping areas between the existing and new shapes.

Merge Shape Components

It is important to note that with the four Combine options explained to the left, the result is the appearance of a single shape, but the original paths of each shape are maintained. You can still manipulate each component path independently.

To make the interaction of overlapping shapes permanent, you can select the paths you want to affect and choose **Merge Shape Components**. This results in a single shape that is the combination of any selected paths; unselected paths are not affected.

The actual result of this command depends on the interaction of the selected paths. In the example below, the top shape has been created with the Intersect Shape Areas operation. After applying the Merge Shape Components operation, anchor points were removed where the original paths did not intersect (as shown in the bottom image).

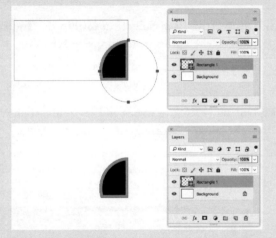

Merging Shape Layers

If multiple shape layers are selected in the Layers panel, you can combine them by choosing Merge Shapes in the Layers panel Options menu.

This command combines the shapes on all selected layers into a single shape layer — basically the same as using the Combine
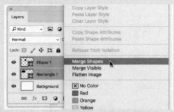
Shapes path operation. The new combined layer adopts the name of the highest layer in the previous selection.

Important note: Don't confuse this Merge option with the Merge Shape Components option in the Path Operations menu. The Merge Shapes option in the Layers panel actually combines the various shapes into a single layer, but maintains all of the existing paths.

18. **In the lower half of the Properties panel, makes sure the four corner radius fields are linked.**

When the link icon is highlighted (active), changing any one radius value affects the other three corners.

19. **Type 10 in the top-left field, then press Return/Enter to apply your changes.**

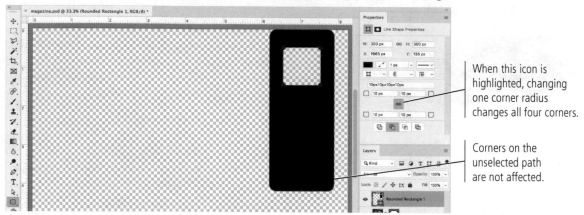

When this icon is highlighted, changing one corner radius changes all four corners.

Corners on the unselected path are not affected.

20. **Choose the Path Selection tool in the Tools panel, then click the outer path of the compound shape to select it.**

Each component path of the overall shape is still an independent vector path, which means you can select and edit its properties in the Properties panel at any time.

21. **Unlink the four corner radius fields, then change the top-left and top-right corner radius fields to field to 0 px.**

Although rounded-corner shapes always start with four identical corners, you can use this panel to change each corner radius individually.

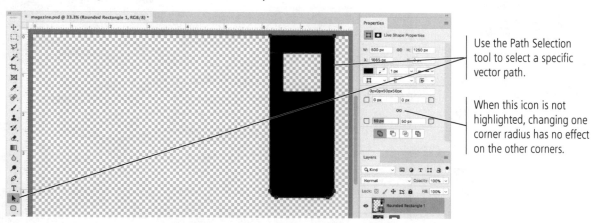

Use the Path Selection tool to select a specific vector path.

When this icon is not highlighted, changing one corner radius has no effect on the other corners.

22. **Save the file and continue to the next exercise.**

Selecting and Modifying Paths

When you draw vector paths, you can use the Path Selection tool to select and move specific paths on a layer.

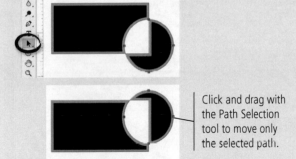

Click and drag with the Path Selection tool to move only the selected path.

You can also select a specific shape to change the path operation that applies to it (in either the Options or Properties panel). In the example below, the rectangle was created first, and then the oval was created with the Combine Shapes path operation. We then used the Path Selection tool to select the oval, and chose the Intersect Front Shape operation. Unless you merge the paths into a single shape, you can always select an individual path and change the way it interacts with underlying shapes.

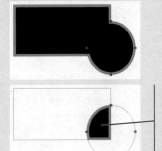

Changing the path operation of the selected path changes the way it interacts with the bottom path.

Because the path operations affect underlying shapes, you should also understand the concept of **stacking order**. When you create multiple shapes on the same shape layer, they exist from bottom-to-top in the order in which you create them — the first shape is on the bottom, and then the next shape is above, and so on, until the last shape created is at the top of the stack. You can use the **Path Arrangement** menu to control the stacking order of selected paths on the same shape layer.

• Bring Shape To Front
• Bring Shape Forward
• Send Shape Backward
• Send Shape To Back

Clone and Align Layers

If you need more than one version of the same layer, you can create a copy by choosing Duplicate Layer in the layer's contextual menu. This command results in a copy of the original layer in exactly the same position as the original.

You can also use the Move tool to **clone** a layer, which results in a duplicate copy of the original, in the position where you drag to make the clone. In this exercise, you will use cloning to create three rectangle shape layers across the bottom of the canvas. You will then distribute those shape layers evenly across the canvas.

Note:

These shapes will be used to hold additional inset photos to enhance the visual interest of the overall composition.

1. **With magazine.psd open, click the empty area at the bottom of the layers panel to deselect the existing shape layer.**

   If you don't first deselect the shape layer, your stroke color changes in the next few steps would affect the existing shape.

2. **Choose the Rectangle tool (nested under the Rounded Rectangle tool if you continued directly from the previous exercise). In the Options bar, define the following settings:**

Fill Color:	White
Stroke Color:	Dark Red
Stroke Width:	15 px

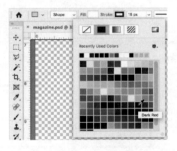

3. **Open the Path Operations menu and review the options.**

   The Path Operations menu defaults to the New Layer option if an existing shape layer is not selected.

4. **Open the Set Additional Shape and Path Options menu. Define a 1 px thickness and use the Default color.**

   Because you are creating a shape with an actual red stroke, the red path you defined earlier is not a good choice. In this case, the thinner Default (blue) option will be far less distracting.

5. **Click and drag to create a rectangle in the lower half of the canvas. Using the Properties panel, define the new shape's parameters as:**

   W: 600 px   H: 500 px

   X: 200 px   Y: 2430 px

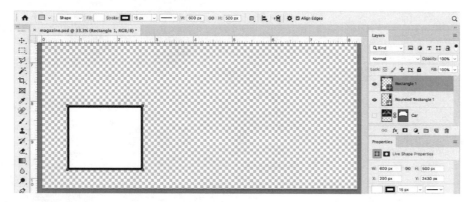

6. **Choose the Move tool in the Tools panel. Press Option/Alt, then click inside the smaller rectangle shape and drag right to clone it.**

   Pressing Option/Alt while dragging a selection clones that selection. Because the shape layer is the active selection, the entire shape layer is cloned. The Smart Guides help you maintain the cloned layer's horizontal alignment to the original. If you decide to hide Smart Guides, pressing Shift constrains the movement to 45° angles.

   The new cloned layer appears immediately above the original in the Layers panel, with the name, "Rectangle 1 Copy."

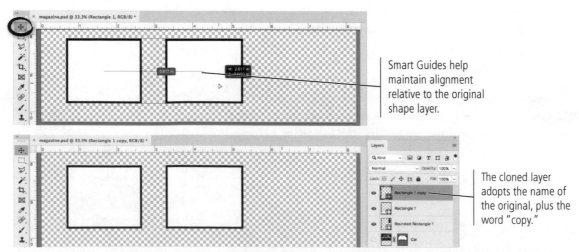

Smart Guides help maintain alignment relative to the original shape layer.

The cloned layer adopts the name of the original, plus the word "copy."

7. **Double-click the name of the Rectangle 1 layer to highlight it. Type** `Left Inset`**, then press Return/Enter to change the layer name.**

   Even though you will have only three copies of this shape layer, it could become very confusing later if you don't use meaningful names to differentiate the layers.

8. **Double-click the name of the cloned layer to highlight it. Type** `Center Inset`**, then press Return/Enter to change the layer name.**

9. **Repeat Step 6 to create a third shape layer at the bottom of the canvas. Name this new layer** `Right Inset`**.**

10. **In the Properties panel, change the X position of the active shape to** `1700 px`**.**

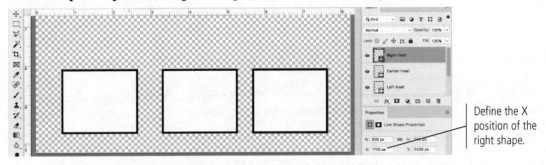

Define the X position of the right shape.

11. **In the Layers panel, Shift-click to select all three Inset shape layers.**

   When multiple layers are selected in the Layers panel, a number of alignment options become available in the Options bar. These are very useful for aligning or distributing the content of multiple layers relative to one another.

12. **With the Move tool active, click the Distribute Horizontal Centers button in the Options bar.**

   When the Move tool is active and multiple layers are selected, you can use the Options bar to align the contents of the selected layers relative to one another. The Distribute Horizontal Centers option places an equal amount of space between the center pixel of each selected layer; the positions of layers containing the outermost pixels in the selection are not affected.

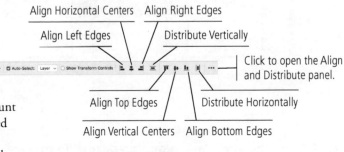

Align Horizontal Centers   Align Right Edges
Align Left Edges   Distribute Vertically
Click to open the Align and Distribute panel.
Align Top Edges   Distribute Horizontally
Align Vertical Centers   Align Bottom Edges

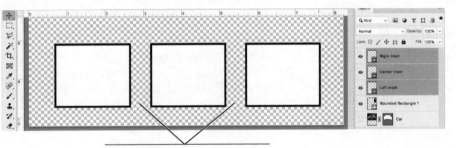

Distribute Horizontal Centers creates equal space between selected layers.

Note:

You can click the Align and Distribute button to access options for distributing based on specific edges or centers.

13. **Save the file and continue to the next exercise.**

Auto-Select Layers

When your files have more than a few layers — a common occurrence — selecting exactly the layer you want can be difficult. As you already learned, the Move tool defaults to affect the layer that is selected in the Layers panel. Using the Auto-Select option, you can automatically select a specific layer by clicking pixels in the document window, rather than manually selecting a layer in the panel first.

1. **With magazine.psd open, choose File>Place Embedded.**

2. **Navigate to inset1.jpg (in your WIP>Cars folder) and click place. When the image appears on the canvas, press Return/Enter to finalize the placement.**

   New Smart Object layers appear immediately above the previously selected layer. In this case, it is at the top of the layer stack.

3. **In the Layers panel, drag inset1 to appear immediately above the Left Inset layer.**

4. **Repeat Steps 1–3 to place inset2.jpg as an embedded file, and position the inset2 layer immediately above the Center Inset layer.**

   Unfortunately, you can only select one file at a time in the Place dialog box.

5. **Repeat Steps 1–3 to place inset3.jpg as an embedded file, and position the inset3 layer immediately above the Right Inset layer.**

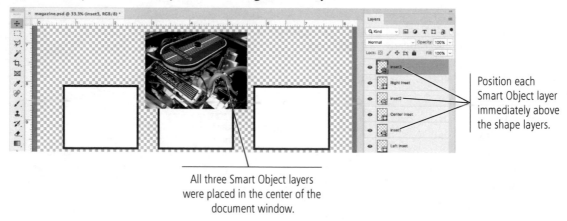

Position each Smart Object layer immediately above the shape layers.

All three Smart Object layers were placed in the center of the document window.

6. **Choose the Move tool in the Tools panel. In the Options bar, check the Auto-Select option.**

7. **Click in the area of the placed images and drag until the inset3 image entirely obscures the bottom-right rectangle shape.**

When Auto-Select is active, clicking in the canvas automatically selects the layer containing the pixel where you clicked. Because the inset3 image is on top of the other two, clicking in the area of the placed images automatically selects the inset3 layer.

Check the Auto-Select option.

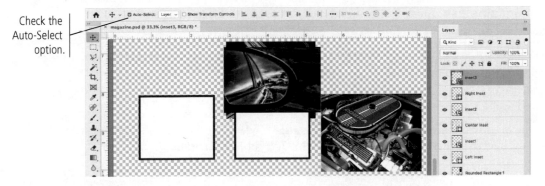

8. **Click again in the original area of the placed images, and drag to move the inset2 image until it entirely obscures the center rectangle.**

Again, clicking automatically selects the relevant layer. Using the Auto-Select option makes it easier to manage layer contents, even when you are not sure which layer contains the pixels you want to affect.

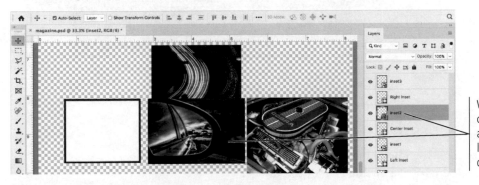

When Auto-Select is checked, clicking automatically selects the layer containing the pixel on which you clicked.

9. **Move the inset1 image until it entirely obscures the left rectangle.**

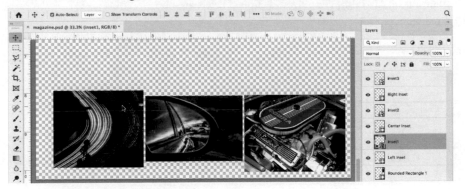

Note:

Remember, if the Auto-Select option is checked in the Options bar, you can simply click pixels of the layer you want to move without first selecting the layer.

10. **Save the file and continue to the next exercise.**

Create Clipping Masks

As you can see, the placed images completely hide the underlying layer content. To make the inset images appear only within the area of the underlying shapes, you need to create clipping masks. This task is relatively easy to accomplish.

1. **With magazine.psd open, Control/right-click the inset1 layer to open the layer's contextual menu.**

   Remember, to access the contextual menu for a specific layer, you have to Control/right-click in the area to the right of the layer name.

2. **Choose Create Clipping Mask from the contextual menu.**

   A clipping mask is another way to show only certain areas of a layer; in this case, using the shape of one layer (Left Inset) to show parts of the layer above it (inset1).

   The Layers panel shows that the inset1 layer is clipped by the Left Inset layer.

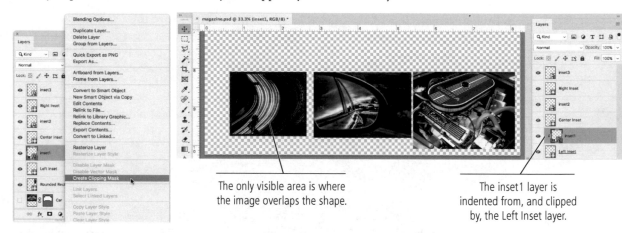

The only visible area is where the image overlaps the shape.

The inset1 layer is indented from, and clipped by, the Left Inset layer.

3. **With the Move tool active, click in the area of the left inset image and drag until you are satisfied with the visible area of the image.**

   Even though a layer is clipped, you can still move it without affecting the position of the clipping layer. Unlike a layer mask, the clipping and clipped layers are not automatically linked.

Use the Move tool to reposition the clipped image.

The clipping layer still defines the visible area of the clipped image.

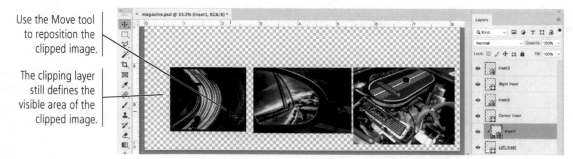

As with layer masks, clipping masks do not permanently modify the pixels in the layer. You can choose Release Clipping Mask in the clipped layer's contextual menu to undo a clipping mask, without altering the affected layers.

4. **Repeat Steps 1–3 to clip the inset2 and inset3 images to their underlying layers.**

5. **In the Layers panel, show the Car layer, and then move it to the top of the layer stack.**

6. **Using the Move tool, position the car so it slightly overlaps the three shape layers at the bottom of the page.**

   Use the following image as a guide.

Move the Car layer to the top of the stack.

Move the car to slightly overlap the three shape layers.

7. **Save the file, and then continue to the next stage of the project.**

STAGE 3 / Applying Styles and Filters

Photoshop includes a large number of options for creating artistic effects, including built-in patterns, styles, and filters. You can add texture to the flat fill color of a vector shape layer or apply effects, such as drop shadows or beveling, to add the appearance of depth. You can make images look like pencil sketches, paintings, or any of the dozens of other options. You can even compound these filters and styles to create unique effects that would require extreme skill in traditional art techniques, such as oil painting. In this stage of the project, you will use a number of these options to enhance your overall composition.

Add Texture to a Shape Layer

Aside from their usefulness as scalable vector paths, shape layers can be filled with solid colors (as the background shape is now), with other images (as the smaller inset shapes are now), or with styles or patterns (which you will add in this exercise).

1. **With magazine.psd open, choose Window>Styles to open the Styles panel.**

   This panel shows the predefined styles that can be applied to a shape layer. The icons give you an idea of what the styles do, but these small squares can be cryptic.

2. **Click the button in the top-right corner of the Styles panel and choose Large List from the Options menu.**

   We prefer the list view because the style names provide a better idea of what the styles do. The Large List option displays a bigger style thumbnail than the Small List view.

By default, styles appear in Small Thumbnail view.

Click here to open the panel Options menu.

3. **Open the Styles panel Options menu again and choose Web Styles near the bottom of the list.**

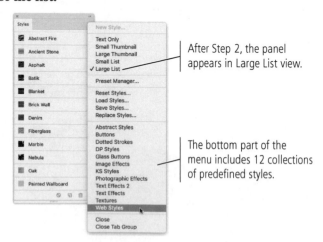

After Step 2, the panel appears in Large List view.

The bottom part of the menu includes 12 collections of predefined styles.

Note:

In the default set, a word in parentheses next to a style name identifies the collection in which that style exists.

4. Click OK to replace the current set with the Web Styles set.

When you call a new set of styles, Photoshop asks if you want to replace the current set or append the new set to the existing set(s).

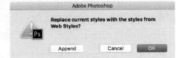

If you select Append, the new styles will be added to the existing ones. This can result in a very long list, which makes it difficult to find what you want. By replacing the current set, you will only see the styles in the texture set. This does not delete the previous styles, it only removes them from the panel. You can recall the previous styles by choosing Reset Styles in the panel Options menu.

Note:

Some users report seeing a message asking if they want to save changes to the current styles before replacing them, even if they did not make changes to the default set. This is a minor bug in the software. If you see this message, click Don't Save.

5. Select the Rounded Rectangle 1 shape layer in the Layers panel, then click the Black Anodized Metal style in the Styles panel to apply the style to the shape layer.

The layers panel shows that a series of effects (those which make up the style) has been applied to the layer.

Photoshop styles are nondestructive, which means you can change or delete them without affecting the original layer content. You can temporarily disable all effects by clicking the eye icon to the left of the word, "Effects" or disable individual effects by clicking the icon for a specific item in the panel.

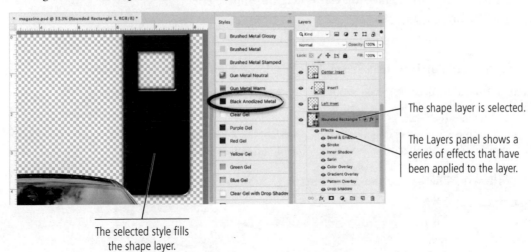

The selected style fills the shape layer.

The shape layer is selected.

The Layers panel shows a series of effects that have been applied to the layer.

6. In the Layers panel, click the arrow to the right of the fx icon of the Rounded Rectangle 1 layer.

This collapses the list of applied effects, which helps keep the Layers panel easier to manage.

Click here to collapse or expand the list of applied effects.

7. Save the file and continue to the next exercise.

Apply Custom Layer Effects

A style is simply a saved group of effects that can be applied with a single click. You can also create your own styles using the Layer Effects dialog box, which you will do in this exercise.

1. **With magazine.psd open, choose the Left Inset layer.**

2. **Choose Layer>Layer Style>Drop Shadow.**

3. **In the resulting dialog box, make sure the Preview option is checked.**

    The Preview option allows you to see the results of your settings while the dialog box is still open.

4. **In the Layer Style dialog box, make sure the Use Global Light option is checked.**

    This option is checked by default, so you should not have to make any change.

    The Angle field defines the position of the effect in relation to the layer. When the Global Light option is checked, changing the style Angle applies the same change to any other layer for which an effect using the Use Global Light option is applied.

5. **Make the following changes to the default settings in the dialog box:**

Opacity:	**50%**
Distance:	**10 px**
Spread:	**5%**
Size:	**10 px**

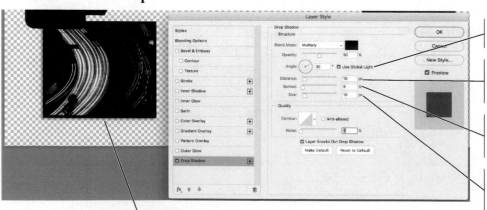

Make sure Use Global Light is checked.

Distance offsets the effect relative to the layer content.

Spread is the percentage the effect expands beyond the layer content.

Size controls the amount of blurring applied to the effect.

When Preview is checked, the effect is visible behind the dialog box.

6. **Click the + button to the right of the Drop Shadow layer style.**

You can apply more than one instance of certain layer styles (those identified with a "+"). When you click the + button, a new instance of the style appears in the list.

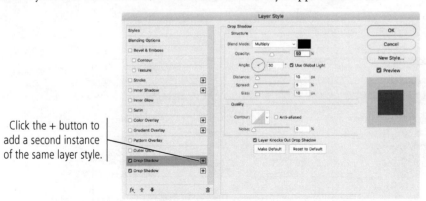

Click the + button to add a second instance of the same layer style.

Note:

You can use the buttons at the bottom of the effects list to change the order of applied effects, as well as delete a specific (selected) effect.

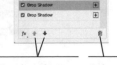

Use these buttons to reorder applied effects. Delete Effect

7. **With the top Drop Shadow item selected in the list, click the color swatch to the right of the Blend Mode menu.**

8. **When the Color Picker appears, move the mouse cursor over the dark blue color on the car's windshield and click to sample that color. Click OK to close the Color Picker dialog box.**

Click the swatch to open the Color Picker for the style.

Click to sample a color that you want to use for the style.

9. **Uncheck the Use Global Light option, then change the Angle field to -150°.**

If you change the angle field while the Use Global Light option is checked, you would change the global angle and that change would apply to any other applied layer style that uses the global light angle. You want to change the angle for only this style instance, so you must uncheck Use Global Light *before* changing the angle field.

10. **Make the following changes to the settings in the dialog box:**

Opacity:	75%
Distance:	20 px
Spread:	10%
Size:	20 px

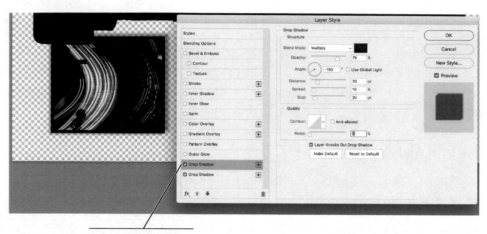

Changes affect only the
selected style instance.

11. **Click OK to apply the layer style.**

In the Layers panel, the drop shadow styles appear as effects for the Left Inset layer. As with the built-in style you applied in the previous exercise, custom layer styles are nondestructive.

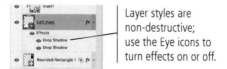

Layer styles are
non-destructive;
use the Eye icons to
turn effects on or off.

12. **Press Option/Alt, then click the word "Effects" in the Layers panel and drag it to the Center Inset layer.**

Just as you cloned a layer in an earlier exercise, pressing Option/Alt allows you to clone effects from one layer to another. This offers an easy way to apply exactly the same effects to multiple layers in your file.

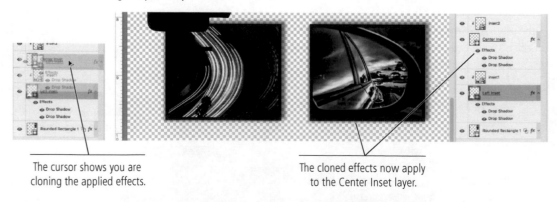

The cursor shows you are
cloning the applied effects.

The cloned effects now apply
to the Center Inset layer.

13. **Repeat Step 12 to add the Drop Shadow effects to the Right Inset layer.**

Bevel and Emboss

This style has five variations:

- **Outer Bevel** creates a bevel on the outside edges of the layer contents.
- **Inner Bevel** creates a bevel on the inside edges.
- **Emboss** creates the effect of embossing the layer contents against the underlying layers.
- **Pillow Emboss** creates the effect of stamping the edges of the layer into the underlying layers.
- **Stroke Emboss** applies an embossed effect to a stroke applied to the layer. (The Stroke Emboss effect is not available if you haven't applied a stroke to the layer.)

Any of these styles can be applied as **Smooth** (blurs the edges of the effect), **Chisel Hard** (creates a distinct edge), or **Chisel Soft** (creates a distinct but slightly blurred edge).

You can change the **Direction** of the bevel effect. **Up** creates the appearance of the layer coming out of the image; **Down** creates the appearance of something stamped into the image.

The **Size** slider makes the effect smaller or larger, and the **Soften** slider blurs the edges of the effect.

In the Shading area, you can control the light source **Angle** and **Altitude** (think of how shadows differ as the sun moves). You can also apply a **Gloss Contour** (see the following explanation of Contours). Finally, you can change the Blending Mode, Opacity, and Color settings of highlights and shadows created in effects.

When a Bevel and Emboss style is applied, you can also apply Contour and Texture effects.

Stroke

The **Stroke** style adds an outline of a specific number of pixels to the layer. The Stroke effect can be added at the outside or inside of the layer edge, or it can be centered over the edge (half the stroke will be inside and half outside the actual layer edge). You can adjust the Blending Mode and Opacity setting of the stroke, and you can also define a specific color, gradient, or pattern to apply as the stroke.

Satin

The Satin options apply interior shading to create a satiny appearance. You can change the Blending Mode, Color, and Opacity settings of the effect, as well as the Angle, Distance, and Size settings.

Drop Shadow and Inner Shadow

Drop Shadow adds a shadow behind the layer. **Inner Shadow** adds a shadow inside the edges of the layer's content. For both types, you can define the blending mode, color, opacity, angle, distance, and size of the shadow.

- **Distance** is the offset of the shadow, or how far away the shadow will be from the original layer.
- **Spread** (for Drop Shadows) is the percentage the shadow expands beyond the original layer.
- **Choke** (for Inner Shadows) is the percentage the shadow shrinks into the original layer.
- **Size** is the blur amount applied to the shadow.

You can also adjust the Contour, Anti-aliasing, and Noise settings in the shadow effect. (See the Contours section later in this discussion for further explanation.)

When checked, the Layer Knocks Out Drop Shadow option removes the drop shadow underneath the original layer area. This is particularly important if you convert a shadow style to a separate layer that you move to a different position, or if the layer is semi-transparent above its shadow.

Global Light. The Use Global Light check box is available for Drop Shadow, Inner Shadow, and Bevel and Emboss styles. When this option is checked, the style is linked to the "master" light source angle for the entire file. Changing the global light affects any linked style applied to any layer in the entire file. You can change the Global Light setting in any of the Layer Style fields, or by choosing Layer>Layer Style>Global Light.

Outer Glow and Inner Glow

Outer Glow and **Inner Glow** styles add glow effects to the outside and inside (respectively) edges of the layer. For either, you can define the Blending Mode, Opacity, and Noise values, as well as whether to use a solid color or a gradient.

- For either kind of glow, you can define the **Technique** as Precise or Softer. **Precise** creates a glow at a specific distance. **Softer** creates a blurred glow and does not preserve detail as well as Precise.
- For Inner Glows, you can also define the **Source** of the glow (Center or Edge). **Center** applies a glow starting from the center of the layer. **Edge** applies the glow starting from the inside edges of the layer.
- The **Spread** and **Choke** sliders affect the percentages of the glow effects.
- The **Size** slider makes the effect smaller or larger.

Contours

Contour options control the shape of the applied styles. Drop Shadow, Inner Shadow, Inner Glow, Outer Glow, Bevel and Emboss, and Satin styles all include Contour options. The default option for all but the Satin style is Linear, which applies a linear effect from solid to 100% transparent.

The easiest way to understand the Contour options is through examples. In the following series of images, the same Inner Bevel style was applied in all three examples. In the top image, you can clearly see the size and depth of the bevel. In the center and bottom images, the only difference is the applied contour. If you look carefully at the shape edge, you should be able to see how the applied contour shape maps to the beveled edge in the image.

The Linear contour is applied to the bevel.

The Gaussian contour is applied to the same bevel.

The Cone contour is applied to the same bevel.

When you apply a contour, the **Range** slider controls which part of the effect is contoured. For Outer Glow or Inner Glow, you can add variation to the contour color and opacity using the **Jitter** slider.

Textures

The Textures options allow you to create texture effects using the built-in patterns.

- The **Scale** slider varies the size of the applied pattern.
- The **Depth** slider varies the apparent depth of the applied pattern.
- The **Invert** option (as the name implies) inverts the applied pattern.
- If you check the **Link with Layer** option, the pattern's position is locked to the layer so you can move the two together. If this option is unchecked, different parts of the pattern are visible if you move the associated layer.
- When you create a texture, you can drag in the image window (behind the Layer Style dialog box) to move the texture. When the Link with Layer option is checked, clicking the **Snap to Origin** button positions the pattern origin at the upper-left corner of the layer. If Link with Layers is unchecked, clicking the Snap to Origin button positions the pattern at the image origin point.

Color Overlay, Gradient Overlay, Pattern Overlay

A **color overlay** is simply a solid color with a specific Blending Mode and Opacity value applied. A color overlay can be used to change an entire layer to a solid color (with the Normal blending mode at 100% opacity), or to create unique effects using different Blending Mode and Opacity settings.

A **gradient overlay** is basically the same as a color overlay, except you use a gradient instead of a solid color. You can choose an existing gradient or define a new one, change the Blending Mode and Opacity value of the gradient, apply any of the available gradient styles (Linear, Radial, etc.), or change the Angle and Scale values of the gradient.

A **pattern overlay** is similar to the Texture options for a Bevel and Emboss style. You can choose a specific pattern, change the Blending Mode and Opacity value, or change the applied pattern scale. You can also link the pattern to the layer and snap the pattern to the layer or the file origin.

14. Press Option/Alt, then click the second (bottom) instance of the Drop Shadow and drag it to the Car layer.

If you remember, you edited the top instance to use blue as the shadow color. The bottom instance — the one you are cloning here — applies a black shadow at a 30° angle (the global angle).

You can clone an entire set of effects by Option/Alt-dragging the word "Effects," or clone only specific effects by Option/Alt-dragging an individual item in the list.

The cursor shows you are cloning only one drop shadow effect.

The single cloned effect now applies to the Car layer.

15. In the Layers panel, double-click the Drop Shadow effect for the Car layer.

Double-clicking an effect in the panel opens the dialog box, where you can make changes to the settings that define the effect for the active layer.

16. Click in the document window (behind the dialog box) and drag down until the drop shadow is much more prominent behind the car layer.

When you drag in the document window, the dialog box dynamically changes to reflect the new angle and distance for the effect.

As you dynamically change the angle, you should also notice the effect on the three Inset layers. Because the Use Global Light option is checked for all four layers, changing the angle for one of these layers applies the same change to all four layers.

You should also notice, however, that the altered Distance value does not apply to the other three layers in which the Drop Shadow effect is applied. Only the Angle of the effects is synchronized between the various layers.

Changing the angle for one effect changes the angle for all that use the Global Light option.

Click and drag in the document window to dynamically change the effect settings.

17. **Change the size field to 50 px, then click OK to apply the changed settings.**

18. **In the Layers panel, click the arrow buttons to the right of each fx icon to collapse the effects for all layers.**

Note:

If you double-click the word "Effects" in the Layers panel, the dialog box opens to the Blending Options: Default screen. Double-clicking a specific effect opens the dialog box directly to the settings for the effect on which you clicked.

19. **Save the file and continue to the next exercise.**

 ## Use the Filter Gallery

You can apply filters to specific selections, individual layers, or even individual channels depending on what you need to accomplish. If you combine filters with Smart Objects, you can apply nondestructive filters, and then change the settings or turn off the filters to experiment with different results.

In addition to the options in the Filter Gallery, a wide range of other filters can be accessed in the various Filter submenus. We encourage you to explore the various settings. Any filter that includes an ellipsis (...) in the menu command opens a secondary dialog box, where you can control the filter's specific settings.

Keep the following points in mind when you use filters:

Note:

Photoshop ships with more than 100 filters divided into 13 categories; some of these are functional while others are purely decorative.

• Filters can be applied to the entire selected layer or to an active selection.

• Some filters work only on RGB images. If you are in a different color mode, some (or all) filter options — including the Filter Gallery — will be unavailable.

• All filters can be applied to 8-bit images but options are limited for 16- and 32-bit images.

1. **With magazine.psd open, select the inset3 layer in the Layers panel.**

   Like styles and effects, filters apply to the selected layer, not to the entire file.

2. **Choose Filter>Filter Gallery.**

   If the Filter menu includes the Filter Gallery at the top of the list, the top command applies the last-used filter gallery settings to the selected layer. To open the Filter Gallery dialog box, you have to choose the Filter Gallery command at the third spot in the menu.

This command applies the last-used filter without opening the Filter Gallery dialog box.

This command opens the Filter Gallery dialog box with the last-used settings applied.

3. **If necessary, adjust the view percentage and position in the dialog box so you can see the inset3 image.**

4. **In the middle pane of the dialog box, expand the Artistic collection of filters and click the Plastic Wrap thumbnail.**

The left side of the dialog box shows a preview of the applied filter(s). You can use the options in the bottom-left corner to change the preview view percentage.

In the middle column, available filters are broken into six categories. Inside each folder, thumbnails show a small preview of each filter.

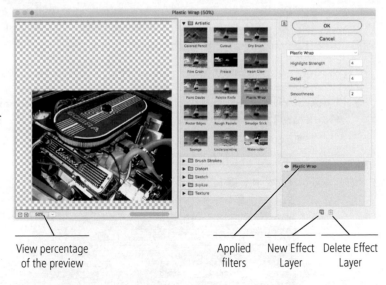

On the right, the top half shows settings specific to the selected filter (from the middle column). The bottom shows the filters that are applied to the selected layer.

You can apply more than one filter to a layer by clicking the New Effect Layer button in the bottom-right corner of the Filter Gallery dialog box.

View percentage of the preview

Applied filters

New Effect Layer

Delete Effect Layer

5. **Adjust the filter options until you are satisfied with the result, then click OK to apply the filter.**

Because the inset3 layer is a Smart Object layer, the filter is applied nondestructively as a Smart Filter. If you apply a filter to a regular layer, it is destructive, and cannot be changed or turned off.

The filter is applied to the Smart Object layer as a Smart Filter.

6. **Press Option/Alt, then click the Filter Gallery listing in the Layers panel and drag it to the inset2 layer.**

As with layer styles, this method allows you to apply the same Smart Filter to multiple layers, without opening any dialog boxe.

The cursor shows you are cloning the Smart Filter.

7. **Repeat Step 6 to apply the Smart Filter to the inset1 layer.**

The Smart Filters have been cloned, but the lists do not automatically expand in the panel.

8. **Collapse the Smart Filters listing for the inset3 layer.**

9. **Save the file and continue to the next exercise.**

Duplicate a Layer

The next piece of this project is a custom background, which you will create from a provided image. In this exercise, you will use the Duplicate method to move layer content from one file to another.

1. **With magazine.psd open, open tires.jpg from your WIP>Cars folder.**

2. **Control/right-click the Background layer in the tires.jpg file and choose Duplicate Layer in the contextual menu.**

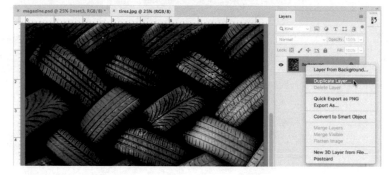

3. **In the resulting dialog box, choose magazine.psd in the Destination Document menu, then click OK.**

   The Duplicate command provides an easy method for copying an entire layer — either in the current file, any other open file, or a new file. If you choose the current file as the destination, you can define a new name for the duplicated layer.

Choose where you want the duplicate layer in this menu.

4. **Close the tires.jpg file and review the current magazine.psd file.**

   The Background layer from the tires file is copied into the magazine file. It is placed immediately above the previously selected layer. Although it is still named "Background" because of the file from which it was copied, it is neither locked nor placed at the bottom of the layer stack.

The duplicated layer is placed above the previously selected layer.

5. **Click the Background layer in the Layers panel and drag it to the bottom of the layer stack.**

6. **Double-click the layer name to highlight it. Type Tires as the new layer name, then press Return/Enter to finalize the new name.**

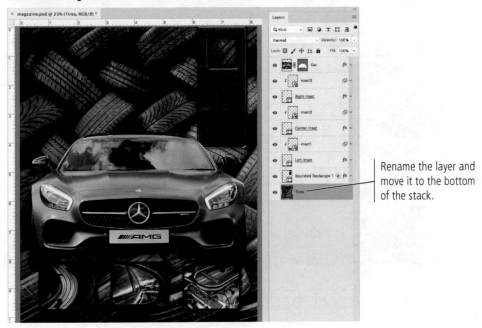

Rename the layer and move it to the bottom of the stack.

7. **Save the file and then continue to the next exercise.**

Liquify a Layer

Rather than just using the image of stacked tires as the background, you are going to create something less patterned and recognizable. In this exercise, you use the Liquify filter to push around layer pixels in a freeform style to create a unique background for the magazine cover.

1. **With magazine.psd open, hide all but the Tires layer.**

   You can Option/Alt-click the eye icon for a layer to hide all other layers.

2. **With the Tires layer selected in the Layers panel, choose Filter>Liquify.**

   The Liquify filter has its own interface and tools. Depending on which tool you select, different options become available in the right side of the dialog box.

3. **In the bottom-left corner of the dialog box, open the View Percentage menu and choose Fit In View.**

4. **On the left side of the dialog box, choose the Forward Warp tool.**

5. **On the right side of the dialog box, define a large brush with medium density.**

   For any of the distortion tools, you have to define a brush size, density (feathering around the edges), and pressure. Some tools also allow you to define the brush rate (how fast distortions are made).

6. Make sure the Pin Edges option is checked.

When checked, this option prevents transparent pixels from appearing at the canvas edges.

7. Click and drag in the preview to warp the tire pattern away from the neat stack in the original image.

Forward Warp tool

The tool cursor reflects the brush size.

When Pin Edges is active, you can't push pixels away from the canvas edge.

Use this menu to change the view percentage.

Check this option to avoid creating transparent areas at the canvas edges.

8. Continue clicking and dragging to push pixels until you are satisfied with your results.

If necessary, you can press Command/Control-Z to undo your last brush stroke in the Liquify dialog box.

9. Click OK to return to the image.

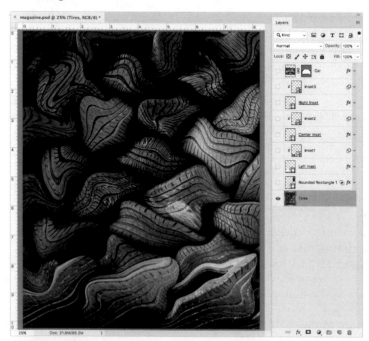

Depending on the size of the layer you are liquifying, the process might take a while to complete; be patient.

The Liquify filter is not a smart filter, and cannot be applied to a Smart Object layer; it permanently alters the pixels in the layer to which it is applied.

10. Save the file and continue to the next exercise.

Tools in the Liquify filter distort the brush area when you drag. The distortion is concentrated at the center of the brush area, and the effect intensifies as you hold down the mouse button or repeatedly drag over an area. (The **Hand** and **Zoom tools** function the same as they do in the main Photoshop interface.)

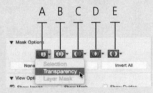

A. The **Forward Warp tool** pushes pixels as you drag.

B. The **Reconstruct tool** restores distorted pixels.

C. The **Smooth tool** smoothes jagged edges.

D. The **Twirl Clockwise tool** rotates pixels clockwise as you hold down the mouse button or drag. Press Option/Alt to twirl pixels counterclockwise.

E. The **Pucker tool** moves pixels toward the center of the brush, creating a zoomed-out effect if you simply hold down the mouse button without dragging.

F. The **Bloat tool** moves pixels away from the center of the brush, creating a zoomed-in effect.

G. The **Push Left tool** moves pixels left when you drag up, and right when you drag down. You can also drag clockwise around an object to increase its size, or drag counterclockwise to decrease its size.

H. The **Freeze Mask tool** protects areas where you paint.

I. The **Thaw Mask tool** removes the protection created by the Freeze Mask tool.

J. The **Face tool** reveals on-screen controls for changing the shape of various facial features. For example, you can click and drag to change the shape of the forehead, chin height, jawline, and face width when the overall face shape is selected.

Face-Aware Liquify Options

If an image includes faces, the Liquify filter automatically recognizes them, and provides options for manipulating the individual eyes, nose, mouth, and overall face shape. You can use the controls on the right side of the dialog box, or use the Face tool to drag on-screen controls in the preview area.

If more than one face exists in the overall image, you can use the Select Face menu to determine which one you want to edit using the slider controls.

Mask Options

Mask Options allow you to freeze areas in the Liquify preview to protect them from distortion. You can use the Mask options to freeze areas based on existing selections, transparent areas, or layer masks in the original image.

A. **Replace Selection**

B. **Add to Selection**

C. **Subtract from Selection**

D. **Intersect with Selection**

E. **Invert Selection**

You can click the **None** button to thaw all masked areas. Click the **Mask All** button to mask the entire image or the **Invert All** button to reverse the current mask.

Brush Reconstruct Options

When the Liquify dialog box is open, pressing Command/Control-Z undoes your last brush stroke. Clicking **Restore All** has the same effect as using the Undo keyboard shortcut.

You can also use the **Reconstruct** button to affect the last-applied stroke. Rather than undoing the entire stroke, you can use the resulting dialog box to lessen the effect by a specific percentage.

View Options

Show Image, active by default, shows the active layer in the filter's preview area. If you check the **Show Mesh** option, the preview also shows a grid that defaults to small, gray lines. You can use the Mesh Size and Mesh Color menus to change the appearance of the grid.

When **Show Mask** is checked, any mask you paint with the Freeze Mask tool appears in the filter's preview area. You can use the Mask Color menu to change the color of that mask.

When **Show Backdrop** is checked, you can include other layers in the filter's preview area. The Use menu also lists individual layers in the file so you can show only a certain layer in the preview. You can use the Mode and Opacity menus to change how extra layers appear in the preview.

Use the Eyedropper Tool

In Photoshop, there is almost always more than one way to complete a task. In this exercise, you use the Eyedropper tool to change the Foreground and Background colors by sampling from the original car image. You will then use those colors to create a gradient background for the overall composition.

1. **With magazine.psd open, hide all but the Car layer.**

   You can hide multiple layers by clicking and dragging over the eye icons of each layer that you want to hide.

2. **Choose the Eyedropper tool in the Tools panel.**

3. **In the Options bar, choose 5 by 5 Average in the Sample Size menu and choose All Layers in the Sample menu. Make sure the Show Sampling Ring option is checked.**

   The default Eyedropper option — Point Sample — selects the color of the single pixel where you click. Using one of the average values avoids the possibility of sampling an errant artifact color because the tool finds the average color in a range of adjacent pixels.

   By default, the sample will be selected from All [visible] Layers. You can choose Current Layer in the Sample menu to choose a color from only the active layer.

4. **Move the cursor over the light silver color near the left edge of the car (as shown in the following image). Click to change the foreground color.**

   When you click with the Eyedropper tool, the sampling ring appears and shows the previous foreground color on the bottom, and the current sample color on the top half.

   If you hold down the mouse button, you can drag around the image to find the color you want. The sampling ring previews which color will be selected if you release the mouse button.

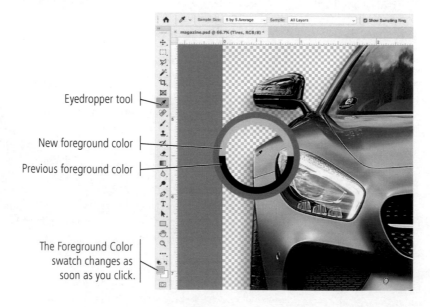

Eyedropper tool

New foreground color

Previous foreground color

The Foreground Color swatch changes as soon as you click.

5. **Move the cursor over the yellowish tones in the bottom part of the headlight (as shown in the image below). Option/Alt-click to change the background color.**

Pressing Option/Alt while you click with the Eyedropper tool changes the Background color. In this case, the sampling ring shows the previous background color on the bottom and the current selection on the top.

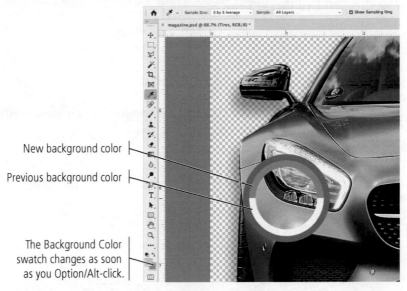

New background color

Previous background color

The Background Color swatch changes as soon as you Option/Alt-click.

6. **Save the file and continue to the next exercise.**

 ## Create a Custom Gradient

A **gradient** (sometimes called a blend) is a fill that creates a smooth transition from one color to another or across a range of multiple colors. Photoshop can create several different kinds of gradients (linear, radial, etc.) from one color to another, and you can access a number of built-in gradients. You can also create your own custom gradients, which you will do in this exercise.

1. **With magazine.psd open, choose the Gradient tool in the Tools panel.**

2. **In the Options bar, click the arrow to the right of the gradient sample bar to show the Gradient Picker panel.**

The Gradient Picker panel shows a set of predefined gradients, including black-to-white, foreground-to-transparent, foreground-to-background, and several other common options. You can also access additional gradient libraries in the panel Options menu.

3. **Open the Gradient Picker panel Options menu and choose Small List view.**

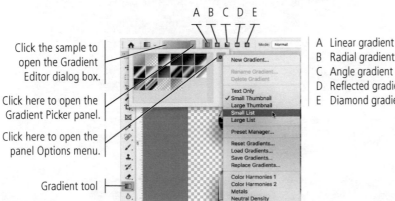

Click the sample to open the Gradient Editor dialog box.

Click here to open the Gradient Picker panel.

Click here to open the panel Options menu.

Gradient tool

A Linear gradient
B Radial gradient
C Angle gradient
D Reflected gradient
E Diamond gradient

4. **Open the Gradient Picker panel again (if necessary) and choose Foreground to Background from the list of gradients. Press Return/Enter to close the Gradient Picker panel.**

5. **Click the gradient sample in the Options bar to open the Gradient Editor dialog box.**

You can use this dialog box to edit existing gradients or create new ones.

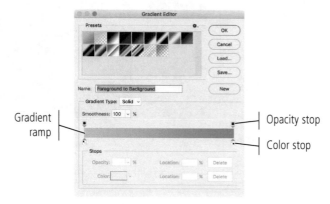

Gradient ramp

Opacity stop

Color stop

6. **Click the right color stop below the gradient ramp. Drag left until the Location field shows 60%.**

As soon as you click the color stop, the name changes to Custom because you're defining a custom gradient.

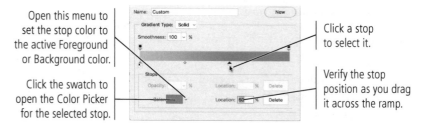

Open this menu to set the stop color to the active Foreground or Background color.

Click the swatch to open the Color Picker for the selected stop.

Click a stop to select it.

Verify the stop position as you drag it across the ramp.

7. **Double-click the moved stop to open the Color Picker dialog box. Change the stop color to C: 25%, M: 40%, Y: 80%, K: 5%, then click OK.**

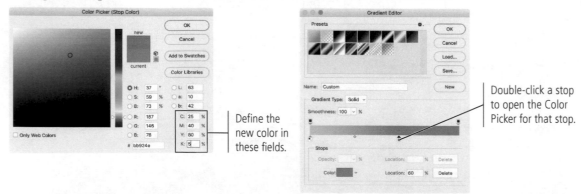

Define the new color in these fields.

Double-click a stop to open the Color Picker for that stop.

8. **Click the left stop to select it. Drag right until the Location field shows 30%.**

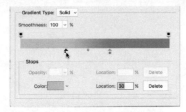

9. **Click the small diamond icon between the first and second stops. Drag right until the Location field shows 80%.**

This point indicates where the colors of the two surrounding stops are equally mixed. Dragging this point extends the gradient on one side of the point and compresses the gradient on the other.

Drag this icon to change the midpoint between the two surrounding stops.

10. **Click below the right side of the ramp. Drag the new stop until the location field shows 80%.**

Clicking below the ramp adds a new stop to the gradient, using the same color settings as the last-selected stop.

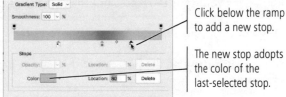

Click below the ramp to add a new stop.

The new stop adopts the color of the last-selected stop.

11. **Click below the left end of the gradient ramp to add a new stop. Set its location to 0%.**

12. **Double-click the new stop to open the Color Picker dialog box. Change the stop color to white, then click OK.**

Note:

Whenever the Color Picker dialog box is open, you can use the Eyedropper cursor to sample a color from the image in the document window.

13. **Click the left stop to select it, then click below the right end of the gradient ramp to add another new stop. Set its location to 100%**

If you didn't click the leftmost stop first, the new stop from this step would have the same color settings as the last-selected stop (from Step 10).

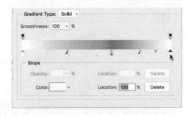

14. Type **Car Background** in the Name field and click the New button.

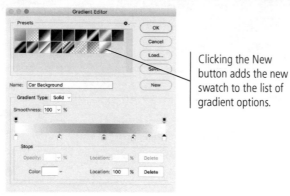

Clicking the New button adds the new swatch to the list of gradient options.

Note:

Drag a stop off the gradient ramp to remove it from the gradient.

15. Click OK to close the dialog box.

16. Save the file and continue to the next exercise.

Create a Gradient Fill Layer

Once you define the gradient you want, applying it is fairly easy: add a layer (if necessary), select the type of gradient you want to create, and then click and drag.

1. With **magazine.psd** open, make sure the Tires layer is selected.

2. Click the Create a New Layer button at the bottom of the Layers panel. Name the new layer **Shading**.

   When you add a new layer, it is automatically added directly above the selected layer.

Create a New Layer button

3. Show all layers, and then click the Shading layer to select it.

4. Make sure the Gradient tool is selected. In the Options bar, make sure the Car Background gradient is selected and the Linear Gradient option is active.

5. **Click in the top edge of the cutout area and drag to the bottom outside edge of the cutout layer (as shown in the following image).**

The Car Background gradient is selected.

The Linear Gradient option is selected.

The Gradient tool is active.

Click here…

…and drag to here.

When you release the mouse button, the layer fills with the gradient. Areas before and after the line drawn with the Gradient tool fill with the start and stop colors of the gradient (in this case, they're both white).

6. **Save the file and continue to the next exercise.**

Adjust Blending Mode and Layer Opacity

The final step to creating your custom background is to blend the gradient you just created into the liquified tires. Photoshop includes a number of options for making this type of adjustment.

1. **With magazine.psd open, select the Shading layer in the Layers panel.**

2. **Open the Blending Mode menu in the Layers panel and choose Overlay.**

Photoshop provides access to 27 different layer blending modes; the default is Normal, or no blending applied. As you move your mouse cursor over each option in the menu, the document window shows a dynamic preview of that mode. Using the Overlay mode, colors in the gradient are blended onto the pixels in the underlying Tires layer.

Blending Mode menu

3. **Select the Tires layer in the Layers panel, then change the Opacity field to 10%.**

Reducing the layer opacity reduces the strength of the layer content so that it no longer overpowers other elements in the composition. You can now better see the effect created by the blended gradient.

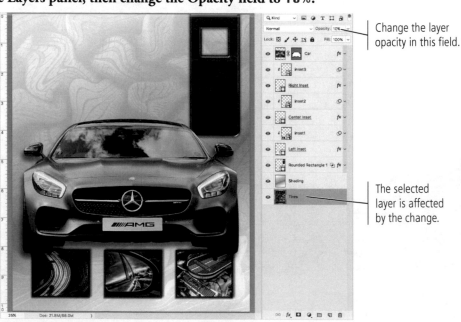

Change the layer opacity in this field.

The selected layer is affected by the change.

4. **Save the file and continue to the next exercise.**

Distinguishing Photoshop Blending Modes

When working with blending modes, think of the top layer as the "blend" layer and the next lowest layer as the "base."

- **Normal** is the default mode (no blending applied).

- **Dissolve** results in a random scattering of pixels of both the blend and base colors.

- **Darken** returns the darker of the blend or base color. Base pixels that are lighter than the blend color are replaced. Base pixels that are darker than the blend color remain unchanged.

- **Multiply** multiplies (hence, the name) the base color by the blend color, resulting in a darker color. Multiplying any color with black produces black. Multiplying any color with white leaves the color unchanged (think of math — any number times 0 equals 0).

- **Color Burn** darkens the base color by increasing the contrast. Blend colors darker than 50% significantly darken the base color by increasing saturation and reducing brightness. Blending with white has no effect.

- **Linear Burn** darkens the base color similar to Color Burn. Using Linear Burn, the brightness is reduced about twice as much for blend colors in the mid-tone range.

- **Darker Color** compares the channel values of the blend and base colors, resulting in the lower value.

- **Lighten** returns whichever is the lighter color (base or blend). Base pixels that are darker than the blend color are replaced. Base pixels that are lighter than the blend color remain unchanged.

- **Screen** is basically the inverse of Multiply, always returning a lighter color. Screening with black has no effect; screening with white produces white.

- **Color Dodge** brightens the base color. Blend colors lighter than 50% significantly increase brightness. Blending with black has no effect.

- **Linear Dodge (Add)** is similar to Color Dodge, but creates smoother transitions from areas of high brightness to areas of low brightness.

- **Lighter Color** compares channel values of the blend and base colors, resulting in the higher value.

- **Overlay** multiplies or screens the blend color to preserve the original lightness or darkness of the base.

- **Soft Light** darkens or lightens base colors depending on the blend color. Blend colors lighter than 50% lighten the base color (as if dodged). Blend colors darker than 50% darken the base color (as if burned).

- **Hard Light** combines the Multiply and Screen modes. Blend colors darker than 50% are multiplied, and blend colors lighter than 50% are screened.

- **Vivid Light** combines the Color Dodge and Color Burn modes. Blend colors lighter than 50% lighten the base by decreasing contrast. Blend colors darker than 50% darken the base by increasing contrast.

- **Linear Light** combines the Linear Dodge and Linear Burn modes. If the blend color is lighter than 50%, the result is lightened by increasing the base brightness. If the blend color is darker than 50%, the result is darkened by decreasing the base brightness.

- **Pin Light** preserves the brightest and darkest areas of the blend color. Blend colors in the mid-tone range have little (if any) effect.

- **Hard Mix** pushes all pixels in the resulting blend to either all or nothing. The base and blend values of each pixel in each channel are added together (e.g., R 45 [blend] + R 230 [base] = R 275). Pixels with totals over 255 are shown at 255; pixels with a total lower than 255 are dropped to 0.

- **Difference** inverts base color values according to the brightness value in the blend layer. Lower brightness values in the blend layer have less of an effect on the result. Blending with black has no effect.

- **Exclusion** is very similar to Difference, except that mid-tone values in the base color are completely desaturated.

- **Subtract** removes the blend color from the base color.

- **Divide** looks at the color information in each channel and divides the blend color from the base color.

- **Hue** results in a color with the luminance and saturation of the base color, and the hue of the blend color.

- **Saturation** results in a color with the luminance and hue of the base color, and the saturation of the blend color.

- **Color** results in a color with the luminance of the base color, and the hue and saturation of the blend color.

- **Luminosity** results in a color with the hue and saturation of the base color, and the luminance of the blend color (basically, the opposite of the Color mode).

Finish the Magazine Cover

The final piece required for this job is the nameplate and text treatment, which is created every month from a template in Adobe Illustrator. In this exercise, you will place and position the required file to complete the project.

1. **With magazine.psd open, choose File>Place Linked.**

   You are using the Place Linked option so that any changes in the cover treatment file (a common occurrence in professional design environments) will automatically reflect in your Photoshop file.

2. **Navigate to driver-mag.ai (in your WIP>Cars folder) and click Place.**

3. **Choose Bounding Box in the Crop To menu of the Open as Smart Object dialog box, then click OK.**

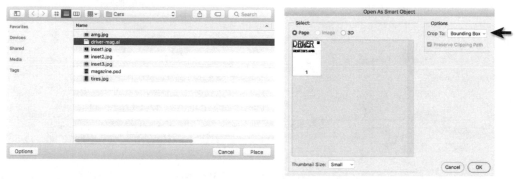

   When you place files in Photoshop, either linked or embedded, they are commonly placed at slightly other than 100%. You should always verify — and correct, if necessary — the scaling of the placed content.

4. **In the Options bar, change the W and H values to 100%, then press Return/Enter to finalize the placement.**

5. **In the Layers panel, move the driver-mag layer to the top of the layer stack.**

6. **Using the Properties panel, change the position of the placed content to X: 0.375 in, Y: 0.375 in.**

   The Properties panel only displays two decimal values, so after typing the new position, the fields show only "0.38 in". This is a minor flaw in the software, but one that is worth noting.

7. **Save the file and then continue to the final exercise.**

Sharing Photoshop Files

If you are connected to the Internet, you can use the Share an Image button to easily send a JPEG version of your file through a variety of communication media. If you choose Mail in the menu, for example, the image automatically appears in a new mail message in your email client software. If you choose one of the social media outlets, you can create your post directly through a window in the Photoshop interface; you do not need to interact with a browser or separate application to share an image from Photoshop. Keep in mind that you must have defined accounts in your system preferences for each of the various social media outlets. If an account is not defined, you will be prompted to add one before you can use these options in Photoshop.

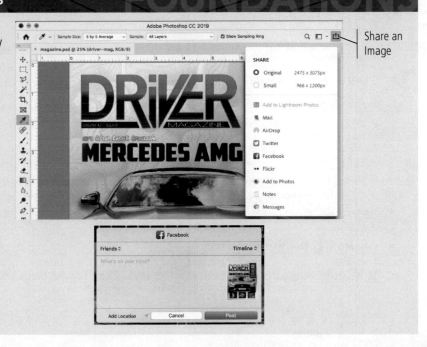

Print a Composite Proof

The last stage of most jobs — after the client has approved the work — is printing a proof. A printed proof is basically the output provider's roadmap of how the final job should look. As more processes move to all-digital workflows, a printed proof is not always required — especially if you're submitting files digitally. But some output providers still require a printed proof, and you might want to print samples of your work at various stages of development.

To output this file at 100%, you need a sheet at least tabloid size (11″ × 17″). If you don't have that option, you can use the Photoshop Print dialog box to fit the job onto letter-size paper. Keep in mind, however, that many of the effects that you created with filters will lose some of their impact when you reduce the file to fit onto a letter-size page.

1. **With magazine.psd open, choose File>Print.**

2. **In the Printer menu of the Print dialog box, choose the printer you're using.**

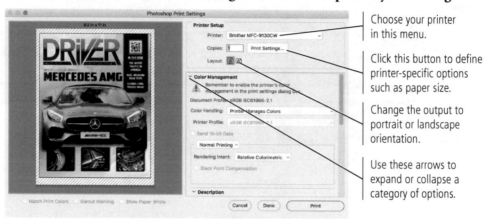

Choose your printer in this menu.

Click this button to define printer-specific options such as paper size.

Change the output to portrait or landscape orientation.

Use these arrows to expand or collapse a category of options.

3. **Choose the Portrait layout option (below the number of copies).**

   Ideally, you should always print proofs at 100%. If this is not possible, however, you can print a sample content proof by scaling the page to fit the available paper size.

4. **Review the options in the scrolling pane below the Printer Setup options.**

   Different types of output jobs require different settings. If you are simply printing a desktop proof, you can leave most of these options at their default values.

   As a general rule, proofs should be printed at 100% of the actual file size. If you are printing a file that is larger than the paper size your printer can handle, you can use the Scaled Print Size options to fit the job on the available paper size. Alternatively, you can use the Print Selected Area option to output different portions of the image onto separate sheets, and then manually assemble the multiple sheets into a single page.

5. **Click Print to output the file.**

6. **When the output process is complete, close the file without saving.**

Note:

If you submit a scaled proof with a print job, make sure you note the scale percentage prominently on the proof.

Color Management Options

- **Color Handling** determines whether color management is applied by the printer or by Photoshop.
- **Printer Profile** defines the known color characteristics of the output device you are using.
- **Normal Printing** simply prints the file to your printer, using no defined output profile for color management.
  - **Rendering Intent** defines how colors are shifted to fit inside the printer's output capabilities.
  - **Black Point Compression** adjusts for differences in the black point (the darkest possible black area) between the file and the output device.
- **Hard Proofing** simulates the color output properties of another printer, based on the defined profile in the Proof Setup menu.
  - **Simulate Paper Color** applies the absolute colorimetric rendering intent to simulate the appearance of color on the actual paper and output device that will be used (for example, newsprint on a web press).
  - **Simulate Black Ink** simulates the brightness of dark colors as they would appear on the defined output device. If not checked, dark colors are printed as dark as possible on the actual printer you are using.

Position and Size Options

- **Position** defines the location of the output on the paper. It is centered by default. You can use the Top and Left fields to position the output at a specific distance from the paper corner. You can also click in the preview area and drag to reposition the image on the paper.
- **Scale** defaults to 100%, creating a full-size print. The **Height** and **Width** fields define the size of the image being printed. If you change the Scale field, the Height and Width fields reflect the proportional size. You can also define a specific size in the Height and Width fields; in this case, the Scale field is adjusted accordingly.
- If you check **Scale to Fit Media**, the image is automatically scaled to fit inside the printable area on the selected paper size.
- **Print Resolution** defines the resolution that will be sent to the output device. Remember the principle of effective resolution: if you print a 300-ppi image at 200%, the printer has only 150 ppi with which to work.
- If you check **Print Selected Area**, handles appear in the preview area. You can drag those handles to define the image area that will be output.

Printing Marks

- **Corner Crop Marks** adds crop marks to show the edges of the image where it should be cut.
- **Center Crop Marks** adds a crop mark at the center of each edge of the image.
- **Registration Marks** adds bulls-eye targets and star targets that are used to align color separations on a printing press. Calibration bars and star target registration marks require a PostScript printer.)
- **Description** adds description text (from the File>File Info dialog box) outside the trim area in 9-pt Helvetica.
- **Labels** adds the file name above the image.

Functions

- **Emulsion Down** reverses the image on the output. This option is primarily used for output to a filmsetter or imagesetter.
- **Negative** inverts the color values of the entire output. This option is typically used if you are outputting directly to film, which will then be used to image a photo-sensitive printing plate (a slowly disappearing workflow).
- The **Background** option allows you to add a background color that will print outside the image area.
- The **Border** option adds a black border around an image. You can define a specific width (in points) for the border.
- The **Bleed** option moves crop marks inside the image by a specific measurement.

PostScript Options

- **Calibration Bars** adds swatches of black in 10% increments (starting at 0% and ending at 100%).
- The **Interpolation** option can help reduce the jagged appearance of low-resolution images by automatically resampling up when you print. This option is only available on PostScript Level 2 or 3 printers.
- The **Include Vector Data** option sends vector information in the output stream for a PostScript printer, so the vector data can be output at the highest possible resolution of the output device.

If your printer is not PostScript compatible, the PostScript options will not be available.

1. _____ sharpens an image by increasing contrast along the edges in an image.

2. _____ refers to the overall image area, like the surface used by traditional painters.

3. The _____ tool is used to draw freeform, vector-based shapes and paths.

4. A _____ is a special type of Photoshop layer that retains vector path information.

5. _____ control the shape of a curve between two anchor points.

6. The _____ option is used to link the angle of styles to the "master" angle for the entire file. Changing it affects any linked style applied to any layer in the entire file.

7. A _____ is a smooth transition from one color to another.

8. The _____ command is used to show only areas of one layer that fall within the area of the underlying layer.

9. In the Liquify filter, the _____ tool can be used to protect specific areas from being liquified.

10. The _____ allows you to experiment with different filters and filter settings, and to compound multiple filters to create unique artistic effects.

1. Briefly explain the difference between vectors and pixels.

2. Briefly describe two different tool modes when using a vector drawing tool.

3. Briefly explain the difference between the Path Selection tool and the Direct Selection tool.

PORTFOLIO BUILDER PROJECT

Use what you have learned in this project to complete the following freeform exercise.
Carefully read the art director and client comments, then create your own design to meet the needs of the project.
Use the space below to sketch ideas. When finished, write a brief explanation of the reasoning behind your final design.

art director comments

Against The Clock is considering a new design for the covers of its *Professional Portfolio* series of books. You have been hired to design a new cover comp for the Photoshop CC book.

❑ Measure the cover of the existing Photoshop CC book to determine the required trim size.

❑ Incorporate the same elements that currently appear on the book cover — title, logo, and the text in the bottom-right corner. (The logo file is included in the **Covers_Print19_PB.zip** archive on the Student Files web page.)

❑ Create compelling images and artwork to illustrate the concept of the book title.

❑ Design the cover to meet commercial printing requirements.

client comments

We really like the existing cover design, but after nine editions, we're starting to think a fresh look might be a good thing.

Obviously, the most important element of the cover is the title. Keep in mind that Adobe differentiates each software release using the year instead of a version or edition number, so the year needs to be incorporated somewhere in the cover design.

In the last few version of the covers, we've used an urban theme — cityscapes, museum buildings, architectural macros, and so on — as a representation of places where graphic designers find jobs. We don't really have any set ideas for new imagery, but there should be some connection between graphic design and the imagery you choose.

Finally, keep in mind that the design should allow for repurposing for the other titles in the series.

project justification

Vectors offer an advantage over pixel-based images because they can be freely scaled and edited, without losing quality. This project focused on many different options related to working with vectors in Photoshop — drawing paths, creating shape layers, and editing vector shape properties. You used vectors in this project to create a custom layer mask, as well as vector shapes that you filled with other images and a custom artistic pattern.

This project also introduced some of the creative tools that can turn photos and flat colors into painting-like artwork. You learned to use the Filter Gallery, the Liquify filter, custom gradients, and layer blending modes. You will use these options many times in your career as you complete different types of projects in Photoshop.

Create a compound vector shape layer

Edit corner properties of vector shapes

Apply a style to a vector shape layer

Use a vector mask to remove an image from its background

Use gradients to create a custom background

Liquify pixels to create unique effects

Adjust blending mode and opacity to blend one layer into another

Create clipping masks to isolate specific image areas

Apply filters to images to create artistic effects

Museum Image Correction

6

Your client is curator at the local Museum of Art and History. The institution wants to create a printed brochure of images from a recently acquired collection of antiquities. Your job is to adjust the supplied images as necessary to achieve the best possible result when the final brochure is printed.

This project incorporates the following skills:

❏ Repairing damaged images

❏ Understanding the relationship between tonal range and contrast

❏ Correcting image lighting and exposure problems

❏ Understanding how gray balance affects overall image color

❏ Correcting minor and severe image color problems

❏ Preparing corrected images for printing

❏ Combining exposures into an HDR image

PROJECT MEETING

client comments

The Museum of Art and History recently received a large donation from a wealthy patron's estate. We are going to create a printed catalog that will showcase some of the collection's stars, as well as explain the history behind the various pieces.

We've selected seven photos that we want to include in the catalog. We want you to make sure they will look as good as possible when printed.

We have a photo of one of the family's first American-born descendants, who was responsible for building much of the family's collection. The picture is a bit grainy and has some damage, though, and we'd like you to clean it up as much as possible.

Finally, we also want to include a picture of the new museum on the back of the catalog, along with the contact information, hours, and so on. We are proud of the new space, and would like the photo to also be a work of art.

art director comments

Digital images come from a wide variety of sources — scanned photographs and digital cameras are the two most common — as is the case for the client's images for this project. Some images can be used as is, or with only minor correction.

Unfortunately, not every project involves a professional photographer. Consumer-level digital cameras and smartphones are common sources of photography that is submitted for professional design work. This means many images require a bit of help — and some require a lot.

Even when a professional photographer is involved, not every image comes from a perfectly lit studio. Location shots — where a subject is photographed in a "real-world" setting — can't always be captured perfectly. Those images usually need work, as well. Fortunately, Photoshop provides a powerful toolset for solving most image problems, or at least, improving the worst of- them.

1 - J.R. - Touchup, fix damage
2 - Bezel - Brighten, increase contrast
3 - Drachma - Improve contrast
4 - Vases - Fix underexposure
5 - Bust - Remove yellow cast
6 - Plaque - Remove red cast, fix contrast
7 - Tile - Fix contrast overall
8 - Jar - Check for color shift
9 - Mill - Combine exposures / HDR

project objectives

To complete this project, you will:

- ❏ Remove grain with blur and sharpen techniques
- ❏ Heal severe scratches
- ❏ Clone out major damage
- ❏ Correct minor problems with the Brightness/Contrast adjustment
- ❏ Correct tonal range with the Levels adjustment
- ❏ Correct lighting problems with the Exposure adjustment
- ❏ Correct overall color problems with the Color Balance adjustment
- ❏ Correct precise color values with the Curves adjustment
- ❏ Correct an RGB image to CMYK gamut limits
- ❏ Embed color profile information in a file
- ❏ Combine multiple exposures with the Merge to HDR Pro utility

STAGE 1 / **Retouching Damaged Images**

Image repair is the process of fixing damaged images, while **retouching** is the technique of changing an image by adding something that wasn't there or removing something that was there. Damage can come from a wide range of sources: creases, scratches, water spots, and tape marks, to name just a few. Other image problems, such as photographic grain, are a natural part of photographs (especially older ones), and dust is common (if not inevitable) whenever photographs are scanned.

There are many different ways to approach image repairs. As you complete the exercises in this stage of the project, you will use several tools to clean up damage in a portrait from the 1940s.

Remove Grain with Blur and Sharpen Techniques

Photographic film is made up of microscopic grains of light-sensitive material. These grains capture the image information, which is eventually processed into a print or transparency. While not usually apparent in a standard photographic print, the grain in a photograph can become pronounced when scanned with a high-resolution scanner. Enlarging an image during scanning further enhances any grain that already exists.

When grain is evident in a digital image, it can destroy fine detail and create a mottled appearance in areas of solid color or subtle tone variation.

Blurring and Sharpening techniques are the best methods for removing photographic grain. The techniques you use in this exercise work for any image with grain. Older images — such as the one your client wants to use — almost always have obvious grain problems that can be fixed to some degree, but there are limits to how much can be corrected. The techniques you learn in this project produce very good results if you need to remove grain from modern scanned images.

1. **Download MOAH_Print19_RF.zip from the Student Files web page.**

2. **Expand the ZIP archive in your WIP folder (Macintosh) or copy the archive contents into your WIP folder (Windows).**

   This results in a folder named **MOAH**, which contains the files you need for this project. You should also use this folder to save the files you create in this project.

3. **Open the file rossi.jpg from your WIP>MOAH folder.**

Water damage is evident in the background.

The corner has been torn off.

Scratches cut into the man's jacket.

The image has been creased in storage.

4. Choose View>100% to show the image at the actual size.

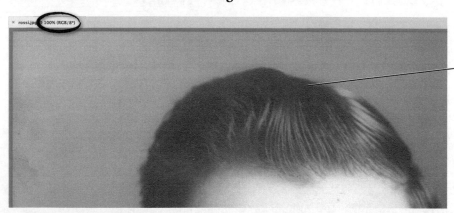

Grain is most obvious when you view the image at 100%.

Understanding the Noise Filters

Noise is defined as random pixels that stand out from the surrounding pixels, either hurting the overall appearance of the image (as in the case of visible grains in an old photograph) or helping to prevent printing problems (as in the case of a gradient that extends across a large area). Photoshop includes several filters (Filters>Noise) that can add or remove noise.

The **Add Noise** filter applies random pixels to the image. Uniform distributes color values of noise between 0 and the defined amount. Gaussian distributes color values of noise along a bell-shaped curve. Monochromatic adds random pixels without affecting the colors in the image.

The **Despeckle** filter detects the edges in an image and blurs everything except those edges.

The **Dust & Scratches** filter reduces noise by comparing the contrast of pixels within the defined radius. Pixels outside the defined threshold are adjusted.

The **Median** filter reduces noise by blending the brightness of pixels within a selection. The filter compares the brightness of pixels within the defined radius, and replaces those that differ too much from the surrounding pixels with the median brightness value of the compared pixels.

The **Reduce Noise** filter provides far greater control over different aspects of noise correction. In Basic mode, you can remove luminance noise and color noise in the composite image. **Luminance noise**, also called grayscale noise, makes an image appear grainy. **Color noise** usually appears as color artifacts in the image.

In Advanced mode, you can remove noise from individual color channels.

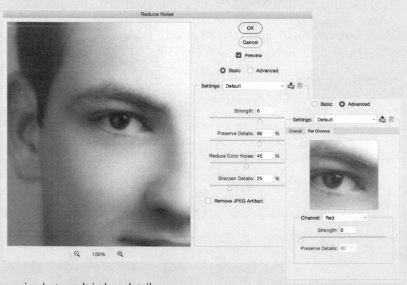

- **Strength** controls the amount of luminance noise reduction.

- **Preserve Details** controls how carefully the filter compares the difference in luminance between adjacent pixels. Lower values remove more noise, but result in less detail.

- **Reduce Color Noise** removes random color pixels from the image.

- **Sharpen Details** sharpens the image. Because the noise reduction process inherently blurs the image, this option applies the same kind of sharpening that is available in the Photoshop Sharpen filters.

- **Remove JPEG Artifact** removes artifacts and halos caused by saving an image with a low JPEG quality setting (in other words, using a high lossy compression scheme).

5. **Choose Filter>Blur>Gaussian Blur.**

6. **In the image behind the dialog box, click the area between the man's right eye and eyebrow.**

    When many filter dialog boxes are open, clicking the image (behind the dialog box) changes the visible preview area in the dialog box. You can also click inside the dialog box preview area and drag to change the visible preview area.

Note:

All Photoshop blur filters work in essentially the same way: they average the brightness values of contiguous pixels to soften the image.

7. **Make sure Preview is checked in the dialog box and change the Radius field to 2.0 pixels.**

    The **Radius** field defines (in pixels) the amount of blurring that will be applied. Photoshop uses this value to average the brightness of a pixel with that of surrounding pixels. A small radius value can soften an image and remove most photographic grain.

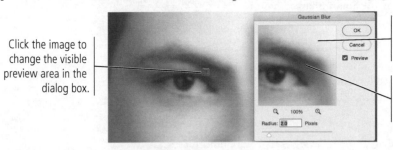

Click the image to change the visible preview area in the dialog box.

A small amount of Gaussian blur removes most of the photographic grain.

Areas of fine detail are also slightly blurred by the Gaussian Blur filter.

8. **Click OK to apply the Gaussian Blur to the image.**

    To remove the photographic grain, you had to blur the entire image. This means that areas of fine detail were also blurred. You can use a second technique — sharpening — to restore some of the lost edge detail.

Understanding the Blur Filters

The Filter>Blur menu includes a number of choices for applying corrective or artistic blurs to an image or selection.

Average finds the average color of an image or selection, and then fills the image or selection with that color to create a smooth appearance.

Blur and **Blur More** smooth transitions by averaging the pixels next to the hard edges of defined lines and shaded areas. When you apply these filters, you have no additional control: Blur is roughly equivalent to a 0.3-pixel radius blur, and Blur More uses approximately a 0.7-pixel radius.

Box Blur averages the color value of neighboring pixels. You can adjust the size of the area used to calculate the average value. A larger radius value results in more blurring.

Gaussian Blur blurs the selection by a specific amount.

Lens Blur adds blur to an image to create the effect of a narrower depth of field, so some objects in the image remain in focus, while others areas are blurred.

Motion Blur includes an option for changing the blur angle, as well as a Distance value, or the number of pixels to blur.

Radial Blur either spins the pixel around the center point of the image, or zooms the pixel around the center point based on the Amount setting. The farther a pixel is from the center point, the more the pixel is blurred. You can drag in the Blur Center window to move the center point of the blur.

Shape Blur uses a specific shape, or **kernel**, to create the blur. Radius determines the size of the kernel — the larger the kernel, the greater the blur.

Smart Blur blurs tones closely related in value without affecting edge quality. Threshold determines how closely pixels must be related in tone before being blurred. You can also specify a Quality level and change the Mode setting. Using Edge Only mode, edges are outlined in white and the image is forced to black. Using Overlay Edges mode, the color image is blurred and edges are outlined in white.

Surface Blur blurs an image, while trying to preserve edges. The Radius option specifies the size of the blur in whole numbers. Threshold controls how much the tonal values of neighboring pixels must differ before being blurred.

9. **Choose Filter>Sharpen>Smart Sharpen.**

The Smart Sharpen filter allows you to sharpen an image based on a specific amount and radius. You can also limit the sharpening that occurs in shadow and highlight areas.

10. **If you don't see the entire dialog box, click the arrow to the left of Shadows/Highlights to show all the available options.**

11. **Make the man's right eye visible in the dialog box preview area.**

12. **Define the following settings in the dialog box:**

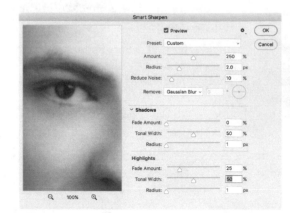

- **Choose Gaussian Blur in the Remove menu.**

  The **Remove** menu defines the type of blur you want to remove. Because you applied a Gaussian blur to remove the heavy noise, you are now using the Smart Sharpen filter to remove that blur and restore image detail.

  Lens Blur detects edges and detail, and provides finer sharpening of detail and reduced halos. Motion Blur attempts to reduce the effects of blur caused by camera movement. You can also define a specific angle of the blur to remove.

- **Set the Amount to 250%.**

  Amount defines how much sharpening to apply. A higher amount increases contrast between edge pixels, giving the appearance of greater sharpness. Be careful — if this is set too high, it can result in halos at apparent edges.

- **Set the Radius to 2.0 px.**

  Radius defines the number of pixels around edge pixels that will be affected by the sharpening. Higher radius values result in more obvious sharpening.

- **Set the Reduce Noise slider to 10%.**

  Reduce Noise helps to avoid sharpening any noise that still exists in the image.

- **In the Highlights section, set the Fade Amount to 25%.**

  In the Shadows and Highlights sections, you can adjust sharpening that will be applied in those areas of the image.

  – **Fade Amount** adjusts the amount of sharpening. By reducing the sharpening in the highlights of this image, you help to further remove the noise that remains in the lighter portions (the faces and background).

  – **Tonal Width** controls the range of tones that will be modified. Smaller values restrict the adjustments to darker regions for shadows, and lighter regions for highlights.

  – **Radius** defines the size of the area around each pixel used to determine whether a pixel is in the shadows or highlights.

13. **Click OK to apply sharpen the image.**

14. **Choose File>Save As. Choose Photoshop in the Format/Save As Type menu, and save the file as a native Photoshop file named rossi.psd in your WIP>MOAH folder.**

You have to choose File>Save As to save the file with a different name or format.

15. **Continue to the next exercise.**

Understanding the Shake Reduction Filter

As the name suggests, the Shake Reduction filter (Filter>Sharpen>Shake Reduction) was designed to reduce blur caused by a shaking camera — for example, images photographed with a slow shutter speed or without a flash.

This filter was not designed to remove blur caused by a moving subject. It also does not work well on images with specular highlights or noise. It works best to reduce shake in specific areas, not over an entire image.

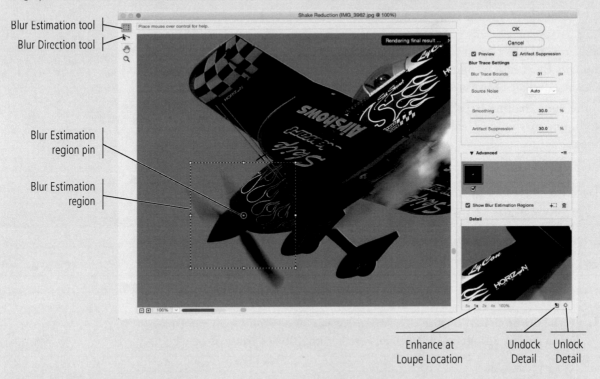

Blur Estimation tool

Blur Direction tool

Blur Estimation region pin

Blur Estimation region

Enhance at Loupe Location

Undock Detail

Unlock Detail

When you first open the filter, the image is automatically analyzed. The software determines a "region of interest," and calculates the shape and direction of the blur.

If necessary, you can adjust the automatically defined settings on the right side of the dialog box:

- **Blur Trace Bounds** is the extent of blur size introduced by the camera shake.

- **Source Noise** defines the noise level of the Source image: Auto, Low, Medium, or High.

- **Smoothing** reduces high-frequency sharpening noise.

- **Artifact Suppression** reduces larger artifacts that might be enhanced by sharpening.

You can use the Blur Estimation tool to add more than one blur estimation region to the image, or use the Blur Direction tool to specify the direction and length of a straight blur.

When Advanced options are expanded, the small icons show previews of the blur shape that was defined for each region.

You can select a specific region to make it active in the larger preview pane. Click the handles on the marquee to resize it, and click the pin in the center of a region to move it.

Using the Detail Loupe

You can use the Detail loupe (pane) to analyze specific areas of the image. You can enlarge the detail preview using the options at the bottom of the pane: .5x, 1x, 2x, or 4x.

To change the preview area, click inside the pane while it is docked. You can also undock the Detail pane and drag it over the image to enhance a specific area.

If you click the Enhance at Loupe Location button, the filter creates a new blur estimation region based on what is visible in the Detail pane.

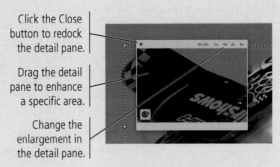

Click the Close button to redock the detail pane.

Drag the detail pane to enhance a specific area.

Change the enlargement in the detail pane.

Heal Severe Scratches

The blur and sharpen routine from the previous exercise improved the client's image — the obvious grain is gone. Even though the edges are slightly less sharp than the original scan, they are sharp enough to produce good results when the image is printed. If you're working with images that aren't 70 years old, you will be able to produce far sharper edges using these same techniques.

There are still a number of problems in the image that require intervention. Photoshop includes several tools for changing the pixels in an image — from painting with a brush or nudging selections on a layer, to using repair tools specifically designed to adjust pixels based on other pixels in the image.

The **Spot Healing Brush tool** allows you to remove imperfections by blending surrounding pixels. The **Healing Brush tool** has a similar function, except you can define the source pixels that will be used to heal an area. The **Patch tool** allows you to repair an area with pixels from another area by dragging the selection area.

Note:

Whenever you need to clean up blemishes on images and make other adjustments that require looking at very small areas, it can be very helpful to clean your monitor so you don't mistake on-screen dust or smudges for flaws in the images.

1. **With rossi.psd open, view the image at 100%. Set up the document window so you can see the man's forehead.**

2. **Select the Spot Healing Brush tool in the Tools panel.**

3. **In the Options bar, choose the Proximity Match option. Open the Brush Preset picker and define a 20-pixel brush with 100% hardness.**

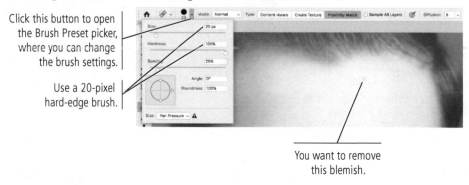

Click this button to open the Brush Preset picker, where you can change the brush settings.

Use a 20-pixel hard-edge brush.

You want to remove this blemish.

The **Proximity Match** method uses the pixels around the edge of the selection to find an image area to use as a patch for the selected area. The **Create Texture** method uses all the pixels in the selection to create a texture for repairing the area. **Content Aware** mode attempts to match the detail in surrounding areas while healing pixels (this method does not work well for areas with hard edges or sharp contrast). If you select **Sample All Layers**, the tool pulls pixel data from all visible layers.

4. **Place the cursor over the orange spot on the man's forehead. Click immediately over the spot to heal it.**

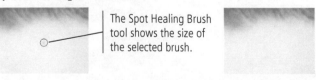

The Spot Healing Brush tool shows the size of the selected brush.

5. **Make the man's chin visible in the document window, then choose the Healing Brush tool (nested under the Spot Healing Brush tool).**

It might help to zoom in when you want to heal small areas such as this white spot on the man's chin. We are working at 200% in the following screen captures.

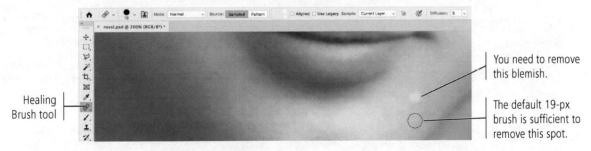

Healing Brush tool

You need to remove this blemish.

The default 19-px brush is sufficient to remove this spot.

For the Healing Brush tool, you can define brush settings just as you did for the Spot Healing Brush tool. As the tool cursor shows in the document window, the default 19-px brush size is sufficient to cover the white spot on the man's chin.

The Mode menu determines the blending mode used to heal an area. The default option (Normal) samples the source color and transparency to blend the new pixels smoothly into the area being healed. The Replace mode preserves texture in the healed area when you use a soft-edge brush. Multiple, Screen, Darken, Lighten, Color, and Luminosity modes have the same function as the blending modes for specific layers and brushes.

Note:

You can use the bracket keys to enlarge (]) or reduce ([) the Healing Brush tool brush size.

6. **Place the cursor directly below the spot you want to heal. Press Option/Alt and click to define the healing source.**

Pressing Option/Alt with the Healing Brush tool changes the cursor icon to a crosshair, which you can click to select the source of the brush (the pixels that will be used to heal the spot where you next click).

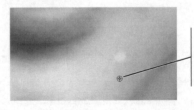

Pressing Option/Alt allows you to define the source pixels that will be used to heal the next spot you click.

7. **Place the cursor over the blemish on the man's chin and click.**

Unlike the Spot Healing Brush tool, the Healing Brush tool allows you to define the source of the healing. By choosing nearby pixels as the healing source, the blemish on the man's chin disappears, and that spot blends nicely into the surrounding pixels.

The Healing Brush tool blends colors from the source pixels (which you defined in Step 6) with colors in the area where you click. You can also change the source from Sampled (the pixels you defined by Option/Alt-clicking) to Pattern, which uses pixels from a defined pattern to heal the area — a good choice for creating artistic effects, rather than healing blemishes in a photo.

After clicking, the spot is healed using the source pixels.

8. **Save the file and continue to the next exercise.**

When you work with the Healing Brush and Clone Stamp tools, you have the option to align the healing source to the cursor. If the Align option is turned off, the source starting point will be relative to the image; each successive click uses the same source point. If the Align option is turned on, the source starting point will be relative to the cursor.

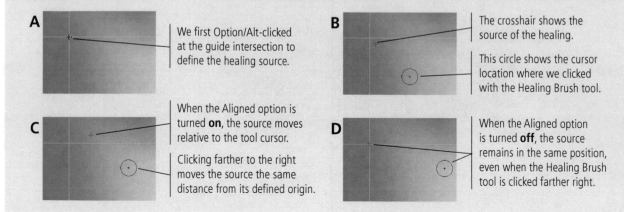

A We first Option/Alt-clicked at the guide intersection to define the healing source.

B The crosshair shows the source of the healing.

This circle shows the cursor location where we clicked with the Healing Brush tool.

C When the Aligned option is turned **on**, the source moves relative to the tool cursor.

Clicking farther to the right moves the source the same distance from its defined origin.

D When the Aligned option is turned **off**, the source remains in the same position, even when the Healing Brush tool is clicked farther right.

Clone out Major Damage

The client's image has definitely been improved by removing the grain and healing the small blemishes, but four major areas of damage still need to be fixed. In this exercise you will use the Fill dialog box to fix the damage in the image background, and then use the Clone Stamp tool to fix the scratch on the man's shoulder.

1. **With the file rossi.psd open, zoom into the top-right of the image (where the corner has been ripped off).**

2. **Using the Rectangular Marquee tool, draw a selection around the torn-off corner.**

3. **With the new marquee active, choose Edit>Fill.**

   In the Fill dialog box, the Contents menu determines what will fill the active selection when you click OK. You can choose any of the following options as the content with which to fill the selection: the active foreground or background color; any Color selected from the Color Picker dialog box when you choose the Color option; white, gray or black; a defined pattern; or a specific state in the History panel. If you use the Content-Aware option, you allow Photoshop to evaluate the image and surrounding pixels to determine what should fill the selection.

   In the case of this image, the backdrop is a slightly mottled gradient. The Content-Aware option is an excellent choice for fixing the torn-off corner.

4. **Choose Content-Aware in the Contents menu, then click OK.**

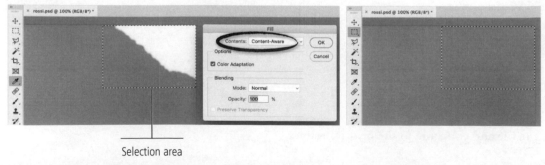

Selection area

5. **Choose Select>Deselect to turn off the active selection marquee.**

6. **Repeat the process from Steps 2–5 to remove the crease on the right edge and the water damage on the left edge of the image.**

Note:

Press Command/ Control-D to turn off a selection marquee.

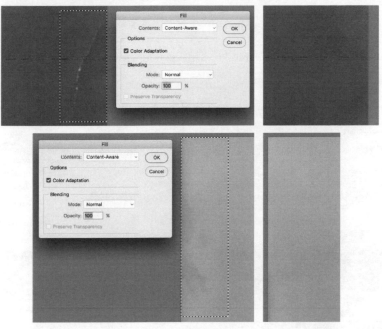

7. **Make the man's shoulder visible in the document window, then choose the Clone Stamp tool.**

   Content-Aware Fill works very well on areas of subtle shading, such as the backdrop in this image, or other areas where you do not need to maintain fine detail or edges in the selected area. If you try to use this option on a sharp edge, however, the Content-Aware Fill results are unpredictable. Other tools, such as the Clone Stamp tool, work better for retouching distinct edges.

   The Clone Stamp tool paints one part of an image over another, which is useful for duplicating objects or removing defects in an image. When you are using the Clone Stamp tool, the Options bar combines brush options (brush size, blending mode, opacity, and flow) with healing options (alignment and sample source, which you used in the previous exercise).

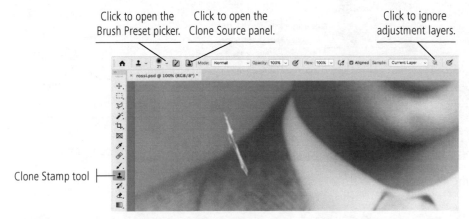

Click to open the Brush Preset picker.   Click to open the Clone Source panel.   Click to ignore adjustment layers.

Clone Stamp tool

8. **Open the Brush Preset picker in the Options bar. Define a 50-pixel brush with 50% hardness.**

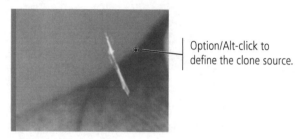

   This brush size is large enough to cover the scratch on the man's shoulder.

   When using the Clone Stamp tool, hard-edge brushes can result in harsh lines where you clone pixels. The reduced hardness creates a soft-edged brush, which will help to prevent hard edges in areas where you clone pixels.

Note:

You can use the bracket keys to enlarge (]) or reduce ([) the Clone Stamp brush size.

9. **In the Options bar, make sure the Aligned option is turned on (checked).**

   As with the Healing Brush tool, you can define the source that will be cloned when you click with the Clone Stamp tool; the difference is that whole pixels are copied, not just their color values.

10. **Place the cursor over the edge you want to reproduce and Option/Alt-click to define the source.**

   Option/Alt-click to define the clone source.

Note:

When you are cloning, it's usually a good idea to clone in small strokes, or even single clicks. This can help you avoid cloning in patterns or "railroad tracks" that do more damage than good. When cloning large areas, it's also a good idea to frequently resample the clone source to avoid cloning the same pixels into a new, noticeable pattern.

11. **Place the cursor over the scratched pixels on the man's shoulder.**

   As you move the Clone Stamp tool cursor, the source pixels move along with the tool cursor to give you a preview of what will happen when you click.

12. **Click without dragging when the cloned pixels appear to align properly with the area behind the scratch.**

   Clicking without dragging clones a 50-pixel area. Because the brush we chose has 50% hardness, the center (the edge of the man's shoulder) is clear, but the outside parts of the brush are feathered into the surrounding area.

   Before clicking, use the cursor preview to align the cloned pixels to the edge in the original.

Note:

If you're not happy with the result of a clone, simply undo the action (Command/Control-Z, or using the History panel) and try again. Cloning — especially edges — often takes more than one try to achieve the desired result.

13. **Choose the Lasso tool in the Tools panel. Draw a marquee around the scratches in the background, above the man's shoulder.**

   Be careful to avoid the man's shoulder in the selection area.

14. **Choose Edit>Fill. Choose Content-Aware in the Contents menu and click OK.**

Photoshop evaluates the image and determines what should be created inside the selection area. The fill might take a few seconds to process, so be patient.

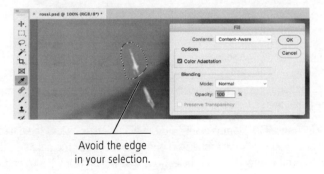

Avoid the edge
in your selection.

15. **Turn off the active selection (Select>Deselect).**

16. **Use the same method from Steps 13–15 to remove the scratches from the man's coat.**

17. **Choose File>Save As. Change the file name to rossi-fixed.psd and save it in your WIP>MOAH folder.**

18. **Close the file and continue to the next stage of the project.**

The Clone Source Panel in Depth

The Clone Source panel (Window>Clone Source) allows you to store up to five sources for the Clone Stamp or Healing Brush tool. These sources can be from any layer of any open image, which allows you to combine pixels from multiple layers or multiple files.

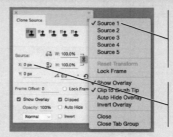

Store and access up to five sources from any layer of any open image.

The Show Overlay options show (at the defined opacity) the source pixels on top of the area where you are cloning. Say you want to clone a parachutist onto a plane photo. You would first define a clone source in the parachutist image and then make the plane image active.

Transform the offset, size, and angle of the clone source.

With the Show Overlay option checked, placing the Clone Stamp cursor over the plane image shows the parachutist on top of the plane image. When you click in the plane image with the Clone Stamp tool, that area of the parachutist image will be cloned into the plane image. The overlay allows you to preview the source areas that will be cloned into the plane image.

If the Auto Hide option is checked, the overlay is only visible when the mouse button is not clicked. The Invert option reverses the overlay into a negative representation of the source image. You can also change the blending mode of the overlay from the default Normal to Darken, Lighten, or Difference.

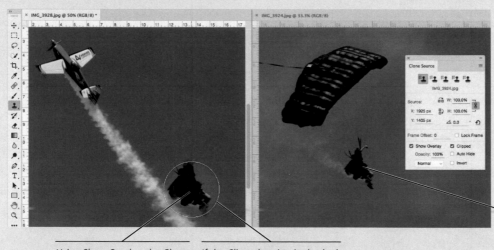

Using Show Overlay, the Clone Stamp cursor shows the pixels that will be cloned by clicking.

If the Clipped option is checked, the clone source appears only within the tool cursor area.

We defined a clone source here.

We turned off the Clipped option and reduced the opacity to 50% to show the entire source file over the image where the cloning is taking place.

STAGE 2 / Correcting Lighting Problems

Before you start correcting problems with lighting and color, you should understand the different parts of an image, as well as the terms used to describe these areas.

- **Highlights** are defined as the lightest areas of the image that include detail. Direct sources of light, such as a light bulb or reflected sunlight on water, are called **specular highlights**; they should not be considered the highlights of an image.

- **Shadows** are the darkest areas of the image that still contain some detail. Areas of solid black are not considered shadow tones.

- The shades between the highlights and shadows are the **midtones** (or **gamma**) of the image.

Contrast and saturation play an integral role in reproducing high-quality images. **Contrast** refers to the tonal variation within an image. An image primarily composed of highlights and shadows is a high-contrast image, while an image with more detail in the midtones is a low-contrast image.

Saturation refers to the intensity of a color or its variation away from gray. The saturation of individual colors in an image, and the correct saturation of different colors in relation to one another, affects the overall image contrast. If an image is under- or oversaturated, the contrast suffers.

 Correct Problems with Brightness/Contrast

Several tools are available for correcting problems related to images that are either too dark or too light. The most basic adjustment option — Brightness/Contrast — can fix images that need overall adjustment to brightness, contrast, or both.

1. **Open the file bezel.jpg from your WIP>MOAH folder.**

   This image has an overall dark feel, probably caused by poor lighting or underexposure. The Brightness/Contrast adjustment can correct this problem.

2. **Choose Image>Adjustments>Brightness/Contrast and make sure the Preview option is checked.**

3. **Make sure the Use Legacy option is not checked, and then drag the Brightness slider to 35.**

   Increasing the overall brightness creates an immediate improvement in this image, although some areas of detail are still muddy.

Note:

Image adjustments can be applied directly to the image pixels or as nondestructive adjustment layers using the Adjustments panel. In this project, you edit the actual image pixels.

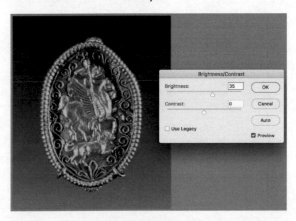

4. Drag the Contrast slider to 15.

Increasing the contrast brings out more detail in the overall object.

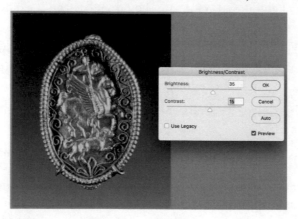

5. Click OK to apply the change.

6. Save the file in your WIP>MOAH folder as a native Photoshop file named bezel-fixed.psd.

7. Close the file and continue to the next exercise.

Correct Contrast and Tonal Range with Levels

The **tonal range** of an image is the amount of variation between the lightest highlight and the darkest shadow in a particular image. A grayscale image can contain 256 possible shades of gray. Each channel of a color image can also contain 256 possible shades of gray. To achieve the best contrast in an image, the tonal range of the image should include as many levels of gray as are available.

While the Brightness/Contrast option is a good choice for making basic adjustments, the Levels adjustment is the best approach for enhancing image detail throughout the entire tonal range. Using Levels, adjusting contrast is a three-step process:

- Determine the image's highlight areas (the lightest areas that contain detail).

- Determine the image's shadow areas (the darkest areas that contain detail).

- Adjust the gamma (the contrast in midtones of an image) to determine the proportion of darker tones to lighter tones.

1. **Open the file drachma.jpg from the WIP>MOAH folder.**

2. **Display the Histogram panel (Window>Histogram), and then choose Expanded View from the panel Options menu.**

   The Histogram panel shows the distribution of pixels — or, more accurately, the tonal values of those pixels — from the darkest to the lightest portions of an image, for the entire image or for individual color channels. The Histogram panel can help identify problems that need to be corrected.

   When you first display the panel, it probably appears in Compact view, which shows only the graphs for the individual color channels and the composite image. In Expanded view, you can see more information about how pixels are distributed in the image (from shadows on the left to highlights on the right).

   - The **Mean** value is an average point of the brightness values. A Mean of 128 usually identifies a well-balanced image. Images with a Mean of 170 to 255 are light; images with a Mean lower than 90 are very dark.

     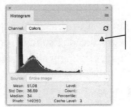

     If you see a warning icon, click it to reset the cache.

   - The **Standard Deviation** (Std Dev) value represents how widely the brightness values vary.

   - The **Median** value shows the middle value in the range of color values.

   - The **Pixels** value displays the total number of pixels used for the graphic displayed on the histogram.

   - The **Level** statistic displays the intensity level of the pixels below the mouse cursor.

   - **Count** shows the number of pixels in the area below the cursor.

   - **Percentile** represents the percentage of pixels below, or to the left, of the cursor location. Zero represents the left edge of the image and 100% is the right edge.

   - The **Cache Level** is determined by the Performance preferences, and is related to the Cache Refresh and Warning icons. The larger your cache, the more you can do before the image and disk cache don't match. On the other hand, a larger cache requires more RAM for the application to run smoothly.

3. **In the Histogram panel, change the Channel menu to RGB.**

The histogram — the chart that shows the distribution of tones — can display a single graph for the entire composite image (all channels combined) or for individual channels. The white space at the left and right sides of the histogram indicate that some of the tones in the available range are not being used in this image.

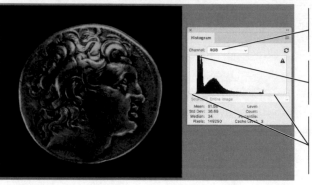

Choose from this menu to view the histogram for individual channels.

These shadows are pushing out of the "container," indicating a problem in the shadow tones.

Empty spaces on the left and right of the histogram indicate that some tones are not being used.

4. **If you see a Warning icon in the upper-right corner of the Histogram panel, click it to reset the cache.**

Every time you zoom in or out of an image, Photoshop stores the results of the display in a **cache** (a drive location that keeps track of what you're doing). The image you're looking at on the histogram often doesn't match the results on the drive. The Warning icon shows there's a problem; clicking it resets the image and rereads the cache.

Note:

You can use the Channels menu in the Histogram panel to view the histogram for individual channels.

5. **Choose Image>Adjustments>Levels and make sure Preview is checked.**

The Levels dialog box shows a histogram like the one shown in the Histogram panel.

Two sets of sliders control input and output levels. Each set has a black slider for adjusting the shadows and a white slider to adjust highlights. The Input Levels slider also has a gray triangle in the center of the slider bar for adjusting gamma or midtones.

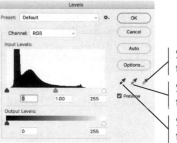

Sample in image to set White Point

Sample in image to set Gray Point

Sample in image to set Black Point

The Input sliders in the Levels dialog box correspond to the tonal range of the image. Any pixels that exist to the left of the Input Shadow slider are reproduced as solid black, and have no detail. Any pixels that exist to the right of the Input Highlight slider are reproduced as pure white.

Note:

You can use the Channel menu in the Levels dialog box to access and adjust the levels for a specific color channel.

6. **Move the Input Shadow slider to the right until it touches the left edge of the curve.**

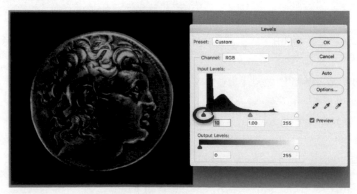

Note:

You can change input and output levels by moving the sliders, entering actual values in the boxes below the slider sets, or by using the eyedroppers to select the brightest and darkest points in the image.

7. Move the Input Highlight slider to the left until it touches the right edge of the curve.

The adjustments in Steps 6 and 7 extend the colors in the image to take advantage of all 256 possible tones.

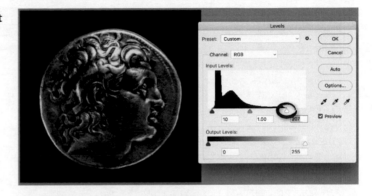

8. Move the Input Gamma slider to the left until the middle box below the slider shows approximately 1.35.

The Input Gamma slider controls the proportion of darker to lighter tones in the midtones of an image. If you increase gamma, you increase the proportion of lighter grays in the image. This effectively increases contrast in lighter shades and lightens the entire image. If you decrease gamma, you extend the tonal range of darker shades. This allows those areas of the image to be reproduced with a larger range of shades, which increases the contrast in darker shades.

Dragging the Input Gamma slider extends the range between the midtone and the highlights, creating greater contrast and showing more detail throughout the image.

To decrease contrast in an image, you can adjust the Output sliders. This method effectively compresses the range of possible tones that can be reproduced, forcing all areas of the image into a smaller tonal range. Areas originally set to 0 are reproduced at the value of the Output Shadow slider. Areas originally set to 255 are output at the value of the Output Highlight slider.

9. Click OK to close the Levels dialog box.

10. Save the file in your WIP>MOAH folder as a native Photoshop file named `drachma-fixed.psd`.

11. Close the file and then continue to the next exercise.

Identifying Shadows and Highlights

When you move the Shadow and Highlight sliders in the Levels dialog box, you change the **black point** and **white point** of the image — the points at which pixels become black or white. The goal is to find highlight and shadow points that maintain detail. Choosing a point that has no detail causes the area to turn totally white (highlight) or black (shadow), with no detail reproduced. In some images, it can be difficult to visually identify the black and white points. In these cases, you can use the Levels dialog box to help you find those areas.

If you press Option/Alt while dragging the Input Shadow or Input Highlight slider, the image turns entirely white or black (respectively). As you drag, the first pixels that become visible are the darkest shadow and the lightest highlight.

Once you identify the highlight and shadow points in the image, select the White Point eyedropper and click the highlight, then select the Black Point eyedropper and click the shadow to define those two areas of the image.

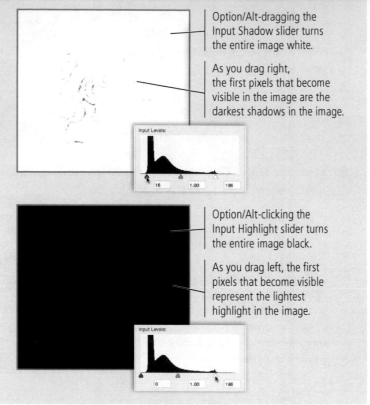

Option/Alt-dragging the Input Shadow slider turns the entire image white.

As you drag right, the first pixels that become visible in the image are the darkest shadows in the image.

Option/Alt-clicking the Input Highlight slider turns the entire image black.

As you drag left, the first pixels that become visible represent the lightest highlight in the image.

Correct Lighting Problems with the Exposure Adjustment

Many images are either over- or underexposed when photographed. If an image is underexposed, it appears dark and lacks detail in the shadows. If an image is overexposed, it appears too light and lacks detail in the highlights. You can use the Exposure adjustment to correct exposure, and thus, the overall detail and contrast in the image.

Keep in mind, however, that Photoshop cannot create information that doesn't exist. If you have an underexposed image with no detail in the shadow areas, Photoshop cannot generate that detail for you. Some problems are simply beyond fixing.

The Exposure dialog box is designed to make tonal adjustments to 32- and 64-bit HDR (high dynamic range) images, but it also works with 8- and 16-bit images. The Exposure adjustment works by performing calculations in a linear color space (gamma 1.0), rather than the image's current color space.

Note:

HDR refers to high-dynamic range (32- or 64-bit) images.

1. **Open vases.jpg from your WIP>MOAH folder.**

2. **Choose Image>Adjustments>Exposure and make sure Preview is checked.**

3. **Choose the White Point eyedropper in the dialog box, and then click the white area on the edge of the center vase.**

The eyedroppers in the Exposure dialog box adjust the image's luminance (or the degree of lightness, from white to black). By adjusting the luminance only, you can change the lightness of the image, without affecting the color.

- Clicking with the Black Point eyedropper shifts the point you click to black (0 luminance).
- Clicking with the White Point eyedropper shifts the point you click to white (100 luminance).
- Clicking with the Gray Point eyedropper shifts the point you click to gray (50 luminance).

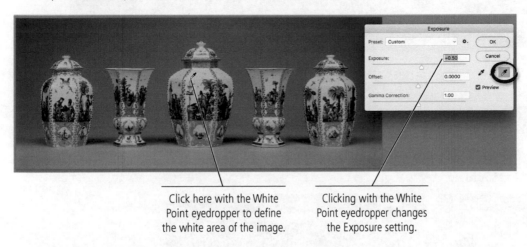

Click here with the White Point eyedropper to define the white area of the image.

Clicking with the White Point eyedropper changes the Exposure setting.

4. **Drag the Gamma Correction slider left to extend the midtone range, which increases contrast and brings out detail in the image. (We used a setting of 1.20.)**

The Gamma slider adjusts the image midtones. Dragging the slider left lightens the image, improving contrast and detail in the midtones and highlights. Dragging the slider right darkens the image, extending the range and increasing detail in the shadows.

Extending the Gamma Correction value into the shadow range brings out more detail in the midtones.

5. **Click the Offset slider and drag very slightly left to add detail back into the midtones and shadows.**

   The Offset slider lightens (when dragged to the right) or darkens (when dragged to the left) the shadows and midtones of the image. The white point (highlight) remains unaffected, but all other pixels are affected.

   Decreasing the Offset value adds
   detail back into the shadows.

6. **Click OK to finalize the adjustment.**

7. **Save the file as a native Photoshop file named vases-fixed.psd in your WIP>MOAH folder.**

8. **Close the file and continue to the next stage of the project.**

STAGE 3 / **Correcting Color Problems**

You can't accurately reproduce color without a basic understanding of color theory, so we present a very basic introduction in this project. Be aware that there are entire, weighty books written about color science. We're providing the condensed version of what you absolutely must know to work effectively with files in any color mode.

Before starting to color-correct an image, you should understand how different colors interact. There are two primary color models — RGB and CMYK — used to output digital images. Other models, such as LAB and HSB, have their own purposes in color conversion and correction, but they are not typically output models.

Additive vs. Subtractive Color

The most important thing to remember about color theory is that color is light, and light is color. Without light, you can't see — and without light, there is no color.

The **additive color** model (RGB) is based on the idea that all colors can be reproduced by combining pure red, green, and blue light in varying intensities. These three colors are considered the **additive primaries**. Combining any two additive primaries at full strength produces one of the **additive secondaries** — red and blue light combine to produce magenta; red and green combine to produce yellow; and blue and green combine to produce cyan. Although it is considered a "color," black is the absence of light, and therefore, also the absence of color.

Additive color model

White is the sum of all colors, produced when all three additive primaries are combined at full strength. Additive color theory is practically applied in computer monitors, which are black when turned off; when the power is turned on, light in the monitor illuminates at different intensities to create the range of colors that you see.

Printing pigmented inks on a substrate is a very different method of reproducing color. Reproducing color on paper requires **subtractive color theory**, which is essentially the inverse of additive color theory. Instead of adding red, green, and blue light to create the range of colors, subtractive color begins with a white surface that reflects red, green, and blue light at equal and full strength. To reflect (reproduce) a specific color, you add pigments that subtract or absorb only certain wavelengths from the white light. To reflect only red, for example, the surface must subtract (or absorb) the green and blue light.

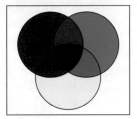

Subtractive color model

Remember that the additive primaries (red, green, and blue) combine to create the additive secondaries (cyan, magenta, and yellow). Those additive secondaries are also called the **subtractive primaries**, because each subtracts one-third of the light spectrum and reflects the other two-thirds:

- Cyan absorbs red light, reflecting only blue and green light.

- Magenta absorbs green light, reflecting only red and blue light.

- Yellow absorbs blue light, reflecting only red and green light.

A combination of two subtractive primaries, then, absorbs two-thirds of the light spectrum and reflects only one-third. As an example, a combination of yellow and magenta absorbs both blue and green light, reflecting only red.

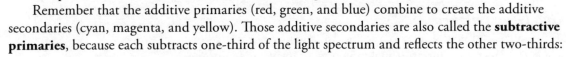

Color printing is a practical application of subtractive color theory. The pigments in the cyan, magenta, yellow, and black (CMYK) inks are combined to absorb different wavelengths of light. By combining different amounts of the subtractive primaries, it's possible to produce a large range (or gamut) of colors.

Although the RGB and CMYK models handle color in different ways, these two color models are definitely linked. RGB colors are directly inverse (opposite) to CMY colors, referring to the position of each color on a color wheel. The relationship between primary colors is the basis for all color correction.

Referencing a basic color wheel can help you understand how RGB colors relate to CMY colors. If you center an equilateral triangle over the color wheel, the points of the triangle touch either the RGB primaries or the CMY primaries. Adding together two points of the triangle results in the color between the two points. Red and blue combine to form magenta, yellow and cyan combine to form green, and so on.

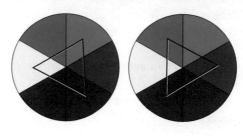

Opposite colors on the color wheel are called **color complements**. Using subtractive color theory, a color's complement absorbs or subtracts that color from visible white light. For example, cyan is opposite red on the color wheel; cyan absorbs red light and reflects green and blue. If you know green and blue light combine to create cyan, you can begin to understand how the two theories are related.

How does all this apply to color correction?

If you want to add a specific color to an image, you have three options: add the color; add equal parts of the color's constituent colors; or remove some of the color's complement color. For example, to add red, you can add red, add yellow and magenta, or remove cyan. Conversely, this means that to remove a color from an image, you can remove the color itself, remove equal parts of its constituents, or add its complement. To remove cyan, for example, you can remove cyan, remove blue and green, or add red.

Make sure you understand the relationships between complementary colors:

- To add red, add yellow and magenta, or remove cyan.
- To add blue, add cyan and magenta, or remove yellow.
- To add green, add cyan and yellow, or remove magenta.
- To remove cyan, remove blue and green, or add red.
- To remove yellow, remove green and red, or add blue.
- To remove magenta, remove blue and red, or add green.

Understanding Gray Balance

Understanding the concept of neutral gray is also fundamental to effective color correction. Once you correct the contrast (tonal range) of an image, many of the remaining problems can be, at least partially, fixed by correcting the **gray balance**, or the component elements of neutral grays.

In the RGB color model, equal parts of red, green, and blue light combine to create a shade of gray that is equal to the percentage of each component — R=0 G=0 B=0 creates pure black; R=255 G=255 B=255 creates pure white. To correct an image in RGB mode, you should evaluate and correct the neutral grays so that they contain equal percentages of the three primary colors.

Using the CMYK color model, equal percentages of cyan, magenta, and yellow *theoretically* combine to produce an equal shade of gray. For example, C=0 M=0 Y=0 creates white; C=100 M=100 Y=100 creates black. In practice, however, the impurities of ink pigments (specifically cyan) do not live up to this theory. When you print equal parts cyan, magenta, and yellow, the result is a muddy brown because the cyan pigments are impure. To compensate for those impurities, neutral grays must be adjusted to contain equal parts of magenta and yellow, and a slightly higher percentage of cyan.

Note:

Because white is a combination of all colors of light, white paper should (theoretically) reflect equal percentages of all light wavelengths. However, different papers absorb or reflect varying percentages of some wavelengths, thus defining the paper's apparent color. The paper's color affects the appearance of inks printed on it.

Note:

It might seem easiest to simply add or subtract the color in question. However, a better result might be achieved by adding one color and subtracting another. For example, if an image needs less blue, simply removing cyan can cause reds to appear pink or cyan to appear green. Adding magenta and yellow to better balance the existing cyan often creates a better result.

Note:

An important point to remember is that any color correction requires compromise. If you add or remove a color to correct a certain area, you also affect other areas of the image.

Correct Color Cast with the Color Balance Adjustment

Color cast is the result of improper gray balance, when one channel is significantly stronger or weaker than the others. An image with improper gray balance has an overall predominance of one color, which is most visible in the highlight areas. The image that you will correct in this exercise has a strong yellow cast that needs to be removed.

1. Open the file **bust.jpg** from your WIP>MOAH folder.

2. Display the Info panel (Window>Info).

3. If you don't see both RGB and CMYK color modes in the Info panel, choose Panel Options in the Info panel Options menu. In the resulting dialog box, choose Actual Color for the First Color Readout and CMYK Color for the Second Color Readout, then click OK.

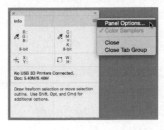

Note:

This exercise relies purely on numbers to correct gray balance. To see an accurate preview of image color on screen, you should calibrate your monitor and create a monitor profile that you can load into Photoshop.

4. Choose the Color Sampler tool (nested under the Eyedropper tool).

5. In the Options bar, choose 3 by 3 Average in the Sample Size menu.

Instead of correcting based on individual pixel values, you can average a group of contiguous pixels as the sample value. Doing so prevents accidentally correcting an image based on a single anomalous pixel (a dust spot, for example).

6. Click the cursor on the bust's right shoulder to place a color sample.

As you can see in the Info panel, the sample shows a significantly lower percentage of blue, which leads to a strong yellow color cast.

Note:

The Color Sampler tool can place up to ten sample points per image.

Note:

To delete an existing sample point, make the Color Sampler tool active, press Option/Alt, and click a point when the cursor icon changes to a pair of scissors.

Use this menu to define the sample size.

Color Sampler tool

Color samples are numbered in order of creation.

The Info panel shows color values for the current cursor location, in both RGB and CMYK modes.

The Info panel shows the values associated with the sample point you created.

7. **Choose Image>Adjustments>Color Balance.**

   Color Balance is a basic correction tool that can effectively remove overall color cast. The Color Balance dialog box presents a separate slider for each pair of complementary colors. You can adjust the highlights, shadows, or midtones of an image by selecting the appropriate radio button. The Preserve Luminosity check box ensures that only the colors shift, leaving the tonal balance of the image unchanged.

8. **Click the Highlights radio button in the Tone Balance section at the bottom of the Color Balance dialog box.**

9. **Drag the Yellow/Blue slider right until the right field shows +25.**

   Remember, adding a color's complement is one method for neutralizing that color. Increasing blue in the highlight areas neutralizes the yellow color cast.

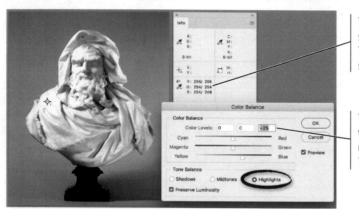

The values after the slash (/) show the result of the changes. These will become the actual sample values if you click OK.

These fields correspond to the three color sliders. The right field shows the Yellow/Blue adjustment.

10. **Click the Midtones radio button in the Tone Balance section at the bottom of the Color Balance dialog box.**

    The focus of this image — the bust — primarily occupies the highlight and midtone ranges. You are adjusting the color balance in both ranges to minimize the yellow cast.

11. **Drag the Yellow/Blue slider right until the right field shows +10.**

    Remember, adding a color's complement is one method for neutralizing that color. Increasing blue in the midtone areas further neutralizes the yellow color cast.

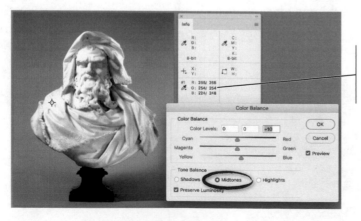

Changing the color balance brings the three values much closer to equal, removing the color cast.

12. **Click OK to apply the adjustment.**

13. **Save the file in your WIP>MOAH folder as a native Photoshop file named bust-fixed.psd.**

14. **Close the file and continue to the next exercise.**

 ## Correct Gray Balance with Curves

The Curves adjustment is the most powerful color-correction tool in Photoshop. If you understand the ideas behind curves, you can use this tool to remove color cast, enhance overall contrast, and even modify color values in individual channels.

The diagram in the Curves dialog box is the heart of the Curves adjustment. When you open the Curves dialog box, a straight diagonal line in the graph represents the existing color in the image.

The horizontal axis represents the input color value, and the vertical axis represents the output color value. The upper-right point is the maximum value for that color mode (255 for RGB images and 100 for CMYK images). The bottom-left corner of the curves grid is the zero point.

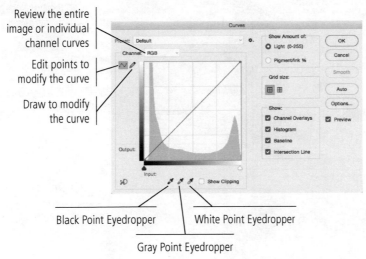

Review the entire image or individual channel curves

Edit points to modify the curve

Draw to modify the curve

Black Point Eyedropper

White Point Eyedropper

Gray Point Eyedropper

The color mode of the image determines the direction of the input and output scales. In both CMYK and RGB, 0 means "none of that color." However, remember the difference between the two color modes:

- The additive RGB color model starts at black and adds values of each channel to produce different colors, so 0, 0, 0 in RGB equals black.

- The subtractive CMYK model starts with white (paper) and adds percentages of each ink (channel) to produce different colors, so 0, 0, 0, 0 in CMYK equals white.

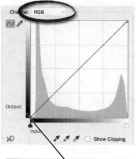 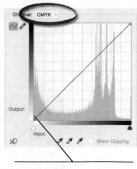

In RGB, the zero point represents the black point, or image shadows.

In CMYK images, the zero point represents the white point, or image highlights.

Every curve is automatically anchored by a black point and a white point. (For RGB, the black point is at the bottom left and the white point is at the top right.) You can add points along the curve by simply clicking the curve. You can also move any point on the curve by clicking and dragging.

When you move points on the curve of an image (whether for the whole image or for an individual channel), you are telling Photoshop to, "Map every pixel that was [this] input value to [that] output value." In other words, using the image to the right as an example, a pixel that was 137 (the input value) will now be 115 (the output value). Because curves are just that — curves, and not individual points — adjusting one point on a curve changes the shape of the curve as necessary.

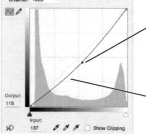

This point changes the input value of 137 to an output value of 115.

On either side of the adjusted point, the curve is adjusted to smoothly meet the other points on the curve (in this case, the black and white points).

Adjusting Curves On-Screen

The On-Image Adjustment tool in the Curves dialog box allows you to make curve adjustments by interacting directly with the image (behind the dialog box).

When the On-Image Adjustment tool is active, clicking in the image places a point on the curve based on the pixel data where you clicked. You can then drag up or down within the image area to move that point of the curve (i.e., to change the output value of the selected input value).

You can add 14 points on a curve, and delete points by pressing Command/Control-delete.

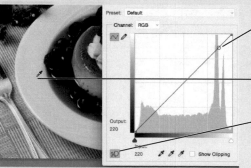

The open circle shows the curve point related to the cursor.

On-Image Adjustment tool cursor

The On-Image Adjustment tool is active.

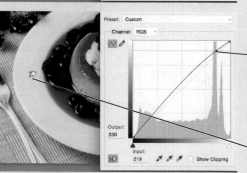

Clicking with the On-Image Adjustment tool adds a point at the appropriate spot on the curve.

Drag up or down in the image to adjust the curve at the added point.

1. **Open the file `plaque.jpg` from the WIP>MOAH folder.**

2. **Using the Color Sampler tool, place a sample point in the empty area outside the plaque.**

   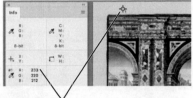

   The sample shows a strong red cast in what should be a neutral area.

   Recognizable "neutral" areas — such as the surrounding area in this image — are the best places to look for global color problems; fixing these will also fix many problem areas that you might not immediately recognize.

   This image has a strong red cast that needs to be neutralized. You can correct cast by removing the cast color or adjusting the other two primaries. The goal is equal (or nearly equal) parts of red, green, and blue in the neutral areas.

   In the Info panel, the sample values show that the red channel has a value of 233, the green channel has a value of 220, and the blue channel has a value of 212. To fix the cast in this image, you will use the middle of these values (the green channel) as the target and adjust the other two curves.

3. **Choose Image>Adjustments>Curves and make sure the Preview option is checked in the Curves dialog box.**

4. **Choose Red in the Channel menu to display the curve for only the Red channel, and then click the line on the graph to place a point near the three-quarter grid intersection.**

   After you adjust a curve (including adding the point, as you did in this step) the Info panel shows two values for the placed color sample. Numbers before the slash are the original values. Numbers after the slash are the values that result from changes in the Curves dialog box.

   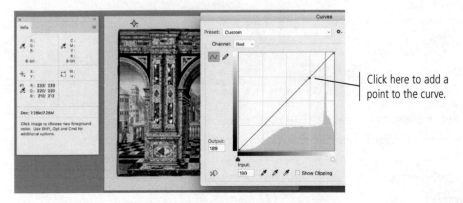

   Click here to add a point to the curve.

   > **Note:**
   >
   > *Your sample might be in a different place, showing slightly different values. Use the values on your screen, rather than the numbers in our screen captures, to complete the following steps.*

5. **With the new point selected on the curve, type the original Red value in the Input field (ours is 233).**

6. **Type the target value in the Output field (ours is the Green value of 220).**

   In the Info panel, the number after the slash shows that the Red value for this sample will be equal to the Green value when you click OK.

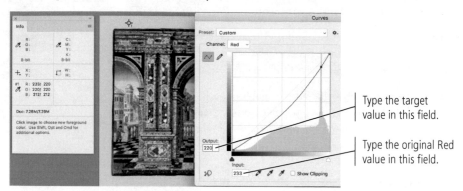

Type the target value in this field.

Type the original Red value in this field.

7. **In the Channel menu, choose the other channel that you need to adjust based on your sample values (ours is Blue). Add a point to the curve, and then adjust the input value to match your target output value (the original Green value, in our example).**

   Using our sample point, we adjusted the Input value of 212 to an Output value of 220.

   You can add the point anywhere along the curve. When you change the Input and Output values, the point automatically moves to that location along the curve.

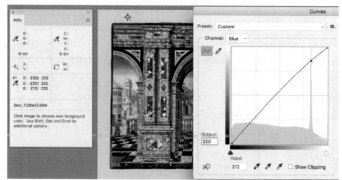

8. **Click OK to apply the changes and close the Curves dialog box.**

   You can see how simply correcting gray balance has a significant impact on the image:

9. **Save the file in your WIP>MOAH folder as a native Photoshop file named plaque-fixed.psd.**

10. **Close the file and continue to the next exercise.**

Correct Contrast with Curves

Remember, contrast is essentially the difference between the values in an image. By adjusting the points on the curve, you increase the tonal range between those points — which means you also increase the contrast in that same range.

In the image to the right, Point A has an Input value of 167 and an Output value of 182. Point B has an Input value of 87 and an Output value of 62. Mathematically:

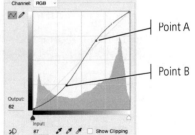

- Original tonal range (Input values): 167 to 87 = 80 available tones

- New tonal range (Output values): 182 to 62 = 120 available tones

Making these two curve adjustments significantly increases the tonal range available for the image's midtones, which means the contrast in the midtones is also significantly increased. A steeper curve indicates increased tonal range and increased contrast. Notice, however, that the curves before Point B and after Point A are much shallower than the original curves, which means this change also significantly reduces the contrast in the shadow and highlight areas.

Understanding Curve Display Options

Options on the right side of the dialog box allow you to control what is visible in the graph.

The Show Amount Of radio buttons reverse the input and output tone scales. Light is the default setting for RGB images; Pigment/Ink % is the default setting for CMYK images.

Use the Show Amount Of options to reverse the tone scales.

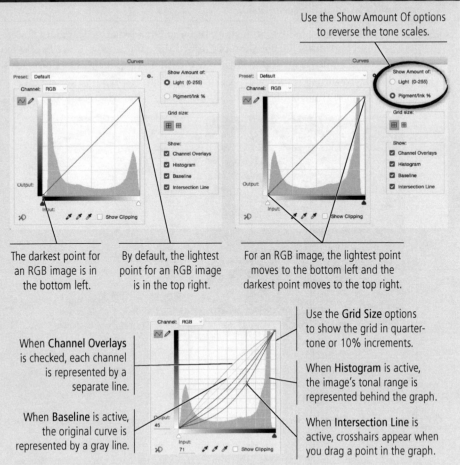

The darkest point for an RGB image is in the bottom left.

By default, the lightest point for an RGB image is in the top right.

For an RGB image, the lightest point moves to the bottom left and the darkest point moves to the top right.

When **Channel Overlays** is checked, each channel is represented by a separate line.

When **Baseline** is active, the original curve is represented by a gray line.

Use the **Grid Size** options to show the grid in quarter-tone or 10% increments.

When **Histogram** is active, the image's tonal range is represented behind the graph.

When **Intersection Line** is active, crosshairs appear when you drag a point in the graph.

Points to Remember about Curves

Curves are very powerful tools, and they can be intimidating. To simplify the process and make it less daunting, keep these points in mind:

- Aim for neutral grays.
- You can adjust the curve for an entire image, or you can adjust the individual curves for each channel of the image.
- The horizontal tone scale shows the Input value, and the vertical tone scale shows the Output value.
- Changes made to one area of a curve affect all other areas of the image.
- The steeper the curve, the greater the contrast.
- Increasing contrast in one area inherently decreases contrast in other areas.

1. **Open the file tile.jpg from the WIP>MOAH folder.**

2. **Choose Image>Adjustments>Curves and make sure Preview is checked.**

3. **Activate the Show Clipping option. Click the white point on the top-right corner of the graph, and drag left until some pixels start to appear in the image (behind the dialog box).**

    We dragged the Input White point just past the point where the histogram shows the lightest highlights in the image. (You performed this same action in the Levels dialog box when you adjusted the Input Highlight slider.) The Input and Output fields show that any pixels with an Input value of 220 will be output as 255. In other words, anything with an Input value higher than 220 will be clipped to solid white.

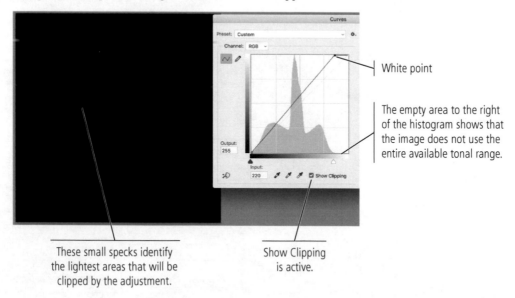

These small specks identify the lightest areas that will be clipped by the adjustment.

Show Clipping is active.

White point

The empty area to the right of the histogram shows that the image does not use the entire available tonal range.

4. **Turn off the Show Clipping option so you can see the actual image behind the dialog box.**

    Even this small change improved the image, but the midtones need some additional contrast. To accomplish that change, you need to steepen the curve in the middle of the graph.

5. **Click the curve to create a point at the quartertone gridline and drag it slightly to the right.**

   We adjusted the curve point from an Input value of 75 to an Output value of 65.

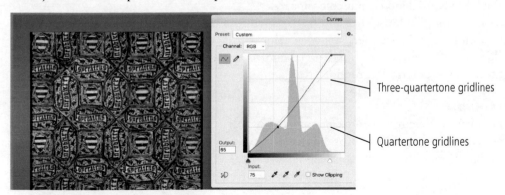

Three-quartertone gridlines

Quartertone gridlines

6. **Click the curve at the three-quartertone gridline and drag the point to the left.**

   We adjusted the Input value of 165 to an Output value of 190.

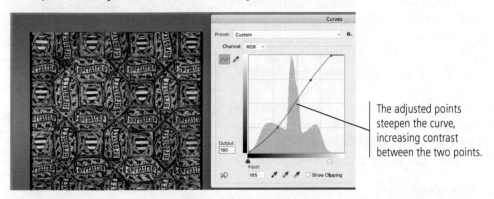

The adjusted points steepen the curve, increasing contrast between the two points.

7. **Click OK to apply the changes and close the dialog box.**

   Adjusting the contrast with curves improved the detail in the image and enhanced the overall image color.

8. **Save the file in your WIP>MOAH folder as a native Photoshop file named tile-fixed.psd.**

9. **Close the file and continue to the next stage of the project.**

STAGE 4 / **Preparing Images for Print**

You might have noticed that all the images for this project are in the RGB color mode. Printing, however, relies on the CMYK mode to output color images.

Although a full discussion of color science and management can be extremely complex, and is beyond the needs of most graphic designers, applying color management in Photoshop is more intimidating than difficult. We believe this foundational information on color management will make you a more effective and practically grounded designer.

Understanding Gamut

Different color models have different ranges, or **gamuts**, of possible colors. The RGB model has the largest gamut of the output models. The CMYK gamut is far more limited; many of the brightest and most saturated colors that can be reproduced using light cannot be reproduced using pigmented inks.

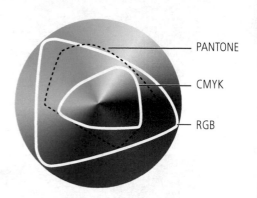

This difference in gamut is one of the biggest problems graphic designers face when working with color images. Digital image-capture devices (including scanners and digital cameras) work in the RGB space, which, with its larger gamut, can more closely mirror the range of colors in the original scene. Printing, however, requires images to first be converted or **separated** into the CMYK color space.

The usual goal in color reproduction is to achieve a color appearance equivalent to the original. Depending on the image, at least some colors in the RGB color model likely cannot be reproduced in the more limited gamut of the CMYK color model. These **out-of-gamut** colors pose a challenge to faithfully reproducing the original image. If the conversion from RGB to CMYK is not carefully controlled, **color shift** can result in drastic differences between the original and printed images.

Color Management in Brief

Color management is intended to preserve color predictability and consistency as a file is moved from one color mode to another throughout the reproduction process. Color management can also eliminate ambiguity when a color is only specified by some numbers. For example, you might create a royal purple in the Photoshop Color Picker, but without color management, that same set of RGB numbers might look more lilac (or even gray) when converted to CMYK for printing. A well-tuned color-management system can translate the numbers that define a color in one space to numbers that can better represent that same color in another space.

It's important to have realistic expectations for color management, and realize that color management isn't a replacement for a thorough knowledge of the color-reproduction process. Even at its best, color management can't fix bad scans or photos — all it can do is introduce consistency and predictability to a process that otherwise, rarely has either.

Color management relies on **color profiles**, which are data sets that define the reproduction characteristics of a specific device. A profile is essentially a recipe that contains the ingredients for reproducing a specific color in a given color space. The color recipes in profiles are known as **look-up tables** (LUTs), which are essentially cross-reference systems for finding matching color values in different color spaces.

Note:

Color shift can also result when converting from one type of CMYK to another, or (though less likely) from one version of RGB to another. Whatever models are being used, color management gives you better control over the conversion process.

Note:

Color profiles are sometimes also called "ICC profiles," named after the International Color Consortium (ICC), which developed the standard for creating color profiles.

Source profiles are the profiles of the devices (scanners, digital cameras, etc.) used to capture an image. **Destination profiles** are the profiles of output devices. LAB (or L*a*b*, or CIELAB) is a theoretical color space that represents the full visible spectrum. This device-independent color space can represent any possible color. By moving device-dependent RGB and CMYK colors into LAB as an intermediary space, you can convert color from any one space to any other space.

The **Color Management Module** (CMM) is the engine that drives color conversions via the LUT numbers. The engine doesn't do much other than look up numbers and cross-reference them to another set of numbers. The mechanics of color-managed conversions are quite simple. Regardless of the specific input and output spaces in use, the same basic process is followed for every pixel:

Note:

Most professional-level devices come with profiles you can install when you install the hardware. A number of generic and industry-specific destination profiles are also built into Photoshop.

1. The CMM looks up the color values of a pixel in the input-space profile to find a matching set of LAB values.

2. The CMM looks up the LAB values in the output-space profile to find the matching set of values that will display the color of that pixel most accurately.

Color Management in Theory and Practice

RGB and CMYK are very different entities. The two color models have distinct capabilities, advantages, and limitations. There is no way to exactly reproduce RGB color using the CMYK gamut because many of the colors in the RGB gamut are simply too bright or too saturated. Rather than claiming to produce an exact (impossible) match from your monitor to a printed page, the true goal of color management is to produce the best possible representation of the color using the gamut of the chosen output device.

A theoretically ideal color-managed workflow resembles the following:

- Image-capture devices (scanners and digital cameras) are profiled to create a look-up table that defines the device's color-capturing characteristics.

- Images are acquired using a calibrated, profiled device. The profile of the capturing device is tagged to every image captured.

- The image is opened in Photoshop and viewed on a calibrated monitor. The monitor's profile is defined in Photoshop as your working space.

- Photoshop translates the image profile to your working space profile.

- You define a destination (CMYK) profile for the calibrated output device that will be used for your final job.

- The image is converted from RGB to CMYK, based on the defined working space and destination profiles.

Notice that three of the "ideal workflow" steps mention a form of the word, "calibrate." To **calibrate** something means to check and correct a device's characteristics. Calibration is an essential element in a color-managed workflow, and it is fundamentally important to achieving consistent and predictable output.

You cannot check or correct the color characteristics of a device without having something with which you can compare the them. To calibrate a device, a known target — usually a sequence of distinct and varying color patches — is reproduced using the device. The color values of the reproduction are measured and compared to the values of the known target. Precise calibration requires adjusting the device until the reproduction matches the original.

As long as your devices are accurately calibrated to the same target values, the color acquired by your RGB scanner will exactly match the colors displayed on your RGB monitor and the colors printed by your desktop printer. Of course, most devices (especially consumer-level, desktop devices that are gaining a larger market share in the commercial graphics world) are not accurately calibrated, and very few are calibrated to the same set of known target values.

Keeping in mind these ideals and realities, the true goals of color management are to:

- Compensate for variations in the different devices
- Accurately translate one color space to another
- Compensate for limitations in the output process
- Better predict the result when an image is reproduced

Bitmap color reproduces all pixels in the image as either black or white; there are no shades of gray.

Grayscale color reproduces all tones in the file as shades of gray. This type of image has only one channel (you were introduced to color channels in Project 4: Music CD Artwork, and will learn more in subsequent projects).

RGB creates color by combining different intensities of red, green, and blue light (collectively referred to as the "additive primaries"). Computer monitors and television sets display color in RGB, which has a **gamut** (or range) of more than 16.7 million different colors. An RGB file has three color channels, one for each of the additive primaries.

LAB color is device independent; the colors it describes don't depend upon the characteristics of a particular printer, monitor, or scanner. In theory, LAB bridges the gap between the various color models and devices. It is used in the background when converting images from one color space to another.

CMYK ("process") **color** is based on the absorption and reflection of light. Four process inks — cyan, magenta, yellow, and black — are used in varying combinations and percentages to produce the range of printable colors in most commercial printing. A CMYK file has four color channels — one for each subtractive primary and one for black.

Theoretically, a mixture of equal parts of cyan, magenta, and yellow would produce black. Pigments, however, are not pure, so the result of mixing these colors is a muddy brown (called **hue error**). To obtain vibrant colors (and so elements, such as type, can be printed cleanly), black ink is added to the three primaries. Black is represented by the letter "K" for "key color."

The problem with using RGB for print jobs is that the RGB colors eventually need to be converted to CMYK separations for a commercial printing press. Photoshop includes sophisticated tools that allow you to control this conversion.

Your client's catalog will be printed, which means the image files ultimately have to be in the CMYK color mode. In this stage of the project, you will learn how to control and correct for the conversion process from RGB to CMYK — a very common process in professional graphic design. (In a professional environment, you would actually have to convert all of the images you have used in this project; we are only working with one for the sake of illustration.)

Define Color Settings

Photoshop's color management system allows you to set up a fully managed color workflow — from input device through output device. You can use Adobe's predefined color settings or create custom settings that pertain to the equipment you use.

1. **With no file open in Photoshop, choose Edit>Color Settings.**

   The Color Settings dialog box defines default working spaces for RGB, CMYK, gray, and spot colors, as well as general color management policies.

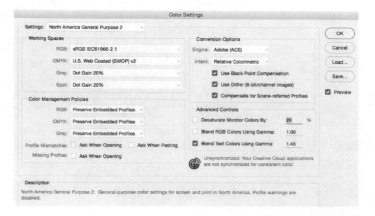

Note:

Your default options might be different than what you see here, depending on what previous users have defined.

2. **Choose North America Prepress 2 in the Settings menu.**

Photoshop includes four saved groups of options that are common in North America, which can be accessed in the Settings menu. You can also make your own choices and save those settings as a new preset by clicking Save, or you can import settings files created by another user by clicking Load.

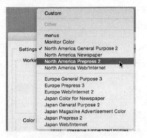

3. **In the Working Spaces area, choose the RGB profile for your monitor. If your specific monitor isn't available, choose Adobe RGB (1998).**

If you use a color-managed workflow, each color mode must be defined as a particular type of color space. Because there are different types of monitors, there are different types of RGB color spaces; the same is true of the other color spaces. The Working Space menus define exactly which version of each space is used to define color within that space.

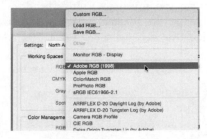

For color management to work properly, you must have accurate, device-specific profiles for every device in the workflow. However, you can use generic settings such as Adobe RGB (1998) in a "better-than-nothing" color environment — which is almost a direct contradiction to the concept of color management. We're showing you *how* to use the tools in Photoshop, but it's up to you to implement true color management by profiling your devices and using those profiles for specific jobs.

Note:

*A **working space** is the default profile used for each of the different color modes.*

Note:

When you choose a profile that isn't part of the saved settings, the Settings menu automatically changes to "Custom."

4. **In the CMYK menu, choose U.S. Sheetfed Coated v2.**

There are many CMYK profiles — each different printer and press has a gamut unique to that individual device.

This is a United States industry-standard profile for a common type of printing (sheetfed printing on coated paper). In a truly color-managed workflow, you would actually use a profile for the specific printing press/paper combination being used for the job. Again, we're using the default profiles to show you how the process works.

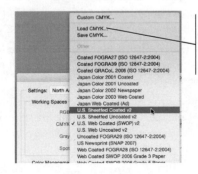

Use the Load CMYK option to access profiles that are supplied by your output provider.

Note:

We assume this catalog will be printed on a sheetfed press. However, always ask your output provider which profile to use for a specific job.

Note:

If you convert an image's color space using the Image>Mode menu, Photoshop converts the image to the default working space for the mode you choose.

5. **Leave the Gray and Spot working space menus at their default settings.**

The Gray working space defines how grayscale images will translate when the images are printed. Gray working space options include:

- **Dot Gain** (of varying percentages). These options compensate for the spread of a halftone dot in a grayscale image.

- **Gray Gamma.** This option allows you to set the monitor's gamma to compensate for differences between the monitor's presentation of an image and the actual grayscale image on press.

The Spot working space is similar to the Gray working space, but you can only specify dot gain percentages (not gamma).

6. **In the Color Management Policies area, make sure RGB is turned off, Preserve Embedded Profiles is selected for CMYK and Gray, and all three check boxes are selected.**

These options tell Photoshop what to do when you open an existing image. When an option here is turned off, color is not managed for that mode. If you choose Preserve Embedded Profiles, images that have a defined profile retain that profile; images with no profile use the current working space. If you choose Convert to Working Space, all images, even those with an embedded profile, are converted to the current working profile; images with no profile are assigned the current working profile.

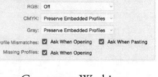

For profile mismatches, you can display a warning when opening or pasting an image with a different embedded profile. When an image doesn't have an embedded profile, you can display a warning by checking the Ask When Opening option.

7. **Review the options in the right side of the dialog box.**

Engine determines the system and color-matching method used to convert between color spaces – **Adobe (ACE)** or Adobe Color Engine; **Apple CMM** (Macintosh only); or **Microsoft ICM** (Windows only).

The **Intent** menu defines how the engine translates source colors outside the gamut of the destination profile.

- **Perceptual** presents a visually pleasing representation of the image, preserving visual relationships between colors. All colors, including those available in the destination gamut, shift to maintain a proportional relationship.

- **Saturation** compares the saturation of colors in the source profile and shifts them to the nearest-possible saturated color in the destination profile. The focus is on saturation instead of actual color value. This method can produce drastic color shift.

- **Relative Colorimetric** maintains any colors that are in both the source and destination profiles; source colors outside the destination gamut shift to fit. This method adjusts for the whiteness of the media.

- **Absolute Colorimetric** maintains colors in both the source and destination profiles. Colors outside the destination gamut are shifted to a color within the destination gamut, without considering the white point of the media.

When **Use Black Point Compensation** is selected, the full range of the source space is mapped into the destination space. This method is most useful when the black point of the source is darker than that of the destination.

When **Use Dither** is selected, colors in the destination space are mixed to simulate missing colors from the source space. This can result in larger file sizes for web images.

Compensate for Scene-Referred Profiles relates to the increasingly popular use of Photoshop to perform color correction (and profile matching) for video enhancement.

Desaturate Monitor Colors is useful for visualizing the full range of color, including colors outside the monitor's range. When this option is deselected, colors that were previously distinct might appear as a single color.

Blend RGB Colors Using Gamma inputs a gamma curve to avoid artifacts. A gamma of 1.00 is considered "colorimetrically correct."

Blend Text Colors Using Gamma applies the defined gamma to text layers.

Note:

Web printing is done on larger presses and fed from huge rolls of paper, with the actual pages being cut off the roll only after the ink has been laid down. Although web presses are typically cheaper to operate for long print runs, they generally do not produce the same quality of color as their sheetfed counterparts.

Sheetfed presses place ink on sheets of paper that have already been cut to press-sheet size from a large roll of paper. Sheetfed presses are typically considered higher quality, with appropriately higher costs associated with the job.

8. **Click Save in the Color Settings dialog box. In the resulting navigation dialog box, change the Save As/File Name field to museum.csf and click Save.**

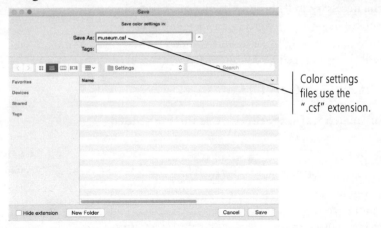

Color settings files use the ".csf" extension.

By default, custom color settings are saved in a Settings folder in a specific location where your system stores user preferences for different applications. Settings files saved in the application's default location are available in the Settings menu of the Color Settings dialog box.

If you are working on a shared computer or a network where you can't save to the system files, you might want to save the custom Color Settings file in your WIP folder. In this case, you would have to click the Load button to locate the CSF file.

9. **In the Color Settings Comment dialog box, type Use this option for Photoshop museum image adjustment project.**

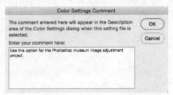

10. **Click OK to return to the Color Settings dialog box.**

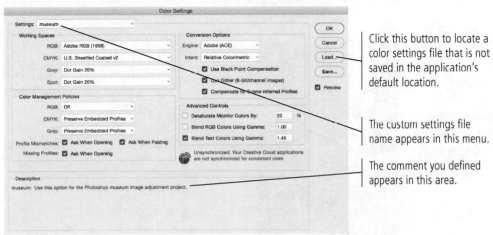

Click this button to locate a color settings file that is not saved in the application's default location.

The custom settings file name appears in this menu.

The comment you defined appears in this area.

11. **Click OK to close the Color Settings dialog box and apply your settings, and then continue to the next exercise.**

Identify Out-of-Gamut Colors

Fortunately, Photoshop contains the necessary tools for previewing out-of-gamut colors, which means you can correct colors *before* converting an image. If you have no out-of-gamut colors, then there is nothing to shift, and you can be fairly confident that your color images will be reproduced as you intended.

1. **Open the file jar.jpg from the WIP>MOAH folder.**

2. **When you see the profile mismatch warning, choose Use the Embedded Profile, and then click OK.**

    Remember, color management relies on profiles to accurately translate color from one model to another. This dialog box shows you the starting point — the embedded image profile. As a general rule, you should use the embedded profile whenever one is available.

Note:

You can choose Edit>Assign Profile to define a specific profile for the active image.

3. **Choose View>Proof Colors to toggle that option on.**

    This toggle provides a quick preview of what will happen when the image is converted to the CMYK working-space profile, without affecting the actual file data. In this case, you do not see significant color shift, suggesting that the image will not need significant correction for four-color printing.

Original color

Proof color

Note:

Command/Control-Y toggles the Proof Colors view on or off.

Shift-Command/ Control-Y toggles the Gamut Warning View.

4. **Choose View>Proof Colors again to toggle the option off.**

5. **Choose View>Gamut Warning.**

    When the Gamut Warning is visible, any areas where color shift will occur are highlighted with a gray overlay. In this case, the highlight shows that only the brightest blue areas on the jar will be affected.

A gray highlight overlays areas where color shift will occur.

Note:

You can change the color of the gamut warning overlay in the Transparency & Gamut pane of the Preferences dialog box.

6. **Continue to the next exercise.**

Adjust Highlight and Shadow Points for Print

For images that will be commercially printed, some allowance must be made in the highlight and shadow areas for the mechanics of the printing process. Images are printed as a pattern of closely spaced dots called a **halftone**. Those dots create the illusion of continuous color. Different sizes of dots create different shades of color — larger dots create darker shades and smaller dots create lighter shades.

There is a limit to the smallest size dot that can be consistently reproduced. The mechanical aspect of the printing process causes anything specified as a 1% dot to drop out, resulting in highlights that lack detail and contrast. The **minimum printable dot** is the smallest printable dot, and should be specified for highlights in a CMYK image. There is some debate over the appropriate highlight setting because different presses and imaging equipment have varying capabilities. To be sure your highlights will work on most printing equipment, you should define the highlight as C=5 M=3 Y=3 K=0.

Maximum printable dot is the opposite of minimum printable dot. Paper's absorption rate, speed of the press, and other mechanical factors limit the amount of ink that can be placed on the same area. If too much ink is printed, the result is a dark blob with no visible detail. Heavy layers of ink also result in drying problems and a number of other issues.

Total ink coverage is the largest percentage of ink that can be safely printed on a single area, and therefore dictates the shadow dot you define in Photoshop. This number, similar to minimum printable dot, varies according to the ink/paper/press combination being used for a given job. The Specifications for Web Offset Publications (SWOP) indicates a 300% maximum value. Many sheetfed printers require 280% maximum, while the number for newspapers is usually around 240% because the lower-quality paper absorbs more ink.

Note:

The larger cyan percentage is to compensate for the typically weaker characteristics of cyan printing ink.

1. **With jar.jpg open and the gamut warning visible, choose Image>Adjustments>Curves.**

2. **Double-click the White Point Eyedropper.**

3. **In the resulting Color Picker (Target Highlight Color) dialog box, change the CMYK values to C=5 M=3 Y=3 K=0, and then click OK.**

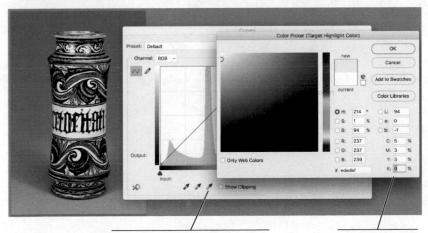

Double-click the White Point Eyedropper to open the Color Picker (Target Highlight Color) dialog box.

Change the Target Highlight Color in these fields.

4. **With the White Point Eyedropper selected, click the lightest highlight in the image where you want to maintain detail.**

We selected this area as the white point.

5. **Double-click the Black Point Eyedropper. Change the target CMYK values to C=80 M=70 Y=70 K=70, and then click OK.**

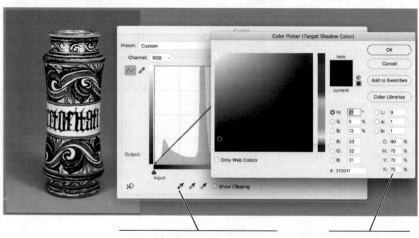

Double-click the Black Point Eyedropper to open the Color Picker (Target Shadow Color) dialog box.

Change the Target Shadow Color in these fields.

6. **With the Black Point Eyedropper selected, click the darkest area of the image where you want to maintain shadow detail.**

   By defining the target highlight and shadow points in the image, you can see that the gray gamut warning is nearly gone in all but the brightest blue areas. As you saw when you used the Proof Colors option, the shift will be minimal. No further correction is required for this image.

Note:

You can turn the gamut warning off and on while the Curves dialog box is open.

We selected this area as the black point.

7. **Click OK to apply your changes.**

8. **Click No in the warning message.**

   If you change the target Black Point, Gray Point, or White Point Eyedropper values, Photoshop asks if you want to save the new target values as the default settings when you click OK to close the Curves dialog box.

9. **Choose View>Gamut Warning to toggle that option off.**

10. **Continue to the next exercise.**

   Because the RGB gamut is so much larger than CMYK, you can expect colors to be far less brilliant (especially in the outer ranges of saturation) when corrected to the CMYK gamut. It's better to know this will happen and control it, rather than simply allowing the color management engine to shift colors where it deems best.

Converting Image Color Modes

Although many modern workflows convert RGB images to CMYK during the output process (called "on-the-fly" or "in-RIP" conversion), there are times when you need to manually convert RGB images to CMYK. This is a fairly simple process, especially if you have corrected your images to meet the requirements of the printing process.

1. **With the corrected jar image open from the previous exercise, choose Image>Mode>CMYK Color.**

   This option converts the image to the CMYK color mode using the current working space. Since you intentionally defined the working profile and corrected the image to that profile, you can safely use this menu option to convert the RGB image to CMYK.

2. **Click OK in the resulting warning dialog box.**

3. **Choose File>Save As. Navigate to WIP>MOAH as the target location.**

4. **Change the Format/Save As Type menu to Photoshop, and then add -CMYK to the end of the existing file name.**

5. **Macintosh users: In the bottom half of the Save As dialog box, make sure the Embed Color Profile: U.S. Sheetfed Coated v2 option is checked.**

   Windows users: In the bottom half of the Save As dialog box, make sure the ICC Profile: U.S. Sheetfed Coated v2 option is checked.

   By embedding the profile into the Photoshop file, other applications and devices with color management capabilities will be able to correctly process the image color data in the file, based on the embedded profile.

 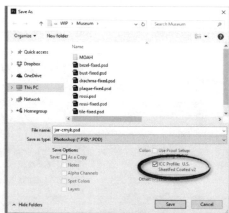

6. **Click Save.**

7. **Close the file, then continue to the final stage of the project.**

Note:

You can also convert an image to a different color model by choosing Edit>Convert to Profile, and then choosing any available profile in the Destination Space Profile menu.

Note

Color mode is not something that should be switched on a whim; rather, it is the final stage of a specific process.

Converting Images to Grayscale

An RGB image has three channels and a CMYK image has four channels. Each channel is a grayscale representation of the tones of that color throughout the image. A **grayscale image** has only one channel, and the grayscale tones in that channel are the tones in the entire image. Choosing Image>Mode>Grayscale simply flattens the component color channels, throwing away the color information to create the gray channel.

The **Desaturate** adjustment (Image>Adjustments> Desaturate) has a similar effect, but maintains the same number of channels as the original image. This adjustment averages the individual channel values for each pixel and applies the average value in each channel. (Remember, equal values of red, green, and blue combine to create a neutral gray value.)

If you need to convert a color image to grayscale, you might want to carefully consider which data to use for generating the gray channel. The **Black & White** adjustment (Image> Adjustments>Black & White) enables you to control the conversion process. In the Black and White dialog box, you can either choose one of the built-in presets, or drag the individual color sliders to determine how dark that color component will be in the resulting image.

If you move the mouse cursor over the image, it changes to an eyedropper. You can click an area in the image to highlight the predominant color in that area. Click within the image and drag to dynamically change the slider associated with that area of the image.

Remember, equal parts red, green, and blue combine to create a neutral gray. Applying the Black & White filter maintains the existing color channels, with exactly the same data in all three channels. Because the adjusted image is still technically in a color mode (not Grayscale), you can also use the Tint options in the Black & White dialog box to apply a hue or saturation tint to the grayscale image. After using the Black & White dialog box to control the conversion of colors to grayscale, you can safely discard the color data by choosing Image>Mode>Grayscale.

STAGE 5 / Working with HDR Images

The human eye is extremely sensitive to subtle changes in light. In general, we can perceive detail in both light and dark areas — and areas in-between — with a single glance. Camera sensors, on the other hand, are not as perceptive. If you look at most photographs, they typically have sharp detail in one of the ranges — highlights, midtones, or shadows — depending on the exposure and other settings used to capture the image. If a photograph favors highlights, details in shadow areas are lost (and vice versa).

To solve this problem, the concept of HDR (**high dynamic range**) images combines multiple photographs of different exposures into a single image to enhance the detail throughout the entire image. HDR images combine highlight, shadow, and midtone detail from various exposures to create an image more like what the human eye is capable of observing, rather than the more limited range that characterizes a digital camera's sensors.

The phrase "dynamic range" refers to the difference between the darkest shadow and the lightest highlight in an image.

- A regular 8-bit RGB photo has a dynamic range of 0–255 for each color channel (2^8 or 256 possible values). In other words, each pixel can have one of 256 possible values to describe the lightness of that color in that specific location.

- A 16-bit RGB photo allows 16 bits of information to describe each pixel, allowing a dynamic range of 2^{16} or 65,536 possible values in each color channel.

- A 32-bit, or HDR, image allows 2^{32} possible values — more than 4 billion, which is signficantly larger than the visible spectrum of 16.7 million colors (thus, 32-bit dynamic range is sometimes referred to as "infinite").

Use Merge to HDR Pro

The last piece required to complete this project is an image of the new museum's exterior. The photographer suggested using high dynamic range (HDR) photo techniques to capture the most possible detail in the scene, and has provided you with five photos taken at the same time, using different exposure settings.

1. **With no file open, choose File>Automate>Merge to HDR Pro.**

2. **In the resulting Merge to HDR Pro dialog box, choose Folder in the Use menu and then click the Browse button.**

   This option makes it easy to identify the folder that contains all component images for the HDR merge.

3. **Navigate to WIP>MOAH>Museum, and then click Open/OK.**

Note:

You can merge up to seven images with the Merge to HDR Pro utility.

4. **Make sure the Attempt to Automatically Align Source Images box at the bottom of the dialog box is checked, then click OK.**

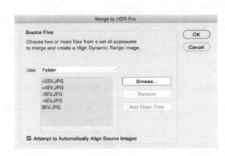

Because you are merging multiple images into one, there is a chance that one or more images might be slightly misaligned. Even using a tripod, a stiff breeze can affect the camera just enough to make the different exposures slightly different. When Attempt to Automatically Align Source Images is checked, Photoshop compares details in each image and adjusts them as necessary to create the resulting merged image.

5. **If you don't see a histogram on the right side of the dialog box, open the Mode menu and choose 32 Bit.**

The resulting dialog box shows each selected image as a thumbnail at the bottom. By default, all selected images are included in the merge. You can exclude specific exposures by unchecking the box for that image.

If you work with HDR, you need to realize that most computer monitors are not capable of displaying 32-bit image depth. When you merge to a 32-bit image, you can use the White Point Preview slider to change the dynamic range that is visible on your screen, but this has no effect on the actual data in the file — it affects only the current display of the image data.

6. **Check the Remove Ghosts option on the right side of the dialog box.**

When an HDR image contains movement, merging the individual exposures can blur the areas where that movement occurs. When you check Remove Ghosts, the software uses one of the exposures (highlighted in green) to define detail in the area of motion, such as the moving car in this image. You can change the key exposure by simply clicking a different image in the lower pane.

Note:

The merge process might take a minute or two to complete, so be patient.

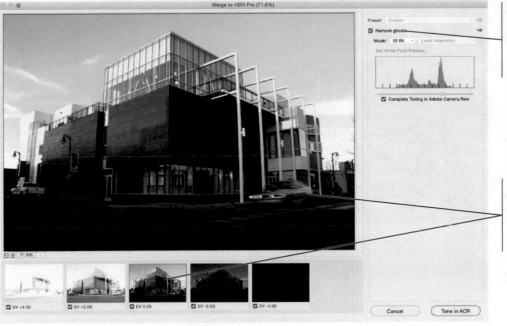

Check Remove Ghosts to eliminate blurring in areas that differ from one exposure to another.

When Remove Ghosts is checked, details in areas of movement are defined by the selected exposure.

7. Open the Mode menu and choose 8 Bit.

32-bit images can store a tremendous amount of information, which creates images with far more detail than you see in a conventional 8-bit photograph. However, one significant disadvantage of such images is that they cannot be separated for commercial printing. If you're going to use an HDR image in a print application — such as the cover of this catalog — you need to apply the process of **tone mapping** to define how the high dynamic range will be compressed into the lower dynamic range required by the output process.

8. Leave the secondary menu set to Local Adaptation.

You can use the other options to apply less specific tone mapping to the image. Equalize Histogram and Highlight Compression have no further options. The Exposure and Gamma option allows you to define specific values for only those two settings.

When the Local Adaptation method is selected, you can change the values for a number of specific options to map the tones in the HDR image to a lower dynamic range.

9. Open the Preset menu and choose Surrealistic.

The application has a number of standard settings, including several variations of monochromatic, photorealistic, and surrealistic. Each preset changes the values of the Local Adaptation sliders to create the desired effect.

You can create your own presets by clicking the button to the right of the Preset menu and choosing Save Preset in the resulting menu.

10. **Experiment with the different sliders until you are satisfied with the result.**

Tone mapping is a largely subjective process, and different end uses can influence the settings that you apply to a specific image. You should understand the following information as you experiment with the various settings:

- **Radius** defines the size of the glowing effect in areas of localized brightness.

- **Strength** determines the required tolerance between tonal values before pixels are no longer considered part of the same brightness region.

- **Gamma** values lower than 1.0 increase details in the midtones, while higher values emphasize details in the highlights and shadows.

- **Exposure** affects the overall lightness or darkness of the image.

- **Detail** increases or decreases the overall sharpness of the image.

- **Shadow** and **Highlight** affect the amount of detail in those areas of the image. Higher values increase detail and lower values reduce detail.

- **Vibrance** affects the intensity of subtle colors, while minimizing clipping of highly saturated colors.

- **Saturation** affects the intensity of all colors from –100 (monochrome) to +100 (double saturation).

11. **Click OK to finalize the process.**

Because you chose 8 Bit in the Mode menu of the Merge to HDR Pro dialog box, the resulting image is an 8-bit RGB image (as you can see in the document tab).

Note:

The original exposures for this image were captured by Charlie Essers.

12. **Save the file in your WIP>MOAH folder as a native Photoshop file named museum-merged.psd, and then close it.**

1. The _____ filter blurs an image by a selected pixel radius.

2. _____ is defined as random pixels that stand out from the surrounding pixels.

3. The _____ blends colors from user-defined source pixels with colors in the area in which you click.

4. The _____ paints one part of an image over another part, which is useful for duplicating specific objects or removing defects in an image.

5. _____ are direct sources of light such as a light bulb or reflected sunlight on water; they should not be considered the highlights of an image.

6. _____ refers to the tonal variation within an image.

7. A _____ is a visual depiction of the distribution of colors in an image.

8. The _____ is the darkest point, beyond which no shadow detail is maintained.

9. The _____ is the lightest point, beyond which no highlight detail is maintained.

10. Images are printed as a pattern of closely spaced dots called a _____.

1. Explain the concept of neutral gray.

2. List three important points to remember when working with curves.

3. Briefly explain the concepts of minimum printable dot and maximum ink coverage.

Use what you have learned in this project to complete the following freeform exercise.
Carefully read the art director and client comments, then create your own design to meet the needs of the project.
Use the space below to sketch ideas. When finished, write a brief explanation of the reasoning behind your final design.

art director comments

The director of the local tourism board recently saw your work for the museum, and has hired you to work on a new project about local architecture.

To complete this project, you should:

❑ Find at least 10 photos of different architectural styles throughout the Los Angeles metropolitan area.

❑ Use photo retouching techniques to clean up any graffiti and trash that is visible in the images.

❑ Use correction techniques to adjust the tonal range and gray balance of the images.

❑ Correct and convert all images based on the U.S. Sheetfed Coated v2 CMYK destination profile.

client comments

Over the next year, we're planning on publishing a series of promotional booklets to show tourists that L.A. is more than just Hollywood.

Each issue will focus on an "area of interest" such as architecture, which is the first topic. The city has a diverse architectural mix, from eighteenth-century Spanish missions and 1920s bungalows, to the Disney Concert Hall designed by Frank Gehry in the 1990s.

We'd like at least 10 pictures of different landmarks or architectural styles, corrected and optimized for printing on a sheetfed press. If possible, we'd also like some historical images to include in a "building a metropolis" section on the first couple of pages.

Of course, Los Angeles is a large city, and cities have their problems — not the least of which are graffiti and garbage. We are trying to attract tourists. Make sure none of the images show any graffiti or blatant litter. If these problems are visible in the images you select, give them a good digital cleaning.

project justification

PROJECT SUMMARY

As with many other skills, it takes time and practice to master image correction techniques. Understanding the relationship between brightness and contrast, and how these two values affect the quality of reproduction in digital images, is the first, and possibly, most critical factor in creating a high-quality image. An image that has too much contrast (a "sharp" image) or not enough contrast (a "flat" image) translates to an unsatisfactory print.

A basic understanding of color theory (specifically, complementary color) is the foundation of accurate color correction. Effective color correction relies on the numbers, rather than what you think you see on your monitor. As you gain experience in correcting images, you will be better able to predict the corrections required to achieve the best possible output.

Remove photographic grain with blur and sharpen techniques

Use the Healing Brush and Spot Healing Brush tools to correct scratches

Use the Clone Stamp tool to remove major damage

Use Merge to HDR Pro to find detail in multiple exposures

Correct lighting problems with the Exposure adjustment

Correct minor problems with the Brightness/ Contrast adjustment

Correct contrast with the Curves adjustment

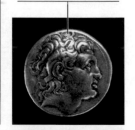

Correct and convert an image using the defined destination CMYK profile

Correct contrast and tonal range using the Levels adjustment

Correct contrast and gray balance using the Curves adjustment

Correct overall color cast using the Color Balance adjustment

Letterhead Design

7

Your client has hired you to create a letterhead design that incorporates the corporate logo and a set of images representing the kind of products that are available at the client's retail location. They are going to have the letterhead printed commercially so they can use it to print letters, invoices, and other business correspondence.

This project incorporates the following skills:

❏ Creating a new file to meet defined project requirements

❏ Using the basic InDesign drawing tools to develop visual interest

❏ Selecting objects and object contents

❏ Creating and formatting basic text attributes

❏ Placing and manipulating external graphics files

❏ Printing a desktop proof sample

client comments

Until now, we've just added the logo and address at the top of a Word document whenever we sent out correspondence. The business has been growing lately, and we want something more professional.

I sent you our logo, which was created in Adobe Illustrator. I also selected a bunch of images that represent the different stores at the market; I want to include at least a few of those on the letterhead.

Can you get our address information from our website, or do we need to send that to you as a separate document?

art director comments

I've looked over the client's images, and I think we should use all of them. InDesign has everything you need to create the necessary graphics directly on the page layout.

I already reviewed the size of the photos. They should be fine to place into the layout as they are; you won't need to manipulate the actual image files.

I also copied the client's contact info into a file for you. I noticed they have a tagline — Grand Cuisine. Grand Culture. Grand Central. — fairly prominent throughout the site, so I think we should include that in the print design work, as well.

It might feel like there's a lot involved in creating this piece, but it's not too complicated. The client liked the initial sketch, so putting in the effort at this point will be worth it.

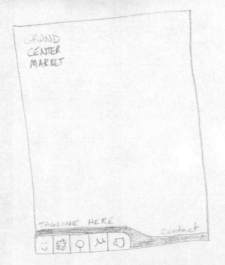

project objectives

To complete this project, you will:

- ❏ Create a new document based on the requirements of a commercial printer.
- ❏ Place ruler guides to define "safe" areas on the page.
- ❏ Draw basic shapes using native InDesign tools.
- ❏ Use a variety of methods to arrange multiple objects.
- ❏ Work with anchor points and handles to create a complex shape.
- ❏ Apply color to fills and strokes.
- ❏ Create and format basic text elements.
- ❏ Import external text and graphics files.
- ❏ Print a desktop proof.

STAGE 1 / **Setting up the Workspace**

As you learned in the Interface chapter, InDesign gives you extensive control over your workspace — you can choose where to place panels, whether to collapse or expand open panels, and even to save workspaces with sets of panels in specific locations. Because workspace issues are largely a matter of personal preference, we tell you what tools to use, but we don't tell you where to keep the various panels. Many of our screen captures show floating panels so we can clearly focus on a specific issue. Likewise, we typically don't tell you what view percentage to use; you should use whatever you are comfortable with to accomplish the specific goal of an exercise.

Define a New Layout File

Some production-related concerns will dictate how you design a letterhead. If letterhead is being printed commercially, it's probably being printed with multiple copies on a large press sheet from which the individual letterhead sheets will be cut. Most commercial printing happens this way. This type of printing typically means design elements can run right off the edge of the sheet, called **bleeding**.

If you're designing for a printer that can run only letter-size paper, you have to allow enough of a margin area for your printer to hold the paper as it moves through the device (called the **gripper margin**); in this case, you can't design with bleeds.

The most basic process in designing a layout is creating a new InDesign file. The New Document dialog box has a large number of options, and the following exercise explains them. Don't be overwhelmed by the length of this process; in later projects, we simply tell you what settings to define without re-explaining every field.

> **Note:**
>
> *Some desktop printers have a minimum margin at the page edges; you're usually safe with 3/8".*
>
> *Many newer inkjet printers have the capability to print 8.5 × 11" with full bleed. Consult your printer documentation to be sure.*

1. **Download GCMarket_Print19_RF.zip from the Student Files web page.**

2. **Expand the ZIP archive in your WIP folder (Macintosh), or copy the archive contents into your WIP folder (Windows).**

   This results in a folder named **GCMarket**, which contains all the files you need for this project. You should also use this folder to save the files you create in this project.

   If necessary, refer to Page 1 of the Interface chapter for specific information on expanding or accessing the required resource files.

3. **In InDesign, choose File>New>Document.**

   You have several options for creating a new file:

   - Choose File>New>Document
   - Use the associated keyboard shortcut Command/Control-N
   - Click the Create New button in the Start workspace

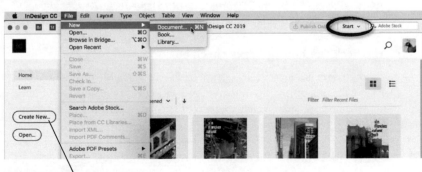

If the Start workspace is visible, click the Create New button to open the New Document dialog box.

4. **Click the Print option at the top of the resulting New Document dialog box.**

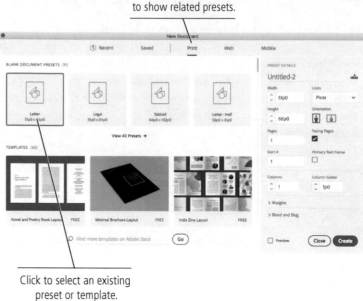

Click a category name to show related presets.

Click to select an existing preset or template.

5. **Choose the Letter preset on the left side of the dialog box.**

The New Document dialog box presents a number of preset sizes and prebuilt starter templates, broken into categories based on the intended output.

When you choose the Print category, you see common page sizes such as Letter and Legal. The Print presets automatically default to the CMYK color mode, which is required for commercial printing applications. For all the Web and Mobile categories of presets, the new document defaults to the RGB color mode.

6. **On the right side of the dialog box, type gcm-letterhead in the Name field.**

Because you selected the Letter preset in Step 5, the Width and Height fields default to 8.5 inches and 11 inches respectively.

7. **Make sure the Portrait Orientation option is selected.**

Portrait documents are higher than they are wide; **landscape** documents are wider than they are high. If you click the Orientation option that is not currently selected, the Width and Height values are automatically reversed.

Click here to highlight the field, then type to define a new file name.

Landscape

Portrait

8. **Leave the Number of Pages field set to 1.**

A letterhead is a single page, usually printed on only one side. This project needs only a single layout page in the InDesign file.

9. **Leave the Start Page # field set to 1.**

This option is useful when you work with multi-page files. Odd-numbered pages always appear on the right, as you see in any book or magazine; you can define an even-numbered starting page to force the first page of a layout to the left.

10. **Uncheck the Facing Pages check box.**

Facing pages are used when a printed job will be read left to right like a book, with Page 1 starting on the right, then Page 2 facing Page 3, and so on. Facing-page layouts are based on **spreads**, which are pairs of left-right pages as you flip through a book (e.g., Page 6 facing Page 7).

11. **Leave the Primary Text Frame option unchecked.**

When this option is checked, InDesign creates a text frame that automatically fills the area created by the defined page margins. A letterhead design primarily focuses on the area outside the margins, so you don't need to add a primary text frame to this file.

12. Choose Inches in the Units menu.

By default, InDesign uses picas as the unit of measurement for print documents; measurements in this dialog box are shown in picas and points, using the "ApB" notation (for A picas and B points).

If you choose Web or Digital Publishing, InDesign changes the default unit of measurement to pixels, which is more appropriate for web design.

Regardless of which unit of measurement you choose when you create a new file, you can change the setting for a specific file in the Units and Increments pane of the Preferences dialog box. InDesign supports all modern units of measurement, including points, picas, inches, millimeters, centimeters, and pixels (as well as a few others from historic typography).

You can also type different measurement units, such as "2cm", in a dialog box or panel field. As long as you include the unit in your entry, the software accurately translates the value you type into the default unit for the active file.

13. Expand the Margins section of the preset details.

14. If the chain icon to the right of the Margin fields shows two connected links, click the icon to break the link between the fields.

When the chain icon is active (connected links), all four margin fields will be the same; changing one field changes all margin values to the same value. For this project, the top and bottom values need to be different from the left and right values, so you need to unlink (unconstrain) the fields.

Click here to expand or collapse the Margins section.

Click this icon to unlink the four Margin fields.

15. Highlight the first Margins field (Top) and type 2.

When you define values using the default unit of measurement, it is not necessary to type the unit; you can simply type the numbers.

16. Press Tab to move to the Bottom field.

You can tab through the fields of most dialog boxes and panels in InDesign. Press Shift-Tab to move the highlight to the previous field in the tab order.

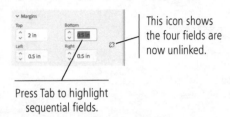

This icon shows the four fields are now unlinked.

Press Tab to highlight sequential fields.

17. Change the Bottom field to 1.75, then press Tab to highlight the Left field.

18. Change the Left field to 0.75, press Tab, and then change the Right field to 0.75.

It is not necessary to type the preceding zero when you define a value. We include it here for clarity.

Note:

Picas are the measuring units traditionally used in typography; they are still used by many people in the graphic communications industry.

1 point = 1/72 inch

12 points = 1 pica

1 pica = 1/6 inch

6 picas = 1 inch

Note:

You should become familiar with the common fraction-to-decimal equivalents:

1/8 = 0.125

1/4 = 0.25

3/8 = 0.375

1/2 = 0.5

5/8 = 0.625

3/4 = 0.75

7/8 = 0.875

Note:

When you work with non-facing pages, the Inside and Outside margin fields change to Left and Right respectively. Technically, non-facing pages do not have an inside (spine edge) or outside (face or trim edge), so there are only left and right sides.

19. **Click the arrow button to the left of the Bleed and Slug heading.**

20. **Make sure the chain icon to the right of the Bleed fields is active (unbroken links), then change the first Bleed field to 0.125 (the decimal equivalent of 1/8). Press Tab to apply the new Bleed value to all four sides.**

    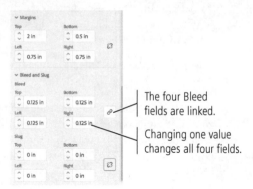

    The four Bleed fields are linked.

    Changing one value changes all four fields.

    Bleed is the amount an object needs to extend past the edge of the artboard or page to meet the mechanical requirements of commercial printing.

    The letterhead for this project will be printed commercially; the printer said the design can safely bleed on all four sides, and its equipment requires a 1/8″ bleed allowance.

21. **Make sure all four Slug fields are set to 0.**

    A **slug** is an area outside the bleed, where designers typically add job information that will not appear in the final printed piece. The slug area can be used for file/plate information, special registration marks, color bars, and/or other elements that need to be printed on the press sheet but do not appear within the job area.

22. **Check the Preview box at the bottom of the New Document dialog box.**

    When this option is active, you can see the result of your choices (behind the dialog box) before you click OK to create the new file.

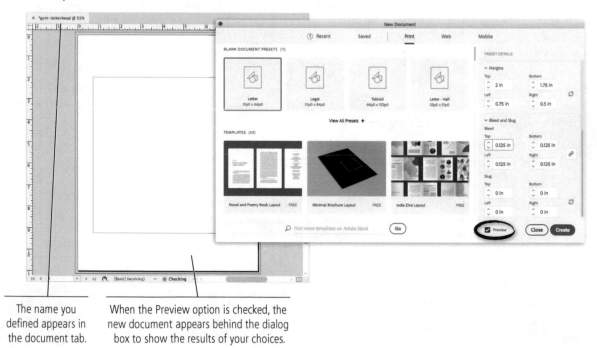

The name you defined appears in the document tab.

When the Preview option is checked, the new document appears behind the dialog box to show the results of your choices.

23. Click Create to create the new document.

The document appears, filling the available space in the document window. (Your view percentage might appear different than what you see in our images.)

The letter-size page edge is represented by a dark black line. Pink/purple lines identify margin guides, and red lines identify bleed guides. The color of the pasteboard (the area around the artboard) defaults to match the brightness of the user interface. You can change this setting to show a white pasteboard by unchecking Match Pasteboard to Theme Color in the Interface pane of the Preferences dialog box.

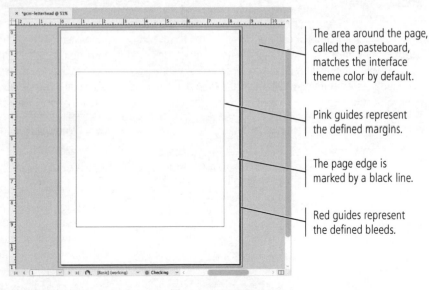

The area around the page, called the pasteboard, matches the interface theme color by default.

Pink guides represent the defined margins.

The page edge is marked by a black line.

Red guides represent the defined bleeds.

As we explained in the Interface chapter, the panels you see depend on what was done the last time you (or someone else) used the application. Because workspace arrangement is such a personal preference, we tell you what panels you need to use, but we don't tell you where to place them. In our screen shots, we typically float panels over the relevant area of the document so we can focus the images on the most important part of the file at any particular point. Feel free to dock the panels, grouped or ungrouped, iconized or expanded, however you prefer.

24. Choose File>Save As and navigate to your WIP>GCMarket folder.

If you assign a name in the New Document dialog box (as you did in Step 6), that name becomes the default file name in the Save As dialog box.

The dialog box defaults to the InDesign CC 2019 (.indd) format, and the extension is automatically added to the name you defined. If the Hide Extension option is checked at the bottom of the dialog box, the ".indd" will not appear in the file name.

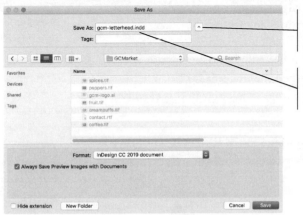

Click here if you don't see the full navigation options on Macintosh.

The extension ".indd" is automatically added to the file name.

Note:

The first time you save a file, the Save command opens the same dialog box as the File>Save As command. After saving the file once, you can use Save to save changes to the file or use Save As to create another file under a new file name.

Note:

The Save As dialog box follows a system-standard format. Macintosh and Windows users see slightly different options, but the basic functionality is the same.

25. Click Save, then continue to the next exercise.

Understanding Document Presets

If you frequently define the same new-document settings, you can click the Save Document Preset button to save those choices as a preset so you can create the same document settings with minimal repetition. You can access your user-defined presets in the Saved pane of the New Document dialog box.

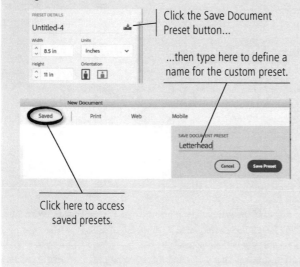

Click the Save Document Preset button...

...then type here to define a name for the custom preset.

Click here to access saved presets.

You can also access and manage your document presets in the File>Document Presets submenu. Choosing one of the existing presets in the menu opens the legacy New Document dialog box, which defaults to the values in the preset that you called.

Choosing Define in the Document Presets submenu opens a dialog box that lists the existing presets.

- Click New to open the New Document Preset dialog box, which is basically the same as the New Document dialog box, except the Preset menu is replaced with a field where you type the preset name instead of clicking the Save Preset button.

- Select a preset and click Edit to change the preset's associated options.

- Select a preset and click Delete to remove the preset from the application.

- Click Load to import presets from another computer.

- Click Save to save a preset (with the extension ".dcst") so it can be sent to and used on another computer.

Create Ruler Guides

In addition to the margin and bleed guides you defined when you created the document, you can also place ruler guides to mark whatever other positions you need to identify in your layout.

The **live area** is the "safe" area inside the page edge where important design elements should reside. Because printing and trimming are mechanical processes, there will always be some variation, however slight. Elements placed too close to the page edge run the risk of being accidentally trimmed off. The printer for this job recommended a 1/4" live-area margin. You defined the margins for this file to describe the area that would typically occupy the content of a letter; in this exercise you will create ruler guides to mark the live area.

1. **With gcm-letterhead.indd open, choose View>Show Rulers if you don't see rulers at the top and left edges of the document window.**

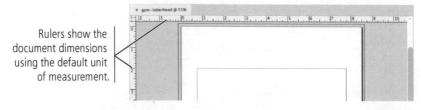

Rulers show the document dimensions using the default unit of measurement.

Note:

You can change the default units of measurement for a file in the Units & Increments pane of the Preferences dialog box or by Control/right-clicking a ruler and choosing a new option. Each ruler (horizontal and vertical) can have a different unit of measurement.

2. **Zoom in to 100% so you can clearly see the top of the page.**

3. **Click the horizontal page ruler (at the top of the document window) and drag down until cursor feedback indicates the guide is positioned at Y: 0.25 in. With the cursor inside the page area, release the mouse button.**

As you drag, the Control panel and cursor feedback show the current position of the guide you are placing; this makes it very easy to precisely position guides.

If the Control panel is not visible, you can show it by choosing Window>Control. If you don't see the cursor feedback, make sure Show Transformation Values is checked in the Interface pane of the Preferences dialog box.

Note:

Y values define vertical (top-to-bottom) position; X values define horizontal (left-to-right) position.

The Control panel, ruler, and cursor feedback all show the location of the guide.

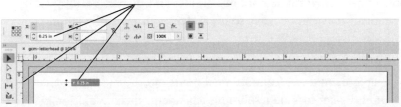

4. **Click the horizontal page ruler again and drag a guide to Y: 10.75 in.**

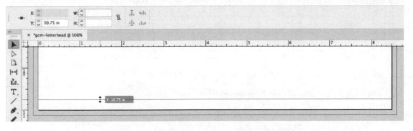

Note:

If you drag a guide outside the page edge, the guide will extend across the entire pasteboard. You can also press Command/Control while dragging a guide onto the page to extend the guide the entire width of the pasteboard.

5. **Click the vertical ruler and drag a guide to X: 0.25 in.**

Watch the marker on the horizontal ruler to judge the guide's position.

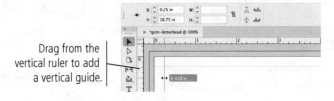

Drag from the vertical ruler to add a vertical guide.

6. **Click the vertical ruler again and drag a second vertical guide to X: 8.25 in.**

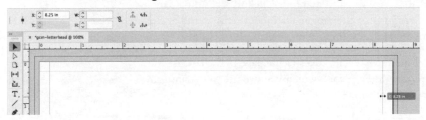

Note:

You can click the intersection of the rulers and drag to reposition the zero point away from the top-left corner of the page. If you do reposition the zero point, you can double-click the ruler intersection to reset the original zero point.

7. **Using the Selection tool, click anywhere in the document space to deselect the guide you just created.**

8. **Save the file and continue to the next stage of the project.**

STAGE 2 / Creating Basic Page Elements

Based on the approved sketch, the client's letterhead includes several elements:

- A logo that was created in Adobe Illustrator

- The client's slogan or "tag line"

- Contact information, which was provided to you as a rich-text file

- A graphic near the bottom of the page, which will serve as a container for a series of client-supplied images

When you build an InDesign file, keep in mind the two primary types of design elements:

- **Vector graphics** are composed of mathematical descriptions of lines and shapes. Vector graphics are resolution-independent; they can be freely scaled and are automatically output at the resolution of the output device. The shapes you create in Adobe InDesign, or in drawing applications such as Adobe Illustrator, are vector graphics.

- **Raster images**, such as photographs or files created in Adobe Photoshop, are made up of a grid of pixels in rows and columns. Raster files are resolution-dependent; their resolution is determined when you scan, photograph, or create the file. (**Line art** is a type of raster image made up entirely of 100% solid areas; the pixels are either all black or all white.)

Create a Simple Line

Although much drawing work is done in a dedicated illustration program such as Adobe Illustrator, you can use drawing tools in InDesign to create vector artwork.

InDesign includes two tools for creating lines: the Line tool for creating straight lines and the Pen tool for creating curved lines called **Bézier curves** (although you can also create straight lines with the Pen tool). In this exercise, you create the most basic element possible: a straight line. You then add anchor points to the line to create a multi-segment path.

1. **With gcm-letterhead.indd open, make sure nothing is selected in the file. Review the Properties panel (Window>Properties).**

   The Properties panel is context-sensitive, which means it provides access to different options depending on which tool is active and what is selected in the document.

   When nothing is selected in the file, you can use the Properties panel to change document-related settings such as page size and margins. Clicking the Adjust Layout button opens a dialog box where you can change the document settings and at the same time adjust layout elements to match the new page size and/or margin.

   You can use the Page Number field to navigate to a specific page in the layout. Clicking the Page button activates the Page tool, which you can use to dynamically change the page size in the document window.

   The three buttons in the Rulers & Grids section toggle the visibility of rulers ( ), the baseline grid( ), and the document grid( ).

   The three buttons in the Guides section toggle the visibility of page guides( ), lock and unlock page guides( ), and toggle the visibility of smart guides( ).

The Control panel combines many common formatting options into a single, compact format. It is context-sensitive, which means different options are available depending on what is selected in the layout. It is also customizable, which means you can change the options available in the panel. (It is also important to note that the options available in the Control panel might be limited by the active workspace and by the width of your monitor or Application frame.)

Default Control panel when a graphics frame is selected on a 21-inch monitor:

Default Control panel when a text frame is selected on a 21-inch monitor:

Default Control panel when text is selected on a 21-inch monitor:

When anything other than text is selected, the panel Options menu includes options for controlling the position of the panel (top, bottom, or floating), as well as how transformations affect selected objects:

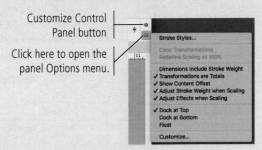

- **Stroke Styles.** This opens a dialog box where you can edit or define custom styles for lines and object strokes.

- **Clear Transformations.** Choosing this option resets an object to its original position (also clearing rotation).

- **Dimensions Include Stroke Weight.** When checked, width and height values include the object width, as well as the defined stroke width. For example, a square that is 72 points wide with a 1-point stroke would be 73 points wide overall (when using the default stroke position that aligns the stroke on the center of the object edge).

- **Transformations are Totals.** When checked, transformations are cumulative for the frame and its contents. For example, say an image frame is rotated 10°.

  – When checked, the frame content also shows a 10° rotation; you can change the content rotation to 0° to return the image (but not the frame) to horizontal.

  – When not checked, the frame content shows 0° because the content is not rotated relative to its container. You have to rotate the content −10° to return it to horizontal without affecting the frame's rotation.

- **Show Content Offset.** When checked, the Control panel shows X+ and Y+ values for a frame's content when the actual content (not the frame) is selected.

- **Adjust Stroke Weight when Scaling.** When checked, resizing an object changes the stroke weight proportionally. For example, resizing an object with a 1-pt stroke to 50% results in a 0.5-pt stroke.

Clicking the Customize Control Panel button, or choosing Customize in the panel Options menu, opens a dialog box where you can define the available options in the panel; anything with a checkmark will be available when it's relevant to the selection in the document.

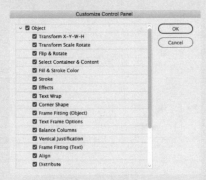

Clicking the Quick Apply button (⚡) opens a special navigation dialog box. This feature enables you to easily find and apply what you want (menu commands, user-defined styles, and so on) by typing a few characters in the text entry field and then clicking the related item in the list.

2. **Choose View>Grids & Guides>Smart Guides to make sure this option is toggled on. If the option is already checked, move the cursor away from the menu and click to dismiss it.**

Smart guides are a useful function of the application, making it easy to create and precisely align objects. Smart guides show the dimensions of an object when you create it, the position of an object when you drag it, the edge and center position of nearby objects and the distance between nearby similar objects.

This option should be checked (active).

3. **Choose the Line tool in the Tools panel, then click the Default Fill and Stroke button at the bottom of the Tools panel.**

The default option for the Line tool is a black stroke with no fill.

4. **Near the bottom of the page, click at the left bleed guide and drag to the right bleed guide. Press Shift, and then release the mouse button.**

As you drag, cursor feedback shows the length of the line you are drawing. The blue line previews what will appear when you release the mouse button. Pressing Shift as you draw forces (constrains) the line to exact 45° angles, including exactly horizontal.

Note:

You can turn off specific Smart Guide functions in the Guides & Pasteboard pane of the Preferences dialog box.

Note:

When drawing lines, cursor feedback shows the length of the segment you are drawing.

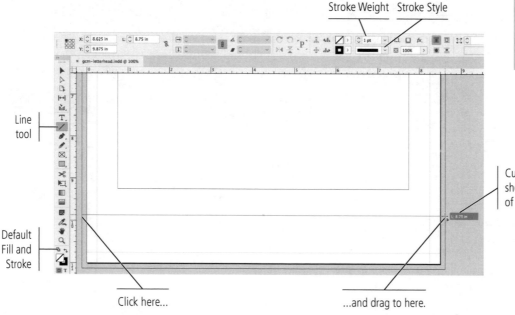

Stroke Weight Stroke Style

Line tool

Default Fill and Stroke

Cursor feedback shows the length of the line.

Click here...   ...and drag to here.

5. In either the Control or Properties panel, open the Stroke Weight menu and choose 2 pt.

Because a line is selected in the layout, both the Control panel and Properties panel present options related to the selected line: stroke weight, style, color, etc. You can choose one of the stroke weight presets from the menu or simply type any value in the field.

Like the Properties panel, the Control panel is context-sensitive; both present options that specifically relate to whatever is selected in the layout.

We primarily use the Properties panel throughout this book, unless a required option is only available in the Control panel. You should realize, however, that the Properties panel options are typically duplicated in the Control panel.

6. In either the Control or Properties panel, change the Y field to 9.75 in and press Return/Enter to apply the change.

X defines the horizontal (left-to-right) position, and Y defines the vertical (top-to-bottom) position. Because you constrained this line to horizontal, changing the Y field moves the entire line.

Remember, you do not need to type the units if you are entering a measurement in the default unit of measurement. We include the units in our steps for the sake of clarity.

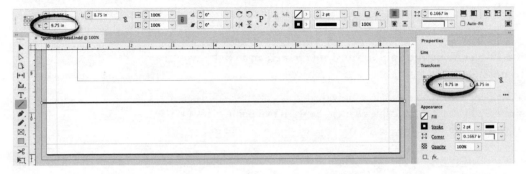

7. **Choose the Pen tool in the Tools panel, then move the cursor over the line you just created.**

When the Pen tool is over an existing, selected line, it automatically switches to the Add Anchor Point tool cursor; clicking adds a new point to the selected line.

If the Pen tool is over a specific point on a selected line, it automatically switches to the Delete Anchor Point tool cursor; clicking removes that point from the line.

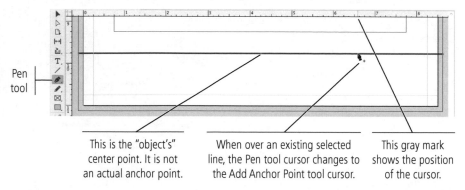

Pen tool

This is the "object's" center point. It is not an actual anchor point.

When over an existing selected line, the Pen tool cursor changes to the Add Anchor Point tool cursor.

This gray mark shows the position of the cursor.

8. **When the cursor is at the 4.5″ mark of the horizontal page ruler, click to add a point to the line.**

The visible center point of the selected line is a bit deceptive. This simply marks the center of the shape (a line, in this case); it is not an actual point on the line.

9. **Move the cursor right to the 6″ mark and click to add another point.**

All vector objects are composed of anchor points and connecting line segments, even if you don't create each point manually. The original line had two regular points (one at each end) and a straight connecting segment. You added two new points for a total of four points and three connecting segments.

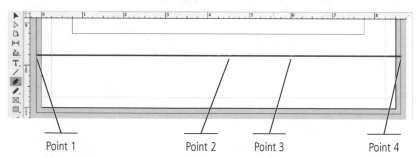

Point 1   Point 2   Point 3   Point 4

10. **Choose the Direct Selection tool in the Tools panel, and click away from the line to deselect it.**

The Direct Selection tool is used to select individual pieces of objects, such as a specific point on a line or a specific line segment between two points. However, you have to first deselect the entire line before you can select only part of it.

11. Move the cursor over the right part of the line.

When the Direct Selection tool cursor shows a small line in the icon, clicking will select the specific segment under the cursor.

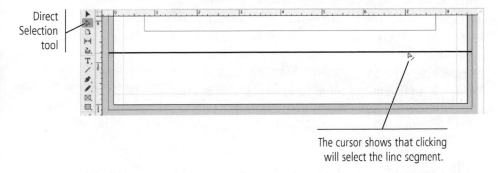

Direct Selection tool

The cursor shows that clicking will select the line segment.

12. Click anywhere between the third and fourth points on the line. Press Shift, and drag down until the cursor feedback shows the Y position of 10.2 in.

The segment you selected moves, and the segment between points 2 and 3 adjusts as necessary to remain connected. The segment between points 1 and 2 is not affected.

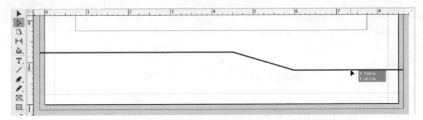

13. Using the Direct Selection tool, click the second point from the left (Point 2).

When the Direct Selection tool cursor shows a small circle in the icon, clicking will select the specific point under the cursor.

14. In the Control or Properties panel, change the X position of the selected point to 4.875 in.

As you can see, you can control the precise position of every point in a shape.

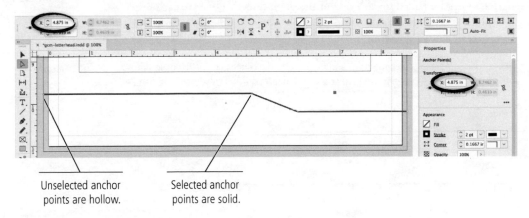

Unselected anchor points are hollow.

Selected anchor points are solid.

15. Save the file and continue to the next exercise.

Create Bézier Curves

As you have learned, every line is composed of anchor points and line segments that connect those points. Even a simple, straight line has two points, one at each end. More sophisticated shapes can be created by adding anchor points and manipulating the direction handles of those points to control the shape of segments that connect the different points. This concept is the heart of Bézier curves and vector-based drawing and can be one of the most challenging skills for new designers to master.

In this exercise you will make very simple manipulations to the straight line you just created. The Pen tool in InDesign works the same as it does in Illustrator and Photoshop; if necessary, refer to Project 2: Regatta Artwork for a refresher on anchor points and curves.

1. **With gcm-letterhead.indd open, make sure the line at the bottom of the page is selected.**

2. **Choose the Convert Direction Point tool nested under the Pen tool.**

   The Convert Direction Point tool changes a corner point to a smooth point (and vice versa). **Smooth points** have handles that control the size and shape of curves connected to that point. You can then use the Direct Selection tool to adjust handles for a selected anchor point.

3. **Click the second point on the line, press Shift, and drag right until the ruler shows the cursor is at 5.625″.**

   When you click a point with the Convert Direction Point tool and immediately drag, you add direction handles to the point. Those direction handles define the shape of the line segments connected to the point. As you drag farther away from the point, the affected segment's curve increases.

   Pressing Shift constrains the new direction handles to 45° angles — in this case, exactly horizontal. If you look closely, you can see the direction handle on the left side of the point is exactly on top of the line.

   By default, clicking and dragging creates a smooth, symmetrical point in which equal-length handles are added to each side of the point directly opposite each other. As long as a point is symmetrical, changing the angle of one handle also affects the handle on the other side of the point.

Click the point and drag right to add handles.   The connected line bends in the direction in which you pull the handle.

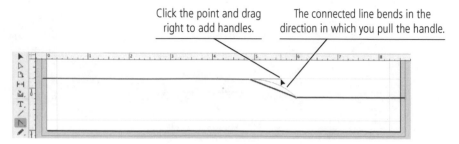

4. **Click the third point, press Shift, and drag right until the ruler shows the cursor is at 6.5".**

As we just explained, the affected curve gets larger as you drag farther away from the point. Because you're dragging exactly horizontally, the horizontal segment on the right is not curving.

On the left side of the point, however, you can see the effect of converting Point 3 to a symmetrical point. Dragging to the right side of the point adds direction handles on *both sides* of the point; the length and position of the left handle defines the shape of the curve on the left side of the point, which is the one you want to affect in this step.

Note:

If you add points to a curved line segment, the new points automatically adopt the necessary direction handles to maintain the original curve shapes.

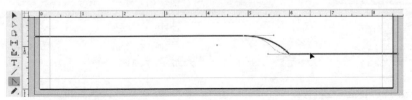

5. **Choose the Pen tool in the Tools panel. It is now nested under the Convert Direction Point tool.**

When you choose a nested tool variation, the nested tool becomes the default option in that position on the Tools panel.

Note:

The lines that connect anchor points based on the angle and length of the control handles are called Bézier curves.

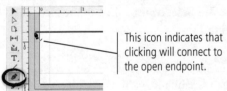

6. **Move the cursor over the left endpoint of the line. When you see a diagonal line in the cursor icon, click to connect to the existing endpoint.**

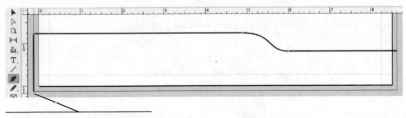

This icon indicates that clicking will connect to the open endpoint.

Note:

When you drag direction handles, the blue lines preview the effects of your changes.

7. **Press Shift, then click at the bottom-left bleed guide.**

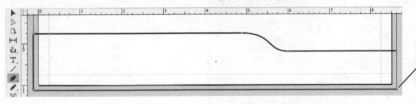

Shift-click to create a vertical line connected to the previous point.

Note:

If you move an anchor point that has direction handles, the handles don't change angle or length. The related curves change shape based on the new position of the point.

8. **Press Shift, then click the bottom-right bleed guide.**

Shift-click to create a horizontal line between the previous point and the point where you click.

9. **Move the cursor over the open endpoint at the right end of the original line. When you see a small circle in the cursor icon, click to close the shape.**

You could have created this shape as a regular rectangle and then modified the top line with the Pen tool. However, our goal was to teach you how to create a basic line and how to perform some basic tasks with the Pen tool and its variations.

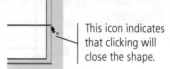

This icon indicates that clicking will close the shape.

It's important to realize there is almost always more than one way to accomplish a specific goal in InDesign. As you gain experience, you will develop personal preferences for the most effective and efficient methods of doing what you need to do.

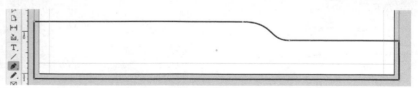

10. **Save the file and continue to the next exercise.**

Change Color Values

Although there are several default color choices built into the Swatches panel of every InDesign file, you are not limited to these few options. You can define virtually any color based on specific values of component colors. Keep in mind that when you are building a page to be printed, you should use CMYK colors.

1. **With gcm-letterhead.indd open, use the Selection tool to make sure the shape at the bottom of the page is selected.**

Every shape you create in an InDesign document has a **bounding box**, which is a non-printing rectangle marking the outer dimensions of the shape. (Even a circle has a square bounding box, marking the largest height and width of the object.) The bounding box has eight handles, which you can drag to change the size of the rectangle. If you can see an object's bounding box handles, that object is selected.

2. **Click the button at the right end of the Control panel to open the panel Options menu.**

3. **If the Dimensions Include Stroke Weight option is checked, click that item to toggle the option off.**

When this option is active, the size of an object's stroke is factored as part of the overall object size. Consider, for example, a frame that is 72 points wide with a 1-point stroke. If you remove the stroke from the frame, the frame would then be only 71 points wide.

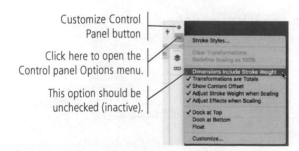

Customize Control Panel button

Click here to open the Control panel Options menu.

This option should be unchecked (inactive).

4. **At the bottom of the Tools panel, click the Swap Fill and Stroke button.**

    The object now has a black fill and a stroke of none. Because you turned off the Dimensions Include Stroke Weight option, removing the stroke has no effect on the object's size.

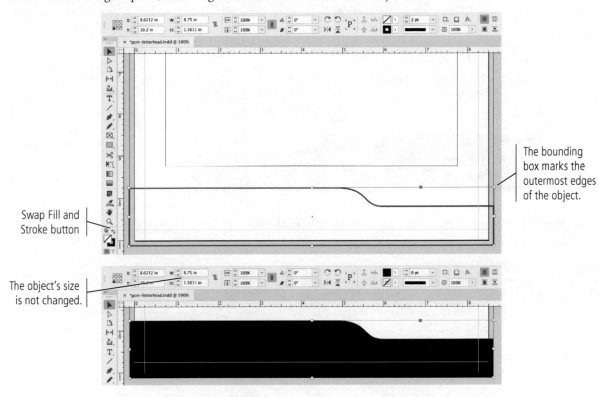

Swap Fill and Stroke button

The bounding box marks the outermost edges of the object.

The object's size is not changed.

5. **Open the Color panel (Window>Color>Color).**

    Remember, all panels can be accessed in the Window menu. Because workspace arrangement is a matter of personal preference, we won't tell you where to place panels.

6. **Click the Fill swatch to bring it to the front (if it isn't already).**

    When you apply color from any of the Swatches panels (including the ones in the Control panel), the Color panel shows a swatch of that color as a single slider. You can use this slider to easily apply a percentage of the selected swatch.

7. **Click the Options button in the top-right corner of the Color panel and choose CMYK from the Options menu.**

    This option converts the single swatch slider to the four process-color sliders. You can change any ink percentage to change the object's fill color.

Click here to open the panel Options menu.

The top swatch indicates which attribute you can change (in this case, Fill).

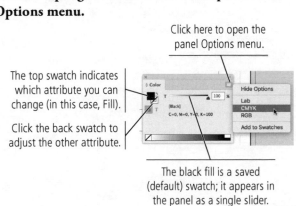

Click the back swatch to adjust the other attribute.

The black fill is a saved (default) swatch; it appears in the panel as a single slider.

8. **Highlight the C (cyan) field and type 85%.**

   You do not need to type the "%" character; we include it here for clarity.

9. **Press Tab to highlight the M (magenta) field, then type 50%.**

10. **Repeat the process from Step 9 to define the Y (yellow) value as 85% and the K (black) value as 40%.**

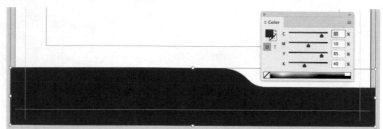

11. **With the object selected and the Fill swatch on the top of the stack, open the Color panel options menu and choose Add to Swatches.**

   This command creates a saved swatch from the active values; the new swatch will appear in the standalone Swatches panel as well as in the pop-up panels attached to the Control panel. After saving the swatch, the Color panel shows the fill color as a single slider of that swatch.

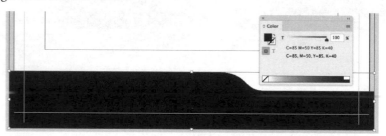

12. **Save the file and continue to the next exercise.**

Create a Basic Graphics Frame

When you place an external image file into an InDesign layout, it is contained in a frame. If you simply place the file into a layout, a containing frame is automatically created for you based on the dimensions of the placed image. You can also create graphic frames *before* placing images, which can be useful if you want to define the available space without using the actual external files.

InDesign includes two groups of tools for creating basic shapes in a layout: the frame tools and the shape tools. There is no practical difference between the shapes created with the two sets of tools (for example, a rectangle created with the Rectangle Frame tool or with the Rectangle tool). The frame tools create empty graphic frames, which are identified by crossed diagonal lines when Frame Edges are visible in the layout (View>Extras>Show Frame Edges). Basic shapes do not have these lines; however, if you place content into a shape created with one of the basic shape tools, it is automatically converted to a graphic frame.

In this exercise, you will create the first of five graphic frames to hold the client's thumbnail images.

1. **With gcm-letterhead.indd open, choose the Rectangle Frame tool in the Tools panel.**

   If you don't see the Rectangle Frame tool, click and hold the default shape tool until the nested tools appear; slide over and down to select the Rectangle Frame tool.

2. **Press Command/Control, then click away from the existing shape to make sure it is deselected.**

   If you don't deselect the existing shape, the changes you make in the next step would affect the selected object.

   Pressing Command/Control temporarily switches to the last-used Selection tool (Selection or Direct Selection). This allows you to easily make selections — or, in this case, deselect an object — without changing the active tool.

Note:

To deselect objects, you can also choose Edit>Deselect All.

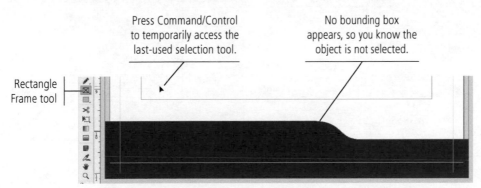

3. **Click the Default Fill and Stroke button at the bottom of the Tools panel.**

In InDesign, the default fill is None, and the default stroke is 1-pt black.

4. **Click anywhere on the page, press and hold the Shift key, then drag down and right to draw a rectangle 1.25″ high and 1.25″ wide.**

As you draw, cursor feedback shows the size of the shape you are creating.

Pressing Shift while drawing a shape constrains the horizontal and vertical dimensions of the shape to have equal height and width — in other words, this creates a perfect square or circle.

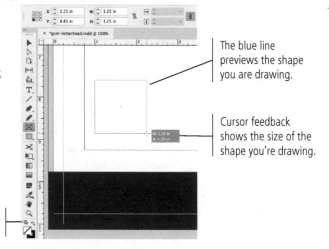

The blue line previews the shape you are drawing.

Cursor feedback shows the size of the shape you're drawing.

Default Fill and Stroke button

Note:

If you simply click a basic shape or frame tool on the page, a dialog box opens so you can define a specific size for the new shape.

5. **Release the mouse button to create the rectangle.**

The new shape appears in the position where you drew it. Notice new frame has both a Fill and Stroke color of None even though you reset the Black stroke color in Step 3.

New graphics frames always default to a Fill and Stroke color of None with a 0-pt stroke weight regardless of the settings you define before creating the frame. Fortunately, you can always change these settings after creating the frame.

Note:

If you use the regular shape tools instead of the frame tools, the Fill and Stroke settings you define before drawing are reflected in the new shape.

Position and dimensions of the selected object

Bounding box handles

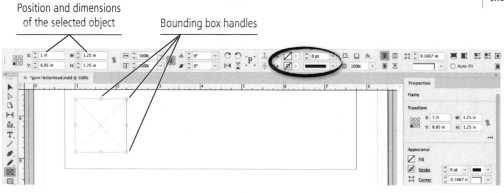

6. **In either the Control panel or Properties panel, select the bottom-left reference point.**

As we already explained, the Control and Properties panels are context-sensitive, which means different options are available depending on what is selected. The Transform section of the Properties panel defaults to show only the position and size of the selected object; clicking the More Options button reveals the other transformations that can be applied.

The **reference point** determines how transformations will occur (in other words, which point of the object will remain in place if you change one of the position or dimension values). These points correspond to the object's bounding box handles as well as to the object's exact center point.

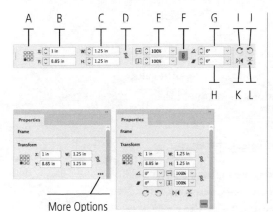

A Transformation reference point
B Object position
C Object dimensions
D Constrain proportions for width & height
E Scale the object by a specific percentage
F Constrain proportions for scaling
G Rotation Angle
H Shear X Angle
I Rotate 90° Clockwise
J Rotate 90° Counterclockwise
K Flip Horizontal
L Flip Vertical

More Options

Note:

You can use math operators to add (+), subtract (-), divide (/), or multiply (*) existing values in the Control panel. This is useful when you want to move or change a value by a specific amount.

Type **+.5** after the value to move the object down half an inch.

7. **Highlight the X field in either panel and type 1, then press Tab to move the highlight to the Y field.**

As in dialog boxes, you can use the Tab key to move through the fields in a panel. The X and Y fields determine the position of the selected object. X defines the horizontal (left-to-right) position, and Y defines the vertical (top-to-bottom) position.

8. **With the Y field highlighted, type 9 and then press Return/Enter.**

Pressing Return/Enter applies your changes. (You can also simply click away from the object to apply the change.)

The bottom-left reference point is selected.

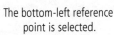

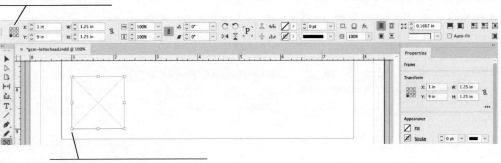

The bottom-left corner of the object is positioned at X: 1 in, Y: 9 in.

9. **Save the file and continue to the next exercise.**

Clone, Align, and Distribute Multiple Objects

As you should have already noticed, there is often more than one way to accomplish the same task in InDesign. Aligning multiple objects on a page is no exception. In this exercise you will explore a number of alignment options as you create the remaining graphics frames for the client's thumbnail images.

1. **With gcm-letterhead.indd open, choose the Selection tool in the Tools panel.**

   The Selection tool is used to select entire objects; the Direct Selection tool is used to select parts of objects or the contents of a frame.

   Using the Selection tool, you can

   - Click and drag a handle to resize selected objects.
   - Shift-click and drag to resize objects proportionally.
   - Command/Control-click and drag to scale selected objects.
   - Command/Control-Shift-click and drag to scale selected objects proportionally.
   - Press Option/Alt with any of these to apply the transformation around the selection's center point.

2. **Click inside the area of the empty graphics frame to select the shape.**

3. **Press and hold Option/Alt, then click the frame and drag right. Release the mouse button when green lines connect the top, center, and bottom edges of the two shapes and when the horizontal ruler shows 1/8″ space between the two objects.**

   Note:

   You might need to zoom in to the object you are dragging to see the Smart Guides.

   Pressing Option/Alt as you drag moves a copy of the selected object (called **cloning**).

   As you drag, a series of green lines marks the top, center, and bottom of the original object. These green lines are a function of InDesign's Smart Guides, which make it easy to align objects to each other by simply dragging.

   Note:

   You can also press Shift to constrain the drag/cloning movement to 45° angles from the original object.

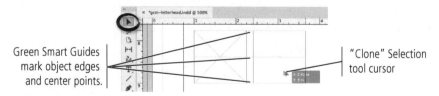

Green Smart Guides mark object edges and center points.

"Clone" Selection tool cursor

4. **Click the second shape, press Option/Alt, and drag right. Release the mouse button when the horizontal edges align and when you see opposing arrows below/between the three frames.**

   In addition to aligning edges, Smart Guides also make it easy to identify and match the distances between multiple objects. Smart Guides also identify equal dimensions when you create a new object near an existing one.

   Note:

   Smart guides do not function when moving objects on the pasteboard (outside the page boundaries).

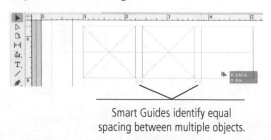

Smart Guides identify equal spacing between multiple objects.

5. With the third object still selected, choose Object>Transform Again>Transform Again.

This command applies the last-used transformation to the selected object. Because you used the cloning movement in the previous step, the result is a fourth copy spaced at the same distance used in Step 4. (The Transform Again command can be used to reapply rotation, scaling, sizing, and other transformations.)

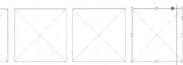

Note:

You can choose Object>Step and Repeat to make more than one copy of an object using specific horizontal and vertical distances for each copy.

6. With the fourth frame selected, choose Edit>Duplicate.

This command makes a copy of the selected object using the last-applied distance.

Note:

If you start by clicking inside an existing shape, you will drag that shape instead of drawing a selection marquee.

7. Zoom out so you can see the entire bottom of the document.

8. Using the Selection tool, click outside the existing shapes and then drag a marquee touching any part of all five frames.

As we stated previously, the Selection tool is used to access and manipulate entire objects; any object partially selected by the marquee will be included in the selection.

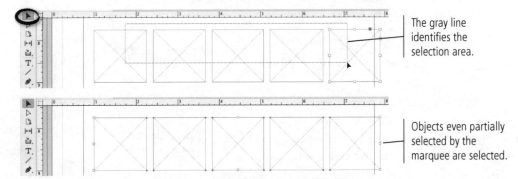

The gray line identifies the selection area.

Objects even partially selected by the marquee are selected.

9. Click the right-center bounding box handle of the active selection. Press and hold the Spacebar, then drag left. When you see no space between the five frames, release the mouse button.

As you drag, the space between the selected objects changes; the size of the actual objects is not affected (called **live distribution**).

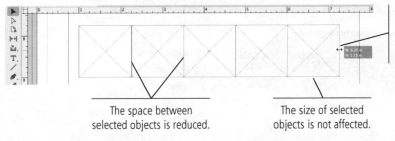

Click the center handle, then press the Spacebar and drag left.

The space between selected objects is reduced.

The size of selected objects is not affected.

10. Click the right-center handle again. Without pressing the Spacebar, drag left until the cursor feedback shows the width of the selection is 5.5″.

Simply dragging the handle resizes the entire selection; the spacing and position of various selected objects relative to one another is not affected.

Note:

Dragging a center handle changes the object size in only one direction.

11. With the five frames selected, choose Object>Group.

Grouping multiple objects means you can treat them as a single unit.

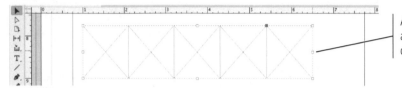

After grouping,
a single bounding box
outlines the entire group.

12. Open the Align panel (Window>Object & Layout>Align).

You can use the Align panel to align multiple objects relative to one another, to the page, or to the spread. The Align Objects options are fairly self-explanatory; when multiple objects are selected, they align based on the edge(s) or center(s) you click.

Note:

Group objects by pressing Command/Control-G.

Ungroup objects by pressing Command/Control-Shift-G.

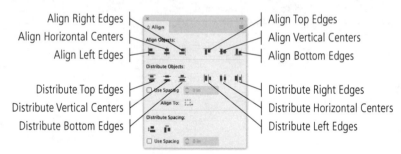

Align Right Edges
Align Horizontal Centers
Align Left Edges

Align Top Edges
Align Vertical Centers
Align Bottom Edges

Distribute Top Edges
Distribute Vertical Centers
Distribute Bottom Edges

Distribute Right Edges
Distribute Horizontal Centers
Distribute Left Edges

13. With the grouped graphics frames selected, press Shift and then click to add the green-filled shape to the active selection.

You can Shift-click an object to select it in addition to the previously selected object(s) or Shift-click an already selected object to deselect it without deselecting other objects.

Note:

When the insertion point is not flashing in text, choosing Edit>Select All selects all objects on the active spread.

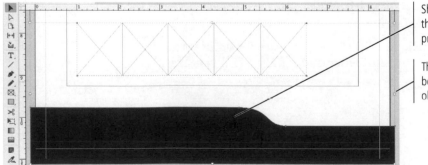

Shift-click to add
this shape to the
previous selection.

The selection bounding
box now surrounds all
objects on the page.

14. **In the Align panel, open the Align To menu and make sure Align To Selection is the active option.**

Using the (default) Align To Selection option, selected objects align to one another based on the outermost edges of the entire selection. In other words, aligning the top edges moves all objects to the same Y position as the highest selected object.

If you use the Key Object option, you can click any object in the selection to designate it as the key. (The key object shows a heavier border than other objects in the selection.)

Because you can align objects relative to the document, the align buttons are also available when only one object is selected, allowing you to align any single object to a precise location on the page or spread.

Note:

Align options are also available in the Properties panel and, depending on the width of your monitor and the workspace you are using, in the Control panel.

15. **With all objects selected, click the Align Left Edges and Align Bottom edges buttons in the Align panel.**

Because you grouped the five graphics frames, they are treated as one object during alignment; their positions relative to each other do not change.

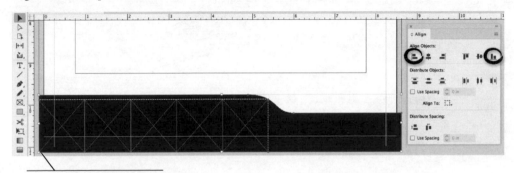

Selected objects are aligned to the bottom-most and left-most edges of the selection.

Understanding Object Distribution

The Distribute Objects options in the Align panel control the positions of multiple objects relative to each other.

Original position   Distribute Horizontal Centers position

By default, objects are equally distributed within the dimensions of the overall selection. You can check the Use Spacing option to space edges or centers by a specific amount.

Distribute Horizontal Centers with 1″ spacing value

Distribute Spacing options place equal space between selected objects, using the value defined in the Use Spacing field. You can also check Use Spacing to add a specific amount of space between the selected objects.

Distributed Spacing with 0.25″ spacing value

16. **Using the Selection tool, click away from the selected shapes to deselect all objects.**

17. **Using the Selection tool, click the right empty graphics frame to select it.**

    Because the frames are grouped, clicking once selects the entire group containing the frame you clicked.

18. **In the Control panel, change the Stroke Weight field to 3 pt.**

19. **Click the arrow button to the right of the Stroke swatch to open the attached Swatches panel. Choose Paper from the pop-up panel.**

    Because the active selection is a group, the new stroke weight and color apply to every object in the group.

    There is a difference between no fill and 0% of a color. The "None" color option essentially removes color from that attribute; underlying objects will be visible in areas where None is applied.

    Using 0% of a color — or using the Paper color — effectively creates a solid "white" fill. (In printing, solid white areas **knock out** or hide underlying shapes.)

Note:

Paper is basically white but more accurately named because the paper for a specific job might not be white.

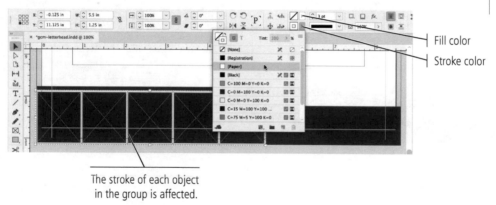

Fill color

Stroke color

The stroke of each object in the group is affected.

You can also use the Properties panel to change an object's stroke and fill attributes. Clicking the fill or stroke swatch opens a pop-up panel where you can define the color of the related attribute. The pop-up panel defaults to show saved swatches; you can click the Color button at the top to show the same options as you see in the stand-alone Color panel or click the Gradient button to show options from the Gradient panel.

Swatches   Color   Gradient

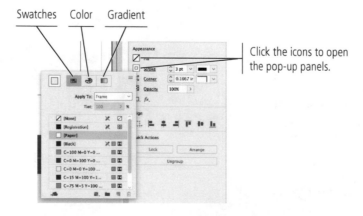

Click the icons to open the pop-up panels.

20. **Save the file and continue to the next exercise.**

Create a Rounded Rectangle

In addition to basic rectangles, you can create frames with a number of special corner treatments. In this exercise, you modify one corner of the right-most graphics frame to smoothly blend with the curve of the underlying background shape.

1. **With gcm-letterhead.indd open, make sure nothing is selected in the layout.**

2. **Using the Selection tool, double-click the right-most graphics frame in the group.**

   Double-clicking a group allows you to select only one object in a group without ungrouping the various objects. This is called "entering into the group."

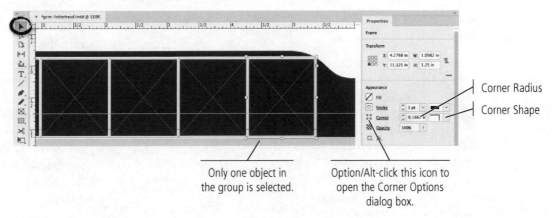

Only one object in the group is selected.

Option/Alt-click this icon to open the Corner Options dialog box.

Corner Radius

Corner Shape

3. **With the single frame selected, Option/Alt-click the Corner Shape icon in the Properties panel.**

   You can also choose Object>Corner Options to access the same dialog box.

   You can use the fields in the Properties panel to change the corner shape and radius of all corners on a selected shape. In this case, however, you want to change the shape of only one corner. Option/Alt-clicking the icon in the panel opens the related dialog box — in this case, the Corner Options dialog box — where you can exercise greater control over various settings.

Note:

Corner radius and shape options are also available in the Control panel.

4. **Check the Preview option in the bottom-left corner of the dialog box.**

   Many dialog boxes in InDesign have a Preview checkbox. When checked, you c see the effects of your selections before finalizing them.

5. **Click the Constrain icon in the dialog box to unlink the four corners.**

6. **Open the Corner Shape menu for the top-right corner and choose Rounded.**

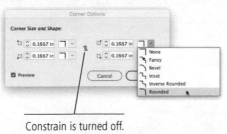

Constrain is turned off.

7. Type 0.45 in the top-right Corner Size field, then press the Tab key.

For the dialog box Preview option to work properly, you have to move the highlight away from the field you changed. Pressing Tab while the dialog box is open allows you to see the results of your changes.

Remember, you don't need to type the unit of measurement as long as the new value is the same unit as the default; we use units in our directions for clarity. We will not continue to repeat this explanation.

A rounded-corner rectangle is simply a rectangle with the corners cut at a specific distance from the end (the corner radius). The two sides are connected with one-fourth of a circle, which has a radius equal to the amount of the rounding.

Radius

Even though the adjusted frame now has one rounded corner, the **bounding box** still marks the outermost corners of the shape.

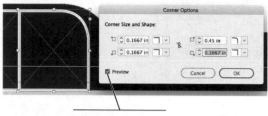

Preview is turned on.

8. Click OK to return to the document.

9. Save the file and continue to the next stage of the project.

Note:

The Polygon Frame and Polygon tools can be used to create odd shapes with a defined number of straight edges (including triangles).

Polygon Frame tool

Polygon tool

Clicking once with either Polygon tool opens the Polygon dialog box, where you can define the size of the new object as well as the number of points on the new shape. Star Inset determines how much closer those inside points will be to the center. (An inset of 0% creates all points at the same distance from the object's center.)

Editing Live Corners

FOUNDATIONS

When a rectangular frame is selected in the layout, a small yellow square appears on the right edge of the shape's bounding box. You can click this button to enter Live Corner Effects edit mode, where you can dynamically adjust the appearance of corner effects for all corners or for one corner at a time. Simply clicking away from the object exits the edit mode.

Click the yellow square to enter Live Corner Effects edit mode.

Drag a yellow corner diamond left or right to change the radius of all four corners.

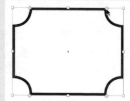

Option/Alt-click a yellow diamond to change the shape of corner effects.

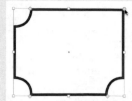

Shift-click a yellow diamond to change the radius of only one corner. Option/Alt-Shift-click to change the shape of one corner.

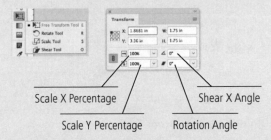

More about Working with InDesign Objects

Transforming Objects Manually

You have a number of options for transforming objects in an InDesign layout. Using the Selection tool, you can

- Click a center bounding-box handle and drag to resize an object in one direction.
- Click a corner handle and drag to resize an object in both directions at once.
- Click outside a corner handle and drag to rotate an object.

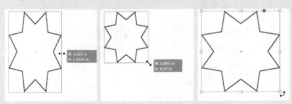

When you drag a handle, you can press Shift to maintain the object's original height-to-width proportions during the transformation. Press Option/Alt while dragging to transform the object around its center point.

You can also use one of the Transformation tools to rotate, scale, or shear an object (or use the fields in the Control, Transform, or Properties panels to apply transformations).

Scale X Percentage   Shear X Angle

Scale Y Percentage   Rotation Angle

Using the Pathfinder

You can apply a number of transformations to objects using the Pathfinder panel (Window>Object & Layout>Pathfinder).

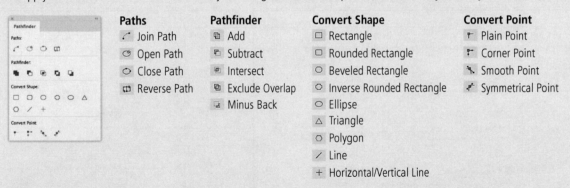

Paths
- Join Path
- Open Path
- Close Path
- Reverse Path

Pathfinder
- Add
- Subtract
- Intersect
- Exclude Overlap
- Minus Back

Convert Shape
- Rectangle
- Rounded Rectangle
- Beveled Rectangle
- Inverse Rounded Rectangle
- Ellipse
- Triangle
- Polygon
- Line
- Horizontal/Vertical Line

Convert Point
- Plain Point
- Corner Point
- Smooth Point
- Symmetrical Point

Path options break (open) a closed path, connect (close) the endpoints of an open path, or reverse a path's direction (start becomes end and vice versa).

Pathfinder options create objects by combining multiple existing objects. When you use the Pathfinder (other than Subtract), attributes of the front object are applied to the resulting shape; Subtract maintains attributes of the back object.

- **Add** results in a single combined shape from selected objects.
- **Subtract** results in the shape of the back object minus any overlapping area of the front object.
- **Intersect** results in the shape of only the overlapping areas of selected objects.
- **Exclude Overlap** results in the shape of all selected objects minus any overlapping areas.
- **Minus Back** results in the shape of the front object minus any area where it overlaps other selected objects.

Convert Shape options change the overall appearance of an object using one of the six defined basic shapes or using the default polygon settings; you can also convert any shape to a basic line or an orthogonal (horizontal or vertical) line.

Convert Point options affect the position of direction handles when a specific anchor point is selected.

- **Plain** creates a point with no direction handles.
- **Corner** creates a point that produces a sharp corner; changing the direction handle on one side of the point does not affect the handle on the other side of the point.
- **Smooth** creates a point with opposing direction handles that are exactly 180° from one another; the two handles can have different lengths.
- **Symmetrical** creates a smooth point with equal-length opposing direction handles; changing the length or position of one handle applies the same change to the opposing handle.

Tips and Tricks for Working with Layout Objects

Copying and Pasting

The standard Cut, Copy, and Paste options are available in InDesign, just as they are in most applications. Whatever you have selected will be copied or cut to the Clipboard, and whatever is in the Clipboard will be pasted. InDesign has a number of special pasting options in the Edit menu:

Paste. If you are pasting an object (frame, etc.), the object will be pasted in the center of the document window. If you are pasting text, it will be pasted at the location of the current insertion point; if the insertion point is not currently placed, the text is placed in a new basic text frame in the middle of the document window.

Paste without Formatting. This command is available when text is in the Clipboard; the text is pasted using the default type formatting options (12-pt black Minion Pro, if it hasn't been changed on your system).

Paste Into. This command is available when an object is in the Clipboard and another object is selected. The pasted object becomes the contents of the object that is selected when you choose this command.

Paste in Place. This command pastes an object at the exact position as the original. If you paste on the same page as the original, you create a second object exactly on top of the first. You can also use this command to place a copy in the exact position as the original but on a different page in the layout.

Managing Stacking Order

The top-to-bottom order of objects is called **stacking order**. When you have multiple stacked objects, it can be difficult to select exactly what you want. Fortunately, the application provides a number of options to make it easier.

When you move the Selection tool cursor over an object, the edges of the object are highlighted. This lets you know what will be selected if you click.

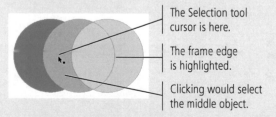

The Selection tool cursor is here.

The frame edge is highlighted.

Clicking would select the middle object.

When an object is already selected, InDesign favors the already selected object. This prevents you from accidentally selecting an object higher in the stacking order (for example, if you want to drag only the middle object).

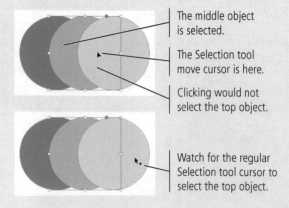

The middle object is selected.

The Selection tool move cursor is here.

Clicking would not select the top object.

Watch for the regular Selection tool cursor to select the top object.

You can select the next object down in the stacking order by pressing Command/Control while clicking within the area of the object stack.

You can use the Object>Select submenu commands (or their related keyboard shortcuts) to access objects relative to their order in the stack.

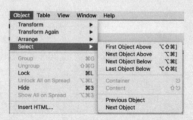

You can use the Object>Arrange submenu commands (or their related keyboard shortcuts) to change the stacking-order position of objects.

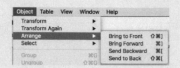

Finally, you can use the individual item listings in the Layers panel to select exactly the object you want or to rearrange objects in the layer stack.

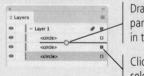

Drag an item in the panel to a new position in the stacking order.

Click this icon to select a specific object.

STAGE 3 / **Placing External Images**

As you saw in the first stage of this project, InDesign incorporates a number of tools for building graphics directly in a layout. Of course, most page-layout projects will include files from other sources. Logos created in Adobe Illustrator, raster-based images created in Adobe Photoshop, digital photographs, stock images, and many other types of files can be incorporated into a larger project.

Place an Adobe Illustrator File

Every image in a layout exists in a frame. You can either create the frame first and place a file into it, or you can simply place an image and create the containing frame at the same time. In this exercise, you are going to place the client's logo, and transform it to fit into the margin space at the top of the layout.

Note:

Artwork in an Illustrator file must be entirely within the bounds of the artboard (page) edge. Anything outside the artboard edge will not be included when you place the file into InDesign.

1. **With gcm-letterhead.indd open, make sure nothing is selected.**

2. **Choose File>Place. Navigate to the WIP>GCMarket folder and select gcm-logo.ai. At the bottom of the dialog box, check Show Import Options.**

   Macintosh users: if you don't see three checkboxes at the bottom of the dialog box, click the Options button to reveal those checkboxes.

   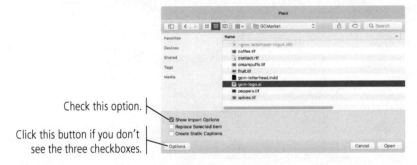

   Check this option.

   Click this button if you don't see the three checkboxes.

3. **Click Open.**

   When Show Import Options is checked, the Place [Format] dialog box opens with the options for the relevant file format. Every file format has different available options.

   If you press Shift when clicking Open in the Place dialog box, the Place [Format] dialog box for the selected file appears even if Show Import Options is not checked.

   When you place a native Illustrator file, the dialog box shows Place PDF options because the PDF format is the basis of Illustrator files that can be placed into InDesign.

4. **In the General tab, choose Art in the Crop To menu.**

You can use the Preview area on the left to determine which page/artboard you want to place.

The Crop To menu determines what part of the file will be placed:

- **Bounding Box** places the file based on the minimum area enclosing the objects on the page. You can also choose to include all layers or only visible layers in the calculation.

- **Art** uses the outermost dimensions of artwork in the file.

- **Crop** uses a crop area defined in the file.

- **Trim** uses trim marks defined in the file.

- **Bleed** uses the defined bleed area in the file.

- **Media** uses the physical size at which a PDF file was created.

When Transparent Background is checked, background objects in the InDesign layout show through empty areas of the placed file. If this option is not checked, empty areas of the placed file knock out underlying objects.

Note:

If Crop, Trim, or Bleed is not defined in a file, the file will be placed based on the defined artboard size.

5. **Click the Layers tab to display those options.**

PDF and native Illustrator files can include multiple layers. You can determine which layers to display in the placed file by toggling the eye icons on or off in the Show Layers list. In the Update Link Options menu, you can determine what happens when/if you update the link to the placed file.

- **Keep Layer Visibility Overrides** maintains your choices regarding which layers are visible in the InDesign layout.

- **Use PDF's Layer Visibility** restores the layer status as saved in the placed file.

6. **Click OK to load the cursor with the placed file.**

By default, the loaded Place cursor shows a small thumbnail of the file you're placing. You can turn off the thumbnail preview feature by unchecking the Show Thumbnails on Place option in the Interface pane of the Preferences dialog box.

7. **Click near the top-left corner of the page to place the image.**

   Every image in an InDesign layout exists in a frame. When you click an empty area of the page to place an image, the containing frame is automatically created for you.

   In the layout, blue handles and frame edges indicate the frame, and not its contents, is selected on the page; values in the Properties panel relate to the actual containing frame.

8. **Using the Properties panel, choose the top-left reference point and then change the frame's position to X: 0.25 in, Y: 0.25 in.**

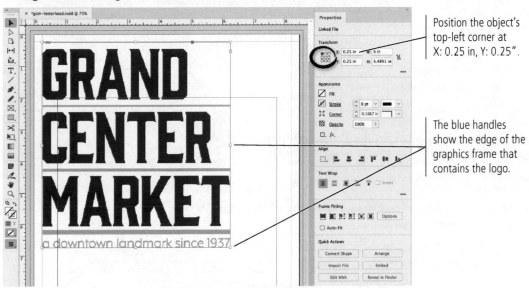

Position the object's top-left corner at X: 0.25 in, Y: 0.25".

The blue handles show the edge of the graphics frame that contains the logo.

9. **Open the Interface pane of the Preferences dialog box. Choose Immediate in the Live Screen Drawing menu, then click OK.**

   Remember, preferences are accessed in the InDesign menu on Macintosh and in the Edit menu on Windows.

   Live Screen Drawing controls the appearance of an image when you move or resize it. The default behavior, Delayed, means the image does not appear inside the frame while you change the frame parameters (position, etc.).

   Using the Immediate Live Screen Drawing option, the image inside the frame always appears inside the frame when you move or resize the frame. If Delayed is selected, you can click and hold down the mouse button for a couple seconds to temporarily access the Immediate preview behavior.

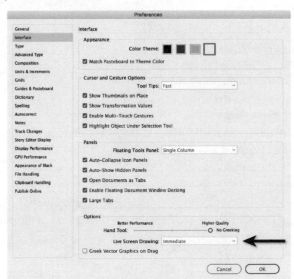

10. **With the placed image selected, check the Auto-Fit option in the Frame Fitting section of the Properties panel.**

11. **Click the bottom-right corner of the frame, then drag up to make the frame smaller. When cursor feedback shows the frame is 1.6 in high, release the mouse button.**

When the Auto-Fit option is checked, resizing the frame automatically resizes the contained image to fit the new frame size; the image remains centered inside the frame. Areas of the image outside the resized frame remain visible, but slightly ghosted, while you hold down the mouse button.

When Auto-Fit is not selected, you can press Command/Control while resizing a frame to also scale the frame's content.

12. **Uncheck the Auto-Fit option in the Properties panel.**

If you don't turn off this option, you will not be able to manually apply other frame fitting commands in the next steps.

13. **With the graphics frame still selected, click the Fit Content Proportionally button in the Properties panel.**

The fitting options can resize the image relative to its frame or resize the frame relative to its content.

Auto-Fit is turned off.

- **Fill Frame Proportionally** resizes content to fill the entire frame while preserving the content's proportions. Some of the image area might be cropped.

- **Fit Content Proportionally** resizes content to fit entirely within its containing frame, maintaining the current aspect ratio of the image. Some empty space might result along one dimension of the frame.

- **Fit Content to Frame** resizes content to fit the dimensions of the container, even if that means scaling the content out of proportion (stretched in one direction or another).

- **Fit Frame to Content** resizes the frame to the dimensions of the placed content.

- **Center Content** centers content within its containing frame, but neither the frame nor the content is resized.

- **Content-Aware Fit** allows the software to evaluate the placed image, then scale the image inside the frame to show what it determines to be the most important part of the image.

In this case, you defined the available frame height; you are using the fitting options to force the content proportionally into that available space.

Note:

Frame fitting options can also be accessed in an object's contextual menu or in the Control panel.

14. **With the Selection tool active, move the cursor inside the resized frame.**

    This reveals the Content Grabber, which you can use to access and manipulate the frame's content without the need to switch tools.

    Content Grabber

15. **Click the Content Grabber in the logo frame.**

    When the frame's content is selected, the X+ and Y+ fields define the position of the image *within the frame* and not to the frame itself. The Scale X and Scale Y fields show the file's current size as a percentage of the original.

    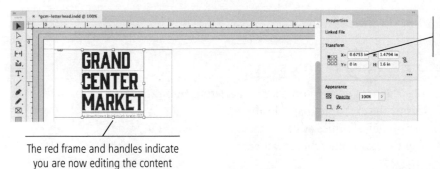

    These fields now show the parameters of the content in the frame.

    The red frame and handles indicate you are now editing the content instead of the containing frame.

    Note:

    You can also use the Direct Selection tool to access and edit the content inside a graphics frame.

16. **With the frame content selected, select the top-left reference point in the Properties panel and change the X+ field to 0.**

    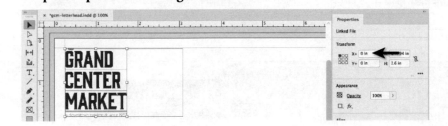

17. **Press Esc to return to the frame of the selected object.**

    The graphics frame is again selected, and the Selection tool is still active.

    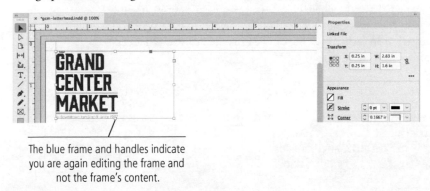

    The blue frame and handles indicate you are again editing the frame and not the frame's content.

18. **With the graphics frame still selected, click the Fit Frame to Content button in the Properties panel.**

19. **Save the file and continue to the next exercise.**

Place Images into Existing Frames

In many cases, you will need to place an image or graphic into an existing frame and then manipulate the placed file to suit the available space. In the previous stage of this project, you created five empty graphics frames at the bottom of the layout; in this exercise, you will place the client's photos into those frames.

1. **With gcm-letterhead.indd open, make the bottom of the page visible in your document window.**

2. **Using the Selection tool, click one of the empty graphics frames.**

   Remember, when objects are grouped, the Selection tool selects the entire group.

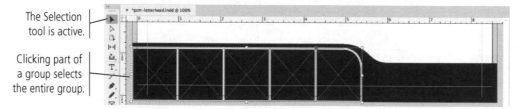

The Selection tool is active.

Clicking part of a group selects the entire group.

3. **Open the Layers panel (Window>Layers), then click the arrow to the left of Layer 1 to expand the layer.**

   Every file has a default layer named "Layer 1" where objects you create exist automatically. Every object on a layer is listed in the Layers panel, nested under the appropriate layer name. Groups, which you created in an earlier exercise, can be expanded so you can access and manage the individual components of the group.

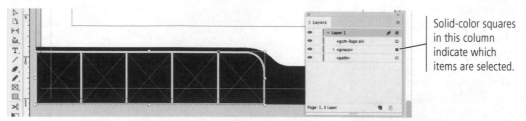

Solid-color squares in this column indicate which items are selected.

4. **Click the arrow to the left of the <group> item to expand the group.**

5. **Click the Select Item button for the first <rectangle> item in the group.**

   This method makes it easy to work with individual items in a group without first breaking apart the group.

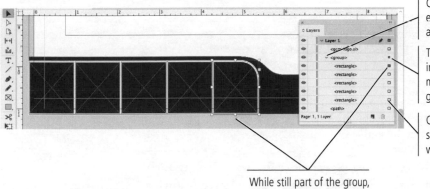

Click the arrows to expand or collapse a layer or group.

The smaller square indicates that one or more objects in the group are selected.

Click this icon to select a specific item within the group.

While still part of the group, only one frame is selected.

6. **In the Properties panel, check the Auto-Fit box, then click the Options button.**

   In this case, you know how much space is available, but you don't yet know the size of the images intended to fill the space. You can use the Frame Fitting options to determine what will happen when you place any image into the existing frames.

Note:

You can also use the Direct Selection tool to select individual objects within a group.

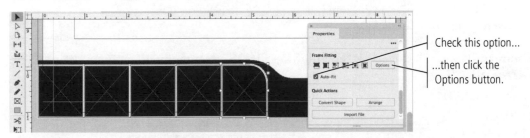

Check this option...

...then click the Options button.

7. **In the Frame Fitting Options dialog box, choose Fill Frame Proportionally in the Fitting menu, choose the top-left point in the Align From proxy, and click OK.**

   When an image is placed into this frame, it will fill the entire frame, and the aspect ratio of the image will be maintained.

   The Align From reference points determine the position of the placed content relative to the frame. In this case, the top-left corner of the content will be anchored to the top-left corner of the frame.

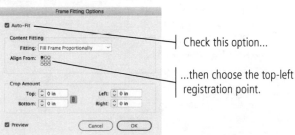

Check this option...

...then choose the top-left registration point.

8. **With the Selection tool still active, click the fourth frame to select it.**

When you are already "inside" a group, you can use the Selection tool to select another individual object within the same group.

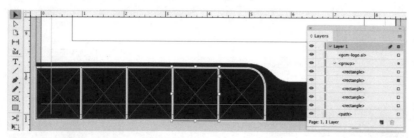

When you use the Auto-Fit checkbox in the Control panel, the center registration point is the default Content Fitting option. To change the registration point for each frame, you need to use the Frame Fitting Options dialog box.

9. **Repeat Steps 6–8 for the remaining placeholder frames, selecting each frame and changing the frame fitting options for the selected frame.**

10. **Choose File>Place. If necessary, navigate to the WIP>GCMarket folder.**

11. **Uncheck all options at the bottom of the dialog box.**

Macintosh users: Remember, you might have to click the Options button to show the Options checkboxes. We will not continue to repeat this instruction.

If you leave Show Import Options checked, you would see the TIFF Options dialog box for each of the selected images. In this case you simply want to place the images so you don't need to review the file options.

12. **Press Command/Control, then click the following files to select them:**

> **coffee.tif**
> **creampuffs.tif**
> **fruit.tif**
> **peppers.tif**
> **spices.tif**

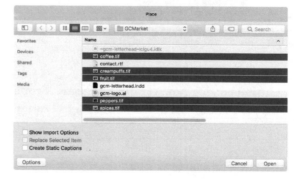

In many cases, you will need to place more than one image from the same location into an InDesign layout. You can streamline the process by loading multiple images into the cursor at once, and then clicking to place each image in the correct location.

Note:

Press Shift to select multiple contiguous files in a dialog box.

Press Command/Control to select multiple non-contiguous files.

Note:

You can press Command/Control to select non-consecutive files in the list, or press Shift to select consecutive files.

13. **Click Open to load the selected files into the Place cursor.**

When you select multiple files in the Place dialog box, the cursor is loaded with all selected pictures; a number in the cursor shows the number of files loaded.

Five images are currently loaded in the Place cursor.

The thumbnail in the cursor shows the active file, which will be placed when you click. You can use the Left Arrow and Right Arrow keys to navigate through the loaded images, watching the cursor thumbnails to find the one you want to place.

Note:

When more than one file is loaded in the Place cursor, the Links panel shows "LP" for the item that is active in the Place cursor.

14. **Click inside the left placeholder frame to place the first image.**

As soon as you place the first file, the next loaded image appears as the cursor thumbnail.

In the Layers panel, the <rectangle> object is replaced with the name of the file you placed into the frame.

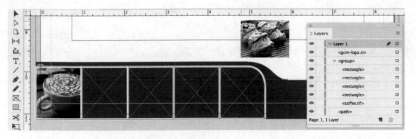

15. **Click inside each empty frame to place the remaining loaded images.**

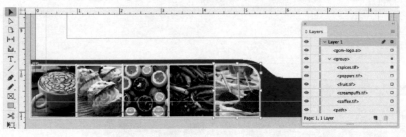

16. **Save the file and continue to the next stage of the project.**

STAGE 4 / Creating and Formatting Basic Text

InDesign is ultimately a page-layout application; **page layout** means combining text and graphic elements in a meaningful way to convey a message. Text can be a single word (as in the logo used in this project) or thousands of pages of consecutive copy (as in a dictionary). Virtually every project you build in InDesign will involve text in one way or another; this letterhead is no exception.

Create a Simple Text Frame

Adding text to a page is a relatively simple process: draw a frame, and then type. In this exercise, you'll create a new text frame and add the client's tag line, then apply some basic formatting options to style the text.

Keep in mind this project is an introduction to creating elements on a layout page; there is far more to professional typesetting than the few options you use here. InDesign provides extremely precise control over virtually every aspect of every letter and word on the page. In the following projects, you will learn about the vast number of options available for setting and controlling type, from formatting a single paragraph to an entire multi-page booklet.

Note:

Remember from the Getting Started section at the beginning of this book: to complete the projects in this book, you should install and activate the ATC fonts provided with the book's resource files.

1. **With gcm-letterhead.indd open, select the Type tool in the Tools panel.**

2. **Click in the empty space above the green-filled shape and drag to create a frame.**

   To type text into a layout, you must first create a frame with the Type tool; when you release the mouse button, you see a flashing bar (called the **insertion point**) where you first clicked to create the text frame.

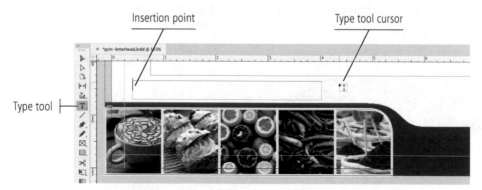

Insertion point

Type tool cursor

Type tool

   The tag line for the letterhead is supposed to appear in the black area to the right of the logo. However, if you click inside that area with the Type tool, it will convert the existing shape to a type area. In this case you want a simple rectangular text frame, so you are creating it in an empty area and then moving it into place.

3. **Type Grand Cuisine. Grand Culture. Grand Central.**

The text appears beginning at the flashing insertion point. Depending on the size of your frame, the text might automatically wrap to a second line within the frame or might not fit into the frame (indicated by a red X, called an **overset text icon**).

New text in InDesign is automatically set in black 12-pt Minion Pro. This font is installed along with the application, so it should be available on your computer unless someone has modified your system fonts. Don't worry if your type appears in some other font; you will change it shortly.

When the insertion point is flashing, the Properties panel includes a fairly large number of text formatting options, consolidated from a variety of other panels and dialog boxes. Depending on the height of your monitor or application frame, you might need to scroll through the panel to find specific formatting options that appear at the bottom of the panel.

Note:

Type defaults to a 100% black fill with no stroke. (You can apply a stroke to type, but you should be very careful when you do to avoid destroying the letter shapes.)

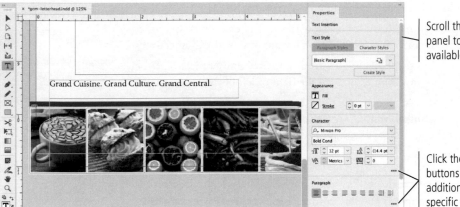

Scroll through the panel to find all the available options.

Click the More Options buttons to show additional options in a specific section.

4. **Choose the Selection tool in the Tools panel.**

You must use the Selection tool to change the position and size of a text frame. You can either drag the handles to manually change the frame or use the Control panel options to define specific parameters.

5. **In the Properties panel, make sure the constrain option is not active for the W and H fields. Choose the top-left reference point, and then change the frame's dimensions to:**

X: 0.25 in	W: 4.5 in
Y: 9.5 in	H: 0.25 in

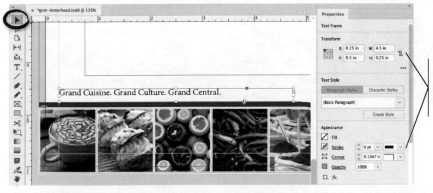

When the frame is selected, frame-specific options become available in the Properties panel.

6. **Choose the Type tool, and click inside the repositioned text frame to place the insertion point.**

7. **Choose Edit>Select All to select all text in the frame.**

   Character formatting such as the font, style, size, and fill color apply only to selected characters.

   In addition to using the Select All command to select all text in a story, you have a number of options for selecting type characters in a frame:

   - Select specific characters by clicking with the Type tool and dragging.
   - Double-click a word to select the entire word.
   - Triple-click a word to select the entire line containing the word.
   - Quadruple-click a word to select the entire paragraph containing the word.
   - Press Shift-Right Arrow or Shift-Left Arrow to select the character to the immediate right or left of the insertion point, respectively.
   - Press Shift-Up Arrow or Shift-Down Arrow to select all characters up to the same position as the insertion point in the previous or next line, respectively.
   - Press Command/Control-Shift-Right Arrow or Command/Control-Shift-Left Arrow to select the word immediately to the right or left of the insertion point, respectively.
   - Press Command/Control-Shift-Up Arrow or Command/Control-Shift-Down Arrow to select the rest of paragraph immediately before or after the insertion point, respectively.

Note:

When a type frame is selected with the Selection tool, you can double-click inside the frame to place the insertion point inside that frame. The Type tool automatically becomes active.

8. **In the Control panel, open the Fill swatch panel and click the custom green swatch at the bottom of the list color. Press Return/Enter to close the pop-up Swatches panel.**

   This is the swatch you defined and saved earlier when you changed the fill color of the green-filled shape. By clicking the swatch, you change the color of all selected text.

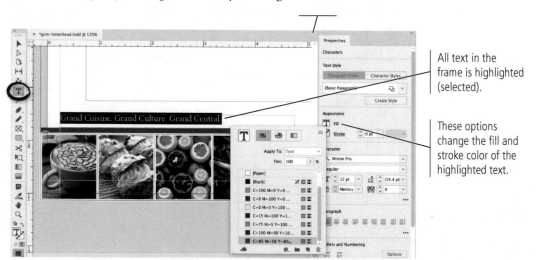

All text in the frame is highlighted (selected).

These options change the fill and stroke color of the highlighted text.

9. **With the text still selected, click in the Font Family field to highlight the current font name.**

10. **With the font name highlighted, type ATC.**

When you type in the Font Family field, the application automatically presents a menu of all fonts that include the letters you type.

By default, the application presents any font that includes the search characters *anywhere in the font name*; a search for "gar" would find both Garamond and Devangari. This kind of search returns all matching fonts in the pop-up menu.

If you click the magnifying glass icon, you can also choose to Search First Word Only. In this case, typing "gar" would automatically change the Font Family field to the first font that begins with those characters; no menu is presented.

11. **Move your mouse cursor over various fonts in the menu.**

You can use this method in the font menu to show a live preview of various fonts before actually applying them to the selected text.

Individual characters do not need to be selected to change text formatting. Changes made while a type *object* is selected apply to all text in that type object.

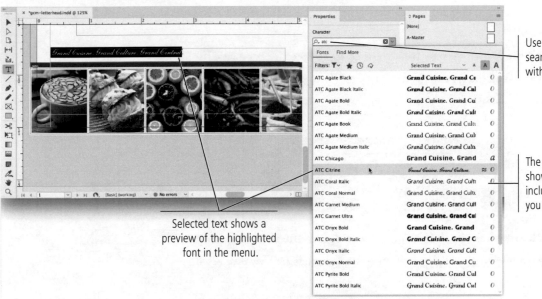

Use this field to search for fonts with specific names.

Selected text shows a preview of the highlighted font in the menu.

The resulting menu shows all fonts that include the characters you type.

12. **Click ATC Coral Normal in the Font menu to select that font.**

After you select the font, you should notice the Font Family menu shows "ATC Coral" and the secondary Font Style menu shows "Normal." When you use the Font Search option (as in Step 10), the resulting menu shows all font variations that include the letters you type — including different styles within the same family.

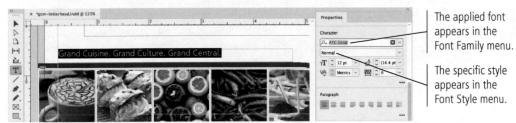

The applied font appears in the Font Family menu.

The specific style appears in the Font Style menu.

13. Click the Up-Arrow button for the Font Size field until you see a red icon on the right edge of the frame.

Each time you click, you increase the type size by one point. The red X is the **overset text icon**; it indicates more text exists than will fit into the frame.

You can also choose from the common preset type sizes in the menu or type a specific size in the field.

If you type in the Font Size field, you don't need to type the unit "pt" for the type size; InDesign automatically applies the measurement for you.

Note:

Press Command/Control-Shift-> to increase the type size by 2 pt, or Command/Control-Shift-< to decrease the type size by 2 pt.

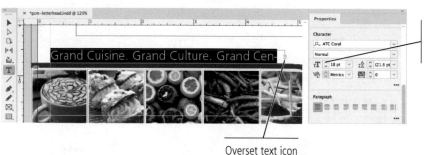

Click these buttons to change the type size by 1 pt.

Overset text icon

14. Click the Down-Arrow button once to reduce the type size by 1 pt.

This allows all the type to fit in the frame.

15. Click anywhere in the selected text to place the insertion point.

This removes the highlight, indicating the characters are now deselected.

16. Save the file and continue to the next exercise.

Place an External Text File

You just learned how to create a text frame and create new text. You can also import text created in an external word-processing application, which is a common situation when creating page-layout jobs (more common, perhaps, than manually typing text in a frame). In this exercise, you import text saved in a rich-text format (RTF) file, which can store type-formatting options as well as the actual text.

1. **With `gcm-letterhead.indd` open, make sure nothing is selected in the layout and then choose File>Place.**

   Remember, you can choose Edit>Deselect All, or simply click in an empty area of the workspace to deselect any selected objects.

2. **Navigate to `contact.rtf` in the WIP>GCMarket folder. Make sure none of the options are checked at the bottom of the dialog box and click Open.**

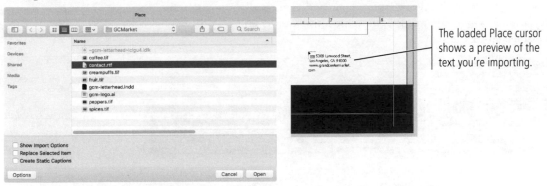

The loaded Place cursor shows a preview of the text you're importing.

3. **Click the loaded Place cursor within the pink margin guides, approximately 0.5″ up from the bottom margin guide.**

   The resulting text frame is automatically created as wide as the defined margin guides and extending down to the bottom margin guide on the page.

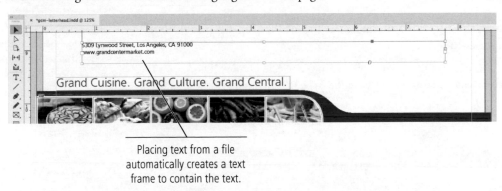

Placing text from a file automatically creates a text frame to contain the text.

4. **Choose the Selection tool. Click the bottom-right corner of the frame and drag until the frame is just large enough to contain the text.**

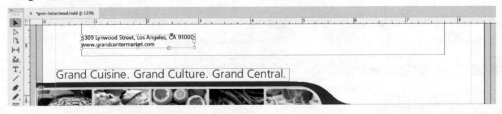

5. **Click and drag the frame until its bottom-right corner snaps to the page guides in the bottom-right corner of the page.**

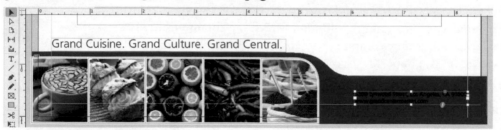

6. **Press Command/Control-Shift, then click the top-left bounding box handle of the frame. While holding down the mouse button, drag to the left. When the Scale X and Scale Y fields in the Control panel show approximately 120%, release the mouse button.**

   As you drag the frame handle, pressing Command/Control allows you to resize the type along with the frame. Pressing Shift constrains the scaling to maintain the original height-to-width ratio.

Note:

The same fields are available in the Properties panel if you click the More Options button in the Transform section.

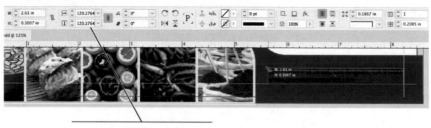

These fields show the percentage to which the frame and its content are being scaled.

Note:

In the standalone Swatches panel, you can use the Formatting Affects Text button to achieve the same result as choosing Text in the Properties panel's Apply To menu.

7. **With the Selection tool still active, open the Fill color pop-up panel in the Properties panel.**

8. **Choose Text in the Apply To menu at the top of the pop-up panel, then click the Paper color.**

   Keep in mind this changes the color of all text in the selected frame; if you want to change only some characters, you must use the Type tool to highlight the characters you want to affect.

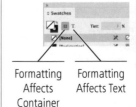

Formatting Affects Container

Formatting Affects Text

The frame is selected.

Choose Text in this menu.

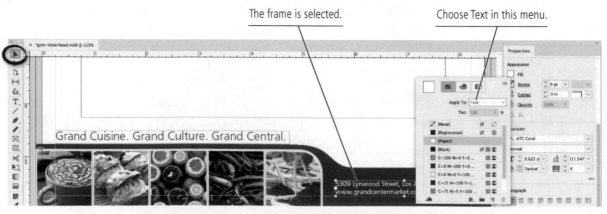

9. **In the Control panel, click the [Paragraph] Align Right option.**

Paragraph formatting (including alignment) applies to all selected paragraphs. If no text is highlighted, it applies only to the paragraph where the insertion point is placed.

In this case, the containing text frame is selected; all paragraphs in the selected frame are also considered selected and will be affected by formatting changes.

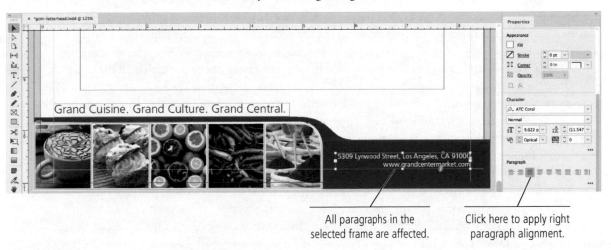

All paragraphs in the selected frame are affected.

Click here to apply right paragraph alignment.

10. **Zoom out so you can see the entire page.**

11. **Use the Screen Mode button in the Application/Menu bar to turn on the Preview mode.**

This mode turns off nonprinting indicators, including guides and the blue borders surrounding every frame. These tools can be very valuable when you're working on a layout, but they can be distracting in other cases.

12. **Save the file and continue to the final stage of the project.**

Note:

You can also toggle off just frame edges in the View>Extras submenu.

When frame edges are hidden, moving the Selection tool cursor over a frame reveals its edges. This frame highlighting can make it easier to find exactly the object you want, especially when working in an area with a number of overlapping or nearby objects.

STAGE 5 / **Printing InDesign Files**

Although the PDF format is the *de facto* standard for submitting files to a commercial printer, you will still need to output printed proofs at some point in your career, whether to show a hard copy to a client or to simply review a document's content away from a monitor. Creating those proofs requires a basic understanding of how software and hardware translate what you see on screen to ink on paper.

For a printer to output high-quality pages from Adobe InDesign, some method of defining the page and its elements is required. These definitions are provided by Page Description Languages (PDLs), the most widely used of which is Adobe PostScript 3.

When a file is output to a PostScript-enabled device, the raster image processor (RIP) creates a file that includes mathematical descriptions detailing the construction and placement of the various page elements; the print file precisely maps the location of each pixel on the page. In the printer, the RIP then interprets the description of each element into a matrix of ones (black) and zeros (white). The output device uses this matrix to reconstruct the element as a series of individual dots or spots that form a high-resolution bitmap image on film or paper.

Not every printer on the market is capable of interpreting PostScript information. Low-cost, consumer-level inkjet printers, common in the modern graphic design market, are generally not PostScript compatible. (Some desktop printers can handle PostScript, at least with an additional purchase; consult the technical documentation that came with your printer to make certain it can print PostScript information.) If your printer is non-PostScript compatible, some features in the InDesign Print dialog box will be unavailable, and some page elements (particularly EPS files) might not output as expected.

If you do not have a PostScript output device, you can work around the problem by first exporting your InDesign files to PDF (see Project 8: Festival Poster) and then opening the PDFs in Acrobat to print a proof. This is a common workflow solution in the current graphic design industry.

Print a Sample Proof

In general, every job you create will be printed at some point in the workflow — whether for your own review, as a client comp, or as a final proof to accompany a file to the commercial printer. So, whether you need a basic proof or a final job proof, you should still understand what is possible in the InDesign Print dialog box.

Composite proofs print all colors on the same sheet, which allows you to judge page geometry and the overall positioning of elements. Final composite proofs provided to the printer should include **registration marks** (special printer's marks used to check the alignment of individual inks when the job is printed), and they should always be output at 100% size.

Note:

It is also important to realize that desktop inkjet and laser printers typically do not accurately represent color.

1. **With gcm-letterhead.indd open, choose File>Print.**

   The Print dialog box includes dozens of options in eight different categories.

   The most important options you'll select are the Printer and PPD (PostScript printer description) at the top of the dialog box. InDesign reads the information in the PPD to determine which of the specific print options are available for the current output.

2. **Choose the printer you want to use in the Printer menu, and choose the PPD for that printer in the PPD menu (if possible).**

3. **Review the options in the General pane.**

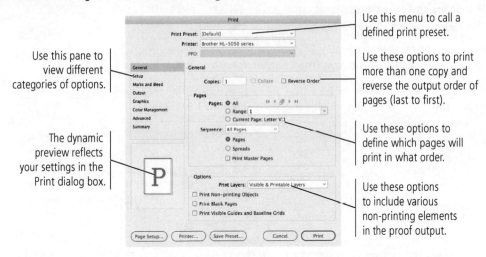

Use this pane to view different categories of options.

Use this menu to call a defined print preset.

Use these options to print more than one copy and reverse the output order of pages (last to first).

The dynamic preview reflects your settings in the Print dialog box.

Use these options to define which pages will print in what order.

Use these options to include various non-printing elements in the proof output.

If you frequently use the same options for printing proofs, simply click the Save Preset button at the bottom of the dialog box after defining those settings. You can then call those same settings by choosing the saved preset in the Print Preset menu.

4. **Click the Setup option in the list of categories.**

These options determine the paper size that will be used for the output (not to be confused with the page size), paper orientation, and page scaling and positioning options relative to the paper size.

5. **If your printer can print to tabloid-size paper, choose Tabloid in the Paper Size menu.**

If you can only print to letter-size paper, choose the landscape paper orientation option, and then activate the Tile check box.

To output a letter-size page at 100% on letter-size paper, you have to tile to multiple sheets of paper; using the landscape paper orientation allows you to tile to two sheets instead of four (as shown in the preview area).

The Offset and Gap fields should only be used when a job is output to an imagesetter or high-end proofing device. They define page placement on a piece of oversized film or on a printing plate.

Check Tile to output the page to multiple sheets of paper.

The overlap area is reflected in the preview; this area will print on both pieces of paper.

6. **Click the Marks and Bleed option in the list of categories.**
   Activate the All Printer's Marks option and change the Offset field to 0.125 in.
   Make sure the Use Document Bleed Settings option is checked.

   You can specify individual printer's marks or simply print them all. For proofing purposes, the crop and bleed marks are the most important options to include.

   The Offset value determines how far from the page edge printer's marks will be placed; some printers require printer's marks to stay outside the bleed area, which means the offset should be at least the same as the defined bleed area.

   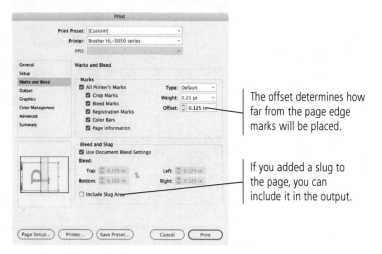

   The offset determines how far from the page edge marks will be placed.

   If you added a slug to the page, you can include it in the output.

7. **Click the Output option in the list of categories.**
   If you can print color, choose Composite CMYK or Composite RGB in the Color menu; otherwise, choose Composite Gray.

   In the Color menu, you can choose the color model you want to use. (If you only have a black-and-white printer, this menu will default to Composite Gray.) The composite options output all colors to a single page, which is appropriate for a desktop proof. If you choose either Separations option in the menu, the Inks list shows which inks (separations) will be included in the output.

   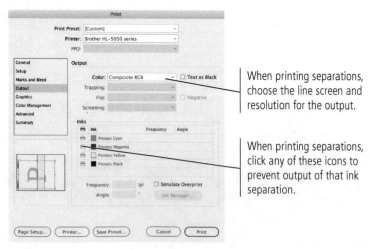

   When printing separations, choose the line screen and resolution for the output.

   When printing separations, click any of these icons to prevent output of that ink separation.

   The Trapping, Flip, Negative, Screening, Frequency, and Angle options should only be used by the output service provider; these options relate to the way separations are imaged on a printing plate for commercial print output.

8. **Click Graphics in the list of categories.**

9. **Choose Optimized Subsampling in the Images Send Data menu.**

This menu determines how much data is sent to the output device for placed images.

- **All**, the default option, sends full-resolution image data.

- **Optimized Subsampling** sends only the necessary data to output the best possible resolution on the printer you are using.

- **Proxy** outputs low-resolution screen previews, which reduces the time required for output.

- **None** outputs all placed images as gray frames with crossed diagonal lines. This is useful for reviewing overall placement when developing an initial layout comp.

If you are using a compatible output device, the Fonts Download menu determines how much font data is downloaded to the printer. (Font data is required by the output device to print the job correctly.)

- **None** sends no font information to the printer. (This can cause output problems, especially if you use TrueType fonts.)

- **Complete** sends the entire font file for every font used in the document.

- **Subset** sends font information only for the characters used in the document.

Professional-quality output devices include a number of resident fonts, from just a few to the entire Adobe type library. If the Download PPD Fonts option is checked, InDesign sends data for all fonts in the document, even if those fonts are installed on the output device. (This can be important because different fonts of the same name might have different font metrics, which can cause text to reflow and appear different in the print than in the file you created.)

The PostScript menu defines which level of PostScript to use. Some older devices cannot process PostScript 3. You should generally leave this menu at the default value.

The Data Format menu defines how image data is transferred. ASCII is compatible with older devices and is useful for cross-platform applications. Binary is smaller than ASCII but might not work on all platforms.

10. **Click Print to output the page.**

11. **When the document comes back into focus, save and close it.**

Note:

We're intentionally skipping the Color Management and Advanced panes in the Print dialog box. We explain them in later projects when they are relevant to the project content.

PROJECT REVIEW

fill in the blank

1. _____ is the area of an object that extends past the edge of a page to compensate for variations in the output process.

2. Shapes created in InDesign are _____, which are resolution-independent and can be freely scaled.

3. The _____ defines the outermost dimensions of an object; it is always a rectangle, regardless of the object's specific shape.

4. _____ are based on the concept of anchor points and their defining control handles.

5. _____ are the four primary colors used in process-color printing.

6. The _____ tool is used to select entire frames or other objects.

7. The _____ tool can be used to select specific segments or individual points on a path.

8. The _____ panel can be used to select and rearrange specific objects in a group.

9. The _____ can be used to access a frame's content when the Selection tool is active.

10. The _____ is context sensitive, reflecting different options depending on what is selected in the document.

short answer

1. Briefly explain how resolution affects a page laid out in InDesign.

2. Briefly explain how Smart Guides help to create a layout.

3. Briefly explain the concept of a reference point relative to a selected object.

PORTFOLIO BUILDER PROJECT

Use what you have learned in this project to complete the following freeform exercise.
Carefully read the art director and client comments, then create your own design to meet the needs of the project.
Use the space below to sketch ideas. When finished, write a brief explanation of the reasoning behind your final design.

The owner of your agency is pleased with your work on behalf of your client. She has decided to create more formal branding for the agency and wants you to create a new logo and accompanying collateral pieces.

To complete this project, you should:

❏ Develop a compelling logo that suggests the agency's purpose (graphic design). Incorporate the agency's name — Creative Concepts — in the logo.

❏ Build a letterhead using the same specifications you used to design the market's letterhead.

❏ Build a business card 3.5″ wide by 2″ high, with 1/8″ bleeds.

❏ Build an envelope layout for #10 business-size envelopes (9.5″ × 4.125″).

For the logo, I want something that really says "graphic design" because how can we convince clients that we can design their logos if we don't have a good design for our own? Find or create some kind of imagery people will immediately recognize as graphics- or art-related.

The letterhead should have the company's mailing address, phone number, and website. The business card needs to include a name, title, mailing address, email, and phone number. The envelope should only have the mailing address and the website. Use your own contact information as placeholder text for everything.

For the envelope, we're going to print pre-folded envelopes, so you can't use bleeds. You need to keep objects at least 0.25″ from the edges.

All pieces should have a consistent look. Whatever you do on the letterhead, you should use similar visual elements on all three pieces.

PROJECT SUMMARY

We designed this project to introduce you to the basics of page layout with InDesign; you will expand on these skills throughout this book. Creating a new document to meet specific project needs — including page size, margins, and the printer's stated bleed requirements — is one of the most important tasks you will complete in InDesign.

After the page structure is created, InDesign has many tools for creating objects: basic shapes, lines, and Bézier curves, placeholder frames, and text frames. The built-in drawing tools can create sophisticated artwork directly on the page (although InDesign should not be considered an alternative to Adobe Illustrator for creating all vector artwork). You can also place external image and text files, and then transform those files to meet the specific needs of a given project.

There are many different methods for managing objects and their content. The Selection and Direct Selection tools, the Content Indicator icon, frame edge highlighting, and the Layers panel all provide ways to access only — and exactly — what you want to edit.

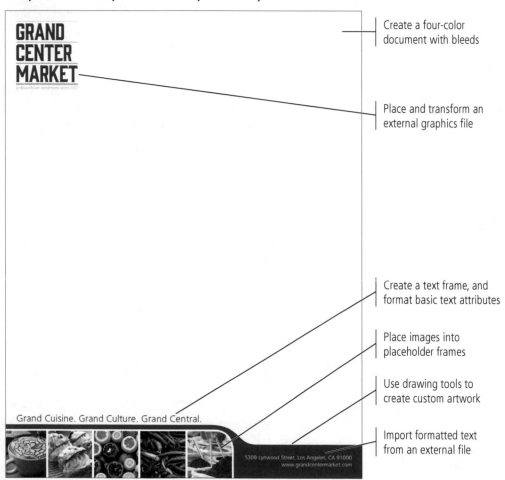

Create a four-color document with bleeds

Place and transform an external graphics file

Create a text frame, and format basic text attributes

Place images into placeholder frames

Use drawing tools to create custom artwork

Import formatted text from an external file

Festival Poster

8

Your client, the marketing director for the city department of parks and recreation, wants a poster and postcard to advertise the opening festival that kicks off the annual Summer Concert Series. She wants to use very little text and large, vivid graphics.

This project incorporates the following skills:

❏ Creating a file with the appropriate settings for a five-color, commercially printed poster

❏ Using gradients, graphics, and effects to attract the viewer's attention

❏ Adding text elements and applying formatting as appropriate

❏ Threading a single text story across multiple text frames

❏ Understanding the options for formatting characters and paragraphs

❏ Adjusting layouts to different page sizes

❏ Creating PDF files that meets the printer's requirements

PROJECT MEETING

client comments

The poster to promote this festival is basically the "play bill," and we will plaster it all over the city. We want the artwork to be very colorful and vivid, so the main focus — and most of the poster real estate — should be on the graphics. But the text also has to be readable; this morning I emailed the text I want to include.

Our posters for past years' festivals have always been 11″ × 17″, but we've been told that 11″ × 8.5″ will fit in the half-page ad space of the local newspaper. We're going to switch to that size for this year's event.

For the postcard, we typically go oversized and use 7″ × 5″ because it stands out a bit more than a typical 6″ × 4.25″ postcard.

art director comments

The client has provided all the pieces you need, so you can get started composing the layout. Most of this job is going to involve compositing multiple images and formatting text, but I want you to go beyond basic image placement. InDesign includes many tools for manipulating images; use some of those to make sure this poster consists of more than just plain pictures.

Finally, I want you to use a special metallic ink for the date and location. That should give the poster just a bit more visual impact than regular flat colors. I think the gold 8005 in Pantone's metallic collection will work well with the other visual elements.

You already know the page sizes. According to the printer the postcard only needs the standard 1/8″ bleed allowance, but the poster needs a 1/4″ bleed just to be safe.

The final files should be saved as PDFs using the printer's specs, which I'll email to you.

project objectives

To complete this project, you will:

❑ Convert the content type of frames.

❑ Create a custom gradient to add visual impact.

❑ Create a frame using an image clipping path.

❑ Apply effects to unify various graphic elements.

❑ Create a QR code.

❑ Thread the flow of text through multiple text frames.

❑ Format text characters and paragraphs to effectively convey a message.

❑ Place inline graphics to highlight important textual elements.

❑ Place text on a path.

❑ Apply a spot color.

❑ Adjust the layout to more than one page size.

❑ Create PDF files for commercial output.

STAGE 1 / **Building Graphic Interest**

Graphics and text are contained in frames, and those objects (including graphics frames) can have stroke and fill attributes. You can use those foundational skills to build virtually any InDesign layout.

InDesign also includes a number of options for extending your artistic options beyond simply compositing text and graphics that were finalized in other applications. The first stage of this project incorporates a number of these creative tools to accomplish your client's stated goal of grabbing the viewer's attention with vivid, attractive graphics.

Set up the Workspace

1. **Download `Concert_Print19_RF.zip` from the Student Files web page.**

2. **Expand the ZIP archive in your WIP folder (Macintosh), or copy the archive contents into your WIP folder (Windows).**

   This results in a folder named **Concert**, which contains the files you need for this project. You should also use this folder to save the files you create in this project.

3. **In InDesign, choose File>New>Document. Choose the Print option at the top of the dialog box, and choose the Letter document preset.**

   Remember, using the Print category of presets automatically applies inches as the unit of measurement and CMYK as the default color model.

4. **In the Preset Details section, make the following changes to the default values:**

Name:	**poster**
Units:	**Inches**
Orientation:	**Landscape**
Facing Pages:	**Unchecked**
Margins:	**0.25 in on all four sides**
Bleed:	**0.25 in on all four sides**

   > *Note:*
   >
   > *If a setting isn't mentioned, leave it at the default setting.*

5. **Click Create to create the new file.**

6. **Save the new file as `poster.indd` in your WIP>Concert folder, and then continue to the next exercise.**

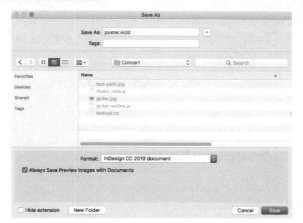

 Define Color Swatches

Before you begin creating colors to use in a layout, you should understand a few basics about the mechanics of designing with color.

Color By Numbers. If you base color choices solely on what you see on your monitor, many colors will probably not look quite right when printed with process-color inks. Even if you have calibrated your monitor, there will always be some discrepancies since monitors display color in RGB and printing uses CMYK.

Every print designer should have some sort of printed process-color chart, which contains small squares of process ink builds so you can see, for example, what a process build of C=10 M=70 Y=30 K=20 will really look like when printed. When you define process colors in InDesign, you should enter specific numbers in the CMYK fields to designate your color choices rather than relying on your screen preview. As you gain experience defining colors, you will become better able to predict the outcome for a given process-ink build.

The same concept also applies when using special ink libraries. You should have, and use, swatch books showing printed samples of the special inks. You cannot rely on the monitor preview to choose a special ink color.

Total Area Coverage. When defining the ink values of a process-color build, you must usually limit your total area coverage (TAC, also called total ink coverage or total ink density), or the amount of ink used in a given color. If you exceed the TAC limits for a given paper-ink-press combination, your printed job might end up with excess ink bleed, smearing, smudging, show-through, or a number of other printing errors because the paper cannot absorb all the ink.

Maximum TAC limits are between 240% and 320% for offset lithography, depending on the paper being used; TAC can be easily calculated by adding the percentages of each ink used to create the color. If a color is defined as C=45 M=60 Y=90 K=0, the total area coverage is 195% (45 + 60 + 90 + 0).

Swatches in InDesign. The Swatches panel (Window>Color>Swatches) is used to apply predefined colors to any element in a layout.

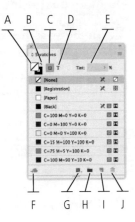

A **Fill** and **Stroke** swatches determine the active attribute; whichever appears at the top of the stack is the one that will be changed by clicking a swatch.

B The **Swap Fill and Stroke** button reverses the current fill and stroke colors.

C The **Formatting Affects Container** option is active by default when an object is selected with the Selection tool; when selected, clicking a color changes the fill or stroke of the selected object.

D If a text frame is selected, you can click the **Formatting Affects Text** button to change the color of text inside that frame. This option is active by default when the insertion point is placed in a text frame.

E Use the **Tint** field to change the tint of the applied color, from 0% to 100%.

F Clicking the **Add Selected Swatch to CC Library** button adds the selected swatch to the active CC Library.

G Use the **Swatch Views** menu to show all swatches, show only color swatches, show only gradient swatches; or show only color groups.

H Click the **New Color Group** button to create a new color group (folder) for organizing swatches. Selected swatches move into the new color group.

I Click the **New Swatch** button to create a new color swatch based on the active color. If the active color is an existing swatch, the new swatch is a duplicate of the existing swatch with "2" appended to the swatch name.

J Click the **Delete Selected Swatch/Group** button to remove selected color swatches/groups; objects where those colors had been applied are not affected.

A number of options are included in the default swatches panel for new print files:

- **None.** This swatch removes any applied color from the active attribute.

- **Registration.** This swatch appears on every separation in a job. This "color" should only be used for special marks and information placed outside the design's trim area.

- **Paper.** In four-color printing, there is no white ink; instead, you have to remove or "knock out" underlying colors so the paper shows through, regardless of whether it is white or some other color. This is why InDesign refers to this swatch as "Paper" instead of "White."

- **Black.** This is a 100% tint of only black ink.

- **Colors.** Six default color swatches represent the subtractive (CMY) and additive (RGB) color models.

The right side of the panel has two columns of icons for each color swatch:

- The left icon identifies whether a swatch is a process (▣) or a spot color (◉).

- The right icon identifies the color model used to define the color: CMYK (▣), RGB (▤), or LAB (▦).

Note:

Using the Fill and Stroke swatches at the top of the Swatches panel, you can apply different colors to the fill and stroke of selected text.

Note:

You cannot edit or delete the None, Registration, or Black color swatches.

You can edit the Paper swatch to more accurately represent the color of paper being used for a specific job. Editing the appearance of the Paper swatch only affects the on-screen preview; it does not appear in the print output.

1. **With `poster.indd` open, open the Swatches panel (Window>Color>Swatches).**

2. **In the Swatches panel, double-click the default blue color swatch (C=100 M=90 Y=10 K=0).**

   Double-clicking a swatch opens the Swatch Options dialog box, where you can change the settings of that swatch. The top of the dialog box shows this swatch is a Process CMYK color named according to the color values.

Note:

Remember, all panels (whether docked or not) can be accessed from the Window menu. If you don't see a specific menu command, choose Edit>Show All Menu Items.

3. **Change the ink percentages to the following:**

Cyan:	70%
Magenta:	80%
Yellow:	0%
Black:	0%

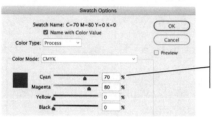

Change the color values in these fields.

4. **Click OK to apply the change.**

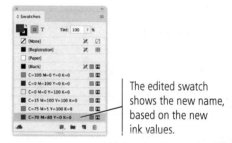

The edited swatch shows the new name, based on the new ink values.

5. **Repeat Steps 2–4 to change the definition of the default red color swatch (C=15 M=100 Y=100 K=0) to:**

Cyan:	20%
Magenta:	100%
Yellow:	100%
Black:	10%

6. **With nothing selected in the layout, click the default green color swatch and drag it to the panel's Delete button.**

   Although it isn't necessary to delete the swatch, you should know how the process works. If you delete a swatch used in the layout, you will be asked what color to use in place of the one you are deleting.

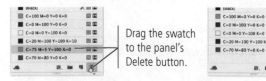

Drag the swatch to the panel's Delete button.

7. Open the Swatches panel Options menu.

This menu has options for creating four types of color swatches: Color, Tint, Gradient, and Mixed Ink.

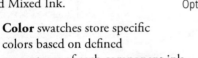 Click here to open the panel Options menu.

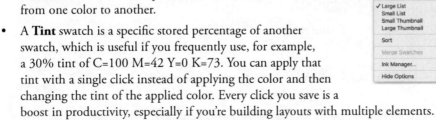

- **Color** swatches store specific colors based on defined percentages of each component ink.

- **Gradient** swatches store specific transitions from one color to another.

- A **Tint** swatch is a specific stored percentage of another swatch, which is useful if you frequently use, for example, a 30% tint of C=100 M=42 Y=0 K=73. You can apply that tint with a single click instead of applying the color and then changing the tint of the applied color. Every click you save is a boost in productivity, especially if you're building layouts with multiple elements.

- **Mixed Ink** swatches allow you to combine percentages of spot and process colors, or of multiple spot colors; this option is only available when at least one spot color exists in the file. The **Mixed Ink Group** option allows you to build multiple swatches at once. Be very careful if you use mixed ink swatches; they can be a source of unpredictable color reproduction and potential output problems.

8. Choose New Color Swatch in the panel Options menu.

9. Leave the Name with Color Value option checked. Make sure the Color Type is set to Process and the Color Mode is set to CMYK.

There is no industry standard for naming colors, but InDesign comes close with the Name with Color Value option when you define a new swatch. This type of naming convention serves several purposes:

- You know exactly what components the color contains, so you can easily see if you are duplicating colors.

- You can immediately tell the color should be a process build rather than a special ink or spot color.

- You avoid mismatched color names and duplicated spot colors, which are potential disasters in the commercial printing production process.

Mismatched color names occur when a defined color name has two different values — one defined in the page layout and one defined in a file you placed into your layout. When the files are output, the output device might be confused by different definitions for the same color name; the imported value might replace the project's value for that particular color name (or vice versa). The change could be subtle, or it could be drastic.

A similar problem occurs when the same spot color is assigned different names in different applications. For example, you define a spot color in InDesign as "Border Color"; another designer might define the same spot color in Illustrator as "Spec Blue." When the illustration is placed into the InDesign layout, two different spot-color separations exist even though the different color names have the same values.

Note:

Use the Load Swatches option to import color swatches from another InDesign file.

Use the Add Unnamed Colors option to find and add colors that are applied in the layout without using a defined swatch (e.g., using the Color panel).

Use the Sort submenu options to sort swatches by name or color value.

10. **Define the swatch color percentages as**

Cyan:	0%
Magenta:	40%
Yellow:	0%
Black:	100%

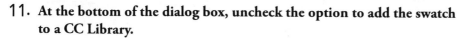

Leave this option checked.

Choose Process color type.

Choose CMYK color mode.

Define ink percentages here.

Uncheck this option.

100% black and some percent of another color is called **rich black** or **super black**. Remember, when the inks are printed, adding another ink to solid black enhances the richness of the solid black. Adding cyan typically creates a cooler black, while adding magenta typically creates a warmer black.

11. **At the bottom of the dialog box, uncheck the option to add the swatch to a CC Library.**

CC Libraries are useful for sharing assets such as color swatches across multiple Adobe CC applications if you have an individual Creative Cloud user account.

12. **Click the Add button to create the new color swatch.**

By clicking the Add button, you can add more color swatches without having to reopen the New Color Swatch dialog box. If you click OK, the swatch is created and the dialog box closes.

13. **In the New Color Swatch dialog box, choose Spot in the Color Type menu.**

14. **Choose Pantone+ Metallic Coated in the Color Mode menu.**

Spot colors are created with special premixed inks to produce a certain color with one ink layer; they are not built from the process inks used in CMYK printing. When you output a job with spot colors, each spot color appears on its own separation.

Spot-color inks are commonly used when an exact color, such as a corporate color, is required. InDesign includes a number of built-in color libraries, including spot-color systems such as the Pantone Matching System (PMS), the most popular collections of spot colors in the United States.

Even though you can choose a color directly from the library on your screen, you should look at a swatch book to verify you are using the color you intend. Special inks exist because many of the colors cannot be reproduced with process inks, nor can they be accurately represented on a computer monitor. If you specify special colors and then convert them to process colors later, your job probably won't look exactly as you expect.

Note:

Spot colors are safely chosen from a swatch book — a book of colors printed with different inks, similar to the paint chip cards used in home decorating.

When choosing spot colors, ask your printer which ink system it supports. If you designate TruMatch but they use Pantone inks, you won't get the colors you expect.

15. Place the insertion point in the Pantone field and type 8005.

You can also scroll through the list and simply click a color to select it.

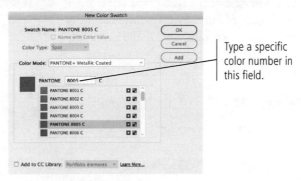

Type a specific
color number in
this field.

16. Click Add, then click Done to return to the document window.

Your panel now has
two edited swatches,
one new process swatch,
and one new spot swatch.

17. Save the file and continue to the next exercise.

Working with Color Groups

Color groups are a convenient way to manage swatches, much as you might organize files in folders on your desktop.

When you click the New Color Group button at the bottom of the Swatches panel, a new group is added to the panel with the default name "Color Group X," where X is simply a sequential number.

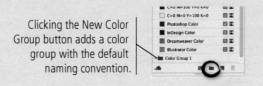

Clicking the New Color
Group button adds a color
group with the default
naming convention.

You can double-click the color group name to open the Edit Color Group dialog box, where you can define a specific name for the group.

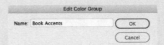

Choosing New Color Group in the panel Options menu automatically opens the Edit Color Group dialog box, where you can name the new group at the time it is created.

If one or more swatches are selected in the panel when you create a new color group, the selected swatches are automatically moved to the new group.

After a group is created, you can drag existing swatches in the group using the following steps:

1a. Click to select a single swatch;
 b. Shift-click to select multiple consecutive swatches; or
 c. Command/Control-click to select multiple nonconsecutive swatches.

2. Release the mouse button.

3. Click one of the selected swatches away from the swatch name.

4. While holding down the mouse button, drag the selected swatches until a heavy line appears immediately below the color group name.

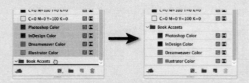

If an existing group, or a swatch inside an existing group, is selected when you create a new swatch, the new swatch is automatically added to the selected group.

Create the Poster Background

The background of this poster is going to be a solid fill of the rich black swatch you defined in the previous exercise. However, an object filling the entire page can cause certain problems. For example, if you try to create a text frame inside the area, you end up converting the frame to a text frame. In this exercise, you use the Layers panel to prevent problems that could be caused by the background shape.

1. **With poster.indd open, choose the Rectangle tool in the Tools panel.**

2. **In the Swatches panel, make sure the Fill swatch is on top and click the C=0 M=40 Y=0 K=100 swatch.**

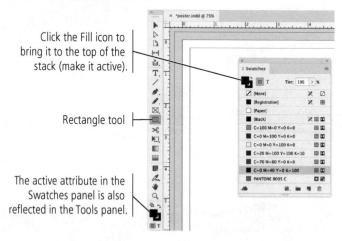

Click the Fill icon to bring it to the top of the stack (make it active).

Rectangle tool

The active attribute in the Swatches panel is also reflected in the Tools panel.

3. **Click the Stroke icon at the top of the panel to activate that attribute, then click the None swatch.**

    By changing the fill and stroke attributes when no object is selected, you define those attributes for the next object you create.

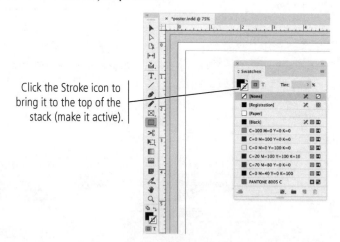

Click the Stroke icon to bring it to the top of the stack (make it active).

4. **Using the Rectangle tool, create a rectangle covering the entire page and extends to the defined bleed guides.**

    You can single-click to define the rectangle size, and then drag it into position with the Selection tool. Alternatively, you can simply click and drag with the Rectangle tool, using the Bleed guides to snap the edges of the shape.

5. **In the Layers panel (Window>Layers), click the arrow to expand Layer 1.**

6. **Click the empty space to the right of the eye icon for the <rectangle> item.**

   The second column in the Layers panel can be used to lock individual items or entire layers. (If you lock a whole layer, all items on that layer are automatically locked.) You can click an existing lock icon in the Layers panel to unlock an object or layer.

Note:

You can also click a lock icon on the page to unlock a specific object.

This icon identifies a locked object.

Click this space to lock a specific object.

7. **With the Rectangle tool still selected, change the stroke color to the custom blue swatch. Using the Control panel, change the stroke weight to 6 pt.**

   When you locked the rectangle in Step 6, it was automatically deselected. This means changing the stroke and fill attributes does not affect the rectangle.

Note:

You cannot use the Properties panel to define settings for the next object you create; in this case you must use the Control panel.

8. **Click and drag to draw a rectangle anywhere on the page.**

9. **Using the Control panel, choose the top-left reference point and then change the frame's dimensions to**

X: -0.25 in	W: 11.5 in
Y: 1 in	H: 6.5 in

   These dimensions create a frame extending the entire width of the layout (including bleeds), with 1″ of space above and below the frame.

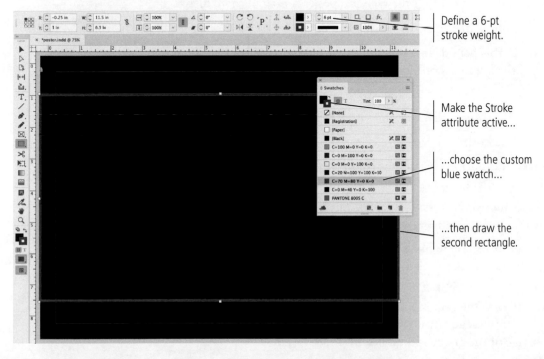

Define a 6-pt stroke weight.

Make the Stroke attribute active...

...choose the custom blue swatch...

...then draw the second rectangle.

10. **In the Layers panel, click the Eye icon to the left of the locked <rectangle>.**

The visible rectangle has the same fill color as the background shape (which is now hidden). To make it easier to see and work with only specific objects, you can use the Layers panel to toggle the visibility of individual objects or entire layers.

Note:

If you hide an entire layer, all objects on that layer are hidden.

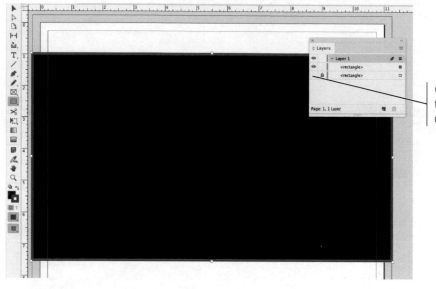

Click an Eye icon to hide a specific object or layer.

11. **Save the file and continue to the next exercise.**

Define and Apply a Gradient

A **gradient**, also called a **blend**, can be used to create a smooth transition from one color to another. You can apply a gradient to any object using the Gradient panel (Window>Color>Gradient), or you can save a gradient swatch if you plan to use it again. The Gradient panel controls the type and position of applied gradients.

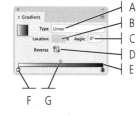

A **Type.** Choose either linear or radial gradient.

B **Location.** This field defines the position (from 0 on the left to 100 on the right) of the selected stop along the gradient ramp.

C. **Angle.** This field defines the angle of the gradient around a circle:

- 0° is horizontal, left to right
- 180° is horizontal, right to left
- 90° is vertical, bottom to top
- −90° (270°) is vertical, top to bottom

D. **Reverse.** This button changes the colors in the gradient left to right, as if flipping it horizontally.

E. **Gradient Ramp.** This shows a sample of the defined gradient. You can click below the ramp to add a new stop.

F. **Gradient Stops.** These show positions where specific colors are defined along the gradient. You can click and drag stops to new positions along the ramp or drag them off the ramp to remove stops from the gradient.

G. **Center Point.** The center point between two stops is the point where the two adjacent stops blend equally. You can drag the center points to change the percentage of the gradient occupied by a specific color.

Note:

You can drag a swatch from the Swatches panel to the gradient ramp in the Gradient panel to add a new color stop or to change the color of an existing stop.

1. **With poster.indd open, choose the Selection tool. Click outside the area of the visible rectangle to deselect it.**

2. **Choose New Gradient Swatch from the Swatches panel Options menu.**

3. **Click the gradient stop on the left end of the gradient ramp to select it.**

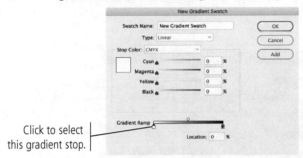

Click to select
this gradient stop.

4. **Make sure Linear is selected in the Type menu, and then choose Swatches in the Stop Color menu.**

You can define gradients using LAB values, CMYK percentages, RGB values, or existing color swatches.

5. **With the first stop selected, click the blue CMYK swatch.**

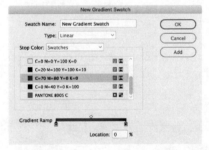

6. **Select the second gradient stop (on the right end of the ramp), and then click the custom red swatch.**

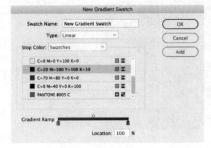

7. Type **Blue to Red** in the Swatch Name field and then click OK.

The new gradient swatch
is selected by default.

8. Using the Selection tool, click the visible rectangle on the page to select it.

9. Make the Fill icon active in the Swatches panel, and then click the Blue to Red gradient swatch.

It is important to remember but easy to forget: make sure the correct attribute (fill or stroke) is active when you change a color.

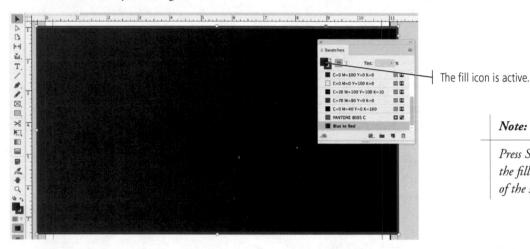

The fill icon is active.

10. Make the Stroke icon active in the Swatches panel, and then click the Blue to Red gradient swatch.

11. Using the Gradient panel (Window>Color>Gradient), change the Angle field to 180° so the stroke goes from red on the left to blue on the right (the reverse of the fill).

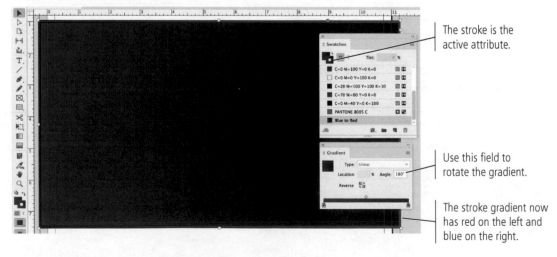

The stroke is the
active attribute.

Use this field to
rotate the gradient.

The stroke gradient now
has red on the left and
blue on the right.

12. Click away from the rectangle to deselect it.

13. **Use the Screen Mode button on the Tools panel or the Application/Menu bar to display the layout in Preview mode.**

This option hides all guides and frame edges, which makes it easier to see the subtle effect created by the opposing gradients.

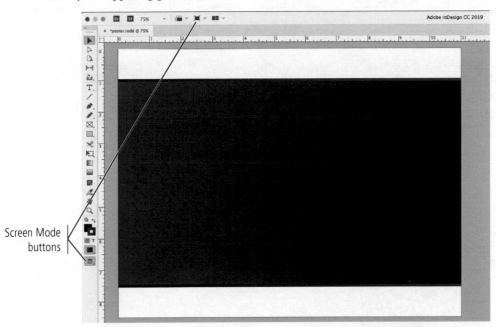

Screen Mode buttons

14. **Restore the document view to the Normal mode in the Screen Mode menu.**

15. **Save the file and continue to the next exercise.**

Using the Gradient Tools

FOUNDATIONS

Clicking a gradient swatch adds a gradient to the selected object, beginning at the left edge and ending at the right edge for linear gradients, or beginning at the object's center and ending at the object's outermost edge for radial gradients. When you drag with the **Gradient tool**, you define the length of the gradient without regard to the object you're filling.

This frame is filled with the Green to Blue gradient.

The Gradient tool defines a new angle, start point, and end point for the gradient.

Start point
End point

The **Gradient Feather tool** has a similar function but produces different results. Rather than creating a specific-colored gradient, the Gradient Feather tool applies a transparency gradient, blending the object from solid to transparent.

The image frame is placed over a cyan-filled frame.

The Gradient Feather tool defines transparency, from 0 at the start point to 100 at the end point.

End point
Start point

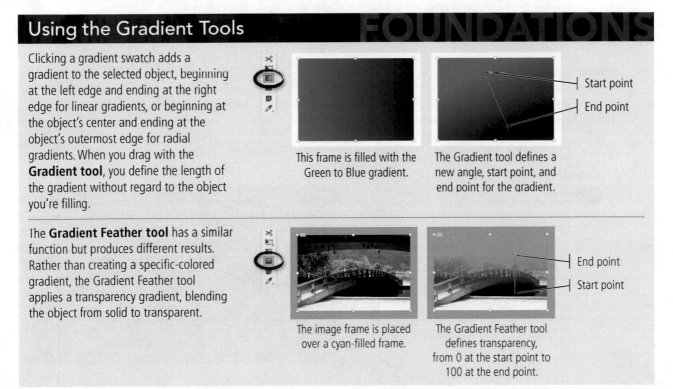

Create an Irregular Graphics Frame

You can create basic graphics frames using the Rectangle, Ellipse, and Polygon Frame tools. You can also create a Bézier shape with the Pen tool, and then convert the shape to a graphics frame, which means you can create a frame in virtually any shape. However, it requires a lot of work to trace complex graphics with the Pen tool; fortunately, you can use other options to create complex frames from placed graphics.

1. **In the open `poster.indd` file, select the gradient-filled rectangle in the layout.**

2. **Choose File>Place. Navigate to `guitar-outline.ai` in the WIP>Concert folder. Check Show Import Options and Replace Selected Item, then click Open.**

   Macintosh users: Remember, you might have to click the Options button to reveal the three options checkboxes. We will not continue to repeat this instruction.

This frame should be selected.

Make sure both options are checked.

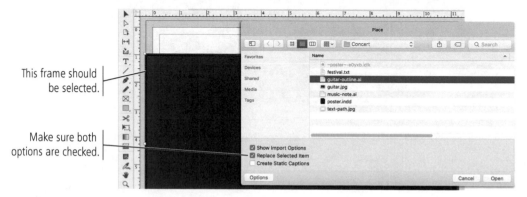

3. **In the resulting dialog box, choose Art in the Crop To menu, then click OK.**

   If Replace Selected Item was not checked in the Place dialog box, the image would be loaded into the cursor.

   Because the existing rectangle was selected and the Replace Selected Item option was checked, the new image automatically appears in the selected frame. If another image had already been placed in the frame, the guitar graphic would replace the existing image (hence the name of the command).

Note:

Refer back to Project 1: Letterhead Design for an explanation of the Crop To options.

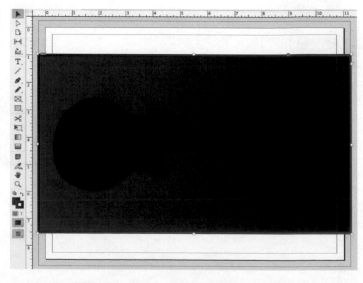

4. Choose Edit>Undo Replace.

If you accidentally replace a selected item, undoing the placement loads the last-placed image into the cursor.

This is an easy fix if you accidentally replace an image. Simply choose Edit>Undo Replace, and then click to place the loaded image in the correct location.

Note:

The Undo command undoes the single last action. In this case, placing the image into the frame — even though it happened automatically — was the last single action.

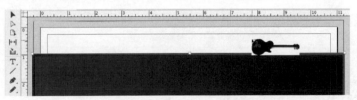

5. Click in the white area near the top-left corner to place the loaded image.

Do not click inside the gradient-filled rectangle; if you do, the loaded image will be placed back into that frame instead of in a new frame.

6. Using the Properties panel, select the top-left reference point and then change the new image frame's position to X: 0.25 in, Y: 4.75 in.

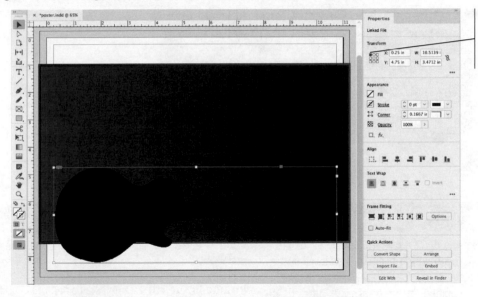

Use the top-left reference point to position the graphics frame.

7. With the same frame selected, choose Object>Clipping Path>Options.

A **clipping path** is a hard-edged outline that masks an image. Areas inside the path are visible; areas outside the path are hidden.

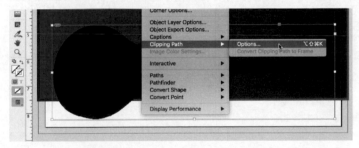

8. **In the resulting dialog box, check the Preview option and then choose Detect Edges in the Type menu.**

InDesign can access Alpha channels and clipping paths saved in an image, or you can create a clipping path based on the image content. Because this graphic is a vector graphic with well-defined edges filled with a solid color, InDesign can create a very precise clipping path based on the information in the file.

Note:

The Include Inside Edges option generates a compound clipping path that removes holes in the middle of the outside path.

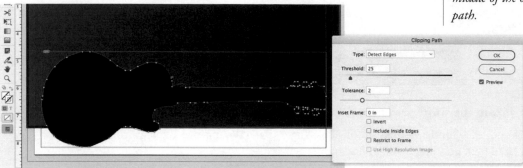

9. **Click OK to close the dialog box and create the clipping path.**

10. **Choose Object>Clipping Path>Convert Clipping Path to Frame.**

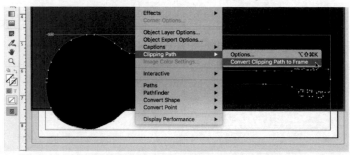

Understanding Clipping Path Options

Threshold specifies the darkest pixel value that will define the resulting clipping path. In this exercise, the placed image is filled with solid black, so you can set a very high Threshold value to define the clipping path. In images with greater tone variation (such as a photograph), increasing the Threshold value removes lighter areas from the clipped area.

Tolerance specifies how similar a pixel must be to the Threshold value before it is hidden by the clipping path. Increasing the Tolerance value results in fewer points along the clipping path, generating a smoother path. Lowering the Tolerance value results in more anchor points and a potentially rougher path.

Inset Frame shrinks the clipping path by a specific number of pixels. You can also enter a negative value to enlarge the clipping path.

Invert reverses the clipping path, making hidden areas visible and vice versa.

Include Inside Edges creates a compound clipping path, removing inner areas of the object if they are within the Threshold and Tolerance ranges.

Restrict to Frame creates a clipping path that stops at the visible edge of the graphic. You can include the entire object, including areas beyond the frame edges, by unchecking this option.

Use High Resolution Image generates the clipping path based on the actual file data instead of the preview image.

11. Using the Direct Selection tool, select the image inside the irregular frame.

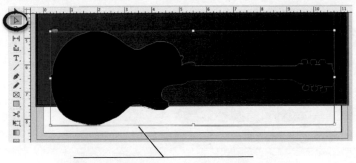

The red bounding box indicates that you have selected the image inside the frame.

12. With the frame content selected, press Delete/Backspace to delete the placed file but leave the frame you created.

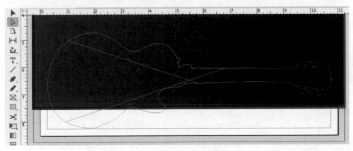

Note:

If you don't see the frame edges, make sure you reset the screen mode to Normal instead of Preview (which you used in the last exercise).

13. Using the Selection tool, click the irregular graphics frame to select it.

14. Choose File>Place and navigate to guitar.jpg in the WIP>Concert folder. Uncheck all options at the bottom of the dialog box and click Open.

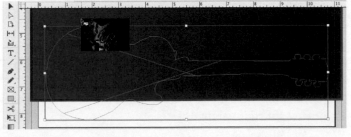

This frame should be selected.

This option should not be checked.

Although the existing frame was selected when you opened the Place dialog box, the new image is loaded into the cursor because you unchecked the Replace Selected Item option.

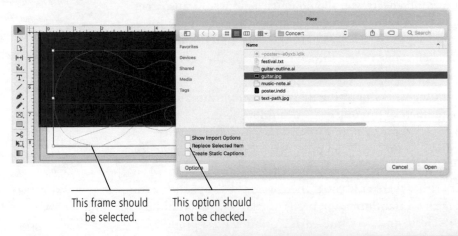

15. **Click inside the empty frame with the loaded cursor to place the image inside the frame.**

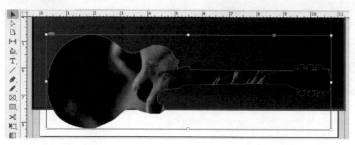

16. **Save the file and continue to the next exercise.**

 Create Visual Impact with Transparency

The image effects and transparency controls in InDesign provide options for adding dimension and depth directly in the page layout. You can change the transparency of any object (or individual object attributes), apply different blending modes, and apply creative effects such as drop shadows and beveling.

Transparency and effects are controlled in the Effects panel. You can change these options for an entire object (fill and stroke), only the stroke, only the fill, the text (if you're working with a text frame), the graphic (if you're working with a graphics frame), or all objects in a group. The selected item in the panel list is referred to as the **target**.

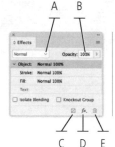

A   Blending Mode
B   Opacity
C   Clear all effects and make object opaque
D   Add an object effect to the selected target
E   Remove effects from the selected target

Technical Issues of Transparency

Before you use these features and effects, you should understand what transparency is and how it affects your output. **Transparency** is the degree to which light passes through an object so that objects in the background are visible. In terms of page layout, transparency means being able to "see through" objects in the front of the stacking order to objects lower in the stacking order.

Because of the way printing works, applying transparency in print design is a bit of a contradiction. Commercial printing is, by definition, accomplished by overlapping a mixture of (usually) four semitransparent inks in different percentages to reproduce a range of colors. In that sense, all print design requires transparency.

But *design* transparency refers to the objects on the page. The trouble is, when a halftone dot is printed, it's either there or it's not. There is no "50% opaque" setting on a printing press. This means a transformation needs to take place behind the scenes, translating what we create on screen into what a printing press produces.

When transparent objects are output, overlapping areas of transparent elements are actually broken into individual elements where necessary to produce the best possible results. Ink values in the overlap areas are calculated by the application and based on the capabilities of the mechanical printing process; the software converts what we create on screen into the elements necessary to print.

When you get to the final stage of this project, you'll learn how to preview and control the output process for transparent objects.

Note:

The Graphic option is only available when a placed graphic within a frame is selected. Group replaces Object in the list only when a group is selected.

Note:

Effects applied to text apply to all text in the frame; you can't apply effects to individual characters.

Note:

Transparency is essentially the inverse of opacity. If an object is 20% transparent, it is also 80% opaque.

1. In the open **poster.indd** file, use the Selection tool to select the gradient-filled rectangle.

2. Choose **Object>Content>Graphic.**

Note:

You can also Control/ right-click an object and change its content type in the contextual menu.

When you create a frame with one of the basic shape tools, it is considered "unassigned" because it is neither a text frame nor a graphics frame. You can convert any type of frame (graphics, text, or unassigned) to another type using this menu.

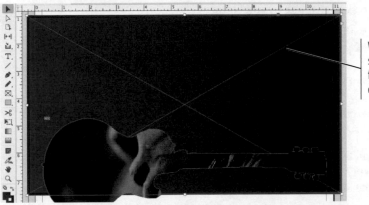

When frame edges are showing, an empty graphics frame shows crossed diagonal lines.

3. With the gradient-filled rectangle still selected on the page, choose **File>Place.** Navigate to the WIP>Concert folder and choose **guitar.jpg.** At the bottom of the dialog box, check the Replace Selected Item option.

This option should be checked.

4. Click Open to place the selected file.

Because Replace Selected Item was active in the dialog box, the image is placed directly into the selected frame.

5. Using the Selection tool, click the guitar-shaped graphics frame to select it.

6. Move the Selection tool cursor over the image frame to reveal the Content Grabber.

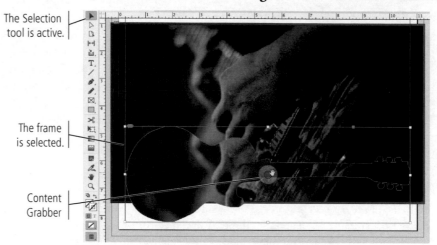

The Selection tool is active.

The frame is selected.

Content Grabber

Note:

You can turn off the Content Grabber by choosing View>Extras> Hide Content Grabber.

7. Click the Content Grabber to access the image in the frame.

Remember, when you select an image within a frame using either the Content Grabber or the Direct Selection tool, the Control panel fields define the position of the graphic *relative to* its containing frame. Negative numbers move the graphic up and to the left from the frame edge; positive numbers move the graphic down and to the right.

8. Using the Properties panel, change the image's position inside the frame to X: -0.75 in, Y: -4.5 in (based on the top-left reference point).

This position aligns the image in the guitar-shaped frame with the image in the rectangle frame, giving the impression of a single image in both frames. In the next few steps, you will use transparency effects to differentiate the two versions of the image.

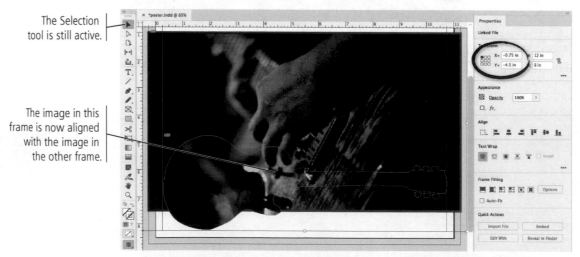

The Selection tool is still active.

The image in this frame is now aligned with the image in the other frame.

9. Press ESC to restore the frame (not the frame content) as the active selection.

10. **In the Properties panel, click the *fx* button and choose Drop Shadow from the menu.**

When a frame is selected, you can use this menu to apply effects to the entire object. The Effects dialog box opens to show options for the effect you selected in the menu.

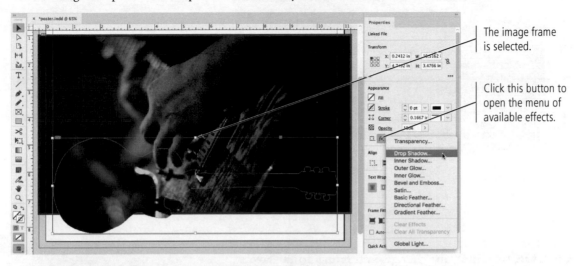

The image frame is selected.

Click this button to open the menu of available effects.

11. **In the resulting dialog box, check the Preview option so you can preview your results before accepting/applying them.**

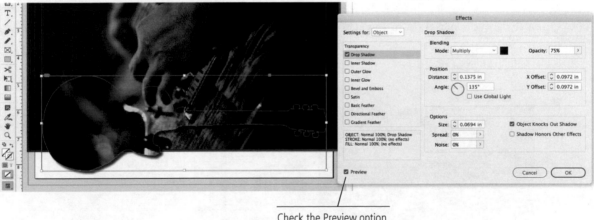

Check the Preview option.

12. **With the Drop Shadow options showing in the dialog box, click the color swatch in the Blending section to open the Effect Color dialog box.**

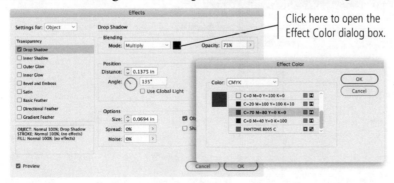

Click here to open the Effect Color dialog box.

13. **Select the custom blue swatch in the list, then click OK.**

If the Preview option is checked in the Effects dialog box, you should see the result of changing the drop shadow color.

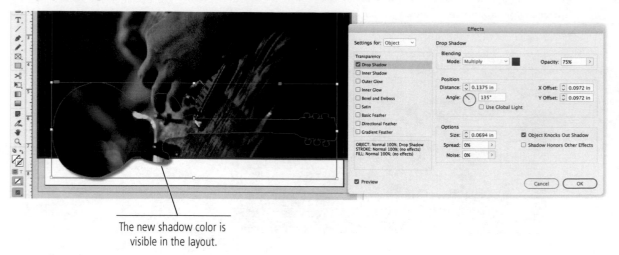

The new shadow color is
visible in the layout.

14. **Click OK to apply your changes and return to the layout.**

15. **Using the Direct Selection tool, click to select the image inside the rectangular graphics frame.**

16. **Open the Effects panel (Window>Effects).**

When the content inside a graphics frame is selected, you can apply effects to the image itself, independent of the frame.

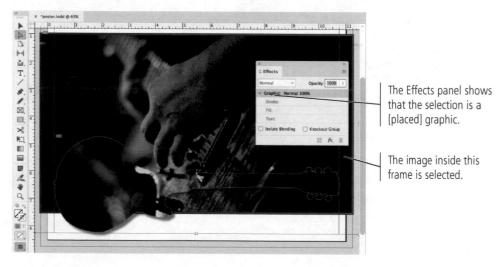

The Effects panel shows
that the selection is a
[placed] graphic.

The image inside this
frame is selected.

17. **With the Graphic option selected in the Effects panel, choose the Multiply option in the Blending Mode menu.**

The image now blends into the gradient background.

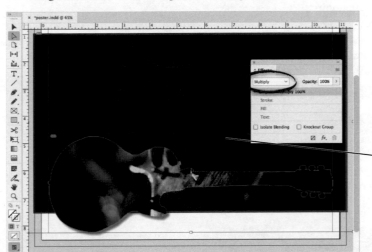

Note:

Effects in InDesign are non-destructive, which means they have no effect on the physical file data.

The Multiply blending mode merges the image colors into the object's gradient fill.

Understanding Blending Modes

Blending modes control how colors in an object interact with underlying colors.

- **Multiply** multiplies the base color by the blend (top) color, resulting in a darker color. Multiplying with black produces black; multiplying with white has no effect.

- **Screen** is basically the inverse of Multiply, always returning a lighter color. Screening with black has no effect; screening with white produces white.

- **Overlay** multiplies or screens the blend color to preserve the original lightness or darkness of the base.

- **Soft Light** darkens or lightens base colors depending on the blend color. Blend colors lighter than 50% lighten the base; blend colors darker than 50% darken the base.

- **Hard Light** combines the Multiply and Screen modes. Blend colors darker than 50% are multiplied, and blend colors lighter than 50% are screened.

- **Color Dodge** brightens the base color. Blend colors lighter than 50% significantly increase brightness; blending with black has no effect.

- **Color Burn** darkens the base color by increasing the contrast. Blend colors darker than 50% significantly darken the base color by increasing saturation and reducing brightness; blending with white has no effect.

- **Darken** returns the darker of the blend or base color. Base pixels lighter than the blend color are replaced; base pixels darker than the blend color do not change.

- **Lighten** returns whichever is the lighter color. Base pixels darker than the blend color are replaced; base pixels lighter than the blend color do not change.

- **Difference*** inverts base color values according to the brightness value in the blend layer. Lower brightness values in the blend layer have less of an effect on the result; blending with black has no effect.

- **Exclusion*** is similar to Difference, except that midtone values in the base color are completely desaturated.

- **Hue*** results in a color with the luminance and saturation of the base color and the hue of the blend color.

- **Saturation*** results in a color with the luminance and hue of the base and the saturation of the blend color.

- **Color*** results in a color with the luminance of the base color and the hue and saturation of the blend color.

- **Luminosity*** results in a color with the hue and saturation of the base color and the luminance of the blend color (basically the opposite of the Color mode).

*Avoid applying the Difference, Exclusion, Hue, Saturation, Color, and Luminosity modes to objects with spot colors. It could create unpredictable results when the file is separated for commercial print requirements.

18. **Click the *fx* button at the bottom of the Effects panel, and choose Gradient Feather.**

The Gradient Feather effect creates a transparency gradient so an object blends into underlying objects instead of leaving a hard edge. The effect is created using a gradient that shifts from 100% opacity to 0% opacity. The levels of opacity in the gradient determine the opacity of the object to which the feather effect is applied.

19. **In the Effects dialog box, click the button to the right of the gradient ramp sample to reverse the gradient.**

20. **Click in the Angle circle and drag until the field shows 90°. The line should point straight up.**

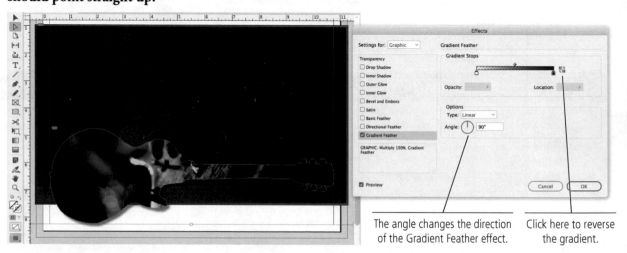

The angle changes the direction of the Gradient Feather effect.

Click here to reverse the gradient.

21. **Drag the right gradient stop until the Location field shows approximately 85%.**

Extending the solid black part of the gradient extends the entirely visible part of the image.

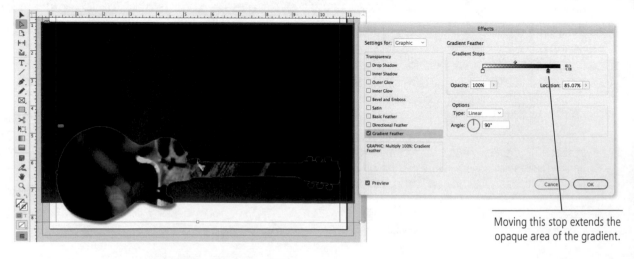

Moving this stop extends the opaque area of the gradient.

Nine different InDesign effects can be applied by clicking the *fx* button at the bottom of the Effects panel, by clicking the *fx* button in the Control panel, or by choosing from the Object>Effects menu.

Drop Shadow and Inner Shadow

Drop Shadow adds a shadow behind the object. **Inner Shadow** adds a shadow inside the edges of the object. For both types, you can define the blending mode, color, opacity, angle, distance, offset, and size of the shadow.

- **Distance** is how far away the shadow will be from the original object. The **Offset** fields allow you to define different horizontal and vertical distances.

- **Size** is the blur amount applied to the shadow.

- **Spread** (for Drop Shadows) is the percentage that the shadow expands beyond the original object.

- **Choke** (for Inner Shadows) is the percentage that the shadow shrinks into the original object.

- **Noise** controls the amount of pixels added to the effect.

When the **Object Knocks Out Shadow** option is checked, areas of the shadow under the object are knocked out or removed. This option is particularly important if the original object is semitransparent above its shadow.

Use Global Light is available for the Drop Shadow, Inner Shadow, and Bevel and Emboss effects. When this option is checked, the style is linked to the "master" light source angle for the entire file. Changing the global light setting affects any linked effect applied to any object in the entire file. (You can also change the Global Light settings by choosing Object>Effects>Global Light.)

Outer Glow and Inner Glow

Outer Glow and **Inner Glow** add glow effects to the outside and inside edges, respectively, of the original object. For either kind of glow, you can define the blending mode, opacity, noise, and size values.

- You can define the **Technique** as **Precise**, which creates a glow at a specific distance, or **Softer**, which creates a blurred glow and does not preserve detail as well.

- For Inner Glows, you can define the **Source** of the glow: **Center** applies a glow from the object center, and **Edge** applies the glow starting from the object's inside edges.

- The **Spread** and **Choke** sliders affect the percentages of the glow effects.

Satin

Satin applies interior shading to create a satiny appearance. You can change the blending mode, color, and opacity of the effect, as well as the angle, distance, and size.

Bevel and Emboss

This effect has four variations or styles:

- **Inner Bevel** creates a bevel on an object's inside edges.

- **Outer Bevel** creates a bevel on an object's outside edges.

- **Emboss** creates the effect of embossing the object against the underlying layers.

- **Pillow Emboss** creates the effect of stamping the edges of the object into the underlying layers.

Any of these styles can be applied as **Smooth** (blurs the edges of the effect), **Chisel Hard** (creates a distinct edge to the effect), or **Chisel Soft** (creates a distinct, slightly blurred edge to the effect).

You can change the **Direction** of the bevel effect. **Up** creates the appearance of the layer coming out of the image; **Down** creates the appearance of something stamped into the image. The **Size** field makes the effect smaller or larger, and the **Soften** option blurs the edges of the effect. **Depth** increases or decreases the three-dimensional effect of the bevel.

In the **Shading** area, you can control the light source's **Angle** and **Altitude** (think of how shadows differ as the sun moves across the sky). Finally, you can change the blending mode, opacity, and color of both highlights and shadows created with the Bevel and Emboss effect.

Basic Feather, Directional Feather, Gradient Feather

Basic Feather equally fades all edges of the selection by a specific width. The **Choke** option determines how much of the softened edge is opaque (higher settings increase opacity). **Corners** can be **Sharp** (following the outer edge of the shape), **Rounded** (according to the Feather Width), or **Diffused** (fading from opaque to transparent). **Noise** adds random pixels to the softened area.

Directional Feather applies different feather widths to individual edges of an object. The **Shape** option defines the object's original shape (First Edge Only, Leading Edges, or All Edges). The **Angle** field allows you to rotate the effect.

Gradient Feather creates a transparency gradient that blends from solid to transparent. This effect underlies the Gradient Feather tool. You can move the start and end stops to different locations along the ramp or add stops to define specific transparencies at specific locations. You can also choose from a Linear or Radial Gradient Feather effect and change the angle of a Linear Gradient Feather effect.

22. **Click OK to close the Effects dialog box and apply your choices.**

The *fx* icon to the right of the "Graphic" listing indicates effects have been applied to the selected graphic. You can double-click the *fx* icon in the Effects panel to open the Effects dialog box, where you can change the settings of the applied effects.

This icon indicates that effects have been applied to the selected graphic.

23. **Click away from the active image to deselect it and its containing frame.**

24. **Save the file and continue to the next exercise.**

 ## Create a QR Code

A **QR code**, short for Quick Response code, is a type of bar code that provides easy access (using a special QR code reader app) to additional information programmed into the code. InDesign includes a built-in option for creating QR codes in a layout, which makes it simple to incorporate this kind of marketing tool.

1. **With poster.indd open, create a new rectangle frame in the bottom-right corner of the image area. Define the frame parameters (based on the object's top-left reference point) as**

X: 0.25 in	W: 0.8 in
Y: 7.45 in	H: 0.8 in

2. **Using the Properties panel, change the frame's stroke weight to 3 pt, change its fill color to Paper, and change its stroke color to the custom blue swatch.**

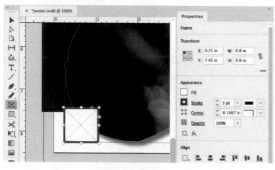

Note:

You can edit the properties of a QR code by choosing Object>Edit QR code (or by choosing Edit QR Code in the object's contextual menu.)

3. **With the new frame selected, choose Object>Generate QR Code.**

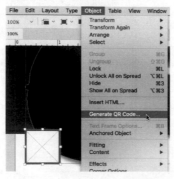

Note:

Keep in mind that distorting the code graphic might prevent it from working.

4. **In the resulting dialog box, choose Web Hyperlink in the Type menu and type www.westonsummerconcertseries.com in the URL field.**

You can use the Type menu to define what the QR code does:

- **Web Hyperlink.** If you choose this option, you can define the specific URL that appears when a user scans the code.

- **Plain Text.** If you choose this option, you can define a plain-text message that appears when a user scans the code.

- **Text Message.** If you choose this option, you can define the phone number and message content sent.

- **Email.** If you choose this option, you can define the email address, subject, and email body included in the resulting email.

- **Business Card.** If you choose this option, you can define the specific fields common in digital contact applications (name, company, address, etc.).

5. **Click the Color tab at the top of the dialog box. Choose C=0 M=40 Y=0 K=100, then click OK.**

The color you define here determines the color of the QR code object. Keep in mind high contrast between the QR code object and the frame background color assures the code will work on all devices and apps.

InDesign automatically generates the QR code inside the frame. The resulting graphic is centered in the frame and scaled to leave a 10-pixel inset from the nearest frame edges. The QR code is actually created as an embedded EPS graphic (although it does not appear in the file's Links panel). If you select the graphic inside the frame, you can scale it as you would any other placed graphic.

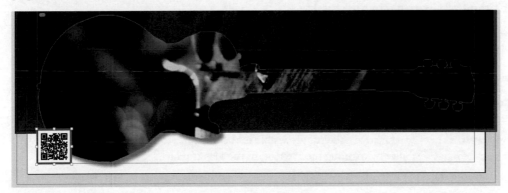

6. **Save the file and continue to the next stage of the project.**

Placing text is one of the most critical functions of page-layout software, whether you create the text directly within InDesign or import it from an external file. InDesign provides all the tools you need to format text, from choosing a font to automatically creating hanging punctuation.

 ## Define Multiple Layers

You are going to create a second layer to hold the text frames for this poster. This allows you to work without distraction from the existing graphics as well as protect the graphics from being accidentally altered while you are working on the text.

1. **With `poster.indd` open, open the Layers panel.**

2. **Expand Layer 1 in the panel if necessary, then click the empty space to the left of the bottom <rectangle> to show that object.**

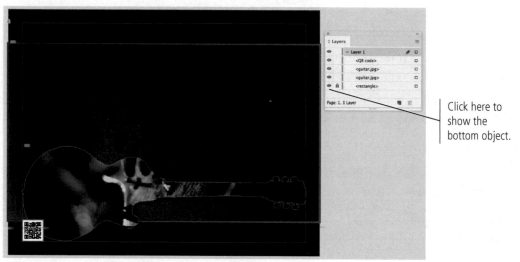

Click here to show the bottom object.

3. **Double-click the Layer 1 name in the panel.**

   The default in every file is named "Layer 1," which is not terribly useful when you use multiple layers. Descriptive names are far better for any asset, including layers.

4. **Change the Name field to `Graphics` and review the other options.**

   - The **Color** menu determines the color of frame edges and bounding box handles for objects on that layer.

   - If **Show Layer** is checked, the layer contents are visible in the document. You can also change visibility by toggling the eye icon in the Layers panel.

   - If **Lock Layer** is checked, you can't select or change objects on that layer.

   - If **Print Layer** is checked, the layer will output when you print or export to PDF.

   - The **Show Guides** option allows you to create and display different sets of guides for different layers; this is a more versatile option than showing or hiding all guides (which occurs with the View>Grids & Guides>Show/Hide Guides toggle).

   - The **Lock Guides** option allows you to lock and unlock guides on specific layers.

   - If **Suppress Text Wrap When Layer is Hidden** is checked, text on underlying layers reflows when the layer is hidden.

5. **Check the Lock Layer option, then click OK to close the Layer Options dialog box.**

The layer and all objects on it are now locked.

Create New Layer

Delete Selected Layers

Note:

The Layers panel only shows objects on the active page or spread.

6. **In the Layers panel, click the arrow to the left of the Graphics layer to collapse it.**

7. **Click the eye icon for the Graphics layer to hide that layer.**

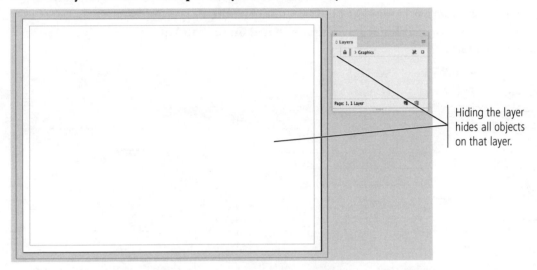

Hiding the layer hides all objects on that layer.

8. **Click the Create New Layer button at the bottom of the Layers panel.**

9. **Double-click Layer 2 in the Layers panel. Change the layer name to Text.**

10. **Click OK to create the new layer.**

The new layer is active, which means objects you create from this point will appear on that layer unless you intentionally create or select another layer in the layout file. Objects on the new layer will have red bounding box handles, matching the layer color as defined in the Layer Options dialog box.

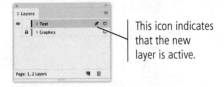

This icon indicates that the new layer is active.

11. **Save the file and continue to the next exercise.**

Control Text Threading

Some layouts require only a few bits of text, while others include numerous pages. Depending on how much text you have to work with, you might place all the layout text in a single frame, or you might cut and paste different pieces of a single story into separate text frames. In other cases, you might thread text across multiple frames, maintaining the text as a single story but allowing flexibility in frame size and position.

1. With **poster.indd** open, zoom into the empty area at the top of the page.

2. Use the Type tool to create a text frame filling the horizontal space between the margin guides.

3. With the text frame active, choose the Selection tool. Use the Properties panel to change the selected frame's parameters (based on the top-left reference point) to

X: 0.25 in	W: 10.5 in
Y: 0.25 in	H: 0.625 in

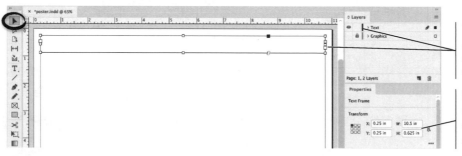

The frame's handles and edges match the color of the layer where it resides.

With Selection tool active, use the Properties panel to change the position and dimensions of a text frame.

4. Create two more text frames using the following parameters:

Frame 2	X: 5.75 in	W: 5 in
	Y: 1.5 in	H: 4.25 in

Frame 3	X: 4.5 in	W: 6.25 in
	Y: 7.9 in	H: 0.35 in

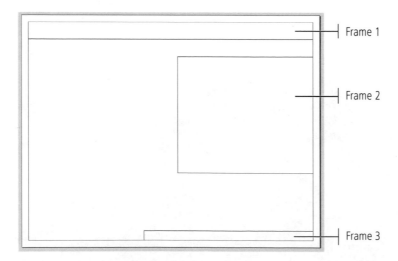

Frame 1

Frame 2

Frame 3

5. **Choose the Type tool, and click inside the first text frame to place the insertion point.**

When you click in a text frame with the Type tool, you see a flashing insertion point where you click or, if there is no text in the frame, in the top-left corner. This insertion point marks the location where text will appear when you type, paste, or import it.

6. **Choose File>Place. Navigate to the file named festival.txt in the WIP>Concert folder.**

7. **Make sure the Replace Selected Item option is checked and then click Open.**

The insertion point is in the first frame.

This option should be checked.

When Replace Selected Item is checked, the text file is automatically imported at the location of the insertion point. If this option is not checked, the text is imported into the cursor.

8. **Choose the Selection tool in the Tools panel.**

When a text frame is selected, you can see the In and Out ports that allow you to link one text frame to another. In this case, the Out port shows the **overset text icon**, indicating the placed file has more text than can fit within the frame.

It might help to zoom in to better see the in and out ports. The overset text icon is visible even when the In and Out ports are not.

In port

Out port

Overset text icon

9. **Click the Out port of the first text frame.**

Clicking the Out port loads the cursor with the rest of the text in the story. When the loaded cursor is over an existing frame, you can click to place the next part of the story in that frame. When the cursor is not over a frame, you can click and drag to create a frame containing the next part of the story. You can do this with the Selection tool (as you just did) or the Direct Selection tool.

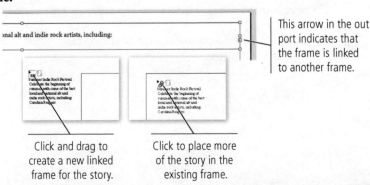

This arrow in the out port indicates that the frame is linked to another frame.

Click and drag to create a new linked frame for the story.

Click to place more of the story in the existing frame.

10. Click inside the second frame to link it to the first frame.

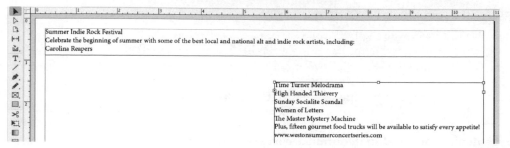

11. Repeat this process to link from the second frame to the third.

You can define the thread of text frames even when there is no text to fill those frames. Simply use the Selection or Direct Selection tool to click the Out port of one frame, and then click anywhere within the next frame to add to the thread.

You can also press Command/Control while the Type tool is active to click a text frame Out port and thread the frames.

12. Choose View>Extras>Show Text Threads.

When this option is toggled on (and you are in Normal viewing mode), you can see all threading arrows whenever any text frame in the thread is selected.

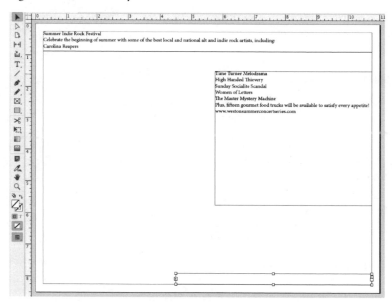

13. Choose View>Extras>Hide Text Threads.

14. Save the file and continue to the next exercise.

Note:

When you load the cursor with overset text, the loaded cursor shows the text from the beginning of the story even though the beginning is already placed. This is a quirk of the software; when you click with the loaded cursor, the text will flow into the new frame at the proper place in the story.

Note:

*Text that appears as a series of gray bars is called **greeked text**. By default, text smaller than 7 pt (at 100%) is greeked to improve screen redraw time. You can change the greeking threshold in the Display Performance pane of the Preferences dialog box.*

View percentage is part of the determination for greeking text; in other words, if your view percentage is 50%, 12-pt text appears as 6-pt text on screen, so it would be greeked using the default preferences.

Define Manual Frame Breaks

When you thread text from one column or frame to another, you often need to control exactly where a story breaks from frame to frame. InDesign includes a number of commands for breaking text in precise locations.

1. **In the open `poster.indd` file, use the Type tool to click at the end of the first line (after the word "Festival") to place the insertion point.**

   As you complete the following exercises, feel free to zoom in as necessary to work with specific areas of your layout.

2. **Choose Type>Insert Break Character>Frame Break.**

   InDesign provides several special break characters that allow you to control the flow of text from line to line, from column to column, and from frame to frame. The Frame Break character forces all following text into the next frame in the thread.

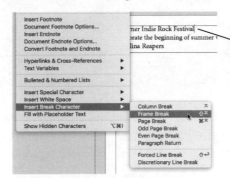

The insertion point is at the end of the first paragraph.

3. **Choose Type>Show Hidden Characters.**

   Each paragraph is separated by a paragraph return character (¶). A paragraph can be one or two words or multiple lines. The important thing is to realize a paragraph is technically any copy between two paragraph returns (or other break characters).

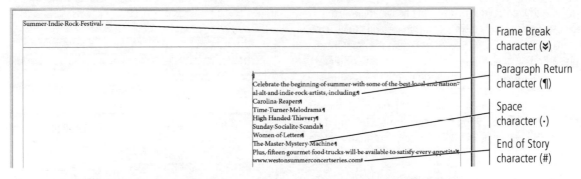

Frame Break character (⊻)

Paragraph Return character (¶)

Space character (·)

End of Story character (#)

When you placed the Frame Break character in Step 2, everything following the insertion point was pushed to the next frame, including the paragraph return character that was at the end of the first line. This created an "empty" paragraph that should be deleted.

4. **With the insertion point flashing at the beginning of the second frame, press Forward Delete to remove the extra paragraph return.**

   The Forward Delete key is the one directly below the Help key on most standard keyboards. If you don't have a Forward Delete key (if, for example, you're working on a laptop), move the insertion point to the beginning of the next line ("Celebrate the beginning...") and press Delete/Backspace.

Note:

You can also toggle the visibility of hidden characters using the View Options button in the Application/Menu bar.

Note:

Press Enter (numeric keypad) to add a Column Break.

Press Shift-Enter (numeric keypad) to add a Frame Break.

Press Command/Control-Enter (numeric keypad) to add a Page Break, which pushes all text to the first threaded frame on the next page.

5. **With hidden characters visible, highlight the paragraph return character at the end of the next-to-last sentence in the second frame (before the web address).**

6. **Choose Type>Insert Break Character>Frame Break to replace the highlighted paragraph return with a frame break character.**

   When text is highlighted — including hidden formatting characters — anything you type, paste, or enter using a menu command replaces the highlighted text.

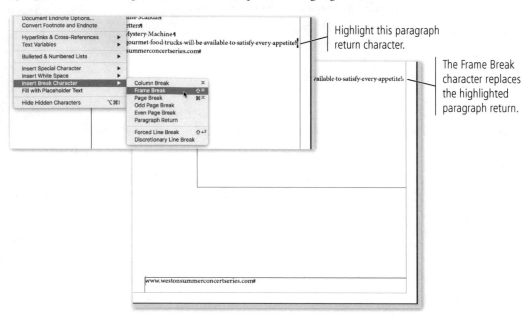

Highlight this paragraph return character.

The Frame Break character replaces the highlighted paragraph return.

7. **Save the file and continue to the next exercise.**

Designing with Placeholder Text

With the insertion point placed in a text frame, choosing Type>Fill with Placeholder Text fills the active frame with **lorem text** (supposedly from a Latin treatise on ethics written by Cicero more than 2,000 years ago) using the default text-format settings. If a text frame is linked to other text frames, the placeholder text fills the entire series of linked text frames.

Lorem placeholder text is valuable for experimenting with the appearance of paragraph text, giving you a better idea of what blocks of copy will look like when real content is placed in the layout.

If you press Command/Control while choosing Fill with Placeholder Text, you can define a different language to use for the placeholder text. These options are useful if you want to experiment with a design for a layout in which the text does not use the Roman alphabet — again, the placeholder more accurately represents what the final copy will look like.

Three threaded text frames are filled with Roman placeholder text.

Three threaded text frames are filled with Japanese placeholder text.

Apply Character Formatting

Once text is in a frame, you can use character formatting attributes to determine the appearance of individual letters, such as the font and type size. These attributes can be controlled in the Character panel (Window>Type & Tables>Character), Control panel, or Properties panel. In the Properties panel, you have to click the More Options button to access some of these options.

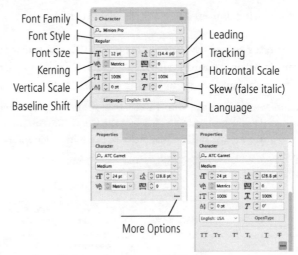

Options in the InDesign Character panel are the same as those in the Illustrator Character panel. (If necessary, refer to Project 3: Identity Package for a refresher on the various options.)

More Options

Several additional styling options are also available in the panel Options menu.

- **All Caps** changes all the characters to capital letters. This option only changes the appearance of the characters; they are not permanently converted to capital letters. To change the case of selected characters to all capital letters — the same as typing with Caps Lock turned on — use the Type>Change Case menu options.

- **Small Caps** changes lowercase letters to smaller versions of the uppercase letters. If the font is an Open Type font containing true small caps, InDesign uses the true small caps.

- **Superscript** and **Subscript** artificially reduce selected character(s) to a specific percentage of the point size; these options raise (superscript) or lower (subscript) the character from the baseline to a position that is a certain percentage of the leading. (The size and position of Superscript, Subscript, and Small Caps are controlled in the Advanced Type Preferences dialog box.)

- **Underline** places a line below the selected characters.

- **Strikethrough** places a line through the middle of selected characters.

- **Ligatures** are substitutes for certain pairs of letters, most commonly fi, fl, ff, ffi, and ffl. Other pairs such as ct and st are common for historical typesetting, and ae and oe are used in some non-English-language typesetting.

Note:

Choosing Underline Options or Strikethrough Options in the Character panel Options menu allows you to change the weight, offset, style, and color of the line for those styles.

1. **With poster.indd open, choose the Type tool in the Tools panel. Triple-click the first line of text in the story to select it.**

   Character formatting options apply only to selected characters.

2. **In the Character panel (Window>Type & Tables>Character), highlight the existing font name and type atc o. Click ATC Onyx Bold in the resulting menu to apply the new font.**

   The characters you type in the Font Family field result in a menu with all fonts that include the letters you type. After you select the font in the menu, ATC Onyx appears in the Font Family menu, and Bold appears in the Font Style menu.

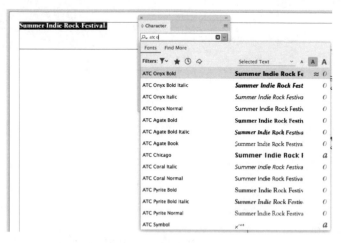

3. **Open the Font Size menu and choose 60 pt.**

   You can choose one of the built-in font sizes, type a specific value in the field, or click the arrow buttons to change the font size by 1 pt.

4. **Change the value in the Horizontal Scale field to 80%.**

   Horizontal and vertical scaling are useful for artificially stretching or contracting fonts that do not have a condensed or extended version. Be careful using these options, though, because artificial scaling alters the character shapes and can make some fonts very difficult to read (especially at smaller sizes).

5. **Open the Character panel Options menu and choose the All Caps option.**

6. **Click four times to select the first paragraph in the second frame, hold down the mouse button, and then drag down to select the other lines in the same frame.**

   Clicking twice selects an entire *word,* clicking three times selects an entire *line,* and clicking four times selects the entire *paragraph.*

7. **Change the selected text to 20-pt ATC Onyx Normal.**

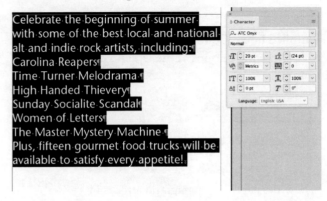

Note:

When you use mouse clicks to highlight text, dragging up or down selects additional text above or below the text you first clicked. If you quadruple-click to select an entire paragraph, for example, dragging down selects entire paragraphs after the first selected.

8. **Highlight the entire last paragraph (in the third frame), and change the text to 24-pt ATC Garnet Medium.**

9. **Save the file and continue to the next exercise.**

Apply Paragraph Formatting

Paragraph formatting options, available in the Paragraph panel (Window>Type & Tables>Paragraph), affect an entire paragraph, or everything between two paragraph return characters. In the Properties panel, only the paragraph alignment options are available by default; clicking the More Options button shows the hidden paragraph formatting fields.

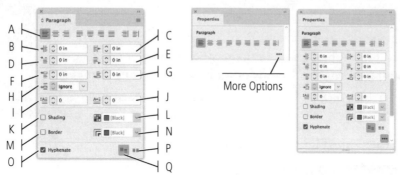

More Options

Paragraph formatting can also be controlled in the Control panel; depending on the width of your monitor, you might have to use the buttons at the left end of the panel to access the paragraph formatting options.

Click this button to show paragraph formatting options.

Click this button to show character formatting options.

A **Paragraph Alignment** determines how the edges of a paragraph appear in relation to the containing frame. Align Left, Align Right, and Align Center are self-explanatory.

The Justify options force the lines in a paragraph to extend the entire width of the containing frame or column with no ragged edges on either side; if you justify a paragraph, you can also determine the alignment of the last line in the paragraph (left, right, center, or justified).

Align Towards Spine and Align Away from Spine change the paragraph alignment from left to right, depending on the paragraph's position in a facing-page layout.

≡ Align Left
≡ Align Center
≡ Align Right
≡ Justify with Last Line Aligned Left
≡ Justify with Last Line Aligned Center
≡ Justify with Last Line Aligned Right
≡ Justify All Lines
≡ Align Towards Spine
≡ Align Away from Spine

B **Left Indent** defines the distance a paragraph is moved from the left edge of its containing frame or column.

C **Right Indent** defines the distance a paragraph is moved from the right edge of its containing frame or column.

D **First-Line Indent** defines the distance the first line of a paragraph is moved in from the left edge of the overall paragraph.

E **Last-Line Indent** defines the distance the last line of a paragraph is moved in from the left edge of the overall paragraph.

F   **Space Before** defines space separating a paragraph from the previous one in the same story.

G   **Space After** defines space separating a paragraph from the next one in the same story.

H   **Space Between Paragraphs Using Same Style** can be used to override the Space Before and Space After values for consecutive paragraphs using the same defined paragraph style. For example, you define 10 pts of space after every paragraph of body copy to enhance visual separation and readability. For a list of items, however, you want the 10 pts above and below the overall list but not in between each individual list item. In this case you can use the Space Between... option to define 0 pts of space between the consecutive list item paragraphs without affecting the space above or below the overall list.

I   A drop cap is a stylistic option that enlarges the first one or more characters in a paragraph (usually the first paragraph in a story or section of a story). **Drop Cap Line Count** defines the number of lines drop cap characters extend.

J   **Drop Cap Character Count** defines the number of characters enlarged at the beginning of the paragraph.

K   **Shading** places a color behind the entire paragraph when this box is checked, as if each paragraph was contained in a separate frame.

L   **Shading Color** defines the color of the shading behind the paragraph. Option/Alt-clicking the Shading icon (⊞) opens a dialog box where you can define specific settings for the shading, such as how far the color extends past the edges of the actual paragraph.

M   **Border** places a border around the entire paragraph when this box is checked.

N   **Border Color** defines the color of the border around the paragraph. Option/Alt-clicking the Border icon (⊩) opens a dialog box where you can define specific settings for the borders, such as border thickness and which edges of the paragraph will be bordered.

O   **Hyphenate**, when checked, allows automatic hyphenation at the ends of paragraph lines.

P/Q **Align to Baseline Grid** and **Do Not Align to Baseline Grid** determine how lines in a paragraph interact with the defined baseline grid, which is explained on Page 483.

1. In the open **poster.indd** file, place the cursor anywhere in the paragraph in the first frame.

2. In the Paragraph panel, click the Justify All Lines button.

   Paragraph formatting applies to the entire paragraph where the insertion point is placed or to any paragraph entirely or partially selected. A paragraph does not have to be entirely selected to change its paragraph formatting attributes.

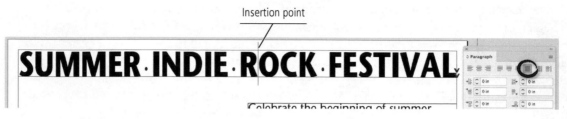

Insertion point

3. Place the cursor anywhere in the paragraph in the third frame, then apply right paragraph alignment.

Insertion point

4. In the second frame, select any part of the first through seventh paragraphs.

   If you want to apply the same formatting to more than one consecutive paragraph, you can drag to select any part of the target paragraphs. Any paragraph even partially selected will be affected.

5. In the Paragraph panel, change the Space After field to **0.125 in.**

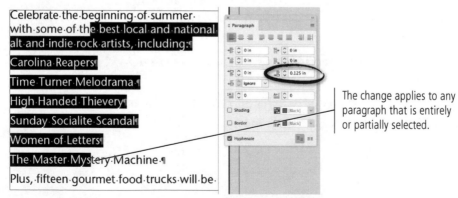

The change applies to any paragraph that is entirely or partially selected.

Note:

Remember, a paragraph is defined as all text between two paragraph return characters (¶).

6. Select any part of the second through sixth paragraphs in the same frame. In the Paragraph panel, click the down-arrow button for the Space After field one time.

   When inches is the unit of measurement, arrows in the Paragraph panel change the values by 1/16″ (0.0625″).

Note:

The arrow buttons for paragraph formatting options step through values in increments of 0.0625 in.

7. **With the same text selected, change the Left Indent field to 0.3 in.**

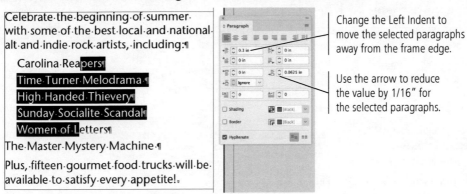

Change the Left Indent to move the selected paragraphs away from the frame edge.

Use the arrow to reduce the value by 1/16" for the selected paragraphs.

8. **Place the insertion point at the beginning of the sixth paragraph (before the words "The Master...") and press Delete/Backspace.**

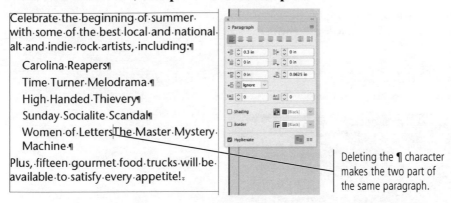

Deleting the ¶ character makes the two part of the same paragraph.

9. **Press Return/Enter to separate the two paragraphs again.**

When you break an existing paragraph into a new paragraph, the attributes of the original paragraph are applied to the new paragraph.

This is an easy way to copy paragraph formatting from one paragraph to the next. When you re-separate the two paragraphs, the "The Master..." paragraph adopts the paragraph formatting attributes of the "Women of..." paragraph.

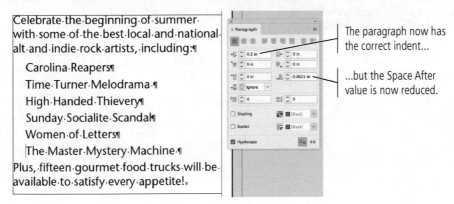

The paragraph now has the correct indent...

...but the Space After value is now reduced.

10. **With the insertion point at the beginning of the seventh paragraph, change the Space After value back to 0.125 in.**

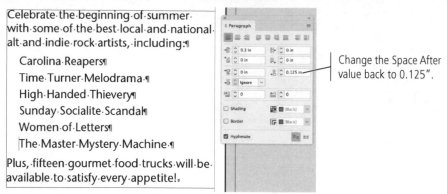

Change the Space After value back to 0.125".

11. **Press Command-Option-I/Control-Alt-I to toggle off the hidden characters.**

Many designers frequently toggle the visibility of hidden characters while working on any given layout. You should become familiar with the keyboard shortcut for this command.

12. **In the Layers panel, click the empty space to the left of the Graphics layer to make that layer — and all its objects — visible again.**

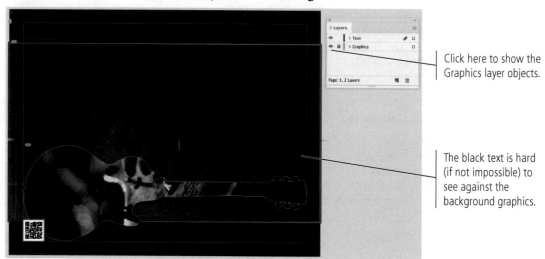

Click here to show the Graphics layer objects.

The black text is hard (if not impossible) to see against the background graphics.

13. **With the insertion point still flashing in the now-obscured text, choose Edit>Select All to select all text in the series of linked frames.**

The Select All command selects all text in the story, whether that story exists in a single frame or threads across multiple frames.

Note:

The Select All command also selects overset text that doesn't fit into the current frame or thread of frames.

14. **In the Swatches panel, make sure the Text icon is selected at the top of the panel, and then click the Paper swatch.**

This "T" icon means you are changing the text color instead of the object color.

Understanding the Baseline Grid

The **baseline grid**, a series of light blue non-printing guides that extends down the page at specific intervals, is used for controlling and aligning type. You can show the baseline grid by choosing View>Grids & Guides>Show Baseline Grid.

You can force paragraphs to align to the baseline grid, which overrides the defined leading. When **Do Not Align to Baseline Grid** is active, line spacing is defined solely by the applied leading:

When **Align to Baseline Grid** is active, line spacing is defined by the baseline; if the type size or leading is too large to fit lines on sequential baselines, text skips every other baseline:

You can change the baseline grid in the Grids pane of the Preferences dialog box. The Start position can be relative to the top of the page (default) or the top margin, and you can change the increment between lines. View Threshold determines the smallest view percentage at which the grid is visible.

You can also change the baseline grid for a specific frame in the Baseline Options tab of the Text Frame Options dialog box (Object>Text Frame Options).

15. **Select only the first paragraph and change the type fill color to Pantone 8005 C.**

Remember, type color is a character attribute. Only the highlighted characters are affected by the change.

16. **Repeat Step 15 for the web address in the third frame.**

17. **Click away from the text to deselect it. Use the button at the bottom of the Tools panel to turn on the Preview mode and review the results.**

18. **Return the file to the Normal viewing mode.**

19. **Save the file and continue to the next stage of the project.**

Applying Optical Margin Alignment

At times, specific arrangements of text can cause a paragraph to appear out of alignment even though it's technically aligned properly. Punctuation at the beginning or end of a line, such as commas at the end of a line, often causes this kind of optical problem. InDesign includes a feature called **optical margin alignment** to fix this type of problem.

Optical margin alignment is applied in the Story panel (Window>Type and Tables>Story). When this option is turned on, punctuation marks move outside text margins — either to the left for left-aligned text or right for right-aligned text. (Moving punctuation outside the margins is often referred to as **hanging punctuation**.) The field in the Story panel tells InDesign what size type needs to be adjusted. The best effect is usually created using the same size as the type that needs adjustment.

Optical margin alignment option applies to an entire story (including all text frames in the same thread) and not just the selected paragraph. If necessary, you can toggle on the **Ignore Optical Margin** option (in the Paragraph panel Options menu) for individual paragraphs so that a specific paragraph is not affected by optical margin alignment.

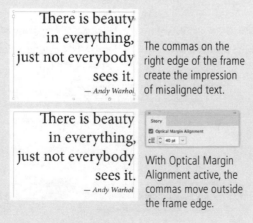

The commas on the right edge of the frame create the impression of misaligned text.

With Optical Margin Alignment active, the commas move outside the frame edge.

STAGE 3 / **Working with Text as Graphics**

Now that you're familiar with the basic options for formatting characters and paragraphs, you can begin to add style to a layout using two techniques: flowing text along a path and placing graphics inline with text. (You will, of course, learn much more about working with text as you complete the rest of the projects in this book.)

Place Inline Graphics

Any graphics frame you create on a page floats over the other elements in the layout. You can position graphics frames over other objects to hide underlying elements, or you can apply a **runaround** so text will wrap around a picture box.

You can also place images as inline graphics, which means they will be anchored to the text in the position in which they are placed. If text reflows, inline objects reflow with the text and maintain their correct positioning.

There are two methods for creating inline objects. For simple applications, such as a graphic bullet, you can simply place the graphic and format it as a text character. (An inline graphic is treated as a single text character in the story; it is affected by many of the paragraph-formatting commands such as space before and after, tab settings, leading, and baseline position.) For more complex applications, you can use the options in the Object>Anchored Object menu.

1. **With `poster.indd` open, place the insertion point at the beginning of the second line in the third frame (before the word "Carolina").**

2. **Choose File>Place and navigate to `music-note.ai` in the WIP>Concert folder.**

The insertion point is at the beginning of this paragraph.

This option should be checked.

3. **Make sure the Replace Selected Item option is checked, and then click Open.**

   If the insertion point is flashing in a story when you place a graphic using the Replace Selected Item option, the graphic is automatically placed as an inline object.

The line spacing adjusts to fit the placed image.

Note:

You can also select an existing object, cut or copy it, place the insertion point, and then paste the object inline where the insertion point flashes.

4. **Select the inline graphic with the Selection tool.**

5. **In the Transform section of the Properties panel, click the More Options button.**

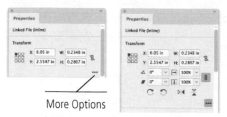

More Options

Note:

When you select the frame with the Selection tool, resizing the frame also resizes the frame content.

6. **Using the Properties panel, scale the selected inline graphic and frame to 60% proportionally.**

   Although inline graphics are anchored to the text, they are still graphics contained in graphics frames. You can apply the same transformations to inline graphics you could apply to any other placed graphics.

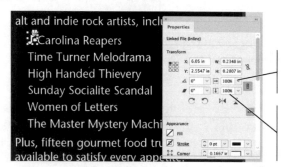

Use these fields to scale the placed graphic and the containing frame.

After you finalize the scaling, the fields show 100% when the frame is selected with the Selection tool.

Note:

For the dialog box Preview option to work properly, you have to move the highlight away from the field you changed. Pressing Tab while the dialog box is open allows you to see the results of your changes.

7. **Choose Object>Anchored Object>Options. Check the Preview option at the bottom of the dialog box.**

8. **With the Inline option selected, change the Y Offset to –0.05 in. Press the Tab key to show the result in the document.**

   A negative number moves the anchored object down; a positive number moves it up.

Note:

You can also open the Anchored Object Options dialog box by Option/Alt-clicking the Anchor icon on the top edge of an anchored graphic.

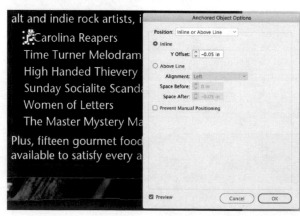

9. **Click OK, and then use the Type tool to place the insertion point between the anchored object and the letter "C." Using the Properties panel, change the Kerning field to 200.**

    Because an anchored graphic is treated like a single character, you can use kerning to add space between the anchored graphic and the following character.

Insertion point

10. **Press Shift-Left Arrow to select the anchored object, and then choose Edit>Copy to copy the highlighted object/character.**

    You can select an inline graphic just as you would any other text character. Copying text in InDesign is the same as copying text in other applications.

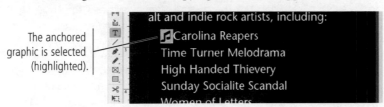

The anchored graphic is selected (highlighted).

Note:

You can also press Command/Control-C to copy selected text.

11. **Place the insertion point at the beginning of the next paragraph and paste the copied object.**

    As with copying, pasting text — including inline graphics — in InDesign is the same as in other applications: choose Edit>Paste, or press Command/Control-V.

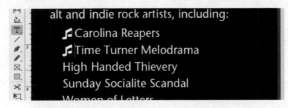

12. **Paste the anchored graphic again at the beginning of the remaining indented paragraphs.**

13. **Save the file and continue to the next exercise.**

The Anchored Object Options dialog box controls the position of an anchored object relative to text where it is placed.

Using the **Inline** option, the object aligns to text baseline; you can move it up or down relative to the baseline by adjusting the Y Offset value.

Using the **Above Line** option, the object can be anchored to the left, right, or center of the frame. If you're using facing pages, you can also choose Toward Spine or Away from Spine so the object will be placed relative to the spread center. Space Before defines an object's position relative to the bottom of the previous line. Space After defines position relative to the first character in the next line.

By default, you can use the Selection tool to drag an anchored object (in other words, change its position relative to the text to which it is anchored). If **Prevent Manual Positioning** is checked, you can't drag the anchored object in the layout.

When text threads are visible (View>Show Text Threads), a dashed blue line identifies the position of anchored objects relative to the text in which they are anchored.

For complex applications such as moving an anchored object outside a text frame, you can choose Custom in the Anchored Object Options Position menu.

The **Relative to Spine** option, which aligns objects based on the center spread line, is only available if your layout has facing pages. When selected, objects on one side of a spread (such as a sidebar in the outside margin) remain on the outside margin even if the text reflows to a facing page.

The **Anchored Object Reference Point** defines the location on the object that you want to align to the location on the page.

The **Anchored Position Reference Point** defines the page location where you want to anchor an object.

The **X Relative To** field defines what you want to use as the basis for horizontal alignment — Anchor Marker, Column Edge, Text Frame, Page Margin, or Page Edge. The **X Offset** setting moves the object left or right.

The **Y Relative To** field specifies how the object aligns vertically — Line (Baseline), Line (Cap Height), Line (Top of Leading), Column Edge, Text Frame, Page Margin, or Page Edge. The **Y Offset** setting moves the object up or down.

When **Keep Within Top/Bottom Column Boundaries** is checked, the anchored object stays inside the text column if reflowing the text would otherwise cause the object to move outside the boundaries (for example, outside the top edge of the frame if the anchoring text is the first line in a column). This option is only available when you select a line option such as Line (Baseline) in the Y Relative To menu.

Creating Anchored Placeholders

You can use the Object> Anchored Object>Insert option to define an inline placeholder object. You can create a frame (unassigned, graphics, or text) with a specific size and apply object and paragraph styles. The **Position** options are the same as those in the Anchored Object Options dialog box. (You can always resize and reposition the object later.)

The anchored object is outside the text frame; it is positioned with custom values.

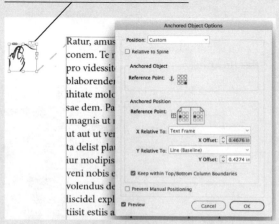

Create Type on a Path

Instead of simply flowing text into a frame, you can also create unique typographic effects by flowing text onto a path. A text path can be any shape you can create in InDesign, whether using one of the basic shape tools, a complex graphic drawn with the Pen tool, or a path created by converting a clipping path to a frame.

1. **With poster.indd open, deselect all objects in the layout.**

   As we explained previously, you can choose Edit>Deselect All or use the Selection tool to click an empty area of the workspace. If you use the click method, make sure you don't click a white-filled object instead of an empty area.

2. **Choose File>Place. Select text_path.jpg in the WIP>Concert folder and click Open. Position the top-left corner of the placed graphic at X: 0 in, Y: 0 in.**

   When this image is loaded into the cursor, click outside the defined bleed area to place the image and not replace the content in one of the existing frames. Then use the Control panel to position the image correctly. (The image you are placing is simply a guide you will use to create the shape of the text path for this exercise.)

3. **Click away from the placed graphic to deselect it.**

4. **Choose the Pen tool. Using the Control panel, change the stroke value to 3-pt Cyan (C=100 M=0 Y=0 K=0), and change the fill value to None.**

   The line in the placed image is magenta, so you're using cyan to help differentiate your line from the one in the image. The white background in the JPEG file makes it easy to focus on the line instead of the elements you have already created.

5. **Using the Pen tool, click once on the left end of the line in the placed image.**

   This first click establishes the first point of the path you're drawing.

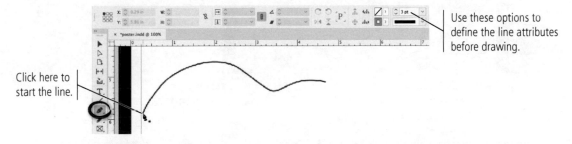

Use these options to define the line attributes before drawing.

Click here to start the line.

6. **Click near the top of the first arc and drag right to create handles for the second anchor point.**

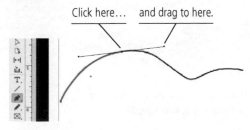

Click here... and drag to here.

7. **Continue clicking and dragging to add the necessary points and handles that create the rest of the line.**

Use what you learned in earlier projects to draw the rest of the Bèzier line.

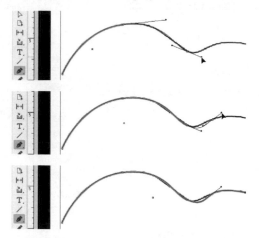

8. **Using the Direct Selection tool, adjust the points and handles until your line closely resembles the one in the placed image.**

9. **Choose the Type on a Path tool. Move the cursor near the path until the cursor shows a small plus sign in the icon, and then click the path.**

This action converts the line from a regular path to a type path; the insertion point flashes at the beginning of the text path.

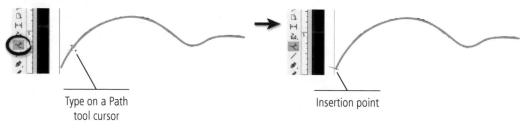

Type on a Path
tool cursor

Insertion point

10. **Type Weston Summer Concert Series. Choose Edit>Select All to select all text on the path, then format the type as 24-pt ATC Garnet Medium.**

11. **Using the Selection tool, click the text_path.jpg image you used as a guide. Press Delete/Backspace to remove it from the layout.**

12. **Click the text path with the Selection tool to select the actual line.**

13. **Click the bar at the left edge of the text path and drag to the right about 3/8″ (use the following image as a guide).**

When you release the mouse button, the left edge of the text moves to the point where you dragged the line. This marks the orientation point of the text on the path.

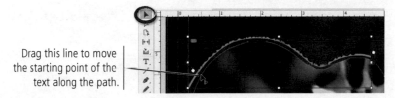

Drag this line to move the starting point of the text along the path.

14. **With the type-path object still selected, use the Swatches panel to change the object's stroke color to None.**

A text path can have a fill and stroke value just like any other path. (When a text path has no stroke color, you can still view the path by choosing View>Extras>Show Frame Edges.)

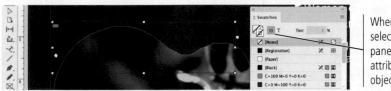

When the actual path is selected, the Swatches panel defaults to show attributes of the path object, not the type.

15. **Click the Text Color button at the top of the Swatches panel, and then click the Pantone 8005 C swatch to change the text color.**

You don't have to select the actual text on a path to change its color. You can use the buttons in the Swatches panel to change the color attributes of either the path or the text.

Click here to change the type fill and stroke colors.

16. **Using the Type tool, place the insertion point immediately before the word "Series" on the path.**

17. **Change the kerning as necessary to separate any letters that run into one another in the type on a path.**

Although your file might be slightly different than ours, depending on the exact path you created and distance you moved the start bar (Step 13), you should probably see some of the lettershapes run or "crash" into each other when the path dips down.

Remember, kerning adjusts the space between two specific characters wherever the insertion point is placed. You should place the insertion point between any crashing letter pairs and adjust the kerning for that pair to separate the lettershapes.

Adjust kerning as necessary.

18. **Save the file and continue to the next stage of the project.**

You can control the appearance of type on a path by choosing Type>Type on a Path>Options. You can apply one of five effects, change the alignment of the text to the path, flip the text to the other side of the path, and adjust the character spacing around curves (higher Spacing values remove more space around sharp curves).

The **Rainbow** (default) effect keeps each character's baseline parallel to the path.

The **Skew** effect maintains the vertical edges of type while skewing horizontal edges around the path.

The **3D Ribbon** effect maintains horizontal edges of type while rotating vertical edges to be perpendicular to the path.

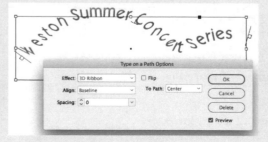

The **Stair Step** effect aligns the left edge of each character's baseline to the path.

The **Gravity** effect aligns the center of each character's baseline to the path, keeping vertical edges in line with the path's center.

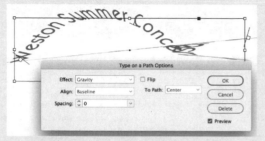

The **Align options** determine which part of the text (Baseline, Ascender, Descender, or Center) aligns to which part of the path (Top, Bottom, or Center).

STAGE 4 / **Adjusting Layout Size**

Many design projects include more than one required piece. In the case of this project, you also need to create a postcard with the same graphics as the poster you just finished. InDesign's Adjust Layout options makes this process far easier than manually recreating the layout for each required piece.

Adjust the Layout Size

Creating different versions of a layout used to require numerous steps to manually adjusting the page size, bleeds, margins, and layout elements. The new Adjust Layout option consolidates a number of those steps with a single dialog box, allowing the software to calculate adjustments as necessary to create a different page size.

1. **With poster.indd open, choose File>Save As. With WIP>Concert as the destination folder, change the file name to postcard.indd, then click Save.**

   You are going to make substantial changes to the file in this exercise. Saving with a different name before making those changes avoids the potential of overwriting the work you already completed to make the client's poster.

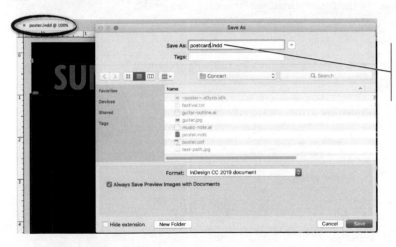

You are re-saving the file with a different name before making significant changes.

2. **With postcard.indd open, choose File>Adjust Layout.**

3. **In the resulting dialog box, change the Width field to 7 in and the Height field to 5 in.**

   You can use this dialog box to define any new Page size, whether larger or smaller than the original. The software will attempt to make the best possible changes based on a comparison of the old and new page aspect ratios (width-to-height comparison).

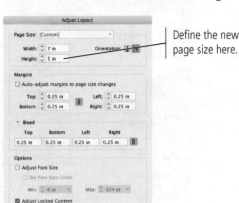

Define the new page size here.

Note:

Click the Adjust Layout button in the Document Setup dialog box (File>Document Setup) to open this dialog box.

4. **Make sure the Constrain icon is active between the Margin fields, then change the Top Margin field to 0.125 in.**

If you check the Auto-Adjust Margins to Page Size Changes option, InDesign will automatically calculate new margins for the

Activate the Constrain icon to change all four fields at once.

adjusted layout. In this case you have been told you need a 1/8″ margin, so you are defining the value rather than letting the software do it for you.

5. **Make sure the Constrain icon is active between the Bleed fields, then change the Top Bleed field to 0.125 in.**

Again, the postcard has different output requirements than the poster. This dialog box allows you to automatically adjust the page settings

Activate the Constrain icon to change all four fields at once.

in one step rather than manually adjusting each setting in different places.

6. **In the Options settings, check the Adjust Font Size box.**

The rather large font sizes you defined in the poster would not be appropriate for the smaller postcard size. Checking this option allows the software to calculate a font size better suited to the adjusted layout size.

When Adjust Font Size is active, you can also determine minimum and maximum Font Size Limits to keep adjusted type within a defined size range.

7. **Make sure the Adjust Locked Content option is checked.**

Before you started working on the poster text, you locked the Graphics layer to protect it from accidental adjustments. If this option is not

Check both these options.

checked, all objects on the graphics layer would remain at their original sizes and positions rather than scaling to fit the new layout size.

8. **Click OK to apply your settings and adjust the layout.**

The adjusted layout is smaller than the original poster, but the page aspect ratio is fairly close to the original. The software's automatic adjustments do a reasonably good job of converting the larger poster elements to fit the smaller postcard size. You will make any necessary fixes in the next exercise.

9. **Save the postcard file, then continue to the next exercise.**

Fine-Tune the Adjusted Layout

As you saw in the previous exercise, changing the layout size is a fairly simple process using the Adjust Layout feature. However, it is important to realize most automatic software functions are not foolproof. Graphic design is a subjective, visual process. Whenever you use automatic adjustments such as Adjust Layout, you should carefully review the results before calling the job finished.

1. **With postcard.indd open, review the adjusted layout.**

   You might notice several problems that were created when the software adjusted the various elements to fit the new page size.

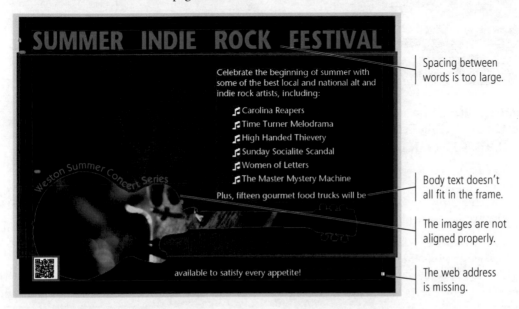

Spacing between words is too large.

Body text doesn't all fit in the frame.

The images are not aligned properly.

The web address is missing.

2. **Using the Selection tool, click the second text frame to select it. Drag the top-center handle up until the Y position is 0.7 in.**

   The body text again fits in the third frame, allowing the web address to move back into place in the third frame.

Drag this handle up.

All body text fits in the frame.

The web address is again visible.

3. **Using the Type tool, click to place the insertion point in the heading (in the first frame) at the top of the layout.**

   This paragraph uses justified alignment. In the adjusted layout and font size, this results in large spaces between words in the heading.

4. **Open the Paragraph panel Options menu and choose Justification.**

The insertion point is in this paragraph.

Click here to open the panel's Options menu.

5. **In the resulting dialog box, activate the Preview option. Change the Maximum Letter Spacing field to 20%, and change the Maximum Glyph Scaling to 150%. Click OK to finalize the change.**

   The Justification dialog box allows you to control the minimum, desired, and maximum spacing applied to create justified paragraph alignment.

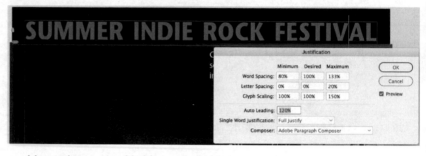

- **Word Spacing** defines the space that can be applied between words (where spaces exist in the text). At 100% (the default Desired amount), no additional space is added between words.

- **Letter Spacing** defines the space that can be added between individual letters within a word. All three values default to 0%, which allows no extra space between letters; at 100%, an entire space would be allowed between characters, making the text very difficult to read.

- **Glyph Scaling** determines how much individual character glyphs can be scaled (stretched or compressed) to justify the text. At 100%, the default value for all three settings, characters are not scaled.

- In narrow columns, single words sometimes appear on a line by themselves. If the paragraph is set to full justification, a single word on a line might appear to be too stretched out. You can use the **Single Word Justification** menu to center or left-align these single words instead of leaving them fully justified.

- The **Composer** menu defines how InDesign controls the overall flow of text (called composition) within a paragraph: Adobe Paragraph Composer (the default) and Adobe Single-line Composer. Both methods create breaks based on the applied hyphenation and justification for a paragraph.

   The settings you defined in this step result in larger spaces throughout the line instead of only stretching the space between whole words. Allowing the software to scale individual glyphs helps reduce the space between individual letters, making the text more readable while still occupying the entire horizontal space.

Note:

By changing these two settings, you are basically telling InDesign, "Increase the amount of letter spacing up to 20% of the normal spacing that would be applied by the pressing the spacebar. Also increase the width of individual glyphs up to 150% of their original scale."

6. **In the Layers panel, click the Lock icon for the Graphics layer to unlock that layer.**

The original poster layout has a distinct combination of two frames with the same image, carefully aligned to create a specific visual effect. When you reduced the page size, the software automatically adjusted the two frames to fit the new layout size. The software did not, however, consider the visual relationship between the two graphics frames, so they do not properly align in the adjusted layout.

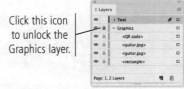

Click this icon to unlock the Graphics layer.

7. **Using the Direct Selection tool, click to select the placed background image in the gradient-filled frame.**

8. **In the Transform section of the Properties panel, click the More Options button to show the scaling percentage of the placed image.**

When the More Options are visible, you can see this image has been reduced to fit into the reduced page size.

The image in the background frame is selected.

More Options button

9. **Change the placed image size to 63% proportionally.**

In the next step you will change the second instance of this graphic to match this one. You are simply rounding the scale percentage to make it easier to exactly match the two images.

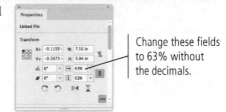

Change these fields to 63% without the decimals.

10. **Still using the Direct Selection tool, click to select the placed image in the guitar-shaped frame.**

The image in the guitar frame is selected.

This image was scaled to a different percentage when the layout was adjusted.

11. **In the Properties panel, change the placed image size to 63% proportionally.**

When the scale percentage matches the background version, the two images align properly.

12. **Save the postcard file, then continue to the final stage of the project.**

STAGE 5 / **Outputting PDF Files**

If your layout contains transparency or effects, those transparent areas will typically need to be flattened for output. **Flattening** divides transparent artwork into the necessary vector and raster objects. Transparent objects are flattened according to the settings in the selected flattener preset, which you choose in the Advanced options of the Print dialog box (or in the dialog box that appears when you export as PDF, EPS, or another format).

When you work with transparency, InDesign converts affected objects to a common color space (either CMYK or RGB) so transparent objects of different color spaces can blend properly. To avoid color mismatches between different areas of the objects on screen and in print, the blending space is applied for on-screen display and in the flattener. You can define which space to use in the Edit>Transparency Blend Space menu; for print jobs, make sure the CMYK option is selected.

Using the Flattener Panel Preview

You can use the Flattener Preview panel (Window>Output>Flattener Preview) to highlight areas that will be affected by flattening. You can use the Highlight menu to preview different areas and determine which preset to use. Clicking Refresh updates the preview based on your choices (or choose Auto Refresh Highlight).

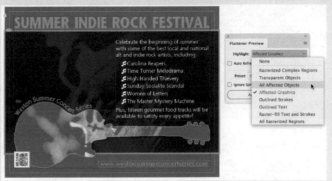

- **None** displays the normal layout.

- **Rasterized Complex Regions** highlights areas that will be rasterized based on the Raster/Vector Balance of the applied preset.

- **Transparent Objects** highlights objects with opacity of less than 100% as well as objects with blending modes, transparent effects, or feathering.

- **All Affected Objects** highlights all objects affected by transparency, including the transparent objects and objects overlapped by transparent objects.

- **Affected Graphics** highlights all placed image files affected by transparency.

- **Outlined Strokes** highlights all strokes that will be converted to filled objects when flattened.

- **Outlined Text** highlights all text that will be converted to outlines when flattened.

- **Raster-Fill Text and Strokes** highlights text and strokes that result in rasterized fills from flattening.

- **All Rasterized Regions** highlights objects (and parts of objects) that will be rasterized when flattened.

Flattener Presets

InDesign includes three default flattener presets:

- **Low Resolution** works for desktop proofs that will be printed on low-end black-and-white printers and for documents that will be published on the web.

- **Medium Resolution** works for desktop proofs and print-on-demand documents that will be printed on PostScript-compatible color printers.

- **High Resolution** works for commercial output on a printing press and for high-quality color proofs.

You can create your own flattener presets by choosing Edit> Transparency Flattener Presets and clicking New in the dialog box. You can also use the Transparency Flattener Presets dialog box to load presets created on another machine, such as one your service provider created for its specific output device and/or workflow.

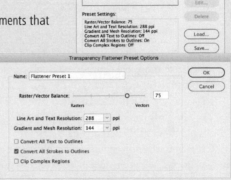

Export a PDF File for Print

1. **Open poster.indd from your WIP>Concert folder.**

2. **Choose File>Export. Navigate to your WIP>Concert folder as the target destination and choose Adobe PDF (Print) in the Format/Save As Type menu.**

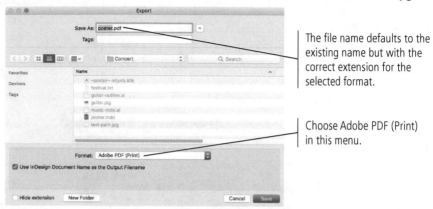

The file name defaults to the existing name but with the correct extension for the selected format.

Choose Adobe PDF (Print) in this menu.

3. **Click Save.**

   Before the PDF is saved, you have to define the settings that will be used to generate the PDF file.

4. **Choose [High Quality Print] in the Adobe PDF Preset menu.**

   The Adobe PDF Preset menu includes six PDF presets that meet common industry output requirements.

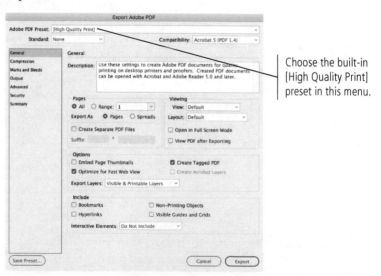

Choose the built-in [High Quality Print] preset in this menu.

Because there are so many ways to create a PDF — and not all of those ways are optimized for the needs of commercial printing — the potential benefits of the file format are often undermined. The PDF/X specification was created to help solve some of the problems associated with bad PDF files entering the prepress workflow. PDF/X is a subset of PDF specifically designed to ensure files have the information necessary for the digital prepress output process. Ask your output provider whether you should apply a PDF/X standard to your files and, if so, which version to use.

5. **Review the options in the General pane, and make sure Visible & Printable Layers is selected in the Export Layers menu.**

- **Pages** options determine which pages to output and whether to output facing pages on a single page. You can also choose to export individual pages or spreads (facing pages) as a single page in the resulting PDF.

- **Create Separate PDF Files** can be used to create individual PDFs of each page included in the Pages section above. When you check this option, you can define the suffix added to the end of the file name to distinguish each exported PDF:

    - **Incremental Numbers** (sequential, beginning with 01 for the first exported page)

    - **Page Number** (the default option, including a preceding "_" character)

    - **Page Size** (useful if you use a single layout to design multiple versions of the same content)

- **View** options determine the default view percentage of the exported PDF file. You can cause the file to open at actual size, fit the page into the Acrobat window based on a number of dimensions, or choose a specific percentage (25, 50, 75, or 100).

- **Layout** determines how spreads appear in the resulting PDF file.

    - The **Single Page** options export each spread separately.

    - The **Continuous** options export files so users can scroll through the document and view parts of successive pages at the same time. Using the non-continuous options, scrolling has the same effect as turning a page; you can't view successive spreads at once.

    - The **Two-Up Facing** options export two spreads side by side.

    - The **Two-Up Cover Page** options export the first spread as a single page and then the remaining spreads two at a time side-by-side. This allows the pages to appear as they would in a book, with even-numbered pages on the left and odd-numbered pages on the right.

- **Open In Full Screen Mode** opens the resulting PDF without showing Acrobat's menus or panels. You can then use the Flip Pages Every field to automatically change pages after a defined interval.

- **View PDF after Exporting** opens the PDF file after it has been created.

- **Embed Page Thumbnails** creates a thumbnail for each page being exported or one thumbnail for each spread if the Spreads option is selected.

- **Optimize for Fast Web View** optimizes the PDF file for faster viewing in a web browser by allowing the file to download one page at a time.

- **Create Tagged PDF** automatically tags elements based on a subset of Acrobat tags, including basic formatting, lists, and so on.

- **Create Acrobat Layers** saves each InDesign layer as an Acrobat layer within the PDF. Printer's marks are exported to a separate "marks and bleeds" layer. Create Acrobat Layers is available only when Compatibility is set to Acrobat 6 (PDF 1.5) or later.

- **Export Layers** determines whether you are outputting All Layers (including hidden and non-printing layers), Visible Layers (including non-printing layers), or Visible & Printable Layers.

- **Include** options can be used to include specific non-printing elements.

6. Review the Compression options.

Compression options determine what and how much data will be included in the PDF file. This set of options is one of the most important when creating PDFs since too-low resolution results in bad-quality printing and too-high resolution results in extremely long download times.

Before you choose compression settings, you need to consider your final goal. In a file for commercial printing, resolution is more important than file size. If your goal is a PDF to be posted on the web, file size is at least equally important as image quality.

You can define a specific compression scheme for color, grayscale, and monochrome images. Different options are available depending on the image type:

- **JPEG compression** options are lossy, which means data is thrown away to create a smaller file. When you use one of the JPEG options, you also define an Image Quality option (from Low to Maximum).

- **ZIP compression** is lossless, which means all file data is maintained in the compressed file.

- **CCITT compression** was initially developed for fax transmission. Group 3 supports two specific resolution settings (203 × 98 dpi and 203 × 196 dpi). Group 4 supports resolution up to 400 dpi.

- **Run Length Encoding** (RLE) is a lossless compression scheme that abbreviates sequences of adjacent pixels. If four pixels in a row are black, RLE saves that segment as "four black" instead of "black-black-black-black."

Note:

Since you chose the High Quality Print preset, these options default to settings that will produce the best results for most commercial printing applications.

Resolution Options for PDF

When you resize an image in the layout, you are changing its effective resolution. The **effective resolution** of an image is the resolution calculated after any scaling has been taken into account. This number is actually more important than the original image resolution. The effective resolution can be calculated with a fairly simple equation:

$$\text{original resolution} \div \frac{\%\ \text{magnification}}{100} = \text{effective resolution}$$

If a 300-ppi image is magnified 150%, the effective resolution is

$$300\ \text{ppi} / 1.5 = 200\ \text{ppi}$$

If you reduce the same 300-ppi image to 50%, the effective resolution is:

$$300\ \text{ppi} / 0.5 = 600\ \text{ppi}$$

In other words, the more you enlarge a raster image, the lower its effective resolution becomes. Reducing an image results in higher effective resolution, which can result in unnecessarily large PDF files.

When you create a PDF file, you also specify the resolution that will be maintained in the resulting PDF file. The Resolution option is useful if you want to throw away excess resolution for print files or if you want to create low-resolution files for proofing or web distribution.

- **Do Not Downsample** maintains all the image data from the linked files in the PDF file.

- **Average Downsampling To** reduces the number of pixels in an area by averaging areas of adjacent pixels. Apply this method to achieve user-defined resolution (72 or 96 dpi for web-based files or 300 dpi for print).

- **Subsampling To** applies the center pixel value to surrounding pixels. If you think of a 3 × 3-block grid, subsampling enlarges the center pixel — and thus, its value — in place of the surrounding eight blocks.

- **Bicubic Downsampling To** creates the most accurate pixel information for continuous-tone images. This option also takes the longest to process, and it produces a softer image. To understand how this option works, think of a 2 × 2-block grid — bicubic downsampling averages the value of all four of those blocks (pixels) to interpolate the new information.

7. **In the Marks and Bleeds options, check the Crop Marks option and change the Offset field to 0.25 in. Check the Use Document Bleed Settings option.**

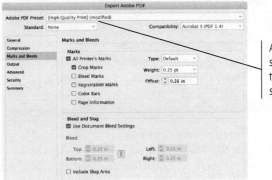

As soon as you choose a setting that is not part of the preset, the preset name shows "(modified)".

8. **In the Compatibility menu, choose Acrobat 4 (PDF 1.3).**

The Compatibility menu determines which version of the PDF format you will create. This is particularly important if your layout uses transparency. PDF 1.3 does not support transparency, so the file will require flattening. If you save the file to be compatible with PDF 1.4 or later, transparency information will be maintained in the PDF file.

9. **In the Advanced options, choose High Resolution in the Transparency Flattener Preset menu.**

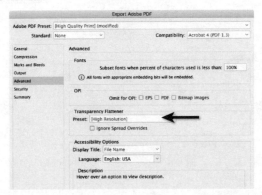

10. **Click Export to create your PDF file. If you see a warning message, click OK.**

Your PDF file will be flattened, so some features (hyperlinks, bookmarks, etc.) will be unavailable. You didn't use those features in this project, so you don't have to worry about this warning.

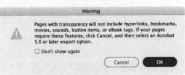

11. **Choose Window>Utilities>Background Tasks.**

The PDF export process happens in the background, which means you can work on other tasks while the PDF is being created. This panel shows how much of the process has been completed as a percentage and will list any errors that occur. When the PDF file is finished, the export process is no longer listed in the panel.

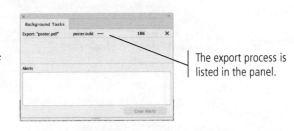

The export process is listed in the panel.

12. **Save the poster file and close it.**

13. **With the postcard.indd file active, choose File>Export. If necessary, navigate to your WIP>Concert folder as the target destination. Choose Adobe PDF (Print) in the Format/Save As Type menu, then click Save.**

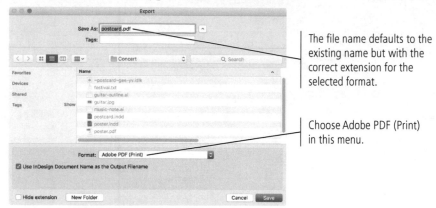

The file name defaults to the existing name but with the correct extension for the selected format.

Choose Adobe PDF (Print) in this menu.

14. **Review the options in the Export Adobe PDF dialog box.**

This dialog box remembers the last-used settings. Because you just defined the required settings for the poster file, those same settings are already selected here.

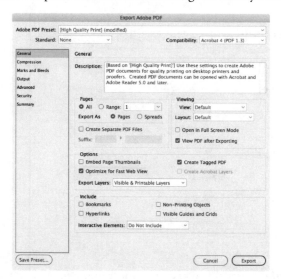

15. **Click Export, then click OK to dismiss the warning message and create the postcard PDF file.**

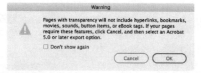

16. **Save the postcard file and close it.**

PROJECT REVIEW

fill in the blank

1. The _____ tool can be used to draw the direction and position of a gradient within a frame.

2. The _____ menu command reveals characters such as paragraph returns and tabs.

3. _____ is the space between specific pairs of letters. To change this value, you have to place the insertion point between two characters.

4. The _____ is the theoretical line on which the bottoms of letters rest.

5. The _____ indicates more text exists in the story than will fit into the available frame or series of linked frames.

6. A/an _____ is defined as all text between two ¶ characters.

7. The _____ panel is used to apply optical margin alignment.

8. _____ are objects that are attached to specific areas of text.

9. _____ is the resolution of an image after its scaling in the layout has been taken into account.

10. _____ compression for raster images is lossy, which means data is thrown away to reduce the file size.

short answer

1. Briefly explain how transparency is applied to objects in an InDesign page layout.

2. Briefly define a clipping path; provide at least two examples of how they might be useful.

3. Briefly explain the difference between character formatting and paragraph formatting.

PORTFOLIO BUILDER PROJECT

Use what you have learned in this project to complete the following freeform exercise.
Carefully read the art director and client comments, then create your own design to meet the needs of the project.
Use the space below to sketch ideas. When finished, write a brief explanation of the reasoning behind your final design.

art director comments

Your local community theater is planning a summer production of "Down the Yellow Brick Rabbit Hole," a satirical mash-up of "The Wizard of Oz" meets "Alice in Wonderland." You have been hired to create several pieces to advertise the play in local media and in the community.

To complete this project, you should:

❑ Design a half-page advertisement for the local newspaper (11.5″ × 10.5″ trim size).

❑ Design a full-page advertisement for the community arts and entertainment magazine (8.5″ × 11″ trim size).

❑ Design a poster that can be placed in local storefronts and other public venues (11″ × 17″ trim size).

❑ Find or create artwork that appropriately illustrates the concept of the play.

client comments

As the director and playwright, I was inspired by Gregory Maguire's interesting rewrites of classic fairy tales. But then I started to think about what would happen if the characters from different books met somehow... and this play is the result.

Some real sparks fly when the Queen of Hearts and the Wizard of Oz get together! And the wicked witch, well, she's got her hands full trying to escape the clutches of an army of talking caterpillars.

This play is one-third mystery, one-third dramedy, and one-third just plain silly! It's got star-crossed lovers, an evil villain, an inept magician, a rather foolish prince, and even a mad flying monkey that wears some very strange hats.

The only text in the ad should be

> Down the Yellow Brick Rabbit Hole
> by Stacey Wrightwood
> at the Preston Theater this August
> 800-555-PLAY for ticket information

project justification

PROJECT SUMMARY

This project combined form and function, presenting the client's information in a clear, easy-to-read manner while using graphic elements to grab the viewer's attention and reinforce the message of the piece. Completing this poster involved adjusting a number of different text formatting options, including paragraph settings and the flow of text across multiple frames. You should now understand the difference between character and paragraph formatting and know where to find the different options when you need them.

The graphics options in InDesign give you significant creative control over virtually every element of your layouts. Custom colors and gradients add visual interest to any piece while more sophisticated tools like non-destructive transparency and other effects allow you to experiment entirely within your page layout until you find exactly the look you want to communicate your intended message.

Create custom swatches and gradients

Control text flow across multiple text frames

Control various character and paragraph formatting attributes

Place graphics as anchored inline objects

Create and format text on a path

Create a custom graphics frame from an image's clipping path

Use blending modes and effects to blend images in different frames

Generate a QR code to provide additional customer information

Adjust the layout to use a different page size

Make corrections as necessary to clean up automatic adjustments

Aerospace Newsletter

9

Your client is a nonprofit foundation that focuses on preserving the history of American innovation in aerospace. It publishes a monthly newsletter for people on various mailing lists, which are purchased from a list-management vendor. The editor wants to change the existing newsletter template, and wants you to take over the layout once the template has been revised.

This project incorporates the following skills:

❑ Opening and modifying an existing layout template

❑ Managing missing font and link requests

❑ Replacing graphics files to meet specific color output needs

❑ Formatting text with template styles

❑ Controlling text-frame inset, alignment, and wrap attributes

❑ Creating a table with data from a Microsoft Excel worksheet

❑ Preflighting the final layout and creating a job package

PROJECT MEETING

client comments

Our newsletter was printed using two spot colors in our logo. However, the printer told us we can save money if we use four-color printing instead.

We also want to go from four columns to three on the front page. Each issue has a highlight image at the top of the front page, which relates to the feature story. The bottom of the front page is a series of photos from one of our affiliates, which are put together by that organization's staff. Half of the back is an ad, and the other half features the same affiliate who provides the photos for the front. If there is room (depending on the content they submit), we can include a table with our ArAA contact information.

We'd like you to modify the template, and then use the template to create the current issue. We sent you all of the files that will be required to complete July's newsletter — photos, ads, three text files (the main article, a sidebar for the front, and the story for the back), and the Microsoft Excel table with our contact information.

art director comments

Whenever you work with a file that someone else created, there is always the potential for problems. When you first open the template, you'll have to check the fonts and images and make whatever adjustments are necessary. Make sure you save the file as a template again before you build the new issue.

The printer said they prefer to work with native application files instead of PDF, so when you're finished implementing the layout, you'll need to check the various elements, and then create a final job package.

project objectives

To complete this project, you will:

❑ Handle requests for missing fonts and images

❑ Edit master page elements to meet new layout requirements

❑ Save a layout file as a template

❑ Access master page elements on the layout pages

❑ Format imported text using template styles

❑ Build and format a table using data from a Microsoft Excel spreadsheet

❑ Create a final job package for the output provider

STAGE 1 / **Working with Templates**

InDesign templates are special types of files that store the basic structure of a project. Well-planned templates can store layout elements, such as nonprinting guides, to mark various areas of the job; placeholder frames that will contain different stories or images in each revision; elements that remain the same in every revision, such as the nameplate; and even formatting information that will be applied to different elements so they can be consistent from one issue to the next.

Manage Missing Fonts

When you work with digital page layouts — whether in a template or in a regular layout file — it's important to understand that fonts are external files of data that describe the font for on-screen display and for the output device. The fonts you use in a layout need to be available on any computer that will be used to open the file. InDesign stores a reference to used fonts, but it does not store the actual font data.

Note:

Missing fonts are one of the most common problems in the digital graphics output process. This is one of the primary advantages of using PDF files for output — PDF can store actual font data so you don't need to include the separate font files in your job package. However, PDF can't solve the problem of missing fonts used in a layout template.

1. **Download Aerospace_Print19_RF.zip from the Student Files web page.**

2. **Expand the ZIP archive in your WIP folder (Macintosh) or copy the archive contents into your WIP folder (Windows).**

   This creates a folder named **Aerospace**, which contains the files you need for this project. You should also use this folder to save the files you create in this project.

3. **Choose File>Open. Select araa-newsletter.indt in the WIP>Aerospace folder, and choose the Open [As] Original option.**

   Macintosh users: As with placing images, you might need to click the Options button in the bottom-left corner to reveal the options for opening a template file. We will not repeat this instruction.

   You have several options when you open an existing template file:

   - If you choose **Open [As] Normal** to open a regular InDesign file (INDD), the selected file appears in a new document window or tab. When you use this option to open a template file (INDT), InDesign creates and opens a new untitled file that is based on the template.

   - When you choose **Open [As] Original**, you open the actual InDesign template file so that you can make and save changes to the template.

   - You can use **Open [As] Copy** to open a regular InDesign file as if it were a template; the result is a new untitled document based on the file you selected.

Macintosh

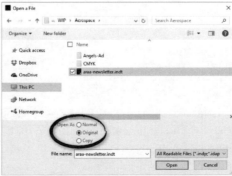

Windows

4. **Click Open, then review the warning message.**

InDesign stores links to images placed in a layout; the actual image data is not stored in the InDesign file. If placed files are not available in the same location as when they were placed, or if they have been resaved since you placed them, you'll see a warning message when you open the file. You'll correct these problems shortly.

5. **Click Don't Update Links. If you get a Profile or Policy Mismatch warning, click OK.**

6. **Review the information in the Missing Fonts dialog box.**

When you open a file that calls for fonts that are not installed on your computer system, you see this warning. You could blindly fix the problem now (without knowing what will be affected), but we prefer to review problem areas before making changes.

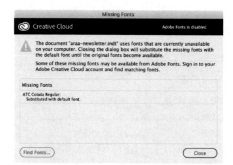

Note:

If you have the ATC fonts from previous editions installed, ATC Colada might not appear in the list of missing fonts.

7. **Click Close to dismiss the Missing Fonts dialog box.**

8. **Open the Pages panel (Window>Pages).**

The Pages panel makes it very easy to navigate through the pages in a layout, including master pages. You can navigate to any page by simply double-clicking the page's icon, or navigate to a spread by double-clicking the spread page numbers (below the page icons).

The document tab shows you are editing the actual template file.

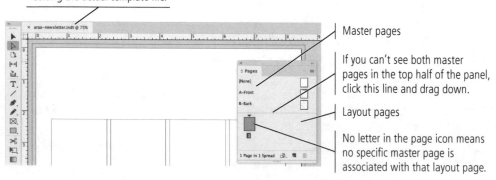

Master pages

If you can't see both master pages in the top half of the panel, click this line and drag down.

Layout pages

No letter in the page icon means no specific master page is associated with that layout page.

Think of master pages as templates for different pages in the layout. This file, for example, has two master pages: Front Page and Back Page. The letters preceding each master name are automatically added and used to identify which layout pages are associated with which master page.

9. **Double-click the A-Front icon to display that layout.**

   The top area of the newsletter (the **nameplate** area) includes the newsletter logotype, as well as the "Published by…" line and the issue date. A pink highlight around the type shows that the font used in this area is not available.

   The Missing Font highlighting is only a visual indicator on your screen; it is not included when the job is output. If the nameplate information is not highlighted, open the Composition pane of the Preferences dialog box and make sure the Highlight Substituted Fonts option is checked.

10. **Using the Type tool, click the frame with the missing font to place the insertion point.**

    The Control panel shows the missing font name in brackets. Any time you see a font name in brackets, you know you have a potential problem.

Note:

The missing-font highlighting only appears if you are in the Normal viewing mode.

Missing fonts are listed in brackets.

Highlighting indicates an area where the required font is not available.

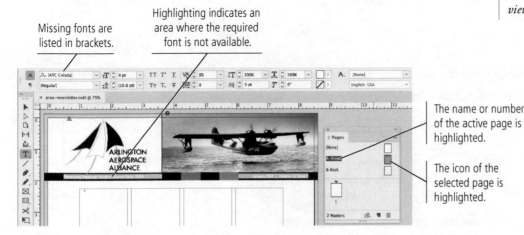

The name or number of the active page is highlighted.

The icon of the selected page is highlighted.

11. **Choose Type>Find Font.**

    The Find Font dialog box lists every font used in the layout — including those that are missing (with a warning icon). You can use this dialog box to replace any font with another that is available on your system.

12. **Highlight ATC Colada Regular in the Fonts in Document list. In the Replace With area, choose ATC Onyx in the Font Family menu and choose Normal in the Font Style menu.**

13. **Check the option to Redefine Style When Changing All.**

    When this is checked, the font replacement will be applied in paragraph and character style definitions, even if those styles are not currently applied in the layout.

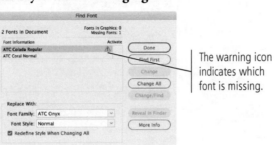

    The warning icon indicates which font is missing.

    If you don't check the Redefine Style option, you might later introduce another missing-font problem when you apply a style that calls for a missing font.

Note:

If you select a font that is used in a placed graphic, you can click the Find Graphic button to navigate to the location of the graphic where the font is used.

Note:

If you click the More Info button, you can see specific details about the selected font, such as what type it is and where it is used.

14. **Click Change All to replace all instances of ATC Colada Regular.**

   You could also click the Find Next button to review individual instances of a missing font, or click the Change or Change/Find button to replace and review individual instances of the selected font.

   When the Redefine Style option is checked and you use the Change All option, InDesign provides a warning when overrides have been applied to existing styles.

15. **Click OK to dismiss the warning message.**

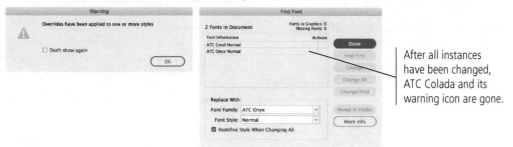

After all instances have been changed, ATC Colada and its warning icon are gone.

16. **Click Done to close the Find Font dialog box.**

   Once you have replaced the missing font, the pink highlighting disappears.

17. **Choose File>Save to save your changes to the template file, and then continue to the next exercise.**

   Because you used the Open Original option, you are editing the actual template file; this means you can simply use the regular Save command to save your changes to the template. If you used the Open Normal option to open and edit a template file, you would have to use the Save As command, and then save the edited file with the same name and extension as the original template to overwrite it.

More About Managing Missing Fonts

It is important to understand that fonts are external files of data that describe the font for the output device. The fonts you use in a layout need to be available on any computer that opens the file. InDesign stores a reference to used fonts, but it does not store the actual font data.

When you open a file that uses fonts you don't have installed on your computer, a Missing Fonts dialog box shows which fonts should be installed.

The software scans the Adobe Font (Typekit) library to locate missing fonts. Missing fonts that exist in the Adobe Font library are automatically checked in the list. Clicking the Activate button syncs the required fonts in your Creative Cloud (CC) account, making them available in your desktop version of InDesign.

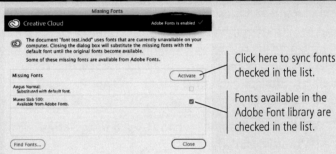

Click here to sync fonts checked in the list.

Fonts available in the Adobe Font library are checked in the list.

Using the Find Font Dialog Box

You can also use the Find Font dialog box (accessed by clicking the Find Font button in the Missing Fonts dialog box or by choosing Type>Find Font) to replace one font with another throughout a layout.

The top half of the dialog box lists every font used in the file. Missing fonts are identified by a warning icon in the list. If a missing font is available in the Adobe Font library, it is automatically checked in the top list. You can click the Activate button to sync those fonts in your CC account.

Before changing a specific font, you can use the Find First button to locate the first instance where the font selected in the top list appears in the layout.

In the lower half of the dialog box, you can use the Replace With menus to choose any available font to use in place of the one selected in the top list.

The Change, Change All, and Change/Find buttons affect only the font that is selected in the top list. If you click the Change/Find button, the first instance of the selected font will be changed and the software identifies the next instance (if any).

If you check the Redefine Style When Changing All button, a missing font used in a style definition will also be replaced if you click the Change All button.

Replace Missing and Modified Graphics

Placed graphics can cause problems if those files aren't where InDesign thinks they should be. Placed graphics files can either be **missing** (they were moved from the location from which they were originally placed in the layout, or the name of the file was changed) or **modified** (they were resaved after being placed into the layout, changing the linked file's "time stamp," but not its location or file name). In either case, you need to correct these problems before the file can be successfully output.

Note:

The issue of missing and modified images is a common problem if you zip a job folder into an archive. When you unzip a job folder and open the InDesign file, you will often see a warning about missing/ modified images (especially on Windows).

To avoid this problem in the resource files for this book, we embedded most of the placed images into the layout files.

1. **With araa-newsletter.indt open in InDesign, display the Links panel (Window>Links).**

   The Links panel lists every file that is placed in your layout. Missing images show a red stop-sign icon. Modified images show a yellow yield sign.

   If you don't see the Missing and Modified icons in the layout, choose View>Extras>Show Link Badge.

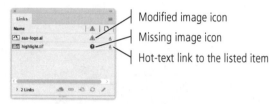

   Modified image icon
   Missing image icon
   Hot-text link to the listed item

2. **Click the hot-text page link for the modified aaa-logo.ai file in the panel.**

   You can also use the Go to Link button in the middle (if the link information section is expanded) or at the bottom (if the link information section is collapsed) of the panel.

   The Pages panel shows that the A-Front master layout is now active because that is where the selected instance exists.

   This icon identifies a modified image.   This icon identifies a missing image.   Click the hot-text link to navigate to a specific instance.

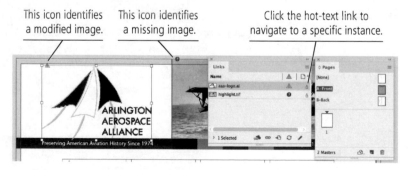

   You can easily use the Links panel to navigate to selected images.

3. **Using the Direct Selection tool or the Content Grabber, click the placed logo on the page.**

   As part of the Adobe Creative Suite, InDesign supports native Adobe Illustrator files (with the ".ai" extension) that have been saved to be compatible with the PDF format. Illustrator files can include both raster and vector information, type and embedded fonts, and objects on multiple layers in a variety of color models (including spot colors, which are added to the InDesign Swatches panel when the AI file is imported).

The Links panel lists all files that have been placed into a layout.

A   The **Name** column shows the name of each linked file. If more than one instance of a file is placed in the same layout, they are grouped together by default. You can click the arrow button to expand the list and review individual instances.

B   The **Status** column shows special icons to identify whether an image file is missing, modified, embedded, or linked from a CC Library.

C   The **Page** column shows a hot-text link to the page on which an image is placed. Letters in this column identify master page layouts. Numbers identify regular document pages.

D   **Show/Hide Link Information** expands or collapses the Link Information section of the panel, which shows details — file name, format, size, etc. — about the selected link.

E   **Relink from CC Libraries** allows you to change a link to a file that is stored in a CC Library on your Creative Cloud account.

F   **Relink** opens a navigation dialog box in which you can locate a missing file or link to a different file.

G   **Go to Link** selects and centers the file in the document window.

H   **Update Link** updates modified links. If the selected image is missing, this button opens a navigation dialog box so you can locate the missing file.

I   **Edit Original** opens the selected file in its native application. When you save the file and return to InDesign, the placed file is automatically updated.

You can click any column head in the panel to sort the list of links based on that column. For example, clicking the Status heading moves all missing and modified links to the top of the list so you can more easily find and address those issues.

When expanded, the Link Information section of the panel shows useful metadata related to the selected file.

Click this bar and drag to change the height of the Link Information area.

Click here and drag to resize the entire panel.

If you open the Panel Options dialog box (from the Links panel Options menu), you can change which information appears in each section of the panel.

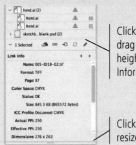

- Use the **Row Size** menu to change the size of item thumbnails in the panel.

- Uncheck **Collapse Multiple Links to Same Source** to list multiple instances of the same file separately, instead of grouped together (as they are by default).

- In the lower section of the dialog box you can use the checkboxes to determine the information that appears in the main Links panel (**Show Column**) and in the Link Information section of the panel (**Show in Link Info**). For example, you might want to include the Effective PPI as a column in the top half of the panel so you can easily monitor link resolution as you work.

Embedding Links

To avoid the problem of missing links, you can embed images directly into the layout file by Control/right-clicking an image in the Links panel and choosing Embed Link in the contextual menu.

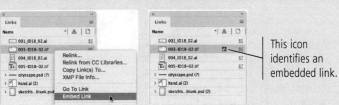

This icon identifies an embedded link.

When links are embedded, there is no longer any relation to the original source file. This means the source files do not need to be included in the job package, and you will not see a missing-link error if the original source file is moved. It also means, however, that any changes in a source file will not result in a modified link warning. To edit an image, you have to manually open the original source file in its native application, save it, and then manually replace the embedded image with the edited file.

4. Open the Transform panel (Window>Object & Layout>Transform).

The options in the Transform panel are the same as those on the left side of the Control panel. As you can see, the selected graphic is placed at approximately 44%.

Note:

Make sure you use the Direct Selection tool, or the Content Grabber, to select the actual placed logo. If you select the frame instead, the Transform panel shows the values for the frame instead of the graphic placed in the frame.

5. Click the Modified icon in the top-left corner of the image frame.

The Missing and Modified icons provide an easy, on-screen method for identifying and correcting image-link problems.

You can also double-click the Modified icon in the Links panel, or select the file in the panel and click the Update Link button to update selected modified files.

6. Click the updated image with the Direct Selection tool.

When you update or replace an existing placed image, the new file adopts the necessary scaling percentage to fit into the same space as the original. In this case, the new file is scaled to approximately 54% — the size that is necessary to fit the same dimensions as the original.

This icon identifies a linked image that is up to date.

7. Click the Missing icon in the top-left corner of the grayscale image.

You can also click the Relink button in the Links panel to replace a missing image link.

8. In the resulting Locate dialog box, uncheck Show Import Options at the bottom of the dialog box, if necessary.

If the Search for Missing Links option is checked, InDesign will scan the selected folder to find other missing image files.

9. Navigate to **highlight-july.tif** in the WIP>Aerospace folder, then click Open.

After you identify a new source image, the graphics frame and the Links panel no longer show the Missing warning. The new image preview appears in the same frame.

The frame shows the new image, which replaced the missing image file.

10. **Save the file and continue to the next exercise.**

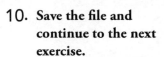 Edit Margin and Column Guides

Your client wants to make several changes to the layout, including fewer and wider columns on the front page. These changes will recur from one issue to the next, so you should change the template instead of simply changing the elements in each issue.

1. **With araa-newsletter.indt open, double-click the A-Front icon to show that layout in the document window.**

Every layout has a default setup, which you define when you create the file. Each master page has its own margin and column settings, which can be different than the default document settings.

2. **Choose Layout>Margins and Columns, and make sure the Preview option is checked in the resulting dialog box.**

Many InDesign dialog boxes have a Preview option, which allows you to see the effects of your changes before finalizing them.

3. **Change the Left and Right Margins fields to 0.5 in, change the Columns field to 3, and change the Gutter field to 0.2 in.**

Notice that changing the margin and column guides has no effect on the text frame; you have to change the text frame settings independently.

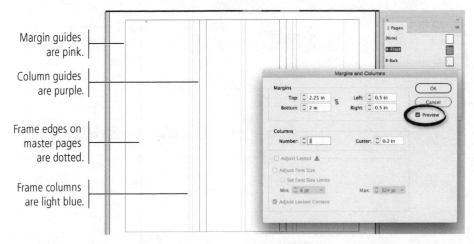

Margin guides are pink.

Column guides are purple.

Frame edges on master pages are dotted.

Frame columns are light blue.

Note:

You can change the default margins and columns for a layout by choosing File>Document Setup.

4. Click OK to apply the change and close the dialog box.

5. Using the Selection tool, click to select the 4-column text frame in the layout.

6. Click and drag the outside-center handles to extend the frame edges to match the modified margin guides.

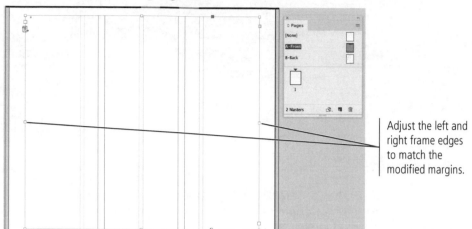

Adjust the left and right frame edges to match the modified margins.

7. With the text frame selected, locate the Text Frame options in the Properties panel.

Note:

You can also access the Text Frame Options dialog box from the Object menu, or by pressing Command/Control-B.

8. Change the Number of Columns field to 3 and the Gutter field to 0.2 in to match the changes you made to the column guides.

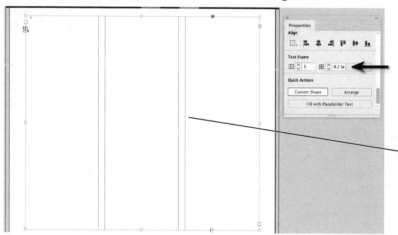

Text frame columns now match the adjusted margin and column guides.

9. Save the file and close it.

Note:

The Columns options might also be available in the Control panel:

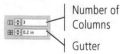

Number of Columns

Gutter

Understanding Master Pages

There are two kinds of pages in InDesign:

- **Layout pages**, which appear in the bottom of the Pages panel, are the pages on which you place content.

- **Master pages**, which appear in the top of the Pages panel, are the pages on which you place recurring information, such as running headers and footers (information at the top and bottom of the page, respectively).

Master pages are one of the most powerful features in page layout software. Think of a master page as a template for individual pages. Anything on the master appears on the related layout page(s). Changing something on a master layout applies the same changes to the object on related layout pages (unless you already changed the object on the layout page, or detached the object from the master).

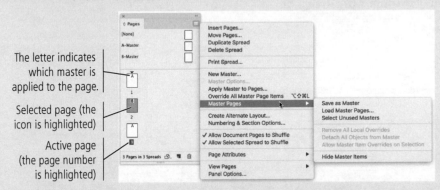

The letter indicates which master is applied to the page.

Selected page (the icon is highlighted)

Active page (the page number is highlighted)

The Pages panel Options menu has a number of indispensable options for working with master pages:

- **New Master** opens a dialog box where you can assign a custom prefix, a meaningful name, whether the master will be based on another master page, the number of pages (from 1 to 10) to include in the master layout, and the size of the master layout (InDesign supports multiple page sizes within a single document).

- **Master Options** opens a dialog box with the same options you defined when you created a new master.

- **Apply Master to Pages** allows you to apply a specific master to selected pages. You can also apply a specific master to a layout by dragging the master icon onto the layout page icon in the lower half of the panel.

- **Override All Master Page Items** allows you to access and change master items on a specific layout page. You can also override individual objects by pressing Command/Control-Shift and clicking the object you want to override. It's important to realize that this command functions on a page-by-page basis.

In the Master Pages submenu:

- **Save as Master** is useful if you've built a layout on a layout page and want to convert that layout to a master. Instead of copying and pasting the page contents, you can simply activate the page and choose Save as Master.

- **Load Master Pages** allows you to import master pages from one InDesign file to another. Assets (styles, swatches, etc.) used on the imported masters will also be imported.

- **Select Unused Masters** highlights all master pages not associated with any layout page (and not used as the basis of another master page). This can be useful if you want to remove extraneous elements from your layout.

- **Remove All Local Overrides** reapplies the settings from the master items to related items on the layout page. This option toggles to **Remove Selected Local Overrides** if you have an object selected in the layout.

- **Detach All Objects from Master** breaks the link between objects on a layout page and objects on the related master. In this case, changing items on the master has no effect on related layout page items. This selection toggles to **Detach Selection from Master** if you have a specific object selected in the layout.

- **Allow Master Item Overrides on Selection**, active by default, allows objects to be overridden on layout pages. You can protect specific objects by selecting them on the master layout and toggling this option off.

- **Hide/Show Master Items** toggles the visibility of master page items on layout pages.

Create a New File Based on the Template

Every issue of the newsletter has one front page and one back page. These layouts are already prepared as master pages, but you have to apply those master pages to the layout pages for individual issues. Since this occurs for every issue, it will remove a few more clicks from the process if you set up the layout pages as part of the template.

1. **Choose File>Open and navigate to your WIP>Aerospace folder. Select the araa-newsletter.indt template file and choose the Open [As] Normal option at the bottom of the dialog box.**

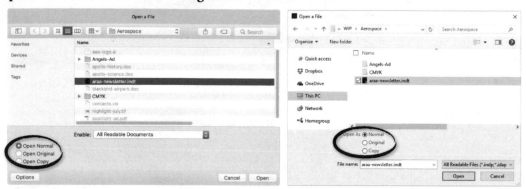

Macintosh   Windows

2. **Click Open to create a new file based on the template.**

   Opening a template using the Open [As] Normal option creates a new untitled document that is based on the template.

   The result is a new, untitled document.

   If you double-click a template file on your desktop, the template opens as if you chose the Open [As] Normal option. To use the Open [As] Original or Open [As] Copy feature, you must choose File>Open from InDesign.

3. **Double-click the Page 1 icon in the Pages panel.**

4. **In the Pages panel, drag the A-Front master icon onto the Page 1 icon in the lower half of the Pages panel.**

   When a master page is applied to a layout page, everything on the master page is placed on the layout page.

Assign a master layout to a specific page by dragging the master icon onto the page icon.

Alternatively, you can choose Apply Master to Pages in the Pages panel Options menu. In the resulting dialog box, you can determine which master page to apply to specific layout pages. Some find this easier than dragging master page icons onto layout page icons in the panel. It is also useful if you want to apply a specific master layout to more than one page at a time.

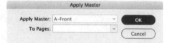

> *Note:*
>
> *You can change the size of page icons in the Pages panel by choosing Panel Options at the bottom of the panel Options menu.*

5. **Click the B-Back icon and drag it into the bottom half of the Pages panel (below the Page 1 icon).**

   You can add new pages to your layout by dragging any of the master page icons into the lower half of the panel.

Add pages to a layout by dragging any master page icon to the lower half of the Pages panel.

   You can also choose Insert Pages in the Pages panel Options menu. In the resulting dialog box, you can determine how many pages to add, exactly where to add the new pages, and which master page to apply to the new pages. This method makes it easier to add only one page from a master page that includes spreads, or add multiple pages at one time based on the same master.

6. **Choose File>Save As. Navigate to your WIP>Aerospace folder as the location for saving the template.**

   Because you opened the template to create a normal layout file, you have to use the Save As command to overwrite the edited template file.

7. **Change the file name to araa-newsletter. In the Format/Save As Type menu, choose InDesign CC 2019 Template.**

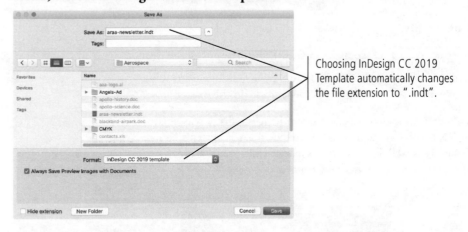

Choosing InDesign CC 2019 Template automatically changes the file extension to ".indt".

8. **Click Save, then read the resulting message.**

   Because you defined the same name as the original template, you have to confirm that you want to overwrite the template file with the new version.

9. **Click Replace/Yes. When the save is complete, close the template file.**

Implement the Newsletter Template

By saving your work as a template, you eliminated a significant amount of repetitive work that would otherwise need to be redone for every issue. There are still some tasks that will need to be done for each issue, such as changing the issue date and adding images to the front and back pages. These elements can't be entirely "templated." However, if you review the layout, you'll see that the template includes placeholders for these elements, so adding them is greatly simplified.

1. **Choose File>Open and navigate to your WIP>Aerospace folder. Select the `araa-newsletter.indt` template file, choose the Open [As] Normal option at the bottom of the dialog box, and click Open.**

   As in the previous exercise, opening the template file creates a new untitled document that is based on the template.

2. **Immediately choose File>Save As and navigate to your WIP>Aerospace folder. Change the file name to `newsletter-july.indd` and click Save.**

   The Format menu defaults to the InDesign CC 2019 Document option, so you do not have to change this menu to save the new file as a regular InDesign document.

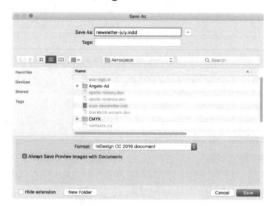

3. **Navigate to Page 1 of the file.**

4. **Using the Selection tool, try to select the text frame that includes the date.**

   This step will have no effect, and nothing will be selected. By default, you can't select master page items on a layout page — changes have to be made on the master page.

   When you change an object on a master page, the same changes reflect on associated layout pages. For example, if you change the red box to blue on A-Front Page, the red box will turn blue on Page 1, as well. Because of this parent-child relationship, it's a good idea to leave objects attached to the master whenever possible.

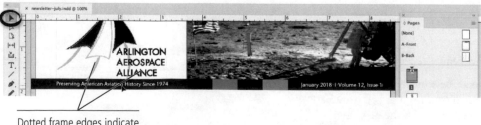

Dotted frame edges indicate that a frame is attached to the related master page.

5. **Command/Control-Shift-click the text frame that contains the issue date.**

   This method detaches an individual object from the master page. It is then no longer linked to the master page, so changes to the same item on the master will not be reflected on the associated layout page.

   If you look carefully, however, you might notice a problem. Detaching the single text frame from the master moves it in front of any object that exists only on the master page. The four color-filled rectangles are now hidden by the text frame's fill color.

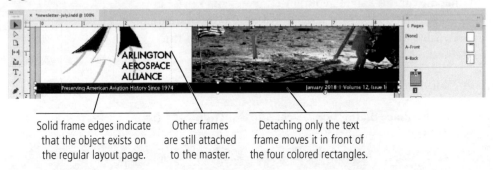

   Solid frame edges indicate that the object exists on the regular layout page. | Other frames are still attached to the master. | Detaching only the text frame moves it in front of the four colored rectangles.

6. **Choose Edit>Undo Override Master Page Items.**

7. **Control/right-click the Page 1 icon in the Pages panel and choose Override All Master Page Items from the contextual menu.**

   Overriding all items from the master page maintains the original stacking order of those objects. You can now see the colored rectangles still on top of the text frame.

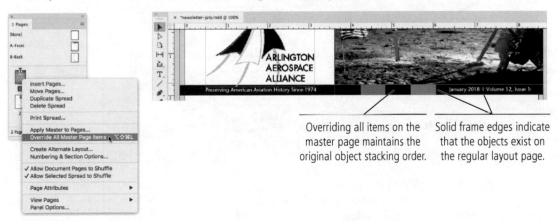

   Overriding all items on the master page maintains the original object stacking order. | Solid frame edges indicate that the objects exist on the regular layout page.

8. **Using the Type tool, change the date in the frame to July 2019 and the issue number to 3.**

Note:

You could have accomplished the same basic result by editing the text on the master page. However, we created these steps so you can understand the concept of detaching master page objects.

9. **Save the file and continue to the next exercise.**

Place a PDF File

PDF (Portable Document Format) files save layout, graphics, and font information in a single file. The format was created to facilitate cross-platform file-sharing so one file could be transferred to any other computer, and the final layout would print as intended. While originally meant for Internet use, PDF is now the standard in the graphics industry, used for submitting completed jobs to a service provider.

You can place a PDF file into an InDesign layout, just as you would place any other image. You can determine which page to place (if the file contains more than one page), which layers are visible (if the file has more than one layer), and the specific file dimensions (bounding box) to use when placing the file.

1. **With `newsletter-july.indd` open, navigate to Page 1 of the newsletter.**

2. **Choose File>Place. In the Place dialog box, select `spotlight-ad.pdf` (in the WIP>Aerospace folder).**

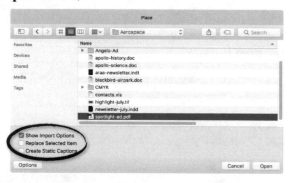

3. **Make sure Show Import Options is checked and Replace Selected Item is not checked, and then click Open.**

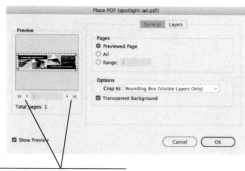

The options in the Place PDF dialog box are exactly the same as the options you saw when you placed the native Illustrator file. However, the options in the General tab are typically more important for PDF files than for Illustrator files.

PDF files can contain multiple pages; you can review the various pages using the buttons below the preview image. You can place multiple pages at once by choosing the All option, or you can select specific pages using the Range option. (Import multiple continuous pages by defining a page range, using a hyphen to separate the first

Use these buttons to navigate the pages in the PDF file.

page and last pages in the range. Import non-continuous pages by typing each page number, separated by commas.) If you place multiple pages of a PDF file, each page is loaded into the cursor as a separate object.

The Crop To options are also significant when placing PDF files. If the file was created properly, it should include a defined bleed of at least 1/8 inch and trim marks to identify the intended trim size.

4. **Choose Bleed in the Crop To menu and click OK.**

Note:

If you place an Illustrator file that contains multiple artboards, you have the same options for choosing which artboard (page) to place.

5. **Click the loaded cursor in the empty graphics frame at the bottom of Page 1 to place the loaded file.**

6. **Access the placed content by clicking the image with the Direct Selection tool or by clicking the Content Grabber with the Selection tool.**

   When you place the image into the frame, it is automatically centered in the frame. If you look carefully, you can see that the text at the bottom of the frame appears very close to the bottom page edge.

   This file was created with 1/8″ bleeds on all four sides. In this context, however, the top bleed allowance is not necessary, because the bleed area on the top causes the image to appear farther down than it should. You need to change the graphic's Y position to eliminate all of the unnecessary bleed at the top of the file.

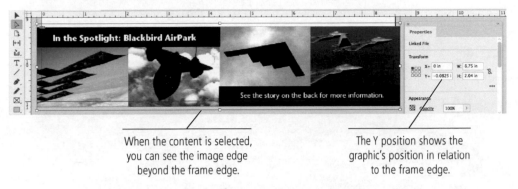

When the content is selected, you can see the image edge beyond the frame edge.

The Y position shows the graphic's position in relation to the frame edge.

7. **With the placed file still selected, make sure the top-left reference point is selected, and then change the picture position (within the frame) to Y+: -0.125 in.**

The image bounding box now shows the extra bleed allowance extending beyond the upper edge of the frame.

8. **Save the file and continue to the next exercise.**

Place an InDesign File

In addition to the different types of images, you can also place one InDesign layout directly into another. As with PDF files, you can determine which page is placed (if the file contains more than one page), which layers are visible (if the file has more than one layer), and the specific file dimensions (bounding box) to use when the file is placed.

1. **With newsletter-july.indd open, navigate to Page 2 and make sure nothing is selected.**

2. **Choose File>Place. In the Place dialog box, select angels-ad.indd (in the WIP>Aerospace>Angels-Ad folder). With the Show Import Options box checked, click Open.**

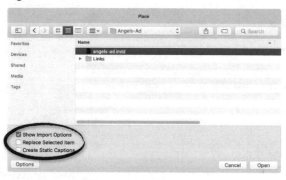

3. **In the General tab of the Place InDesign Document dialog box, choose Bleed Bounding Box in the Crop To menu.**

The options for placing an InDesign file are mostly the same as those for placing PDF files — the only exception is the Crop To menu. When you place one InDesign file into another, you can place the page(s) based on the defined page, bleed, or slug, as described in the Document Setup dialog box.

4. **Click OK. Read the resulting warning message and click OK.**

To output properly, image links need to be present and up to date. Images placed in nested InDesign layouts are still links, so the link requirements apply in those files. (You will fix these problems shortly.)

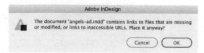

5. **Click the loaded cursor in the empty graphics frame on the left side of Page 2 to place the file.**

6. **Using the Content Grabber or the Direct Selection tool, click to select the new placed content inside the frame.**

As with PDF files, the bleed areas in an InDesign file might not exactly match the needs of the file in which it is placed.

This frame is placed to include the required 1/8" bleed area, but the placed file is centered in the existing frame area. This means that the left edge of the placed content should align to the left edge of the frame.

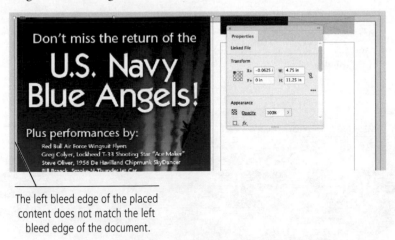

The left bleed edge of the placed content does not match the left bleed edge of the document.

7. **Change the content's position inside the frame to X+: 0 in.**

The left bleed edge of the placed content now matches the left bleed edge of the document.

8. **Open the Links panel and click the arrow to the left of angels-ad.indd to show the nested images.**

When you place one InDesign file into another, the Links panel also lists images in the placed InDesign file, indented immediately below the placed InDesign file.

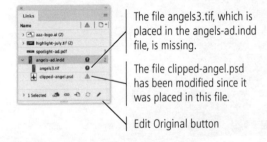

The file angels3.tif, which is placed in the angels-ad.indd file, is missing.

The file clipped-angel.psd has been modified since it was placed in this file.

Edit Original button

9. **Click angels-ad.indd in the Links panel, and then click the Edit Original button.**

   When you open any InDesign file, of course, you are warned if a necessary source file is missing or modified (which you already knew from the Links panel of the newsletter-july.indd file).

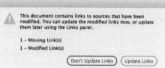

Note:

You can also Control/right-click a specific image in the layout and choose Edit Original from the contextual menu.

10. **Click Don't Update Links to dismiss the warning message.**

    Edit Original opens the file selected in the Links panel. Because angels-ad.indd is a placed InDesign file, that document opens in a new document window. When the file opens, you see the missing and modified image icons — the reason you are editing the file — in the document and in the Links panel.

The angels-ad.indd file is active.

This icon identifies the missing image.

This icon identifies the modified image.

Note:

If you don't see the Missing and Modified icons, choose View>Extras>Show Link Badge.

11. **Click the Modified icon for the placed image in the ad to update that file.**

12. **Click the Missing icon for the missing image in the layout. Navigate to angels-formation.tif in the WIP>Aerospace>Angels-ad>Links folder and click Open.**

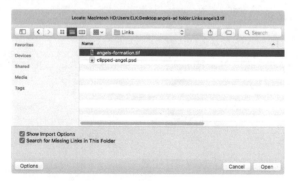

13. **If the Image Import Options dialog box opens, click OK.**

14. **Save the `angels-ad.indd` file and close it.**

When you save and close the angels-ad.indd file, the Links panel for the newsletter file automatically reflects the new placed file.

15. **Save `newsletter-july.indd` and continue to the next stage of the project.**

STAGE 2 / Working with Styles

The principles of good design state that headings, subheadings, body copy, and other editorial elements should generally look the same throughout a single job. In other words, editorial elements should be consistent from one page to another, whether the job is two pages or 200.

For any bit of text, there are dozens of character- and paragraph-formatting options, from the font and type size to the space above and below paragraphs. Whenever you work with longer blocks of copy, you'll apply the same group of formatting options to multiple pieces of text.

If you were to change each element manually, you would have to make hundreds of clicks to create a two-page newsletter. Fortunately, InDesign makes it easy to store groups of formatting options as **styles**, which can be applied with a single click.

The major advantages of using styles are ease of use and enhanced efficiency. Styles ensure consistency in text formatting throughout a publication — rather than trying to remember how you formatted a sidebar 45 pages ago, you can simply apply a predefined Sidebar style. Changes can be made instantly to all text defined as a particular style (for example, changing the font in the Subhead style from Helvetica to Myriad) — when a style definition changes, any text that uses that style automatically changes too.

InDesign supports both character styles and paragraph styles. **Character styles** apply only to selected words. This type of style is useful for setting off a few words in a paragraph, without affecting the entire paragraph. **Paragraph styles** apply to the entire body of text between two ¶ symbols. This type of style defines the appearance of the paragraph, combining the character style used in the paragraph with line spacing, indents, tabs, and other paragraph attributes.

In this project, the client's original template included a number of styles for formatting the text in each issue. Because the text frames already exist in the template layout, you only need to import the client's text and apply the existing styles.

Note:

Paragraph styles define character attributes and paragraph attributes. Character styles define only the character attributes. In other words, a paragraph style can be used to format text entirely — including font information, line spacing, tabs, and so on.

Working with Microsoft Word Files

Microsoft Word files can include a fairly sophisticated level of formatting attributes, from basic text formatting and defined paragraph and character styles to automatically generated tables of contents. When you import a Word file into InDesign, you can determine whether to include these elements in the imported text.

You can use options in the **Include** section to import tables of contents, index text, footnotes, and endnotes that exist in the Word file.

If **Use Typographer's Quotes** is checked, quote marks in the Word file will be converted to typographically correct "curly" quotes in InDesign.

In the Formatting section, you can check the option to **Remove Styles and Formatting from Text and Tables** to import a file as plain text, with none of the Word-applied formatting maintained. When you place the file in InDesign, it is formatted with the [Basic Paragraph] style that defines the default appearance of text in a layout (12-pt black Minion Pro, by default).

If **Preserve Styles and Formatting from Text and Tables** is active, you can choose a number of additional options related to translation between Microsoft Word and InDesign.

The **Manual Page Breaks** menu determines how page breaks in Word translate to InDesign. You can preserve them, convert them to column breaks, or ignore them.

If graphics have been placed into a Word file, **Import Inline Graphics** allows you to include those as anchored objects in the InDesign story. (It is important to understand that these graphics will likely be embedded into the story instead of linked to the original data file.)

If you choose **Import Unused Styles**, all styles in the Word file will be imported into the InDesign layout. The most significant issue here is that styles might require fonts that you have not installed.

Word includes a collaboration tool called **Track Changes**, which allows one person to review another person's changes to a file. If you check the Track Changes option, any tracked changes from the Word file will be included in your InDesign layout. This can cause a lot of items to show up in your text that aren't supposed to be there (corrected typos, for example).

Convert Bullets & Numbers to Text allows you to convert automatically generated numbering and bullet characters into actual text characters.

The **Style Name Conflicts** area warns you if styles in the Word file conflict with styles in the InDesign file. In other words, they have the same style names, but different definitions in the two locations. You have to determine how to resolve these conflicts.

Import Styles Automatically allows you to choose how to handle conflicts in paragraph and character styles.

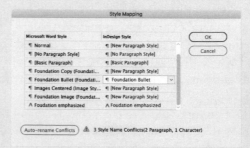

- **Use InDesign Style Definition** preserves the style as you defined it; text in the Word file that uses that style is reformatted with the InDesign definition of the style.

- **Redefine InDesign Style** replaces the layout definition with the definition from the Word file.

- **Auto Rename** adds the Word file to the InDesign file with "_wrd_1" at the end of the style name.

If you choose **Customize Style Import**, the Style Mapping button opens a dialog box where you can review and control specific style conflicts. Click an option in the InDesign Style column to access a menu where you can choose which InDesign style to use in place of a specific Word style.

If you always receive Microsoft Word files from the same source, you can save your choices (including Style Mapping options) as a preset, or even click the Set as Default button in the Import Options dialog box.

Apply Template Styles

Most InDesign jobs incorporate some amount of client-supplied text, which might be sent to you in the body of an email or saved in any number of text file formats. Many text files will be supplied from Microsoft Word, which includes fairly extensive options for formatting text (although, not quite as robust or sophisticated as InDesign). Many Microsoft Word users apply **local formatting** (selecting specific text and applying character and/or paragraph attributes). More sophisticated Microsoft Word users build text formatting styles similar to those used in InDesign.

1. **With newsletter-july.indd open, double-click the Page 1 icon in the Pages panel to make that page active in the document window.**

2. **Choose File>Place and navigate to the file apollo-history.doc.**

   All text files for this project are in the WIP>Aerospace folder; we will not continue to repeat the entire path for each file.

3. **Check the Show Import Options box at the bottom of the dialog box and make sure Replace Selected Item is not checked. Click Open.**

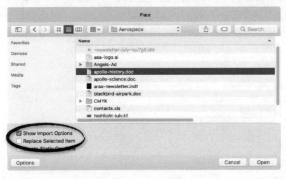

4. **In the resulting dialog box, make sure the Preserve Styles and Formatting option and the Import Styles Automatically radio button are selected. Choose Auto Rename in both conflict menus, and then click OK.**

   When you import a Microsoft Word file into InDesign, you can either preserve or remove formatting saved in the Microsoft Word file (including styles defined in Microsoft Word).

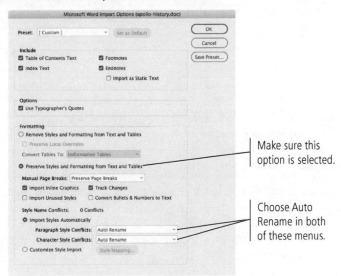

Make sure this option is selected.

Choose Auto Rename in both of these menus.

5. **If you get a Missing Font warning, click Close.**

   You're going to replace the Microsoft Word formatting with InDesign styles, which will correct any problems of this sort.

6. Click the loaded cursor in the empty, three-column text frame.

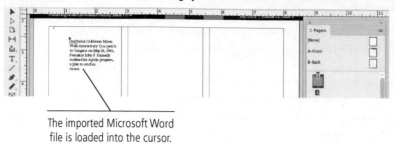

The imported Microsoft Word file is loaded into the cursor.

At this point, the story does not fit into the frame because you haven't yet applied the appropriate styles to the imported text.

Overset text icon

7. Open the Paragraph Styles panel (Window>Styles>Paragraph Styles).

8. Using the Type tool, click to place the insertion point in the first paragraph of the imported story (the main heading) and look at the Paragraph Styles panel.

The imported text appears to be preformatted, but the Paragraph Styles panel tells a different story. This paragraph is formatted as "Normal+."

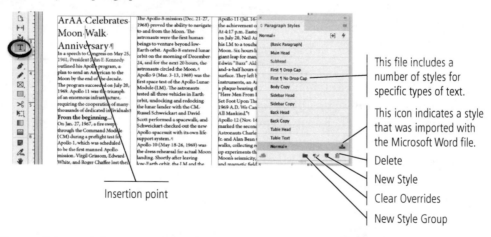

Insertion point

This file includes a number of styles for specific types of text.

This icon indicates a style that was imported with the Microsoft Word file.

Delete

New Style

Clear Overrides

New Style Group

When you imported the Microsoft Word file, you preserved the formatting in the file; this is usually a good idea so you can see what the writer intended. Now that the text is imported into your layout, however, you want to apply the template styles to make the text in this issue consistent with others.

When you import text into InDesign, any number of new styles might appear in the Styles panels. The most common imported style is Normal. Text in a Microsoft Word file is typically formatted with the Normal style, even if you don't realize it. User-applied formatting is commonly local, meaning it is applied directly to selected text instead of with a defined style.

9. **With the insertion point still in place, click the Main Head style in the Paragraph Styles panel.**

A number of styles existed in the original newsletter template, so they also exist in any files that are based on that template. You should be able to guess the purpose of these styles from their names. It's always a good idea to use indicative names when you create styles or other user-defined assets.

The Main Head style has been applied to the active paragraph.

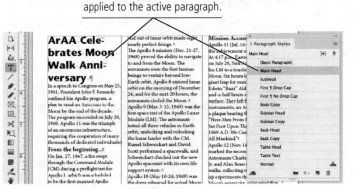

Using styles, you can change all formatting attributes of selected text with a single click. Because you are working with paragraph styles, the style definition applies to the entire paragraph in which the insertion point is placed.

10. **Place the insertion point in the next paragraph of copy, and then click the First ¶ Drop Cap style in the Paragraph Styles panel.**

11. **Format the next paragraph ("From the beginning...") with the Subhead style.**

12. **Format the next paragraph with the First ¶ No Drop Cap style.**

13. Select any part of the next four paragraphs (up to but not including the "Mission Accomplished" paragraph), then click the Body Copy style in the Paragraph Styles panel.

Paragraph styles apply to any paragraph that is partially or entirely selected. You don't have to select an entire paragraph before applying a paragraph style.

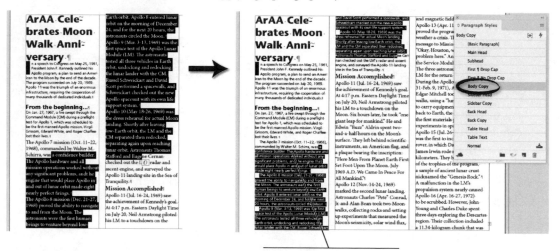

Any paragraph that is partially selected will be formatted with the applied paragraph style.

14. Continue applying styles to the remaining copy (use the style names as a guide).

Some text in the story will be overset until you apply the required paragraph styles. As you format each paragraph, more of the story will be visible. When all paragraphs are formatted, the entire story fits into the frame.

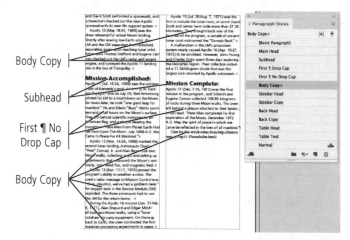

15. Save the file and continue to the next exercise.

Manage Local Formatting Overrides

Local formatting overrides — formatting outside the definition of the applied paragraph style — are common, especially when importing text from external sources such as Microsoft Word. This is usually caused by formatting options in the word processing application that are not supported in InDesign. It is important to realize, however, that if a paragraph includes local formatting, simply clicking a new style name might not work perfectly. You should be aware that you often need to clear overrides in the imported text before the InDesign style is properly applied.

1. **With newsletter-july.indd open, place the insertion point in the last paragraph of body copy on Page 1.**

2. **Look at the Paragraph Styles panel.**

The Body Copy style, which you applied to the active paragraph, shows a "+" next to the style name. This indicates that formatting other than what is defined in the style has been applied to the selected text. This is called a **local formatting override**.

Insertion point

The plus sign indicates that some formatting other than the style definition has been applied.

3. **In the Paragraph Styles panel, click the Style Override Highlighter button.**

In this case, the override is fairly obvious — a different font is applied. In other cases, however, the overrides are not always so easy to spot.

The Style Override Highlighter button toggles this feature on and off, so you can quickly and visually identify text in which formatting outside the style definition has been applied.

Style Override Highlighter button

All text with local formatting overrides is highlighted in the layout.

4. **With the insertion point in the last paragraph of body copy, click the Clear Overrides in Selection button at the bottom of the Paragraph Styles panel.**

The **Clear Overrides in Selection** button removes local formatting that is not defined in the applied style. As the name suggests, it only applies to *selected* text.

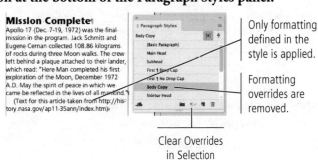

Clear Overrides in Selection

Only formatting defined in the style is applied.

Formatting overrides are removed.

5. **Highlight the last paragraph of body copy, and then change the Font Style menu to Italic.**

6. **Click to place the insertion point anywhere in the last paragraph, removing the highlighting.**

In many cases, local formatting overrides are intentional. As you can see here, the Override Highlighting again appears in the layout as soon as you change the Font Style to something that is not defined in the Body Copy paragraph style.

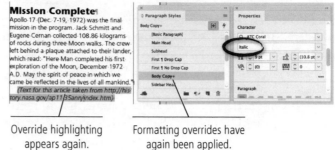

Mission Complete¶
Apollo 17 (Dec. 7-19, 1972) was the final mission in the program. Jack Schmitt and Eugene Cernan collected 108.86 kilograms of rocks during three Moon walks. The crew left behind a plaque attached to their lander, which read: "Here Man completed his first exploration of the Moon, December 1972 A.D. May the spirit of peace in which we came be reflected in the lives of all mankind."¶
(Text for this article taken from http://history.nasa.gov/ap11/35anny/index.htm)

Override highlighting appears again.

Formatting overrides have again been applied.

7. **In the Paragraph Styles panel, click the Style Override Highlighter button to toggle the feature off.**

8. **Save the file and continue to the next exercise.**

Edit a Paragraph to Span Columns

As a general rule, headlines in newsletters and newspapers extend across the top of the entire related story. In previous versions of the software, this required a separate frame that spanned the width of the multicolumn body frame. InDesign includes a paragraph formatting option that makes it easy to span a paragraph across multiple columns *without* the need for a separate frame. This can be applied to individual paragraphs, or defined as part of a paragraph style.

1. **With newsletter-july.indd open, make sure Page 1 is active.**

2. **Place the insertion point in the first paragraph of the story (the main head) and then open the Paragraph panel (Window>Type & Tables>Paragraph).**

3. **With the insertion point still in the same paragraph, open the Paragraph panel Options menu and choose Span Columns.**

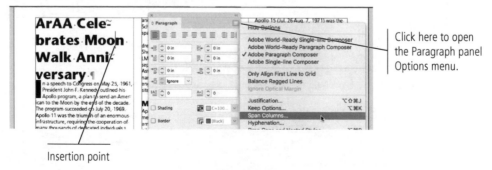

Click here to open the Paragraph panel Options menu.

Insertion point

4. **Click the Preview option on the right side of the dialog box, then choose Span Columns in the Paragraph Layout menu.**

When the Preview option is active, you can see the result of your choices before you finalize them.

5. **Make sure the Span field is set to All.**

   You can use the Span field to extend a paragraph over only a certain number of columns.

6. **Click the Up Arrow button once for the Space After Span field.**

   The Space Before and Space After Span fields determine how much space is placed between the span paragraph and those above or below it. The arrow buttons increase or decrease the related values by 0.0625". (This is the same concept used in the Space Above and Space Below options for regular paragraph formatting.)

Note:

The Split Column option can be used to divide a specific paragraph into multiple columns within a frame's defined column.

7. **Click OK to finalize your changes.**

8. **Save the file and continue to the next exercise.**

 Control Automatic Text Frame Size

Many page layouts have a primary story, as well as related stories called **sidebars**. These elements are not always linked to the main story, and are often placed in their own boxes with unique formatting to draw attention.

1. **On Page 1 of newsletter-july.indd, create a new text frame with the following dimensions (based on the top-left reference point):**

X: 5 in	W: 3.625 in
Y: 7 in	H: 2 in

   To create the new text frame, begin by clicking and dragging outside the boundaries of the existing frames. You can then select the new frame with the Selection tool and use the Control or Properties panel to define the frame's position and size.

2. **Fill the text frame with a 20% tint of Pantone 194 C.**

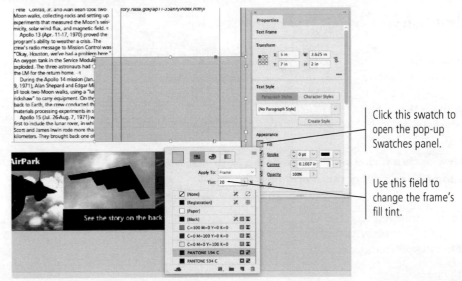

Click this swatch to open the pop-up Swatches panel.

Use this field to change the frame's fill tint.

3. **Choose File>Place. Select `apollo-science.doc`, uncheck the Show Import Options box, then click Open. Click Close if you get a Missing Font warning.**

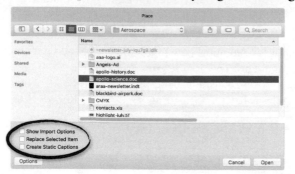

4. **Click the loaded cursor inside the tinted frame you just created.**

Because you turned off the Show Import Options box in the Place dialog box, the file is imported with the last-used import options. In this case, the formatting is maintained, styles are imported, and conflicting styles are automatically renamed — resulting in the new Normal_wrd_1 style, which conflicted with the previously imported Normal style.

You should notice several problems with the imported text:

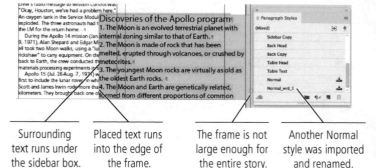

Surrounding text runs under the sidebar box. | Placed text runs into the edge of the frame. | The frame is not large enough for the entire story. | Another Normal style was imported and renamed.

- The frame is not large enough to show all of the text in the story.

- Surrounding text runs under the sidebar frame.

- Placed text in the sidebar frame runs into the edge of the containing frame.

Amateur designers often create three separate elements to achieve the desired effect, which adds an unnecessary degree of complexity to the layout. You will fix each of these problems by changing the options for the single sidebar text frame.

5. **Select the sidebar frame with the Selection tool, and then locate the Text Frame options in the Properties panel.**

6. **Click the Options button to open the Text Frame Options dialog box.**

You can also choose Object>Text Frame Options or press Command/Control-B to open the Text Frame Options dialog box. If the Type tool is active, the Text Frame Options dialog box opens for the frame in which the insertion point is placed.

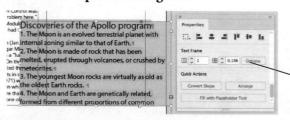

Click this button to open the Text Frame Options dialog box.

7. **Make sure the Preview option is checked, and click the Auto-Size button at the top of the dialog box to display those options.**

Auto-size options allow a text frame to expand or shrink as necessary to fit the contained text. You are going to use these options to dynamically change the sidebar box to fit the entire story, regardless of formatting options.

8. **Choose Height Only in the Auto-Sizing menu and choose the bottom-center reference point.**

The reference points determine which point will remain fixed when the box changes size. In this case, you want the bottom edge to remain in place, so you are choosing the bottom reference point. Because you are only allowing the box's height to change, the left and right reference points are not available.

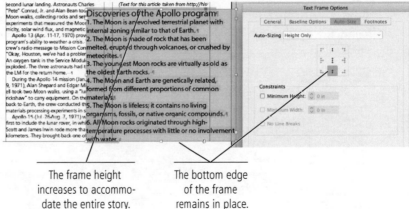

The frame height increases to accommodate the entire story.

The bottom edge of the frame remains in place.

You can also use the Constraints options to define a minimum height and width — in other words, the smallest possible size the frame can be. If you allow the frame to change width, you can check the No Line Breaks option to enlarge the frame as much as necessary to fit the entire text on one line.

9. **Click OK to apply your changes.**

10. **Format the first line of the sidebar with the Sidebar Head style, and format the rest of the text in this frame using the Sidebar Copy style.**

The type sizes in the applied styles are considerably smaller, which requires less space for the sidebar. As you can see, the Auto-Size feature shrinks the height of the frame as necessary to exactly fit the contained text.

The frame height shrinks because the new formatting requires less space.

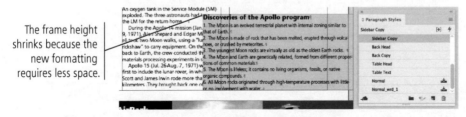

11. **Save the file and continue to the next exercise.**

Edit Text Inset and Wrap Settings

A number of frame attributes can affect the appearance of text both within, and around, a text frame. In this exercise, you adjust the text inset and text wrap to force text into the proper position.

1. **With newsletter-july.indd open, select the sidebar box with the Selection tool, and then open the Text Frame Options dialog box again.**

2. **With the Preview option checked, make sure the chain icon for the Inset Spacing fields is active.**

Like the same chain icon in other dialog boxes, this forces all four inset values to the same value.

3. **Change the Top Inset field to 0.125 in, and then press Tab to move the highlight and apply the new Inset Spacing value to all four fields.**

Text inset spacing is the distance text is moved from the inside edge of its containing frame. You can define different values for each edge or constrain all four edges to a single value.

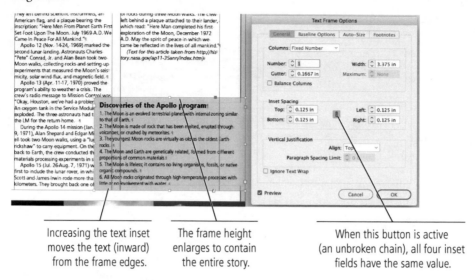

Note:

If you check the Ignore Text Wrap option in the Text Frame Options dialog box, the frame is not affected by wrap attributes of overlapping objects.

Increasing the text inset moves the text (inward) from the frame edges.

The frame height enlarges to contain the entire story.

When this button is active (an unbroken chain), all four inset fields have the same value.

4. **Click the Chain icon in the Inset Spacing area to break the link, and then change the Right field to 0.625 in.**

The different right inset value accommodates for the right page margin.

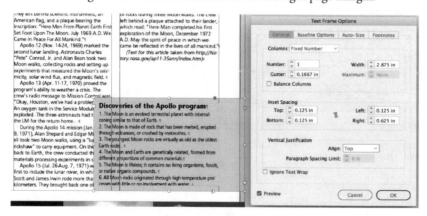

5. **Click OK to close the dialog box and apply your choices.**

6. **With the sidebar frame selected, click the second button from the left in the Text Wrap panel (Window>Text Wrap).**

   Text wrap is the distance around the edge of an object where surrounding text will flow.

7. **Make sure the chain icon is active so all four offset values are the same. Change the Top Offset field to 0.1875 in, then press Tab to apply the value.**

   Clicking the up- or down-arrow buttons changes the offset values by 0.0625″ for each click. Because the fields are linked, you could click the up-arrow button for any field to increase all four values by 0.1875″.

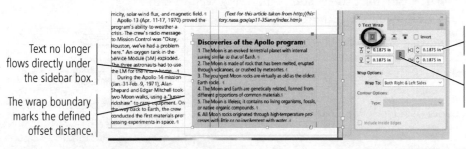

Text no longer flows directly under the sidebar box.

The wrap boundary marks the defined offset distance.

Use the offset fields to define the wrap distance.

When this button is active, all four offset fields have the same value.

8. **Save the file and continue to the next exercise.**

Understanding Text Wrap Options

InDesign provides five options for wrapping text around an object. Wrap attributes are controlled in the Text Wrap panel.

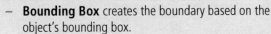

A **No Text Wrap** allows text to run directly under the object.

B **Wrap Around Bounding Box** creates a straight-edged wrap around all four sides of the object's bounding box.

C **Wrap Around Object Shape** creates a wrap in the shape of the object. You can define which contour to use in the Contour Options menu:

   – **Bounding Box** creates the boundary based on the object's bounding box.

   – **Detect Edges** creates the boundary using the same detection options you use to create a clipping path.

   – **Alpha Channel** creates the boundary from an Alpha channel saved in the placed image.

   – **Photoshop Path** creates the boundary from a path saved in the placed image.

   – **Graphic Frame** creates the boundary from the containing frame.

   – **Same as Clipping** creates the boundary from a clipping path saved in the placed image.

   – **User-Modified Path** appears by default if you drag the anchor points of the text wrap boundary.

D **Jump Object** keeps text from appearing to the right or left of the frame.

E **Jump to Next Column** forces surrounding text to the top of the next column or frame.

Regardless of which wrap you apply, you can define the offset value (the distance that any surrounding text will remain away from the object). If you use the Object Shape wrap, you can define only a single offset value. For the other types, you can define a different offset for each edge.

If you use the Bounding Box or Object Shape wrap option, you can also define the Wrap To options — whether the wrap is applied to a specific side (right, left, right and left, or the largest side), or toward or away from the spine.

By default, text wrap attributes affect all overlapping objects, regardless of stacking order. You can turn this off by checking the Text Wrap Only Affects Text Beneath option in the Composition pane of the Preferences dialog box.

Format Numbered and Bulleted Lists

Many page-layout projects include lists — resources referenced in an article, people involved in planning an event, ingredients in a recipe, steps to take in accomplishing a specific task, to name only a few. InDesign includes the ability to easily format both bulleted and numbered lists. You will use both of these options in this exercise.

1. **With newsletter-july.indd open, select all but the first paragraph in the sidebar on Page 1.**

2. **In the Properties panel, locate the Bullets and Numbering section and click the Numbered List button (the second one).**

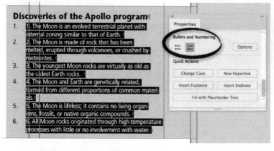

When you apply a numbered list, sequential numbers are automatically added to the beginning of each selected paragraph. The Numbering Style section of the dialog box defines how the numbers appear:

- **Format** determines what type of numbers are used (Arabic numbers, Roman numerals, etc.).

- **Number** defines the format of the list numbers; the default is "number, period, tab" (^# and #t are the special character codes for the list number and the tab character, respectively.)

- **Character Style** can be used to apply a defined style to characters in the paragraph number. Other characters in the paragraph are not affected.

- **Mode** determines how a paragraph is numbered — whether it continues from the previous numbered paragraph or begins at a specific, defined number.

- If you have more than one level of list items, you can use the **Restart Numbers...** option to reset the numbering each time you begin a new level of list items.

As you can see, each numbered paragraph now includes a number, a period, and a tab character (the same sequence that is defined in the Number field) before the actual paragraph copy. The added number characters are not selected because they do not technically exist as characters in the text.

Original numbers in the numbered paragraphs are still in place because they are simply characters in the imported text. If you apply actual numbered-list formatting to specific paragraphs, you might have to delete the original numbering characters from the layout.

The text of each numbered paragraph begins 0.5" from the left frame inset edge, as defined by default in the **Tab Position** field (in the Bullet or Number Position section). The number and period characters still appear at the left edge of the frame or frame inset.

The **Alignment** menu defines how numbers in a list align to one another. This is especially useful for aligning the periods in a regular numbered list that includes more than nine items, or a list using certain numbering formats that have different numbers of characters in each number (such as Roman numerals):

Left	Center	Right	Left	Center	Right
8.	8.	8.	vii	vii	vii
9.	9.	9.	viii	viii	viii
10.	10.	10.	ix	ix	ix
11.	11.	11.	x	x	x

Note:

You can use the Level menu at the top of the dialog box to create nested lists. For example, you could create a list of departments in a business, and then create secondary lists after each department to show the hierarchy of employees in each department:

1. *Marketing*
   a. *Harry*
   b. *Ron*
   c. *Julia*
2. *Production*
   a. *Roger*
   b. *Edward*
   c. *Caitlyn*
3. *Administration*
   a. *Stephanie*
   b. *Justin*
   c. *Betty*

3. **Click the Options button in the Properties panel to open the Bullets and Numbering dialog box.**

4. **In the Bullet or Number Position section, change the First Line Indent field to -0.125 in, and then change the Left Indent field to 0.125 in.**

You have to change the First Line Indent field first because you cannot define a left indent that is smaller than the first-line indent.

A negative first-line indent moves the first line to the left of the others in the same paragraph, sometimes called a **hanging indent**. When applied to a numbered list, the negative first-line indent defines the position of the number character(s) relative to the actual text in each list item.

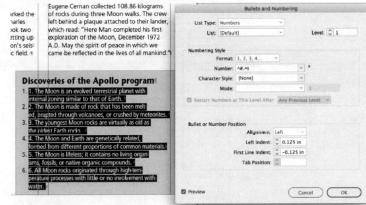

If you define a negative first-line indents the Tab Position field is cleared. The left-indent value becomes the default first tab position and the position of text immediately following the number character(s).

5. **Click OK to finalize the list formatting and return to the layout.**

6. **Delete the extra numbers, periods, and spaces from the beginning of each list item.**

7. **Navigate to Page 2 of the layout and make sure nothing is selected.**

8. **Choose File>Place. Select `blackbird-airpark.doc`, uncheck the Show Import Options box, and then click Open. Click Close if you get a Missing Font warning.**

9. **Click the loaded cursor within the margin guides on the right side of Page 2.**

10. **Format the first paragraph with the Back Head style and the remaining copy with the Back Copy style.**

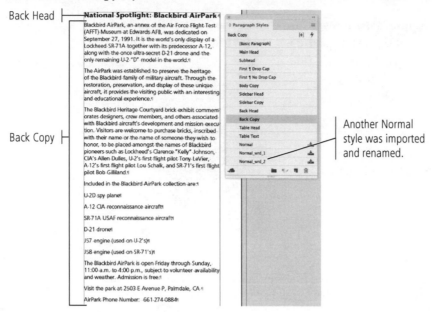

Back Head

Back Copy

Another Normal style was imported and renamed.

11. **Select the six paragraphs as shown in the following image. In the Properties panel, click the Bulleted List button.**

12. **Click the Options button in the Properties panel to open the Bullets and Numbering dialog box.**

13. **In the Bullet Character section, choose the small star character.**

In addition to the options you saw for numbered lists, you can also choose the specific glyph to use as the bullet character. InDesign includes several common bullet characters by default. You can click the Add button to add different characters from any available font.

14. **In the Bullet or Number Position section, change the First Line Indent field to -0.125 in.**

Keep in mind that you can't define a negative First Line Indent unless the Left Indent field is greater than 0. Because the Left Indent field defaults to 0.25 in you can simply change the First Line Indent field.

15. **Click OK to close the dialog box and return to the document window.**

16. **Save the file and continue to the next stage of the project.**

STAGE 3 / Working with Tables

Many page layouts incorporate tables of information, from basic tables with a few rows and columns to multipage catalog spreadsheets with thousands of product numbers and prices. InDesign includes a number of options for building tables directly in a page layout.

If the insertion point is placed in an existing text frame, you can create a new table by choosing Table>Insert Table. If the insertion point is not placed, you can choose Table>Create Table. These methods allow you to define your own table parameters, including the number of rows and columns, the number of header and footer rows (top and bottom rows that appear in every instance of the table if it breaks across multiple columns or frames), and even a defined style for the new table (table styles store formatting options, such as gridline weight and other attributes that will you learn about in this stage of the project). Using the Insert Table command, the new table is placed at the current insertion point. Using the Create Table command, the resulting table is loaded into the Place cursor — you can click and drag to create the text frame and place the loaded table.

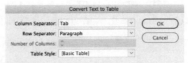

You can also create a table by selecting a series of tab-delimited (meaning, each column is separated by a tab) text in the layout and choosing Table>Convert Text to Table. Using this method, the new table becomes an inline object in the text frame that contained the original text.

Finally, you can create a new table by placing a file created in Microsoft Excel (the most common application for creating spreadsheets). You'll use this method to complete this stage of the newsletter project.

Place a Microsoft Excel Table

Microsoft Excel spreadsheets can be short tables of text or complex, multipage spreadsheets of data. In either case, Microsoft Excel users tend to spend hours formatting their spreadsheets for business applications. Those formatting options are typically not appropriate for commercial printing applications, but they give you a better starting point in your InDesign file than working from plain tabbed text.

1. **With newsletter-july.indd open, navigate to Page 2. Click the pasteboard area to make sure nothing is selected.**

2. **Choose File>Place and navigate to the file contacts.xls in the WIP>Aerospace folder.**

3. **Uncheck the Replace Selected Item option, make sure Show Import Options is checked, and then click Open.**

Note:

4. **Review the options in the resulting dialog box. Make sure your options match what is shown in the following image, and then click OK.**

If you see a warning about missing fonts, click OK — you're going to reformat the table text shortly.

5. **With the table loaded into the cursor, click in the pasteboard area to the right of Page 2 (near the top of the page edge).**

This table will eventually occupy the empty space in the bottom-right corner of Page 2. You are simply using the pasteboard as a temporary workspace.

When you place a table into a layout, a text frame is automatically created to contain it. The new frame matches the width of the defined page margins, regardless of the actual table width. If the page has multiple columns defined, the frame matches the defined column width.

Obviously this table needs some significant modification to make it a cohesive part of the newsletter layout. Some placed tables require more work than others, but be prepared to do at least some clean-up work whenever you place a spreadsheet or table.

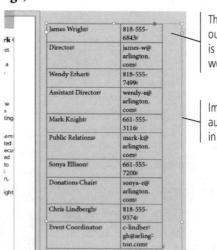

The pasteboard outside the page area is a good temporary workspace.

Imported tables are automatically placed in a text frame.

Note:

If you select the text frame containing a table, you can choose Object>Fitting>Fit Frame to Content to match the text frame dimensions to the table contained in the frame.

6. **Select the Type tool and click in the top-left cell of the table.**

You can use the Type tool to select table cells, either individually or as entire rows/columns.

7. **Move the cursor to the top-left corner of the table. When you see a diagonal pointing arrow, click to select the entire table.**

The heavy diagonal arrow indicates that clicking will select the entire table.

The insertion point must be placed in the table to access the selection cursors.

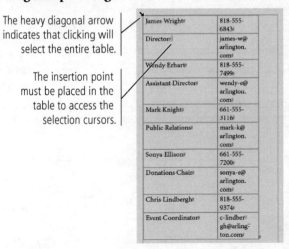

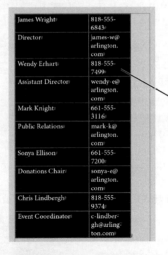

After clicking, all cells in the table are selected.

Note:

Text is still text, even though it's placed inside a table cell. You can apply all of the same text-formatting options to table text that you can apply to text in a regular text frame.

8. **Click Table Text in the Paragraph Styles panel to format all the text in the selected table cells.**

When you work with tables in InDesign, think of the table cells as a series of text frames. Text in a table cell is no different than text in any other text frame — it can be formatted using the same options you've already learned, including with paragraph and character styles.

9. **Click any cell to deselect all table cells.**

10. **Save the file and continue to the next exercise.**

Note:

Your table might not look exactly like what you see in our screen captures. You will be adjusting the formatting in the next exercises.

 ## Format Cell Attributes

As we mentioned in the previous exercise, table cells are very similar to regular text frames. Individual cells can have different attributes, such as height and width, text inset, vertical positioning, and text orientation.

1. **With newsletter-july.indd open, click in the top-left cell of the table with the Type tool.**

2. **Place the cursor over the top edge of the first column of the table. When you see a down-pointing arrow, click to select the entire column.**

You can also select rows by placing the cursor immediately to the left of a row and clicking when the cursor changes to a right-facing arrow.

The down-pointing arrow means clicking will select the entire column.

3. **Open the Table panel (Window>Type & Tables>Table).**

4. **With the left column selected, change the Column Width field to 1.25 in.**

Resizing the width of a cell resizes the entire column. Resizing the height of a cell resizes the entire row.

You don't need to select the entire column to change its width. However, in the next step you are going to change the height of each row — you are selecting all cells in the column now, so that they will all be affected by the height change in the next step.

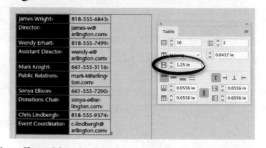

5. **Choose Exactly in the Row Height menu, then change the field to 0.235 in.**

Table row height uses the At Least method by default, which means they expand or shrink (down to the defined minimum) to accommodate the text in the cells.

Because you defined a row height using the Exactly method, the row height is now a specific value. The email addresses in the right column no longer fit in the existing cell width, as you can see from the overset text icons in every other cell.

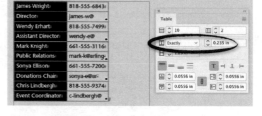

6. **Click to place the insertion point in any cell in the right column.**

The column does not need to be selected to change its width, either by dragging or using the field in the Table panel.

7. **Place the cursor over the right edge of the second column until the cursor becomes a two-headed arrow.**

When you see this cursor, you can drag the gridline to resize a column or row.

8. **Click and drag right until all of the overset text icons are gone.**

You have to release the mouse button to see the results. If you still see the overset text icons after you release the mouse button, click and drag the edge again until the overset text icons are gone.

The two-headed arrow means you can drag to resize a row or column.

9. **Place the insertion point in any cell in the left column, then choose Table>Insert>Column.**

The insertion point should be placed in any cell in the first column.

10. **In the resulting dialog box, make sure the Number field is set to 1 and choose the Left option.**

11. **Click OK to return to the table.**

As you can see, one new column is added to the left of the previous selection.

12. **Place the insertion point in the top cell of the new column and type ArAA CONTACTS.**

13. **Click Table Head in the Paragraph Styles panel to format the new text.**

The overset text icon shows that the text, with the Table Head formatting applied, does not fit into the cell.

14. **Select the entire first column in the table. In the Properties panel, locate the Cell Divisions options and click the Merge Cells button.**

This function extends the contents of a single cell across multiple cells. You can also choose Table>Merge Cells, or use the same command in the Table panel Options menu.

All cells in the active selection are now combined.

A Split Cells Horizontally
B Split Cells Vertically
C Merge Cells
D Unmerge Cells

15. **Click to place the insertion point in the merged table cell. In the Table panel, click the Rotate 270° button.**

The Text Rotation buttons rotate text clockwise within a cell. Icons on each button indicate the resulting orientation of text in the selected cells.

16. **Click the top cell of the second column, hold down the mouse button, and drag down to also select the second cell in that column.**

You can use the click-and-drag method to select any range of consecutive cells, including cells in more than one row or column.

17. **Click the Merge Cells button in the Properties panel.**

When you merge cells, the content in each selected cell is combined into the merged cell. Each cell's content is separated by a paragraph return.

Click here...

...then drag to here.

18. **Repeat Steps 16–17 for the other name/title cells in the second column.**

19. **Select all cells in the table, then click the Align Center vertical alignment button in the Table panel.**

Because the text in the left column is rotated, this option actually aligns the text between the left and right cell edges. It is important to remember that the vertical align options are based on the orientation of the text.

20. **Save the file and continue to the next exercise.**

Manage a Table as an Anchored Character

Tables in InDesign are always contained in a text frame. The table itself is an anchored object, and is treated as a single character in the text frame's story. Rather than using multiple frames to contain different elements in the newsletter layout, you are going to move the table into the story on Page 2 of the existing layout.

1. **With newsletter-july.indd open, make sure the Type tool is active.**

2. **Click inside the text frame that contains the table, but below the actual table.**

   This places the insertion point in the frame, but not in the table.

3. **Press Command/Control-A to select everything in the text frame.**

   The table is placed in the frame, but it exists as a single character in that frame (just like anchored graphics).

The character representing the table is selected.

4. **Press Command/Control-X to cut the selected element and store it in the clipboard.**

5. **Click with the Type tool to place the insertion point in the last paragraph on Page 2 of the newsletter layout.**

   The end-of-story character appears on its own line, indicating that an empty paragraph exists after the one with the phone number. You should place the insertion point in that empty paragraph.

Place the insertion point in the empty paragraph at the end of Page 2.

6. **Press Command/Control-V to paste the table that you cut in Step 4. If necessary, drag down the bottom-center handle of the containing text frame until the table is visible.**

If necessary, extend the containing frame's height to fit the table.

7. **Using the Type tool, click to place the insertion point in any cell in the table.**

8. **Place the cursor over the right edge of the left column, then click and drag until the right edge of the table matches the margin guide. If you see an overset text icon in the cell, drag the edge slightly right until the icon is gone.**

   It's a good idea to make a table fit into the overall layout. In this case, you are adjusting the table to better match the margin guides of the page on which it is placed.

Drag the right edge of the left column.

Watch the right edge of the table to see when it aligns to the margin guide.

9. **Place the cursor over the bottom edge of the bottom row, then click and drag until the bottom edge of the table matches the margin guide.**

   When you reduce the height of the final row, two things happen. First, the text in the bottom-right cell no longer fits into the adjusted cell height. Second, the rows are no longer the same height, which looks like an error.

Drag up the bottom edge of the last row.

The last row is no longer the same height as the others.

Text no longer fits based on the adjusted row height.

10. **Select the entire right column, then choose Table>Distribute Rows Evenly.**

    This command calculates the overall height of the selection, and then divides that space evenly over all selected rows — the height of the overall table does not change. All rows in the selection now have the same height, and all text fits.

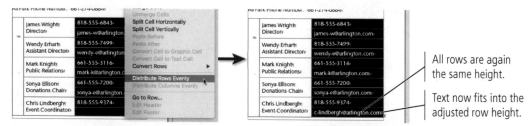

All rows are again the same height.

Text now fits into the adjusted row height.

   If more than one column is selected, you can choose Table>Distribute Columns evenly to make multiple columns the same width.

11. **Using the Selection tool, click the empty frame on the pasteboard to select it, and then press Delete/Backspace.**

    Although not strictly necessary, it's a good idea to remove unnecessary elements from the file, including the pasteboard around the actual layout pages.

12. **Save the file and continue to the next exercise.**

Define Table Fills and Strokes

Like text frames, table cells can have fill and stroke attributes. InDesign includes a number of options for adding color to tables, from changing the stroke and fill of an individual cell to defining patterns that repeat over a certain number of rows or columns.

1. **With newsletter-july.indd open, place the insertion point anywhere in the table on Page 2. Open the Table panel Options menu and choose Table Options>Table Setup.**

Note:

You can also choose Table>Table Options> Table Setup to access this dialog box.

2. **In the Table Setup tab, apply a 0.5-pt solid border of 100% Pantone 194 C.**

3. **In the Fills tab, choose Every Second Row in the Alternating Pattern menu. Set the First field to 2 rows and apply 20% Pantone 194 C. Set the Next field to 2 rows and apply None as the color.**

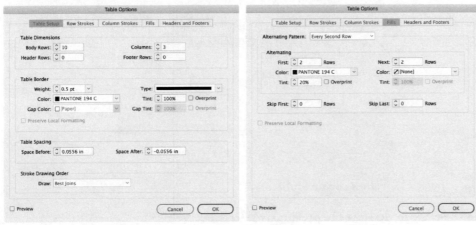

Step 2   Step 3

4. **Click OK to apply your choices.**

   When frame edges are visible, it's difficult (if not impossible) to see the table border and cell strokes.

5. **Select the left column in the table. Using the Swatches panel, change the cell fill tint to 100% of the Pantone 194 C swatch.**

   You can change the color of cell fills and strokes using the Swatches panel, and you can change the cell stroke attributes using the Stroke panel.

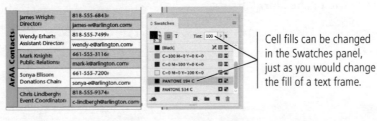

Cell fills can be changed in the Swatches panel, just as you would change the fill of a text frame.

6. **Select all cells in the table. Open the Table panel Options menu and choose Cell Options>Strokes and Fills.**

7. **In the preview area of the dialog box, click to make sure all lines in the preview area are active.**

The preview area shows which strokes you are affecting in the dialog box. When a line is blue, it is active, which means your changes will affect those lines in the selection. If a line is black, it is not active and your changes will not affect those lines.

You can click any line in the preview to toggle it between active and inactive.

8. **Apply a 0.25-pt, 100% Pantone 194 C stroke value, using the Solid stroke type.**

These settings change the attributes of all gridlines for all selected cells.

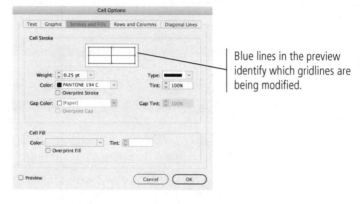

Blue lines in the preview identify which gridlines are being modified.

9. **Click OK to apply the stroke values to your table.**

10. **Click any cell in the table to deselect the previously selected cells.**

11. **Using the menu at the bottom of the Tools panel, activate the Preview option.**

The Preview option hides all non-printing elements, including guides, invisible characters, and frame edges. This makes it easier to get an accurate preview of your table.

12. **Restore the file to the Normal view mode.**

13. **Save the file and continue to the next stage of the project.**

Moving Table Rows and Columns

When a table row or column is selected, moving the cursor over any cell in the selection shows a special Move cursor. You can click and drag the selection to reposition it elsewhere in the table. As you drag, a heavy blue line indicates where the moved selection will be placed when you release the mouse button.

Drag a selected row or column.

Release the mouse button to move the selection.

Managing Table Setup

The Table Setup tab of the Table Options dialog box defines the table dimensions, table border, spacing above and below the table, and how strokes are applied to the table. The **Stroke Drawing Order** option allows you to control behavior where gridlines meet. If Best Joins is selected, styled strokes such as double lines result in joined strokes and gaps.

Best Joins

Row Strokes in Front

Column Strokes in Front

Creating Graphic Cells

When you select one or more cells with no existing content (or the insertion point is placed in a cell with no content), you can choose Table>Convert Cell to Graphic Cell. The active cells become empty graphics cells, identified by crossed diagonal lines when frame edges are visible (View>Extras>Show Frame Edges).

Empty graphics cells show crossed diagonal lines.

Controlling Cell Attributes

Basic attributes of table cells can be defined in the Text tab of the Cell Options dialog box. Most of these are exactly the same as those for regular text frames — the only choice unique to tables is **Clip Contents to Cell**. If you set a fixed row height that is too small for the cell content, an overset text icon appears in the lower-right corner of the cell. (You can't flow text from one table cell to another.) If you check the Clip Contents to Cell option, any content that doesn't fit in the cell will be clipped.

As with any text frame, a table cell can have its own fill and stroke attributes. These attributes can be defined in the Strokes and Fills tab (or using the Swatches and Stroke panels). You can turn individual cell edges (strokes) on or off by clicking specific lines in the preview.

The Rows and Columns tab controls row height and column width. If **At Least** is selected in the Row Height menu, you can define the minimum and maximum possible row height. Rows change height if you add or remove text, or if you change the text formatting in a way that requires more or less space. If **Exactly** is selected, you can define the exact height of the cell.

If you're working with an extremely long table, you can break the table across multiple frames by threading (as you would for any long block of text). **Keep Options** can be used to keep specific (selected) rows together after a break, and to determine where those rows will go, based on your choice in the Start Row menu.

You can add diagonal lines to specific cells using the Diagonal Lines tab. You can apply lines in either direction (or both), and choose a specific stroke weight, color, style, and tint. The Draw menu determines whether the line is created in front of, or behind, the cell's contents.

Working with Table Styles

If you've spent any amount of time refining the appearance of a table, and you think you might want to use the same format again, you can save your choices as a style. InDesign supports both table and cell styles, which are controlled in the Table Styles and Cell Styles panels.

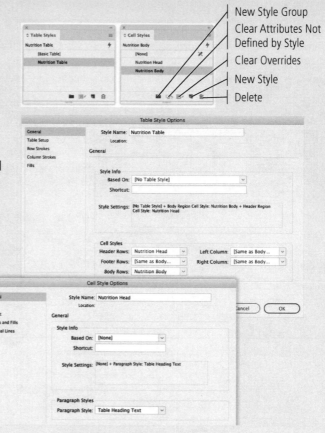

New Style Group

Clear Attributes Not Defined by Style

Clear Overrides

New Style

Delete

Table and cell styles use the same concept as text-formatting styles. You can apply a cell style by selecting the cells and clicking the style name in the Cell Styles panel. Clicking a style in the Table Styles panel applies the style to the entire selected table.

Table styles store all options that can be defined in the Table Setup dialog box (except the options for header and footer rows). You can also define cell styles (called **nesting styles**) for specific types of rows, as well as the left and right columns in the table.

Cell styles store all options that can be defined in the Cell Options dialog box, including the paragraph style that is applied to cells where that style is applied.

Creating Table Headers and Footers

You can break a table across multiple frames, using repeating headers and footers for information that needs to be part of each instance of the table (for example, headings). Repeating headers and footers eliminate the need to manually insert the repeating information in each instance of the table.

Repeating header and footer rows are dynamically linked, meaning that changing one instance of a header or footer — either its content or formatting — changes all instances of that header or footer.

Finally, this capability also means the headers and footers remain at the top and bottom of each instance, even if other body rows move to a different instance.

You can add new header and footer rows to a table when you create it, or by changing the options in the Headers and Footers tab of the Table Options dialog box. You can also convert existing rows to headers or footers by selecting one or more rows, and choosing Table>Convert Rows>To Header or To Footer. These elements can be defined in the Headers and Footers dialog box.

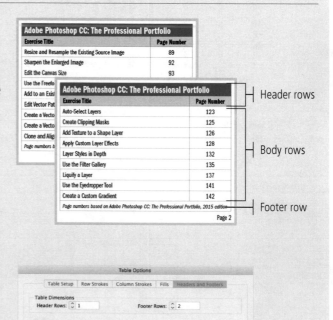

STAGE 4 / **Preflighting and Job Packaging**

When you submit an InDesign layout to a commercial output provider, you need to send all of the necessary pieces of the job — the layout file, any placed (linked) graphics or other files, and the fonts used in the layout. Before you copy everything to a disk and send it out, however, you should check your work to make sure the file is ready for commercial printing.

When you opened the original template at the beginning of this project, you replaced missing fonts and graphics — two of the most common problems with digital layout files. However, successful output on a commercial press has a number of other technical requirements that, if you ignore them, can cause a file to output incorrectly — or not at all. InDesign includes a preflighting utility that makes it easy to check for potential errors, as well as a packaging utility that gathers all of the necessary bits for the printer.

Define a Preflight Profile

InDesign includes a built-in preflighting utility that can check for common errors as you build a file. If you introduce a problem while building a file, the bottom-left corner of the document window shows a red light and the number of potential errors. In the following exercise, you define a profile to check for errors based on the information you have. This is certainly not an exhaustive check for all possible output problems. You should always work closely with your output provider to build responsible files that will cause no problems in the output workflow.

> **Note:**
>
> *Ask your output provider if they have defined an InDesign preflight profile that you can load into your application to check for the problems that will interrupt their specific workflows.*

1. **With newsletter-july.indd open, look at the bottom-left corner of the document window.**

2. **Click the arrow to the right of the No Errors message and choose Preflight Panel from the menu.**

   The message currently shows no errors, but at this point you don't know exactly what is being checked. The Preflight panel provides an interface for defining preflight profiles, as well as reviewing the specific issues identified as errors.

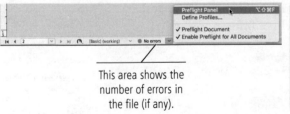

This area shows the number of errors in the file (if any).

Click this button to embed the current profile into the active document.

The Preflight panel shows which profile is being used to check for errors.

3. **Open the Preflight panel Options menu and choose Define Profiles.**

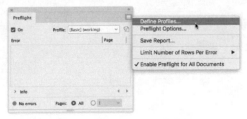

4. **In the Preflight Profiles dialog box, click the "+" button in the left side of the dialog box to create a new profile.**

Rather than relying on generic, built-in profiles, you should be aware of and able to control exactly what is (and is not) flagged as an error.

You can use these buttons to create a new preflight profile (+) or delete an existing preflight profile (−). The preflight profile menu(≡) has options to load an external profile, export an existing one, or embed one into the active document.

5. **Type ArAA Check in the Profile Name field, and then click the empty area below the list of profiles to finalize the new name.**

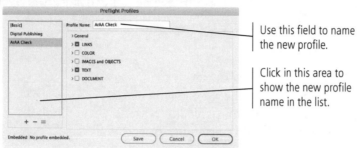

Use this field to name the new profile.

Click in this area to show the new profile name in the list.

6. **With the ArAA Check profile selected on the left side of the dialog box, expand the General category on the right. Highlight the existing text in the Description field, and then type Verify newsletter for 4c press.**

Use these arrows to expand the various categories.

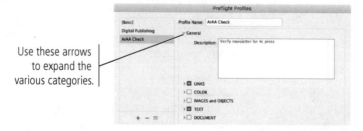

Note:

This description is simply a reminder of the profile's intent.

7. **Collapse the General category and expand the Links category. Check the Links Missing or Modified option, and uncheck all other options.**

Image files placed in a layout need to be available when the job is output. By checking this option, you are warned if any placed image has been moved or modified since it was placed into the layout.

Note:

Some users have reported difficulty expanding various categories in the Preflight Profiles dialog box. Try clicking inside the arrow shape to work around this minor bug.

Click inside the arrow shape.

8. **Collapse the Links category and expand the Color category. Uncheck all options in this category, then check and expand the Color Spaces and Modes Not Allowed option. Check only the RGB and Spot Color options.**

Note:

Some output processes use a method called in-RIP separation to convert RGB images to CMYK during the output process. However, the conversion process can cause significant color shift if it is not controlled.

You know this newsletter is going to be output as a four-color job. Spot colors will create an extra separation, which can be a very costly error. By setting these options, you will receive a warning if you create a spot color in a job that should be output as four-color.

To achieve the best-quality, predictable output, it's a good idea to check for RGB images and control the conversion process in an image-editing application (i.e., Photoshop).

9. **Collapse the Color category and expand the Images and Objects category. Uncheck all but the Image Resolution option, and then expand the it. Check the three Minimum Resolution options. Change the Color and Grayscale minimums to 300 and change the 1-bit option to 1200.**

Remember, commercial output devices typically require at least 300 ppi to output raster images at good quality. By setting these minimum restrictions, you will receive a warning if your (or your client's) images do not have enough resolution to output at good quality using most commercial printing processes.

Note:

Remember that required resolution is actually two times the line screen (lpi) used for a specific job. If possible, always ask your service provider what resolution to use for your job. If you don't know the lpi (and can't find out in advance), 300 ppi is a safe choice for most printing projects.

10. **Collapse the Images and Objects category and expand the Text category. Check only the Overset Text and Font Missing options.**

Overset text could simply be the result of extra paragraph returns at the end of a story. However, you should always check these issues to be sure that some of the client's text has not been accidentally overset.

11. **Collapse the Text category and expand the Document category. Check the Number of Pages Required option. Expand that option, choose Exactly in the menu, and then type 2 in the field.**

You know that every issue of the newsletter should be exactly 2 pages. If your file has fewer, or more than, 2 pages, you will receive an error message.

12. **Click OK to save the profile and close the dialog box.**

13. **Continue to the next exercise.**

The Preflight Profiles dialog box includes a number of options for identifying potential errors. If you are going to build responsible files, you should have a basic understanding of what these options mean. The following discussion is by no means an exhaustive one of all potential problems in digital page-layout files; rather, it's a list of the problems Adobe included in the Preflight Profile dialog box. Other problems are beyond the scope of most graphic designers and are better left to prepress professionals to correct, given the specific equipment conditions in their workflows.

You should also realize that some of these issues are not necessarily errors, but nonetheless should be reviewed before a job is output. For example, blank pages might be intentionally placed into a document to force a chapter opener onto a right-facing page, which would not be an error. In other cases, a blank page might be left over after text is edited, and the blank page would be an error.

Links

- **Links Missing or Modified.** Use this option to receive a warning if a placed file has been moved (missing) or changed (modified) since it was placed into a layout. If a placed file is missing, the output will use only the low-resolution screen preview. If a placed file has been modified, the output will reflect the most up-to-date version of it, which could be drastically different from the original.

- **Inaccessible URL Links.** Use this option to find hyperlinks that might cause problems if you are creating an interactive PDF document.

- **OPI Links.** OPI is a workflow tool that allows designers to use low-resolution FPO (for placement only) files during the design stage. When the job is processed for output, the high-resolution versions are swapped out in place of the FPO images. Although not terribly common anymore, some larger agencies still use OPI workflows.

Document

- **Page Size and Orientation.** Use this option to cause an error if the document size is not a specific size. You can also cause an error if the current document is oriented in a way other than the defined page size (i.e., portrait instead of landscape, or vice versa).

- **Number of Pages Required.** Use this option to define a specific number of pages, the smallest number of pages that can be in the document, or whether the document must have pages in multiples of a specific number.

- **Blank Pages.** Use this option to find blank pages in the document.

- **Bleed and Slug Setup.** Use this option to verify the document's bleed and slug sizes against values required by a specific output process.

- **All Pages Must Use Same Size and Orientation.** Because InDesign supports multiple page sizes in the same document, you can check this option to verify that all pages in the file have the same size.

Color

- **Transparency Blending Space Required.** Use this option to define whether CMYK or RGB should be used to flatten transparent objects for output.

- **Cyan, Magenta, or Yellow Plates Not Allowed.** Use this option to verify layouts that will be output with only spot colors, or with black and spot colors.

- **Color Spaces and Modes Not Allowed.** Use this option to create errors if the layout uses RGB, CMYK, Spot Color, Gray, or LAB color models. (Different jobs have different defined color spaces. The option to flag CMYK as an error can be useful, for example, if you are building a layout that will be output in black only.)

- **Spot Color Setup.** Use this option to define the number of spot colors a job should include, as well as the specific color model that should be used (LAB or CMYK) when converting unwanted spot colors for process printing.

- **Overprinting Applied in InDesign.** Use this option to create an error if an element is set to overprint instead of trap.

- **Overprinting Applied to White or [Paper] Color.** By definition, White or [Paper] is technically the absence of other inks. Unless you are printing white toner or opaque spot ink, white cannot, by definition, overprint. Use this option to produce an error if White or [Paper] elements are set to overprint.

- **[Registration] Applied.** The [Registration] color swatch is a special swatch used for elements, such as crop and registration marks. Any element that uses the [Registration] color will output on all separations in the job. Use this option to find elements that are incorrectly colored with the [Registration] color, instead of (probably) black.

Images and Objects

- **Image Resolution.** Use this option to identify placed files with too little or too much resolution. As you know, commercial output devices typically require 300 ppi to output properly. The maximum resolution options can be used to find objects that, typically through scaling, result in unnecessarily high resolutions that might take considerable time for the output device to process.

- **Non-Proportional Scaling of Placed Object.** Use this option to find placed files that have been scaled with different X and Y percentages.

- **Uses Transparency.** Use this option to find any element affected by transparency. You should carefully preview transparency flattening before outputting the job.

- **Image ICC Profile.** Use this option to find placed images that have embedded ICC profiles. Typically used in color-managed workflows, placed images often store information — in the form of profiles — about the way a particular device captured or created the color in that image. You can cause errors if the image profile results in CMYK conversion, or if the embedded image profile has been overridden in the layout.

- **Layer Visibility Overrides.** Use this option to find layered Photoshop files in which the visibility of specific layers has been changed within InDesign.

- **Minimum Stroke Weight.** There is a limit to the smallest visible line that can be produced by any given output device. Use this option to find objects with a stroke weight smaller than a specific point size.

- **Interactive Elements.** Use this option to find elements with interactive properties.

- **Bleed/Trim Hazard.** Use this option to find elements that fall within a defined distance of the page edge or spine for facing-page layouts (i.e., outside the live area).

- **Hidden Page Items.** Use this option to create an error if any objects on a page are not currently visible.

Text

- **Overset Text.** Use this option to find any frames with overset text.

- **Paragraph Style and Character Style Overrides.** Use this option to find instances where an applied style has been overridden with local formatting.

- **Font Missing.** Use this option to create an error if any required font is not available on the computer.

- **Glyph Missing.** Use this option to identify glyphs that aren't available.

- **Dynamic Spelling Detects Errors.** Use this option to cause an error if InDesign's dynamic spelling utility identifies any errors in the document.

- **Font Types Not Allowed.** Use this option to prohibit specific font types that can cause problems in modern output workflows.

- **Non-Proportional Type Scaling.** Use this option to identify type that has been artificially stretched or compressed in one direction (i.e., where horizontal or vertical scaling has been applied).

- **Minimum Type Size.** Use this option to identify any type set smaller than a defined point size. You can also identify small type that requires more than one ink to reproduce (a potential registration problem on commercial output devices).

- **Cross-References.** Use this option to identify dynamic links from one location in a file to another. You can cause errors if a cross-reference is out of date or unresolved.

- **Conditional Text Indicators Will Print.** Use this option to create an error if certain visual indicators will appear in the final output.

- **Unresolved Caption Variable.** Use this option to find dynamic caption variables for which there is no defined metadata.

- **Span Columns Setting Not Honored.** Use this option to find paragraphs with a defined column-span setting that is prevented by other objects on the page.

- **Tracked Change.** Use this option to find instances of text that has been changed, but not accepted when Track Changes is enabled.

Evaluate the Layout

Now that you have defined the issues that you know are errors, you can check your file for those and make the necessary corrections.

1. **With newsletter-july.indd open, click the Profile menu in the Preflight panel and choose ArAA Check as the profile to use.**

2. **In the bottom of the panel, make sure the All radio button is checked.**

   When the All option is active, the entire document is checked. You can use the other radio button to define a specific page or range of pages to preflight.

   As soon as you call the ArAA Check profile, the panel reports 13 errors.

This pane lists the problem categories that caused the errors.

The now-active profile results in 13 errors.

Use this option to check only certain pages.

Note:

Preflight profiles become part of the application, but are not linked to or saved in a specific document unless you intentionally embed the profile.

3. **Expand the Info section of the Preflight panel.**

   This area offers information about a specific error and suggestions for fixing the problem.

4. **Click the arrow to expand the Color list, and then click the arrow to expand the Color Space Not Allowed list.**

5. **Click the first text frame listing to select it, and then click the hot-text page number for that item.**

   The hot-text link on the right side of the Preflight panel changes the document window to show the specific item that caused the error.

Click the hot-text link to navigate to a specific instance of the problem.

6. **In the Swatches panel, Control/right-click the Pantone 534 C swatch and choose Swatch Options from the contextual menu.**

You can also double-click the swatch name to open the Swatch Options dialog box for that swatch.

Note:

Spot colors are not always errors. Check the project's specifications carefully before you convert spot colors to process. Also, be aware that spot colors are often outside the CMYK gamut — converting a spot color to process can result in drastic color shift.

7. **In the Swatch Options dialog box, choose CMYK in the Color Mode menu and then change the Color Type menu to Process.**

Because this swatch exists only in the layout file and not in any of the placed images, you can change the swatch color mode, type, and name.

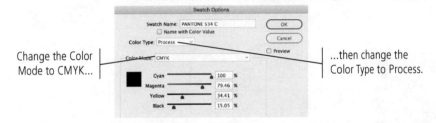

Change the Color Mode to CMYK...

...then change the Color Type to Process.

Note:

If a spot-color swatch was used in a placed file, you would only be able to change the Color Type menu in InDesign.

8. **Click OK to apply the new swatch options.**

Four of the errors have been corrected by fixing this single issue.

The former spot color now shows the process-color icon.

9. **Repeat Steps 6–8 for the remaining spot color in the InDesign file.**

10. **Select the remaining color problem instance in the Preflight panel and click the hot-text link to show that element in the layout.**

When you overrode all master page items on Page 1, you created two instances of the placed highlight-july.tif file — the original one on the master page and the one on Page 1 of the layout. The Preflight panel shows only the item on Page 1 as an error because that is the file that will be used for output.

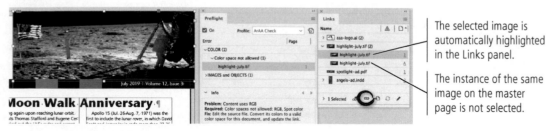

The selected image is automatically highlighted in the Links panel.

The instance of the same image on the master page is not selected.

11. **In the Links panel, click the Relink button. Navigate to highlight-july-cmyk.tif (in the WIP>Aerospace>CMYK folder) and click Open. If you see the Image Import Options dialog box, click OK to accept the default options.**

After the image has been relinked, all of the color problems have been corrected. Because the preflight process only considers elements that will be included in the actual output, the original highlight-july.tif file (which is still an RGB file) is not considered an error as it exists only on the master page. The Color listing no longer appears in the Preflight panel.

12. **Expand the Images and Objects category, and then expand the Image Resolution listing. Click the page link to navigate to the problem file.**

This image is a placed PDF file, supplied by your client. The Links panel shows that the image is 280 ppi, which is lower than the minimum 300 that you defined for this file.

In this case, the 280 ppi will probably be enough to produce good quality. However, in many instances, supplied-image resolution will be far below what you need for commercial printing. Low resolution is a common problem with client-supplied images. Because the placed image is a PDF file, you can't access the individual components and make changes — you would have to contact the client to resolve the problem.

The placed PDF file does not meet the minimum resolution that you defined in the profile.

13. **Save the file and continue to the next exercise.**

Create the Job Package

After you have corrected potential output problems, you can package the project for the output provider. As we have already stated, the images and fonts used in a layout must be available on the computer used to output the job. When you send the layout file to the printer, you must also send the necessary components. InDesign includes a Package utility that makes this process very easy.

1. **With newsletter-july.indd open, choose File>Package.**

2. **Review the information in the Package dialog box and then click Package.**

    If you had not preflighted the file before opening the Package dialog box, you would see warning icons identifying problems with image color space or missing fonts. Because you completed the previous exercise, however, potential errors have been fixed, so this dialog box simply shows a summary list of information about the file you are packaging. You can use the list on the left to review the specifics of individual categories.

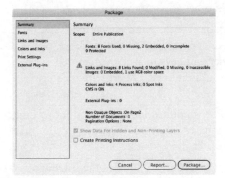

Note:

If you check the Create Printing Instructions option, clicking the Package button opens a secondary dialog box where you can define those instructions.

3. **If you see a message asking you to save, click Save.**

4. **In the resulting dialog box, navigate to your WIP>Aerospace folder as the target location.**

5. **Change the Save As/Folder Name field to Newsletter July Finished.**

    This field defines the name of the folder that will be created. All files for the job will be copied into this folder.

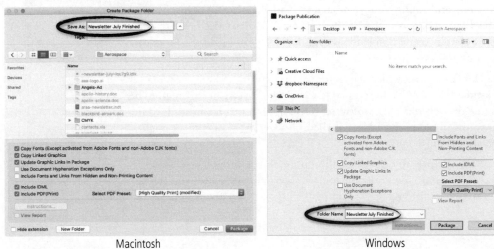

Macintosh   Windows

6. **Review the options at the bottom of the dialog box.**

These options determine what will be included in the packaged job folder.

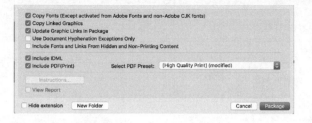

- **Copy Fonts (Except Activated Adobe Fonts and non-Adobe CJK Fonts).** When checked, this option results in a secondary Document Fonts folder to contain the font files that are used in the InDesign file. If placed graphics require specific fonts, those will also be copied into the job package.

   If you hand off the job package folder to another user (or if someone sends you a job package), the fonts in the collected Document Fonts folder will be available in InDesign when you open the packaged INDD file — even if those fonts are not installed at the computer's system level. These **document-installed fonts** are installed when the related document is opened and uninstalled when you close that file. These fonts supersede any existing font of the same PostScript name within the document. Document-installed fonts are not available to other documents or in other applications.

   As the name of this item suggests, Adobe (Typekit) and non-Adobe CJK (Chinese/Japanese/Korean) fonts are not copied into the job package. If you send a file to other InDesign users, they will have to sync the required Typekit fonts using their own Creative Cloud subscriptions, or license the required CJK fonts.

- **Copy Linked Graphics.** When checked, all linked files are copied into a Links folder in the job package folder. If you have placed InDesign files in your main layout, any graphics used in those files will also be copied into the job package.

- **Update Graphic Links in Package.** When checked, links in the InDesign file are changed to refer to the new copied link files (in the job package Links folder). If this option is not checked, the links still point to the original placed file, which might cause a missing-file warning when you send the job package to another user (or open the file at a later time).

- **Use Document Hyphenation Exceptions Only.** If another user opens your InDesign file, hyphenation exceptions in that user's version of InDesign will automatically apply to the file. If you have defined custom hyphenation exceptions, you can check this option to prevent another users settings from overriding the ones you define in a specific layout.

- **Include Fonts and Links from Hidden and Non-Printing Content.** This option packages elements that are either not visible, or have been set to not print (for example, content in hidden conditional text, or on a layer for which the Print option has been disabled).

- **Include IDML.** IDML, which stands for InDesign Markup Language, is a special format that allows a file created in the current release of InDesign to be opened in older versions of the software. Keep in mind that features added in later versions will not be available in earlier software, so the document might lose elements of the design.

- **Include PDF (Print).** You can check this option to automatically create a PDF at the same time you create the job package. When checked, you can also choose the specific PDF Preset containing the export settings you want to use.

7. **At the bottom of the dialog box, make sure the Copy Fonts, Copy Linked Graphics, and Update Graphic Links options are checked.**

8. **Uncheck the Include IDML and Include PDF (Print) options, and then click Package.**

    When you create a job package, InDesign automatically creates a new folder for the job.

9. **Read the resulting warning and click OK.**

    As with any software, you purchase a license to use a font — you do not own the actual font. It is illegal to distribute fonts freely, as it is illegal to distribute copies of your software. Most (but not all) font licenses allow you to send your copy of a font to a service provider, as long as the service provider also owns a copy of the font. Always verify that you are not violating font copyright before submitting a job.

    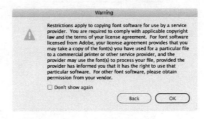

    When the process is complete, the necessary job elements appear in the job folder (in your WIP>Aerospace folder).

10. **Close the InDesign file.**

PROJECT REVIEW

fill in the blank

1. An image file that has been renamed since it was placed into an InDesign layout shows the status of _____.

2. The _____ is used to monitor the status of images that are placed into a layout.

3. _____ is the distance between the edge of a frame and the text contained within that frame.

4. _____ is the distance between the edge of an object and text in other overlapping frames.

5. _____ apply only to selected text characters; this is useful for setting off a few words in a paragraph without affecting the entire paragraph.

6. _____ apply to the entire body of text between two ¶ symbols.

7. While working in a table, the _____ key has a special function; pressing it does not insert the associated character.

8. When the _____ row height method is selected, table rows change height if you add or remove text from the table cells, or if you change the text formatting in a way that requires more or less space.

9. A(n) _____ is a special kind of table row that repeats at the top of every instance of the same table.

10. _____ is the process of checking a layout for errors before it goes to print.

short answer

1. Briefly explain the significance of a Missing Font warning.

2. List three advantages of using templates.

3. Briefly define "styles" in relation to text formatting.

PORTFOLIO BUILDER PROJECT

Use what you have learned in this project to complete the following freeform exercise.
Carefully read the art director and client comments, then create your own design to meet the needs of the project.
Use the space below to sketch ideas. When finished, write a brief explanation of the reasoning behind your final design.

art director comments

Your client is a local food market that sells gourmet and specialty products. To help promote the business, the owners have hired you to create a series of flyers that can be handed out at art festivals and farmers markets.

To complete this project, you should:

❑ Design an 8.5″ × 11″ template that can be reused to feature different sections of the store. The flyer can be printed on both sides of the paper, but should not include bleeds.

❑ Include some type of category identifier that will change for each flyer in the series.

❑ Use the content that has been provided in the **CenterMarket_Print19_PB.zip** archive on the Student Files web page. You can use some or all of the images that were provided by the client.

client comments

Center Market includes an artisanal cheese market, an old-world bakery with craft breads and desserts, a butcher shop that features wild game meats, and a large international section with hard-to-find ingredients for just about any type of cuisine.

Our target customers are the home-gourmet "foodie" types, so we want the flyers to speak to that higher-end market. We definitely prefer a classier approach than the "Sale! Sale! Sale!" flyers that you see in regular weekly grocery ads.

We already have text and images for the artisanal cheese, so start with that one. Once we've approved what you come up with, we'll gather up everything you will need for the other pieces.

Other than the text that we already provided you, be sure to include the store name, address, and phone number prominently on the flyer:

4127 West Alton Drive, Los Angeles, CA 90016
800-555-3663

project justification

PROJECT SUMMARY

This project introduced a number of concepts and tools that will be very important as you work on more complex page-layout jobs. Importing text content from other applications — specifically, Microsoft Word and Microsoft Excel — is a foundational skill that you will use in most projects. This newsletter showed you how to control that content on import, and then reformat it as appropriate in the InDesign layout.

Templates, master pages, and styles are all designed to let you do the majority of work once, and then apply it as many times as necessary. Virtually any InDesign project can benefit from these tools, and you will use them extensively in your career as a graphic designer.

Correct missing and modified graphics

Replace or locate missing fonts

Edit master page layouts

Import formatted text from a Microsoft Word file

Apply style sheets from the template

Control text wrap to move surrounding text away from frame edges

Control text frame inset to move contained text away from frame edges

Place PDF and INDD files as images

Format bulleted and numbered lists

Check for and correct spelling errors

Import and format a table from Microsoft Excel

Preflight a file and make corrections based on four-color printing requirements

Combined Brochure

10

Your client is trying to promote tourism in a newly redeveloped downtown area. As the production artist, your job is to complete the brochure layout, verify that everything is correct, and create the final file for print output.

This project incorporates the following skills:

❏ Managing color in layout files and placed images

❏ Controlling import options for a variety of image file types

❏ Searching and replacing text and special characters

❏ Searching and changing object attributes

❏ Outputting a color-managed PDF file

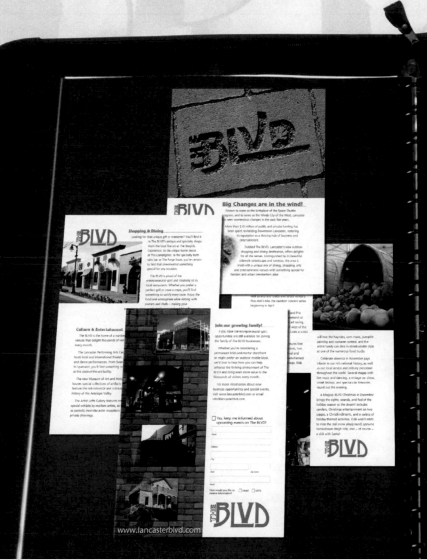

PROJECT MEETING

client comments

We just heard from the printer that we can only use one spot color based on the quote he provided. The logo uses two different spot colors, and those are used throughout the layout, as well. We decided to keep the metallic gold, but we need you to change the other one.

Now that it's official, we'd also like to use the actual name "The BLVD" rather than just saying "Downtown Lancaster" in most places.

We have a lot of great pictures from Charlie Essers, a local photographer. We'd like to use as many of those as possible in the layout.

art director comments

The text has already been placed into the template for this brochure, but the original designer had to move on to a different project. As the production artist, your job is to assemble the rest of the pieces and check the text and images for errors or technical problems.

When everything is in place and verified, you will export a color-managed PDF file using high-quality settings for the commercial printer.

project objectives

To complete this project, you will:

- ❏ Define application color settings
- ❏ Assign color settings to an existing file
- ❏ Replace a native Illustrator file
- ❏ Place a TIFF file with Alpha transparency
- ❏ Place multiple JPEG images
- ❏ Place a native InDesign file
- ❏ Place a native Photoshop file
- ❏ Preview color separations in a file
- ❏ Convert spot color in Illustrator
- ❏ Track changes during the development process
- ❏ Find and change specific text, with and without formatting attributes
- ❏ Find and change object formatting attributes
- ❏ Check document spelling
- ❏ Export a color-managed PDF file

STAGE 1 / **Controlling Color for Print**

In Project 6: Museum Image Correction, you worked with color management in Photoshop to correct an image based on a color profile for sheetfed printing. InDesign's color-management options allow you to integrate InDesign into a color-managed workflow. This includes managing the profiles of placed images, as well as previewing potential color problems on-screen before the job is output.

 ## Define Application Color Settings

There are two primary purposes for managing color in InDesign: previewing colors based on the intended output device and converting colors to the appropriate space when a file is output (whether to PDF or directly to an output device).

As with Photoshop, the first required step in a color-managed workflow is to define the color settings that apply to the file you are building.

1. **With no file open in InDesign, choose Edit>Color Settings.**

   The Color Settings dialog box defines default working spaces for RGB and CMYK colors, as well as general color management policies.

   The RGB working space defines the default profile for RGB colors and images that do not have embedded profiles. The CMYK working space defines the profile for the device or process that will be used to output the job.

2. **Choose North America Prepress 2 in the Settings menu.**

   InDesign includes a number of common option groups, which you can access in the Settings menu. You can also make your own choices and save those settings as a new preset by clicking Save, or you can import settings files created by another user by clicking Load.

   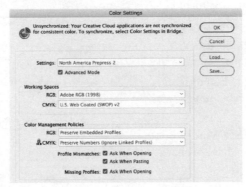

   A working space is a specific profile that defines color values in the associated mode. Using Adobe RGB (1998), for example, means new RGB colors in the InDesign file and imported RGB images without embedded profiles will be described by the values in the Adobe RGB (1998) space.

3. **In the CMYK menu, choose U.S. Sheetfed Coated v2.**

   There are many CMYK profiles, and each output device has a gamut unique to that individual device. U.S. Sheetfed Coated v2 is an industry-standard profile for a common type of printing (sheetfed printing on coated paper). In a truly color-managed workflow, you would actually use a profile for the specific press/paper combination being used for the job. (We're using one of the default profiles to show you how the process works.)

4. **In the Color Management Policies, make sure Preserve Embedded Profiles is selected for RGB, and Preserve Numbers (Ignore Linked Profiles) is selected for CMYK.**

These options tell InDesign what to do when you open existing files, or if you copy elements from one file to another.

- When an option is turned off, color is not managed for objects or files in that color mode.

- **Preserve Embedded Profiles** maintains the profile information saved in the file. Files with no profile use the current working space.

- If you choose **Convert to Working Space**, files automatically convert to the working space defined at the top of the Color Settings dialog box.

- For CMYK colors, you can choose **Preserve Numbers (Ignore Linked Profiles)** to maintain raw CMYK numbers (ink percentages), rather than adjusting the colors based on an embedded profile.

5. **Check all three options under the Color Management Policies menus.**

The check boxes control InDesign's behavior when you open an existing file or paste an element from a document with a profile other than the defined working space (called a profile mismatch), or when you open a file that does not have an embedded profile (called a missing profile).

6. **If it is not already checked, activate the Advanced Mode check box (below the Settings menu).**

The Engine option determines the system and color-matching method for converting between color spaces:

- **Adobe (ACE)**, the default, stands for Adobe Color Engine.

- **Apple CMM** (Macintosh only) uses the Apple ColorSync engine.

- **Microsoft ICM** (Windows only) uses the Microsoft ICM engine.

The **Intent** menu defines how the engine translates source colors outside the gamut of the destination profile.

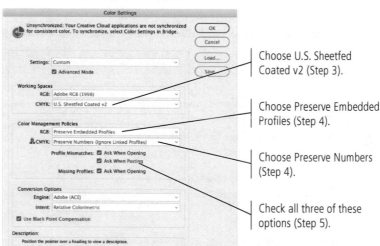

Choose U.S. Sheetfed Coated v2 (Step 3).

Choose Preserve Embedded Profiles (Step 4).

Choose Preserve Numbers (Step 4).

Check all three of these options (Step 5).

When the **Use Black Point Compensation** option is selected, the full range of the source space is mapped into the full-color range of the destination space. This method can result in blocked or grayed-out shadows, but it is most useful when the black point of the source is darker than that of the destination.

7. **Click OK to apply your settings, and then continue to the next exercise.**

Assign Color Settings to an Existing File

This project requires working on a file that has already been started, so some work has been completed before the file was handed off to you. To manage the process throughout the rest of this project, you need to make sure the existing file has the same color settings that you just defined.

1. **Download `Downtown_Print19_RF.zip` from the Student Files web page.**

2. **Expand the ZIP archive in your WIP folder (Macintosh) or copy the archive contents into your WIP folder (Windows).**

   This results in a folder named **Downtown**, which contains the files you need for this project. You should also use this folder to save the files you create in this project.

3. **Open the file `boulevard.indd` from the WIP>Downtown folder. Click Update Links if asked.**

4. **In the Profile or Policy Mismatch dialog box, select the second option: Adjust the document to match current color settings.**

   The existing file has neither a defined RGB nor CMYK profile. Because you activated the Ask When Opening option in the Color Settings dialog box, InDesign asks how you want to handle RGB color in the file.

   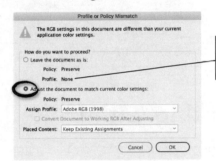

   "None" means that the file you're opening does not have a defined RGB profile.

   This option assigns the existing RGB color settings (which you defined in the previous exercise) to the existing file.

5. **Leave the remaining options at their default values and click OK.**

   Again, your choice in the Color Settings dialog box was to Ask When Opening if a file was missing a CMYK profile. Because the file does not have a defined CMYK profile, you see that warning now.

6. **In the second warning message, choose the second radio button: Adjust the document to match current color settings.**

   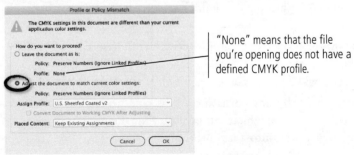

   "None" means that the file you're opening does not have a defined CMYK profile.

7. **Click OK to open the file.**

   This file contains the layout for a four-page brochure. Some content has already been placed; your job is to place the supplied images and prepare the final PDF file for printing.

8. **Save the file and continue to the next stage of the project.**

Assigning and Converting Color Profiles

If you need to change the working RGB or CMYK space in a document, you can use either the Assign Profiles (Edit>Assign Profiles) or Convert to Profile (Edit>Convert to Profile) dialog box. Although these two dialog boxes have slightly different appearances, most of the functionality is exactly the same.

In the Assign Profiles dialog box:

- **Discard (Use Current Working Space)** removes the current profile from the document. Colors will be defined by the current working space, but the profile is not embedded in the document.

- **Assign Current Working Space** embeds the working profile in the document.

- **Assign Profile** allows you to define a profile other than the working one. However, colors are not converted to the new space, which can dramatically change their appearance on your monitor.

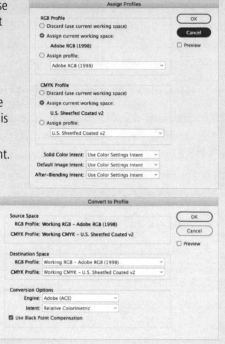

You can also define different rendering intents for solid colors, placed raster images, and transparent elements that result from blending modes, effects, or transparency settings. All three Intent menus default to use the intent defined in the Color Settings dialog box.

In the Convert to Profile dialog box, the menus can be used to change the RGB and CMYK destination spaces. This is basically the same as using the Assign Profile options in the Assign Profiles dialog box.

STAGE 2 / **Working with Linked Files**

Adobe InDesign supports a variety of graphics formats. Your output goal will determine the specific type of graphics used in a particular job. For print applications, such as the brochure you're building in this project, you should use high-resolution raster image files or vector-based graphics files. Depending on what type of file you are importing, you have a number of options when you place a file. This stage of the project explores the most common file formats for print design workflows.

Place a TIFF File with Alpha Transparency

The TIFF format is used only for raster images such as those from a scanner or digital camera. These files can be one-color (bitmap or monochrome), grayscale, or continuous-tone images.

TIFF files can include layers, although InDesign cannot access the individual layers in the file. If you want to manage image layers inside Photoshop, you should use the native Photoshop format (you will do so in a later exercise).

The TIFF format also supports stored clipping paths and Alpha channels. InDesign does provide access to those elements, which can be useful for maintaining transparent image areas when the file is placed into a layout.

1. **With boulevard.indd open, make Page 1 visible in the document window.**

2. **Choose File>Place. Navigate to bloom.tif in your WIP>Downtown>Links folder.**

   All images for this project are located in the WIP>Downtown>Links folder. We will not repeat the entire path in every exercise.

3. **Check the Show Import Options box and uncheck Replace Selected Item, and then click Open.**

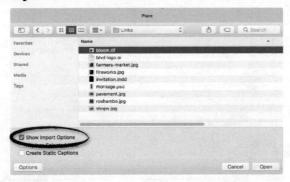

4. **In the Image tab of the Image Import Options dialog box, choose outline in the Alpha Channel menu.**

Remember from Project 4: Music CD Artwork, an Alpha channel stores degrees of transparency. These are commonly used to create gradual transitions at the edges of an image — as in this project.

5. **Click the Color button at the top of the dialog box.**

The Profile menu defaults to the profile embedded in the file. If the file was saved without an embedded profile, the menu defaults to Use Document Default. You can use the Profile menu to change the embedded profile (not recommended) or assign a specific profile if one was not embedded.

When you export the finished layout to PDF, you will use the PDF engine to convert the RGB images to CMYK. This profile tells InDesign how the RGB color is described in the file so it can be properly translated to the destination (CMYK) profile.

6. **Click OK to load the selected image into the cursor.**

Because you unchecked the Replace Selected Item option, the image is loaded into the cursor. It doesn't matter if anything was selected in the layout before you opened the Place dialog box.

7. **Click the empty space in the bottom-left corner of the page to place the loaded image.**

Note:

You can review and change the profile associated with a specific image by selecting the image in the layout and choosing Object>Image Color Settings. Keep in mind, however, that just because you can change the profile doesn't mean you should. If an image has an embedded profile, you should assume that it is the correct one; don't make random profile changes in InDesign.

8. **Using the Selection tool, move the placed image frame until its bottom-left corner snaps to the bottom-left bleed guides.**

As you can see (even in the low-resolution screen preview), the edges of the placed image gradually become more transparent until the underlying text is completely visible.

Because the image is currently obscuring some of the text, you still need to adjust the text wrap settings of the placed image.

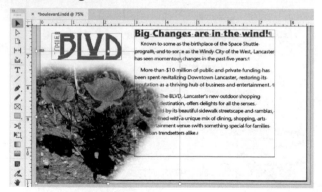

9. **With the placed image selected, open the Text Wrap panel (Window>Text Wrap).**

10. **At the top of the panel, click the Wrap Around Object Shape button. In the Contour Options menu, choose Alpha Channel in the Type menu.**

Rather than wrapping text around the frame, you are using the applied Alpha channel to define a text wrap that allows text to more closely follow the contours in the image.

When you use an Alpha channel as the basis for a text wrap, the initial result is not always exactly what you expect. In this case, you can see the semi-transparent image pixels are still obscuring some of the text.

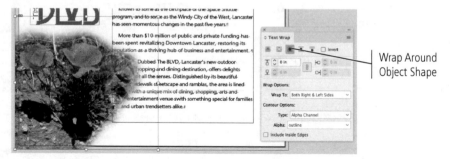

Wrap Around Object Shape

11. **Change the Top Offset field to 0.375 in, then press Return/Enter to apply the change.**

When you use the Wrap Around Object Shape option, you can only define a single offset value that applies to the entire object.

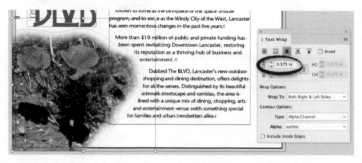

12. **Save the file and continue to the next exercise.**

Place Multiple JPEG Images

The JPEG format is commonly used for raster images, especially images that come from consumer-level digital cameras. Originally used for web applications only, the JPEG format is now supported by most commercial print-design applications (including InDesign).

The JPEG format can be problematic, especially in print jobs, because it applies a lossy compression scheme to reduce the image file size. If a high-resolution JPEG file was saved with a high level of compression, you might notice blockiness or other artifacts (flaws) in the printed image. If you must use JPEG files in your work, save them with the lowest compression possible.

1. **With boulevard.indd open, choose View>Fit Page in Window.**

2. **Open the Links and Pages panels (if they are not already visible).**

3. **Choose File>Place. In the Place dialog box, Command/Control click to select the following files:**

   farmers-market.jpg

   fireworks.jpg

   pavement.jpg

   roshambo.jpg

   shops.jpg

Note:

Remember, pressing Command/Control allows you to select multiple, non-contiguous files in a dialog box.

4. **With the Show Import Options box checked, click Open.**

   In the resulting Image Import Options dialog box, review the Image options.

   JPEG files do not support clipping paths or Alpha channels, so the options in this tab are not available for the selected file.

5. **Click the Color button at the top of the dialog box to show those options.**

   JPEG files do support color profiles. When you open a JPEG file, the options in this tab are the same as those for TIFF files.

6. **Click OK in each of the remaining dialog boxes to load all five selected images into the cursor.**

   When you select multiple files in the Place dialog box and Review Import Options is checked, you will see the Image Import Options dialog box for each selected image.

   When you load multiple files into the cursor, the cursor icon shows the thumbnail of the active file, and the number of files that are loaded.

   In the Links panel, the LP hot-text link identifies the file that is active in the cursor.

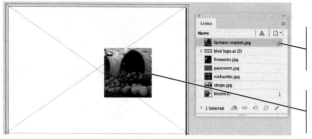

   The active file in the Place cursor is identified in the Links panel.

   The loaded Place cursor shows a thumbnail of the active file.

7. **Press the Right Arrow key twice to make the pavement.jpg file active in the Place cursor.**

   You can use the arrow keys to change the active file in the loaded cursor.

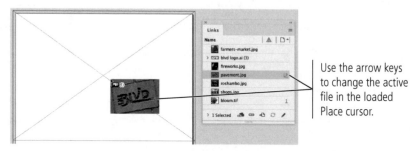

   Use the arrow keys to change the active file in the loaded Place cursor.

Note:

You can press Esc to remove the active file from the loaded Place cursor.

8. **Click inside the empty frame at the top of Page 1 to place the active image.**

   After you place the image, the next file is automatically loaded into the cursor.

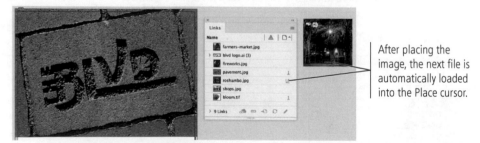

   After placing the image, the next file is automatically loaded into the Place cursor.

9. **Double-click the Page 2 thumbnail in the Pages panel to make that page active in the document window.**

You can still interact with the application interface (panels, menus, etc.) when files are loaded into the Place cursor.

10. **Use the arrow keys to make shops.jpg the active file in the Place cursor.**

Use the arrow keys to make **shops.jpg** the active file in the Place cursor.

11. **Click inside the empty frame at the top of Page 2 to place the loaded image.**

12. **Make roshambo.jpg the active file in the Place cursor, then click in the empty frame at the bottom of the page to place the loaded image.**

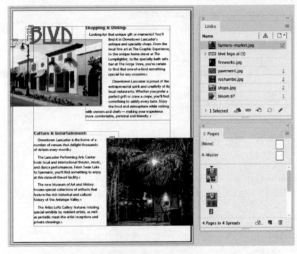

13. **Using the same process as in Steps 9–12, place farmers-market.jpg in the top frame on Page 3, and place fireworks.jpg in the bottom frame on Page 3.**

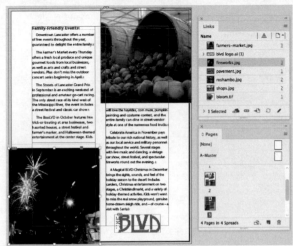

14. **Save the file and continue to the next exercise.**

Place a Native InDesign File

In addition to the different types of image files, you can also place one InDesign layout directly into another InDesign file. As with PDF files, you can determine which page is placed (if the file contains more than one), which layers are visible (if the file has more than one), and the specific file dimensions (bounding box) to use when the file is placed. Placed InDesign pages are managed as individual objects in the file in which they are placed.

1. With **boulevard.indd** open, make Page 4 active in the document window.

2. Choose File>Place, and select the file **invitation.indd**.

3. Make sure Show Import Options is checked, and then click Open.

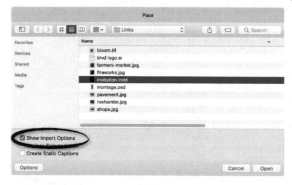

4. In the General tab of the Place InDesign Document dialog box, choose **Bleed Bounding Box in the Crop To menu.**

By default, the first page in the selected file appears as the previewed page that will be loaded into the Place cursor. If you choose to import multiple pages at one time, each page is loaded as a separate file.

When you place a native InDesign file into another InDesign file, you can use the Crop To menu to place pages based on the defined page, bleed, or slug, as described in the Document Setup dialog box.

If a file has more than one page, use these buttons to change the previewed page.

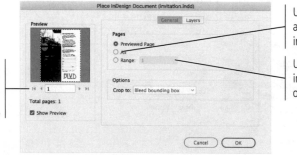

Use this option to load all pages in the file into the Place cursor.

Use this option to import a specific page or range of pages.

5. **Click the Layers button at the top of the dialog box.**

InDesign files can include multiple layers. You can determine which layers to display in the placed file by toggling the Eye icons on or off in the Show Layers list.

In the Update Link Options menu, you can determine what happens when/if you update the link to the placed file.

- **Keep Layer Visibility Overrides** maintains your choices regarding which layers are visible in the InDesign layout in which the file is placed.
- **Use PDF's Layer Visibility** restores the layer status as saved in the placed file.

6. **Click OK. Read the resulting warning message and click OK.**

To output properly, image links need to be present and up to date. Images placed in nested InDesign layouts are still links, so the link requirements apply in those files.

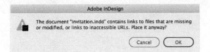

7. **Click to place the loaded file on Page 4 of the active file.**

8. **Using the Selection tool, drag the placed file until the top-left corner snaps to the top and left bleed guides.**

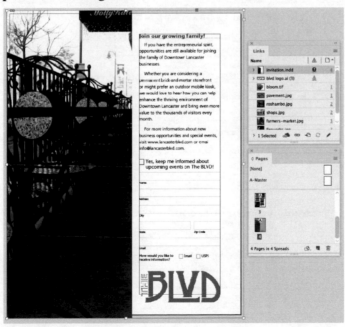

9. **Save the boulevard.indd file.**

10. **In the Links panel, expand the invitation.indd item.**

Expand the placed InDesign file to review the individual links inside that file.

Edit Original

11. **Select invitation.indd in the Links panel, and then click the Edit Original button.**

The Edit Original function opens the file selected in the Links panel. Because invitation.indd is a placed InDesign file, that document opens in a new document window in front of boulevard.indd.

When you open any InDesign file, of course, you are first warned if any necessary source file is missing or modified (which you already knew from the Links panel of the boulevard.indd file).

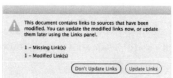

12. **Click Update Links.**

As you saw earlier in this project, The BLVD logo file had been modified after it was placed into these layouts. By clicking the Update Links button in this warning message, you update all modified links in the file without reviewing them in the layout.

13. **In the resulting Profile or Policy Mismatch dialog box, choose the Adjust option and click OK.**

This file (invitation.indd) was created without RGB or CMYK profiles. You need to tell InDesign how to manage color in this file, just as you did when you opened the boulevard.indd file.

14. **In the second Profile or Policy Mismatch dialog box, choose the Adjust option and click OK.**

As you have already seen, the software evaluates RGB and CMYK profiles individually, so you have to define the color behavior separately for each mode.

15. **Continue to the next exercise.**

Place a Native Photoshop File

You can easily place native Photoshop files (with the extension ".psd") into an InDesign layout. You can control the visibility of Photoshop layers and layer comps, as well as access embedded paths and Alpha channels in the placed file. If a Photoshop file includes spot-color channels, the spot colors are added to the InDesign Swatches panel.

1. **With both InDesign files open and invitation.indd active, click the missing image (tables2.jpg) in the Links panel, and then click the Relink button.**

   When an image is missing, you can use this option to identify the new location of the selected file. You can also use it to choose a different file, which will replace the existing file with a new one.

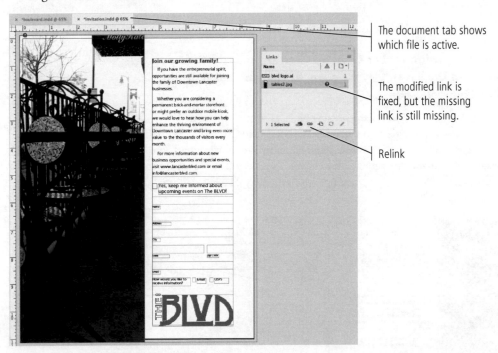

The document tab shows which file is active.

The modified link is fixed, but the missing link is still missing.

Relink

2. **Navigate to montage.psd in the WIP>Downtown>Links folder. Make sure Show Import Options is checked, and then click Open.**

   There is no option to Replace the selected item in this dialog box because you used the Relink button — the file you select automatically replaces the selected file.

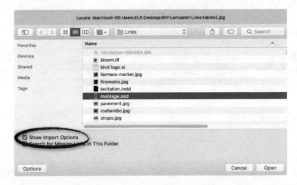

3. **In the resulting Image Import Options dialog box, review the options in the Layers tab.**

Photoshop files can include multiple layers and layer comps (saved versions of specific layer position and visibility). You can turn off specific layers by clicking the Eye (visibility) icon for that layer. If the file includes layer comps, you can use the Layer Comp menu to determine which comp to place.

The Update Link Options you see here are the same as those that are available when you place a native InDesign file.

Note:

The options in the Image and Color tabs are the same as those for TIFF files.

Note:

Unless you know what the different layers contain, it is difficult to decide what you want to place based solely on the very small preview image.

4. **Click OK to replace the missing image with the new one.**

5. **Using the Direct Selection tool or Content Grabber, select the image inside the frame on the left side of the page. Review the image scaling in the Control or Transform panel.**

When you replace one link with another, the new file is automatically scaled proportionally to fit the same space as the original image. In this case, the original image was a bit larger than the defined frame size. The montage, however, was created to match the exact space it was supposed to fill. As you can see, when the image (not the frame) is selected, the new image is scaled to approximately 113% to fill the same space as the original.

Note:

After a Photoshop file has been placed, you can change the layer visibility by choosing Object>Object Layer Options.

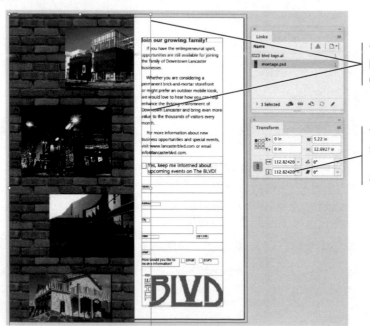

The red bounding box shows the edges of the placed image.

The replaced image is scaled to approximately 113% to fit the same space as the previous image.

Note:

You might want to zoom out to see the entire image bounding box.

6. **In the Control or Transform panel, select the top-left reference point and change the Scale X and Scale Y percentages to 100%.**

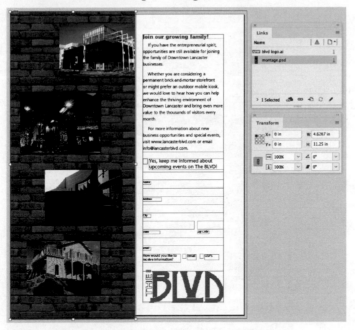

7. **Control/right-click the placed image and choose Edit With>Photoshop CC 2019.**

As you saw in the previous exercise, the Edit Original button opens a file in its native application. You can also use the Edit With option to open the file in any application that can interpret the file's data. The default option — which would apply if you use the Edit Original option — is identified in the menu.

If you have more than one version of an application installed on your machine, each version is listed in the Edit With menu (as you can see in our screen capture).

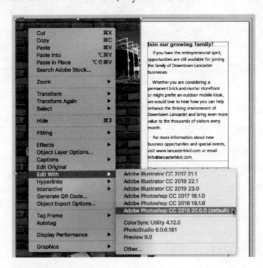

Note:

If Photoshop is not already running, it might take a while for the file to open. Be patient.

8. **If you see an Embedded Profile Mismatch warning, choose the option to use the embedded profile, and then click OK.**

9. **When montage.psd opens in Photoshop, make sure guides are visible (View>Show>Guides).**

10. **Review the Layers panel (Window> Layers).**

    As you saw when you placed the file into InDesign, this image has two hidden layers. You are going to review those layers in Photoshop to make sure you want them to be visible in the final layout.

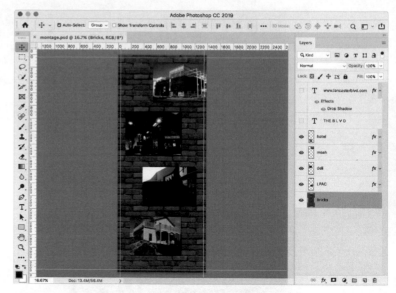

11. **In the Layers panel, click the empty space to the left of the top two layers to make them visible.**

    These two layers are type layers, identified with a "T" in place of the thumbnail. After making them visible, you can see one is used to add visual interest, while the other presents important information (the client's web address).

    When you click with the Type tool in a Photoshop file, a new type layer is automatically created to contain the type that you enter. Each type "object" in Photoshop is managed on separate type layers, which are automatically named based on their content.

    In InDesign, you know that the layout requires 0.125″ bleeds. The image frame correctly extends into the bleed area, and the image was created to match the frame size.

    As you can see, the artist who created the file placed guides 0.125″ from each image edge. The web address sits directly on the bottom guide and is centered horizontally on the canvas. However, based on its position in the InDesign layout, the top, bottom, and left edges of the image will be trimmed from the page. This means the position of the web address is incorrect in the context of the layout in which it is placed. You need to move it up and right so it appears in the correct location within the *trim area* instead of the overall image area. (This is a common problem in placed image files.)

12. **Select the web address layer in the Layers panel and make the Move tool active. Turn off the Auto-Select option in the Options bar.**

    It can be difficult to actually click the pixels in this thin type, so it is easier to move the layer by manually selecting it and turning off the Auto-Select option.

13. Click in the canvas area and drag to move the web address layer content so it snaps to the right guide and there is approximately 1/8″ space between the bottom edge of the type and the bottom guide.

Note:

You might want to zoom in to make this easier.

Auto-Select is turned off.

The Move tool is active.

The web address type layer is selected.

Drag to move the layer content up and right.

14. Save the file, close it, and then return to invitation.indd in InDesign.

15. Save the invitation.indd file and close it.

When you save and close the invitation.indd file, the Links panel for boulevard.indd automatically reflects the new placed file.

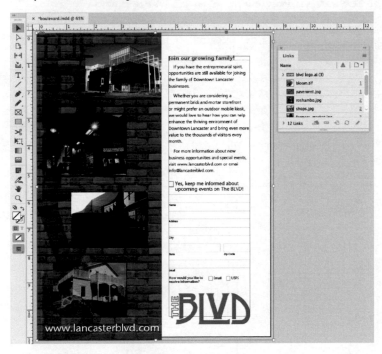

16. Save boulevard.indd and continue to the next exercise.

Preview Separations

To be entirely confident in color output, you should check the separations that will be created when your file is output. InDesign's Separations Preview panel makes this easy to accomplish from directly within the application workspace.

1. **With boulevard.indd open, choose Window>Output>Separations Preview.**

2. **In the View menu of the Separations Preview panel, choose Separations.**

   When Separations is selected in the View menu, all separations in the current file are listed in the panel. You can turn individual separations on and off to preview the different ink separations that will be created:

   - To view a single separation and hide all others, click the name of the separation you want to view. By default, areas of coverage appear in black. You can preview separations in color by toggling off the Show Single Plates in Black command in the panel Options menu.

   - To view more than one separation at a time, click the empty space to the left of the separation name. When viewing multiple separations, each one is shown in color.

   - To hide a separation, click the eye icon to the left of its name.

   - To view all process plates at once, click the CMYK option at the top of the panel.

3. **Click Pantone 875 C in the Separations Preview panel to see where that color is used.**

   As your client stated, the brochure should use a single spot color — the metallic gold in the main logo.

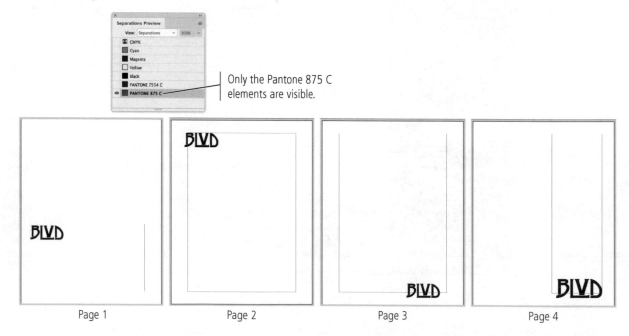

Only the Pantone 875 C elements are visible.

Page 1   Page 2   Page 3   Page 4

4. **Click Pantone 7554 C in the Separations Preview panel to review where that color is used in the layout.**

By reviewing the separation, you can see that the dark brown from the logo is used for all the headings in the text and for the frames on Page 4.

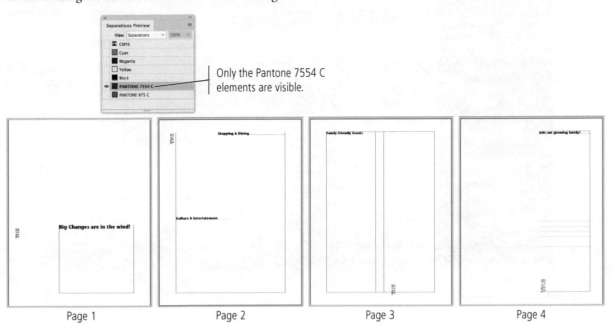

Only the Pantone 7554 C elements are visible.

| Page 1 | Page 2 | Page 3 | Page 4 |

5. **Click the empty space left of CMYK in the Separations Preview panel to view the CMYK separations, in addition to the Pantone 7554 C separation.**

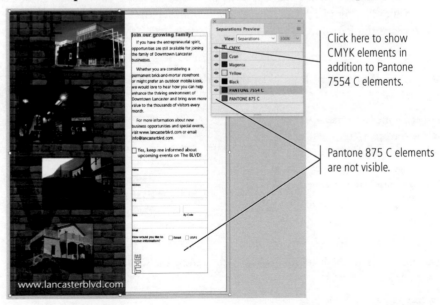

Click here to show CMYK elements in addition to Pantone 7554 C elements.

Pantone 875 C elements are not visible.

6. Choose Off in the View menu at the top of the Separations Preview panel.

When you turn off the separations preview, you again see the frame edges.

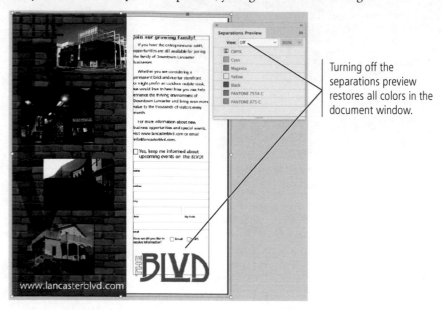

Turning off the separations preview restores all colors in the document window.

7. Continue to the next exercise.

Convert Spot Color in Illustrator

You can't simply delete the extra spot color from the InDesign file because it is used in the placed logo file. Instead, you are going to edit the placed file to remove the extra spot color. You will then replace the Pantone 7554 color with Pantone 875 for all InDesign layout elements.

1. With boulevard.indd open, choose blvd logo.ai in the Links panel, then click the Edit Original button.

Remember, this option opens a file in its native application. In this case, the file opens in Illustrator CC. If multiple instances of the file are placed, you don't need to select any specific instance for the Edit Original option to work.

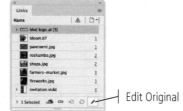

Edit Original

Note:

If Illustrator is not already running when you click the Edit Original button, it might take a while for the file to open. Be patient.

2. In Illustrator, open the Swatches panel.

This file includes two swatches, both of which are spot colors (indicated by the small dot in the corner of the swatch icons).

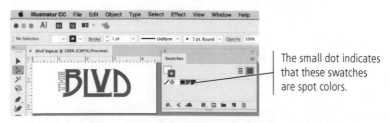

The small dot indicates that these swatches are spot colors.

3. **Double-click the Pantone 7554 swatch (the darker one) to open the Swatch Options dialog box.**

4. **Choose CMYK in the Color Mode menu.**

   After you convert the color to the CMYK mode, it is still set to output as a spot color. To avoid an unwanted separation, you also need to change the color to be a process color build.

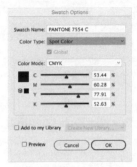

5. **Choose Process Color in the Color Type menu and leave the Global option checked.**

   When you change a spot color from the Book color mode to process, the software uses the nearest-possible ink values in the converted color.

   In this case, the resulting values are a four-color mix that could be a potential problem in the printing process. To achieve the same overall effect with less potential for problems, you are going to use a rich black to reproduce the word "THE" in the logo.

6. **Change the ink values to C: 0%, M: 50%, Y: 0%, K: 100%.**

   Because the Global option is checked, your changes will automatically be applied to any instance in which that color is used.

7. **Click OK to redefine the swatch.**

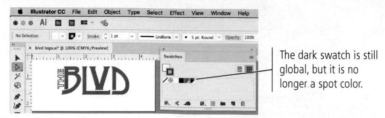

The dark swatch is still global, but it is no longer a spot color.

8. **Save the Illustrator file, close it, and then return to boulevard.indd in InDesign.**

Because you used the Edit Original function to edit the placed logo file, the placed instances are automatically updated when you return to the layout.

This warning icon is caused by the modified image in the placed InDesign file.

The blvd logo.ai file still shows a warning icon. If you expand that item to show individual instances, you see that all instances in the boulevard layout are now up to date.

The problem is the logo instance in the placed InDesign file — the update process does not trickle down to nested files. You still have to open the placed layout and update the link.

9. **Select invitation.indd in the Links panel and click the Edit Original button.**

10. **In the resulting warning dialog box, click Update Links.**

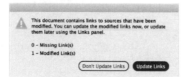

11. **Save the file, close it, and then return to the boulevard.indd file.**

All of the modified warnings — in both the main layout and the nested file — are gone.

12. **Save boulevard.indd, and then continue to the next stage of the project.**

STAGE 3 / **Fine-Tuning Text**

Now that all of the images are in place, you can begin the fine-tuning process for the layout text. As your art director informed you during the project meeting, some of the text work had already been completed before the original designer had to move on to a different project. Your assignment in this stage of the project is to verify that all text in the document is correct.

Some text issues have little to do with typography and more to do with "user error" — common errors introduced by the people (most often, your clients) who created the text. Regardless of how careful you are, some problems will inevitably creep into the text elements of your layouts. Fortunately, InDesign has the tools you need to correct those issues as well.

Enable Track Changes

In many cases, multiple users collaborate on a single document — designers, editors, content providers, and clients all go back and forth throughout the design process. Each person in the process will request changes, from the highlight color in a document to rewriting the copy to fit in a defined space. Because the words in a design are a vital part of communicating the client's message, tracking text changes throughout the process can be useful to make sure that all are accurate and approved before the job is finalized.

1. **With boulevard.indd open, navigate to Page 1, and then use the Type tool to place the insertion point in any story.**

2. **Choose Type>Track Changes>Enable Tracking in All Stories.**

   The Track Changes feature can be activated to monitor text editing during development. This allows multiple users to edit the text without permanently altering it until the changes have been reviewed and approved, or rejected. (After you have made all the changes in this stage of the project, you will review and finalize them.)

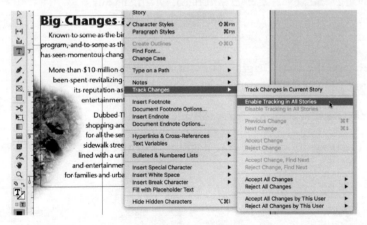

3. **Open the Track Changes pane of the Preferences dialog box.**

4. **Make sure the Include Deleted Text When Spellchecking option is checked at the bottom of the dialog box.**

   It is very easy to make a mistake when spellchecking, so it's a good idea to keep this option checked.

5. **Make sure the Added Text, Deleted Text, and Moved Text options are checked.**

   Remember, preferences are accessed in the InDesign menu on Macintosh or in the Edit menu on Windows.

6. **Choose Underline in the Added Text Marking menu.**

   The Marking options add a visual indicator (strikethrough, underlining, or outlining) so you can more easily identify text that is affected by the Track Changes function.

7. **Choose Red in the Deleted Text Background menu.**

   The Background Color options define the color of highlighting that will identify each type of change. All three options default to the same color. Changing the color for Deleted Text will make it easier to identify this type of change when you review the corrections at the end of this stage of the project.

8. **Click OK to return to the document, save the file, and then continue to the next exercise.**

Find and Change Text

You will often need to search for and replace specific elements in a layout — a word, a phrase, a formatting attribute, or even a specific kind of object. InDesign's Find/Change dialog box allows you to easily locate exactly what you need, whether your layout is two pages or two hundred. For this brochure, you can use the Find/Change dialog box to correct the name of the client's project.

1. **With boulevard.indd open, use the Edit Original function to open invitation.indd (the file that is placed on Page 4).**

2. **Make boulevard.indd the active file, then navigate to Page 1.**

3. **Using the Type tool, place the insertion point at the beginning of the story on that page.**

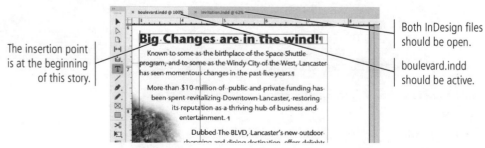

The insertion point is at the beginning of this story.

Both InDesign files should be open.

boulevard.indd should be active.

4. **Choose Edit>Find/Change.**

5. **Place the insertion point in the Find What field, and type** Downtown Lancaster.

6. **Press Tab to highlight the Change To field, and type** The BLVD.

7. **In the Search menu, choose All Documents.**

When the insertion point is placed, you can choose to search the entire Document, All [open] Documents, only the active Story, or only text following the insertion point in the selected story (To End of Story).

Using the Forward Direction option (the default), the search identifies the first instance of the Find What text after the location of the insertion point. If you use the Backward Direction option, the search would identify the first instance preceding the current insertion point.

Note:

If the insertion point is not currently placed, you can only choose to search the active Document or All Documents.

8. **Click Find Next.**

The first instance of the Find What text is automatically highlighted in the document.

Note:

The Find/Change dialog box is one of the few that allow you to interact directly with the document while the dialog box is still open.

9. **Click the Change/Find button.**

The next instance of the Find What text is highlighted in the document.

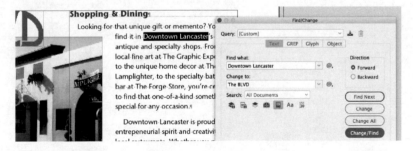

10. **Click Change All.**

11. **When you see the message that the search is completed, click OK.**

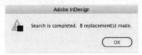

Note:

There is a bug on the Windows version that sometimes causes the Change All function to return a greater number of changes than actually exist. Don't worry if your results messages show a larger number than what you see in our screen captures.

12. **Click Done to close the Find/Change dialog box.**

13. **Save both open files, and then continue to the next exercise.**

As you have seen, the Text tab allows you to search for and change specific character strings, with or without specific formatting options. The Object tab identifies specific combinations of object formatting attributes, such as fill color or applied object effects. In addition to the tools you use in this project, the Find/Change dialog box has a number of options for narrowing or extending a search beyond the basic options. The buttons below the Search menu are toggles for specific types of searches (from left to right):

A When **Include Locked Layers and Locked Objects** is active, the search locates instances on locked layers or individual objects that have been locked. You can't replace locked objects unless you first unlock them.

B When **Include Locked Stories** is active, the search locates text that is locked. You can't replace locked text unless you first unlock it.

C When **Include Hidden Layers and Hidden Objects** is active, the search includes frames on layers that are not visible.

D When **Include Master Pages** is active, the search includes frames on master pages.

E When **Include Footnotes** is active, the search identifies instances within footnote text.

F When **Case Sensitive** is active, the search finds only text with the same capitalization as the text in the Find What field. For example, a search for "InDesign" will not identify instances of "Indesign," "indesign," or "INDESIGN."

G When **Whole Word** is active, the search finds only instances in which the search text is an entire word, not part of another word. For example, if you search for "old" as a whole word, InDesign will not include the words "gold," "mold," or "embolden."

The GREP tab is used for pattern-based search techniques, such as finding phone numbers in one format (e.g., 800.555.1234) and changing them to a different format (e.g., 800/555-1234). Adobe's video-based help system (www.adobe.com) provides some assistance in setting up an advanced query.

The Glyph tab allows you to search for and change glyphs using Unicode or GID/CID values. This is useful for identifying foreign and pictographic characters, as well as characters from extended sets of OpenType fonts.

You can also save specific searches as queries and call those queries again using the Query menu at the top of the Find/Change dialog box. This option is useful if you commonly make the same modifications, such as changing Multiple Return to Single Return (this particular search and replacement is so common that the query is built into the application).

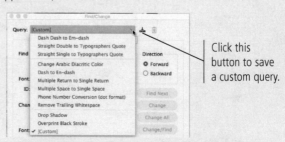

Click this button to save a custom query.

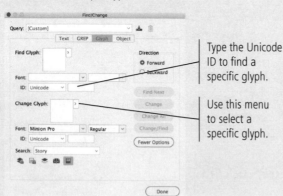

Type the Unicode ID to find a specific glyph.

Use this menu to select a specific glyph.

Find and Change Text Formatting Attributes

In addition to finding and replacing specific text or characters, you can also find and replace formatting attributes for both text and objects. For this project, you need to use the gold spot color as the accent, replacing the brown spot color. The Find/Change dialog box makes this kind of replacement a relatively simple process.

1. **With both InDesign files open and boulevard.indd active, choose Edit>Find/Change (if the dialog box is not already open).**

2. **Delete all text from the Find What and Change To fields.**

3. **Choose Wildcards>Any Character in the menu to the right of the Find What field.**

   Wildcards allow you to search for formatting attributes, regardless of the actual text. In addition to searching for Any Character, you can also narrow the search to Any Digit, Any Letter, or Any White Space characters.

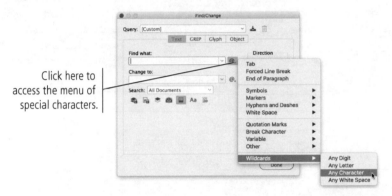

Click here to access the menu of special characters.

4. **Click the More Options button to show the expanded Find/Change dialog box.**

   When more options are visible, you can find and replace specific formatting attributes of the selected text.

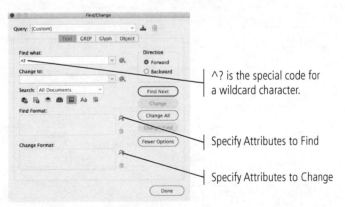

^? is the special code for a wildcard character.

Specify Attributes to Find

Specify Attributes to Change

Note:

The More Options button becomes the Fewer Options button when the extra options are already showing.

5. **Click the Specify Attributes to Find button to open the Find Format Settings dialog box.**

   You can search for and replace any character formatting option (or combination of options) that can be applied in the layout.

Entering Special Characters in Dialog Boxes

You can enter special characters in InDesign dialog boxes using the following special codes, called metacharacters. Note that these metacharacters are case specific — for example, "^n" and "^N" refer to different special characters.

Character	Code (Metacharacters)	Character	Code (Metacharacters)
Symbols		**Break Characters**	
Bullet (•)	^8	Paragraph return	^p
Caret (^)	^^	Forced line break (soft return)	^n
Copyright (©)	^2	Column break	^M
Ellipsis (…)	^e	Frame break	^R
Paragraph	^7	Page break	^P
Registered Trademark (®)	^r	Odd page break	^L
Section (§)	^6	Even page break	^E
Trademark (™)	^d	Discretionary line break	^j
Dashes and Hyphens		**Formatting Options**	
Em Dash (—)	^_	Tab character	^t
En Dash (–)	^=	Right indent tab character	^y
Discretionary hyphen	^-	Indent to here character	^i
Nonbreaking hyphen	^~	End nested style here character	^h
White Space Characters		Nonjoiner character	^k
Em space	^m	**Variables**	
En space	^>	Running header (paragraph style)	^Y
Third space	^3	Running header (character style)	^Z
Quarter space	^4	Custom text	^u
Sixth space	^%	Last page number	^T
Flush space	^f	Chapter number	^H
Hair space	^| (pipe)	Creation date	^S
Nonbreaking space	^s	Modification date	^o
Thin space	^<	Output date	^D
Figure space	^/	File name	^l (lowercase L)
Punctuation space	^.	**Markers**	
Quotation Marks		Section marker	^x
Double left quotation mark	^{	Anchored object marker	^a
Double right quotation mark	^}	Footnote reference marker	^F
Single left quotation mark	^[	Index marker	^I
Single right quotation mark	^]	**Wildcards**	
Straight double quotation mark	^"	Any digit	^9
Straight single quotation mark	^'	Any letter	^$
Page Number Characters		Any character	^?
Any page number character	^#	White space (any space or tab)	^w
Current page number character	^N	Any variable	^v
Next page number character	^X		
Previous page number character	^V		

6. **Show the Character Color options and click the Pantone 7554 C swatch.**

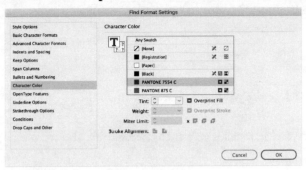

7. **Click OK to return to the Find/Change dialog box.**

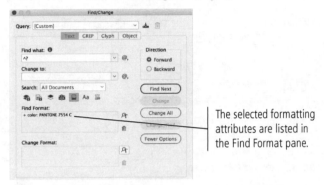

The selected formatting attributes are listed in the Find Format pane.

8. **Click the Specify Attributes to Change button to open the Change Format Settings dialog box.**

9. **Show the Character Color options and click the Pantone 875 C swatch.**

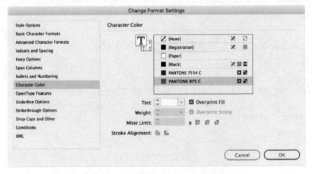

10. **Click OK to return to the Find/Change dialog box.**

11. **Make sure All Documents is selected in the Search menu, then click Change All. Click OK to close the message about the number of replacements.**

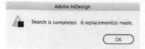

12. **In the Find/Change dialog box, delete the wildcard character from the Find What field.**

   Although clearing the Find What and Change To fields isn't strictly necessary, it is a good habit to develop.

13. **Click the Delete buttons to remove the formatting options from the Find Format and Change Format fields.**

   It can be easy to forget to remove these formatting choices. However, if you leave them in place, your next search will only find the Find What text with the selected formatting. It's a good idea to clear these as soon as you're done with them.

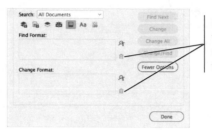

   Click the Delete buttons for both Find Format and Change Format to clear these choices.

14. **Save both open files and continue to the next exercise.**

Find and Change Object Attributes

In addition to searching for specific text formatting attributes, you can also find and replace specific object formatting attributes. In this exercise you will replace all brown-stroked frames with the gold spot color.

1. **With both InDesign files open and boulevard.indd active, open the Find/Change dialog box if necessary.**

2. **Click the Object tab in the Find/Change dialog box to display those options.**

3. **Choose All Documents in the Search menu.**

   When you search objects, you can search the current document, all documents, or the current selection.

4. **In the Type menu, choose All Frames.**

   You can limit your search to specific kinds of frames, or search all frames.

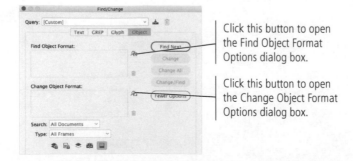

   Click this button to open the Find Object Format Options dialog box.

   Click this button to open the Change Object Format Options dialog box.

5. **Click the button to open the Find Object Format Options dialog box.**

   You can find and change any formatting attributes that can be applied to a frame.

6. **Display the Stroke options and click the Pantone 7554 C swatch.**

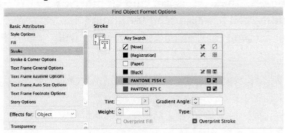

7. **Click OK to return to the Find/Change dialog box.**

8. **Open the Change Object Format Options dialog box and choose the Pantone 875 C swatch in the Stroke options.**

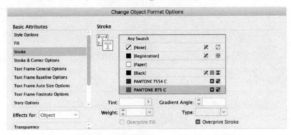

9. **Click OK to return to the Find/Change dialog box.**

10. **Click Change All, and then click OK to dismiss the message about the number of changes.**

11. **Click the Delete buttons for both the Find Object Format and Change Object Format options to clear your choices.**

12. **Click Done to close the Find/Change dialog box.**

13. **Save both open files and continue to the next exercise.**

Note:

There is a bug on the Windows version that sometimes causes the Change All function to return a greater number of changes than actually exist. Don't worry if your results messages show a larger number than what you see in our screen captures.

Check Document Spelling

Many designers carefully monitor the technical aspects of a job, but skip another important check — spelling errors. Misspellings and typos creep into virtually every job, despite numerous rounds of content proofs. These errors can ruin an otherwise perfect print job. InDesign's Spell Check utility can be very useful for finding common problems, although some manual decision making and intervention will also be involved.

1. **With boulevard.indd and invitation.indd both open, make the boulevard.indd file active.**

2. **Open the Dictionary pane of the Preferences dialog box.**

   InDesign checks spelling based on the defined language dictionary — by default, English: USA. You can choose a different language dictionary in the Language menu.

> **Note:**
>
> *The application also includes English: USA Legal and English: USA Medical dictionaries that will be of significant benefit to anyone working for either of those industries. If you work with foreign-language publishing, you can choose one of more than 40 different language dictionaries that are installed with InDesign.*

3. **Make sure English: USA is selected in the Language menu and click OK.**

4. **Choose Edit>Spelling>User Dictionary.**

   When you check spelling, you are likely to find words that, although spelled correctly, are not in the selected dictionary. Proper names, scientific terms, corporate trademarks, and other custom words are commonly flagged, even though they are correct. Rather than flagging these terms every time you recheck spelling, you can add them to a custom user dictionary so that InDesign will recognize them the next time you check spelling.

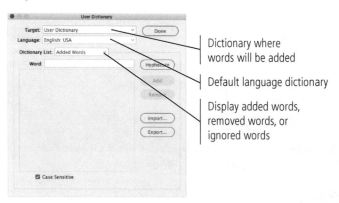

Dictionary where words will be added

Default language dictionary

Display added words, removed words, or ignored words

5. **Make sure User Dictionary is selected in the Target menu.**

   By default, the user dictionary is associated with all documents. You can also define custom words for a specific file by choosing any open file in the Target menu, when you change the user dictionary for a specific file, words you add for that file will still be flagged in other files.

6. **In the Word field, type BLVD.**

   The city's branded name is not a real word. If you know that certain words will be flagged, you can manually add them to the user dictionary at any time.

7. **Check the Case Sensitive option at the bottom of the dialog box, and then click Add.**

   If Case Sensitive is not checked, InDesign will not distinguish between BLVD (which is correct) and Blvd (which is incorrect).

8. **Click Done to close the User Dictionary dialog box.**

9. **Place the insertion point at the beginning of the story on Page 1, and then choose Edit>Spelling>Check Spelling.**

   As soon as you open the Check Spelling dialog box, the first flagged word is highlighted in the layout. The same word appears in the Not in Dictionary field of the Check Spelling dialog box.

10. **Choose All Documents in the Search menu at the bottom of the Check Spelling dialog box.**

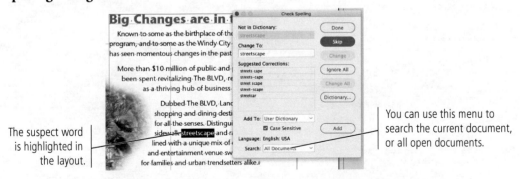

The suspect word is highlighted in the layout.

You can use this menu to search the current document, or all open documents.

The flagged word (streetscape) is not misspelled, but it is not recognized in the defined dictionary. Never simply click Change when checking spelling. Review each flagged word carefully and make the correct choices within the context of the layout.

11. **Click the Dictionary button in the Check Spelling dialog box. Choose boulevard.indd in the Target menu, make sure the Case Sensitive option is checked, and then click Add.**

If you click the Add button in the Check Spelling dialog box, the words are added to the default user dictionary, which applies to all InDesign files on your computer. When you open the User Dictionary dialog box from the Check Spelling dialog box, you can choose the file-specific dictionary in the Target menu, and then click Add to add the word to the dictionary for only the selected file.

Choose boulevard.indd in the Target menu to add the word as a correct spelling in only this document.

12. **Click Done to close the User Dictionary dialog box and return to the Check Spelling dialog box.**

When you return to the Check Spelling dialog box, streetscape still appears in the Word field. You have to click Skip to find the next suspect word.

13. **Click Skip.**

The next suspect is another word that does not appear in the dictionary. According to your client, however, it is spelled correctly.

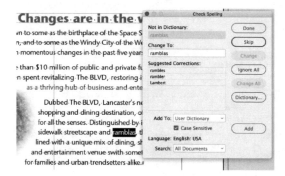

14. **Click the Dictionary button in the Check Spelling dialog box. Choose boulevard.indd in the Target menu, make sure the Case Sensitive option is checked, and then click Add.**

Click Add to remember the word "ramblas" as a correct spelling in only this document.

15. **Click Done to close the User Dictionary dialog box and return to the Check Spelling dialog box. Click Skip to show the next suspect word.**

16. **Review the next error.**

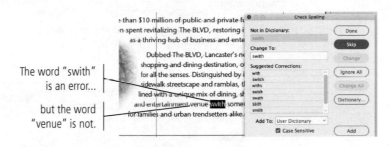

This is an example of a very common typo. The word "swith" is identified as an error, but if you look closely, you can see that the previous word is "venue." If you read the entire sentence, you can see that it should read "venues with," rather than "venue swith." The word "venue" is a grammatical error, not a spelling error, so it is not flagged by the Check Spelling process. You have to correct this problem manually.

The word "swith" is an error...

but the word "venue" is not.

17. **In the layout, place the insertion point before the "s" in "swith," then press the Delete/Backspace key. Add a space after the "s" in "venues."**

As soon as you click to place the insertion point in the story, the Check Spelling dialog box reverts to show the Start button. By interacting directly with the document to manually correct an error that the software can't fix, you have to restart the spell-check process.

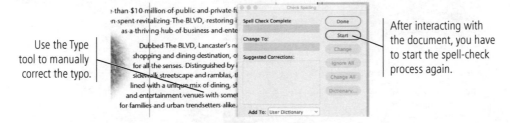

Use the Type tool to manually correct the typo.

After interacting with the document, you have to start the spell-check process again.

18. **Click the Start button in the Check Spelling dialog box.**

The process continues from the current insertion point to the end of the active story.

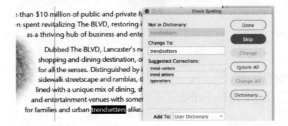

19. **With trendsetters highlighted, click Ignore All.**

When you click Ignore All, the word is added to a special list in the user dictionary so it will not be flagged again.

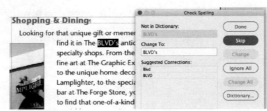

The next suspect is automatically highlighted. Although you added BLVD to the user dictionary, the software does not automatically recognize variations, such as this possessive version of "BLVD".

20. Click Skip.

When you use the Skip option, the same suspect will be flagged every time you check spelling in the document.

After clicking skip, the next suspect is automatically highlighted — in this case, an actual misspelled word ("entrepeneurial").

21. Highlight the correct spelling ("entrepreneurial") in the Suggested Corrections list and click Change.

As you can see in the layout, the misspelled word is replaced with the selected alternative, and the next suspect word is automatically highlighted in the layout.

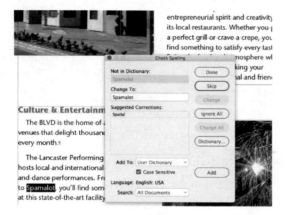

22. Continue checking the spelling in the document. Make the following choices when prompted:

Spamalot	**Ignore All**
artfiacts	**Change to "artifacts"**
Prix	**Ignore All**
BooLVD	**Add to the user dictionary for only the active file**
Christkindlmarkt	**Add to the user dictionary for only the active file**
enviroment	**Change to "environment"**
www.lancasterblvd.com	**Ignore All**
lancasterblvd.com	**Ignore All**

The last three suspects are in the invitation.indd file. Because you chose All Documents in the Search menu, the Spell Check process automatically switches to the secondary file after the process is complete in the first active file.

23. **When you see "Spell Check Complete" at the top of the dialog box, click Done to close it.**

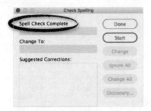

24. **Save invitation.indd and close it.**

25. **With boulevard.indd open, review the Links panel.**

Although you use the Edit Original option to open the invitation.indd file, changes made after the first time you save the linked file do not automatically update in the parent file. You have to manually update the link to the placed file.

26. **Double-click the Modified Link icon in the Links panel.**

27. **Save boulevard.indd, and then continue to the next exercise.**

 # Review Tracked Changes

Earlier in this project, you enabled the Track Changes feature for all stories in this document. You might have noticed, however, that there is no visual indication of those changes in the layout. Tracking editorial changes is useful for monitoring changes in the text, but displaying those in the layout would make it impossible to fit copy and accurately format the text. To avoid this confusion, changes are tracked in a special utility called the Story Editor.

1. **With boulevard.indd open and active, use the Type tool to place the insertion point at the beginning of the text frame on Page 1.**

2. **Choose Edit>Edit in Story Editor.**

The Story Editor opens in a separate window, showing only the current story. A **story** in InDesign is the entire body of text in a single frame or string of linked frames.

Note:

If your deleted text is not highlighted red, you missed a step in the earlier exercise in which you enabled the Track Changes feature (see Page 598). You can open the Track Changes pane of the Preferences dialog box and change the highlight options now.

Note:

You can also Option/Alt click the Accept or Reject Change button to apply the change, and then automatically highlight (find) the next change.

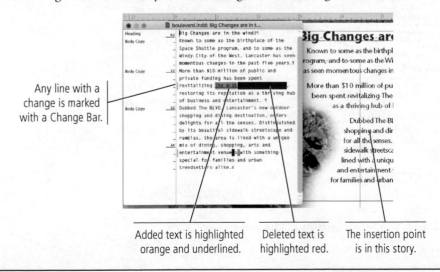

Any line with a change is marked with a Change Bar.

Added text is highlighted orange and underlined.

Deleted text is highlighted red.

The insertion point is in this story.

3. **Open the Track Changes panel (Window>Editorial>Track Changes).**

When the Story Editor window is active, you can use the Track Changes panel to review the tracked changes.

A. Enable/Disable Track Changes in Current Story toggles the track changes function on and off.

B. Show/Hide Changes toggles the visibility of tracked changes in the Story Editor window.

C. Previous Change highlights the first change before the current location of the insertion point.

D. Next Change highlights the first change after the current location of the insertion point.

E. Accept Change makes the highlighted change permanent.

F. Reject Change restores the original text for deleted text, or removes added text.

G. Accept All Changes in Story applies the same result as the Accept Change button, but for all tracked changes in the active story — you do not get to individually review each change.

H. Reject All Changes in Story applies the same result as the Reject Change button, but for all tracked changes in the active story. Again, you do not get to individually review each change.

4. **Click the Next Change button in the Track Changes panel.**

If you read the text, you can see that this instance refers to the area of Downtown Lancaster. The next paragraph goes on to explain that the area was rebranded as "The BLVD," so it wouldn't make logical sense to use the term before it is defined.

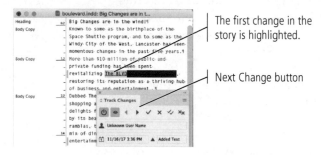

The first change in the story is highlighted.

Next Change button

Note:

This type of decision is usually the client's, so in this exercise, we are assuming the client would agree.

5. **Click the Reject Change button, and then click the Next Change button.**

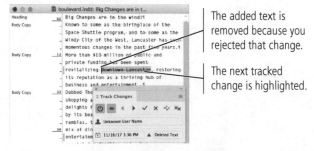

The added text is removed because you rejected that change.

The next tracked change is highlighted.

6. **Click the Reject Change button again.**

Because you did not keep the replacement text, you need to keep the deleted text.

7. **Click the Accept All Changes in Story button at the top of the Track Changes panel.**

8. **When asked to confirm the change, click OK.**

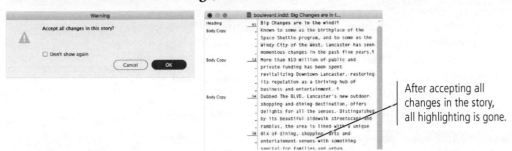

After accepting all changes in the story, all highlighting is gone.

9. **Click the Next Change button.**

Because there were no more changes in the first story, clicking the Next Change button opens the next story in which a change is located. Each story appears in a separate Story Editor window.

Each "story" opens in its own window.

In Step 8 you accepted all changes in the active story, but the second story still has tracked changes that should be reviewed. As you can see, the only changes in this story are the replacement of "Downtown Lancaster" with "The BLVD" and the corrected misspellings. Rather than reviewing each instance separately, you can accept all changes in the story at one time.

10. **Open the Track Changes panel Options menu and choose Accept All Changes>In This Document.**

The In This Document option affects all stories in a file, even if they are not currently open in a Story Editor window.

Accepting all changes without reviewing them essentially defeats the purpose of tracking changes. We are telling you that, in this case, it is safe to do so.

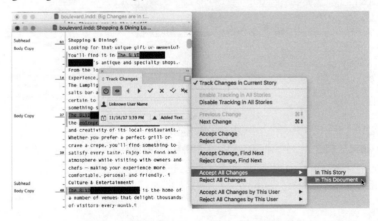

Note:

In a professional environment — and especially if more than one person has been working on the same document — you should be sure to carefully review all tracked changes before finalizing the job.

11. **Click OK to dismiss the Warning dialog box and accept the changes.**

12. **Close both Story Editor windows.**

13. **Save the file and continue to the next exercise.**

Note:

You did not enable Track Changes, so there is nothing to review in the invitation.indd file.

Export a Color-Managed PDF File

As you saw when you placed them, the photos in this layout use the RGB model. InDesign allows you to convert image data to the defined output profile when you create the PDF file for print while still maintaining the RGB images for the digitally distributed formats. However, because the RGB model allows a much greater gamut than CMYK, some color shift might occur when you export the PDF file. It's a good idea to review the potential color shift before you create the final print PDF.

1. **With boulevard.indd open, navigate to Page 1.**

2. **Choose View>Proof Setup>Working CMYK.**

   Remember from the beginning of this project, the working CMYK profile is what you defined as the color characteristics of the intended output device — in this case, a standardized sheetfed press.

3. **Choose View>Proof Colors.**

   This toggle provides an on-screen preview of what will happen when the image is converted to the CMYK working-space profile, without affecting the actual file data. This option, called **soft proofing**, is more valuable with an accurately calibrated monitor; but even with an uncalibrated one, you should be able to see any significant trouble areas.

Note:

If the Proof Colors option is already checked (toggled on), move the mouse cursor away from the menu, and then click to dismiss it.

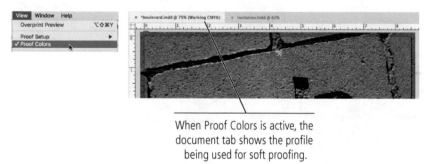

When Proof Colors is active, the document tab shows the profile being used for soft proofing.

4. **Navigate through the layout and review the differences. Toggle the Proof Colors option on and off for each page to look for significant color shift.**

   In many instances, the color shift will be subtle. The most obvious changes will be visible in the brightest colors, such as the blue tarp in the image on the lower half of Page 3.

   We do not include images of the differences here because they do not reproduce well in print. However, you should be able to see the differences on your screen when you toggle the Proof Colors option on and off.

5. **Turn off the Proof Colors option, and then choose File>Export.**

6. Change the file name to **boulevard-print.pdf** and choose Adobe PDF (Print) in the Format menu. Click Save.

7. In the Export Adobe PDF dialog box, choose Press Quality in the Adobe PDF Preset menu.

8. In the Marks and Bleeds options, check the Crop Marks option, and then change the Offset value to **0.125 in**. In the lower half of the dialog box, check the option to Use Document Bleed Settings.

9. In the Output options, choose Convert to Destination in the Color Conversion menu.

You have several options for converting colors when you output a file:

- **No Color Conversion** maintains all color data (including placed images) in its current space.

- **Convert to Destination** converts colors to the profile selected in the Destination menu.

- **Convert to Destination (Preserve Numbers)** converts colors to the destination profile if the applied profile does not match the defined destination profile. Objects without color profiles are not converted.

The Destination menu defines the gamut for the output device that will be used. (This menu defaults to the active destination working space.) Color information in the file (and placed images) is converted to the selected Destination profile.

10. Choose Include Destination Profile in the Profile Inclusion Policy menu.

The **Profile Inclusion Policy** menu determines whether color profiles are embedded in the resulting PDF file. Different options are available, depending on what you selected in the Color Conversion menu.

11. Click the Ink Manager button.

As you already know, this file is only allowed to use one spot color — Pantone 875 C (metallic gold) — when it is printed.

The Ink Manager, which lists all separations in the job, offers control over specific ink separations at output time. Changes here affect the current output, not how the colors are defined in the document.

12. Click the Spot Color icon to the left of the Pantone 7554 C ink.

This converts the individual ink to a process color for the current output. Keep in mind that spot colors are often outside the CMYK gamut and there will almost always be color shift in the resulting CMYK build.

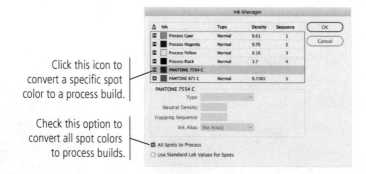

Click this icon to convert a specific spot color to a process build.

Check this option to convert all spot colors to process builds.

13. Click OK to return to the Export Adobe PDF dialog box, and then click Export.

14. If the PDF file opens, close it, and then return to InDesign.

15. Save and close any open InDesign files.

PROJECT REVIEW

1. A(n) _____ describes the color reproduction characteristics of a particular input or output device.

2. The _____ can be used to review the location of specific spot colors in a layout.

3. A(n) _____ can be used to create a smooth transition from solid pixels to transparent pixels in an image.

4. When placing images into a layout, press _____ to select multiple, non-contiguous files in the Place dialog box.

5. When placing a native Photoshop file, you can check the _____ option in the Place dialog box to control layer visibility before the file is placed.

6. When you place an InDesign file as a link, the _____ option in the Place InDesign dialog box determines which area of the file (page, bleed, or slug) is imported.

7. The _____ lists all files that are placed in a layout, including the location and status of each.

8. The _____ can be used to define custom spellings that are not in the main dictionary, such as proper names or trademarked terms.

9. The _____ shows the basic text in a story, without applied formatting; it can be used to review tracked changes.

10. The _____ dialog box can be used to convert specific spot colors to process while the file is being output.

1. Briefly explain the concept of color management, as it relates to building a layout in InDesign.

2. Briefly explain the concept of color separation.

3. Briefly explain how spot colors relate to print separations.

PORTFOLIO BUILDER PROJECT

Use what you have learned in this project to complete the following freeform exercise.
Carefully read the art director and client comments, then create your own design to meet the needs of the project.
Use the space below to sketch ideas. When finished, write a brief explanation of the reasoning behind your final design.

art director comments

Every professional designer needs a portfolio of their work. If you have completed the projects in this book, you should now have a number of different examples to show off your skills using Illustrator, Photoshop, and InDesign CC.

The projects in this book were specifically designed to include a broad range of *types* of projects — your portfolio should use the same principle.

client comments

Using the following suggestions, gather your best work, and then create printed and digital versions of your portfolio:

❏ Include as many different types of work as possible, including illustration, photographic manipulation, and page layout.

❏ Print clean copies of each finished piece that you want to include.

❏ For each example in your portfolio, write a brief (one or two paragraph) synopsis of the project. Explain the purpose of the piece, as well as your role in the creative and production process.

❏ Design a personal promotion brochure. Create a layout that highlights your technical skills and reflects your personal style.

❏ Create a PDF version of your portfolio so you can send it via email, post it on job sites, and keep it with you on a flash drive at all times.

project justification

PROJECT SUMMARY

As you have seen, placing pictures into an InDesign layout is a relatively easy task, whether you place them one at a time or load multiple images at once and then simply click to place them into the appropriate spots. InDesign allows you to work with all of the common image formats. You can even place one InDesign layout directly into another. The Links panel is a valuable tool for managing images, from updating file status or replacing one image with another, to opening an external file in its native application so you can easily make changes in placed files. Fine-tuning a layout requires checking for common errors — both technical and practical, such as spelling errors.

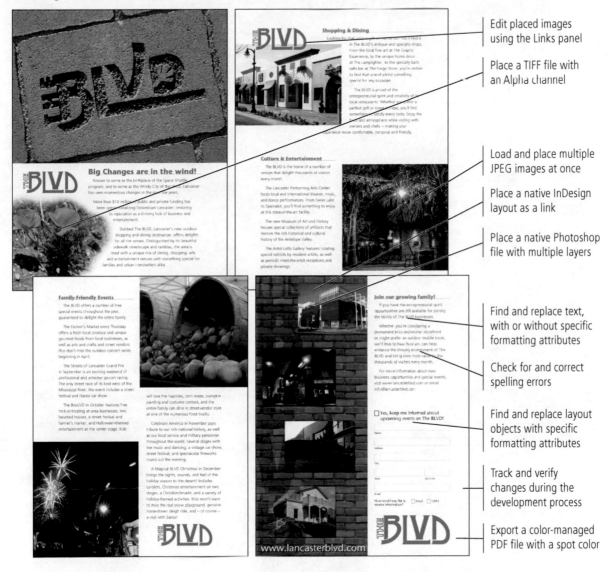

Edit placed images using the Links panel

Place a TIFF file with an Alpha channel

Load and place multiple JPEG images at once

Place a native InDesign layout as a link

Place a native Photoshop file with multiple layers

Find and replace text, with or without specific formatting attributes

Check for and correct spelling errors

Find and replace layout objects with specific formatting attributes

Track and verify changes during the development process

Export a color-managed PDF file with a spot color

INDEX

INDEX

INDEX

INDEX

INDEX

TrueType fonts   164
TruMatch   183
Twirl Clockwise tool   315
type   157
type on a path   489–493
Type on a Path tool   490
Type preferences   158, 164
type scaling   563
Type tool   28, 36, 157–159, 163, 169, 188, 274, 424, 426, 470–473, 513, 548–549, 553, 554
Typekit   568
typical display   17–18

U

unassigned frame   459
underline   162, 475
undo   48, 53, 237, 246, 272, 455
ungrouping   74, 183, 408
unit of measurement   42, 56–57
unite   140
Units & Increments preferences   390
Units & Rulers preferences   205
unlock all   87, 136
unlocking layers   87
unsharp masking   270
update graphic links   569
update link   517, 585, 588

update link options   416
update while dragging   176
use black point compression   368, 576
use classic mode   215
use compression   44
use dither   368
use document bleed settings   503
use global light   304, 309, 465
use InDesign style definition   532
use PDF's layer visibility   416, 585
user dictionary   606, 608
user interface   1–5
User Interface preferences   43
user-modified path   543

V

value [color]   131
vector graphics   23, 41, 149, 203, 223–226, 392
vector mask   286–287
vector shape layer. *See* shape layers
vertical alignment   549
vertical scale   162, 476
vibrance   379
View menu   15, 30, 38, 214, 267, 431
view options   473
view PDF after exporting   501
view percentage   14, 30, 32, 38, 267
Vivid Light blending mode   323

W

web presses   368
white point   350
White Point eyedropper   372
whole word   600
wildcards   602
Window menu   6, 14, 23, 401
word spacing   496
work path   278
working space   367, 575, 578
Workspace switcher   4, 12
workspaces   4, 12
wrap around bounding box   543
wrap around object shape   543

X

x coordinate   211
x-height   157

Y

y coordinate   211

Z

zero point   57, 391
zero-point crosshair   212
ZIP compression   255, 502
zoom all windows   34
Zoom Level field   14–15
Zoom tool   15–16, 30, 34, 38, 243, 267, 315

Use our portfolio to build yours.

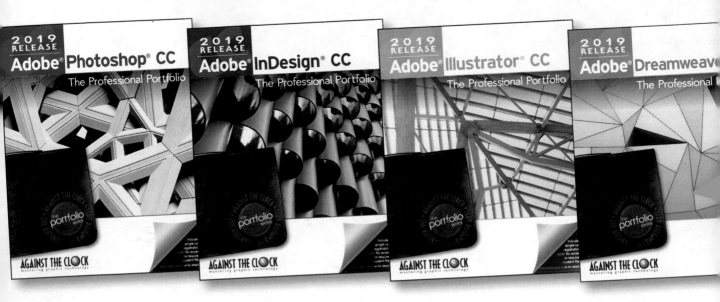

The Against The Clock Professional Portfolio Series walks you step-by-step through the tools and techniques of graphic design professionals.

Order online at www.againsttheclock.com
Use code **ATC2019** for a 10% discount

Go to **www.againsttheclock.com** to enter our monthly drawing for a free book of your choice.